INNOCENT ABROAD

An Intimate Account
of American Peace Diplomacy
in the Middle East

MARTIN INDYK

SIMON & SCHUSTER

NEW YORK LONDON TORONTO SYDNEY

A SABAN CENTER AT BROOKINGS BOOK

 Simon & Schuster
1230 Avenue of the Americas
New York, NY 10020

First Simon & Schuster hardcover edition January 2009

SIMON & SCHUSTER and colophon are registered trademarks
of Simon & Schuster, Inc.

For information about special discounts for bulk purchases,
please contact Simon & Schuster Special Sales at
1-800-456-6798 or business@simonandschuster.com

Designed by Level C
Map pp. x–xi by Paul Pugliese

Manufactured in the United States of America

10 9 8 7 6 5 4 3 2 1

Library of Congress Cataloging-in-Publication Data

Indyk, Martin.
    Innocent abroad : An intimate account of American peace diplomacy in
the Middle East / Martin Indyk. — 1st Simon & Schuster hardcover ed.
        p.   cm.
    Includes bibliographical references and index.
    1. Middle East—Foreign relations—United States.   2. United States—Foreign
relations—Middle East.   3. Arab-Israeli conflict—1993–   4. United States—
Politics and government—1989–   I. Title.
    DS63.2.U5I46   2009
    956.05'3—dc22   2008034835
ISBN-13: 978-1-4165-9429-1
ISBN-10:   1-4165-9429-9

Page 495 constitutes an extension of the copyright page.

To my father, John Indyk,
the healer, who taught me
the value of integrity,
and innocence

Contents

INTRODUCTION   1

PART ONE: THE ASCENT   11

1   Syria First   13

2   Dual Containment   30

3   "That's What Kings Do"   44

4   September 13, 1993   60

5   The Anatomy of Rabin's Oslo Decision   78

6   Detour on the Road to Damascus   92

7   Peace with Jordan   120

PART TWO: THE OTHER BRANCH   147

8   Dual Containment and the Peace Process   149

9   Iran's Breakout   167

10   Saddam Resurgent   182

11   Engaging Iran   215

PART THREE: THE SECOND CHANCE   239

12   Syria Redux   241

13   Shepherdstown Breakdown   253

14   Syrian Denouement   269

15 The Road to the Summit   288

16 Trapped at Camp David   306

17 The Collapse   327

18 Intifada!   341

19 The End of the Peace Process   361

20 Epilogue   377

21 The Lantern on the Stern   391

    APPENDIXES   417

A. The Oslo Agreement   417

B. The Washington Declaration   430

C. Draft Treaty of Peace Between Israel and Syria   434

D. The Clinton Parameters   441

E. The Arab League's Beirut Declaration on the
    Saudi Peace Initiative   446

    NOTES   448

    ACKNOWLEDGMENTS   469

    INDEX   473

These people are naturally good-hearted and intelligent, and with education and liberty, would be a happy and contented race. They often appeal to a stranger to know if the great world will not some day come to their relief and save them.

—Mark Twain,
on first encountering the Arabs of Palestine,
The Innocents Abroad; or, The New Pilgrim's Progress, 1869

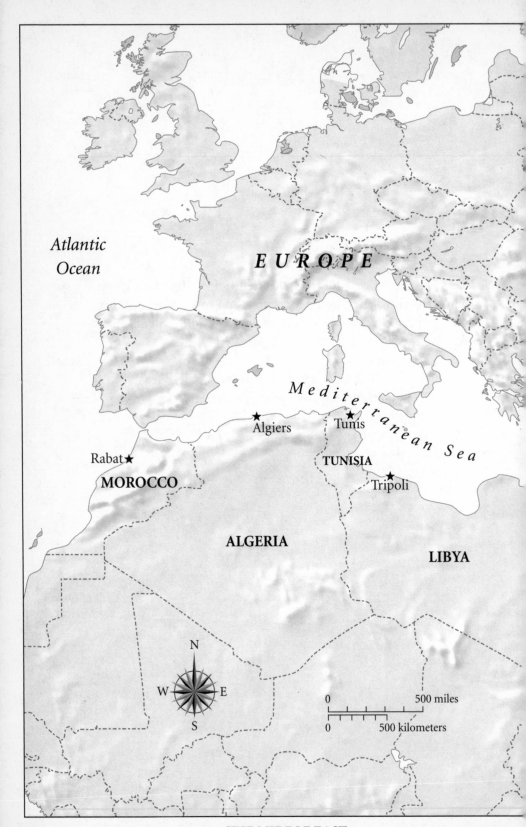

Atlantic
Ocean

E U R O P E

M e d i t e r r a n e a n   S e a

★ Algiers

★ Tunis

Rabat ★

TUNISIA

MOROCCO

★ Tripoli

ALGERIA

LIBYA

N

W ● E

S

| 0 | 500 miles |
| 0 | 500 kilometers |

THE MIDDLE EAST

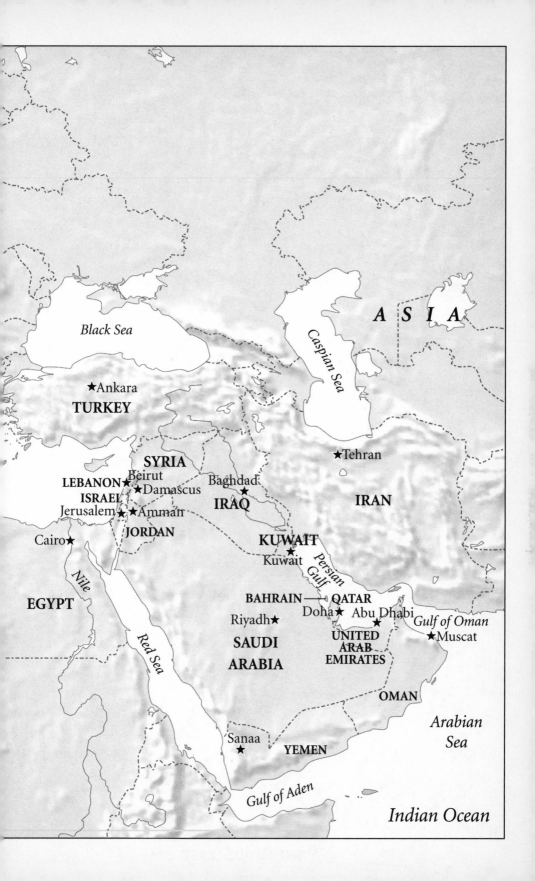

INNOCENT ABROAD

Introduction

If men could learn from history,
What lessons it could teach us!
But passion and party blind our eyes.
And the light which experience gives us
Is a lantern on the stern,
Which shines only on the waves behind us.
                                    —Samuel Taylor Coleridge

Today, with headlines from the Middle East dominated by bloodshed, terrorism, sectarian warfare, civil strife, and threats to destroy Israel, it's hard to imagine that not so long ago the politics of the
region were punctuated by signing ceremonies at the White House
where Arab and Israeli leaders expressed their common commitment
to peace and reconciliation. Critics and cynics would later come to
mock such occasions as mere "photo ops," as if they had no greater
significance. But now, given the deplorable state of Middle Eastern affairs, those ceremonies should be remembered as indicators of what
was possible when Arab and Israeli leaders, under the auspices of an
American president, committed their nations to settle their grievances
through peacemaking.

The handshake between Yitzhak Rabin and Yasser Arafat on the
White House lawn on September 13, 1993, is usually considered the
climactic moment of that era. But that was at the beginning; Rabin
seemed quite reluctant to shake Arafat's hand. The high point of the
peace process actually came two years later, on September 28, 1995,
when Rabin and Arafat came to the White House again, to sign the
"Oslo II Accord," which provided for Palestinian rule to replace the Israeli army in the major cities and towns of the West Bank. Hosni

Mubarak, the always-cautious president of Egypt, turned up this time to bear witness. King Hussein bin Talal of Jordan stood proudly next to Rabin—a year earlier they had signed the Israel-Jordan Peace Treaty. Even the foreign minister of Saudi Arabia in traditional Arab head-scarf and robes was there for the entire world to see.

This time, the audience was treated to a spontaneous gesture quite different to the stiffness of the first occasion: Arafat put an affectionate arm on Rabin's back, and Rabin, a shy and gruff man who normally had no time for demonstrative gestures of affection, had left it there as they departed the room together.

Later that evening, President Bill Clinton hosted a reception for the peacemakers at the Corcoran Gallery, across Seventeenth Street from the White House. In the ornate, Doric-columned main hall, Washington's politicians, diplomats, and lobbyists mingled with representatives of the Jewish and Arab-American communities. After a time, Clinton and Vice President Al Gore appeared with the leaders on a podium at the southern end of the cavernous hall to address the crowd. Arafat and Rabin had not expected to make speeches. Given the opportunity to stray from his usual mantra of demands for justice for the Palestinian people, Arafat actually delivered warm words about the importance of peace with his Jewish cousins.*

Rabin responded in kind. He noted that Jews were not famous for their sporting abilities, except when it came to speechmaking, at which he averred they were Olympic champions. Turning to Arafat, he said, "It seems to me Mr. Chairman, that you might be a little Jewish!" The crowd laughed and a Cheshire-cat grin spread across Arafat's normally pouting lips as he declared: "Yes, yes, Rachel is my aunt!" How exactly Arafat calculated that he was related to the biblical matriarch was a mystery, like so much else about this strange man. But it was emblematic of the occasion that someone who prided himself on being a Muslim world leader would choose publicly to claim Jewish ancestry.

For the first time, Rabin spoke about the right of the Palestinians to self-determination. It may sound strange now, when statehood is commonly accepted as a Palestinian right, that Rabin opposed a Palestin-

---

* Arafat said: "We were, in the past, only cousins, all of us who are the sons of Abraham. And now . . . we have created with our neighbors, our new neighbors and our new partners, a new peace—the peace of the brave. Now, we can say that we have a new Middle East, a new Middle East is in the making . . . We will protect this peace with our souls and our bodies . . . because our peoples need peace. Our children need the peace."

ian state, insisting that the Oslo Accords make no mention of it. But this night was different. Feeling that the Palestinians had committed themselves to living peacefully alongside Israel, Rabin outlined his vision of a peace in which Palestinians would have an independent state of their own. What was needed, Rabin explained, was "separation, not because of hatred, [but] because of respect."

At that moment, many thought the Arab-Israeli peace process had reached a tipping point. It seemed only a matter of time before a Palestinian state would be established in most of the West Bank and all of Gaza. A peace deal between Israel and Syria was also in the works, painstakingly negotiated in secret between Rabin, Clinton, and Syrian president Hafez al-Asad. If it too could be finalized, the Arab-Israeli conflict would be over.

Five weeks later, Yitzhak Rabin would lie dead in the emergency room at Tel Aviv's Ichilov Hospital, murdered by a Jewish religious extremist. The assassination of the principal Israeli architect of peacemaking would set Israelis and Palestinians on a path of destruction that would eventually engulf the whole peace edifice. Try as he might, with Rabin gone, Clinton was unable to salvage the peace process.

HOW FAR WE had traveled in such a short time. Clinton and his peace team—of which I was a member—had entered the White House full of optimism. A student of history, Clinton understood that the stars were aligned for a breakthrough that could end the Arab-Israeli conflict and provide a lasting legacy for his presidency. That heroic endeavor would in the end turn into a blinding obsession to complete the task he started with his slain Israeli friend, and to burnish his own tarnished presidency.

Bill Clinton attempted to transform the Middle East by making peace, committing his energies and prestige to an objective that befitted the idealism and optimism that underpins American foreign policy. He sought to convert far-off provinces bound in conflict and mired in tribalism into a land of peace and harmony. In contrast to his successor, George W. Bush, Clinton chose to operate within the traditional bounds of statecraft, preferring the instruments of diplomacy to the weapons of war, as he attempted to drag the region across the threshold of the twenty-first century.

Clinton was hardly oblivious to the ills that afflicted the Middle East: a rogue predator plotting his revenge in Baghdad; revolutionary mullahs in Tehran using terror and violence to spread their Islamist ideology to the rest of the Middle East; Israeli politicians struggling to survive in the harsh world of coalition politics; and corrupt and unrepresentative Arab regimes that failed to meet the needs of their people and allowed no political space for them to express their disaffection. But Clinton chose to contain and limit the impact of these negative influences rather than confront them, in the belief that a breakthrough to peace would do more than anything else to change them. He did not ignore the American impulse to spread democracy abroad, but he believed that peacemaking would be the catalyst for unleashing the region's potential for political and economic liberalization.

Clinton had some important successes. The negative influences of Iraq and Iran were neutralized and the security of America's oil-rich, Gulf Arab clients enhanced. He helped ensure stable successions in Morocco and Jordan and the eventual defeat of Islamic extremists in Algeria. He persuaded Muammar Qadhafi to get out of the terrorism business, laying the groundwork for Libya's eventual abandonment of its weapons of mass destruction. He brokered a peace treaty between Israel and Jordan, capitalizing on the statesmanship of Yitzhak Rabin and King Hussein. He brought the Israeli-Syrian negotiations to the point where the disposition of barely two hundred meters on the northeastern shore of the Sea of Galilee was all that separated the parties from an agreement. And he took the Oslo Accords, the framework Israeli-Palestinian agreement that had been negotiated behind his back, and diligently translated it into a series of interim accords and parameters for a permanent peace that could have ended the decades-long conflict between Israelis and Palestinians.

It was a wholehearted diplomatic endeavor in which for eight years President Clinton and his peace team invested more time, energy, and prestige than in any other area of American foreign policy. But ultimately it failed.

Instead of peace, Israelis and Palestinians became locked in a bloody conflict, which over the next five years managed to destroy the framework of comity that had taken three decades of dedicated American diplomacy to construct. By the end of President Clinton's second term, the Middle East had already begun to revert to its violent, tribal, fundamentalist tendencies, a trend that erupted in Gaza and the West Bank but found its most explosive expression in the terrorist attacks of September 11, 2001. With Clinton gone, his successor chose to forsake peacemaking for war-making in the belief that it could provide a more effective catalyst for transformation.

This is a story laced with irony. Clinton and his peace team believed they were involved in a noble effort to remake the Middle East in America's image. However, their best efforts were inadequate to the task and the consequences were the opposite of those intended.

I have recounted this tragedy in three parts. In the first, Clinton uses his diplomatic energies to reach the peak, that moment in September 1995 when it actually seemed as if the valley of peace was opening out before us. To reach that point, Clinton developed a strategy that combined the pursuit of peace with a policy of "dual containment" to deal with the Middle East's rogue regimes in Iraq and Iran.

The second part details the fate of "dual containment," that other branch of our strategy, underscoring the symbiotic relationship between developments in the Gulf and the fate of Clinton's primary strategy of peacemaking in the Arab-Israeli arena. The interconnected nature of the political dynamics in the Middle East that this experience reveals provides an important lesson for future American policy makers. And as the policy of regime change pursued by Clinton's successor gives way to new ideas for containment of Iraq's civil strife, and engagement with Iran, Clinton's experience with both those approaches provides salutary schooling.

The third part of this book chronicles the downward spiral that began with Rabin's assassination and culminated in Arafat's rejection of Clinton's parameters for an Israeli-Palestinian final settlement put forward in the last days of his presidency. How we arrived there, via Shepherdstown, Geneva, and Camp David, is a dramatic story in itself. More important, though, are the lessons to be learned from the bold but ultimately unsuccessful attempt to reach the goal of a comprehensive end to the Arab-Israeli conflict.

THE ULTIMATE FAILURE of Clinton's efforts was a very personal one for me. I could never have imagined when I arrived with my wife, Jill, and my infant daughter, Sarah, in America in 1982—as a visiting professor from Australia on sabbatical at Columbia University—that ten years later I would join the White House staff of a new president and become responsible for helping to craft Clinton's Middle Eastern strategy as his special assistant in the National Security Council.

Twenty years earlier, as a student at the Hebrew University in Jerusalem, I had been caught up in the 1973 Yom Kippur War. It was a defining moment in my life. As I lay awake listening to BBC radio broadcasts of Henry Kissinger's efforts to negotiate a ceasefire, I came to understand the pivotal role of the United States as the one party that, through its diplomacy, could help resolve the Arab-Israeli conflict. From that point on, I had become obsessed with the U.S. role in promoting Middle East peace—studying, writing and teaching about it. Suddenly, there I was at the epicenter of that effort.

Even then I could not have imagined that two years later I would become America's first Jewish ambassador to Israel, dispatched by Clinton and Secretary of State Warren Christopher to work with Rabin on completing the Israeli-Syrian peace deal. Two years after that, Madeleine Albright would appoint me as the first Jewish assistant secretary of state for Near Eastern affairs, responsible for developing and implementing Clinton's strategy toward the Arab world. And then in July 1999, on his first visit as Israeli prime minister to Washington, Ehud Barak would ask Clinton to send me back to Israel again as ambassador to work with him on the comprehensive end to the Arab-Israeli conflict that they had set as their common objective.

The climb up that mountain seemed so natural and destined that I never thought of looking down to contemplate how easily and how far we could fall. Like Icarus, only after the wax on my wings finally melted could I begin to understand the precariousness of the whole enterprise.

That getting of wisdom should have begun five months after I arrived in Israel, the night Rabin was assassinated. I was in the emergency ward at Ichilov Hospital with Leah Rabin on that fateful night, just as I had been privileged to be with President Clinton for every meeting he had held with the slain Israeli leader. But I convinced myself that Rabin's decisions had rendered the peace process irreversible. Even the electoral defeat seven months later of Shimon Peres, Rabin's peace partner, with whom I had worked closely, did little to dent my assumption of inevitability. The subsequent Netanyahu era became the winter of our peace process discontent, as we struggled to negotiate the Hebron and Wye agreements, shore up Saddam's containment cage, and chase after an illusory engagement with Iran.

But just as spring's warmth so quickly erases the memories of winter's chill, so too did Barak's election rekindle my belief in manifest destiny as I returned to Israel for a second chance to complete the deal. It was only as George W. Bush's interim ambassador, working with Ariel Sharon, the newly elected Israeli prime minister, did I begin to appreciate the real impact of Rabin's assassination and the profound implications of our inability to complete the peace deals in Clinton's last year.

Because I was intimately involved in Clinton's peacemaking efforts and in his wider strategy for the Middle East, I have felt a keen sense of personal responsibility, not least to understand and explain from an insider's perspective what went wrong. That journey has been a difficult and humbling one. Along the way, I came to appreciate that good intentions backed by America's immense influence are on their own inadequate to the complex task of shaping the course of Middle Eastern history. One also needs to imagine the possible consequences beyond the ones we hoped for. Indeed, hope and optimism are critical components of the innocence that is the hallmark of America's engagement with the Middle East. Why would we bother to try to transform such a troubled region unless we somehow believed we could, and should? But the dark side of that innocence is a naïveté bred of ignorance and arrogance that generate a chronic inability to comprehend the multiple ironies of the Middle East. Bill Clinton tried to make comprehensive peace there and ended up with the intifada instead. George Bush tried to make the Middle East democratic, and look at the result.

Of course, Bush had no intention of following in Clinton's wake. He was convinced he could achieve better results by setting course in the opposite direction. To make the Middle East over in America's democratic image, Bush stepped outside the bounds of traditional statecraft and deliberately eschewed time-honored American concerns for stability in a volatile region of vital interest.

Like Clinton, Bush had some important successes along the way, removing Saddam Hussein, one of the most effective practitioners of the Middle East's violent ways, and pressing Bashar al-Asad, one of the most ineffective, to end Syria's thirty-year occupation of Lebanon. But the unintended consequences of Bush's ambitions are already in plain view: the chaos and sectarian warfare in Iraq, the paralysis and rising tension in Lebanon, an Iranian bid for hegemony in the Arab world backed by its defiant pursuit of nuclear enrichment, a Sunni-Shiite divide opening up across the region, and the filling of the political space that George Bush helped open by armed Islamist groups, notably Hezbollah in Lebanon and Hamas in Gaza, both of which reject Israel's right to exist.

What is it about the United States that its leaders feel obliged to sally forth with such virtuous determination to transform the bazaars and back alleys of the Middle East? And what is it about the Middle East that holds them up, sets them back, and sucks them down into its swamps? My purpose here is to answer those questions, illuminating them with my own experience during the Clinton years.

By dissecting the successes and failures of Clinton's diplomacy in the Middle East, by examining what happened when American and Middle Eastern cultures, values, and power met on the diplomatic battlefield, my purpose is to provide an understanding of why this region is so resistant to the transformational change that America is so insistent on promoting—an understanding that has practical applications for any future effort.

In one sense, Clinton's use of traditional statecraft was inadequate to the task of transformation because it meant that he had to work within the existing Middle Eastern order. On the rare occasions when Arab and Israeli leaders chose to break with that order, Clinton's diplomacy could achieve breakthroughs. But most of the time he had to work with Arab leaders paralyzed by their lack of legitimacy or preoccupied with their own survival rather than the well-being of their people, and elected Israeli leaders constrained by the dictates of fractious coalition politics and a suspicious public. That was the heart of the problem, notwithstanding the missteps of Clinton and his peace team.

In another sense, however, the conclusion George W. Bush reached— that the only way to effect the transformation is through regime change—was more fundamentally mistaken than any of Clinton's errors. A new Middle Eastern order could not be created merely by the ripple effect of the removal of one of its most egregious leaders. War-making could reshape the strategic context and thereby create opportunities for the United States to attempt the transformation we seem bound to seek. But agile and astute American diplomacy must be used to exploit it, as Bush learned the hard way.

In the process, all hope of resolving the Arab-Israeli conflict through negotiated compromise seemed to evaporate. Years of blood-soaked confrontations between Israelis and Palestinians, while Bush lectured from the sidelines, generated the opposite of the peace process that Rabin had championed and Clinton had relentlessly pursued. Instead of the "separation because of respect" that Rabin foresaw, Israelis and Palestinians are separating out of the very hatred that he sought to expunge.

Future American administrations will have to devote a good deal of their energies to digging out of the crater left by the Bush administration's dangerous and costly war. However, peacemaking must also be an urgent priority because seven years of neglect have led to such a deterioration that the chances for peace are now receding at a dangerous pace. And pursuing Arab-Israeli peace, as Clinton's experience demonstrates, can have a broad and positive impact across the region. If taken up effectively by future American presidents peacemaking could do much to reverse the deleterious impact of Bush's mistakes.

The success of such efforts will depend heavily on the resurrection of U.S. diplomacy. Neglected for much of the last decade, it will be sorely needed in the years ahead. The Iraq experience has demonstrated the limitations of force while severely straining the U.S. military. The U.S. recession and the vast transfer of wealth to oil-producing countries have also reduced America's economic leverage and left its people wary of new commitments. That leaves diplomacy to bridge the gap between U.S. interests and ambitions and the means available to protect and promote them. Working with allies, building coalitions, resolving conflicts—the stuff of statecraft—will have to take precedence over an arrogant insistence on the American way. In his second term, George W. Bush's secretary of state, Condoleezza Rice, came to understand this reality, repairing transatlantic relations, rebuilding an Arab-Israeli peace process, and pursuing negotiations with North Korea and Iran on their nuclear programs. Even Bush, after criticizing Clinton's peacemaking efforts, convened his own Arab-Israeli peace conference at Annapolis, Maryland, in November 2007 to endorse the relaunching of Israeli-Palestinian negotiations.

With the time therefore upon us again for serious diplomatic endeavors in the Middle East, the Clinton administration's experience will be important in illuminating the way forward. The lessons detailed here point to a strategy that depends less on the use of force and more on backing diplomacy with the threat of force. They point to a course that tempers America's instinct to spread democracy with its interest in preserving stability. It will need to be a way that is less naïve in its assumptions, more modest in its ambitions, more humble in its approach, and more imaginative in its anticipation of what can go wrong; a way that takes into account the region's tardy tempo, unsuited to the calendar of American presidential terms; a way that is cognizant of the reactionary undertow that operates beneath the surface; a way more sensitive to the crosscurrents of internecine and sectarian rivalries that reach across the region.

Clinton's experience also demonstrates that future presidents will not be able to achieve America's vision of a peaceful Middle East absent leaders with the courage, vision, and statesmanship of an Anwar Sadat, a Menachem Begin, a Hussein bin Talal, or a Yitzhak Rabin. The United States cannot create such statesmen but it can use its immense power to alter the strategic context in which Middle Eastern leaders function and thereby influence their motivations. Should those leaders emerge to take advantage of the moment, future presidents must be ready to grab their outstretched hands and guide them to a safe shore with a firm and steady grip. That is when they will most need America's help but it is also when the United States will be in the best position to achieve the peace it seeks for those troubled lands.

In deriving the lessons of Clinton's attempt to use diplomacy to transform the Middle East into a peaceful realm, I was much influenced by Barbara Tuchman's seminal analysis, *The March of Folly*. In that book she drew on the concept of "the lantern on the stern" to illuminate the causes of history's major foreign policy disasters. Sharing my experience of what occurred, I have tried here to use the lantern on the Clinton administration's stern as a guide to those who will have to deal with the roiling wake generated by the Bush administration's mistakes.

PART ONE

THE ASCENT

1

Syria First

On January 23, 2001, Bill Clinton was in his final hours as president. There was one piece of unfinished business he was determined to take care of: it was payback time for Yasser Arafat.

Three months earlier, the two of them had met at an urgent summit hosted by Egypt's President Hosni Mubarak in Sharm el-Sheikh at his favorite resort hotel, the Marriott Golf. Israeli prime minister Ehud Barak, King Abdullah II of Jordan, U.N. Secretary-General Kofi Annan, and the European Union diplomatic chief, Javier Solana, were there, as well.

Clinton was trying to persuade Arafat and Barak to end the intifada that had erupted two weeks earlier. The escalating violence was destroying Clinton's chance of achieving a negotiated peace agreement before he left office. As he was preparing for his meeting with Arafat, his advisers had urged him to take a tough line, but he was hesitating. When Clinton sat alone with Arafat, gazing out at tailored greens and fairways framed by the Red Sea and the Sinai Desert, his resolve melted. Arafat, sensing that Clinton's real priority was the peace deal, made him a solemn promise to conclude the final status agreement with Israel before the president left office. Clinton was buoyant afterward. "He really does want to do the deal," he told us.

In the final days of his presidency, Clinton had still been waiting for Arafat to make good on his promise. In December 2000, the president had put forward his far-reaching set of parameters on all the final status issues to serve as a basis for an agreement. He was even prepared to spend his last four days in office negotiating the deal. A desperate Barak was waiting for the call to a final summit meeting. Barak's foreign minister, Shlomo Ben-Ami, was so keen to reach agreement that he had gone beyond his instructions and informed Arafat that he could even have sovereignty over the Jewish Holy of

Holies, the Temple Mount in Jerusalem. But at the last moment, Arafat reneged.

Now Clinton wanted to make it clear to the incoming administration just who they would be dealing with. He had already dwelt at length on Arafat's perfidy while briefing George W. Bush and Dick Cheney that morning. Now he called Colin Powell, the secretary of state–designate, who had earlier served as Clinton's chairman of the Joint Chiefs of Staff. When the phone rang, Powell was dressing for a pre-inaugural concert. He was surprised to hear Clinton's voice. "I just wanted to wish you all the best in your new position," the president said. Then he launched into a vituperative, expletive-filled tirade against Arafat. Powell understood the real motive for the call. As he would recount it to me, the president warned him, "Don't you ever trust that son of a bitch. He lied to me and he'll lie to you." Arafat had failed his people and destroyed the chances for peace, Clinton emphasized. "Don't let Arafat sucker punch you like he did me."

THE FIRST TIME I had heard Clinton talk about sucker punching was on August 11, 1992. As the Democratic candidate for president, he was about to have his first meeting with Yitzhak Rabin, the recently elected prime minister of Israel. Clinton knew little of Rabin, but what he did know made him nervous. The hero of Israel's Six-Day War, Rabin had served as Israel's ambassador in Washington while Richard Nixon was president. He had developed a close relationship with Henry Kissinger, then Nixon's national security adviser, and together they had forged a strategic relationship between Israel and the United States. On the eve of the 1972 presidential election, Ambassador Rabin had ignored diplomatic protocol by endorsing Nixon as Israel's best friend.* Clinton feared Rabin might do something of the sort this time around, too.

Rabin would be coming to the meeting from Kennebunkport, Maine, where President George H. W. Bush had just announced, with much fanfare, the release of a $10 billion loan guarantee for Israel to finance its absorption of immigrants from the former Soviet Union. It

---

* In a Washington interview broadcast by Israel Radio and reported on the front page of the *Washington Post*, Ambassador Rabin was quoted as saying, "While we appreciate support in the form of words we are getting from one camp, we much prefer support in the form of deeds we are getting from the other camp."

was an obvious effort by Bush to repair the damage he had done to his relationship with American Jews by attempting to end Israeli settlement activity through withholding this aid. If Rabin now endorsed Bush, as he had Nixon, it might help change attitudes in the Jewish community, a core base of political and financial support for Clinton.

To prepare Clinton for this meeting with Rabin, his foreign policy advisers met him on the campaign trail at the Doral Country Club in Miami. Anthony "Tony" Lake and Samuel "Sandy" Berger had brought me into the campaign to work on Middle Eastern issues. I was then the director of the Washington Institute for Near East Policy, a think tank I had founded with support from the pro-Israel community eight years earlier.

Clinton was late, as usual, having just delivered a speech to the Southern Legislative Conference's convention—a group of Democratic state representatives. The candidate surged into the room where we were waiting, excited, red-faced, larger than life. Immediately, he began to recount how he had brought a huge audience to its feet by warning them repeatedly not to be "sucker punched" by George H. W. Bush's assertion that he was a "crazy, wild-eyed liberal anxious to spring radical ideas on an unsuspecting public."

Clinton had been pumped up by the encounter. He asked one of his aides to get Hillary on the phone so that he could recount the event to her. With that finished, what he really wanted to do was eat, and play golf. His brothers-in-law, Hugh and Tony Rodham, were waiting for him outside on the driving range. But Sandy Berger, who would become Clinton's national security adviser in his second term, was determined to prepare him for what could be a critical encounter with Rabin. Sandy put his hand on Clinton's shoulder and pressed him to sit down and listen.

As Clinton devoured a full plate of food from the buffet, I quickly gave him a thumbnail sketch of the prime minister, explaining that Rabin had won a mandate from the Israeli people to pursue peace and that as a general who had seen too many wars he now intended to end them. Rabin was a strategic thinker, well aware of the profound shifts in the Middle East's balance of power. The Soviet Union's collapse had deprived Arab states that still believed in making war on Israel of their superpower patron. The defeat of Saddam Hussein's army in the Gulf War had punctured the Arab "military option" by destroying the po-

tential for an anti-Israeli eastern front coalition between Syria and
Iraq. For the first time, all of Israel's Arab neighbors were conducting
direct negotiations with the Jewish state.

I told Clinton we were witnessing a rare moment in Middle Eastern
history when a window of opportunity opens wide. To capitalize on
the moment, if he were elected president, he would just need to put his
immense influence as the leader of the dominant power in the Middle
East behind Rabin as he moved forward. I boldly predicted that if
Clinton put his mind to it, he could achieve four Arab-Israeli peace
agreements in his first term as president. Clinton, who had been listening intently, stopped his ravenous eating, looked me in the eye, and
said, "I want to do that."

As SIMPLE AS that; at least we thought so at the time. Five weeks after he entered the White House, on March 3, 1993, Clinton convened
his first National Security Council (NSC) meeting. Middle Eastern
peacemaking was the only item on the agenda.

With the president already preoccupied with domestic issues and
overwhelmed by controversy—at the time of this meeting, he was
dealing with a political storm over the issue of gays in the military—
meetings of the president's NSC were normally chaired by Tony Lake,
his national security adviser, in the underground Situation Room. But
on this day the president wanted to signal his commitment to peacemaking by chairing the meeting in the Cabinet Room.

Warren Christopher, the genteel secretary of state, perfectly
groomed in his Savile Row suit and Turnbull & Asser tie, sat next to
Secretary of Defense Les Aspin, the eccentric intellectual in his rum-
pled Lieutenant Columbo–style clothes. Tony Lake was seated on the
other side of the president. Tony was a low-key, bookish academic
whose experience in the Nixon and Carter administrations had rendered him determined to avoid confrontations with the cabinet secretaries. Colin Powell, then the chairman of the Joint Chiefs of Staff,
showed up in his uniform greens. He was the only cabinet-level hold-
over from the previous administration and was using his considerable
charm to establish himself as part of the new team. CIA director James
Woolsey brooded at the end of the table. A neoconservative wooed
back to the Democratic Party by Clinton, he was constrained by Lake's
insistence that he stick to intelligence assessments rather than opining
on policy; that constraint soon led him to resign. Vice President Al

Gore was the last to enter the room; the president would come to rely on his judgment when making difficult foreign policy decisions, especially those involving force.

They were a diverse crew who would not work easily together as a team even though they were not divided by the ideological disputes that would dominate discussion in the next Bush administration. In this first meeting they were determined to demonstrate conviviality. Lake discussed baseball with Aspin; the vice president exchanged jokes with Leon Fuerth, his national security adviser; Warren Christopher chatted with Colin Powell.

There I was, too, with my own name tent, sitting opposite the secretary of state and the chairman of the Joint Chiefs—I was the special assistant to the president for Middle Eastern affairs. We all sat in oversize brown leather armchairs around a huge oval mahogany table. As my awestruck eyes wandered around the room, I noticed that each of the chairs had a brass plaque on the back engraved with the name of a current cabinet secretary. The president's chair stood at the middle of the table, a few inches taller than all the others, with its back to the long wall of French doors that opened out to the Rose Garden, and facing portraits of Abraham Lincoln and Andrew Jackson.

The president arrived late and wasted no time opening the meeting by expressing his satisfaction with his first five weeks in office. On the foreign policy front, Bosnia, Somalia, and Haiti were presenting problems. But in the Middle East the prospects seemed good for quickly resuming peace negotiations. He turned to Christopher to report on the regional tour he had just completed.

On this trip—the first of nineteen Christopher shuttles through the Middle East—the secretary of state had succeeded in brokering an agreement that would bring all the Arabs back to the negotiating table with Israel.* Christopher reported on his discussions with Syrian president Hafez al-Asad, who had made clear that Israel would have to engage in a full withdrawal from the Golan Heights. If it did so, Asad would agree to a "full" peace and the necessary security arrangements. When Christopher relayed this to Rabin, he was encouraged. Rabin approached problems in a cold, analytical manner; realism was his

---

* The immediate impediment to the resumption of negotiations had been Israel's deportation of four hundred Hamas members from the West Bank and Gaza. Christopher succeeded in convincing Rabin to allow some of the deportees to return immediately and the others over time.

hallmark. In this case, Rabin concluded that Israel should focus on the Syrian track. He explained to Christopher that Asad was a leader who could make decisions and that peace with Syria would be a strategic achievement for Israel, dramatically reducing the danger of war. Rabin would not define the extent of Israeli withdrawal, however, until the Syrians specified the nature of peace and accepted that the agreement would "stand on its own feet" (that is, not be linked to progress on the Israeli-Palestinian track). Rabin then added a coda that, in retrospect, can be seen as an indication of his own calculations: "If the Palestinians see Syria moving it might encourage them."

Christopher invited Rabin to Washington for an official visit. In accepting, Rabin said that when he met the president he would ask him, Would Israel have to make a full withdrawal from the Golan? If so, what would the United States be prepared to do, especially in the event of Asad's death? Would the president be prepared to put American troops on the Golan to replace the Israeli army there? He needed to hear the answers from Clinton before he engaged the Syrians.

Christopher concluded his presentation with uncharacteristic forcefulness. There was, he argued to Clinton, a tremendous opportunity to make progress, an unusual moment to achieve Middle Eastern peace, and he was recommending it as a good place for the president to invest his prestige and influence.

Clinton asked Colin Powell for his professional view of what it would take to secure Israel if it withdrew from the Golan. "No military officer would want to give this up," Powell replied. He then surprised everyone by arguing that the only way Israel could be convinced to withdraw from the Golan Heights would be if the United States were prepared to insert a *brigade* of American troops—some four thousand GIs—on the Golan. Unlike the Israel-Egypt peace treaty observer force deployed in the Sinai, which contained only one battalion of American troops, he said the Golan deployment would need to be a full-fledged fighting force to signal Syria and the Arab world that if they broke the peace agreement they would have to tangle with the U.S. Army.

"It would be worth it," the president responded. He expressed confidence that the traditionally pro-Israel U.S. Congress would go along because it meant securing an Israeli-Syrian peace agreement. If Syria were brought into the peace camp, he said, the risk of regional conflict would be reduced significantly, Israel's northern border with Lebanon would be stabilized, the Palestinian conflict would be more easily managed, and peace with Jordan would be facilitated. Clinton knew that asking Israel to give up the high ground of the Golan Heights to an implacable adversary would involve tangible, life-threatening risks. But the president had made his judgment clear. "We shouldn't minimize the advantage of concentrating on Syria first," he said. "If we have a chance to do that we ought to take it while pushing on the other tracks, too."

THE PRESIDENT HAD based his judgment on an assessment of the situation he inherited in the Middle East. The combined effects of the collapse of the Soviet Union, the rout of Saddam Hussein's forces in the Gulf War, and the elimination of what the U.N. inspectors could find of his weapons of mass destruction capability had made the United States the dominant power in the Middle East. Even though the Gulf War left Saddam in power in Iraq, and even though the Iranian ayatollahs still portrayed us as the "Great Satan," they were all much weakened in their ability to challenge the United States or counter American influence. The destruction of the Iraqi army and the disappearance of their Soviet patron had left the Arab states with only one recourse: to follow the example of Egypt's Anwar Sadat and negotiate with Israel under American auspices to try to recover on the diplomatic front what they had failed to gain by conflict. Clinton had inherited from the Bush administration an ongoing negotiation on all tracks and a new Israeli government with a mandate to pursue agreements urgently.

Looking back on this first Cabinet Room discussion, it is remarkable that the Palestinian dimension of the Arab-Israeli negotiations received barely a mention. At the outset of his presidency, the man who would end up hosting Yasser Arafat in the White House more than he hosted any other foreign leader was little interested in the Palestinian cause. This was partly a reflection of the low standing of the Palestinians in Washington at that time. The Palestine Liberation Organization (PLO), which Arafat led, was on the State Department's terrorism list. U.S. officials were prohibited by law from shaking hands, let alone engaging in negotiations, with any member of the PLO.

The first Palestinian intifada, which raged in the territories from 1987 to 1991, had brought the Palestinian cause into focus, but Yasser Arafat's decision to side with Saddam after his invasion of Kuwait had done the Palestinians tremendous damage. Among America's Gulf allies, especially Saudi Arabia, Arafat was viewed as perfidious. Palestinians who had worked in the Gulf for decades were now rendered suspect, too, and were summarily evicted.

So low had Palestinian standing sunk that their Israeli-approved representatives were only allowed to attend the 1991 Madrid Middle East peace conference that launched Arab-Israeli negotiations as part of the Jordanian delegation. In the subsequent negotiations, conducted at the State Department, the negotiators had spent the first six months arguing about whether there could be a separate Palestinian negotiation.*

Once in the room, the Palestinian delegation had refused to begin negotiations until the Israelis committed in advance to freeze settlement activity and include Jerusalem in the agenda. It was clear that the Palestinian negotiators were taking their instructions from Arafat and that, as long as the United States and Israel ignored him, he would block any progress. Yet given his recent behavior and existing law, the United States had no interest in dealing with him, or ability to do so.

This affected Clinton's perspective. He believed the United States had a strong interest in resolving the Arab-Israeli conflict to stabilize a region of vital concern, strengthen our relations with the Arab world, and fulfill a long-standing commitment to the security of Israel. But on the strategic level, who ruled over whose well in Nablus was a local issue of no great import to the United States, especially compared to the strategic importance of who ruled over whose oil wells in the Persian Gulf. Clinton had no intention of ignoring the Palestinians; he just felt it would be easier to make progress on their issues if he were able to make progress with the Syrians.

No one imagined that Asad would be an easy customer. But as Henry Kissinger had argued after one of his many shuttle trips to Damascus, "You cannot make war in the Middle East without Egypt and you cannot make peace without Syria." As Asad was fond of reminding his guests, Syria was the "beating heart of pan-Arabism." It had led the Arab world's rejection of Sadat's peace with Israel, isolating Egypt for more than a decade. If the "lion of Damascus," as Asad was known in the Arab world, were now to lie down with the Israeli "lamb," then

---

* The dismal prospects were symbolized by the image of the Israeli, Palestinian, and Jordanian delegation heads conducting their negotiating sessions on a sofa in the State Department lobby because the Palestinians refused even to enter the negotiating room.

no Arab nationalist would be able to question the legitimacy of making peace with Israel.

Because of Syria's influence on Lebanon, peace with Israel's northern neighbor was expected to follow immediately, calming the northern border and removing that source of chronic instability. Jordan could then go ahead and conclude a peace deal with Israel. And the more distant Arab states in North Africa and the Gulf would then be free to normalize their relations with Israel. All this momentum could also help Rabin sell the more politically difficult compromises with the Palestinians to a risk-averse Israeli public.

The dispute between Israel and Syria was strictly related to territory and security. There were no religious issues like Jerusalem to complicate the negotiations.* Nor was there a refugee problem to resolve— those Syrian Druze who had left the Golan could return to their villages (many Druze had stayed, living quietly but uneasily under Israeli occupation). And Syria, of course, was a stable state, unlike the Palestinians, who had no state at all.

Syria was on the U.S. terrorism list because it hosted Palestinian rejectionist groups in Damascus and allowed them to train and operate in Lebanon. But when it came to respecting their treaty obligations, the Syrians were puritans. Asad had scrupulously observed the Golan Heights Separation of Forces Agreement, which Kissinger negotiated in 1974: there had been only one minor violent incident in almost twenty years. On the other hand, the Palestinians in the West Bank and Gaza were under Israeli occupation; they had no effective institutions of their own. Their PLO leadership was in exile in Tunis, still engaged in terrorism against Israel. Moreover, as I said, the law banned U.S. officials from talking to it.

Whereas Israelis viewed the Golan in strictly practical terms of holding the high ground, they had developed an ideological rationale for retaining the Palestinian-inhabited West Bank. For many religious and right-wing nationalists this was the land God gave to the Jews, the land of their forefathers, the promised land. No such biblical injunction attached to Israel's hold on the Golan.

A peace agreement with Syria required the negotiation of water rights, effective early warning systems, a demilitarized Golan, and

---

* In one conversation with Christopher in 1994, Asad actually referred to Jerusalem as Israel's capital.

other security arrangements. A peace with the Palestinians required taking back what these politically potent Israelis had come to regard as their birthright. While Israeli settlers would have to be evacuated from the Golan under an agreement that ceded control there back to the Syrians, they were mostly pragmatic farmers who voted for the Labor Party—they could be compensated and relocated. The West Bank settlers were led by people passionately committed to resettling the biblical holy land. They would not be bought off easily with compensation.

Moreover, peace with Syria would neutralize the last hostile Arab army on Israel's borders. The balance of power would then shift decisively toward the peace camp in the Arab world. Iraq and Iran and any other state in the region that remained hostile to U.S. interests would find themselves isolated.

If the strategic benefits to the United States were clear, could we assume that Asad was serious about peacemaking? We knew that he calculated the balance of power like a computer. By the end of the 1980s, he had concluded that his Soviet patron was no longer reliable—the Russians had already refused to supply Syria with advanced weapons systems. After Saddam Hussein, Asad's archrival, invaded Kuwait in 1990, the Syrian leader had seized the moment to realign with the American-led camp. Once Kuwait had been liberated, Saddam's army had been destroyed, and the Soviet Union had collapsed, Asad understood that the balance of power had tipped decisively in America's favor. He could no longer hope to wield the threat of Soviet intervention to deter Israel's use of its superior military capabilities. His urgent priority was to build a relationship with the United States that would give it an interest in restraining Israel. And the only way to achieve that was by engaging in the peace process with Israel, which is what he did when President George H. W. Bush invited Syria to send a negotiating delegation to the Madrid Peace Conference in October 1991.

The negotiations with Israel under the Madrid auspices had gone nowhere until the advent of the Rabin government, which in October 1992, signaled its willingness to consider a territorial withdrawal from Syrian territory. The Syrian negotiators had responded by proposing a draft declaration of principles for an Israeli-Syrian peace agreement. Although the game still had nine innings and extra ones to run, the Syrians and Israelis were at least in the same ballpark, which was much more than could be said for the Palestinians. And in the Middle East context that gave us reason to believe that an agreement was possible. Given the prevailing circumstances back then, it was a proposition clearly worth testing.

ALTHOUGH IT WAS my job to see that the bureaucracy implemented the president's will, I agreed with his assessment that we should focus on Syria first and was impressed that he would so readily commit American troops to a Golan deployment. While I harbored an idealist's desire to bring peace to the Middle East, my upbringing in Australia inclined me to approach it with a realist's mind-set. As a Western outpost in an Asian arena, Australia exists in a strategic environment. Strategic thinkers had heavily influenced my higher education there. I was first drawn to the Middle East through my Jewish identity and connection to Israel. But to this day, it also holds an intellectual fascination, precisely because the interplay of power politics is at its most complex there. Kissinger, Sadat, and Rabin had long been my heroes because of their ability to manipulate those interactions in their efforts to settle the Arab-Israeli conflict. Trying to approach the problem with a similar strategic methodology, "Syria First" became my conviction.

Warren Christopher was also comfortable with this priority. A shy, punctilious lawyer with an iron will, he preferred manipulating the legal language of a draft treaty to massaging the egos of complicated Middle Eastern potentates. So he was happier taking on the Syrians at their own game of legalistic interpretation of U.N. Security Council resolutions than coping with the complaints of powerless Palestinian negotiators. Later he developed such a strong aversion to Arafat's manipulative manner that he insisted Dennis Ross deal with him on substantive matters.

At the outset of the Clinton administration, Dennis was not a significant player. He had been George H. W. Bush's foreign policy adviser in his first presidential campaign and Jim Baker's right-hand man in the second, and was supposedly transitioning out of the government (to take my job at the Washington Institute). Six months later, in a quiet coup, Christopher would appoint him the Special Middle East Coordinator (SMEC) with overall responsibility for the peace process. This was a considerable political feat, testimony to Dennis's political skills and to the wisdom of Clinton and Christopher in understanding the importance of continuity.* Dennis had been educated at the University of California at Los Angeles in the ways of the Middle East by one of its greatest American experts, Malcolm Kerr.† We had become friends when he worked on the Middle East in the Reagan White House.

Dennis tended to be tactical rather than strategic in his approach. His apprenticeship under Secretary of State James Baker had taught him about the importance of timing and leverage. I would marvel at the way he could always come up with another step in his process-driven game plan. And with simultaneous negotiations with Syria, Lebanon, Jordan, and the Palestinians, this was particularly important, since progress in one negotiation could prompt progress in another. If the Israeli-Syrian negotiation showed promise, Dennis would pursue it but he had no particular preference for it.

In Washington, no policy decision goes uncontested, not even one driven by a presidential decision and supported by the secretary of state. While Dennis was not totally convinced the approach was the right one, two other players in the peace team, Daniel Kurtzer and Aaron Miller, felt that it was clearly the wrong one. Kurtzer, an Orthodox Jew and graduate of Yeshiva University in New York, served initially as the deputy for the negotiations in the State Department's Near Eastern Bureau. Miller, also Jewish, had worked on the peace process for Dennis under James Baker. He would subsequently become Dennis's deputy in the SMEC office. Miller and Kurtzer felt keenly that the United States could not hope to resolve the Arab-Israeli conflict unless it treated the "core" Israeli-Palestinian problem first.

Dan would soon leave the peace team in frustration when Dennis was given control. Aaron, however, would push his view for the next eight years. He would eventually be joined in his approach by Robert Malley, also Jewish. The son of a French journalist and intellectual who maintained close relations with the Palestinians, Malley handled the peace process in the NSC during Clinton's second term.

Partisans on each side of the Arab-Israeli conflict tend to caricature the State Department either as the preserve of "Arabists" who view Israel as a liability and want to pressure it to make concessions to the

---

* Contrast this with Bush and Powell, who either dismissed or sidelined everybody who had worked on Clinton's peace team.
† Kerr later became President of the American University of Beirut, where he was killed by some of the very people he had spent his life trying to understand and help.

Arabs, or as controlled by "Zionists" who care only for Israel's interests and follow the dictates of its leadership. Those who believed the latter, including much of the Arab world, were quick to focus on the fact that all the members of Clinton's peace team were Jewish; reflecting this point of view, one particularly acerbic Arab journalist labeled us "the five rabbis." The fact that I had begun my Washington career eleven years earlier working at the American Israel Public Affairs Committee (AIPAC, often referred to as "the Israel Lobby") only reinforced the image in much of the Arab world and among pro-Arab Americans that Clinton's policy had been taken over by a Jewish cabal. On the other side of the partisan divide, some pro-Israelis considered our Jewishness a liability since they believed it would lead us to bend over backward to befriend the Arabs in an effort to avoid the charge of dual loyalty.

Behind that stereotyping lay the reality that our Jewish identities generated a deep desire in all of us to make peace since we all believed that Israel's security depended on ending the conflict with its Arab neighbors and that American interests would be well served by doing so. But we were deeply divided about the best way to achieve that peace. And that division was deepened when Dennis, recognizing we had an image problem, promoted Gamal Helal, the State Department's Egyptian-American translator, to the position of his senior adviser. Like Aaron and Rob, Gamal also was convinced of the need to focus on the Palestinian issue and developed very close relations with some of them.

IN RETROSPECT, THE president's decision to focus on Syria first, hoping it would lead to a wider rapprochement, proved to be an accurate strategic assessment but it was not sufficiently sensitive to how local politics in the Middle East could affect an approach designed in Washington. The horizons and focus of superpowers and smaller powers are inevitably divergent no matter how much they might have in common. As a distant superpower, the United States has a broader perspective and will tend to have a less intense interest in a particular issue than Middle Eastern players who can be affected in much more direct and significant ways. While Clinton's approach was Syria-centric, he discovered the regional players were actually preoccupied with the Palestinians.

This turned out to be as true for Israel as it was for the Arabs, for whom the Palestinian cause had been a dominant factor in their politics for decades. As a strategic thinker Rabin agreed with our approach, but as an Israeli politician he could not ignore his public opinion, which in early 1993 strongly believed that reaching an agreement with the Palestinians in the troublesome and seething West Bank and Gaza should be the top priority.

Leading up to the June 1992 elections, Rabin had declared he would never come down from the Golan but that he would solve the problem in the West Bank and Gaza with an agreement that would grant the Palestinians substantial autonomy within nine months of taking office. This was an ambitious and politically dangerous deadline. By the time Clinton entered the White House in January 1993, Rabin had only three months left to fulfill his campaign pledge. When he paid his first visit to the Clinton White House, we were eager to hear how he planned to reconcile these competing approaches.

During official visits to Washington, with the whole world watching, the leaders confer according to a well-structured agenda coordinated in advance by their staffs. However, politics in the Middle East are personal. All the Arab leaders are autocrats, and many of them depend on a cult of personality to enhance their legitimacy. The Israeli prime minister wields immense personal authority, too. They all inhabit a dangerous neighborhood which at times requires them to make life-and-death decisions. They depend heavily on their personal relationships and none more than their friendship with the president of the United States. Thus, given the infrequency of opportunities to meet, the official visits to Washington take on a special importance, particularly in the first year of a new presidency.*

According to well-established protocol, one of the first visitors in a new administration is the Israeli prime minister, a tradition reflecting the special nature of the U.S.-Israel relationship and Israel's political weight in Washington. He is usually followed over the next few months by the Egyptian president and the monarchs of Jordan and Saudi Arabia.

Clinton's aides had decided early on that his White House would be austere, a reflection of his determination to distinguish his presidency from what they viewed as the profligate times of the Reagan-Bush

---

* It was a sign of how badly George W. Bush had alienated America's major Arab allies that only King Abdullah of Jordan would agree to visit him in Washington during his second term.

years. Rabin, Mubarak, and King Hussein were therefore invited for working visits, rather than state visits with all their pomp, ceremony, and expensive official dinners.

It had become standard practice for the secretary of state to visit each leader in advance to prepare for the meeting with the president. In this case, Christopher and his aides went to see Rabin at the Westin Grand Hotel in downtown Washington, D.C., expecting to discuss Syria. Instead, Rabin wanted to float an idea for invigorating negotiations with the Palestinians. He suggested to Christopher that the United States propose adding Faisal Husseini to the Palestinian negotiating delegation as its official head. Since Husseini had independent legitimacy as the leader of Jerusalem's Palestinians, Rabin thought this might enable the Palestinian delegation to reject Arafat's leadership and strike a deal on autonomy before Rabin's political deadline expired. Rabin insisted the proposal could not come from him because the Likud opposition in Israel would then attack him for making a concession on Jerusalem, the issue of greatest sensitivity to Israelis. Christopher eagerly embraced Rabin's idea.*

In Rabin's penchant for analysis, he resembled a scientist, carefully observing the reaction to an experiment. In this case, he was trying to test a hypothesis that he had developed during the first intifada when, as Israel's defense minister, he had to respond to the stone-wielding *shabab* (Palestinian youths). Rabin viewed the uprising as a sign that the inhabitants of the Palestinian territories were prepared to take matters into their own hands and not wait for Arafat in Tunis to issue orders. So for the first time, but by no means the last, the Clinton administration took an Israeli idea and turned it into an American proposal to make it more palatable to the Arabs.

Even as Rabin pursued this experiment, he revealed his doubts about the likelihood of its success. This came in an unusual format: a breakfast meeting with the American peace team in which, with a characteristic wave of his right arm, he dismissed the very Palestinian

---

* Rabin's predecessor, Yitzhak Shamir, had excluded Faisal Husseini from the Palestinian delegation at Madrid. But we were already treating Husseini as its de facto head. The president had taken the unusual step of including him in the list of Arab leaders to whom he wrote, at the beginning of his administration, to express his commitment to peacemaking. Ironically, Husseini was the son of Abdel Qader al-Husseini, the leader of Palestinian irregular forces in the 1948 War of Independence. Rabin had responsibility for breaking the siege of Jerusalem in that war and his forces had fought and killed Husseini's father.

delegation he was hoping to empower. "They don't make the decisions. . . . I start to think that Arafat decided to foil the negotiations by all means."

Sam Lewis, the sage former longtime ambassador to Israel who had become head of Christopher's Policy Planning Staff, suggested that the obvious solution to this was for Rabin to talk to Yasser Arafat directly. Rabin surprised us by indicating that he had already considered the proposition. The problem, he argued, was that he could only offer Arafat an interim agreement that would empower the "insiders" at his expense. "I can't meet his requirement for a Palestinian state," he declared.

It would take only two months for Rabin to find that his ploy to boost the authority of the Palestinian negotiating delegation had failed. Husseini proved too scared to come to Washington for the negotiations, preferring to wait with Arafat in Tunis to hear the delegation's reports. With his political clock ticking, Rabin would decide instead to test directly whether Arafat would be willing to defer his demand for statehood. Perhaps because he was apparently only thinking about dealing with Arafat at the time he came to Washington, he did not bother to mention it in his meeting with Clinton.

The two leaders instead spoke in grand historical terms about the importance of peace with Syria. Clinton was immediately drawn in by Rabin's analytical approach. Rabin for his part had been impressed by Clinton's empathy for Israel and his intense interest in Rabin's political circumstances. The prime minister explained that the Israeli people had given him a mandate to take risks for peace. Clinton responded, "If you're going to do that, my role is to help you minimize those risks." He echoed that in his public remarks. The two men had quickly and easily reached a simple but profound pact.

Clinton, however, needed to know how far Rabin was prepared to go in helping with his Syria-first strategy. He reserved his question for their one-on-one meeting: "Do you believe that it will be possible to achieve a peace agreement with Syria without full Israeli withdrawal from the Golan Heights?" the president asked. Rabin gave an uncomplicated response: "No."

Rabin argued, however, that his people would only support full withdrawal if they felt Asad was genuinely interested in peace with Israel. So he needed Asad to do something akin to what Sadat did in journeying to Jerusalem to demonstrate his commitment to peace. He also emphasized that the Syrian agreement would have to "stand on its own feet" and not be linked to whatever might happen on the Palestinian track.

The president responded that the United States would be prepared to guarantee the peace agreement by inserting a brigade of American troops on the Golan. Rabin acknowledged the dramatic offer in his backhanded way: "I know it can't be done without U.S. forces, but I hate the idea."

Clinton then laid out a hypothetical question to Rabin: "If you have adequate security arrangements as you have in the Sinai—backed up by American forces—if you have a genuine Syrian offer of peace, and if the agreement stands alone, would Israel then be prepared to withdraw fully from the Golan?" "I don't exclude the possibility," Rabin said.

From that point in March 1993, Clinton knew that if Asad was ready for peace, Rabin was ready to come down from the Golan Heights. It would prove to be the best-kept secret in Washington, only revealed after Rabin's assassination. Our Syria-first strategy could now be pursued in earnest.

The two leaders joined their delegations in the Cabinet Room. I asked the president as he walked past me, "How did we do?" He gave me a thumbs-up sign, bit on his lip, and said, "We did well."

2

Dual Containment

Although Bill Clinton had decided to make peacemaking his priority, he knew he could not ignore the other dynamics in the region. The fact that Israel's Arab neighbors were willing to negotiate peace was linked directly to the liberation of Kuwait and the destruction of Saddam Hussein's army. But Saddam had not disappeared, and Iran with its aggressive clerical regime was attempting to destabilize the Arab leaders Clinton was depending on. Iraq's and Iran's hostility to peacemaking could jeopardize his whole effort. Clinton's choices were straightforward: he could try to overthrow the Iraqi and Iranian regimes, contain them, or engage with them.

George H. W. Bush's decision in February 1991 to leave Saddam's regime in place, even though American troops had cornered the Iraqi army with over 700,000 coalition forces in a position to demand Saddam Hussein's surrender, would have dramatic consequences for Iraqis and Americans alike. When Bill Clinton assumed office, those troops had already been withdrawn, replaced by Security Council resolutions that mandated comprehensive sanctions and U.N. weapons inspections. These were supposed to constitute a "cage" in which Saddam would be confined until he gave up his weapons of mass destruction. This containment strategy enabled Saddam to regain his equilibrium and consolidate his grip on power, but the sanctions kept his regime weak and preoccupied with internal strife and economic troubles. Meanwhile, the U.N. weapons inspectors were destroying huge arsenals of Iraq's chemical weapons and discovering large-scale nuclear facilities.

By the end of the George H. W. Bush administration, however, Saddam had started rattling the cage. In December 1992, Iraq began challenging coalition aircraft policing a no-fly zone established south of the 32nd parallel.* Days before Clinton entered office in January 1993, American, British, and French aircraft had launched punishing retaliatory strikes.

Although Clinton publicly supported Bush's decision to hit Saddam hard, in his first postelection foreign policy interview, with Thomas L. Friedman of the *New York Times*, the president-elect signaled a willingness to change policy. "If [Saddam] wants a different relationship with the United States and the United Nations," he said, "all he has to do is change his behavior." This statement came as a shock to the president's foreign policy advisers. When we had briefed Clinton during the campaign, he had taken a very hard line.†

Within twenty-four hours, Sandy Berger had flown to Little Rock to talk to the president-elect, after which Clinton stated forcefully at a news conference that he had "no intention of normalizing relations" with Saddam and was "astonished" that such a conclusion could have been drawn from what he had told the *New York Times*.

Clinton had revealed an ambivalence he would retain about using force to contain Saddam. He certainly appreciated the domestic political advantages of being tough on Saddam but he did not want the early days of his administration to be consumed by a confrontation with Iraq. He had pledged to the American people that he would concentrate on righting the economy at home; abroad, he planned to reshape the post–Cold War order through multilateral cooperation rather than unilateral policing actions.

But there was a deeper source of ambivalence. Clinton believed that no differences were so profound that reasonable people working together could not resolve them. As he noted in the *Times* interview, if Saddam were "sitting here on the couch, I would further the change in his behavior." This instinct for dialogue, even with the worst of the world's leaders, however, was counteracted by his desire to demonstrate his toughness as president. As a man who had not served in the military and who had been accused of dodging the Vietnam draft, he

---

* The southern no-fly zone was instituted to provide a measure of protection for Iraqi Shiites in southern Iraq who were being brutally suppressed by Saddam's forces.
† Tony Lake, Sandy Berger, and I had flown down to New Orleans to brief Clinton at one of his campaign stops on policy toward Iraq and Iran. I had argued that both nations were hostile to our interests and we should therefore work to contain them while we pressed ahead with Arab-Israeli peacemaking. Clinton had responded that containing them was not a tough enough policy. We had to find a way to change their behavior or change the regimes, he said.

needed to show that he would not shrink from using force when necessary. Clinton feared that America's adversaries would try to test him early on, much as Khrushchev had tested John F. Kennedy's resolve by attempting to place nuclear missiles in Cuba.

Through much of his two terms as president, when Saddam challenged Clinton with aggressive moves, he would respond with punitive force. But for most of the time, Clinton was content to keep Saddam contained in the hope that the pressure of sanctions and some covert action would eventually change his behavior or topple his regime.

Clinton had a similar attitude to the clerical revolutionaries in Iran. Their regime had survived defeat in an eight-year war with Iraq and the passing of its supreme leader, Ayatollah Khomeini. Tehran's unremitting hostility to America as the "Great Satan" rendered engagement an unrealistic option at the beginning of the Clinton administration. Only a handful of romantic dreamers believed that the regime could be overthrown. Containment was our only realistic option. This was particularly the case since the Bush administration had tried a benign approach, offering to reward constructive behavior by indicating to the Iranians that, in the words of President Bush, "goodwill begets goodwill." But the Iranians had spurned this offer.

Nevertheless, true to the instincts Clinton had revealed in that pre-incumbent *New York Times* interview, when the opportunity arose to engage leaders of rogue states, Clinton was quick to choose that option. He had already decided on that path in the case of the Syrian dictator. When Rabin embraced Arafat, Clinton would be quick to take on the challenge of reforming that rogue, too. Even Muammar Qadhafi, when he demonstrated in 1998, a desire to forsake terrorism, became a candidate for transformation into a constructive member of the international community. When Iranians elected a reformist president at the beginning of Clinton's second term, Clinton moved quickly to engage. The notable exception was Saddam Hussein.

CLINTON'S IMMEDIATE CHALLENGE was to develop an approach to protecting American interests in the Gulf that would bolster his peacemaking priorities in the Arab-Israeli arena. The traditional U.S. approach pursued over the previous three decades had proved to be a miserable failure. Geostrategic calculations had seemed to require a realist's deployment of balance of power diplomacy. The Gulf region contained 65 percent of the world's proven oil reserves. Given their size, populations, and military strength, Iraq and Iran dominated a host of weaker, oil-rich Arab states—Saudi Arabia, Kuwait, Bahrain, the United Arab Emirates, Qatar, and Oman—that were incapable of protecting themselves from these stronger neighbors. The United States had long identified a vital strategic interest in protecting the free flow of oil from these weaker states, which fed the Western and Asian economies. To protect that vital interest, the United States needed to prevent each of the two stronger regional powers from achieving a hegemonic position in the Gulf that would enable it to dictate the policies of the lesser states.

One way to achieve this would have been to base American forces in the weaker states. However, prior to Saddam's invasion of Kuwait, these Gulf Cooperation Council (GCC) states were reluctant to host U.S. forces.* So successive administrations had relied on the more moderate regional power to counterbalance the more radical one and in that way protect the weaker states.

In the days of Shah Reza Pahlavi, this maxim translated into depending on Iran's power to balance Iraq's. The Shah may have been a corrupt and autocratic ruler to his people, but he was one of the "twin pillars" on which the United States based its strategic position in the region (oil-rich Saudi Arabia was the other one). Given Iran's military capabilities (enhanced by lucrative sales of American weapons systems), and its good relations with moderate Arab regimes across the Gulf, the United States was able to depend on Iran to maintain stability through the first half of the 1970s without much difficulty.

However, Washington became so committed to the Shah that it lost sight of his shortcomings, misjudged the growing discontent among his people, and remained oblivious to the potent alliance building between a radicalized Shiite clergy and the bazaar merchants who had the capability to finance the revolution. The Carter administration recognized the problem too late. Once the Shah was swept away in January 1979, it was inevitable that the revolution would turn on the United States, his best friend. The anti-Americanism of the Iranian revolution manifested itself both in the taking of American hostages

---

* The Gulf Cooperation Council (GCC) comprised Saudi Arabia, Kuwait, the United Arab Emirates, Bahrain, Qatar, and Oman. Before Saddam invaded Kuwait, only Bahrain was prepared to host the U.S. Navy, which maintained its Naval Forces Central Command headquarters there. Oman provided access to the U.S. Air Force for its B-52 bombers.

and in efforts to export the Shiite Islamic revolution to Sunni Arab states across the Gulf that were aligned with the United States.

The Khomeini regime, however, chose Iraq as the prime target for spreading its Islamic revolution.* Saddam, meanwhile, saw in the turmoil left by the Iranian revolution an opportunity to extend his influence to Iran while projecting himself as the protector of the lesser Arab states. There was little to restrain the war dynamic that these competing expansionist ambitions generated.

The Iran-Iraq War broke out in September 1980 and lasted for eight years. The Reagan administration's realists calculated that war between the two regional powers would keep them preoccupied and debilitate their military power, leaving both little time or energy to prey on their weaker neighbors. But this balance of power approach required the United States to back the losing side to ensure that neither emerged victorious. Accordingly, the Reagan administration "tilted" to Iraq when the Iranians succeeded in repulsing Saddam's invasion and laid siege to Basra, Iraq's second-largest city. Despite the fact that Baghdad was a Soviet ally, Reagan simply removed Iraq from the State Department's terrorism list in order to provide Saddam with critical intelligence data. By the end of the war, this intelligence relationship had blossomed into a full-fledged liaison arrangement. Washington also provided Saddam with access to U.S. "dual use" technology and billions of dollars of credit to purchase American agricultural products so he could spend his oil revenues on arms from the United States and its allies.

The Reagan administration was even prepared to overlook an Iraqi attack on an American frigate that killed thirty-seven sailors, and Saddam's use of chemical weapons against the Kurds in northern Iraq, which killed some two hundred thousand of them and led to the forcible resettlement of 1.5 million others. The Reagan administration also found itself steadily dragged into a combatant role as its protection of Kuwaiti oil tankers led to clashes with the Iranian navy.

With American backing, Iraq eventually prevailed over Iran, devastating its army, destroying much of its heavy equipment, and killing more than 300,000 of its soldiers. Saddam emerged with the largest

---

* The Shiite majority in Iraq had been brutally suppressed by Saddam Hussein. Moreover, six of the holiest Shiite shrines were on Iraqi territory. And, because of Iraq's influence as a regional Arab power, an Islamic revolution there could easily have a domino effect throughout the Gulf.

army in the Middle East: 1.2 million soldiers equipped with ballistic missiles and weapons of mass destruction.

A balance of power strategy would now have required the United States to tilt back toward Iran. Yet to turn American policy around would have necessitated engaging with an Iranian regime that remained deeply antagonistic and abandoning an Iraqi regime that was selling the United States discounted oil, cooperating with our Arab allies, supposedly toning down its hostility to Israel, and using U.S. government supplied credits to purchase American agricultural goods. Instead, the "realists" in George H. W. Bush's administration, which included Richard Cheney (then secretary of defense), decided in 1989 to try to moderate Iraqi behavior through the provision of additional agricultural credits. Even when it was revealed that Iraq had used these credits illegally to purchase weapons and proscribed technology, Washington still extended Baghdad another $1 billion worth. The Bush administration overlooked these and other Iraqi transgressions in the belief that Saddam was at heart a pragmatist who could be tamed.

Easier said than done. It didn't take long for the supposed protector of the Gulf Arab states to turn on them, consuming Kuwait in August 1990 like a snake in one quick gulp. This presented a far greater threat to American strategic interests in the free flow of oil than revolutionary Iran had ever posed. To right the balance, Bush had to dispatch 500,000 troops to liberate Kuwait and destroy much of Saddam's army. But then, as noted earlier, Bush made another strategic miscalculation. Because he feared the consequences of occupying an Arab capital, he left Saddam in place, in the assumption that the Iraqi people would get rid of him without American help. Inexplicably, Saddam was allowed to use his army helicopters to help suppress a Shiite uprising in southern Iraq after Bush had called on the Iraqi people to rise up against the dictator. Saddam's loyalists slaughtered some sixty thousand Iraqi Shiites while American forces looked on. From there, Saddam's surviving Republican Guard divisions moved north against the Iraqi Kurds, killing some twenty thousand of them and forcing some 2 million to flee to the border with Turkey.

Little wonder, then, that by the time President Clinton took office, the idea of playing one regional power off against the other to maintain a stable equilibrium in the Gulf was no longer credible. But it was also no longer necessary: the Iran-Iraq War had seriously weakened

Iran; the Gulf War had all but destroyed Iraq's army; and the collapse of the Soviet Union had left the United States as the dominant super-power in the Middle East. Clinton no longer needed to play a balance of power game.

CLINTON TASKED TONY Lake with developing a new strategy. In the interagency discussions that I chaired on his behalf, I was surprised to find that these experiences had traumatized the bureaucracy in Washington. Disliking open-ended commitments that dissipated budgets and wore out standing forces, the Joint Chiefs proposed that Clinton engage in a dialogue with Saddam if he demonstrated some signs of good faith. Conversely, the civilian side of the Pentagon, under Secretary of Defense Les Aspin, favored an approach in which the United States would ratchet up the pressure on Saddam each time he challenged us, and deploy force to ensure that he was worse off both militarily and politically.

The CIA was comfortable with this harder-line approach. After the Gulf War, President Bush had authorized them to conduct a covert campaign to overthrow Saddam. But they had no confidence that he would be toppled anytime soon. They had seen how ruthlessly effective he had been in reestablishing his control and they had a realistic view of their own capability to get rid of him. They sought as much pressure as possible from sanctions and the use of force to complement their coup-making efforts. As their Middle East chief explained it to me, it was like bending a pencil by putting pressure on both ends— you could not predict exactly when it would snap, but at some point you could be certain it would.

The State Department was still living under the shadow of the perception that April Glaspie, the U.S. ambassador in Iraq before the war had failed to stand up to Saddam, and State's Near Eastern bureau, represented by Mark Parris, its principal deputy assistant secretary, wanted to show toughness.* He preferred to pursue regime change, but the more the United States emphasized regime change, Parris argued, the less support we could hope to garner from the international com-

---

* In a rare personal audience with Saddam, Glaspie had told him, "we have no opinion on the Arab-Arab conflicts, like your border disagreement with Kuwait." (Glaspie maintains that her statement related clearly, and only, to peaceful conflict resolution.)

munity, since many governments were wary of endorsing America's impulse to change regimes not to its liking—they feared that the principle might one day be applied to them.

Moreover, if the intention was to contain Saddam, Parris pointed out that the U.N. resolutions were a flawed instrument for doing so, since they specified that the sanctions would be lifted when he complied with their requirements. Mark therefore proposed that we deemphasize the intention to overthrow Saddam, leaving that to the CIA's covert program. Instead, at the United Nations we would seek to raise the barrier for compliance as high as possible, invoking the resolutions' requirement that Saddam end the repression of the Iraqi people. There was no way he was going to do that.

In the course of the strategic review, State's Iraq experts voiced real concern about the possible fragmentation of Iraq, a view shared by the other agencies. If the Iraqi people managed to overthrow the central authority, Shiites and Kurds could well take their revenge on their Sunni oppressors. Then the Iranians might intervene, raising the specter again of Iranian-Shiite dominance in southern Iraq, which would threaten Kuwait and Saudi Arabia. In other words, the same argument that had been used to justify backing Saddam during the Iran-Iraq War and to allow him to suppress Iraq's Shia after the Gulf War, was invoked again to oppose backing any uprising by the Iraqi people. When it came to choosing between supporting the human rights of the Iraqi people and preventing the spread of Iranian influence to the Arab side of the Gulf, U.S. policy makers opted repeatedly for the latter, honoring a tradition of favoring stability over freedom. George W. Bush chose later to upend that practice, only to return to it at the end of his administration; Clinton would adhere to it from the beginning of his. Today, after Saddam's toppling and the spread of Iranian influence to Iraq during the ensuing chaos and bloodshed, one can better understand Clinton's caution.

The options that emerged from this interagency discussion were clear-cut: engage Saddam; try to overthrow him through a coup; or contain him through sanctions and the occasional resort to force. At the NSC staff level, we favored this latter approach, dubbing it "aggressive containment." We accepted the CIA's assessment that if we pressed Saddam's regime hard enough, it would eventually collapse.

The policy-making process required the NSC principals—Lake,

Aspin, Christopher, Powell, Fuerth, and Woolsey—to review the options and agree on a policy to recommend to the president. There was little contention in their meetings in February 1993.

The principals first decided to recommend that Clinton reauthorize the "findings" that President Bush had signed directing the CIA to seek the overthrow of Saddam Hussein. The Agency wanted to promote an officer-led coup that would avoid all the problems involved in sparking an insurrection. Tony Lake, the national security adviser, was concerned that the CIA not involve the Clinton administration in a "Bay of Pigs" operation, in which the president would be forced to choose between intervening militarily once the coup plotters found themselves in difficulty, or abandoning them to their fate at the hands of Saddam. Any requests for military support, Lake insisted, would have to be brought to the White House before any commitments were made.

The principals then addressed the overt policy options. Colin Powell, chairman of the Joint Chiefs, in a harbinger of the position he would adopt as secretary of state in the second Bush administration, described Saddam as "a toothache" that we could live with. The other principals dwelled on the dangers of Iraqi disintegration. They had already begun to grapple with the problems in Bosnia generated by the disintegration of Yugoslavia and were loath to contemplate the same issues of intervention if Iraq started coming apart at the seams. So they settled for the middle way: a covert coup effort and an overt policy of "aggressive containment." In its public posture, the Clinton administration would clothe its policy in international legitimacy by demanding Saddam's full compliance with all U.N. Security Council resolutions.

Consistent with this policy, the principals also decided to provide political support for the Iraqi National Congress, an opposition group led by Ahmed Chalabi, and to launch an effort to bring Saddam to justice through an Iraqi War Crimes Tribunal. The no-fly zones in northern and southern Iraq would be maintained to provide a modicum of protection to the Kurds and Shia respectively. Clinton would also continue assistance to the Kurds to enable them to survive (and eventually prosper) in the now autonomous regions of northern Iraq.

The policy of containment of the Soviet Union, first articulated by George Kennan, was based on the idea that the Soviet system was rotten to the core and would collapse of its own weight if the United States could only keep the pressure on it. Containment of Iraq was based on a similar calculation. But the Clinton administration's critical assumption was that the combination of sanctions and covert operations would force the collapse of Saddam's regime in five years, not the five decades that it took for the Soviet Union to collapse. And that would prove to be a fatally flawed judgment about the Iraqi dictator's staying power.

THE POLICY OPTIONS toward Iran were more limited. In the interagency discussions, a consensus quickly emerged that Iran was the archetype of a hostile, rogue regime—the most important state sponsor of militant Islamic terrorism. The evidence was clear: active subversion of pro-American governments across the Arab world; assassination of Iranian dissidents abroad; and the surveillance of Americans, presumably for similar treatment. Ayatollah Khomeini had issued a fatwa which commanded the faithful to kill Salman Rushdie, the Indian Muslim whose sin was writing a novel about Islam that the mullahs considered blasphemous. Iran's treatment of women and religious minorities was egregious. In breach of its obligations as a signatory to the Nuclear Non-Proliferation Treaty, it was attempting to develop nuclear weapons and missile delivery systems and was expected to succeed by the end of the decade. It was also engaged in a conventional military buildup intended to make Iran the dominant regional power in the Gulf. And it was directly involved in sponsoring terrorist actions by Hezbollah and Palestine Islamic Jihad designed to subvert the Arab-Israeli peace process.

Overthrow was not a serious option. The revolution had succeeded in conferring on the clerical regime a legitimacy that nobody in Iran seemed willing or able to challenge. There was no organized opposition and the regime maintained the formidable Revolutionary Guards to suppress all protest. The United States no longer had any intelligence assets in the country, so there was no covert option to consider. Yet the Clinton administration needed to develop an effective method for persuading Iran to modify its bad behavior, including its subversion of the Middle East peace process.

Our interagency review considered three options: positive incentives, sanctions and isolation, or military action. The first suggestion was immediately eliminated—the consensus view was that the regime had too strong an animus toward the United States. Military action, however, would bring retaliation—Iran could disrupt the flow of oil from the Gulf and might authorize terrorist attacks on American targets. The Iranians had established a formidable international terrorist network using the combined capabilities of their intelligence services, the Iranian Revolutionary Guard Corps, and the international branch of Hezbollah.* The risks seemed too great and the benefits too uncertain.

Sanctions and isolation seemed the only logical way forward. However, unlike Saddam, the Iranian clerics had been careful to conceal their seditious activities across the Middle East. Consequently, U.N. sanctions were not available at the time as a lever to influence the regime's behavior. That would only come thirteen years later when evidence was found to declare Iran in breach of its obligations under the Non-Proliferation Treaty. And even then it proved difficult to forge a consensus among the Security Council's permanent members on a minimal set of punitive sanctions.

Clinton's advisers therefore decided that he should maintain the unilateral American sanctions that had already been imposed on Iran for its sponsorship of terrorism and work energetically to persuade our allies to avoid commercial dealings with Iran as long as it threatened our common interests. We would block loans to Iran by international organizations. We would press Russia, China, and our European allies to cease cooperating with Iran in nuclear energy and ballistic missile development. And we would attempt to curtail Iran's efforts to purchase conventional weapons that would tip the regional balance in its favor or threaten American forces deployed in the Gulf.

We recognized in adopting this approach that Iran's intentions were more threatening than its capabilities. Its economy was suffering from 20 to 30 percent inflation and 30 percent unemployment. It was some $5 billion in arrears on its short-term international debt repayments. It was in real need of American technology to maintain its existing oil fields or develop new ones. And, as far as could be established, it was still at least five years from attaining a medium-range ballistic missile capability and eight to ten years from developing a nuclear device.

However, unlike the containment of Iraq, which depended on U.N.

---

* Hezbollah had held American hostages in prolonged captivity in Lebanon and had carried out the 1992 terrorist attack on the Israeli embassy in Buenos Aires, which had killed twenty-nine people and wounded 242. They had hijacked TWA flight 847 in June 1985 and beaten and killed U.S. Navy diver Robert Stethem.

sanctions, the containment of Iran depended on the Clinton administration's ability to convince America's allies in Europe and Japan not to do business there. Since Iran was pursuing policies that were inimical to Western interests, not just American concerns, we felt we had at least as much chance of persuading our allies of the correctness of our approach as Iran had of splitting them off from us by offering lucrative contracts.

Dubbed "active containment," our policy also envisaged that, over time, elements in the regime would begin to argue that Iran's international isolation was too much of a burden. To try to speed that day, Clinton would offer to enter into an official dialogue with the government of Iran, an offer that was in itself designed to signal that he did not seek to overthrow the regime and that, if it were willing to moderate specific objectionable policies, he would be prepared to reciprocate by moderating U.S. sanctions.

Although President Clinton was briefed on the conclusions reached by the policy review process, he did not participate in any of these policy discussions. He did sign the covert action findings aimed at overthrowing Saddam and approved the National Security Decision Directives establishing the new policies toward Iraq and Iran, but I only became confident that he felt comfortable with the overall approach when, in a White House meeting in April 1993 with President Mubarak, he argued that we had to contain both Iraq and Iran.

POLICY PRONOUNCEMENTS ARE normally the preserve of the president or secretary of state; sometimes the national security adviser will do it; occasionally, their deputies will fill in for them. But it is rare for a lesser official to announce a new policy. Bruce Riedel, then my deputy for Gulf issues at the NSC, and I had written a speech outlining Clinton's new Middle Eastern strategy for Tony Lake to deliver to the annual symposium of the Washington Institute for Near East Policy, the Middle East think tank that I had helped establish. But as the appointed day came around, neither Lake nor Sandy Berger, his deputy, was available to deliver the speech. So the task fell to me.

A few days before, I had been talking to Elaine Sciolino, then chief diplomatic correspondent for the *New York Times*, and explained our policy of "aggressive containment" of Saddam and "active containment" of Iran. She suggested that it sounded like a policy of "parallel containment." The thought stayed with me and emerged in my speech as "dual containment." The speech, which was cleared by the State Department and the Pentagon, received little immediate attention, since the press assumed that if it were a major policy address, somebody more senior would have delivered it. But soon both the *New York Times* and the *Washington Post* reported that the Clinton administration had adopted a new policy of "dual containment" of Iraq and Iran; inadvertently, I had managed to brand Clinton's policy. Baghdad and Tehran promptly denounced it, and embassies sought briefings on it. Within a month, it seemed all of the Middle East was debating "dual containment." I had managed to combine critics who wanted Clinton to engage with Iran with those who wanted him to overthrow the regime in Iraq. "Dual containment" was denounced as a failure even before it had taken effect.

Not surprisingly, the Iraqi and Iranian regimes did not appreciate their new designations as rogues subject to American policies of isolation and containment. Iraq's foreign minister, in a letter to the U.N. secretary-general that was subsequently debated in the Security Council, denounced me as a Zionist who had taken control of U.S. foreign policy. The Iranian ayatollahs chose a more threatening route to express their displeasure.

As I outlined in the speech, the Clinton administration viewed the Middle East as finely balanced between two alternative futures: "one in which extremists, cloaked in religious or nationalist garb would hold sway across the region," and the other future "in which Israel, its Arab neighbors and the Palestinians would achieve an historic reconciliation."

Bill Clinton, I explained, had concluded that both the Iraqi and Iranian regimes were hostile to American interests in the region but with the United States now dominant in the Middle East he had rejected the bankrupt notion of relying on either one to balance the other. Instead, his administration would seek Iraq's full compliance with all the relevant Security Council resolutions and use pressure to modify Iran's hostility. I made clear that Clinton had no interest in reconciliation with Saddam; on the contrary, the administration would seek his indictment as a war criminal to demonstrate unequivocally that "the current regime in Iraq is . . . *irredeemable*." That word was deliberately deployed to end speculation that the president, despite subsequent denials, had signaled his real intentions toward Saddam when he had spoken to Thomas Friedman about a possible reconciliation.

Containing Iran, the speech noted, would be a more difficult undertaking. I laid out the program the principals had agreed on, emphasizing that "the Clinton administration was not opposed to Islamic government in Iran," only specific aspects of the regime's behavior. While Clinton would boycott the Iraqi regime, he was ready for an official dialogue with Iran. Although the speech emphasized the different approaches to Iraq and Iran, my use of the words *dual containment* created the false impression that we would deal with both rogue regimes in the same way.

What should at least have been clear from the explication of Clinton's policy was that dual containment was one branch of a broader strategy designed to generate a dramatic shift in the regional balance of power that we hoped would result from the achievement of a comprehensive Arab-Israeli peace. If Clinton succeeded in that primary objective, containment of Iraq and Iran would be rendered much more effective. An Israeli-Syrian peace would drive a wedge between Syria and Iran. Moreover, Iran's Hezbollah proxy in Lebanon would be neutralized by Syria's agreement to disarm it as a necessary requirement of the peace deal. Iraq would also find itself without regional friends if we could succeed in moving the Arab world toward peace with Israel.

In short, I argued, we hoped to take advantage of a symbiotic relationship between peacemaking and dual containment. The more we succeeded in brokering a comprehensive Arab-Israeli peace, the more isolated Iraq and Iran would become; the more effective we were in containing the destabilizing activities of these two rogue regimes, the easier it would be for Israel's Arab neighbors to make peace with the Jewish state. It was a neat and logical design.

What we failed to foresee was that a reverse symbiosis could also take hold. If Clinton failed at peacemaking, the rogue states would become less isolated and contained, and if he failed at dual containment, peacemaking would become that much more difficult.

3

"That's What Kings Do"

Dennis Ross and I were beginning to wonder why the motorcade wasn't moving. We had alighted from the secretary of state's Boeing 707, the same plane that, three decades earlier, had ferried President Kennedy's body back from Dallas to Washington. In December 1993, it had just brought Christopher and his peace team to Rabat, Morocco. We had dutifully followed the secretary of state down the obligatory red carpet, past the white-uniformed Moroccan honor guard, into the VIP lounge. We were now waiting in a lightly armored Chevy sedan, two cars behind the heavily armored black Cadillac holding Christopher and Marc Ginsberg, the U.S. ambassador to Morocco. As we sat there, the secretary's security detail became increasingly nervous. After fifteen minutes, the word was finally passed along on their communications net: "The man is not in his house." It seemed the king was not at the palace to receive the secretary of state.

Earlier that evening, as we departed Cairo, the State Department's advance staff had called the plane from Rabat to inform us that His Majesty had invited the secretary of state and his delegation to dine with him at the palace. I was salivating at the prospect of an exquisite Moroccan meal prepared by the royal kitchen. Christopher, a gourmet, should have been salivating, too. But he had developed an aversion to eating in the Arab world. His Middle Eastern trips were structured where possible to avoid staying overnight in any Arab capital. When that proved impossible, Christopher's secretary, Liz Lineberry, would bring canned soup from the plane and heat it for him in his hotel suite kitchenette. Instead, he made Jerusalem his base camp. He particularly savored meals at the Israeli prime minister's residence, where he would wax lyrical about Leah Rabin's home-style cooking. At one such dinner, Christopher made a toast to "Leah's beans," leading Shimon Peres, the foreign minister at the time, to respond: "Mr. Secretary, we have been praised for many things, but never our fine Israeli cuisine."

Moroccan cuisine was a different story. When Christopher heard the king's invitation, he immediately declined and despite our efforts to tempt him, he was immovable. Back-to-back meetings and jet lag had taken their toll. Already exhausted, Christopher had no interest in sitting through a laborious meal with another Arab potentate. This was bound to cause the king offense. The airport wait was just the first indication of the consequences.

MOROCCO IS AT the western extremity of the Arab world. Its diplomatic relations with the United States date back to 1786, when the Treaty of Marrakech was signed. It is a country known for a unique mix of African and Arab cultures that has produced a fine aesthetic sense manifested both in its decorative arts and cuisine.

King Hassan II had played a unique role in the peace process, hosting secret talks between Egyptian and Israeli envoys that paved the way for Sadat's historic visit to Jerusalem in 1977. After the signing of the Oslo Accords, he had invited Yitzhak Rabin to stop in Rabat on his way back from Washington for the first official visit by an Israeli prime minister. The king also maintained a special relationship with the 600,000-strong Moroccan Jewish community, most of whom now lived in Israel.

A visit to Morocco for a secretary of state whose mission was peacemaking was mandatory. But Christopher was always reluctant to add another Middle Eastern capital to his itinerary, and since Cairo, Jerusalem, Amman, and Damascus were compulsory stops and Riyadh next in line, Morocco usually got short shrift. This visit was to check the box.

After a half-hour, the motorcade eventually departed at a snail's pace, while we awaited word that the king was ready to receive the secretary of state. At the palace we were ushered into His Majesty's presence past courtiers wearing pointy bright yellow slippers and burgundy fezzes. Some of their heads were covered with hoods that were attached to the white cotton capes they draped on their shoulders, making them look like Moroccan-style Klansmen. The king, a slender, diminutive figure, received us in black velvet smoking jacket and matching slippers embroidered with gold monograms of the royal crest—hardly the appropriate protocol for such an official occasion. He gestured to the secretary to sit on his right at the head of a long boardroom table; he then sat down on an office version of his throne, an aqua leather desk chair with a gold-embossed crest, and lit a cigarette.

The American delegation took its seat on one side of the table and the king signaled to one of his assistants, who opened the heavy mahogany double doors to let in the king's delegation. First came his two adolescent sons, Crown Prince Mohamed and Prince Moulay. They were followed by the strangest assortment of advisers: a one-eyed general who had apparently left his eye patch at home; a foreign minister with one side of his face and torso rendered inactive by a stroke; an interior minister who was suffering a bad hair day and looked more like David Ben-Gurion than the much-feared suppressor of Moroccan dissent; and last in line, as his status required, André Azoulay, the king's Jewish adviser, elegantly outfitted in a French suit. One by one they literally groveled in front of the king, kissing his hand as he pushed them away with a dismissive gesture.

This did not improve Christopher's mood. He wasted no time on pleasantries. In order to justify his visit to Morocco at the end of a grueling trip that had taken him to six Middle Eastern capitals in seven days we had negotiated an understanding in advance with the Moroccans that would enable him to point to some concrete achievements from his visit—Washington bureaucrats call them "deliverables." By the time of the visit, Arafat and Rabin had already shaken hands on the White House lawn and the peace process was moving ahead. So it was agreed that Christopher would announce after his meeting with the king that Morocco was willing to establish direct flights between Tel Aviv and Casablanca and direct telephone and mail links with Israel. These were modest achievements but they signaled the thawing of relations between Israel and the broader Arab world following the signing of the Oslo Accords with the Palestinians.

Christopher told the king he was glad to be in Morocco and pleased to have the opportunity to announce the beginning of normalization of relations with Israel. The king gave him a sour look and then blew smoke from his expensive, hand-tailored cigarette across the table in Christopher's direction. Speaking in French though he knew English quite well, he embarked on a laborious discourse on the inappropriateness of an American official announcing in Rabat decisions that Moroccans were perfectly capable of announcing themselves. No meal, no announcement. As simple as that.

As we walked Christopher to his limousine in the palace parking lot, Dennis Ross and I apologized to him, explaining that the king's advisers had assured us that he wanted the secretary of state to announce and embrace Morocco's contribution to the peace process. The king had obviously changed his mind. The secretary of state just smiled, shrugged and said, "That's what kings do."

CHRISTOPHER'S SANGFROID IN the face of King Hassan's backtracking disguised a deeper disdain for the rulers of the Arab world. He was a quiet, mild-mannered gentleman, always impeccably attired, his salt-and-pepper hair carefully groomed. Christopher was a democrat of deep conviction. As a child growing up in the tiny town of Scranton, North Dakota, during the Depression, he had been exposed to human suffering, which had bred in him stoicism in the face of adversity and an antipathy toward ostentatious wealth. He had little time for despots and less respect for royalty. Neither his personality nor his predilections suited him well to the task of dealing with Arab leaders whose customs were impediments to the efficient conduct of American-style business.

Hospitality is at the heart of Arab culture. Every meeting begins with the ritual serving of coffee or tea. In Saudi Arabia and Jordan, tribesmen, their chests crossed with bulleted bandoliers, pour cardamom coffee from elaborate brass pots into small china cups. In Oman, the sultan accompanies it with a bowl of sticky, sweet jelly that the guest is required to scoop out with his fingers. In Algeria, guests are invited to partake of a *meshwe* in which they stand in front of a whole roasted lamb and pick at it with their fingers.

Things move more slowly in the Arab world. We would joke that *bukra* means *mañana* in Arabic, only with less urgency. Work hours are much shorter than in the West, leaving plenty of time for coffee, water pipes, and backgammon in the local cafes. And Arab leaders tend to have all the time in the world for meetings with important visitors.

Christopher, by contrast, approached meetings like a lawyer with too many clients. They were to last only for the time allotted and when it came close to that moment Chris would invariably look at his watch and start to wind up the conversation. This was particularly disconcerting to President Asad, who enjoyed taking circumlocutory excursions into history to make his point. Meetings with Asad usually lasted between three and five hours. Jim Baker called the combination of marathon meetings with rounds of coffee, tea, and lemonade "bladder diplomacy." Christopher wanted none of it. He also struggled in Saudi Arabia, where meetings not only were scheduled for double the usual time because translation back and forth from Arabic was necessary, but also rarely took place before midnight because the Saudi leaders worked at night and slept during the day. It was a deeply ingrained Bedouin habit from the pre-air-conditioning days in the desert kingdom. The effect was to disrupt Christopher's carefully protected timetable for sleep.

Bill Clinton, by contrast, was a perfect match for his Arab hosts. He craved personal contact. He enjoyed schmoozing for hours, if only his staff would let him. He rarely would go to sleep before 3 A.M. Where Christopher approached a problem with a lawyer's precision, Clinton approached it with all the nuance of a master politician. He was at home in the land of the veils, where things were never quite what they seemed, where a yes meant maybe and a maybe meant no and a straight answer was considered impolite. And of course, he loved food, of practically any description.

During his presidency, Clinton made four trips to the Middle East, more than any other American president—a reflection of his deep commitment to the transformation he was trying to effect there. But the president simply could not conduct the kind of shuttle diplomacy that the region had come to expect since Henry Kissinger first introduced it in 1973. Middle Eastern diplomacy was properly the responsibility of the secretary of state, and Christopher did not shrink from it. But the nature of his engagement with Arab leaders serves as a metaphor for the interaction between the United States and the Arab world.

The Arab environment is far harsher than the American land of opportunity. Before the oil boom of the 1970s filled the coffers of the Gulf Arabs with riches beyond the dreams of avarice, they eked out their lives in a harsh, desert environment, where a squabble over a well could become a tribal blood feud. Meanwhile, in the great capitals of the Arab world—Cairo, Damascus, and Baghdad—the people were ruled by a procession of autocrats, from pharaohs in ancient times, to Ottoman caliphs, to Arab kings appointed by British and French colonial offices, to military officers who took power by force. All of them maintained control through a patronage network that encouraged fealty, and a *mukhabarat* (intelligence) service that imposed it. Whether they were Bedouins from the desert or cosmopolitan Arabs from these large metropolises, their societies were deeply traditional and atavistic. Thus dignity, honor, respect, tribal loyalty, and revenge tended to be the values that dominated relations between people and between states, in contrast to the American values of freedom, equality, democracy, and the rule of law.

U.S. foreign policy, when it seeks to intervene in the affairs of other states and regions, is often inspired by an idealism that leads Americans to want to extend the bounteous beneficence they have experienced in their own lives to other people. But in the Middle East this do-good impulse is greeted with a cynicism that is the product of the Arab experience in competing for scarce resources in societies where opportunity is determined by tribal or family connections rather than on merit.

American good fortune has also bred a "can-do," problem-solving attitude to complex challenges. The prevailing assumption among Americans is that every problem has a solution. Among Arabs—and increasingly among Israelis, too—the prevailing assumption is that most Middle Eastern problems are too complex to lend themselves to ready, man-made solutions. And since authoritarian leaders who are detached from their people have always made the decisions, the average citizen tends to accept his or her fate rather than try to change it.

Americans know something of the history of the Middle East but they lack awareness of these disparities in culture and the complexities of local politics. We tend to approach the people there with an innocence and ignorance that can often be mistaken for arrogance and insensitivity. We know that they are not like us, but we imagine that they would want to be if they only had the chance. Christopher was an accomplished lawyer and experienced diplomat who had traveled the world. Clinton was a voracious reader of history and perhaps the most intelligent person to have inhabited the Oval Office. But how could they know or understand the intersecting influences of Arab culture, politics, and experience that determine the attitudes of one Arab leader to another and all of them toward the American superpower?

As Clinton and his peace team were exposed more to the ways of the Middle East, we became better at understanding the importance of pride, dignity, and the impact of local rivalries. On occasion we were even able to exploit these to our advantage. Still, time and again we would fail to anticipate the impact of our words or actions on the parochial concerns and calculations of the region's leaders. The innocence that is a hallmark of America's encounter with the Middle East would characterize Clinton's approach, too, notwithstanding the careful strategic calculations on which it was based. It was at heart a contest between American naïveté and Middle Eastern cynicism, and in the end the cynics won.

BILL CLINTON'S EFFORTS to end the Arab-Israeli conflict inevitably pitted him against the established order in the Arab world. Morocco's King Hassan was an important upholder of that status quo but its two principal custodians were Egypt's Hosni Mubarak and Saudi Arabia's King Fahd. As the leaders of the most populous and the wealthiest Arab states respectively, they wielded considerable influence in the region. However, both saw their survival as dependent on maintaining the status quo that Clinton intended to change.

On the surface both Mubarak and Fahd seemed to welcome Clinton's commitment to seek lasting peace. If the Arab-Israeli conflict escalated, as it had so often, it would inflame the passions of the Arab street and threaten their hold on power. Nevertheless, the Arab-Israeli conflict also served a useful purpose for them in that it deflected their publics from focusing on their failings as leaders, while ending the conflict would require them to stand up for compromises with Israel that would expose them to criticism. So what Mubarak and Fahd really wanted was a peace process that would attenuate the conflict but never quite resolve it. By the end of his administration, Clinton would come to recognize this reality. In the meantime, Egyptian and Saudi officials would always manage to convince us that the gap between their encouraging rhetoric and their disappointing support for peace was all a function of our inadequacies rather than theirs. If only we would press Israel or their Arab adversaries harder, they claimed, they would be able to do more to help us.

The desire to maintain the status quo also led Mubarak and Fahd to oppose the overthrow of the Iraqi and Iranian regimes. That is why both Mubarak and King Abdullah, Fahd's successor, warned George W. Bush against invading Iraq to topple Saddam and are now scrambling to deal with the destabilizing consequences for their own regimes of his decision to ignore them.

On the other hand, if left unfettered, Saddam and Ayatollah Ali Khamenei, who became Iran's supreme leader in 1989, could have destabilized the Arab status quo in even more threatening ways. Not surprisingly, then, on Christopher's first encounter with Mubarak and Fahd he found them eager to embrace the concept of "dual containment."

EGYPT IS THE largest and militarily most powerful Arab state. One in four Arabs is an Egyptian, but unlike most other Arab states, which have mixed ethnic and religious communities, Egypt has a homogeneous population of 70 million Sunni Muslims coexisting with only a small, ancient minority community of Coptic Christians. Unlike all the other Arab states, Egypt's borders have remained more or less intact for thousands of years, housing a proud and ancient civilization of extraordinary mathematical and engineering genius. Egypt is home to the oldest and most important Islamic educational institution, al-Azhar University, and its teachers, media, doctors, singers, and movie stars have had a profound influence on Arab life beyond Egypt's borders.

Since the days of the pharaohs, Egypt has also had a long tradition of centralized authority. The dependence of Egyptians on their government for the regulation of the Nile River to ensure their livelihood has accustomed them to obeisance to authoritarian leaders.

Hosni Mubarak had ruled supreme in his realm since he became the president after Anwar Sadat's assassination in October 1981. Until 2005, when he yielded to pressure from the Bush administration and tolerated some independent candidates, he ran for reelection each time unopposed in a referendum on his candidacy in which he, like the Arab world's other authoritarian leaders, regularly garnered over 90 percent of the vote.* By the end of the Bush administration, Mubarak, debilitated by old age and preoccupied with the succession of his son, Gamal, saw his pharaonic power begin to wane. But during the Clinton years he was in full command.

An air force commander trained in the Soviet Union, Mubarak had

---

* Even in 2005, Mubarak won with 88.6 percent. His nearest rival, Ayman Nour, of the Ghad (Tomorrow) party, secured only 7.5 percent. Mubarak subsequently jailed Nour for "election irregularities."

been appointed vice president in part because he posed no threat to Sadat. This was the way Sadat had become president, too, presenting himself as a somewhat quirky lightweight until President Gamal Abdel Nasser had passed from the scene. In Sadat's case it was a shrewd performance that cloaked a formidable statesmanship. In Mubarak's case there was no such talent hidden in the shadows of Sadat's aura and perhaps for that reason he has never dared to designate a vice president. He governs as a straightforward, conservative military commander who rarely wavers from certain essential precepts: don't let Egypt be dragged back into war with Israel; make sure the military is always taken care of; maintain close relations with the United States; support the Palestinians but don't get out in front of your public opinion; protect, and where necessary assert, Egypt's leadership role in the Arab world; and rely on the innate patience and acquiescence of the Egyptian people.

For the United States, Egypt's geostrategic importance lies in its influence in the Arab world and its location at the crossroads of Africa and Asia, astride the Suez Canal, which provides the vital sea link between Europe, the Gulf, and the Far East. During the Cold War, when Nasser's Egypt aligned itself with the Soviet Union, Moscow was able to secure a critical foothold in the Middle East. In 1972, Anwar Sadat ejected the Soviet military advisers and then turned to the United States for support. This dramatically tilted the Cold War Middle East scales in Washington's favor. And when Sadat made peace with Israel in 1979, he completely altered the Arab-Israeli military balance. It became impossible for other Arab states to contemplate war on Israel without Egypt's involvement. Since then, Egypt has provided the strategic cornerstone for America's involvement in the Middle East, anchoring the Arab-Israeli peace process, moderating the politics of the Arab world, and providing ready access to essential military facilities for the deployment of American forces.*

Mubarak was deeply offended when Saddam Hussein transgressed the Arab order by invading neighboring Kuwait. He told Secretary of State Christopher, on their first encounter in Cairo in February 1993, that Saddam had twice promised him that he did not intend any such thing. Saddam, according to Mubarak, had even proposed at an Arab

---

* Egypt's Cairo West Air Base provides a critical logistical waypoint for flowing huge amounts of equipment into Iraq. The Suez Canal is a vital route for the movement of U.S. Navy ships, including aircraft carriers, into the Persian Gulf.

League summit that all Arab leaders be obliged to oppose any among them who invaded another Arab country. Mubarak would never forgive the betrayal: "He is irredeemable; I will never trust him."

However, precisely because Mubarak saw himself as the defender of the Arab status quo, he was preoccupied with the risks involved in trying to remove Saddam from power. It was essential, he thought, to maintain the territorial integrity of Iraq. Otherwise Iran would take advantage of the situation. Rather than overthrow Saddam, Mubarak preferred that Clinton ignore him.

Mubarak's view of the Iranians was similarly jaundiced because they too were seeking to disrupt the status quo by exporting their Islamist revolution to the Arab world. The Iranian Revolutionary Guard Corps (IRGC) and the Iranian Ministry of Intelligence and Security (MOIS) had established links with the Egyptian Gamyat Islamiya. This precursor of al-Qaeda, led by the "blind Sheikh" Omar Abdel Rahman, had denounced Mubarak as an apostate and vowed to overthrow his regime. Its affiliates had already succeeded in assassinating President Sadat; Mubarak had every reason to take them seriously. Moreover, the rise to power of an Islamic militant regime in the Sudan, which bordered Egypt to the south and controlled the headwaters of the Nile, Egypt's only source of fresh water, compounded the threat. Iran had found common cause with Sudan's strongman and ideological guide, Hassan al-Turabi, too.

Mubarak worried that Iran intended to destabilize Egypt because it stood in the way of converting Arab countries to Shiite Islam. Egypt's Islamic militants, who had flocked to Afghanistan during the jihad against the Soviet Union, had come home from that war well trained but penniless. The Iranians were now paying their salaries and were picking up the tab for al-Turabi too. As far as Mubarak was concerned, Iraq and Iran were "two of a kind."

THE UNITED STATES had come to depend upon Saudi Arabia, the other pillar of the Arab status quo, for ensuring that the oil necessary to fuel the Western and Japanese economies flowed out of the Gulf at reasonable prices. Saudi Arabia, which holds the largest oil reserves in the world, is a deeply conservative and religious desert kingdom whose riches have generated a twenty-first-century gold-plated, physical infrastructure housing a seventh-century orthodox Islamic social structure.

While Mubarak was the self-appointed custodian of the Arab status quo, King Fahd was the anointed custodian of the religious sites in Mecca and Medina, the holiest places in Islam. All Muslims are required to make a pilgrimage at least once in their lifetimes to Mecca, which gave the Saudi king a special role in Islam. He and his brothers and half-brothers and their sons, the descendants of Abdul Aziz al-Saud, controlled their country through a pact with the orthodox Wahhabi religious establishment. The pact dates back to the mid-eighteenth century, when Muhammed bin Saud made an alliance with Muhammad Abd al-Wahhab, a religious reformer who espoused strict adherence to the tenets of Islam. This political-religious partnership made it possible in the early twentieth century for Abdul Aziz al-Saud, with the aid of the Ikhwan—the Wahhabi warriors—to evict the Hashemite rulers of the Hejaz region and unite the far-flung Bedouin tribes in one entity.

From then on, the House of Saud let the Wahhabi establishment run the religious, social, and educational institutions of the state while the extended royal family took care of the economy, security, and foreign relations. This division of responsibility worked well for both sides: the Saudi sheikhs gained religious legitimacy, with the king taking on the title of "Custodian of the Two Holy Mosques," while the Wahhabis successfully controlled the social consequences of the rapid modernization that vast oil wealth was generating. Occasionally things would get out of hand: for example, the intolerance preached by the Wahhabis spawned a religious fanatic who assassinated King Faisal, and others who took over the Kaaba, the holy of holies in Mecca, in 1979. But for the most part, the compact worked, lubricated by oil revenues large enough to keep most Saudis quiescent.

Unable to defend such a vast, oil-rich kingdom against its larger neighbors in Iraq and Iran, the Saudi royals had also used their money to purchase security. In the 1970s, they paid hundreds of billions of dollars to American, British, and French defense contractors to supply the kingdom with an arsenal of modern weapons, and the "trainers" to operate them. During the Iran-Iraq War, they paid from $35 to 50 billion to Saddam Hussein to prevent Iranian forces from crossing the Shatt al-Arab waterway and advancing south along the Arabian Peninsula. They preferred to keep American forces "over the horizon" because the Wahhabis vehemently objected to the idea that "infidel" troops might become the occupiers of Islamic holy ground. But King Abdul Aziz had forged a pact with President Franklin Roosevelt back in 1945 when they met on the USS *Quincy*: the United States would protect Saudi Arabia's security in return for access to its oil. This understanding was seriously strained in 1973, when King Faisal joined the Arab oil embargo of the West as part of a concerted effort to support Sadat's war against Israel. But by the 1980s, King Fahd had repaired the relationship with a combination of lucrative defense contracts and Saudi funding for a variety of common causes including the Afghan resistance to Soviet occupation, the Nicaraguan Contras, and Balkan relief operations.

By this stage, Saudi Arabia had developed enough excess capacity in its oil production that it was able to play the role of "swing producer" among the OPEC oil exporting states, increasing or decreasing production to ensure that the price remained within reasonable limits. Saudi Arabia had also discounted its oil for the American market to build a heavy American dependence that the king calculated would help ensure the United States would come to Saudi Arabia's defense when the chips were down.

All this looked as if it would suddenly come to an end when, in August 1990, Saddam invaded neighboring Kuwait. Overnight, the Saudis discovered the Iraqi army sitting just north of Saudi Arabia's oil-rich eastern province, al-Hasa, with nothing except the limitations of extended lines of communication preventing it from invading. Saddam had given the Saudi royal family the fright of its life. King Fahd urgently turned to the United States, agreeing for the first time in Saudi Arabia's history to host U.S. forces in whatever numbers were necessary not only to defend the kingdom but also to evict the Iraqi army from Kuwait.

As Fahd explained to Christopher in their first meeting, he too felt betrayed by Saddam. "We were convinced Saddam wanted Saudi Arabia as well. As long as he is there, there can be no stability in the region." And like Saddam, he argued, the Iranian rulers were not interested in creating peaceful relations with the world community, either. He detailed how the Iranians were creating trouble for moderate Sunni regimes across the Arab world. He counseled that Bill Clinton should watch the Iranians carefully. Fahd emphasized the similarities between Saddam's Iraq and Khomeini's Iran and vowed to work together to stop the danger.

This common theme, sounded by America's two most important allies in the Arab world, made a strong impression on Warren Christopher, who made clear he agreed with them. The United States had no intention of reconciling with Saddam and was also very concerned about Iran. We would contain both, he promised them.

EGYPT PITCHED IN early on by helping to bring the Palestinians back to the negotiating table in Washington. After the Oslo deal was signed, Mubarak would work closely with Clinton and Rabin, using his influence with Arafat to ease the process of implementation.

The Saudis helped us more quietly on the peace process front, where they were willing to provide funding for the Palestinian Authority but were wary of engaging with Israel, preferring to open a secret channel rather than indulge our preference for a more visible, public embrace (although they did attend all the multilateral forums with Israelis that became part of the peace process).

Early evidence of Saudi usefulness in promoting "dual containment" came when we had trouble convincing our European allies that they should forgo commercial deals with Iran. Iran Air was desperately in need of new aircraft for its commercial fleet and was ready to spend up to $4 billion on them. Boeing was competing furiously with Airbus for the business. Clinton was highly sensitive to the potential impact on American jobs, particularly on the West Coast, where California would be critical to his reelection bid in 1996. But if Clinton allowed Boeing to bid on the Iran Air deal, we could hardly expect the Europeans to forgo commercial dealings with Iran.

Enter the Saudis. Saudia Airlines was also due to replace its commercial fleet of some fifty civilian aircraft over the next five years and Boeing and McDonnell Douglas expected a tough fight with Airbus for the business. If Clinton could convince King Fahd to commit to buying all American replacements for his commercial fleet, the deal would be worth at least $6 billion.

Prince Bandar bin Sultan, the Saudi ambassador to the United States, loved aircraft deals.* He had developed a close personal relationship with the first president Bush, who treated him like a son. But because of that he had not found it easy to achieve the same entrée to

---

* One possible reason surfaced in June 2007, when the British press reported allegations of an official cover-up of $2 billion in payments to a Washington bank account controlled by Prince Bandar in connection with a $40 billion aircraft deal between BAE Systems and the Saudi government.

the Clinton White House. The potential Saudia Airlines deal presented Bandar with a ready-made door opener.

King Fahd had a soft spot for Bandar, too, and was predisposed to demonstrate his support for the new president.* So Fahd conveyed to Clinton, through Bandar, a willingness to purchase all American aircraft, provided the United States did not sell aircraft to Iran. The president's announcement of the Saudi commitment to purchase five 747-400s, twenty-three 777s, twenty-nine MD-90s, and four MD-11s did not come until February 16, 1994. But Fahd's commitment to this huge sale was conveyed to the White House in mid-1993, which made it easier for Clinton to introduce the policy of "active containment" of Iran without fear that American commercial interests would be jeopardized.

THE SAUDI AND Egyptian quid pro quo for this kind of support was for Clinton to leave them alone to deal with their internal problems as they saw fit. This tacit bargain meant that at a time when the Clinton administration was vigorously promoting democratic change in every other corner of the world, our Arab allies were exempted from this campaign.

The Clinton administration did not ignore political reform in the Middle East; we just focused our efforts on the periphery of the Arab world. We supported the right of women to vote in Qatar, Oman, and Kuwait; we pressed the Algerian regime to allow greater political openness for its people and engage its Islamic fundamentalists in dialogue (provided they abandoned violence); we supported successful efforts by the kings of Morocco and Jordan to co-opt their political oppositions into government and parliament. And we made a significant effort to support political reform in Yemen in the hope that, over time, change there might spur similar reforms in the rest of the Arabian Peninsula. We also enlisted Vice President Al Gore in a sustained effort to encourage the liberalization and privatization of Egypt's econ-

---

* Fahd also treated Bandar like a son, lavishing on him an ostentatious palace in Riyadh and a four-engine, wide-bodied Airbus 3000 jet so that he could fly nonstop between Washington and Riyadh in the comfort to which he was accustomed. The aircraft, which was readily visible at Washington's Dulles Airport whenever the ambassador was in his Washington residence, had three bedrooms as well as a sumptuous wide-bodied lounge where blond British hostesses served martinis and cigars to the ambassador's guests.

omy, with Mubarak's support. But the process stalled when Mubarak discovered he would actually have to cede some control to market forces.

Otherwise, the Clinton administration made a conscious decision to leave well enough alone in Egypt and Saudi Arabia. At the time, we were particularly worried that the Algerian malady would spread to Egypt, where Islamic fundamentalists were already using terror and assassination in an attempt to bring down the regime. Instead, Clinton would focus his energies on peacemaking, hoping to usher in an era in which political and economic reform could take place with less threatening consequences for our other interests. We calculated that once we had put an end to the Arab-Israeli conflict, these Arab authoritarian regimes would be deprived of their excuse for delaying much-needed domestic reforms. And once peace was established, resources that had previously been devoted to war could be freed up for that process. Conversely, if Clinton pushed hard for political change at the same time as he sought to promote peace, we feared that he might only succeed in generating instability in what were deeply repressed societies. Such instability might not only complicate the search for peace, it could also advantage Iraq and Iran.

It would prove to be a flawed approach, not just because the September 11 terrorists were products of the Egyptian and Saudi systems, but because, along the way, Islamist terror was able to strike withering blows to the peace process, too. At the time, we thought making peace would end the terrorism because we would be turning the key sponsors of terror in the Middle East heartland—Arafat and Asad—into peacemakers. This was another example of our naïveté. Just as Mubarak and Fahd had an interest in diverting American attention to peacemaking rather than internal reform of their societies, we would discover that Arafat and Asad were quite capable of talking peace and encouraging terror at the same time.

We were wed to an idealistic vision of a new, more peaceful Middle East. The leaders of the old Middle East had something else in mind for us.

THIS PURPOSEFUL CHOICE of "stability over freedom" would later be pilloried by George W. Bush, who argued that such a preference, as manifested by successive administrations prior to his—including his father's—had helped spawn the 9/11 terrorists. But it was far more complicated than that, as he would soon discover. As long as the United States has a vital interest in the free flow of oil at reasonable prices from the Persian Gulf, it will have an interest in maintaining stability in such a volatile region. And stability can only be maintained by depending on the pillars of America's influence in the Arab World— Egypt and Saudi Arabia.

Ignoring that reality helped send oil prices through the roof during the Bush administration, with adverse consequences for the American and global economies. It also badly discredited America's image as a promoter of democratic change. By eschewing stability in favor of promoting freedom, Bush gave hope to those thin, small liberal voices in Egyptian and Saudi society. No sooner had they begun to speak out against the repressive policies of the regimes, however, than they found the Bush administration pulling the rug out from under them by making common cause with the regimes themselves, the better to counter the destabilizing consequences of Bush's misadventure in Iraq. Consequently, the United States ended up with the worst of both worlds— neither stability nor freedom!

The lesson lies in finding a middle way between the two poles. The United States cannot ignore the stabilizing contribution that our authoritarian Arab allies make to protecting Western interests. By the same token, the United States cannot abandon the cause of freedom without contradicting its basic purposes and values. And it cannot continue to exempt these regimes from pressure to reform their political systems without risking the overthrow of the very leaders the United States depends upon to maintain stability.

That was the lesson of the Shah's overthrow in Iran. The United States waited too long to promote reform there; when President Carter finally came around to pressing the Shah to make fundamental changes, it was too late. Carter's insistence on his human rights agenda probably only helped to undermine the Shah's resolve to hold on to power.

Conversely, George W. Bush's willful dismissal of the concerns of the Egyptian and Saudi regimes only succeeded in generating cynical responses. They made minor concessions to Bush's demands and then quickly adopted methods that vitiated the impact.

For Clinton, however, the choice was clear—he intended to transform the Arab order through peacemaking. The contradiction between depending on the Egyptian and Saudi custodians of the status quo to transform the existing order would only emerge much later.

4

September 13, 1993

Bill Clinton, Yitzhak Rabin, and Yasser Arafat had just stepped up to the podium on the South Lawn. It was 11:15 A.M. Framed by the rounded colonnades of the White House, against a clear blue sky, and flanked by Warren Christopher, Russian foreign minister Andrey Kozyrev, Israeli foreign minister Shimon Peres, and PLO executive committee secretary general Mahmoud Abbas, the leaders of Israel and the Palestinians were about to enter into an agreement. It was a moment that would capture the imagination of the world—two sworn enemies reaching across a divide of hatred to make peace.

Bill Clinton was at his best at such moments. As president, he relished them. He had awoken at 3 A.M. and checked the weather forecast. Unable to sleep, he had read the Bible verses on Joshua and the battle of Jericho because in the agreement that was about to be signed the descendants of the Israelites would give Jericho back to the modern-day Canaanites. To mark the occasion, he had donned a blue tie with a pattern of gold trumpets to symbolize the crumbling of the walls of hatred that would be heralded by this agreement.

Earlier in the day he had worked on his speech with his advisers, adding an eloquent prophesy from Isaiah, "that the cry of violence shall no more be heard in your land, nor rack nor ruin within your borders." He had wanted to put greater emphasis on security for Israelis so he wrote into the draft: "We dare to pledge . . . that the security of the Israeli people will be reconciled with the hopes of the Palestinian people, and there will be more security and more hope for all." The president particularly liked a line that George Stephanopoulos—then his media adviser and spokesman—had inserted: "Throughout the Middle East, there is a great yearning for the quiet miracle of a normal life." Clinton intended to commit the power and prestige of his presidency to achieving it.

Yitzhak Rabin, a shy man by nature who did not relish such grand public occasions, looked awkward as he stood next to Yasser Arafat and contemplated shaking the hand of the man most Israelis identified with the murder of their athletes at the Munich Olympics in 1972 and their schoolchildren in the Israeli village of Ma'alot in 1974. It was Rabin's decision to enter into the agreement with Arafat that had generated this moment. But he spoke as Israel's everyman as he admitted to the world, "This signing . . . today is not so easy."

Rabin wanted to express the mixture of sorrow for the past and hope for the future that was captured in this ceremony:

> Let me say to you, the Palestinians, we are destined to live together on the same soil in the same land. We . . . who have come from a land where parents bury their children, we, who have fought against you, the Palestinians, we say to you today in a loud and clear voice: Enough of blood and tears! Enough!

Yasser Arafat was clearly in his element, standing there in his signature fatigues and checkered kaffiyeh, his face stubbled as always. He symbolized the long struggle of the Palestinian people for recognition of their nationhood, but I wondered if he shared Rabin's passion for ending the bloodshed, if he intended to help create Clinton's vision of normalcy for his people. It was impossible to know, of course, which is why Clinton referred to the agreement in his speech as "a brave gamble."

Arafat had just pulled off an extraordinary resurrection. Only days before, he was prohibited from coming to the United States because his organization, the PLO, was on the State Department's terrorism list. He was a man vilified and despised by most of the Arab regimes represented in the audience because he threatened their stability. His coffers were empty; his people had been evicted from Kuwait and the Gulf Arab states; his political standing had been at its lowest point. Yet here he was, the consummate actor who had found a new role for himself as peacemaker. He spoke of the beginning of an age of peace, coexistence, and equal rights, of a common Palestinian and Israeli desire for peace, but this came after his people's demand for justice. If there was no justice, in the minds of the Palestinians, would there be no peace for Israelis? Notably absent was any ringing renunciation of terror and violence.

With Clinton standing between them, his arms spread wide, Yitzhak Rabin reluctantly shook Arafat's hand and a gasp went up from the crowd of assembled dignitaries. At that moment, they could not have appreciated the great irony in that historic handshake: from the perspective of Clinton's Middle Eastern strategy, the wrong Arab leader was on the podium. The handshake we had been working for was meant to be between Rabin and Syria's Hafez al-Asad.

"THIS IS AN *amazing* sight!" I said to CNN's television audience, offering my commentary as CNN White House correspondent Wolf Blitzer and I watched the handshake from a broadcasting platform at the back of the White House lawn. For me, it was amazing in more ways than one. Just twelve days before, I had been in Sydney with my family to attend my nephew's bar mitzvah. It was the end of summer and the peace team had scattered to various vacation destinations. Dennis Ross and Warren Christopher were on the West Coast; the president was on Martha's Vineyard. Out of the blue, Dennis had called me from Point Mugu in California, where he and Christopher had met with Shimon Peres for a hastily arranged briefing about the agreement Peres had just reached with the PLO. After consulting with Clinton, Christopher had offered the White House for the signing ceremony. Dennis had called to tell me that I needed to return immediately to Washington to help organize the event.

A week after that, during a frenzy of activity, Tony Lake called me into his office to discuss the briefing he wanted to give the president, who had just returned to Washington from his vacation. We needed to review with him the plans for the ceremony he was about to host. In particular, Clinton had to decide who would be invited to attend for the Israeli and Palestinian sides and who would sign the agreement.

I was suffering from policy whiplash. Christopher had just completed his second trip to the Middle East. In what I had believed was the truly historic move, the secretary of state had told Syria's president that Clinton had in his pocket a conditional commitment from Prime Minister Rabin to a full Israeli withdrawal from the Golan Heights. We were making arrangements for secret Israeli-Syrian negotiations to commence in Washington at the beginning of September. I had departed for Australia fully expecting that we would achieve a framework agreement for Israeli-Syrian peace by the end of the year. Instead, I now found myself organizing a signing ceremony for a declaration of principles between Israel and an arch-terrorist with whom we had previously been banned from dealing. "We can't have Yasser Arafat in the White House," I insisted to Tony. "The American people are not ready to have their president embrace a leader of an organization that pioneered terrorism in the Middle East. He's still on our terrorism list!"

"I agree with you," Tony responded. "Yasser Arafat will come to the White House over my dead body!"

Actually, I had expected Tony to disagree with me. He was already in the process of quietly reaching out to the Irish Republican Army as part of an effort to resolve the conflict in Northern Ireland. But he was as adamant as me.

We shared our view with the president a few minutes later when we briefed him in the Oval Office. "Who then will be coming for the PLO?" Clinton asked. I told him that Arafat intended to send Mahmoud Abbas, known as Abu Mazen, his senior deputy in the PLO and the man who had overseen the negotiations for the Palestinians. Eitan Haber, Rabin's office director, and Itamar Rabinovich, Israel's ambassador in Washington, had informed us that Rabin would be sending his foreign minister, Shimon Peres. These aides had emphasized that Rabin was not coming because he did not want to be seen with Arafat in the White House. In protocol terms, I explained to the president, a symmetrical arrangement was emerging. Peres had overseen the negotiations for the Israelis, and Abu Mazen was his equivalent since Peres was the number two in Rabin's government.

The president listened carefully to the briefing but said nothing. He was about to phone Rabin, the first contact between the two leaders since Peres briefed Christopher on the agreement at Point Mugu. Tony and I monitored the call as Rabin came on the line. The president told him that he believed this agreement was historic but its success was by no means certain. He had agreed to host the signing ceremony to demonstrate America's backing for it, but since it was Israel's agreement, he argued emphatically, Rabin needed to be there for the event, too, to demonstrate his commitment to his people.

Rabin responded that he did not want to create problems for the president. He understood that if he came, Arafat would insist on coming, and that would put the president in an awkward position.

We were all taken by surprise. The president said, "I thought it would be awkward for you." He reassured Rabin, "It won't be awkward for me. I'll take care of all the arrangements." Looking at me across his desk, Clinton told Rabin that he had understood that he didn't want to come because it would be difficult for him to be seen with Arafat. Rabin again responded with the same concern: he didn't want to put the president in an awkward position.

The president became agitated, "Don't worry about me! I'll be all right. But I really think you need to be there."

As Clinton hung up the phone, his face reddened. He turned to me and fumed, "You're the Middle East expert but I'm telling you, Rabin wants to come! You get on the phone to his people and tell them that I'm inviting him, that I want him to be here, and that we'll work together to take care of any problems with Arafat." I was taken aback. Eitan Haber had insisted that Rabin did not want to come and did not want Arafat at the White House, either.

I would later discover that Rabin's aides had been divided. Haber worried that the agreement would be hard enough for Israelis to digest without them having to cope with the image of their prime minister shaking hands with Yasser Arafat. But Shimon Sheves, the director of the prime minister's office, agreed with Clinton's political instinct. He felt that if Rabin did not manifest his overt support for the agreement he would have a harder time selling it to the Israeli public. It would look as if Rabin had reluctantly gone along with an agreement negotiated by Shimon Peres, who was known in Israel for his visionary rhetoric and political maneuvering rather than the hardheaded realism they looked to their prime minister to provide.

The rivalry between Peres and Rabin was deep-seated and bitter and played an important role in Rabin's calculus. He did not want his long-time competitor for Labor Party leadership to steal the show, however controversial. What had started out as a signing ceremony between negotiators was quickly turning into the event of the decade. The White House was planning to invite 1,500 guests, including world leaders, the entire Congress, and every living president, secretary of state, and national security adviser. As Rabin got word of this, his dilemma became more acute. He had revealed to the president, in an indirect way, his desire to be part of the performance.

Nevertheless, we heard nothing more from Rabin until three days before the signing ceremony was set to take place. On Friday, September 10, Arafat sent Rabin a letter committing the PLO to recognition of Israel's right to exist in peace and security and to the resolution of all outstanding disputes through negotiations. In the letter, Arafat also made a solemn undertaking to end violence.*

Our lawyers judged this written renunciation as sufficient grounds for the president to take Arafat and the PLO off the State Department's terrorism list. So on that Friday morning, Tony, Dennis, and I were back in the Oval Office briefing the president before he went out into the Rose Garden to announce that he was clearing the way for the PLO to come to the signing ceremony.

At the Rose Garden event, the president would be in front of the press for the first time since the Israeli-Palestinian agreement had been made public. We told him that he would inevitably be asked whether he had invited Arafat to the signing ceremony. I suggested, and Tony and Dennis concurred, that he should preempt the question by saying that we had sent invitations to the government of Israel and the PLO and that they had informed us Shimon Peres and Abu Mazen would be representing them.

The president listened but did not respond. We left him in the Oval Office and went out to take our seats in front of the podium. It was a glorious fall morning. The Rose Garden looked picture perfect: the blue presidential podium, with the president's gold insignia in front of it, was framed by the imperial white Roman colonnade that wrapped around the Oval Office and the Cabinet Room. The president came out through the French doors and read to the assembled press a prepared announcement declaring the PLO no longer a terrorist organization from the U.S. government's perspective and announcing his intention to resume contacts. Then he paused for questions.

The second one came from Andrea Mitchell, NBC's White House correspondent: "Mr. President, are there any circumstances under which Yasser Arafat might come to this ceremony?"

Clinton shot back: "We have sent invitations to the government of Israel and the Palestine Liberation Organization."

So far, so good, I thought. But then he continued: "In terms of the ceremony, the people who will be here representing the PLO and Israel are the people that the PLO and Israel decide will come. That is en-

---

* Arafat wrote, "The PLO renounces the use of terrorism and other acts of violence and will assume responsibility over all PLO elements and personnel in order to assure their compliance, prevent violence, and discipline violators."

tirely up to them. . . . Whoever they decide will be here is fine with us, and we will welcome them."

I grimaced and then whispered in Dennis's ear, "It looks like Yasser Arafat will be coming after all." By the time we had returned to our offices there was a message from Hanan Ashrawi, the peace team's Palestinian interlocutor, informing us that Arafat had been watching the president's announcement in Tunis and had decided to accept the president's invitation to attend the event.

Arafat craved international recognition. He had sustained the Palestinian cause all these years in part by keeping it in the international spotlight. To be hosted at the White House with the leaders of Israel and other world statesmen, after being treated as a pariah by the United States for so many decades, would be a crowning achievement for him personally and for the Palestinian cause. Indeed, three days later, when the Saudi ambassador, in his capacity as the dean of the diplomatic corps, greeted Arafat at Andrews Air Force Base, the port of entry for foreign dignitaries arriving for official visits to Washington, Arafat exclaimed to him, excitedly: "Andrews, Bandar! We're at Andrews!"

The president had clearly decided to open the door to Arafat, knowing he would march right through it. But at that moment, Clinton was more concerned about Israel's politics than his own, a trait that would manifest itself repeatedly in his presidency. He had reached the conclusion that Rabin needed to be there; Arafat's presence was incidental. As he told the New York Times two days before the event, "The pivotal question is what the traffic can bear in Israel."

The politician in the president, just like the politician in Rabin, knew instinctively that they were attempting to break the mold of the Israeli-Palestinian conflict. This was not just another signing ceremony at the White House. The event would symbolize the ending of conflict and the extending of mutual recognition between two peoples who had been feuding for decades. In the president's words, "This is a huge deal." If it was going to work, it had to be supported by the Israeli public, and for that to happen, in the president's judgment, their prime minister had to be seen to be standing behind the agreement. If that meant hosting Arafat, too, so be it. Thus when Christopher informed the president that Arafat wanted to attend, Clinton asked him to call Rabin immediately and make it clear that the president of the United States was personally inviting the Israeli prime minister to come.

By this time, Rabin had already told Peres that he wanted him to represent Israel at the ceremony. Nevertheless, he confided to his wife, Leah, that he was still having second thoughts. As the president had anticipated, Christopher's call, which came around 10 P.M. Israel time, gave Rabin the explanation to reverse his decision. As Christopher tells it, Rabin responded in a gruffer than usual tone, "I will come; I have no choice."

Typical of Rabin's relationship with Peres, instead of informing him of his change of mind—and of Peres's effective relegation to playing second fiddle—Peres heard it first on an Israel Radio news bulletin on Saturday morning. This humiliation triggered a crisis that threatened to split the government, since Peres responded by declaring that he would resign. Haber called me in desperation to make sure Peres would still have a prominent role, both as a speaker and the person who would actually sign the agreement on Israel's behalf.

With Rabin on his way, the president's next order of business was to make sure the Israeli leader would shake Arafat's hand. This was by no means certain—Rabin had sworn never to engage directly with Arafat.

In the Middle East, shaking hands is a symbolic act of recognition. The Syrians, for example, refused to shake hands with their Israeli counterparts in their negotiations, which was understood by both sides as signaling continued enmity. When Saudi Arabia's foreign minister, Saud al-Faisal, came to the 2007 Annapolis peace meeting, he commented in advance that he would not shake Israeli prime minister Ehud Olmert's hand. Similarly, Ariel Sharon, as foreign minister in the Netanyahu government, refused to shake Arafat's hand during the September 1998 Wye negotiations because, he said, Arafat had innocent Israeli blood on his hands. The three-handed grasp between Sadat, Menachem Begin, and Carter after they signed the Israel-Egypt peace treaty on the North Lawn of the White House in 1978 symbolized their new relationship. And while Benjamin Netanyahu used a video clip of Peres and Arafat holding hands in his successful campaign to defeat Peres in the 1996 elections, he was captured for posterity a few months later warmly shaking Arafat's hand at the White House.

On this occasion, with the whole world watching, the president wanted to be sure of the choreography. He instructed me to ask Eitan Haber whether Rabin would shake hands with Arafat. The answer came back in a typical Rabin formulation: he would do what he had to do. However, he said there could be no kissing, no gun, and no uniform.

Arafat was infamous for his kissing on public occasions. When he met Arab leaders, he would perform a kissing spectacle, repeatedly planting his bulging lips on both their cheeks. If he had a particular reason to demonstrate his affection in front of the cameras, he would conclude the ritual by planting a kiss on his counterpart's forehead. We labeled this "the full package." How could we prevent him from showering the president as well as Rabin with kisses? This was a job for the State Department!

I had already informed the Saudi ambassador, Prince Bandar, about the "no kissing rule" and Bandar had agreed to explain to Arafat that in the United States, unlike in the Arab world, leaders shake hands rather than kiss one another. However, as assistant secretary of state for Near East affairs, it fell to Ed Djerejian to be the first American official to greet Arafat when he landed at Andrews Air Force Base. Lest a precedent be set, we needed to make sure that Ed did not allow Arafat to kiss him before Bandar had the opportunity to deliver the message. Ed and his aides developed a technique for shaking hands with the right hand while placing the left hand firmly on the bicep of Arafat's right arm so that he would be unable to embrace and kiss his greeter.

I watched on CNN as Ed tried out his technique on Arafat when he descended from the executive jet the Algerian government had lent him for the occasion. It worked perfectly. On the morning of the signing, Tony Lake taught the president the same technique in case Arafat tried it on him.* The president demonstrated with a knee to Tony's groin what he might do if the technique failed.

There was still the matter of the gun. On public occasions, Arafat always wore a gun in a hip holster, a symbol of the armed struggle against Israel. He had caused outrage in 1974 when he insisted on wearing it to the United Nations during his first address to the General

---

* From that point on, it actually became policy not to allow Arafat to kiss U.S. officials. The first known violation took place three years later when Agency for International Development director Brian Atwood inadvertently allowed Arafat to peck him on the cheek at a dedication ceremony in Gaza. Arafat was aware of the technique because he would always laugh at me when I put my hand on his bicep. He finally managed to kiss me when my guard was down—at 2 A.M. on January 15, 1997, when the Hebron Agreement was announced at the Erez crossing point in Gaza.

Assembly. As the signing ceremony approached, someone in the Palestinian entourage told us Arafat intended to hand his gun to the president at the event as a symbolic gesture of his renunciation of violence. When I informed the president of this he laughed and said, "If he hands me his gun I'll shoot him!" To make sure that didn't happen, I briefed the international media, emphasizing that the Secret Service would not allow guns in the White House under any circumstances.

I asked Bandar to help me with the problem of getting Arafat out of his uniform. Bandar arranged for some suits to be delivered by a local tailor to the chairman's hotel room. He explained to Arafat that protocol required him to wear a suit like everybody else at the ceremony. When Arafat reluctantly tried on one of the jackets in front of his aides, who had never seen him in anything but his battle fatigues, they burst out laughing. Arafat viewed himself as the embodiment of the Palestinian struggle for nationhood and therefore took his appearance very seriously. He felt humiliated, took off the coat, and insisted that he would only wear his uniform to the ceremony. Bandar, wanting to save face, neglected to let me know he had failed in his mission.

I only discovered it ten minutes before Rabin and Arafat were due to arrive at the White House. Clinton was hosting former presidents Bush and Carter in the Oval Office and Dennis and I were briefing them on the arrangements for the ceremony. One of Clinton's aides pulled me out to take an urgent phone call from Eitan Haber. Eitan told me calmly that Rabin had been watching on television as Arafat left his hotel for the White House. "The chairman is wearing a uniform; tell the president that Rabin is not coming," Haber said.

I exploded: "The whole world is waiting for you. There are three presidents in the Oval Office; ten foreign ministers in the audience. He can't not come. Nobody will understand why. It will cause a major setback to the whole process."

I told Eitan to stay on the line and called Bandar, who was riding with Arafat in his limousine. "Bandar," I said with obvious panic, "Arafat's not wearing a uniform, is he?" Bandar stuttered as he grasped for words, "No, no, it's ah, ah, ah . . . a safari suit."

"A safari suit?" I was incredulous.

"Yes, a safari suit," Bandar said, gaining in confidence.

"Is he wearing medals or insignia on this safari suit?" I asked.

"No, there are no medals on it."

I hung up and got back on the phone with Eitan. I relayed my conversation with Bandar. I said we could not dictate to Arafat what he wore, that Rabin would be late if he didn't move now, and that it would not go down well if Rabin were a no-show merely because of what Arafat was wearing. After checking with Rabin, Eitan said to me with a heavy sigh, "Okay, we're coming. But there had better be no kissing and no gun."

IN RETROSPECT, WE should have been more insistent that Arafat not wear his fatigues. It would have served as a signal to Palestinians that their leader was laying down his gun and taking off his uniform because they were entering a new epoch in which their grievances would be addressed through peaceful negotiations alone.

One can see now that there were warning signs, even at that moment, about the sincerity of Arafat's commitment to renounce terrorism and prevent violence. For example, in the negotiations with the Israelis about the wording of his letter recognizing Israel, Arafat would not make an explicit call for his people to end the violent manifestations of the first intifada.

Indeed, at the time, his call to end the violence was only expressed in a little-noticed letter to the Norwegian foreign minister. His letter to Rabin, in which he forswore terrorism and committed to prevent violence, referred only to actions by "PLO elements and personnel," which excluded Hamas or PIJ militants since they were not part of the PLO.

The Oslo Accords provided for the Palestinian Authority to establish a "strong police force" responsible for guaranteeing public order and internal security for the Palestinians in those areas of Gaza and the West Bank that would come under Arafat's control. Security for Israelis in the West Bank and Gaza, however, was on Rabin's insistence to be Israel's sole responsibility.

It was only after the agreement was initialed in Oslo and negotiators turned to the issue of mutual recognition that the PLO's obligations to renounce terror and prevent violence were spelled out. Dennis Ross suggested to Shimon Peres, when he and Christopher were first briefed on the agreement at Point Mugu, that the Israeli negotiators demand the PLO commit in writing to discipline any constituent group that continued to engage in acts of terrorism. Christopher also raised the issue forcefully with Arafat, after the signing ceremony, in their first bilateral meeting: "The time for calculated ambiguity has passed. Your commitment to stop terror and violence will be watched closely. I urge you in the most sincere way to take action. I know you're not superman but you need to make a serious effort. Our success now depends on you being straightforward in your condemnation of and action against terror."

Arafat's "who me?" response was a sure sign of trouble: he blamed the terror on the bad economic situation, the subversive activities of the Damascus-based Palestinian rejectionist groups, and the refusal of the Gulf sheikhs to give him "my money." It became a frustratingly familiar, ritualistic exchange, repeated on every occasion of high-level American meetings with Arafat. That unwillingness to take responsibility for stopping the violent acts of his own people would come to be recognizable as vintage Arafat. It would do more than anything else to undermine the trust so necessary to the success of his new partnership with Israel. Coming on the day when Arafat had supposedly been transformed from terrorist to statesman, we should have seen it as a bad omen.

CHRISTOPHER COULD DO no more than caution Arafat because we had not been involved in the Oslo negotiations. Conventional wisdom now has it that Clinton pressured a reluctant Rabin to enter into a flawed deal with Arafat. But in fact Rabin took Clinton by surprise: we were only barely aware that official negotiations were taking place in Oslo. Clinton committed the United States to supporting the peace initiative without knowing how the agreement was reached, nor did he have any opportunity to influence its outcome. That might not have mattered if the negotiators had produced a straightforward peace agreement. But all they had achieved was an inexplicit declaration of principles that would guide subsequent negotiations on a four-stage process: first Arafat would take control of Gaza and Jericho; next, an interim agreement would have to be concluded to extend his rule to the West Bank; two further agreements would be needed to govern the Israeli army's further redeployments from parts of the West Bank; and, finally, negotiations would be held on a permanent settlement of the conflict that would resolve the final borders, the disposition of settlements, the status of refugees, Jerusalem's jurisdiction, and control of water resources.

The flaws in the agreement are now quite obvious. Not only did it neglect Palestinian security obligations, it also made no mention of Israeli settlement activity during the interim period. The Palestinians only suggested a freeze on settlement activity after the agreement had been concluded, when the negotiators were composing the letters of mutual recognition. And at that late stage, they were willing to suffice with a nonbinding reference to the Rabin government's 1992 decision to halt new building in West Bank settlements, a moratorium that did not apply to the Jerusalem environs where Rabin stepped up settlement activity. It was as if each side was winking at the other—we Israelis know you Palestinians won't stop violence, and we Palestinians know you Israelis won't stop settlement activity, but let's do the deal anyway and worry about all that later.

These two issues, security and settlements, were structural flaws in the Oslo framework and in all the agreements that flowed from it. But at the time, our peace team barely had a chance to study the document. When Peres presented the agreement to Christopher and Ross at Point Mugu, it had already been initialed. The Israelis and Palestinians had directly negotiated an agreement to end their conflict, something Clinton had explicitly called on them to do. Who were we to second-guess them? Our role was to support the effort. Amidst all the joy of the occasion, that new reality was dawning on us. It was captured in a message to the members of Clinton's peace team from Aaron Miller's father: remember, he warned us, when you dance with a bear, you can never let go.

AFTER THE CEREMONY, Clinton escorted Rabin and Peres from the South Lawn into the Oval Office. Sipping on iced water, Rabin, rather than reflect on the enormity of what had just transpired, wanted to elaborate on the only words he had spoken to Arafat as they stood with Clinton at the White House diplomatic entrance waiting to be summoned to the podium for the signing ceremony. He had told the chairman in a stern voice, "We have a lot of work to do." Now he explained to the president the dire situation of the Gazan economy, its dependence on workers with jobs in Israel, the lack of financial support from the Gulf states, and the huge challenge that awaited Arafat in implementing the agreement they had just signed. He must have spoken for about fifteen minutes without a break. I remember thinking that perhaps the significance of what he had just done was so hard for his mind to digest that he fell back on the familiar territory of statistics, facts, and analysis. Later, at lunch alone in the president's private dining room, Rabin and Clinton would take to whiskey and wine respectively to ease their anxiety.

That was, however, only after Clinton had his first official meeting with Arafat. It had been hastily arranged after presidents Carter and Bush had pressed Clinton to give Arafat a few minutes and Clinton had acquiesced. There had been no time to script the affair. They were left to their own devices.

They met in the Map Room, on the ground floor of the residence. This small room received its name from a display case of maps housed there and because of the two framed historic maps that appear on its walls: the last World War II tactical map prepared for President Franklin D. Roosevelt, on April 3, 1945; and a 1755 French survey map of the American colonies.

As a way of breaking the ice, the president, a history buff, provided a detailed explanation of the maps to a bemused Arafat. Then Clinton tried to joke with him, suggesting that they were both "comeback kids" who had only recently been down and now were back at the center of the world stage. Arafat did not seem to comprehend the sobriquet. The president then said how moving he thought the ceremony had been and asked Arafat how the Palestinian people would react to it. Arafat agreed that it was a historic moment that would help ensure that Palestinians continue to support the process.

Picking up on an idea that Shimon Peres had obviously planted in Arafat's mind when he outlined his vision of a Gaza that would become the Middle East's Singapore, Arafat noted that the Palestinians' choice was "between Soweto and Singapore." If their state was going to become Singapore, they would have to have American support in all aspects of their development. The president promised to work on the practical problems. Then Arafat went into his familiar litany of complaints about how the rich Gulf Arab states were blocking "my money."

The president responded by asking Arafat his opinion about someone who was very much on Clinton's mind even at that moment—Hafez al-Asad.

RELATIONSHIPS BETWEEN ARAB leaders are complicated, a reflection not just of personality differences but of the bitter rivalries beneath the façade of pan-Arab unity. There was none so sour as the relationship between Asad and Arafat. Asad claimed to be the "beating heart of pan-Arabism" and to have filled the "lungs of the Palestinian resistance" with Syrian oxygen. But once he had assumed power, Asad came to see Arafat as a dangerous man who could threaten the interests of the Syrian state. He determined that he would control the Palestinian cause for Syrian purposes.

Arafat, on the other hand, wanted to avoid Asad's influence in order to maintain the "independence of Palestinian decision-making" and to build his own fiefdoms first in Jordan and then in Lebanon. While Asad had no intention of being dragged into a war on someone else's timetable, Arafat sought precisely the opposite, to add to his own meager military capabilities that of a radical Arab state.

Asad first met Arafat in 1966, when Asad was commander of the Syrian air force and one of the strongmen of the new Baathist regime that had come to power in a bloody coup. Asad's intelligence service had arrested Arafat for the murder of a Palestinian political rival in a refugee camp on the outskirts of Damascus. Egypt's president Gamal Abdel Nasser had interceded with Asad to secure Arafat's release. This sparked Asad's curiosity, so Arafat was brought to him. By one account, they had a long discussion, at the end of which Asad returned the murder weapon. Perhaps there was some sense of affinity since neither was averse to killing off his opponents to secure his position of power.

Their paths crossed again four years later, in 1970. Arafat was now chairman of the Palestine Liberation Organization and Asad was Syria's defense minister. The PLO's growing challenge to King Hussein's rule in Jordan finally provoked a military confrontation between the Jordanian army and Arafat's irregulars. Syria's leadership came to Arafat's aid, despatching a column of tanks across the border to help relieve the Jordanian army's siege. However, as defense minister, Asad refused to commit the Syrian air force to the fray, and when the Israeli army mobilized on the Golan Heights and the Jordanian army counterattacked the Syrian tanks, Asad preferred the embarrassment of withdrawal to a confrontation he knew Syria would lose. Arafat felt betrayed by Asad.

Their relationship deteriorated over the next decade as Arafat built a PLO state-within-a-state in Lebanon, challenging Syrian influence there. The Palestinian-Sunni presence threatened the confessional balance, sparking conflict between Lebanon's Maronite Christian and Sunni communities. Asad repeatedly warned Arafat to stay out of the developing civil war, but Arafat saw an opportunity to gain in Lebanon what he had lost in Jordan by throwing the weight of his forces behind the Sunni militias. In June 1976, Asad intervened on the side of the Maronites, sending his army into Lebanon to occupy two-thirds of the country and killing thousands of Palestinians in the process.

Although Asad thus gained effective control over Lebanon, he had also earned the opprobrium of the Arab world. He reached a new modus vivendi with Arafat in which the PLO would be allowed to operate against Israel from southern Lebanon in return for its acceptance of Syrian rule in the rest of the country. In 1982, Arafat's terrorist activities eventually provoked the Israeli government of Menachem Begin and Ariel Sharon into a full-scale invasion of Lebanon that included an assault on Syrian positions. Arafat had again forced Asad to choose between supporting the Palestinian cause and confronting the might of the Israeli army. His forces stood by, licking their wounds, while Sharon laid siege to Beirut and eventually forced the PLO's expulsion from Lebanon. Yet again, Arafat felt betrayed by Asad.

Down and out, Arafat sought asylum in Tunisia, far from Asad's influence, but the rivalry only worsened. In May 1983, Asad backed a challenge to Arafat's leadership from the remnants of the latter's Fatah organization, which had stayed behind in Lebanon and Syria. Arafat excoriated Asad in the Arab press and then joined the remaining Fatah loyalists in the northern Lebanese port of Tripoli. Asad laid siege to him there, eventually forcing him to leave Lebanon for the second time, never to return. For the next decade, Syrian-backed Palestinian dissidents assassinated Arafat loyalists who dared to call for dialogue with Israel. Arafat responded by offering support to Asad's opponents in Lebanon and openly backed Lebanese president Michel Aoun's rebellion against Syrian rule.*

When Saddam Hussein invaded Kuwait in 1990, Arafat sided with him; Asad made the shrewder calculation by siding with the United States. However, in the aftermath of the war, Syrian and Palestinian

---

* Such are the ways of the Arab world that Aoun subsequently allied with Asad's son in his unsuccessful effort to regain the Lebanese presidency in 2007.

delegations joined other Arabs in Madrid in 1991 for the launching of comprehensive negotiations with Israel. Arafat's immediate challenge was to assert control over the Palestinian delegation, from which PLO officials had been excluded; Asad's was to prevent the other Arab delegations from undermining Syria's position by making separate deals with Israel. He had insisted on the establishment of a coordinating mechanism between the Arab delegations as the price for Syrian participation. He easily asserted tight control over the Lebanese negotiators and was able to intimidate the Jordanians.

The Palestinian negotiators seemed to be the least of Asad's problems: first they refused to enter the negotiating room; then they put obstacles in the way of progress. By 1993, Asad found himself in the ironic position of having to exert pressure on the Palestinians to participate in the negotiations so that he could engage with a newly flexible Israel.

Since it was reasonable for him to assume that Israeli antipathy for Arafat mirrored his own, the last thing Asad would have expected was that Arafat and Rabin would do a deal behind his back. It was Arafat's ultimate payback for all of Asad's perceived perfidies.

GIVEN THIS HISTORY, of which Clinton was unaware, Arafat would never have expected to be asked his opinion of Asad by the U.S. president. He responded disingenuously, "He is an old friend, a genius. He's skillful and clever; he understands the changes in the region very well and wants to achieve something for Syria during his lifetime."

Encouraged by Arafat's apparent enthusiasm, Clinton revealed his particular concerns: "Rabin can't make further concessions until he can prove to his people that the agreement he just made with you can work. So the more quickly we can move on your track, the more quickly we'll be able to move on the Syrian track."

The notion that Arafat should speed up implementation of his agreement with the Israelis so that Clinton and Rabin could go off and do a deal with Syria was perfectly logical to the American president, but it must have confirmed Arafat's worst fears. We had made no effort to conceal our intention to pursue a deal with Syria first, and the amount of attention that Clinton and Christopher paid to Asad since coming into office may inadvertently have helped convince Arafat to do his own deal with the Israelis ahead of Syria.

Now that Arafat had used that deal to open up a relationship with

Washington, he did not want to let Clinton shift his attention back to Syria. And the more he managed to involve us in the details of his agreement with the Israelis, the less we would be able to do that. In his good-hearted innocence, Clinton had revealed his preferences. Arafat would not forget them.

5

The Anatomy of
Rabin's Oslo Decision

Unlike Clinton, Rabin was not new to the ways of the Middle East. The Israeli warrior, who had first drawn blood fighting to relieve the siege of Jerusalem in the 1948 War of Independence, was engaged in what would be the final battle of his life and he intended to use America's power and influence to help him achieve the peace deal he had promised his people. Whatever the strategic benefits to the United States, and to Israel, that was not going to be a deal with Syria, at least not yet.

While Clinton was unaware of the rivalry between Arafat and Asad, his peace team had tin ears when it came to understanding what Rabin's true intentions were. We simply assumed that once the United States had decided on a course, at least our friends in the region would go along. This was not quite the arrogance of the George W. Bush administration, which developed the habit of believing that all the United States had to do was will it, and it would happen. But we failed to anticipate that the Middle Eastern players, including our Israeli peacemaking partner, would succeed in bending our efforts to their own advantage, producing a very different result than the one we were aiming for.

It was not as if we neglected the Palestinian negotiations. In May 1993, Christopher had proposed a plan for Palestinian self-government in the West Bank and Gaza that was designed to empower the Palestinians there.* But for Arafat, the American effort to provide these Palestinians with control over their own lives threatened his claim

---

* They would control fiscal policy, health, and education until an autonomy agreement was finalized. Economic development there would be funded by an international donor mechanism to which we were trying to get the Saudis to contribute.

to be their sole, legitimate representative. He had been forced to accept the Madrid provision that a Palestinian delegation from the West Bank and Gaza would negotiate with the Israelis under the auspices of his Jordanian nemesis. But there was no way he would consider an American proposal designed to "empower" these people at his expense.

Rabin's suggestion that the United States invite Faisal Husseini to head the official Palestinian negotiating delegation only exacerbated the situation. Poorly informed at that stage about intra-Palestinian rivalries, we quickly learned that Arafat saw in Husseini a potential threat to his leadership. The scion of a prominent Jerusalem family, Husseini commanded the allegiance of the city's 150,000 Palestinians. Once anointed by Washington, Arafat wasted little time asserting control over him. In this way, Arafat ensured that the Palestinian delegation would not move without his orders, and he would not allow the talks to progress without being directly involved.

Since Rabin was under pressure to make good on his campaign promise to deliver a Palestinian autonomy agreement within six to nine months of his election, he concluded—as Arafat intended him to—that the key negotiating partner was in Tunis, not in Washington, where the negotiations were going nowhere. We, however, did not share Rabin's pressing concern. Since we were more focused on Syria, we were satisfied to mark time with the Palestinian delegation in Washington.

Rabin's public statements actually reinforced us in this approach, even as he was privately dealing with the PLO. In May 1993, at the same time as he authorized official negotiations with Arafat's delegates without informing us, Rabin openly expressed a willingness to undertake a Golan withdrawal and define its depth "according to the depth of peace Israel received in return." Asad's foreign minister, Farouq al-Sharaa, responded with a public offer of "full peace for full withdrawal."

Given the auspiciousness of these opening moves, Clinton had decided, with Rabin's approval, to move the Syrian negotiations forward through higher-level intervention. Because Asad and Rabin were the sole decision makers, it made sense to engage them directly. But since Asad would not deal directly with Rabin, Christopher would have to shuttle between Damascus and Jerusalem, like Kissinger and Baker before him. Thus in early July, Dennis Ross, as the newly appointed Special Middle East Coordinator, and I, as the White House representative, journeyed to Israel and Syria to prepare for Christopher's arrival.

Unbeknown to us, by then the Oslo negotiations between the Israeli government and the PLO were reaching their climax. Yet we found Rabin ready to make a dramatic move toward Syria. He asked Dennis to convey to Asad that he was aware of his requirement of full withdrawal from the Golan and understood that there would be no agreement without it. In return, he wanted to know whether Syria was ready to meet Israel's needs. Asad responded warmly to Rabin. He said he was committed to "real peace" and that it was "understandable" that Rabin had political requirements, too. Now, Asad said, it was up to the United States to define the details of both sides' requirements.

Our meeting in Damascus had occurred two days after Rabin had authorized a ninth round of the Oslo negotiations; he would authorize a tenth round while Christopher was in the region a week later. In retrospect, it is possible to see that both Rabin and Peres were dropping broad hints in their presentations to us during those visits. They both briefed us on the idea of "Gaza first plus Jericho," that is, giving Palestinians working control of Gaza and a toehold in the West Bank, the very things they were negotiating in Oslo with Arafat's representatives. Rabin also repeatedly emphasized his red lines to us: an agreement that didn't touch Jerusalem or the settlements and left responsibility for security in Israel's hands. What he omitted to tell us was that he was in the midst of persuading Yasser Arafat to accept his requirements.

We were aware that since the beginning of 1993 a "track II" dialogue had been taking place in Norway between PLO officials and two Israeli academics, Yair Hirschfeld and Ron Pundak. They had provided regular briefings to Dan Kurtzer. However, we had considered that a sideshow. What we did not know—and no Israeli official informed us—was that in mid-May 1993 that informal dialogue had been transformed into an *official* negotiation when Rabin and Peres sent Uri Savir, the director general of Israel's Foreign Ministry, to the Oslo talks.

We were so unaware of these events that in our July meeting with Rabin, Dennis actually proposed launching a secret, official dialogue between Israel and the PLO. Rabin vetoed it categorically. With the Oslo talks ongoing, Rabin probably had no interest in or need for another channel. But because we had no knowledge of what was transpiring in Oslo, we took his rejection to indicate his continued opposition to dealing with the PLO.

After we returned from Damascus with Asad's initial positive response to Rabin's overture, Rabin showed Dennis a letter he had received from Arafat via Ahmed Tibi (an Israeli-Arab physician and Knesset member) and Haim Ramon (then minister for health and a Rabin confidant). The letter specifically answered Rabin's concerns about Jerusalem, settlements, and security. At that moment we should have connected the dots. This letter indicated that Rabin was both communicating directly with Arafat and that the chairman was ready to accept an interim phase before final status issues were negotiated as well as Rabin's requirements on the other "red line" issues.

I believe now that Rabin shared this letter with Dennis as his way of signaling us that he was dealing with Arafat and that these contacts were yielding important results. He avoided revealing to us what was taking place in Oslo, however, because he compartmentalized everything he did in the peace process.

Rabin was innately suspicious of his fellow Israelis because he believed they were incapable of keeping anything secret. Indeed, leaks are the lifeblood of the Israeli political system. Its fragmented character, dating from the splintered nature of Zionist politics before Israel's birth, means that the struggle for power between the multiple political parties and within each of them is particularly intense. Consequently, nothing of political value stays secret for long in Israel.*

Acutely sensitive to leaks because of their potential political consequences, Rabin strictly limited the number of people with knowledge of the negotiations. Itamar Rabinovich was the only other Israeli to know when Rabin made a conditional commitment to full withdrawal from the Golan.† The first time Peres heard about it was from Rabinovich on the evening of Rabin's funeral, more than two years later, immediately prior to his first meeting with Clinton as prime minister. Similarly, Rabin did not inform any of his closest aides about the Oslo talks, using Joel Singer, a former Ministry of Defense lawyer who was working in a Washington law firm, as his sole watchdog in those negotiations.

Rabin always preferred to keep the United States out of direct en-

---

* The notable exception was the silence imposed in September 2007, when the Israeli air force attacked a Syrian nuclear reactor. In its aftermath, no one in the know in the Israeli political echelon said a word.

† At Rabin's request, on the American side the president restricted the knowledge of Rabin's commitment to Christopher, Tony Lake, Dennis Ross, and me.

gagement in his negotiations with Arab adversaries. He knew from his experience with Kissinger during the Israel-Egypt disengagement negotiations in the 1970s that once Washington became the "honest broker" in any Middle East talks, it would seek to build its credibility with the Arab side by taking a more middle-of-the-road position than Israel preferred. And because the United States had more influence with its Israeli ally, its mediators would inevitably make more demands of Israel. Rabin's strong preference, therefore, was for direct negotiations with the Arabs; the United States would only help implement an agreement once it had been struck. In the Syrian case, he had no alternative but to work through Christopher because Asad would not engage him directly, but he made it clear to us that he didn't like it. The Oslo process, however, allowed direct engagement with Arafat. But he knew this negotiation would be problematic for Clinton, given U.S. laws that banned dealing with the PLO. There would be time enough to inform us if the deal were ever done.*

Rabin probably wanted to leave a trail so that at least we could not accuse him of double-dealing, but he left it to us to draw the appropriate conclusion and we failed to do so. That was partly because a mere ten days before he sent Peres to Stockholm and Oslo to finalize the agreement with the PLO he asked Christopher to take to Damascus the vital concessions necessary to launch a bold and far-reaching initiative with Syria.

Apparently encouraged by the response Dennis had brought him from Asad, on August 3, 1993, Christopher formally conveyed to Syria's president Rabin's willingness to withdraw fully from Syrian territory provided his requirements were met. For the first time since the Israeli army conquered the Golan Heights in 1967, a prime minister of Israel had committed to relinquish all that territory.†

---

* Rabin's strict compartmentalization also manifested itself in his request to Christopher not to discuss with Shimon Peres, his foreign minister and Christopher's counterpart, any peace process issue other than the multilateral negotiations (on water, economic development, and refugees), which made for many awkward moments in their meetings.

† Rabin outlined four requirements: 1) their peace treaty would "stand on its own feet" (that is, not be dependent on any other Arab-Israeli agreement); 2) peace meant normalized relations, including embassies and borders open to people and trade; 3) the deal would be implemented in three phases over four to five years with elements of normalization in the first phase and Golan settlements only evacuated in the last phase; and 4) satisfactory security arrangements would have to include the safeguarding of Israel's water needs and the U.S. manning of early warning sites on the Golan.

In two meetings with Asad in Damascus, on August 3 and August 6, Christopher learned that Asad was willing to accept what we referred to as the "core" bargain of full withdrawal for "normalization" of relations. He argued that the withdrawal could be done in one phase over six months rather than Rabin's preference for three phases over five years, and he wanted all the settlements to be withdrawn at the beginning rather than at the end of the process, as Rabin preferred. But Asad approved a secret channel between the Israeli and Syrian ambassadors in Washington under American auspices to work out these details.

Although Christopher would remember Asad's response as a "series of nitpicking questions and contentious pronouncements," this did not reflect the mood at the time. After Christopher reported to Rabin on his meeting with Asad, Rabin went out to the assembled press and declared: "I believe that you have brought certain good news from Damascus." His top aides backgrounded the Israeli press in fulsome terms: "Now we are convinced that Damascus genuinely wants to reach a peace accord with Israel."

We felt we were on the threshold of a momentous breakthrough. Had we realized at the time that Rabin had decided to go for an interim agreement with the Palestinians rather than pursue a potentially long, drawn-out peace negotiation with the Syrians, we might have acted differently. Instead of heading off for summer vacation, Christopher might have returned to Damascus to press Asad to be more immediately forthcoming, warning that if he failed to move more quickly he might be left behind. But in our excitement for the Syrian deal, we had missed what was really going on.

Rabin had helped us reach the wrong conclusion. He had not told Christopher that Asad's response was insufficient; sharing his satisfaction with the press was a strange way to show disappointment. Moreover, when Christopher asked Rabin for his assessment of what we thought were unofficial discussions in Oslo during his August 2 meeting, Rabin dismissed them with a typical wave of his right hand. He described the Gaza-Jericho idea as "not a real approach" and negotiations with the Palestinians as "still a mess," suggesting "there may be a better opening with Syria."

It would have been out of character for Rabin purposely to mislead us. Rather, he was using the United States to his advantage. With several sets of negotiations with the Arabs moving at the same time, he knew well the benefit of playing one off against the other. Asad was particularly paranoid about this possibility because he would never forget when Sadat chose to make a separate peace with Israel in 1977 without informing him. This had significantly undermined Syria's leverage over Israel; without Egypt's military power to back him, Asad could not threaten force to extract political concessions.* Since Madrid, the Syrians had tried to use a coordinating mechanism among the four Arab negotiating teams (Syria, Jordan, Lebanon, and the Palestinians) as a way of monitoring and controlling progress in the other negotiations. Syrian insecurity was underscored by its constant rhetorical emphasis in public statements on the need for a "comprehensive peace"—meaning that no Arab party was allowed to make a separate deal with Israel.

Given Palestinian weakness, however, it was much more likely that their cause would be sacrificed on the altar of some separate Syrian-Israeli deal. From the initial establishment of the PLO in 1964, it had been used as a pawn by Arab states that would give it rhetorical support but act in their own interests. In 1993, given the parlous condition of the PLO due to the post–Gulf War loss of Arab support, the Palestinians feared Jordan and Syria would make their own deals with Israel, leaving them on the sidelines. That made them particularly sensitive to any suggestion that Israel was about to do a deal with Syria.

Rabin understood all this. During his March 1993 visit to Washington, he had noted that a peaceful gesture toward Syria could put pressure on the Palestinians to be more flexible. On July 26, when the tenth round of the Oslo negotiations had ended in an impasse, he applied that pressure, without our knowledge. Uri Savir warned his Palestinian counterpart, Abu Ala (Ahmed Qurei), that if they didn't conclude the deal Israel would turn to the Syrians, "which is what the Americans prefer." Then, at the beginning of August, Shimon Peres wrote to the Norwegian foreign minister, Jorgen Holst—a letter meant for Arafat's eyes—to warn of an impending Syrian deal. Once Peres arrived in Stockholm for what he hoped would be the concluding round of negotiations, he asked Terje Roed-Larsen, the Norwegian mediator, to warn the Palestinians "that Israel might yet go for a quick deal with Syria instead of concluding the accord with the P.L.O." It was one or the other, said Peres.

---

* This strategic reality remains true to this very day and explains why the Golan has remained essentially conflict-free since 1974.

When Rabin publicly announced the "good news from Damascus" after his meeting with Christopher on August 4, his real intention was probably to put pressure on the Palestinians, though he encouraged us to believe that his primary focus was Syria.

Rabin could have treated Syria in a similar fashion, threatening through Christopher that he would make a deal with the Palestinians unless he received a more favorable response to his offer. The Syrians certainly didn't want the Israelis to conclude a deal with Arafat just when Rabin had offered them full withdrawal from the Golan. But if Rabin had tried to use the Oslo negotiations as leverage with Asad, the Syrians might well have exposed and thwarted them. According to Rabinovich, that's why Rabin did not reveal the status of the Oslo talks during Christopher's August meetings in Jerusalem.

THE KEY TO understanding what happened in the summer of 1993 is that Bill Clinton's highest priority was Syria and Yitzhak Rabin's was not. Rabin had always been clear that he intended to pursue negotiations with Syria and the Palestinians simultaneously to determine which offered the more promising path. During his first meeting with Clinton in Washington in March, when the president had been pressing him on the Syrian issue, Rabin had reminded him that there was a Palestinian problem to deal with, too.

Rabin was probing for the softer spot. That is why he wanted us to appoint Faisal Husseini head of the Palestinian delegation, why he wanted to test Asad's flexibility, and why he sent Uri Savir to Oslo to see whether Arafat was prepared to accept Rabin's red lines for an agreement. It was clear he was weighing in his own mind which approach held out the better promise of a breakthrough. On July 13, when Dennis reported Asad's positive response to his initial message, Rabin again warned him: "I don't think I can move on two fronts at once—that will combine my opposition."* He made the same point to Christopher on August 2. We of course felt the better approach was toward Syria.

Rabin may have been leaning in that direction in early August be-

---

* He had also told us on July 8: "We have to find out on which track to move. . . . I thought it would be easier with the Palestinians but . . . the PLO has managed to get control. . . . On the Syrian track, you should know better than me. But Asad doesn't look like he is in a hurry. He wants to build relations with the United States. Peace with Israel is not a burning issue for him. . . ."

cause the Oslo talks were, at that stage, in crisis. Rabin's open skepticism about Israeli talks with the Palestinians in that meeting conformed to Christopher's own experience because he went directly from Rabin's office to a surreal meeting with Faisal Husseini and the Palestinian delegation in East Jerusalem. Husseini said he required more time before responding to our "early empowerment" proposal. Then he said Arafat had actually approved a response, but he refused to provide it to us. Uncharacteristically, Christopher exploded in frustration, demanding a response before he left the region.*

From our perspective, the Palestinian negotiations were hardly going as well as our talks with Syria. But Rabin was reaching the opposite conclusion. The Oslo talks had stalled in late July, but Rabin then received the letter from Arafat transmitted through Haim Ramon, which signaled that he was desperate for the deal. After another round of talks in Oslo on August 13 and 14, it became clear the remaining gaps were bridgeable. Two days later, Rabin told Peres to try to conclude the deal with the aim of initialing it in Oslo on August 19.

Rabin was essentially choosing between a quick and advantageous deal with the Palestinians, albeit with Arafat, and a drawn-out negotiation with Asad; between an agreement with the Palestinians that deferred for at least three years the toughest political issues for Israel (settlements, statehood, and Jerusalem), and an agreement with the Syrians that would require Israelis to pay a large price, up front (acceptance of full withdrawal from the Golan Heights, including the evacuation of all settlements).

Israelis had just been through seven years of a Palestinian intifada and no longer wanted to determine the day-to-day lives of the Palestinians. Rabin had promised them a quick solution. Moreover, most Israelis agreed with Rabin's bluntly expressed sentiment that Gaza could sink into the sea. For all he cared, Arafat was welcome to it. The West Bank was another matter entirely, but except for tiny Jericho, the Oslo Accords would put that issue off for the time being.

By contrast, the militarily valuable Golan Heights had been tranquil since the Kissinger-brokered 1974 separation of forces agreement, and few Israelis wanted to change the status quo. That took precedence for them over the chance of a peace treaty with Syria meant to isolate Iraq

---

* The Palestinian delegation was, at that point, aware that something else was going on. One of them told me privately that Arafat had asked for written comments on the idea of a "Gaza first" deal.

and Iran. At that point, they were willing to absorb the costs of a low-intensity conflict with Syrian-sponsored Hezbollah in southern Lebanon to maintain control over the Golan.

The Golan had relatively few settlers in comparison to the West Bank, but a majority of them were Labor Party voters who supported Rabin. Indeed, Rabin's first government had been responsible for expanding the Golan settlements. It was therefore almost inconceivable for Rabin, both politically and personally, even to think of sacrificing the Golan settlements unless the Israeli public could feel the benefit from peace with Syria before the settlements had to be evacuated. He had promised voters during the election campaign in 1992 that he would not withdraw from the Golan. If Asad had been prepared, like Sadat, to engage in some act of public diplomacy that would convince Israelis of Syria's real desire for peace, Rabin might have seen things differently. But Asad viewed Sadat's visit to Jerusalem in 1977 as a reprehensible act; he would make no such gesture until Israel returned "every inch" of Syrian land. He was unwilling to help Rabin influence Israeli public opinion through his own overt gestures. That was, in Asad's view, Rabin's responsibility.

Rabin's rivalry with Shimon Peres also influenced his choice. Peres still had considerable support within the Labor Party but had offered Rabin a moratorium on efforts to challenge his leadership in return for allowing him to pursue seriously an agreement with the Palestinians. If Rabin abandoned the Palestinian deal Peres had brought him for a Syrian deal Peres knew little about, his longtime rival may have mutinied against him.

THE MOST IMPORTANT factor in Rabin's calculus, however, was time. Rabin was in a hurry. He knew he had to achieve a breakthrough in the peace process during his first year, because Israeli governing coalitions had a way of falling apart soon afterward. Indeed, by August 1993, the end of his first year in office, his coalition had already become unstable.*

Asad, by contrast, was in no hurry at all. The Golan Heights was a

---

* Rabin needed the six seats of the Shas Sephardi religious party to maintain a slim two-seat majority in the Knesset. In August 1993, the police sought to indict Aryeh Deri, the leader of the party, on corruption charges. Consequently, Shas left Rabin's government in September, on the eve of Rabin's departure for the Oslo signing in Washington. Rabin now ruled with a minority government.

relatively unimportant piece of real estate to Syria, with no meaningful economic value. The hundred thousand refugees generated by the
1967 war had been easily absorbed. Peace with Israel, however, could
generate pressures on Asad to open up the economy and loosen his
grip over Syrian society and politics; he would also be open to criticism for selling out the Arab cause, especially from the Sunni majority
in Syria, which had been denied power. He also understood that to be
seen as short of breath put one at a considerable disadvantage in negotiations. He would remind his American interlocutors of the Arab
proverb "Haste is from the devil."

By mid-1993, though, Yasser Arafat was in a desperate hurry. He
had lived on the margins of Arab politics since being evicted from Beirut in 1982 but was attempting to move back toward center stage
through verbal renunciation of terrorism and a willingness to acknowledge the existence of Israel. He had succeeded in securing American recognition at the end of the Reagan administration, only to be
ostracized by the United States soon afterward for his failure to prevent PLO terrorist attacks. His standing fell even lower after his support of Saddam Hussein's invasion of Kuwait.

Arafat had been forced to accept a humiliating role at the October
1991 Madrid Peace Conference and because the PLO's coffers were
empty, he was no longer able to pay for his far-flung diplomatic missions. Arafat had long relied on a patronage system to retain the allegiance of his followers. If he couldn't pay them, he feared he would
lose control over them to Arab rulers with much deeper pockets. This
explains his preoccupation with "my money."

Arafat had burned his bridges with the Bush administration by siding with Saddam. Now, if Bill Clinton was successful in helping achieve
an Israeli-Syrian peace agreement, Arafat feared that Jordan would
then make peace with Israel, leaving the Palestinians without any pa-
trons. Clinton was also trying to promote the local West Bank, Gaza,
and Jerusalem leadership at Arafat's expense.

Given the circumstances, Arafat had little to lose by reaching out to
his archenemy. Rabin soon learned that he could virtually dictate his
own terms as long as he gave Arafat a foothold in "Palestine." This
clearly came as a welcome surprise to Rabin; he told us in Washington
in March 1993 that he felt he could not meet Arafat's requirements.
But within five months it had become clear that Arafat was ready for
the time being to give up his supposedly cherished objective of an in-

dependent Palestinian state with its capital in Jerusalem. One of Arafat's closest advisers confided to me afterward that Arafat was so desperate he did not even bother to read the Oslo agreement!

As Rabin told us when we visited him in Jerusalem a month later, "Asad didn't give us a clear answer but we got a clear answer from Arafat." So he went with the track that offered the cheaper deal in the short run, even though the other track would have provided greater strategic benefits over time. Rabin also calculated that the Palestinian agreement might actually facilitate progress with the Syrians; Asad could no longer be accused of betraying the Palestinians. If Rabin's government held together, he would have another two or three years to make peace with Syria—assuming the Palestinian agreement proved successful. Rabin's contingent offer of full withdrawal from the Golan Heights could serve as a placeholder in the meantime, encouraging Asad to believe he would regain the Golan eventually. As Rabin told Clinton on September 8, after he had made his decision to go ahead with the Palestinian deal, he had taken "the best option available."

From a Washington perspective, the choice would have looked very different. There were many strategic advantages to the United States in our "Syria-first" approach and very few strategic advantages to getting caught up in the weeds of a "Gaza/Jericho-first" agreement with Yasser Arafat. At best, Clinton felt it might facilitate the Syrian deal. But the choice was not his to make. The United States was the peace facilitator, not the peacemaker. Clinton would have to adjust his strategy accordingly.

RABIN HAD SHOWN how effectively the Israeli tail could wag the American dog. This asymmetrical relationship between the American superpower and a small, dependent ally is not supposed to be that way. As Anwar Sadat pointed out when he decided to dump the Soviet Union and turn to Washington after the Yom Kippur War in 1973, the United States gives Israel everything "from a Phantom jet to a loaf of bread." In his mind, as in the minds of most Arab leaders, Washington merely needs to tell Jerusalem to jump and Israeli prime ministers will respond by asking "how high?" That view took hold in the Arab world in 1957 when President Eisenhower demanded that Israel withdraw from the Sinai Peninsula after the 1956 Suez Crisis and David Ben-Gurion reluctantly acquiesced.

Since then, however, there have been few occasions when the president has been prepared to take a stand against Israel and when he does, he usually ends up backing down. This has led some analysts to conclude that the "Israel lobby" in America has grown so strong since 1957 that it is able to deter presidents from pressuring Israel and, worse, has proved so capable of influencing American policy that the national interest has been distorted. What these analysts willfully overlook is the logic of their own realist analysis, which assumes nations pursue their interests.

In the U.S.-Israel case, there are many shared interests, based on democratic values, a Judeo-Christian ethic, and a commitment to ensure the well-being of the Jewish state. Over time, that has produced close coordination between the two allied governments and intense working relationships, especially between intelligence agencies. It has also generated strong bipartisan support in Congress, which has been substantially reinforced by the effectiveness of the American Israel Public Affairs Committee (the actual Israel lobby). In recent years, the evangelical community has also mobilized in opposition to any hint of pressure on Israel out of a biblical conviction that God gave the Holy Land to the Jews.

Moreover, there is a natural tendency for American presidents to sympathize with the political travails of their Israeli counterparts because they can instinctively relate to the difficulties of coalition politics in a democratic society. By contrast, presidents tend to assume that authoritarian Arab leaders are capable of acting independently of public opinion since they are not accountable to their people. This of course is a misperception because the very fact that they rule without popular consent makes these Arab leaders particularly sensitive to the attitudes of their people and more fearful of them. Nevertheless, the fact that Israel is a vibrant, fractious democracy tends to make American presidents reluctant to push Israeli prime ministers beyond the limits dictated by their often vociferous opponents.

Consequently, when American and Israeli interests diverge, as is natural even in the closest alliance, the president is only likely to prevail when he has as intense an interest in the outcome as his Israeli counterpart does. That is rarely the case because as a superpower, the United States has broader horizons and much larger margins for error; Israel, conversely, is intensely focused on its survival in a hostile neighborhood.

In the pursuit of Arab-Israeli peace, the United States has an inherent tendency to defer to Israel because its smaller ally is the one that has to make the tangible concessions of territory.* The president also has to be careful not to puncture the Arabs' belief in the value to them of American influence on Israel. To attempt to pressure Israel on their behalf and to fail to deliver reduces their incentive to work with Washington.

In these prevailing circumstances, it will always be easier and more effective for an American president to get behind an Israeli peace initiative and help shape it and sell it to the Arab side, than to press Israel to produce an initiative if its government is unwilling to do so. However, this process tends to create the suspicion among Arabs that the United States is only acting as Israel's lawyer, taking its ideas and repackaging them in American wrapping. But the Arabs cannot have it both ways: if they want the United States to use its influence with Israel they should not complain when that effort results in a coordinated response. The alternative of driving a wedge between the United States and Israel may provide some psychic satisfaction but it will not make Israel more willing to take the risks involved in relinquishing territory.

In the Rabin case, Clinton had it easy. The prime minister made it clear from the outset that he had a mandate to pursue peace and he intended to use it. We thought we had agreement on the way forward—a common effort to achieve peace with Syria first, based on full Israeli withdrawal from the Golan. It was typical of our naïveté that we never expected Rabin would use U.S. influence for his own purposes. The problem in this case was a failure of coordination, not too much of it. Clinton had promised Rabin not to surprise him but had failed to make clear that in return the United States expected not to be surprised by Israel. Coordination needed to be a two-way street.

---

* This point can be better understood by reference to the joke about the chicken and the pig discussing how to meet their owner's requirement for a breakfast of bacon and eggs; the pig notes that for the chicken it only requires a contribution, but for the pig it's a total commitment.

6

Detour on the
Road to Damascus

Clinton had become the adopted parent of a newborn agreement conceived in a Norwegian test tube. That conferred certain obligations beyond hosting the signing ceremony.* But by no means had Clinton abandoned his primary interest in pursuing a Syria-Israel agreement. On September 9, four days before the Oslo signing ceremony, Clinton called Asad to reassure him that the United States remained committed to working with Syria. He also promised Asad that he would work to build a bilateral relationship with Damascus and host his foreign minister in Washington.

Asad said he was still determined to continue with the peace process, though he reminded the president, "If there is no comprehensive peace, this agreement will not stand." Clinton was encouraged by the conversation. Now he was confident that if he helped ensure tangible benefits for the Israelis from the agreement with the PLO, peace with Syria was even more likely. On September 11, two days before the Oslo signing ceremony, the president again gave a lengthy interview to Thomas Friedman of the *New York Times* in which he spoke of the need to help make Israelis feel more secure, emphasizing that was the key to making progress with Syria.

We expected that Asad would view Arafat's separate deal with Israel as an act of betrayal. Instead, after his talk with Clinton he agreed to send Ambassador Walid Mouallem to the ceremony. Ironically, Asad

---

* We quickly organized an international donors' conference, convened within three weeks at the State Department, which raised $2.5 billion in pledges to support Palestinian self-government. We also successfully pressed for an end to the secondary and tertiary Arab boycotts of Israel and for acts of normalization from Arab states in the Maghreb and the Gulf.

felt the Oslo Accords had taken the Palestinians off his back, betrayal or not, freeing Syria to make its own compact with Israel. As a senior Syrian diplomat noted to me at the signing ceremony, "Arafat has now been taken off our shoulders and he's been firmly placed on yours!"

On September 20, encouraged by Asad's decision to send his ambassador to the ceremony, Arafat went to Damascus to explain himself. According to a diplomat familiar with what transpired in the meeting, Asad interrogated Arafat about the Oslo agreement.* He then told Arafat, "You have taken care of your interests and now we are free to take care of ours." From that point on Asad publicly defined the "comprehensive peace" he sought as excluding the Palestinians since they had gone their own way.

Given Asad's reasonableness and his delinking of the Syrian and Palestinian negotiations, Clinton now believed he had found an effective way to adjust his strategy to the new realities. We were moving from a "Syria-first" to a "Syria-second" approach. He had Rabin's commitment to full withdrawal in his pocket. All he had to do now, we thought, was to get Asad to fill up his other pocket with Syrian commitments to real peace and normalization, and work out the security arrangements, and he would have a strategic achievement and a peace agreement to call his own.

After the signing ceremony at the White House, the president vowed to Asad that he would resume the effort to pursue an Israeli-Syrian agreement by the end of the year. Accordingly, in October 1993, Dennis Ross and I were dispatched to Jerusalem and Damascus to prepare for the secretary of state's reengagement with Syria. We were in for another surprise.

On October 6, Yitzhak Rabin had been invited to a clandestine meeting with King Hussein at his summer palace in Aqaba. Although Israel and Jordan were technically in a state of war, such meetings had become routine over the years. This covert relationship had originated

---

* According to this account, the Syrian president asked Arafat three questions about the agreement.
  1. Would this interim agreement lead to a final status agreement? Arafat responded that the agreement provided for final status negotiations to begin within three years.
  2. Is Jerusalem assured? Gilding the lily, Arafat responded that yes it was because the Israelis had agreed to put Jerusalem on the agenda for the final status talks.
  3. Is it part of a comprehensive solution or is it a separate deal? Arafat swore disingenuously that it was part of a comprehensive deal and that he wanted to help Syria reach its own agreement, too.

in the tumultuous days of the British withdrawal from Palestine, when the Israeli state had been established. Golda Meir, head of the Jewish Agency's political department, had established official contact with Hussein's grandfather, King Abdullah. Since then, Jordan had used intelligence channels to maintain the relationship.*

Rabin had become involved with Hussein in 1970, when he was Israel's ambassador in Washington. In that year, when the PLO challenged the king's rule and Syrian tanks crossed the border to assist them, Hussein had called on the Nixon administration for assistance. Henry Kissinger, Nixon's national security adviser, had turned to Rabin, who quickly arranged for the Israel Defense Forces (IDF) to mobilize tanks on the Golan Heights while the Pentagon dispatched the Sixth Fleet to the eastern Mediterranean. The Syrian tanks promptly withdrew.

Hussein would never forget the debt he owed Rabin, nor the danger posed by Syria. In August 1974, the king had his first opportunity to work with Rabin as prime minister. He had tried through Kissinger to take back control of Jericho and a strip of territory along the west side of the Jordan River. Like all subsequent efforts to reintroduce Jordanian control into the West Bank, the effort failed, in that case because Kissinger and Rabin preferred to focus on a second Sinai disengagement deal with Sadat, which they judged more significant.

Nevertheless, the Rabin-Hussein relationship had been cemented. Hussein had an interest in a strategic alliance with Israel to protect his weak kingdom from its predatory Arab neighbors. Rabin had an interest in a stable Jordan that would police its borders with the West Bank and deny its territory to Iraq and Syria in their efforts to form an eastern front against Israel.

As a strategist, Rabin sympathized with Hussein's security dilemmas, but that would not stop him from playing on them to Israel's advantage in this, their first meeting since Rabin and Arafat had consummated their negotiations. The king expressed his profound displeasure that Rabin had made a deal with Arafat behind his back and without any provision for a Jordanian role. Hussein had thought

---

* The king would helicopter to Israel for occasional meetings with the prime minister, landing at Mossad headquarters near Herzliya. The Mossad had built guest quarters there for the express purpose of hosting the king in the style to which he was accustomed.

he could rely on Rabin to be his strategic partner against the PLO. He accused the Israeli prime minister of betrayal.

Rabin responded in kind, blaming the king for renouncing his claims to the West Bank back in 1988. Peres and Rabin had been in the midst of a reelection campaign then, which had been based on returning the West Bank to Jordan. Rabin said the Labor Party had lost those elections because of the king's retreat from responsibility for the West Bank. The king had left him little choice but to deal with the PLO, Rabin argued, and unless he was now ready to negotiate a full peace treaty with Israel, there would be no role for Jordan in the peace process.

The king protested that he could not risk signing a peace treaty with Israel ahead of the Syrians; he could only adopt a step-by-step approach with implementation after each stage of agreement. In that case, Rabin said, the king could continue to talk to Efraim Halevy, the Mossad agent responsible for liaison with the king, but there was no reason to waste Rabin's own time. There was only one point on which he was willing to offer the king solace: he promised he would not allow Arafat to establish an independent state in the West Bank.

In playing hardball with the king, Rabin was pursuing a calculated strategy. As he explained to us when Dennis and I met him in Jerusalem two weeks later: "Our next partner will be Jordan. . . . There are only minor territorial issues. With Jordan it's much easier and it might complement our agreement with the Palestinians. With Syria it's more complicated."

When Peres told us he had reached the same conclusion, I could not restrain myself. We had already been diverted once by their surprise deal with the Palestinians; now, after the president had made a commitment to Asad, with Rabin's approval, to resume the effort to achieve an Israeli-Syrian agreement, the Israelis were off to Amman! I expressed doubt that the king would risk Asad's ire by making a separate deal with Israel. And if Asad felt Israel was trying to isolate him by dealing with Arafat and King Hussein, he could severely complicate the Palestinian negotiations with Israel. He could also create problems for Israeli forces in southern Lebanon using Hezbollah and Palestinian terrorists as proxies. While conceding that a Syrian deal was more complicated for Israel, I argued to Peres that it would provide political cover for the Palestinians and Jordan to make peace with Israel.

I did not know at the time that Israel's Directorate of Military Intel-

ligence, upon which Rabin relied heavily, had reached the same conclusion. It didn't matter. Peres and Rabin had decided to "storm
Jordan." Accordingly, when Dennis asked Rabin what he could convey
to Asad about his willingness to stand by his offer of full withdrawal
from the Golan, the prime minister responded: "Say you didn't ask
me!" He wasn't joking. Rabin seemed to be backing out of the commitment he had given Christopher in August. We were headed for an
encounter with the always-suspicious Asad with empty pockets.

ONE HUNDRED AND twenty-five years earlier, Mark Twain had observed, "Go back as far as you will into the vague past, there was always a Damascus. . . . She measures time not by days and months and
years, but by the empires she has seen rise and prosper and crumble to
ruin." Damascus is believed to be the oldest continuously inhabited
city in the world. It was once renowned for its crowded souks and the
elaborate Umayyad Mosque, for the exquisite work of its craftsmen
and its dominance of historic trade routes. But the ancient city itself,
like empires of old, was crumbling.

Travelers in earlier centuries who approached Damascus from the
Anti-Lebanon Mountains to the west would recount seeing a shim-
mering white city, fringed by a green oasis, with the dry desert beyond
stretching to the horizon—a breathtaking mirage. But to us, hurtling
toward town from Damascus Airport in a black, armor-plated,
government-owned Mercedes-Benz, along a deserted highway, past
Palestinian refugee camps that had morphed into outlying shantytown
suburbs, Damascus looked like a Stalinist-era Soviet city. The satellite
television dishes adorning every balcony of its austere, dirt-encrusted,
concrete apartment blocks seemed to be its only concession to the
wonders of globalization in the last decade of the twentieth century.

The streets of Damascus in 1993 were full of cars from the 1950s;
there was no foreign currency with which to buy new ones. Posters of
Asad were everywhere—on billboards and in shop windows—mirror-
ing a communist-style cult of personality campaign. One felt trans-
ported into a bygone totalitarian era.

In the 1970s, when I first visited Damascus, Asad's brother Rifat
commanded praetorian guards, the Defense Companies, who seemed
to occupy every street corner in downtown Damascus, lounging in
shiny green Range Rovers, sporting red berets, awaiting any sign of
trouble. A tank company was also conspicuous, its base camp located

in the heart of downtown Damascus between the president's old palace and the Officers Club.

By the 1990s, Asad had so consolidated his rule—in part by ruthlessly suppressing the Islamic fundamentalists who posed a real challenge to it—that this military presence was no longer necessary.*

In ancient days, the great caliphs who established their capitals in Damascus built magnificent mosques open to all the people. By contrast, Asad built his vast palace on a high mountain perch to shut himself off from his people. Everything about the gray marble presidential palace seemed designed to symbolize the power of the state and the insignificance of the individual.

Once past the guardhouse and gate, visiting officials approach the palace on a wide boulevard. The delegation is escorted through a long, cavernous, three-storied hallway, on a red carpet that stretches ahead, rising by intermittent steps the distance of what seems like a city block. As we approached Asad's inner sanctum, his furtive flunkies watched us from their office doorways on either side. At the end of the walkway were large double doors where Asad stood waiting for us, framed by a huge floor-to-ceiling window that afforded a full view of the city below.

As Asad moved carefully to his seat, I noticed that the back and top of the president's head were flat, creating a boxlike look. His cheeks had thinned out so much that when viewed from the front, his head had taken on the shape of a lightbulb. His swollen ankles were wrapped in bandages; his hand felt bony.

Henry Kissinger, who spent many days in Damascus negotiating the 1974 Golan Heights Separation of Forces Agreement, developed a "high regard" for this Syrian leader because of his "first class mind allied to a wicked sense of humor." Jimmy Carter found him to be constructive and flexible even though Carter would later come to see him as doing everything possible to sabotage his efforts to convene Arab-Israeli negotiations. James Baker, who had eleven lengthy meetings with Asad to prepare for the 1991 Madrid conference, which launched Arab-Israeli negotiations, described him as "intellectually engaging, wily and one tough customer," but "not readily prone to take risks in pursuit of his goals."

---

* Indeed, in 1983 Asad discovered it could be used to threaten his hold on power when his brother took advantage of Asad's hospitalization because of a heart ailment to try to take control.

By the time the Clinton peace team engaged him, Asad had lost a lot of his charm but none of his acuity. Although only in his late sixties by then, diabetes and a heart condition had taken their toll. He and his country seemed to be stuck in a rut. Two years earlier, Asad had used the Gulf War adroitly to reposition Syria as a potential Arab partner for the United States. But he then proved unable or unwilling to take the necessary steps to develop the relationship: he would not shut down the Palestinian terrorist groups who operated out of Damascus and Syrian-controlled Lebanon, and he would not end his support for Hezbollah's operations against Israeli forces in southern Lebanon, which often spilled over into Katyusha rocket attacks on northern Israeli townships. He insisted that both steps would have to await a final peace agreement with Israel. That meant, notwithstanding Asad's realignment with the United States, that Syria remained on the State Department's terrorism list with its sanctions and restrictions on bilateral relations.

Asad sat in one of two heavy, square lounge chairs with elaborate mother-of-pearl inlaid designs; behind him was a large, circular, carved marble mosaic. His interpreter, Buthaina Shaaban, and his foreign minister, Farouq al-Sharaa, were sitting at his right hand. At the end of the row of seated officials sat a nervous aide, writing down every word of our conversation.

On this visit in November 1993, we found Asad in a positive mood because of the constructive talks his foreign minister had just completed in Washington, crowned by a meeting in President Clinton's private study. Clinton had begun discussing bilateral relations with Sharaa and Christopher had reached an understanding with him on a humanitarian issue of considerable concern to the American Jewish community and to Israel.

The once great, now tiny community of less than 1,500 Syrian Jews had been allowed to leave in small numbers after Syria joined in the Madrid conference in 1992. But Asad had shut the gates in the last months of the Bush administration. Clinton and Christopher had been pressing Asad and Sharaa to allow all the remaining Jews to leave.

Sharaa, who had served as head of Syrian Arab Airlines, was keen to find replacements for the airline's aging fleet of Russian-made aircraft. The Kuwaitis were prepared to give the Syrians three civilian Boeing 727s but because they were American aircraft and Syria was on the

State Department's terrorism list, the U.S. government had to approve the transfer and Congress had to be consulted. Christopher told Sharaa that if Syria decided to let all the Syrian Jews go, that move would facilitate our ability to secure congressional acquiescence in the transfer of the Kuwaiti 727s to Damascus. The Syrians were always promising that if we took one step toward them they would take two steps toward us—such were the ways of the bazaar, they claimed—so Christopher decided to test them by offering aircraft for exit visas. Sharaa accepted the trade.

In our meeting, Asad was also pleased to hear from Dennis that the president believed Syria was the key to a comprehensive settlement and that he wanted to build a positive bilateral relationship. But Asad quickly zeroed in on the one issue about which we had nothing to tell him: whether Rabin had repeated to Dennis his commitment to full withdrawal from the Golan. Dennis responded with a "yada yada yada" routine, avoiding the question by raising a number of procedural ideas that he claimed Peres and Rabin had suggested to us.

Asad was not buying it. He asked directly whether Rabin had reaffirmed his commitment. "Not exactly" was Dennis's answer. Asad said coldly, "I conclude from what you've said that Rabin is going back on the commitment conveyed by the U.S. This is a dangerous indication." He said that in his view, after the Oslo agreement Rabin was stronger, not weaker as Dennis had claimed, and that nothing now prevented Rabin from making an agreement with Syria. If he became convinced that Rabin was no longer interested, Asad warned us, he would "take a firm stand." But he then expressed sympathy for our predicament and urged us to get a clarification from Rabin. Then he added: "If anybody in Israel believes there can be peace without Syria they're wrong. If we are sure they are backing away, they will have blocked the process with their own hands. . . . We've been moderate; we won't be any longer."

In these sharp words, one could glimpse the thuggish instincts that lay beneath Asad's civil façade. He had ordered the leveling of the Syrian city of Hama to send a clear signal to his people that he would not tolerate an Islamic fundamentalist challenge that had been brewing there. It was widely thought that he ordered the assassination of two Lebanese leaders, Kamal Jumblatt and Beshir Gemayel, for challenging Syria's grip on Lebanon. His threats could not be taken lightly. Yet this minor episode revealed a change in Asad. Despite his tone, he clearly wanted to leave the door open. He was shrewdly putting the onus on Secretary Christopher, who was due to visit, to produce the reaffirmation of Rabin's commitment.

IF ASAD HAD known that at that very moment the Israelis were actively seeking peace with Jordan, he might not have waited for Christopher's clarification. On November 2, 1993, Shimon Peres crossed the Jordan River in disguise to meet with King Hussein. In contrast to his reluctance a few weeks earlier, Hussein now made clear that he wanted to move quickly and secretly on a peace agreement with Israel.

The king's motivation appears to have been fear of what would happen in the West Bank now that Israel was offering Arafat a controlling presence there. His meeting with Rabin had concentrated his thinking. Arafat in the West Bank would pose an existential threat to his regime and he could no longer rely on Rabin to suppress it. As many as two-thirds of Jordan's population were Palestinians whose families came from Israel or the West Bank as refugees following the 1948 and 1967 wars. Because they identified with West Bank Palestinians, what happened there could affect the king's hold on power on the East Bank.

Geographically, Jordan abutted the West Bank along a ninety-seven-kilometer border that had, in years past, provided easy infiltration routes for Palestinian terrorist operations against Israel. The Israelis would hold Jordan responsible and retaliate accordingly. This threatened the kingdom's stability.

Since the PLO had already tried to dethrone him once, in 1970, there was a real danger that Arafat would try again if he were now free to use the West Bank as a launching pad. Hussein wanted to retain some influence over the West Bank even if he could not control it for the time being. It seemed that making peace with Israel was now the best route to achieving that objective.

The king had some other motivations, too. He had inherited Jordanian control over the West Bank and East Jerusalem from his grandfather, King Abdullah, only to lose it to Israel in the 1967 Six-Day War. Hussein harbored a deep desire to undo this humiliation.

The king also had a personal attachment to the al-Aqsa Mosque in Jerusalem, the third-holiest site in Islam. In 1924, his great-grandfather, Sharif Hussein, had lost custodianship of Mecca and Medina, the two holiest sites in Islam, when Ibn Saud conquered the Hejaz and created the Kingdom of Saudi Arabia. His grandfather, King Abdullah, had been given control over the al-Aqsa Mosque by the British. Subsequently, a young Hussein had been by his grandfather's side when Palestinians assassinated him on the steps of al-Aqsa in 1951. As an Arab leader who traced his lineage back forty-two generations to the Prophet Mohamed, he had drawn legitimacy in Jordan and elsewhere in the Muslim world from his role as custodian of Jerusalem's Haram al-Sharif (Temple Mount), where the al-Aqsa Mosque and the Dome of the Rock shrine were situated.

When the Israelis took control of the Old City of Jerusalem during the Six-Day War in 1967, Hussein lost his custodianship just as his great-grandfather had lost custodianship of Mecca and Medina. He nevertheless sought to maintain his influence over the al-Aqsa Mosque through the *waqf* (Islamic trust), which managed the compound under Israeli rule. The Israelis preferred to have King Hussein retain his responsibilities there rather than to have the Palestinians take control. However, the lack of a Jordanian physical presence in Jerusalem made it increasingly difficult for the king to preserve his influence. Through Palestinian clerics, Arafat had already been waging a determined battle to take over the *waqf*. With Arafat's imminent return to the West Bank, the king's custodianship would be even more deeply threatened. Only Israel could help prevent that from happening.

Hussein also feared the development of an "unholy alliance" between the right wing in Israel and the PLO regarding the East Bank. Those Israelis who wanted to retain control of the West Bank argued that Jordan was in fact Palestine and the Palestinians should exercise their self-determination there. The king feared that if a right-wing Israeli government replaced Rabin, it might transfer Palestinians across the Jordan River in an effort to destabilize his regime and create a Palestinian state on the East Bank. A peace agreement with Israel would forestall that possibility, binding future Israeli governments to the maintenance of the Hashemite Kingdom.

As long as the Palestinians did not engage Israel in negotiations, the king could afford to be relaxed about the fate of the West Bank; he knew that Israel would police the Palestinians there. But once negotiations began, the king needed to assert his tutelage over the Palestinians. He had suffered a setback in that effort when, at a summit of Arab leaders in Rabat in 1974, the Arab League designated the PLO as the "sole, legitimate representative of the Palestinian people." However, the king maneuvered adroitly to preserve his role by ensuring that any Palestinian negotiations with Israel took place under the umbrella of a joint Jordanian-Palestinian delegation. He had been able to achieve this at the 1991 Madrid Peace Conference because of Arafat's weakened stature. But now Arafat had done a deal behind his back directly with Israel's leadership. Hussein suddenly felt his ability to regain East Jerusalem or the West Bank was in jeopardy, and his control on the East Bank was threatened, too.

All these concerns found expression in the king's meeting with Peres in Amman in November 1993. Peres had first met Hussein in 1974, when he was defense minister during Rabin's first term as prime minister. At that time, Peres advocated joint Israeli-Jordanian control of the West Bank, expressing adamant opposition to an independent Palestinian state. His proposal foundered when the Labor Party was defeated at the polls.

Hussein and Peres had met again in London in April 1987, when Peres was foreign minister in a national unity government under Likud prime minister Yitzhak Shamir. The two had reached agreement on a Jordanian takeover of the West Bank but Peres then failed to get the Israeli cabinet or the United States to endorse the agreement. This severely embarrassed the Jordanian monarch.

Nevertheless, this time overnight they again reached agreement on a set of principles to govern Israeli-Jordanian peace negotiations. Hussein was likely using Peres's renewed enthusiasm for a deal to soften up Rabin, who three weeks earlier had treated him so harshly. In return for accelerating the Jordan-Israel negotiations to achieve a quick peace agreement, Peres pledged Israel's support for close cooperation between Jordan and the Palestinians, and an immediate role for Jordan in the Palestinian economy, including permission for Jordanian banks to establish branches in the West Bank and Gaza. Beyond the pledge that Rabin had already made to the king that no independent Palestinian state would be established, Peres promised not to allow Arafat to challenge Jordanian control of the *waqf* in Jerusalem.

When Uri Savir briefed Dennis and me on this agreement in Paris two days later, we were impressed by the apparent breadth of the understanding that Peres and Hussein had reached in one night of negotiations. And we were grateful that this time the Israelis had kept us in the loop. Nevertheless, I worried about Asad's reaction. When it leaked, the Peres-Hussein understanding might convince him that Clinton's words had been designed to lull him into passivity while we worked with Israel and Jordan to isolate Syria and weaken his bargaining position.

For once Rabin and Peres were sensitive to these concerns. Rabin indicated to us that when he met with the president in Washington in November he would be more forthcoming about Syria than he had been when we met with him in Jerusalem in October. For his part, Peres started sending positive signals to Syria in his public statements.

Peres had another motivation. In their meeting, King Hussein had stipulated that their understanding and the negotiations that followed needed to be kept secret precisely because he was fearful of Asad's reaction. But the day after Peres's rendezvous with history in Amman, he had told an Israeli TV interviewer in an off-camera aside, "Remember the third of November." It did not take the Israeli press long to establish that Peres had been in Jordan and to speculate that he had already achieved a peace agreement. The king was furious, and Peres was looking for a way to make it up to him. By sending positive signals to Syria, Peres hoped to demonstrate his sensitivity to the king's circumstances.

Contrary to my fears, however, Asad did not create trouble for Hussein. Rather, he waited to see if Secretary of State Christopher would bring him a reaffirmation of Rabin's commitment. Asad was a cautious chess player who carefully calculated the consequences of his moves. To turn on the United States just at the moment his relations with us were improving would have been unwise. Or perhaps it was just that without a superpower patron or a military option against Israel, he understood that he had little choice but to hope the United States would deliver the Golan Heights to him.

In any case, Asad's cautious approach did not assuage the king's fears of how the Syrian leader would react now that Peres had divulged the deal. On November 21, 1993, soon after Peres's faux pas, Hussein visited Damascus to reassure Asad that Jordan would not race ahead of Syria in its negotiations with Israel. He then sent word to Rabin through Efraim Halevy that because of Peres's leak he had no choice but to move at a more measured pace. He insisted that Peres not be involved in the secret negotiations and that there be no talk of quickly concluding a peace treaty. As King Hussein would tell Christopher in

December, he would "build from the bottom up, address all the difficulties, implement what we agree on, and then at the end the peace
treaty will be the 'crowning achievement.' "

It wasn't just fear of the Syrian reaction that slowed him down. The
Palestinian negotiations had by now stalled, removing the urgency to
protect Hashemite interests in the West Bank and Jerusalem.

Rabin, none too pleased with Hussein's prevarications, now concentrated on breaking the impasse with Arafat and determining whether
a breakthrough could be achieved with Syria rather than Jordan. He
told the president on his November visit to Washington that he could
reaffirm to Asad his conditional commitment to full withdrawal.
Christopher was dispatched to Damascus, where he was well received
by Asad. The Syrian leader readily agreed to Christopher's proposal for
meetings in Washington between the Israeli and Syrian heads of delegation. He confirmed that all Syrian Jews who wanted to leave would
be given visas immediately.* In return, Christopher delivered an invitation to a rendezvous with Clinton in Geneva.

ON JANUARY 16, 1994, Clinton arrived in Geneva to meet Asad in
pursuit of his belief that a Syrian-Israeli peace was the key to resolving
the Arab-Israeli conflict. He also saw it as an opportunity to test the
proposition that through dialogue he could change the behavior of one
of the world's more intractable dictators.

The world's press had assembled in the ballroom of Geneva's Inter-
Continental hotel to hear the results. As the two presidents entered the
hall, the frail and older one holding the arm of the younger, both
seemed satisfied. Clinton's peace team was sitting in the front row with
the Syrian delegation. We had been up all night haggling over the
statement Asad was about to read and arguing over how many Israeli
journalists would be allowed in the room. We, too, thought we had
reason to be satisfied. Our Israeli friends had told us on the summit's
eve that the one thing they would be listening for, as a sign of Asad's
intentions, was whether he would speak about normalizing relations
with Israel. Now he read aloud those very words in Arabic:

---

*   Asad also agreed that Syria would receive a congressional staff delegation pursuing new information on three Israeli MIAs who had either been killed or captured at
Sultan Yaqub in southern Lebanon and had possibly been buried in Damascus. And
he promised Christopher to look into the question of what had happened to Ron
Arad, an Israeli navigator who was shot down over Lebanon in 1986.

Syria seeks a just and comprehensive peace with Israel as a strategic choice. . . . We want the peace of the brave, a genuine peace which can survive and last. . . . If the leaders of Israel have sufficient courage to respond to this kind of peace, the new era of security and stability with *normal peaceful relations among all* shall dawn anew.

Barry Schweid, a skeptical curmudgeon who covered the State Department for the Associated Press, asked Clinton the first question. From long experience, Barry was closely attuned to the code words of the peace process and immediately picked up on the reference to normalization of relations. He asked Clinton whether Asad's words meant open borders, free trade, and diplomatic relations. Clinton had raised these issues with Asad and was therefore quite confident in responding, "Yes, I believe President Asad has made a clear, forthright, and very important statement on normal peaceful relations."

Wolf Blitzer of CNN followed up by asking Asad the same question. The Syrian leader responded that Clinton and he had "completely agreed" on the requirements of peace. "We will respond to these requirements," he added.

During their meeting, Clinton had sought to convince Asad that Rabin's commitment to full withdrawal was in his pocket but it wouldn't be taken out until Asad filled up the other pocket with Syrian commitments on security arrangements and normalization. He tried to persuade Asad that engaging in some positive public gestures toward Israel would help lubricate the negotiations by making it easier for Rabin to sell full withdrawal to his people.

Asad wanted something quite different. The evening before his meeting with Clinton, he had sent his foreign minister to meet Christopher to negotiate the terms for a U.S.-Syrian entente. In a polite but tough conversation, Christopher made clear to Sharaa that there was no chance for any serious improvement in bilateral relations unless Syria canceled its support for terrorist organizations. The most Christopher would offer was an improvement in relations if the peace process moved ahead. Sharaa was clearly frustrated and disappointed.

When Asad raised the question of bilateral relations in the next day's summit meeting, the president responded with a well-practiced bureaucratic technique: he offered to establish a joint U.S.-Syria committee under the auspices of the secretary of state and the Syrian foreign minister to explore how to resolve the problems in the bilateral relationship. Asad recognized this for what it was. In return he wouldn't give much, either.

He did not respond to Clinton's offer to place American troops on the Golan in a peacekeeping role. When Clinton pushed him on Israel's need for adequate security arrangements to compensate for ceding the Golan high ground, Asad held forth on the history of Israeli "aggression." Arguing that Damascus was much closer to the 1967 border than either Tel Aviv or Jerusalem, he insisted that the security arrangements would need to be "on both sides" of the border and they would need to be "balanced, reciprocal and on an equal footing." This did not augur well for the negotiations that were about to begin in Washington, since Rabin would find it difficult to accept such concepts. Asad also continued to insist that Israel's withdrawal be in one phase and completed within a year (Rabin was insisting on three phases over five years with embassies established in the first phase and settlements evacuated in the last).

Asad did, however, make two concessions. While insisting that the peace had to be "comprehensive," he confirmed that his definition of comprehensiveness had changed since Arafat had signed the Oslo agreement with Rabin. Now he defined it as final peace agreements with Syria, Lebanon, and Jordan—the Palestinians had made their separate deal and from his point of view were now on their own. This was significant because Asad had always sought to appear as the foremost exponent of the Palestinian cause. Now he indicated a willingness to make peace with Israel regardless of whether the Palestinians had reached a final settlement with the Israelis. In other words, he was prepared to meet Rabin's requirement that the Syrian deal "stand on its own feet."

The second concession was his willingness to accept "normal peaceful relations" with Israel as one of the requirements of the agreement. The very notion of normalization with Israel was anathema to Asad. It could threaten his grip on power in Damascus by forcing the opening of Syria's economy and society. Up to this point, peace with Israel had meant an absence of war. As Patrick Seale, Asad's biographer, put it, Asad's objective in the negotiations had always been to "shrink Israel's influence to more modest and less aggressive proportions." Asad's acceptance at the Geneva summit of the formula of "normal peaceful relations" with Israel therefore represented a significant opening.

. . .

DENNIS AND I were elated. After the Clinton-Asad press conference, we backgrounded the American press to make sure they understood the importance of what Asad had said. Then Clinton dispatched us to brief Rabin. We landed in Israel expecting an enthusiastic reception, but as the leading columnist for Israel's most authoritative daily, *Ha'aretz,* wrote the next morning, Rabin "wiped the smiles off their faces."

What we had failed to consider was the zero-sum nature of the Israeli-Syrian relationship. If the president embraced something Asad had offered, Israelis immediately felt pressured rather than reassured. Since Asad had made a concession, they now expected they would have to do the same and so immediately devalued what we brought from Geneva. This tactical skepticism was enhanced by their inherent mistrust of Syria, which led them to assume Asad's words were a ruse.

Rabin received us at his offices in the Defense Ministry compound in Tel Aviv that evening. From the outset he was completely dismissive of what we brought from Asad. Rabin said that those Israelis who wanted peace were disappointed by Asad's statement; the Israeli press had certainly adopted that point of view. Asad's words on normalization were nothing new, he said. He summoned his head of military intelligence, Uri Saguy, to explain that the Arabic word for "normal" that Asad used (*aadi*) connoted "usual relations" rather than "normal relations" (*tabi'i*). Saguy gave us a citation from a Syrian newspaper of April 1993 to prove Asad had used the words long before the Geneva summit.

Rabin treated Asad's explicit delinking of his negotiations from the Palestinians—something Rabin had previously insisted on—with similar suspicion. He suggested it indicated that Asad was looking to influence the Jordanian track: "I can't buy anything if it's linked to Jordan." He then explained to us again that it would be easier for Israel to make peace with Jordan. "I prefer Jordan—it complements the Palestinians."

Instead of focusing on the meeting Clinton had just completed with Asad, Rabin was more interested in the meeting the president was about to have in Washington with King Hussein: "Therefore, I would prefer that the president ask the king: are you ready to sign with Israel or not? If there is any option to go with Jordan then *forget* about Syria."

It is difficult to convey how adamant Rabin could be once he had decided to reject an idea. He would swing his right arm dismissively, as if he were sweeping the suggestion off the table. Recognizing our frustration, he captured the moment precisely: "You look at it from your point of view; I look at it from my point of view."

Dennis decided to press on with his debriefing nevertheless, explaining at one point that Asad had asked Clinton whether Rabin was using the negotiations with Syria as a device to keep him engaged without ever concluding an agreement. Rabin responded by complaining about our role in the negotiations. The problem, he argued, was that Asad only wanted to hear about full withdrawal from the Golan whereas Israel had other requirements that needed to be addressed. "You committed us [to full withdrawal] but it doesn't stand on its own. If I lose this as a bargaining chip, I am crippled. This is the problem when you work through a mediator: I put it in a context, but when you convey it, the context gets lost and you undermine my bargaining power."

His approach stood in stark contrast to the views expressed by his IDF Chief of General Staff, Lieutenant General Ehud Barak, when Rabin expanded the meeting to include him and other aides. Not privy to Rabin's dismissal of Asad's words, nor his secret negotiations with the Jordanians, Barak expounded on what he viewed as Clinton's "impressive and important achievement." The fact that Asad had mentioned Israel and normal peaceful relations in the same breath and in the presence of the U.S. president was, in Barak's view, very important. In a harbinger of the approach he would take when he became prime minister, Barak expressed frustration with Arafat and portrayed the Syrian negotiations as a strategic opportunity.

Uri Saguy, the chief of military intelligence, argued that Asad had taken a strategic decision to make peace with Israel and understood that he would have to make concessions on security arrangements but would not budge on territory. According to Saguy, Asad had already communicated this strategic decision to the Syrian general staff, who had come to understand that the Golan Heights would have to be demilitarized. Saguy viewed the summit statement as nothing new, but he meant it in the opposite sense to Rabin—Asad, in his assessment, had taken the decision to make peace some time ago. To Saguy, what Asad said in Geneva was just one more confirmation of that choice.

Rabin's most senior military advisers both saw the virtue of a peace agreement with Syria, understanding that it would require in the final analysis a full IDF withdrawal from the Golan Heights. Six years later, with Barak as prime minister and Saguy as his negotiator with Syria, their views would hold more sway, but for now Rabin was running the show and he was unhappy with the Syrian "breakthrough" we thought we had achieved.

RABIN NEVERTHELESS NEEDED Clinton's help. Secret Israeli-Jordanian negotiations had begun in London in the second week of December and had quickly moved to Israel and Jordan, where at the end of 1993 the two sides began twice-weekly sessions using a special helicopter air bridge to enable the negotiators to travel easily between the two capitals. But the king refused to discuss a peace treaty; he wanted to focus instead on the subagenda of bilateral issues: water sharing, displaced Palestinians, return of territory, and economic development projects. Rabin's frustration with the king was best expressed by Peres, who told us in exasperation, "History cannot be made by a lady in waiting."

For Rabin and Peres, the president's meeting with Hussein in Washington, a week after his rendezvous with Asad, had become critical to the achievement of their strategy. But when Clinton, at Rabin's urging, pressed Hussein to move toward a peace treaty, Hussein said that Jordan's concerns had to be addressed first. Like Asad, the king also wanted to lay the groundwork for improving Jordan's bilateral relationship with the United States before he finalized any arrangement with Israel.

The king asked the president whether the United States would be willing to resume the military aid that had been cut off after the Gulf War because of his decision to side with Saddam Hussein. Just as with Asad, the president was noncommittal; he knew he would have a hard time convincing Congress to forgive the king his 1991 trespass on American interests in the Gulf. Unlike Asad, however, King Hussein wasn't looking to rebuild his relations with the United States in order to counterbalance Israel's strength; he was interested rather in knowing if he could again rely on the United States to counterbalance Syria's strength, especially were he to sign a peace agreement with Israel. And if Asad were to make peace with Israel, as appeared likely in early 1994, the king did not want to be left picking up the crumbs as the United States enhanced its relations with Jordan's more powerful Arab neighbor.

This fear of being left out also applied to the king's anxiety over the Palestinian negotiations. By the end of February 1994, Arafat was coming under increasing pressure from Palestinian critics to show something tangible from the Oslo agreement. Concerned that the Clinton-Asad summit in Geneva signaled that Rabin was about to consummate his deal with Syria and abandon him, Arafat started to drop some of his more outlandish demands.

Since the September signing ceremony, we had had little to do with the Israeli-Palestinian negotiations. Rabin was adamant that the United States should not get involved. The Palestinians for their part assumed that if we were brought into the negotiations we would be in Israel's corner. The Israeli and Palestinian negotiators were attempting to reach agreement on the implementation of the Oslo Accords, which would lead to an Israeli army withdrawal from Gaza and Jericho and allow Arafat to establish his rule there. They soon discovered huge gaps between their positions.* Nevertheless, they had managed to come up with creative solutions. That was the great advantage of the interim process—each side could accept a compromise in the short term on the assumption that there would be opportunities later to undo the concession. But it was also the great shortcoming of the process, since issues were never fully resolved and both sides got into the habit of observing their agreements in the breach.

In a series of meetings between Peres and Arafat in late January and early February, the first logjam was broken.† Accordingly, the king instructed his team to reinvigorate the peace negotiations. In Washington, we had reason to think things were now moving forward on all three fronts. Despite the difference in emphasis that Rabin had expressed, the symbiotic relationship between the three sets of negotia-

---

* Arafat insisted on Palestinian control of the border crossing points to Jordan and Egypt; Rabin adamantly refused. Rabin insisted on retaining overriding Israeli security responsibility even in the territory from which Israel would withdraw; Arafat refused. Arafat wanted the Jericho enclave to cover an area ten times larger than what Rabin was prepared to offer.

† Peres convinced Arafat to accept that Israel would retain security control over the border crossing points while the Palestinians would be accorded respect for their dignity there.

tions helped to reinforce the positive dynamics. The peace train was rolling.

IN THE MIDDLE East, you learn quickly to suspect that good news is usually only a harbinger of bad news to follow.

On Friday, February 25, 1994, Dr. Baruch Goldstein, an Israeli settler who had migrated from Brooklyn to the West Bank settlement of Kiryat Arba, donned his army reserve uniform, took his machine gun into Hebron, down to the tomb of Abraham, the patriarch of Jews and Arabs. Goldstein, walked into the mosque where Palestinians were reciting their early morning prayers and massacred twenty-nine of them before he was killed. The peace process stopped in its tracks as outrage spread through the Arab world and precipitated the suspension of all peace negotiations with Israel.

Clinton dispatched the peace team—Dennis Ross, Aaron Miller, Dan Kurtzer, and me—to Tunis to talk to Arafat about what could be done to salvage the negotiations.

Tunis is a tranquil Mediterranean city far from the Middle Eastern cauldron that had just boiled over in Hebron. Arafat had repaired there after his evacuation from Beirut on the advice of Abu Mazen, who had argued that it was time to escape the influence of Arab leaders and intelligence services that had played havoc with Palestinian decision-making for decades.

I had imagined that the chairman of the PLO would be ensconced in some elaborate compound with high walls, guarded by Palestinian fedayeen sporting Kalashnikovs, heads covered in their checkered kaffiyehs. But the Tunisians were not about to let Arafat and his associates establish another state-within-a-state in their capital, as the PLO had done in Lebanon. Security was provided by the Tunisian police alone. Arafat's "compound" was an unassuming villa in need of renovation in a quiet inner-city neighborhood.

Arafat received us in his office, a long narrow room with a desk and adjoining conference table that looked like they had been purchased from a Salvation Army store. A huge photograph of the Dome of the Rock in Jerusalem served as the backdrop. At the other end of the conference table was an old TV set and VCR on which Arafat was rumored to pass the time watching Mickey Mouse cartoons. Maps of Palestine hung on one of the side walls, notably lacking any depiction of Israel.

And there was a large life-size picture of a much younger, uniformed Arafat standing in front of a black Mercedes-Benz next to his swashbuckling comrade in arms, Abu Jihad (Khalil al-Wazir), the military commander of the PLO. Israeli commandos had assassinated Abu Jihad in his Tunis home six years earlier, a month after he had almost managed to pull off a terrorist attack on Israel's nuclear reactor in Dimona.

We were subjected to Arafat's signature theatrical performance, one part conspiratorial, one part paranoid, one part plaintive victimhood, and one part pure mythology, all in the service of extracting the maximum advantage out of the grievous circumstances in Hebron.

First he cataloged the pressures he was under from Palestinians who were asking him what kind of a peace process could result in a Jew massacring Muslims at prayer. Then came an accusation against King Hussein for encouraging Palestinian demonstrators to smash Arafat's portrait in front of TV cameras. After that came the whispered, secretive warning that Goldstein's act was an Algerian-style plot by a "secret army" within the IDF, run by senior officers. Finally came his demands. In order to restore a sense of security to his people in Hebron he needed an international presence in the city; the deployment there of Palestinian police; the evacuation of forty-five Jewish settlers from Tel Rumeida, in the heart of Hebron; and a U.N. Security Council resolution that would condemn Israel and codify these arrangements. Only after all this had been implemented would he consider returning to negotiations.

"We're not asking for the moon!" Arafat said. To us, he sounded as if he were on the moon. Interposing an international force between angry Hebronites and zealous Israeli settlers seemed to us a recipe for endless problems. The evacuation of settlers would be hugely traumatic for Israel—not something we thought Rabin was likely to undertake. But our biggest problem with Arafat's list of requirements was his demand for a U.N. Security Council resolution.

The Clinton administration had a severe allergy to dealing with the Palestinian issue in the Security Council. There, in the spotlight of international public opinion, the Palestinians as the underdog would always enjoy a majority, and the United States would always stand in the dock alongside Israel. Although the United Nations had been instrumental in the establishment of the state of Israel in 1948, since then the General Assembly had become a Star Chamber for anti-Israel activities, the most notorious of which was U.N. General Assembly Resolution 3379, declaring "Zionism is a form of racism." Clinton had made considerable progress since the Oslo agreement in persuading the United Nations to adopt positive and supportive resolutions. But to insert the Security Council into the process now would severely complicate the U.S. role as mediator.

Any effort to pass a new Security Council resolution would also inevitably bring up the issue of Jerusalem. Previous Security Council resolutions treated East Jerusalem as "occupied territory" and rejected Israel's annexation of it. American policy was deliberately more ambiguous: it neither recognized Israel's annexation nor viewed East Jerusalem as "occupied territory." The American Jewish community, as well as an overwhelming majority in Congress, wanted Jerusalem recognized as Israel's capital and the U.S. embassy moved there. Candidate Clinton said Jerusalem should be the capital; President Clinton understood that Jerusalem was the most sensitive issue of the Arab-Israeli conflict; the subject had to be skirted if he was going to help achieve peace.

In any event, the Oslo agreement provided that the final status negotiations would deal with Jerusalem; those talks were still at least two years off. If the Palestinians pushed for a new Security Council resolution that declared Jerusalem to be occupied Palestinian territory, Clinton would have no choice but to exercise America's veto and that would doom our efforts to overcome the impact of the Goldstein massacre. Moreover, the Clinton administration had a strong aversion to wielding its veto, because of its interest in maintaining international consensus as part of its multilateral approach to critical foreign policy issues such as Iraq. Casting our veto on a Palestinian resolution could provide justification for other powers to exercise their veto on an Iraq resolution.

Alas, the reference to Jerusalem as occupied territory had already been included in a draft circulated to members of the Security Council. If Arafat agreed to remove it before a vote he would be charged with selling out Jerusalem as well as the residents of Hebron. Both Clinton and Arafat were boxed in.

After Dennis and I left the meeting with Arafat in Tunis, Dennis received a phone call from Sandy Berger, then the president's deputy national security adviser, instructing him to return to Arafat and tell him in no uncertain terms that the United States would veto the Security Council resolution if he insisted on moving ahead with it. Dennis had already tried to explain to Arafat the dangers of insisting on such a resolution, to no avail. Predictably, when he went back to Arafat with Berger's message, Arafat exploded in rage. A veto would bring disaster on him and us, he said.

Despite the dilemma we now faced, we knew that Israel, Syria, and Jordan all wanted to see the negotiations resume: Rabin wanted to show the settler extremists that they could not undo with violence what had been done at Oslo; Asad and Hussein wanted to prevent Arafat from holding up their negotiations. Still, given the magnitude of Goldstein's massacre, they could hardly continue talking with Israel as if nothing had happened. A Security Council resolution that criticized Israel would give them some cover for resumption; an American veto would make it impossible for them to come back to the table.

While we were struggling for a way out of this predicament, Rabin came to Washington on a previously scheduled visit. He accepted the idea of a symbolic international presence in Hebron and the transfer of Palestinian police to the city, as long as Israel retained overall security control. If Arafat were ready to resume negotiations, Rabin would send Peres to meet him to accelerate the process.

Rabin also proposed that Christopher take a new initiative to Asad offering a package deal involving the timing and phasing of elements of withdrawal and normalization. With this inducement in his hands, Clinton decided to try to obtain Asad's help. If Asad would announce that he was sending his negotiators back to the table in Washington, that would put pressure on Arafat to move. In return, the U.S. would abstain on the U.N. resolution, allowing it to pass and thereby providing Asad with the cover he would need. Understanding that Syria's return to negotiations would increase the pressure on Arafat to find a way to resume negotiations too, Rabin responded enthusiastically, even though Clinton's approach would result in the Security Council passing a resolution critical of Israel. With that, it was relatively easy to win the backing of key pro-Israel senators as well as the American Israel Public Affairs Committee.

Armed with this support, Clinton called Asad, briefed him on his talks with Rabin, and proposed a Christopher shuttle between Damascus and Jerusalem to try to achieve progress. He then asked for Asad's help in winning the support of Arab leaders for resuming all the negotiations. He said that was essential if the United States was to accelerate the Israeli-Syrian negotiations. Without the resumption of all negotiations, Clinton said the United States would be forced to exercise its veto in the Security Council. Asad took the bait. The president of the United States had asked him for a favor and would therefore be indebted to him. The United States was looking to him rather than our traditional partner, Hosni Mubarak, to play the leadership role in the Arab world in this instance. He would be able to claim that his actions averted a U.S. veto of a U.N. resolution on the Palestinian issue. And Christopher turning up in Damascus would underscore Asad's primary role in regional diplomacy.

Within twenty-four hours, Asad informed Clinton that he had spoken with King Hussein and Lebanese president Ilyas Harawi. Not surprisingly, they had agreed to respond positively to Clinton's request that the peace talks resume—Hussein had his own interest in doing so, and Harawi took his orders from Damascus. The White House promptly announced that, after consulting with other Arab leaders, the president of Syria had decided to resume the negotiations.

A few days later Dennis and I returned to Tunis. Our visit coincided with the arrival of an Israeli team led by the IDF deputy chief of staff, Major General Amnon Lipkin-Shahak. We found Arafat a changed man. With Lipkin-Shahak, he performed his rant but then dropped his demand for the evacuation of settlers from Hebron, leaving it to Rabin to decide if he could handle it politically. In return, Lipkin-Shahak agreed to what eventually became known as the Temporary International Presence in Hebron (TIPH), a group of white-uniformed, unarmed observers from Norway, Italy, and Denmark.* No doubt Arafat understood TIPH's limitations but perhaps he hoped it would serve as a precedent, enabling him to interpose more robust international forces between Israel and the Palestinians in the future. Along with the passage of U.N. Security Council Resolution 904, adopted on March 18, 1994, and some other minor Israeli concessions, the package provided a cosmetic solution to Arafat's problems. He agreed to resume negotiations, riding roughshod over those in his entourage who opposed his decision. As he proudly explained to us, "My aides are with me in the morning and against me in the afternoon, but in politics, I am a dictator!"

Rabin had not expected this outcome. Indeed, he had empowered

---

* The TIPH still functions to this very day although its ability to protect Palestinian residents of the city is belied by the myriad incidents of attacks by settlers that have continued over the years.

Lipkin-Shahak to offer Arafat the evacuation of the settlers from Tel Rumeida in the heart of Hebron if that was necessary to satisfy him. But Arafat had not insisted, much to Rabin's subsequent relief—Rabin told Lipkin-Shahak on his return to Israel that he did not have the ability to deliver it politically.

The crisis was over. Within two days, Israeli and Palestinian negotiators were meeting in Cairo. And Christopher and his team went off again to Damascus, where we received a warm reception from Asad, who was very pleased with himself.

ARAFAT'S VOLTE-FACE CAN be explained partially by the way Rabin dealt with him. Rabin called him repeatedly during the crisis, at one time speaking to him for over an hour. From that moment, they began to treat each other as politicians with constituencies: Rabin recognized that the Goldstein massacre had put pressure on Arafat from the Palestinians; Arafat acknowledged that the settler opposition to the peace process posed a political danger for Rabin. By allowing an international presence in Hebron, Rabin was setting a precedent, but he also knew Arafat needed it to calm his people.

Arafat's willingness to drop his demand that Rabin evacuate settlers from Tel Rumeida in downtown Hebron came out of recognition, as Arafat told us, that politically Rabin simply could not evacuate settlers. He expressed admiration for Rabin's decision to place settlers in administrative detention and outlaw the Kach and Kahane Chai right-wing extremist movements that had spawned Goldstein's ideology.

Out of this crisis, then, came the beginnings of a partnership based on a developing trust between the two leaders. That process was greatly facilitated by the role of Amnon Lipkin-Shahak, a tall, handsome Israeli with a winning smile, a sparkle in his eye, and a gentle charm. As an Israeli general, Amnon had a hypnotic effect on Arafat, who wore a general's uniform to remind everybody of his military rank although he had no army. Nevertheless, we should not sentimentalize the bond between Arafat and Rabin. When it suited his purpose Arafat was perfectly capable of betraying Rabin's trust and lying to him. But if he felt respected by his Israeli counterpart he was more likely to respond positively than if he were treated with disdain. His dignity was more important to him than gaining advantage in a negotiation (although he would prefer to have both).

But the most important factor in Arafat's decision to end the stand-off was Asad's announcement of his intention to resume negotiations once the Security Council resolution had passed. Arafat knew how much resentment he had generated by splitting with Asad and King Hussein to make his own deal with Israel. He feared they would want to pay him back. Returning to Gaza was essential for him, but for that he needed to resume the negotiations. While his aides in Tunis were still grandstanding in front of us about the need to remove the settlers from Hebron, Arafat decided to give up on this most important Palestinian demand without a fight when he understood the Syrians were not prepared to wait for him. For American policy makers the lesson was clear: encouraging multiple Arab-Israeli negotiations is preferable to concentrating on only one because that gives the United States the ability to take advantage of the rivalries and differing interests of the Arab players to overcome the obstacles to progress. Yet again, American diplomacy was at its most effective when we wielded our influence to shape the environment for peacemaking, in this case by playing Asad off against Arafat.

The Bush administration would have done well to learn this lesson, too. Its attempt to jump-start Israeli-Palestinian final status negotiations in November 2007 created concern in Damascus that Syria would be left out. Bashar al-Asad sent a delegation to the Annapolis Conference, but when that failed to stimulate Bush's interest in relaunching Israeli-Syrian negotiations, he turned to neighboring Turkey with its strategic relationship with Israel, to play the role of intermediary. After an eight-year hiatus, Israeli-Syrian negotiations were relaunched in May 2008, six months after Annapolis.

There was also a lesson for U.S.-Israeli relations. Clinton's close coordination with Rabin enabled us to make a tactical concession to Arafat in the U.N. Security Council while avoiding the wrath of the pro-Israel community at home.

Ironically, the immediate beneficiaries of Arafat's newfound partnership with Rabin were the extremist settlers who had created the problem for both of them in the first place. Rabin missed an important opportunity during the Hebron crisis to remove members of Israel's radical right wing from their troublemaking community in downtown Hebron. Goldstein's act had outraged most Israelis. Evacuating the settlers to Kiryat Arba on the outskirts of the city would have been controversial because of the Jewish religious attachment to the old city of Hebron, where its patriarch is buried, but it would have struck a blow to the extremists. Because Rabin did not move them when he had the opportunity, we subsequently had to waste four months negotiating a Hebron agreement that would enable them to stay. And in the process they became an aggressive and disruptive factor in every effort to promote coexistence in Hebron, flaunting Israeli law and confronting the Israel Defense Forces. Rabin's assassin, Yigal Amir, was a fellow-traveler of these extremist settlers.

In this crisis Rabin again demonstrated his aversion to altering the status of any of the settlements. He had become a deeply cautious politician during his second term as prime minister. This may seem hard to reconcile with the political risks he took in embracing Arafat, but it was precisely because he had taken those risks that he was not prepared to spend precious political capital on battles that could be postponed until later. His coalition was already fragile. If he ended up forging an agreement with Asad, one consequence would be the formation of an alliance between the settlers on the Golan Heights and the settlers in the West Bank and Gaza Strip. These groups didn't share the same ideology, but they would become natural allies were they confronted with having to leave their homes. Thus Rabin had no interest in igniting a premature battle with the West Bank settlers.

Rabin's lack of political courage on the settlements was matched by Arafat's apparent indifference to the issue. He did not care to deal with settlements in the Oslo agreement, preferring to shelve it until final status talks. Similarly, Arafat did not insist on the evacuation of settlements in Gaza in the subsequent Gaza-Jericho implementation agreement that was signed soon after the Hebron massacre. He preferred to believe that in the final agreement all the settlements would have to be evacuated anyway. But it was also an indication of his cynical disdain for the conditions of Palestinians in the West Bank and Gaza. Though ignoring the settlements issue made the Hebron crisis easier to resolve, the matter would come back to haunt us all later.

A lesson to be drawn from all of this is that the United States should stand up to rather than indulge Israeli leaders when they plead political circumstances to fend off pressure to curb settlement activity. Clinton had been reluctant to do that, partly because as a politician he was sympathetic to their predicament, and partly because George H. W. Bush's confrontation with Prime Minister Yitzhak Shamir over settlement activity had proved politically costly for Bush even though it contributed to Shamir's electoral defeat. Clinton had vowed not to repeat that experience. Arafat's apparent indifference to the settlements only reinforced that judgment. Nevertheless, it would prove to be a costly mistake in the context of the effort to resolve the Arab-Israeli conflict.

7

Peace with Jordan

The world's media were gathering again, this time on May 4, 1994, in the huge auditorium at the conference center complex on the outskirts of Cairo. Dozens of TV cameras were preparing to broadcast the signing ceremony for the Gaza-Jericho agreement, which provided for the implementation of the first stage of the Oslo Declaration of Principles—the opening of the gates of Palestine to Yasser Arafat.

As the negotiators greeted one another, a mood of elation spread among them, even though few had gotten much sleep after the long night of wrangling at President Mubarak's Abdeen Palace. The Palestinian chief negotiator, Nabil Shaath, was slumped back in his chair fast asleep, oblivious to the camaraderie that enveloped him.

The previous day, Arafat had engaged directly in the negotiations, much to the chagrin of his subordinates, since he conceded issues they had been holding back to trade. Israel's negotiators felt the same way about Shimon Peres. They had briefed him before this encounter with Arafat on their carefully developed fallback positions and he had pre-emptively offered them as his opening positions! Their negotiators had drawn up a list of a dozen issues for the principals to resolve in order to wrap up the agreement. Arafat and Peres, meeting alone, had managed to settle most of them,* but Arafat remained unreconciled on several issues and entered the final negotiating session that night intent on improving his position.

Once Clinton had helped break the Goldstein impasse, the Israeli and Palestinian negotiators had made quick progress without American involvement. However, Christopher's presence now was important

---

* Peres conceded to the Palestinians the right to issue their own passports and stamps and agreed to allow the use of the title of *rais* ("president") for their leader, although to avoid conceding the image of a head of state, Arafat would be referred to in the agreement as "Rais of the Palestinian Authority."

to both sides as they finalized their agreement and looked for American support. Mubarak, who had not attended the Oslo signing at the White House, wanted his own grand ceremony to highlight Egypt's role in the peace process. Accordingly, he had invited Christopher to join him in hosting the final negotiating session with Arafat, Rabin, and Peres.

Arafat's main concerns were the size of his Jericho enclave, the lack of Palestinian control over the Gazan coastal area known as Muwassi, and a Palestinian police presence on the bridges across the Jordan River. Every time Rabin and Peres conceded on one of Arafat's additional demands, Mubarak wanted to end the negotiations. But Arafat would interrupt and say, "Just one more thing, Your Excellency?" The third time he did it, members of the Israeli delegation burst out laughing. Arafat took umbrage; he felt they were humiliating him. Rabin scolded his negotiators and made it clear to Arafat that he respected his concerns.

All of this was taking much longer than Mubarak had planned. The palace kitchen had closed earlier, on the assumption there would be no need to feed the president's guests. But now it was approaching midnight and everyone was hungry. Mubarak instructed his aides to go to the corner street vendor and bring back "take out" sandwiches for the three delegations.

The palace staff came back with plastic shopping bags containing pita bread filled with *fuul,* an Egyptian peasant dish of crushed brown fava beans, olive oil, and garlic. As the host, and in celebration of his own birthday, Mubarak insisted that Christopher partake of this humble meal. Christopher hesitated, then ate the first pita sandwich out of diplomatic necessity; the second he consumed out of hunger.

Finally, at 2 A.M., the principals went off to bed, leaving their aides to put all the last-minute additions into the voluminous text of the agreement. Because this was an implementation agreement, the maps of the territory in Gaza and the West Bank that would come under Arafat's control had to be signed by both sides for the agreement to come into force. But there had been no time for the Palestinian negotiators to discuss the final maps with Arafat before the signing ceremony.

The leaders were now filing onto the cavernous stage, taking up their assigned positions in front of a diaphanous curtain behind which lurked a massive papier-mâché replica of the Sphinx. Arafat was on the left; Rabin and Peres were on the right. Mubarak and his foreign minister, Amre Moussa, Russian foreign minister Andrey Kozyrev, and our secretary of state occupied the middle ground. Arafat was called over to a table on the left of the stage where the documents and maps were laid out. He signed the written agreement and initialed every page. But he did not sign the maps. When Rabin came over to sign he noticed the omission. His face reddened as he spoke angrily with Joel Singer, the Israeli lawyer on the negotiating team and their document handler for the signing ceremony.

An extraordinary scene then unfolded as the ceremony departed from its carefully choreographed script. Rabin conferred with Mubarak; Mubarak spoke to Arafat; then Moussa consulted with Arafat; and then Peres tried to convince him. The chairman's left leg was jerking up and down; a visibly angry, red-faced Rabin looked away from Arafat in disgust. The Israelis claimed later that Mubarak had angrily whispered to Arafat in Arabic, "Sign already, you dog!"

During all of this Christopher was an impassive observer. He would have done something if he could, but the *fuul* was taking its revenge. He clearly rued his late-night failure to uphold his rule about not eating in Arab countries. Dennis had the presence of mind to go up onto the stage and suggest to Christopher that he recommend an intermission so that all the parties could try to find a solution offstage. Given his fragile condition, Christopher moved with alacrity to get all the players to exit. It was not a moment too soon. As Christopher was counseling retreat, Eitan Haber came over to inform me that he had been instructed to assemble the Israeli motorcade—Rabin was about to walk out.

Offstage the problem was quickly fixed. Arafat thought that if he signed the maps he would be conceding on some unresolved issues.* Rabin said he would write Arafat a letter referring to the territorial issues as "still to be negotiated." The participants reconvened onstage. Arafat signed the maps, writing next to his signature that it was contingent on receiving the letter from Rabin. Suspicious that Arafat was

---

* In the endgame the night before, Arafat had demanded that a Palestinian policeman be stationed on the Allenby Bridge connecting the West Bank and Jordan. Rabin was determined to prevent any Israeli recognition, symbolic or otherwise, of a Palestinian claim to control the border passage to Jordan. Finally, they had agreed to leave the issue open for subsequent negotiation, along with a review of the size of the Jericho enclave and the arrangements for access to the Muwassi beach area in Gaza.

pulling another fast one, Rabin called Jacques Neriah, an adviser who was fluent in Arabic, onto the stage to translate what Arafat had written next to his signature. Rabin now had Arafat's measure as a manipulator and was determined not to let the newly designated *rais* take advantage of him.

Television viewers across the world had just witnessed an extraordinary performance. Arafat had severely embarrassed his Egyptian host, the Palestinians' most important patron, and he had infuriated the prime minister of Israel, his supposed partner in peace. Perhaps he didn't raise the issue with them before he went onstage because he wanted to show his people that he was struggling for the best deal possible against the overwhelming pressure of Israel, Egypt, and the United States. Perhaps he was trying to divert attention from the shortcomings of the deal, which left Israeli settlements in the heart of Gaza and denied Palestinians control over the border with Jordan. Whatever the case, Arafat had treated his audience to a classic display of the "power of the weak"—the ability to say no and force the stronger players to deal with the consequences. And, in the process, Arafat's character had been revealed—erratic, mercurial, manipulative, yet artful.

As I watched the spectacle Arafat had created in front of the impressive Sphinx, Yeats's discomfiting lines from "The Second Coming," came to mind:

> . . . somewhere in sands of the desert
> A shape with lion body and the head of a man,
> A gaze blank and pitiless as the sun,
> Is moving its slow thighs, while all about it
> Reel shadows of the indignant desert birds.
> . . . .
> And what rough beast, its hour come round at last,
> Slouches towards Bethlehem to be born?

DESPITE ARAFAT'S HISTRIONICS in Cairo, to the senior members of Clinton's peace team it was all actually a sideshow. The main event was in Damascus, where Christopher had just encountered a problem that could well immobilize our diplomacy as effectively as the *fuul* had immobilized him in Cairo.

Two days before the Cairo event, Christopher had put forward a proposal to Asad from Rabin designed to elicit a point-by-point reaction that would delineate the gaps between them. Asad had responded,* but he had also raised a new demand: that Israel withdraw to "the line of June 4, 1967." Previously, in their discussions with the United States, Asad and Rabin had only referred to "full withdrawal" from the Golan Heights. The detail-oriented Christopher noted that Rabin had not specified the June 1967 line in his proposal. Asad claimed (inaccurately) that Christopher and Dennis Ross had both previously affirmed that Rabin would withdraw to the June 4 line. Christopher said he would seek clarification from Rabin. Asad responded with a tirade. If Christopher could not reassure him that all of Syria's land would be returned then he would have to reconsider his position. He said he had always insisted he would never give up an inch of the land Israel occupied; the point was nonnegotiable.

Christopher, fearing a major setback, responded defensively. "Blame me," he said, explaining that he had not been aware there was a distinction between the international border and the June 4, 1967, line.

Asad then detailed how before World War I, Syria encompassed all of Palestine, Jordan, and Lebanon. After the collapse of the Ottoman Empire, he said, the British and French divided Syria into six states under their tutelage, imposing borders without consultation. Consequently, many Syrians were dispossessed of land they owned in what became known as the British Mandate for Palestine. Any reference to "international borders" reminded Syrians of this. Asad said that when he agreed to participate in the peace process with Israel he did so based on U.N. Security Council Resolution 242, which refers to the land occupied in 1967, not the international border. This, in Asad's view, was a concession in itself since it meant Syria recognized that territory it once controlled was now Israeli land. If the Israelis did not withdraw

---

* Where Rabin had proposed Israeli withdrawal from the Golan over a five-year period, Asad had countered that it should be completed in six months. Where Rabin had proposed a withdrawal in three phases, Asad wanted one phase. Where Rabin had insisted that significant elements of normalization, such as the establishment of embassies, should occur in the first phase, Asad wanted peace agreements with Lebanon and Jordan to precede that. Where Rabin's chief of staff, Ehud Barak, had proposed that the Golan be completely demilitarized and only limited Syrian forces be allowed in two additional zones stretching east beyond Damascus, Asad wanted a seven-kilometer-deep limited forces' zone on both sides of the new border. Where Rabin had proposed that a Syrian early warning station inside Israel serve as compensation for his demand for an Israeli early warning station remaining in the Golan, Asad had rejected any ground stations in favor of aerial early warning systems.

from the territory they occupied in 1967 it would be tantamount to Syria agreeing to Israel's further expansion. Asad made clear that would not happen: "Giving up a grain of our soil is treason."

Rabin reacted negatively when Christopher raised the matter. Asad had not only failed to respond to his proposal in a serious way, Rabin said, but was now trying to show the Arab world that he would get a better deal than Egypt did ten years earlier: less normalization, less security restrictions, and more land (Israel had withdrawn to the international border with Egypt).

Insisting on Israel's withdrawal to the June 4 line rather than the international line—a difference of only a few hundred meters—was especially important to Asad because it signaled to the Arab world that he was regaining land taken by conquest; in his mind that represented the difference between dignity and humiliation, patriotism and treason. As the leader of an Alawite minority clan regarded as heretics by the Arab world's Sunni establishment, Asad believed he could not afford to expose himself to the charge that he had abandoned "Arab interests" for the sake of a deal with Israel. As he told Christopher, "It's a matter of life or death. I cannot define my personal history by giving away one meter of land."

Rabin was hardly sympathetic to that argument, knowing that his own political life was endangered by agreeing to full withdrawal from the Golan. Polls showed a sizable majority of Israelis opposed coming down from the heights. But Rabin saw in this new Syrian demand an opportunity to raise one of his own. He asked Christopher to find out whether Asad would accept an interlocking of Israel's phases of withdrawal with Syria's phases of normalization. If the answer was yes, Rabin would consider clarifying the line of withdrawal. In mid-May, Christopher went to Damascus, where Asad agreed with Rabin's request on condition that "the line of June 4, 1967" stood as the line of withdrawal.

Rabin's chief negotiator, Itamar Rabinovich, delivered Rabin's response to Dennis and me over lunch at the Three Arches Restaurant on the terrace of the Jerusalem YMCA, a beautiful stone building that combines the style of the British Mandate with the arched terraces and corridors of traditional Arab architecture. As we ate Moroccan *harira* soup, Itamar read from a piece of paper: "The full withdrawal contemplated in the Israeli package will be from all the Syrian territories occupied as a result of the 1967 war."

When Christopher returned to Damascus to deliver the message to Asad, he added Rabin's stipulation that Israeli requirements would also have to be met. Instead of accepting Rabin's concession gracefully, Asad now interpreted this as a reference to modifying the line of June 4, 1967. Until Rabin's position was further clarified there would be no more negotiations, said Asad.

Christopher, who had now gone back and forth three times between Jerusalem and Damascus to deal with this one issue, was exasperated. He told Asad that he was the mirror image of Rabin; each of them immediately discounted whatever he brought from the other side. Asad was unmoved. "When a farmer is plowing his land and finds a stone, he can stop and remove it or go around it," he said. "If he goes around, he loses the land the stone is sitting on. This is land we were born in."

Yet again Asad seemed more interested in the process than the result. At least that was our conclusion. But he was also sending Clinton a message, which we would have done well to keep in mind in subsequent negotiations. For Asad, the image of Israeli withdrawal to the June 4, 1967, line had become everything.

In the meantime, while Asad was imagining his birthright jeopardized by every new diplomatic formulation, and was no doubt enjoying having the secretary of state do everything possible to assuage his concerns, Rabin had become frustrated by both of them. Little wonder that he decided to direct his attention elsewhere.

IN APRIL 1994, observing that Israel was about to reach an agreement with the PLO that would put Arafat in Jericho, on Jordan's western border, King Hussein had suddenly decided to move ahead again in his own negotiations with Israel. Knowing it would not be long before Arafat took control of the main West Bank cities, a situation that would threaten Jordan's remaining influence across the river, Hussein decided he could no longer afford to wait.

In mid-April, the king summoned Efraim Halevy. Hussein had come to trust this quiet, intelligent, bespectacled Israeli whose signature feature was the strip of hair he combed across his balding scalp, and who, having grown up in London, spoke the King's English. Bearing an uncanny resemblance to John le Carré's master spy, George Smiley, Halevy had an immense capacity for discretion, a rare commodity among Israelis.

In a week of intensive discussions, the king and Halevy developed the outlines of what would become the Israel-Jordan peace treaty. Rabin was impressed by Halevy's progress report and asked him to arrange a meeting with the king. To prepare for that meeting, Halevy and Eli Rubinstein, the chief Israeli negotiator for the agreement with Jordan, met with Crown Prince Hassan in London on May 11, 1994, one week after Arafat's histrionics in Cairo. They too made quick progress on a package in which the Israelis agreed to establish a joint boundary commission that would resolve any disagreements over territory; in turn the Jordanians agreed to work quickly toward a peace treaty.

Compared to the Syrian and Palestinian negotiations, the Jordanian issues with Israel were relatively straightforward: some minor territorial issues, water allocations from the Yarmuk and Jordan rivers to address Jordan's chronic water shortages, and control of the *waqf* administration of Jerusalem's Muslim holy sites. But as the king contemplated jumping ahead of the other negotiations, he also needed America's military backing. He had lost it during the Persian Gulf War and, as the king told his military officers at the time, if Jordan were now endangered, it would have "nobody to back it."

Because of this strategic vulnerability, Hussein had worked hard to establish a friendship with President Clinton. His first visit to Washington in June 1993 had laid the foundations. The king appreciated the warmth of Clinton's welcome, conditioned though it was on Jordan's implementation of sanctions on Iraq. He had responded by writing the president a heartfelt thank-you letter in which he had invoked the name of his slain grandfather, King Abdullah I, to express his personal commitment to peacemaking.

However, Hussein knew only too well that personal affinity and positive sentiments only go so far in the affairs of states. In return for making peace with Israel, he had drawn up a long list of requirements from the United States that would provide tangible manifestations of a new relationship with Washington.* As a weak state, lacking few additional sources of leverage to achieve such an ambitious agenda, the king quickly came to understand that if he could add Israel's influence in Washington to his own he was more likely to succeed. This calcula-

---

* The list included debt relief to the tune of some $900 million, resumption of military assistance, cessation of U.S. maritime inspections in the Gulf of Aqaba that had been imposed to prevent Iraq sanctions evasion, and backing for the joint economic development projects he was negotiating with the Israelis.

tion reversed the lens through which Arab leaders traditionally viewed the U.S.-Israel relationship. As already noted, ever since President Eisenhower had pressured Israel to withdraw from the Sinai after the 1956 Suez Crisis, Arab leaders hankered for American pressure on Israel as the best way to seek diplomatic redress for their grievances.

Hussein understood that Israel's close relationship with the administration and Congress and the support it enjoyed from the American Jewish community gave it a unique ability to do the converse: to pressure the U.S. government on his behalf. If Israel wanted peace with Jordan so badly, he calculated, it should be prepared to use that influence to help rebuild Jordan's relations with the United States.*

The first opportunity to test this proposition had come on October 1, 1993, two weeks after Rabin and Arafat had consummated the Oslo deal, when both Crown Prince Hassan and Shimon Peres turned up in Washington for a donors' conference that focused on raising money for the Palestinians. Peres had come to manifest Israeli support for the Palestinian economy; Hassan had come to remind the world donor community that Jordan was also in dire need. To get the president to focus on those needs, Hassan agreed to a three-way meeting with Peres and Clinton. In the meeting, the Israeli foreign minister lobbied the president on behalf of debt relief for Jordan. In the subsequent press conference with Hassan and Peres, Clinton for the first time publicly committed the United States to supporting the proposition.

In January 1994, the king met again with the president and provided him with a list of military items that his army would desperately need if it were to prevent smuggling across the Iraqi border and terrorist infiltration from Jordan into the West Bank. In his next meeting with Rabin, Christopher heard an aggressive pitch from the Israeli prime minister in favor of the Jordanian arms request.

Securing debt forgiveness and military assistance for Jordan was no simple matter. Congress had neither forgotten nor forgiven the king for his actions during the 1990–91 Gulf crisis. Moreover, new rules required debt forgiveness be covered by newly appropriated dollars. In other words, forgiving Jordan's debt was almost as costly as giving Jordan new economic assistance. And this was at a time when Clinton was under great pressure to reduce the budget deficit. Christopher told

---

* Fifteen years later, Bashar al-Asad would copy this tactic, launching negotiations with Israel in order to improve his relationship with the United States. As one of his advisers told me, "We believe the road to Washington is through Jerusalem."

King Hussein during a meeting in London at the end of April that only if the king signed a peace agreement with Israel would it be possible to convince Congress to provide debt relief and military assistance.

Meanwhile, in every high-level meeting with U.S. officials the Israelis were doing their part to meet the king's requirements. In June, Efraim Halevy's message to the administration was "Help the king!" He was so strident that Dennis asked him whether he represented Jordan or Israel.

When Clinton met with Hussein that month he suggested Hussein take the dramatic step of a public meeting with Rabin to signal to Congress his commitment to peace. The president said he could use that to secure congressional approval of debt forgiveness and military assistance.* The king said he would do that only if there was some tangible progress in the peace negotiations with Israel before then. Rabin's response: "We should make every effort."

In that White House meeting in June, the king left the president with the impression that he would meet publicly with Rabin and Clinton in October, but he soon sent us word that he was actually ready to meet Rabin openly in July. This was not occasioned by progress in the negotiations. Rather, the king's sense of urgency was driving him forward and now the president's promise of U.S. support reduced the risks of doing so.

What about the Syrians? The king had promised Asad back in November 1993 that he would not sign a peace treaty ahead of Syria. However, in mid-May 1994, King Hussein had spent nine hours with Asad in Damascus. He was surprised to hear that Asad was satisfied with his own negotiations with the Israelis. Something Asad said led the king to understand that Rabin had agreed to full withdrawal from the Golan.

If Rabin was about to do a deal with Asad, the king could forget about getting Washington's attention for Jordan's needs; the United States would be preoccupied with the much larger requirements of the Syrian deal. But if Asad was about to reach agreement with Israel, how could he complain if Hussein made his own peace?†

---

* On military assistance, the president would begin to meet the king's request by providing Jordan access to defense materiel that the Pentagon no longer needed but that still had utility for the Jordanian army.

† As the king noted to us during his Washington visit in June, "The Syrians have already covered some ground. We started at the same point but now the opportunity has presented itself to us. I understand that they are doing the same."

Like Sadat when he announced to the Egyptian parliament in November 1977 that he was willing to go "to the ends of the earth . . . even to the Knesset itself" to pursue Egypt's interest in peace, the king now made his move. On July 9, 1994, in an address to the Jordanian parliament broadcast live, he laid out his rationale for a dramatic decision. He explained to his people the "critical and difficult circumstances" their country faced and the necessity of securing support in Washington. If meeting publicly with the Israeli prime minister was the price he had to pay, he told them, he would not hesitate to do it. He emphasized that Jordan was not getting ahead of the Arab states; it was merely catching up with Egypt and the Palestinians, who had already made their separate deals with Israel.

THIS SPEECH REPRESENTED a turning point for Jordan and Israel. Although he had prevaricated, King Hussein was now publicly committed to achieving peace. He would not look back until his death from cancer five years later.

We assumed the Clinton-Hussein-Rabin summit would be held in Washington to have maximum impact on Congress. Rabin, however, wanted the event to take place in Israel or Jordan, which he felt would have more influence on an Israeli public growing ever more skeptical of the benefits of peacemaking as it experienced each new terror attack. In the end the matter was easily resolved. I conveyed to Eitan Haber the simple reality: no event in Washington, no debt forgiveness or military assistance to Jordan. Rabin grudgingly acquiesced, insisting that if it had to be at the White House, it also had to be a more impressive event than the signing ceremony with Arafat.*

We still had to lay the groundwork for the debt forgiveness the president had promised the king. The budget bureaucrats were aghast that without knowing where he would find the money, the president had made the commitment—such was the stringent budget environment in those days. But to their dismay, when they protested directly to Clinton, he told them to find the money, and miraculously they did.†

---

* In short order we organized a welcoming event in the Rose Garden, a signing ceremony in a different location on the South Lawn, a black-tie dinner at the White House, and an unprecedented Rabin-Hussein appearance before a special joint session of Congress, followed by a large reception at the State Department for the Arab-American and American Jewish communities.
† In the process, I discovered a term of budget art that every senior political appointee needs to know about—"headroom," the hundreds of millions of dollars that

Nevertheless, Clinton still placed a higher priority on a peace agreement with Syria than on the breakthrough he now found himself promoting with Jordan. As with the Oslo deal, he calculated that an Israel-Jordan peace might bolster Rabin's support in Israel for the deal with Damascus, but he was concerned about an adverse Syrian reaction. He feared Asad might try to destabilize Jordan and bring pressure to bear on the king in Arab forums. A war of words had already ignited in the Jordanian and Syrian press in the wake of the king's speech to his parliament.

The Syrian ambassador, Walid Mouallem, was certainly upset when Dennis and I informed him of the upcoming summit in Washington. He warned us that Asad might be forced to take a stand since it would be legitimate for him to prevent Jordan from being used by Israel to put pressure on Syria.

On July 15, before Clinton announced the impending summit to the world, he called Asad to explain what he was planning to do. The president gilded the lily with renewed assurances of his own commitment to comprehensive peace and to the achievement of a breakthrough with Syria. Asad, surprisingly, thanked the president for his pledge and said he had no problem with the Hussein-Rabin summit. However, he wasn't so sure what the popular Syrian reaction would be. These last words, of course, were a subtle reminder of his troublemaking ability.

Nevertheless, the king's calculation proved correct. Asad would not try to block other Arab leaders from moving forward in the peace process as long as Syria's interests dictated his continued engagement in it. Had Asad not already secured Rabin's commitment to withdrawal to the June 4, 1967, line, he might have had other thoughts. But with that concession securely in Clinton's pocket, Asad clearly calculated that it was better to incur an obligation from the superpower than to offend it.

WITH ASAD NEUTRALIZED, we focused on what the Washington summit would produce. The actual details of the Israel-Jordan peace treaty would take the negotiators another three months to conclude.

---

result from accounting adjustments to take account of fluctuations in interest and exchange rates. It represents "go-to" funds when the president really needs some extra money. For fiscal year 1995, the Office of Management and Budget managed to come up with $101 million in "headroom" funds that could be used to forgive $160 million of discounted Jordanian debt immediately. The rest was taken care of in the budgets for subsequent years.

Instead, as we headed for the Middle East on Christopher's plane in mid-July 1994, the peace team drafted the "Washington Declaration," which essentially encapsulated the apple-pie rhetoric of peacemaking without any of the substance that would have to appear in the actual peace treaty.

Surprisingly, Christopher made no headway when he sought to negotiate this declaration. In his meeting with Rabin, the prime minister refused to engage, arguing that it had to be prepared "in the proper way." Whatever that meant, it didn't seem to involve the United States. As we rose from the meeting Rabin took me aside and emphasized that the signing event needed to be better than that with Arafat; Israelis would draw comparisons. He also whispered that I should work out the statement with Eitan Haber to avoid leaks.

In Amman the next day, our ideas received the same frosty treatment from King Hussein. As was his habit, the king first took the secretary of state into his private office for a chat. There the king made clear he would prefer to work out a declaration directly with the Israelis. But Secretary Christopher insisted on some involvement, so, out of deference to the summit host, the king suggested that American diplomats stay in Amman to discuss our ideas for the declaration. Christopher and the rest of the U.S. contingent went off to a Dead Sea resort to participate with Shimon Peres and Jordanian prime minister Abdel Salaam Majali in the first ever U.S.-Jordan-Israel ministerial meeting. Since I was responsible for organizing the summit meeting at the White House, Christopher designated me to stay behind to go over our draft declaration with the king's brother, Crown Prince Hassan.

IT IS INCONGRUOUS how thoroughly British are the ways of the Hashemite royal family of Jordan. They speak the King's English. They drink the queen's tea. Their palaces are decorated in the queen's style— probably by the queen's designers. And they behave precisely as if they were to the English manor born. King Hussein did prefer to collect Harley-Davidson motorbikes rather than Thoroughbred horses and corgis, and the palace guard consisted of fierce, mustachioed, Circassian warriors in black uniforms crossed with silver-bulleted bandoliers, rather than the tall, red-coated soldiers of the queen's Coldstream Guards with their signature black busbies. Nevertheless, the Hashimiya Palace in downtown Amman could easily have been transplanted from England—except that the visitor looks over a high wall at a squalid Palestinian refugee camp that covers an adjacent hill, a grim reminder to the royal family of the dangerous neighborhood they actually inhabit. Indeed, in 1970, Palestinian gunmen from that camp had opened fire on the palace during the king's confrontation with Arafat and the PLO.

The king was excessively polite, in the English style, always speaking in such quiet tones that a visitor had to strain to hear him. He added "sir" at the end of every sentence to emphasize his respect, or his point. Crown Prince Hassan, short like his brother but stockier, was irreverent and jovial, although never impolite. Whereas the king always spoke precisely and concisely, his brother had adopted the affectations of an Oxford don; his circumlocutory sentences were interspersed with unintelligible words like *holistic* and *epistemological*. His signature characteristic, however, was a deep, prolonged belly laugh, which usually followed the telling of his own joke.

Whereas the king combined the shrewdness of a desert Bedouin with the charisma of a tribal chieftain and the gait of a Sandhurst-trained officer, the crown prince came across as an effete intellectual more at home with his books and his interfaith dialogue than with ruling a restive population in an avaricious neighborhood.

I suspected the crown prince's jolly façade cloaked a deep and justified insecurity about his position as number two in an uncertain realm.* But over many years he had proved to be a thoughtful and effective manager of the affairs of state. "Sidi" Hassan, as he was known in Jordan because of his descent from the Prophet Mohamed, understood the value of ideas, the importance of staff work, the way to run a bureaucracy. Hassan and Hussein together had worked assiduously to recover after the king's ill-advised decision to side with Saddam.

Lunch with the crown prince consisted of delicate, English-style sandwiches: one slice of beef on buttered white bread, cut into petite triangles. The crown prince and I consumed them as we watched on television the ceremonies at the Dead Sea, Hassan poking fun at Majali, Christopher, and Peres. I was anxious to get down to business, so when the opening presented itself I told the crown prince what we wanted in the Hussein-Rabin joint declaration.

---

* On his deathbed, King Hussein summarily dismissed Hassan as his successor in favor of his first-born son, Abdullah, ostensibly because Hassan would not commit to appointing Hamza—Hussein's son by Queen Noor—as crown prince once he became king. But while he depended on Hassan as his deputy, Hussein had long harbored doubts about the wisdom of making him his successor.

At first he tried to divert me by telling me what he thought the president should say about the U.S. role as the "point of intersection" between the parties and about Jordan's role as the "pivot point" between Israel and oil. When nevertheless I described elements we thought should be included in the declaration, he indulged me a little and then noted nonchalantly that he had already initialed the draft of a declaration with the Israelis the previous day.

I was embarrassed. The ceremony was five days away. The president was busy lobbying Congress on Jordan's behalf. Under constant pressure from Rabin, we were arranging spectacles at the White House and State Department. And now we stumble across the fact that the Israelis and Jordanians were negotiating a joint declaration for the ceremony without our involvement. It was in that respect Oslo all over again.

I at least secured the crown prince's agreement to consider some vague reference to the need for trade liberalization and the end to economic boycotts in the joint declaration. Repairing to my hotel room, I called Eitan Haber. Before I could express my astonishment, he started complaining that not enough Jewish community leaders had been invited to the signing ceremony, that it wasn't going to be as big as the Arafat event. When he said Rabin was very angry, I told him Clinton would be too when he found out that Rabin had circumvented him again. "We are not just the kosher caterers at a Jewish wedding," I shouted at him. Eitan said he would talk to the prime minister. Five minutes later, Rabin was on the phone.

He began by warning me that we had to be careful about what was said on the telephone because others were listening. (He was apparently talking about preventing his own intelligence services from learning what he was doing.) Somewhat defensively, he said he had informed Christopher the day before that he had a direct channel to King Hussein. The negotiations could only be successful if they remained absolutely secret. He was trying to get the king to commit to a nonbelligerency pact but in return he would have to give something on Jerusalem, "which still has to be clarified." He assured me that when the summit convened in Washington, the president would not be disappointed. He warned me that if I talked to anybody about the negotiations, "you will destroy everything!"

As I hung up the phone it finally dawned on me that Jordan and Israel, like the PLO and Israel before them, when they decided to make the deal were quite capable of reaching an agreement without the help of the United States. Clinton's role was as the underwriter of the enterprise.

When we arrived back in Israel, Eitan invited me to come alone to Rabin's office in the Defense Ministry compound in Tel Aviv. There, after Eitan had left the room, Rabin showed me the draft text so I could brief the president and the secretary of state. He said he would give us the final version when he arrived in Washington four days later. No one else should know about it at this stage, he emphasized, especially on the Israeli side.

The draft contained a clear commitment of the two sides to terminate the state of belligerency between them. Legally, that was the penultimate step before achieving a peace treaty (Asad was only offering to terminate the conflict *after* a full agreement with Israel was signed). It was also the way to penetrate the hearts and minds of common Israelis. King Hussein understood much better than Asad that his willingness to offer Israelis a "warm peace" was worth a great deal to Rabin at that point when the latter was trying to convince his people of the wisdom of his deal with Arafat while preparing them for full withdrawal from the Golan. For that, Rabin would be prepared to pay.

According to the draft document, Rabin had promised the king that the preservation of Jordan's historic role in the Muslim holy sites of Jerusalem would be accorded a "high priority." Arafat, who had designs on Jerusalem that had not yet been addressed, would not be happy.* Rabin had promised Arafat in the Oslo Declaration of Principles that Jerusalem would be dealt with in final status negotiations. Now, before those negotiations with the Palestinians had even begun, Rabin was promising a role to Arafat's archrival.

After memorizing as much of the draft as possible, I congratulated Rabin on the breakthrough.† The only missing item for the United

---

* Arafat wasn't the only other Arab leader with ambitions regarding Jerusalem: as the custodian of the two Muslim holy sites in Mecca and Medina, the Saudi king harbored a desire to spread his ambit to the third-holiest site in Jerusalem. King Hassan II of Morocco did, too; his special association with the Jerusalem mosque was recognized by the Organization of the Islamic Conference in his appointment as chairman of its Jerusalem Committee.

† In the declaration, Jordan and Israel committed vigorously to pursue their negotiations to arrive at a state of peace; they recognized each other's right to live in peace within secure and recognized boundaries and committed to thwarting terrorism. They also undertook a number of tangible steps to normalize their relations, including establishing direct telephone lines, linking the electricity grids, and opening border crossings and an international air corridor between the two countries.

States, I said, was some reference to ending the Arab economic boycott of Israel, which affected American companies doing business in the Arab world. While inconsequential to Rabin, it was significant for the Clinton administration because, in response to the unrelenting urging of Israel's congressional supporters, we were engaged in a major effort to persuade Arab governments to remove at least the secondary boycott. Rabin shrugged and told Eitan to take care of it. In the final version of the Washington Declaration it dutifully appeared in anemic form.

Rabin and King Hussein were less concerned about denying the United States a role than they were obsessed with keeping the document secret to shut out their rivals: Arafat from competing with Hussein over Jerusalem; Peres from taking credit away from Rabin for the declaration.

In its aftermath, Arafat tried in vain to convene an emergency Arab summit that would declare the PLO the sole Arab party with rights in Jerusalem. Eventually he would get his revenge by successfully wresting control of the *waqf* from pro-Jordanian hands.

Peres remained ignorant of the contents of the declaration to the very last moment. In a meeting Christopher held with him and Rabin at the Mayflower Hotel in Washington the day before the summit meeting, Peres was still introducing ideas for the declaration. Christopher, caught in an awkward spot, argued that the headline reporting the meeting would be more important than any fine print.

Nobody's fool, Peres knew something was afoot. I had the misfortune of running into him taking a stroll down Connecticut Avenue as I headed to the Hay-Adams hotel to go over the final text of the declaration with Eli Rubinstein and Fayez Tarawneh, the king's chief negotiator. Peres asked me whether I had seen the declaration, a copy of which I was carrying in my portfolio. I mumbled something about asking Rabin and excused myself, explaining I was late for a meeting (at least that was true). Rabin only showed the document to Peres in the formal trilateral meeting with King Hussein and President Clinton, five minutes before it was made public.

Peres was humiliated. He had worked for a peace agreement with Jordan for more than a decade; he had proposed the strategy of "storming Jordan"; and he had crossed the river in November to lay the foundations for the breakthrough that had now been produced without him. He was further stung when Rabin told the Israeli press in Washington that his foreign minister had not been involved at all in the secret negotiations. Before boarding the plane to return to Israel, Peres told the political correspondent for *Yedioth Ahronoth*, "I will not let him assail my dignity or my credibility ever again."

Rabin claimed he cut out Peres on the insistence of King Hussein, who no longer trusted him after his slip of the tongue the previous November. That may have been a factor, but more important was Rabin's desire for an agreement he could call his own. He wanted to show Israelis, including Shimon Peres, that he too was capable of negotiating a secret agreement with an Arab leader, and that he was able to get a better deal from Hussein than Peres negotiated with Arafat. More than Israelis might want to admit, the rivalry between Rabin and Peres resembled the rivalry between Arab leaders.

THE WARMTH OF the prolonged handshake between King Hussein and Yitzhak Rabin on the South Lawn of the White House on July 25, 1994, stood in marked contrast to the reluctant grasp between Rabin and Arafat on September 13 the previous year. But its symbolic value was hardly as great, given the fact that friendly relations between the leaders of Jordan and Israel had been established decades ago. The rhetoric of signing ceremonies had also become quite predictable with its references to the suffering inflicted by past conflict and the hope of a better future for the children of the region. The high point, however, came in King Hussein's speech, when he noted that in Arabic and in Hebrew there was no word for the concept of nonbelligerency that appeared in the English text of the Washington Declaration the three leaders had just signed. Instead he proposed a clearer form of words: "What we have accomplished and what we are committed to is the *end of the state of war* between Jordan and Israel." Eli Rubinstein, who had spent many hours arguing with his Jordanian counterpart about the meaning of nonbelligerency, could not restrain himself. He let out an exuberant cheer and the crowd broke out in extended applause.

The side-by-side appearance of the Jordanian monarch and the Israeli prime minister before an unprecedented joint session of Congress the next day was actually more inspiring than the White House ceremony, notwithstanding the breakthrough the Washington Declaration represented. There were prolonged and repeated standing ovations for the two Middle Eastern peacemakers as they stood together at the podium in front of Speaker of the House Tom Foley and Vice President Al Gore.

Although Rabin was deeply unhappy with the sentimentalism of the speech Eitan Haber had written for him, its emotional content overwhelmed his hesitant delivery. He spoke of the role of leaders and the responsibility they bore to represent their people's desire for peace: "We have the power to decide. And we dare not miss this great opportunity."

King Hussein, whose delivery was always flawless though he spoke without notes, referred in his speech to his grandfather, King Abdullah I, as he had in his first letter to Clinton, noting emotionally, "I have pledged my life to fulfilling his dream of peace." He emphasized the need to make normalcy and humanity the prevailing order in the Middle East, of putting an end to the unnatural state of affairs where leaders could not meet openly to resolve their differences, of the desire to secure peace for "all the children of Abraham." He spoke of Jerusalem, too, asserting that "sovereignty over the holy places in Jerusalem resides with God, and God alone," a formula that we would have done well to invoke when we came to negotiating Jerusalem's holy places at Camp David six years later. And then the king turned to Tom Foley sitting behind him and succinctly declared, "Mr. Speaker, the state of war between Israel and Jordan is over."

The applause and cheers from hundreds of appreciative senators and congressmen was thunderous. The king had redeemed himself. With his words of peace he had assured congressional support for debt forgiveness and military assistance. Jordan was back in America's good graces and peace was again at hand.

THE PRESIDENTIAL STUDY aboard Air Force One was designed to portray the image of a flying Oval Office. The president sat behind a large, varnished mahogany desk with a presidential seal on its front; his aides sat on mushroom-colored leather banquettes across from him. Three months had passed since King Hussein and Yitzhak Rabin stood before the joint session of the United States Congress. It was October 26, 1994. The president was en route to the Jordanian port city of Aqaba to bear witness to the signing of the Israel-Jordan Peace Treaty, which had been finalized in the meantime.

Clinton had summoned his staff to review the protocol for the ceremony that would take place later that day in the Wadi Araba desert, just north of Aqaba on the borderline between Israel and Jordan. He read out loud: "Two-fifteen P.M.: the president and the first lady exchange gifts with His Majesty King Hussein and Her Majesty Queen Noor." He turned to me and asked, "What are we giving the king and queen?"

I had no idea. While the president had been sleeping, I had spent the last four hours of the flight negotiating whether he would ride from the airport to the ceremony in the king's car. The Secret Service insisted that the president only ride in his own armored black stretch Cadillac with its Secret Service driver. Royal Jordanian protocol insisted that, as a personal gesture, the king drive the president himself in his metallic-gray Mercedes with the queen and first lady in the rear seats. They didn't dare tell His Majesty that the president had turned down this invitation. But Clinton simply wasn't prepared to override the advice of his lead agent, who worried that if the president set the precedent of riding in the king's car, he would end up riding in the limousines of Arab leaders in Syria, Egypt, Kuwait, and Saudi Arabia—the other stops on his first presidential trip to the region. That presented too grave a threat to the president, in their view.*

In my preoccupation with this last-minute snafu and others of the kind that always seem to precede historic events, I had not had time to pay attention to the protocol order of ceremonies. So now I excused myself and went looking for the White House social secretary, who was responsible for the official gifts. She explained to the president that King Hussein would be giving him an ancient pottery vessel from the Nabataean era, discovered at Petra. The queen would give Hillary a silver brooch with antique jewels found in Petra.

"So what are we giving them?" asked the president.

"You'll present the king with a glass paperweight and Hillary will give the queen a key ring," the social secretary responded.

The president exploded: "A key ring! Don't you know that they don't

---

* Prince Bandar solved the limousine problem. With King Fahd, he had been watching the television broadcast of Clinton's arrival in Aqaba. The Saudi king was horrified to see Clinton and King Hussein reach the end of the red carpet and then leave the airport in separate cars. Bandar tracked me down through the White House switchboard to make sure there wouldn't be a problem like that when Clinton landed in Riyadh. When I explained the problem to him, he suggested putting Saudi license plates on the president's limo. Since the king had a black Cadillac similar to the president's, nobody could tell that the president was not riding in the king's car. We did the same thing in Damascus with Asad's license plates, underscoring the point that in the Middle East, appearance is often more important than reality.

let women drive in this part of the world?" The U.S. Constitution in its Emoluments Clause forbids any government official including the president from accepting gifts "from any king, prince or foreign state." Subsequent legislation allowed officials to keep gifts worth no more than $260 in 1994 dollars. That also became the standard for the budget the White House staff could spend on the president's gifts during foreign visits.

Clinton was angry. "That's typical! They give us gifts we're not allowed to keep and we give them gifts they wouldn't want to keep," he noted indignantly.

Thankfully, in the ceremony itself the gift exchange was upstaged by another more symbolic transaction between the Israeli and Jordanian chiefs of the armed services. In a carefully choreographed act, Israeli and Jordanian generals faced one another five abreast on either side of the borderline in front of the podium where the treaty was to be signed. In unison, they saluted, shook hands, and swapped gifts, a gesture intended to symbolize the transition from war to peace or, as the king put it poetically, "the end of a chapter of darkness and the opening of a book of light."

Hussein's and Rabin's speeches were extraordinary in their common commitment to make their shared desert bloom, to clear mine fields "and supplant them with fields of plenty," to rid their people of hatred, and to bequeath to their children what Clinton declared as "a peace for the generations." These speeches were much different from those delivered a year earlier when Arafat and Rabin signed their accord. Hussein and Rabin were old colleagues now basking in the warmth of a Clintonian embrace.

THE ISRAEL-JORDAN PEACE Treaty was certainly an important milestone in the annals of the Arab-Israeli conflict. It removed one more of Israel's Arab neighbors from the arena of that conflict. At the time it looked as if only Syria and Lebanon remained, and they appeared to be well on their way to peace agreements with Israel. The treaty solidified the strategic role of Israel and Jordan in each other's defense.* Israelis achieved the warm peace they had craved; Jordan received territory, water, and protection, along with the commitment of

---

* Through Jordan's treaty commitment not to allow the stationing of foreign forces on its territory, the Hashemite Kingdom became a strategic buffer for Israel against an attack from Iraq. And in Israel's commitment not to permit the transfer of Pales-

the American superpower to the well-being of the Hashemite dynasty. Within a decade, Jordan would become the third-largest recipient of U.S. aid in the world (behind Israel and Egypt); the first Arab country to have a free trade agreement with the United States; and the only poor Arab country to have all its foreign debt either forgiven or rescheduled on favorable terms.

The expected political benefit for Rabin, however, would prove short-lived. Palestinian terror incidents quickly extinguished the peace treaty's glow. According to a poll taken three weeks after the signing of the peace treaty, the right-wing Likud party would have won elections if they were held at that point, gaining nine seats, while Rabin's Labor Party would have lost four seats.

For Syria, King Hussein's breaking of ranks proved to be an irritant worthy only of some scathing press attacks. However, it confirmed Asad's suspicion that his Israeli and American negotiating partners had been intent on stealing the Palestinian and Jordanian cards from his pocket to isolate and pressure him. That only made him less flexible, as the president would discover when he visited Damascus two days later. Asad did make three tactical concessions to compensate Clinton for making the journey.* But their joint press conference was dominated by Asad's refusal to condemn Palestinian terrorist attacks and Hezbollah rocket firings on northern Israeli villages, which had formed the violent backdrop for the signing ceremony in Jordan. On the flight from Damascus to Jerusalem, Clinton called Dennis and me into his study to inform us of his judgment that Asad was "the most constipated" leader he had ever met. "You work on the details of the peace deal; I'm going to work on his head."

Ironically, the Arab country that felt most threatened by the breakthrough was Egypt, the only other Arab state to have signed a peace treaty with Israel. For the first time since the signing of the Israel-Egypt peace treaty in March 1979, Mubarak now had to compete with another Arab leader for Washington's favor. Egypt's determinedly cool relations with Israel would henceforth be contrasted unfavorably in

---

tinians in ways that could jeopardize Jordan's security, the Hashemite Kingdom gained Israeli protection from its worst nightmare.

* Asad agreed to two phases for Israel's withdrawal (previously, he had offered only one), sixteen months for the completion of the withdrawal (previously, he had said twelve months), and an Israeli diplomatic presence, but not an embassy, four months before the completion of the withdrawal (previously, diplomatic relations were to come after Israel completed its full withdrawal).

American and Israeli eyes with the warm peace and normalization of relations to which Hussein had committed his kingdom. Moreover, Egypt had been happy that Israel's isolation in the Arab world left it no choice but to use Cairo as its gateway. Jordan now provided an alternative opening, even if it was less influential than Egypt's.*

IF THE ISRAEL-JORDAN peace treaty had limited implications for the broader balance of power in the region, it nevertheless held some important lessons for Arab-Israeli peacemaking and the U.S. role in fostering it.

First, there was the all-important time factor in the calculations of Arab leaders. As autocrats without term limits, they tend to have a built-in preference for a status quo that ensures their own survival; the needs of their people usually come later. Over time they have perfected the means to maintain that status quo, minimizing the risks to their rule. Only when an Arab leader concludes that time is not on his side, that the risks of clinging to the status quo are more dangerous than the consequences of change, is he likely to move. This is especially true of making peace with Israel, which is inherently unpopular among an Arab leader's people.

The king clearly calibrated the pace of his negotiations to the other tracks, but when he saw the Palestinians reach an agreement that would put Arafat in the West Bank, and he suspected that Asad was about to do his deal with Israel, too, Jordan's circumstances became urgent and the king decided to plunge ahead.

Another lesson for U.S. peacemaking diplomacy is to be sensitive to the impact of inter-Arab rivalries on the calculations of Arab leaders. Beneath the façade of Arab unity, they put their parochial national interests above those of the mythical Arab nation. Arafat raced to reach agreement with Rabin in the summer of 1993 because most of the Palestinians' Arab sponsors had sent him to perdition and because he feared being sidelined by a Syrian-Israeli deal. King Hussein had good reason to fear the intentions of Asad and Arafat since they both had

---

* This competition manifested itself at the 1995 Middle East North Africa Economic Summit in Amman, when Egyptian foreign minister Amre Moussa publicly accused Jordan of "rushing" toward normalization with Israel. The Arabic word he used connoted begging. Insulted, Crown Prince Hassan responded by pointing out that Egypt had made its peace with Israel twelve years earlier, so if anybody could be accused of "rushing" it was Cairo, not Amman.

tried to destabilize his kingdom. Rabin understood this rivalry, and he played on it to pressure the king to move forward.

A third lesson lies in the way King Hussein demonstrated his peaceful intentions to a skeptical Israeli public. That was critical to producing the Israeli concessions that made the deal possible. Sadat grasped this instinctively; King Hussein followed in his footsteps.* Both understood basic Israeli psychology: a battered and insecure people whose collective Jewish psyche had hungered for acceptance after centuries of harsh oppression would respond positively to visible indications of peaceful intentions. It was a lesson in peacemaking with Israel that Asad would refuse to acknowledge, to his country's detriment.

The process of making Israeli-Jordanian peace established once again that America's greatest contribution to peacemaking lies in shaping the environment, rather than engaging in the details of the negotiations. Those specifics are always better left to the parties themselves, if they are willing to deal directly with each other. They are more familiar with the issues, they have a greater stake in the outcomes generated by the negotiations, and, if they can arrive at solutions through a direct give-and-take, it increases the likelihood that they will be prepared to honor the deal.

Conversely, the United States, with its immense power and resources, can do much more than any local party to shape a positive and supportive environment for peacemaking. This was captured by President Clinton's early commitment to "minimize the risks" of those who would make peace. In this regard, Rabin and Clinton worked effectively to orchestrate the dynamics of King Hussein's calculus: Rabin used progress with Arafat to press the king to move forward; Clinton used his relationship with Asad and America's resources to ease the king's way. And behind all this was Clinton's overall effort to use American capabilities to maintain a favorable regional balance of power through containment of radical forces and rogue regimes.

Another lesson is that when Arab leaders resolve to make peace deals with Israel, the establishment of a secret, back-channel mechanism for doing so becomes both possible and critical. Secret engagement is an essential indicator of seriousness because it shields the

---

* King Hussein reinforced his public embrace of Rabin in Washington by an additional gesture: nine days later, on his way home, piloting his own plane, he flew for the first time through Israeli airspace with an Israeli Air Force escort, circling over Jerusalem while he spoke to Rabin and the people of Israel via his cockpit radio.

discussion from the glare of hostile scrutiny. It also makes it much easier to do business, since if the talks remain secret they boost mutual confidence, build personal relations between the closeted interlocutors, and enable each to act in the knowledge that the other will reciprocate, thereby building a virtuous cycle of give-and-take.

Sadat established a secret back channel using his national security adviser, Hassan Tuhami, who met twice with Moshe Dayan, Israel's foreign minister, in secrecy in Morocco. Rabin used Yossi Ginossar, a former Shin Bet security service operative who did business with the Palestinian Authority, as his secret back channel to Arafat. In the king's case, clandestine meetings facilitated by the Mossad had been his long-established way of doing business with Israel. Efraim Halevy's discreet relationship with the king was essential to the deal.

Direct engagement by the leaders themselves is another critical ingredient. Rabin, Peres, and Arafat met regularly after signing the Oslo Accords and learned to do a good deal of business together. Rabin and King Hussein developed a close friendship. Through such summitry, Israeli and Arab leaders grew to respect one another and learned to listen to their respective concerns and constraints. They could size one another up and gauge the sincerity of their intentions. They each would have to assume responsibility for selling any agreement to their people and would need help from the other leader to do that successfully. It was an obvious reality—Human Relations 101—and King Hussein took to it naturally. Asad, by contrast, seemed incapable of grasping this basic truth.

Just as important as direct contact between the Arab and Israeli leaders was direct engagement with the president of the United States. Peacemaking in the Middle East is risky business, often involving life-and-death decisions—as the fates of Sadat and Rabin underscore. In these circumstances, Middle Eastern leaders need to know that they can rely on the United States as they embark on a treacherous path. In order to establish that trust, there can be no substitute for direct engagement by the president himself. Jimmy Carter's personal involvement was critical to the achievement of the Israel-Egypt peace treaty; without it, Sadat would not have taken the huge risks involved in making a separate peace with Israel. Clinton's ability to master the details of his brief and establish empathy with his interlocutors was a formidable asset in the peacemaking effort. Arab and Israeli leaders alike were caught in his spell. They knew they had a friend in the White

House on whom they could depend, a fact that was deeply reassuring to King Hussein as well as Yitzhak Rabin.

Finally, and perhaps most importantly, there was the essential ingredient of leadership, without which none of the other factors would matter. Leadership in Middle Eastern peacemaking manifests itself in the form of courage to break the mould of conflict, the willingness to take large but calculated risks. Successful statesmanship, however, must combine it with an ability to set an achievable if ambitious goal, to develop a realistic strategy for attaining it, and to maintain tactical flexibility along the way. Sadat, Begin, Rabin, Hussein, Peres, and subsequently Ariel Sharon, each possessed these leadership characteristics, towing their people along in their wake.

King Hussein learned well the lessons of his earlier mistaken decisions to allow his country to be dragged into war by Egypt in 1967 and to side with Saddam after his invasion of Kuwait. After these debacles, Hussein developed an astute ability to read the map of the balance of power and accurately calculate the risks of breaking ranks. Like Sadat and Rabin, he acquired a profound conviction that his course was the right one for his people, despite all the opposition and criticism. His legacy is a secure Jordan, guaranteed by the United States, at peace with Israel. His statesmanship explains why the Israel-Jordan peace treaty is still standing while Arafat's "peace of the brave" has been destroyed, and Asad's was never achieved.

Bill Clinton's statesmanship was also on display. Though his objective had been a breakthrough with Syria, he accepted that he could not impose his American agenda on the Middle East's leaders; his role was to support the peacemakers whenever they stepped forward. He made peace where he could, rather than where he preferred.

PART TWO

THE OTHER BRANCH

8

Dual Containment
and the Peace Process

Clinton's diplomatic strategy consisted of two branches. Two years into his presidency, the first branch—peacemaking—was not working exactly as he intended, but he had reason to be satisfied. In the second branch—dual containment of Iraq and Iran—he hoped that pressure on both would eventually produce Saddam's overthrow and the modification of Iran's behavior. In the meantime, with peacemaking his primary goal, Clinton wanted to neutralize the negative impact of their hostility on the peace process. He was playing defense against Iraq and Iran while he pursued a diplomatic offensive with Israel and its Arab neighbors. At the outset of his presidency, that defense worked well.

Its first test came in the spring of 1993. Just after the National Security Council principals had finalized the policy of "aggressive containment" they discovered that Iraqi intelligence was planning to assassinate former President George H. W. Bush during his visit to Kuwait to commemorate the anniversary of its liberation.* After two nights of deliberations, Clinton decided on direct military retribution to deter Saddam from any further aggression. It would be the first time he ordered the use of force in his presidency. But Clinton decided only to attack the Iraqi intelligence headquarters in Baghdad and to do it in the middle of the night, when the offices would be deserted. He had followed the advice of the chairman of the Joint Chiefs of Staff, Gen-

---

* Before Bush's visit, the Kuwaitis had arrested sixteen people, including eleven Iraqis who had crossed the border with an SUV loaded with a concealed bomb and detonators. One of the defendants testified that Iraqi intelligence had recruited him, and the detonator found in the car was identical to those used by Iraqi intelligence in another bombing mission that the United States had intercepted.

eral Colin Powell, who was confident that a little force would go a long way to deter Saddam.

My NSC colleagues and I thought Clinton should retaliate against targets of importance to Saddam himself, such as his presidential palaces, to drive home the point that if Saddam came after one of our presidents, the United States would consider itself free to come after him. While Clinton was sympathetic to this tougher approach, he was already engulfed in a controversy with the military over the treatment of gays in the armed services. He was not inclined to overrule Powell. He was also wary of inflicting civilian casualties. And he knew Saddam would like nothing better than to distract him from his primary purpose of peacemaking.

On June 26, 1993, twenty-three Tomahawk missiles were launched from American warships in the Persian Gulf at Mukhabarat intelligence headquarters in Baghdad. They destroyed the building but, notwithstanding the president's caution, four missiles went astray, killing eight civilians in nearby residences, including a famous Iraqi artist. Nevertheless, Powell proved correct in his assessment that the strike would deter more such schemes by Saddam. For the next seven years, we saw no evidence that his intelligence services were involved in any terrorist or assassination activities against American or Western targets. That is why the American intelligence community so doubted George W. Bush's claim that Saddam was linked to Osama bin Laden and the 9/11 attacks. It knew that since the 1993 retaliation, Saddam had ordered his intelligence services to focus instead on building up a network of front companies and financial arrangements that would help him circumvent the sanctions imposed on Iraq in 1990. That successful enterprise kept Iraq's intelligence services busy.

The June 1993 retaliation was a test case for Clinton's application of the strategy of "aggressive containment." It was one thing for the president's advisers to agree on a policy that would require sustained use of force; it was another for that policy to be applied by a president who was conscious of how blunt a weapon a military strike could turn out to be. In his first decision to use force, Clinton revealed that his emphasis would be more on containment and less on aggressive action. Force would be used to deter Saddam, but not in a way that might produce his overthrow.

This was underlined in October 1994, when Clinton faced another Iraqi crisis and again chose the more limited response. Into 1994, the peace process had gained considerable momentum. Arafat had staged a triumphant return to Gaza and Clinton, as we have seen, was intensively engaged in peace negotiations on the Syrian and Jordanian fronts. Just as Clinton's advisers had calculated, the strategy of "dual containment" had facilitated progress on peacemaking, which in turn increased the isolation of both Iraq and Iran.

This proved to be a particular source of discomfort for Saddam. King Hussein, previously his ally, not only moved back into the American orbit, he also began to cooperate in our covert efforts at regime change. Having lost Jordan, Saddam might have reconciled with Iraq's sister ruling Baath party in Syria. Iran and Syria had already developed a strategic partnership; if Iraq were to join them, the United States would find itself facing an axis of potentially hostile powers across the Middle East from the Persian Gulf to the Mediterranean (ironically, an axis that has now been facilitated by George W. Bush's overthrow of Saddam). But Clinton was able to exploit a longtime personal antagonism between Asad and Saddam and use his engagement with Syria in the peace process to drive a deeper wedge between them. Asad had no intention of jeopardizing his relationship with the United States and his prospects for regaining the Golan Heights for Saddam's sake. This ensured that, during a period of intensive U.S.-Syrian engagement over the peace process, Asad strictly enforced the sanctions on Iraq. This stands in contrast with his son's facilitation of the Iraqi insurgency after Saddam's overthrow, in the absence of any interest from George W. Bush in an Israeli-Syrian peace process.

The other option for Saddam to break out was to make a tactical reconciliation with Iran. But, despite some efforts by both sides to deal with issues from their eight-year war, mutual antagonism and distrust made any reconciliation impossible.*

By mid-1994, Saddam found himself isolated internationally at a time when the sanctions were beginning to create internal stresses that destabilized his regime. The sanctions never prohibited him from importing food and medicines to alleviate the stress on his people. However, Saddam at this stage refused to accept a U.N. arrangement that would allow him to sell oil in exchange for importing humanitarian

---

* Overtures in 1993 had led to official visits and discussion of the POW issue, including an Iranian acknowledgment that it held twenty thousand Iraqi prisoners. Yet Iraq consistently denied that it was holding Iranian POWs and the talks eventually collapsed.

goods. Consequently, four years after the imposition of sanctions, the widespread shortages of basic commodities, medicines, and spare parts were causing frequent electrical blackouts, inadequate hospital treatment, and problems with water and sanitation.

In those days I would measure the decline of Saddam's fortunes by the reduction in the value of the Iraqi dinar and the rise in the number of reported coup or assassination attempts. By mid-1994, Saddam's regime had resorted to printing money to stave off economic disaster and the dinar had fallen from 140 to the U.S. dollar to 700. Saddam was facing discontent in the Sunni Ubayd tribe, one of the mainstays of the regime, and had survived two assassination attempts. In 1994, the regime was also trying to cope with CIA–inspired bombings in and around Baghdad organized by Ayad al-Allawi and officers who had defected from the Iraqi army (Allawi would become interim prime minister of Iraq after the 2003 invasion).

Finding himself in an increasingly tight corner, Saddam had sought relief from the sanctions by beginning to comply with the demands of the United Nations Special Commission (UNSCOM) weapons inspectors.* With his cooperation, Saddam's long-range missiles and stockpiles of chemical agents and munitions were destroyed. The International Atomic Energy Agency (IAEA) removed all fissionable material from Iraq, and the equipment for Iraq's clandestine nuclear weapons program was also destroyed.

In this context of Iraqi cooperation with UNSCOM, Saddam's officials had started relentlessly pressuring the commission's chief, Rolf Ekéus, to report progress on Iraqi disarmament to the Security Council. At the same time Saddam was pressuring the Russians, who had a strong interest in salvaging the debts owed them by Iraq, to push for language in a new Security Council resolution that would promise early sanctions relief.

Ekéus was an experienced and skillful Swedish diplomat committed to disarming Iraq. By mid-1994, Saddam's bullying had convinced him that he had to offer the Iraqi leader some hope of sanctions relief if he were to secure Iraq's continued cooperation with UNSCOM. However, Ekéus also understood that Clinton would not countenance any move

---

* The U.N. resolutions specified that when UNSCOM reported that all Saddam's missile, weapons of mass destruction (WMD) programs, and ordnance had been accounted for and destroyed, the sanctions on oil exports and the importation of non-military goods would be lifted.

on sanctions until and unless there was a full and complete account- ing by Saddam of all his weapons programs because U.S. containment strategy depended on keeping those sanctions in place.

In July 1994, Ekéus reported to the Security Council that UNSCOM was making progress on Iraq's disarmament. The Russians promptly proposed that a deadline be set for a transition to long-term monitor- ing and the lifting of sanctions. The United States had little difficulty in blocking that effort. But in a subsequent meeting with Tony Lake, Ekéus warned that he needed to give the Iraqis a timetable for lifting sanctions. Tony responded that until there was a complete accounting of all of Saddam's WMD, the United States would block any attempt in the Security Council to transition to long-term monitoring.

When Saddam heard from Ekéus that there would be no sanctions relief, he decided to provoke a crisis around Ekéus's upcoming October 10, 1994, report to the Security Council. First he threatened another Iraqi assault on Kuwait unless the Security Council agreed to a time- table for lifting sanctions. Then he mobilized his elite Hammurabi and al-Nida Republican Guard armored divisions and dispatched their lead elements south toward the Kuwaiti border. By October 8, 1994, Iraq's troop strength in the south had risen to 64,000. The Hammu- rabi armored division, which had led the 1990 invasion of Kuwait, was only twenty kilometers from the Kuwaiti border.

This seemed like a godsend to the proponents of "aggressive con- tainment" in the White House. We had been anticipating a tough battle in the Security Council when the sanctions came up for review in Oc- tober. But now, in a ham-fisted effort to pressure the Security Council to lift sanctions, Saddam had managed only to underscore that he still retained aggressive impulses backed by dangerous capabilities. This be- havior offered Bill Clinton an opportunity to tighten the screws.

IT TAKES A crisis for the president's National Security Council to as- semble on a Sunday morning in the Situation Room. On this particu- lar Sunday in early October, the White House staff, including the national security adviser, turned up in blue jeans. The secretary of defense, William Perry, who had succeeded Les Aspin when he re- signed earlier in the year, and the chairman of the Joint Chiefs, John Shalikashvili ("Shali"), who had succeeded Colin Powell, were both dressed in uniform blue sports jackets, button-down shirts, khaki pants, and loafers. They looked slightly out of place, the ramrod-backed Shali usually sporting a green, medal-bedecked uniform, the bookish Perry a Brooks Brothers suit. Their matching outfits, however, suited their matching intellects. They were probably the most intelligent combination of civilian and military chiefs their respective posts had known since the days of George Marshall and General Omar Bradley. They not only commanded the respect of the other principals, but together tended to dominate the meetings.

After the nondescript acting CIA chief, Admiral William Studeman, informed the meeting that two Republican Guard armored divisions were heading for the Kuwaiti border and the Iraqi army was on full alert, Shali added that three additional divisions seemed to be assembling in possible preparation for a move to the south. If they advanced, by the end of the week Saddam would be in the same position as in August 1990, just before he invaded Kuwait. Shali said we had to assemble the forces necessary to get Saddam to pull back his divisions and, if he invaded Kuwait, to defeat them decisively, quickly, and with minimum casualties.

Strobe Talbott, the deputy secretary of state, was sitting in Warren Christopher's chair since he happened to be en route to Kuwait at that moment. He asked: "How do we define 'defeat'? Is it taking out Saddam?"

"That would be my judgment," Perry responded immediately. "We don't want to have to go back and do this yet again."

Shali then outlined a plan to dispatch 350 aircraft to the Gulf, including B-52s and Stealth F-117s, which the president would have to decide on immediately. Saudi Arabia would have to agree to host the bulk of the aircraft. The president would then have to decide whether to move additional troops to the theater. He would also need to authorize the use of airpower to attack Iraqi forces if they crossed the border into Kuwait.

Tony Lake asked Shali, "What happens if he just sits there on the Kuwaiti border?"

"That's not acceptable," Shali responded. "If he leaves them there, we will not be able to withdraw our forces. We need to demand that he move his forces back. And then we have to have something that will ensure that he doesn't do this again." He laid out a series of options for preventing a recurrence of the crisis, including extending the no-fly zone to the entire airspace of Iraq.

That afternoon, President Clinton gave Shali the authorizations he requested and added his own request—the preparation of a list of high-value, strategic targets that the air force would hit if Saddam initiated military action. And then he called King Fahd to secure permission to use Saudi bases and airspace.

KING FAHD HAD come to see Saudi Arabia's security as entirely dependent on the United States. Saddam's invasion of Kuwait in 1990 had put Iraqi forces on his border, threatening Saudi Arabia's main oil fields in the Eastern Province. Fahd was therefore predisposed to say yes to a direct request from the president to access Saudi military facilities, especially when it looked like Saddam might invade Kuwait again. But it was much easier for him to do so this time because the United States was actively engaged in an effort to bring Syria into the peace process and resolve the Palestinian problem—a hot-button issue for his people.

However, if the king were to expose himself to Arab criticism that he was facilitating the bombing of Iraqis, he wanted to know that this time the United States would get rid of Saddam.

The president was direct and forthright in saying to Fahd that if Saddam attacked, the United States would finish the job. Fahd was clearly satisfied; after the call, he told Ray Mabus, our ambassador in Riyadh, that even though he would have to consult with his brothers, we should act as if the decisions had already been made.

Mubarak felt just as strongly when Clinton spoke to him. "This man Saddam is unreliable," the Egyptian president declared. "You can never believe him." He then made a point of noting that he had spoken to Asad, who expressed his satisfaction with the way Syria's negotiations with Israel were moving forward. "Don't worry about it, Mr. President," he said. "We'll support you strongly against Saddam." Clinton could now rely on access to Egypt's air bases and transit for the U.S. Navy through the Suez Canal.

The symbiosis we had hoped for was clearly at work. Certainly Fahd and Mubarak were willing to support Clinton out of concern that Saddam would attack Kuwait again. But the fact that Clinton was so heavily engaged in an Arab-Israeli peacemaking effort that was yielding positive results advantaged his strategy for countering Saddam's aggressive tendencies. Nowhere was this clearer than with King Hussein, who was finalizing his peace agreement with Yitzhak Rabin as the crisis unfolded. He would not be caught on the wrong side again.

While Clinton was calling King Fahd, Hussein was meeting with Iraqi deputy prime minister Tariq Aziz and upbraiding him for Saddam's actions. He told Aziz to take a clear message back to Saddam: "Jordan will not support Iraqi aggression!"

ON MONDAY, OCTOBER 10, 1994, the National Security Council gathered again in the West Wing basement. The principals had decided eighteen months earlier on a "ratchet" strategy—whenever Saddam challenged us militarily, we would use the opportunity to increase the pressure on him. At Tony Lake's request, Bruce Riedel and I had drafted an options paper for their consideration that reflected this approach: it began with the demand that Iraq withdraw all the forces it had inserted in the south to their previous positions north of the 32nd parallel. The paper then discussed the option of demanding that Iraq remove all ground forces from the south, making the area below the 32nd parallel a "no-drive zone." The third option was to extend the no-fly zone to all of Iraq's airspace.

Shali, however, responded to Tony Lake's faithful rendition of these options by cautioning, "We shouldn't overreach and end up with nothing." He argued that from a military perspective, the destabilizing factor in the current events was the reinforcement of Iraqi forces in the south with Republican Guard units. They should be removed from the south. We had to deliver the message that any subsequent deployment of such forces below the 32nd parallel would be treated as a hostile act and dealt with appropriately.

"Makes sense to me," Lake responded. Suddenly a consensus had formed around the minimalist option. Tony then turned to me and asked me to present the "no-drive zone" option. This was, to say the least, an unusual way of proceeding. Tony always pushed his senior directors forward, often preferring that they brief the president and attend to his meetings or phone calls with foreign leaders, while Tony stayed at his desk. But to have a senior director present to the principals an option for action was different; he was signaling them that he didn't support it himself.

Put on the spot, I made the best case I could muster. We needed to take advantage of the moment to increase the pressure on Saddam. Preventing him from deploying any tanks or heavy artillery in the south would replicate the situation in the north, showing Iraqis that he had less and less control over them. Most importantly, I argued, it would stop his campaign against the Marsh Arabs.

For the past year, Saddam had been waging a counterinsurgency campaign in the south against Iranian-backed, Iraqi Shia who were using the camouflage of the vast southern marshes to assist their efforts. Saddam had dammed the rivers that fed the marshes, drying up huge tracts of marshland, burning villages, and forcing the Marsh Arabs, who had maintained their unique lifestyle for thousands of years, to abandon their homes. Now Clinton had an opportunity to help them in a meaningful way. The "no-drive" option would increase the pressure on Saddam and serve a humanitarian purpose as well.

Madeleine Albright, as our ambassador at the United Nations, had taken up the cause of the Marsh Arabs but in this instance she sided with Shali. The Russians were already adamantly opposed to the "no-fly zones" as an infringement on Iraqi sovereignty. A "no-drive zone" would not pass in the Security Council, she concluded.

It was left to Shali to deliver the coup de grâce. He said that by preventing Saddam from deploying any ground forces in the south we would be leaving the area wide open to the Iranians.* The principals were familiar with the fact that the Reagan administration had backed Saddam in his eight-year war with Iran to prevent Iranian forces from taking southern Iraq, where they could threaten the oil fields of Kuwait and Saudi Arabia. The principals had not forgotten how George H. W. Bush had allowed Saddam to suppress the Shia uprising in the south in 1991 for fear that the Iranians would gain control there. None of them was prepared to open this Pandora's box.

It would prove ironic that, a decade later, Bush's son would open the gates wide to Iranian influence in southern Iraq. But Clinton's national security team was made of more cautious stuff. We were operating within the constraints of the existing Middle Eastern order, not seeking to destroy them. Clinton and his advisers believed that transformation would come through peacemaking. In the meantime, they viewed the containment of Iran as important as containing Iraq.

---

* Shali also argued that enforcing a "no-drive zone" would require large resources to monitor Iraqi troop movements in the south. Saddam could easily provoke us into a tit-for-tat game by moving a few forces into the forbidden area wherever and whenever he chose. Airpower could not stop an advancing army in the south so we would need ground forces in the area ready to intervene.

When Clinton met with his national security team on October 14 and October 16, these instincts were manifest. By then Mohammed al-Sahhaf, the Iraqi foreign minister, who would later distinguish himself by his buffoonery as information minister during the 2003 U.S.-led invasion, had announced in Baghdad that Saddam was pulling his army units back "for further training." Clinton outlined the principles that should guide U.S. policy: Saddam must get no reward for his misconduct, and we should make sure that a new Security Council resolution would allow for the use of force if Saddam misbehaved again. However, Clinton was categorical that we should be satisfied with the withdrawal of Saddam's reinforcements from the south.

Within days, the ambassadors of the United States, Britain, and France at the United Nations would issue a joint ultimatum to the Iraqi head of mission demanding that Saddam withdraw all units he had moved south and declaring that if he ever attempted to move them south again, the coalition would reserve the right to respond in "a manner of its own choosing." By October 13, our intelligence agencies were reporting that virtually every unit that Saddam had put into the south since late September had now pulled back beyond the 32nd parallel. By October 15, the Security Council had passed Resolution 949, which codified these demands under Chapter VII of the U.N. Charter.

Clinton, in forcing Saddam to back down, had followed Shali's injunction not to overreach. But the president had left Saddam free to rattle his cage again whenever he liked. Some might criticize Clinton for having chosen "stability over freedom," much as George W. Bush dismissed Franklin Roosevelt's meeting with Stalin and Churchill in Yalta at the close of World War II. But Clinton was making a calculated decision to hold Saddam at bay while he pursued Arab-Israeli peace, an objective he thought far more attainable in the prevailing circumstances.

The outcome of the October 1994 Iraq crisis represented a victory for Clinton's policy of "dual containment." The United States had demonstrated, through its ability to move large forces rapidly to Iraq's borders, that it could effectively deter Saddam from threatening or attacking his neighbors. For the next ten years, until his overthrow, Saddam would not threaten any other neighbor again.

The policy of ratcheting up the pressure on Saddam, however, had now been unofficially abandoned in favor of a more defensive containment strategy based on deterrence and the maintenance of sanctions.

There was, however, a structural flaw in the modified policy: international support for sanctions would inevitably erode, making it harder to maintain the containment over time. This made the covert campaign to overthrow Saddam all the more important.

THE BASEMENT OFFICES in the West Wing known collectively as the Situation Room have two conference rooms: the one that the principals had used in their Iraq crisis deliberations, and another in the back, which the NSC staff used for secure videoconferences with officials from other parts of the government.

On this Thursday morning in March 1995, one screen displayed three uniformed members of the Joint Chiefs of Staff; the other showed the faces of two senior CIA officials, looking like they'd just been caught red-handed raiding the fridge. At the other end of the conference table sat George Tenet, then the NSC's senior director for intelligence; Ellen Laipson, who had replaced Bruce Riedel as my deputy for the Gulf and South Asia; and me.

I had convened an urgent videoconference because Riedel, who had returned to the Agency to work on Middle East assessments, had called at 7 A.M. to alert me that Saddam was mobilizing his elite Republican Guard units for military action in northern Iraq. The Iraqi army was on full alert, all leaves had been cancelled, and reserves were being called up. Having failed to move on Kuwait five months earlier, Saddam now seemed intent on moving against the Kurds.

Any indication that Saddam might be planning to send his forces into northern Iraq set off alarm bells in Washington. Clinton had taken on a special commitment to protect the Iraqi Kurds but we were doing so with only a squadron of aircraft at Incirlik Air Base in eastern Turkey.* The whole exercise was essentially a bluff; the United States had no ground forces in the vicinity that could intervene rapidly to stop an Iraqi ground assault.

Bruce's report indicated that Saddam was responding to information about a coup plot. Six months earlier, consistent with Clinton's decision to seek the covert overthrow of Saddam's regime, the White

---

* This was a commitment that grew out of the Kurdish refugee crisis of 1991. In the wake of the Gulf War, Saddam had forced tens of thousands of Kurds to flee toward the Turkish border. The first Bush administration then launched Operation Provide Comfort to stop the Iraqi army from moving north and to help the refugees return to their homes.

House had authorized the dispatch of a small team of CIA agents into northern Iraq. Tony Lake had made clear that they were not to do anything without coordinating with the NSC. He did not want the president involved in a Bay of Pigs–style coup plot.

As Lake's Middle East staffer, I was to make sure his instructions were followed. I thought I had made myself clear to the Middle East chief in the CIA Directorate of Operations (DO) and to Bob Baer, the leader of the team he was inserting in northern Iraq, when they came to see me on the eve of Bob's departure.

Baer, as he would later admit, viewed himself as a "cowboy" engaged in derring-do around the world on behalf of the U.S. government. I admired his courage but I specifically warned him and his boss that no commitments could be made on behalf of the U.S. government to putative coup plotters unless the White House explicitly approved them. At a minimum, they would need air cover, but if the United States gave such a commitment, they would effectively have the ability to commit U.S. forces to combat. I made clear that the White House needed to vet the coup plotters, assess the seriousness of their intentions and capabilities, and make sure they were not worse than Saddam.

I was therefore flabbergasted on that Thursday morning to hear Baer's boss say the CIA was aware of the coup plot that Saddam was now preparing to crush, and that the coup leader, General Wafiq al-Samarrai, was "known to the CIA."

When I asked incredulously what exactly the CIA knew, he prevaricated. When I pressed him, he admitted that Samarrai, who had been Saddam's intelligence chief, was communicating with disaffected Iraqi commanders who controlled three Iraqi combat units. The coup attempt was supposed to begin with an attack on the Iraqi army by Kurdish forces near Salah ad-Din in northern Iraq. While Saddam's attention was diverted, the disaffected Iraqi army units would move on Baghdad, forcing Saddam to flee to his stronghold of Auja, near his hometown of Tikrit, where other units planned to capture him.

Baer's boss admitted that Samarrai had asked whether the United States would support a post-Saddam regime and continue to patrol the northern no-fly zone. "When he went beyond that, we asked for a conversation," the Middle East chief explained in the cryptic jargon of the CIA. God only knew what had been promised or what Samarrai might have thought had been promised in such a "conversation," presumably with Bob Baer.

On the other TV monitor, the staff of the Joint Chiefs now briefed us on what they were picking up about the military situation in northern Iraq. They noted that Iranian intelligence and security personnel were flowing into Iraqi Kurdistan. Apparently, Jalal Talabani, the head of the Patriotic Union of Kurdistan (PUK), one of the two major Kurdish parties, and subsequently the first president of post-Saddam Iraq, had committed his Pesh Merga troops to the coup effort. He was relying on the Iraqi Shiite Badr Brigade, which was trained, supplied, and supported by Iran, to join in his attack on Iraqi troops. Iranian armor had also moved to the Iraqi border to support these pro-Iranian forces. According to the briefers from the Joint Chiefs, there were also indications that the Turkish armed forces were preparing to move into Kurdistan from the north. It seemed that everybody—even Saddam—was in on this coup except Clinton, in whose name it was being launched.

George, Ellen, and I stormed out of the windowless Situation Room and up a narrow flight of stairs into the large, light-filled West Wing corner office of the national security adviser. Sitting behind his desk littered with baseball paraphernalia and files, Tony Lake absorbed our report with surprising equanimity. It was as if he had expected that one day we would turn up in his office with just such a story. When Ellen produced a black-and-white photograph of General Samarrai, which showed a corpulent, swarthy, mustachioed coup plotter, direct from central casting, we all burst out laughing.

But it wasn't funny. A lot of people were about to get themselves killed for no good purpose. Tony jabbed the button on the console of his large white secure phone set, which connected him directly to Admiral Studeman. It was possible that the secretive DO had not bothered to inform Studeman either; he was not one of them. Tony spoke to the admiral in measured tones that barely disguised his sarcasm. "Bill, I have just been informed by my staff that we are involved with somebody who is launching a coup against Saddam Hussein. It seems that we've had discussions with him, possibly made commitments to him. The Iraqis, Iranians, Turks, and Kurds all know about it and believe we are behind it. And the first time the White House finds out about it is today, not from a report from the CIA, but from an intercept!"

I could not hear Studeman's response, but Tony clearly felt he hadn't effectively conveyed the gravity of the situation. He decided to spell it out for him. "This puts the president in a position when it leaks to the press that he launched a coup and then let it fail. And it *will* leak to the press because, having denied us the information, your agency is now going around briefing the whole U.S. government! I would appreciate it if you would send your people over here to give me a full and complete briefing too."

Tony turned to us with precise instructions: "We need to turn this thing off, now! We have to warn off the Iraqis and the Turks. We have to get a message to the Kurds to tell them that their mission has been compromised. We have to get the CIA under control, now!"

We warned the Iraqis through their ambassador in New York that any movement north would be met by American force. We warned the Turkish general staff through military channels that any move south would be unwelcome in Washington. To warn the Kurds and their fellow coup plotters, however, we had to go through CIA channels. We took the unusual step of sending Bob Baer instructions directly from the White House. He was to inform his friends immediately, "The action you have planned for this weekend has been totally compromised. We believe there is a high risk of failure. Any decision to proceed will be on your own."

Twenty-four hours later, the DO's Middle East chief turned up in Lake's office with his tail between his legs to provide the "full" briefing that he should have given us a month earlier. According to his account, Samarrai first briefed Baer about his plans at the end of January and had elaborated on them in two subsequent meetings in February. Tony asked what Baer had promised Samarrai. Amazingly, Baer's boss didn't seem to know, or perhaps he didn't want to say. Instead he responded that Baer had been ordered immediately to provide a definitive statement of what was promised in a cable. He then claimed he had just found out that Ahmed Chalabi, the head of the CIA-funded Iraqi National Congress opposition group, had brought Samarrai into his organization and had sought and received Iranian support for the coup attempt. Chalabi had now conveyed to the CIA a message from the Iranians, who wanted to know what the U.S. position was on the coup and whether we would attack their forces if they participated in the fighting. Six years later, Chalabi would become the man that Vice President Dick Cheney and Defense Secretary Donald Rumsfeld designated to replace Saddam. For that purpose, the Pentagon flew him into Iraq with his band of merry men, hard on the heels of the U.S. Army's occupation of Baghdad. U.S. government officials subsequently alleged that he had provided highly sensitive classified information to Iran.

(Chalabi denied the charge.) That Iranian connection was already manifesting itself back in March 1995: he was trying to orchestrate a joint Iranian-U.S. operation against Saddam.

Baer has claimed he "outlined the coup, chapter and verse, for the folks back home. . . . But Washington had simply ignored everything we'd reported, letting preparations go forward as if there was a green light." Baer admits he was "operating at the edge of my orders, out where the bright fires burn." But since he had heard nothing from Washington he assumed that he should proceed. After all, his instructions were to foment a coup against Saddam and he claims he was reporting to his headquarters on the progress he was making. Either Baer did not tell all to his CIA bosses or they were incompetent, obtuse, furtive, or worse. Whatever the case, the fact is the White House was, as they say in Washington jargon, "out of the loop."

Although Talabani's Pesh Merga forces acquitted themselves well, routing two Iraqi infantry brigades and capturing a disaffected Iraqi army battalion, Saddam rounded up Samarrai's accomplices and sent in elite Republican Guard units to crush the Kurdish penetration. Warned by Washington, Talabani's forces withdrew and everybody in Iraq went back to business as usual: the Kurds to fighting one another, Chalabi to spinning a new coup plot, and Saddam to recalculating his strategy for breaking out of the containment box we had put him in.

The March 1995 coup debacle, however, did more than just reveal the fecklessness of certain CIA officials and their agents. It highlighted the contradiction inherent in Clinton's Iraq policy: the overt objective was to contain Saddam while covertly we were seeking to overthrow him. But if a credible coup attempt manifested itself, would Clinton be prepared to intervene militarily to ensure its success? The only overthrow effort that would not need active American military intervention was a "palace coup," but that was the least likely scenario since Saddam relied on loyalists from his family and tribe to staff his inner circle. Any other scenario for regime change would require the United States to go to war again with Saddam Hussein. As long as he was contained effectively and posed no threat to his neighbors, there was little appetite in the White House and among the American public for such a conflict.

This created a dilemma only evident in retrospect. Containment of Saddam was originally designed as a short-term strategy to increase the prospects for a covert coup. But it had now morphed into a longer-term strategy for leaving Saddam in place as sanctions kept him weak.

However, a containment policy that depended on international enforcement of a draconian sanctions regime had a limited shelf life.

By 1995, notwithstanding the policy's success, discomfort with the sanctions was already growing in the international community. Arab leaders had begun to express reluctance to provide open-ended support for Clinton's containment efforts because public opinion in the Arab world increasingly identified with the suffering of the Iraqi people. At the same time, France and Russia were beginning to use their privileged positions as permanent veto-wielding powers in the Security Council to distance themselves from Clinton's strategy.

At the United Nations, Madeleine Albright tried to counter this erosion, using photographs of Saddam's huge and ornate palaces to show that he had enough money to spend on his people. But she made little headway against the statistical evidence of increasing hardship. Particularly devastating to her case were the rising rates of infant mortality. Saddam was deliberately exacerbating the problem by denying Iraqi hospitals desperately needed medical supplies and equipment. Still, it was increasingly accepted worldwide that sanctions were responsible for inflicting undue suffering on the Iraqi people. Albright's photographs of Saddam's palaces were trumped by Saddam's photographs of baby-size coffins being paraded around Baghdad on the roof racks of Iraqi taxicabs.

In April 1995, in an attempt to stem the erosion of sanctions support, the United States introduced a resolution in the Security Council that would allow Iraq to export oil to pay for the importation of food and medicine. U.N. Security Council Resolution 986 passed unanimously and won resounding approval internationally. This was the genesis of the now notorious "oil-for-food" arrangements. It was designed to help relieve the hardships of the Iraqi people while raising the comfort level of the international community about maintaining the sanctions regime. The oil revenues would also be used to fund UNSCOM's inspections, the Kurdish enclave, and the Kuwaiti victims of Saddam's invasion.*

The mechanism required that all the proceeds be placed in a

---

* U.N. Security Council Resolution 986 provided for Iraq to sell $1 billion of oil every three months. The revenues generated would be divided as follows: 53 percent for the needs of the Iraqi people; 30 percent for a fund to compensate the victims of Saddam's aggression; 13 percent to meet Kurdish needs in northern Iraq; and 4 percent for U.N. operations, especially UNSCOM.

U.N.-controlled escrow account and only released to pay for contracts approved by the U.N. Sanctions Committee (where the United States could use its veto to block suspect contracts). We never imagined that the people chosen by the United Nations to administer the arrangements—including the son of Secretary-General Kofi Annan—would subsequently abuse them for their own gain. But in any case, at this stage Saddam indignantly rejected the resolution, making the United States look reasonable to the world while he proved once again that he cared little for his people's welfare. Clinton had regained the moral high ground and had not yet had to concede on the issue of Iraq's oil exports.

Nevertheless, it would only take one clean report from UNSCOM's chairman about the state of Saddam's WMD programs to isolate the United States in the Security Council. Clinton always had the option of wielding the veto but he had to consider the impact on the willingness of other states to uphold the sanctions regime if he did—that was the downside of working within the conventions of the international system.

By 1995, UNSCOM and the IAEA had made considerable progress in identifying and eliminating Saddam's WMD stockpiles and capabilities. Ekéus believed the rest could be taken care of by transitioning to a long-term monitoring and verification regime. So the threat to the sanctions regime was real. However, in August 1995, Hussein Kamel, Saddam's son-in-law and the head of Iraq's unconventional weapons programs, defected to Jordan. Saddam panicked. In an attempt to pre-empt anything Kamel might reveal, the regime suddenly provided UNSCOM with more than half a million pages of documents that revealed Iraq had produced massive quantities of anthrax, botulinim toxin, and other biological substances. Saddam tried to make it appear that Kamel had done all this behind his back, by planting the boxes of documentation at Kamel's chicken farm and then leading the UNSCOM inspectors to the location. But that only induced Kamel to implicate his father-in-law further. He gave UNSCOM details of Saddam's program to weaponize biological agents during the Gulf War and his crash program in 1990 to enrich uranium for a nuclear device.

Saddam had thoroughly deceived UNSCOM about his biological weapons program. Now Ekéus had a whole new pile of information to verify and a large amount of materiel to account for. Those who had become impatient with sanctions and inspections had just had the rug pulled out from under them. Clinton's Iraq policy had gained a reprieve. But that was bound to be temporary; eventually sanctions fatigue would again play to Saddam's advantage. If we could use the limited time available to promote a successful coup against Saddam when his grip on power was weakening and the international consensus was against him, we might have avoided subsequent trouble.

To exploit this opportunity, in early 1996 the principals approved a more aggressive covert effort to overthrow Saddam. This time the CIA hoped to use the newfound willingness of King Hussein to put his extensive relationships with the tribes of western Iraq at our disposal. With the help of a group of Sunni generals in exile that the Agency had been cultivating, the principals decided to promote a military putsch rather than an uprising. The plan required only U.S. air cover, without a ground intervention. John Deutsch, the new director of central intelligence, took personal responsibility for managing the project to assuage White House doubts about CIA freelancers.

For a short time, the approach looked quite promising. The Iraqi National Accord (al-Wifaq al-Watani), headed by Ayad al-Allawi, succeeded in recruiting a significant number of midlevel operational officers. The coup was scheduled to be launched in August 1996, but the wider the conspiracy spread, the greater the opportunity for Saddam's agents to discover it. Sure enough, in June Saddam ordered the arrest of more than one hundred officers and then summarily executed the ten ringleaders.

It was a dramatic setback. Saddam had dealt a body blow to the CIA's operational effectiveness in Iraq, as well as its morale. His detection system in the Iraqi armed forces and security services had proved so effective that any dissenters now had to operate on the assumption that they would be discovered, which effectively deterred them from even trying. Without an effective covert option, it was now only a matter of time before Clinton's containment strategy would start to come apart.

9

Iran's Breakout

Containing Iran would prove even more difficult. Tehran had interpreted the enunciation of the dual containment policy in May 1993 as a declaration of hostile intent. Given Iranian paranoia and mistrust of American purposes, they did not take seriously repeated declarations by Clinton's spokesmen that the president did not seek the overthrow of the Iranian government but rather was ready for an official dialogue with it. Instead they focused on Clinton's declared intention to contain, isolate, and sanction Iran, to discourage foreign investment in its oil industry, and to prevent it from acquiring nuclear weapons, missile delivery systems, and offensive conventional weapons.

Tony Lake and I had worried that Iran would respond to our strategy by seeking a rapprochement with Iraq. The Iranians embarked on just such an effort in October 1993 by dispatching their deputy foreign minister, Javad Zarif, to Baghdad, but as noted earlier it soon became clear that we had little to fear.

The Iranians neutralized the impact of our dual containment strategy in a more sophisticated way than we had imagined. They studied our strategy carefully, identified its two weak points, and exploited those vulnerabilities with considerable skill.

First, they focused on the tension between the United States and Europe over Iranian sanctions. While we wanted to exact a price for Iran's malevolent behavior, the European states had made a collective decision to engage with Iran instead, through what they called a "critical dialogue." Given its large market, vast oil resources, and geostrategic location, the Europeans judged Iran too important to be isolated and punished. Moreover, Iran had not been indicted for transgressing the rules of the international order. The regime had managed successfully to keep its fingerprints off the major terrorist operations that it was believed to have sponsored, and the IAEA had not yet raised the alarm about its nuclear program. Unlike Iraq, it was therefore not subject to mandatory U.N. sanctions; those would only come a decade later.

Clinton's efforts to persuade the Europeans to conform to his approach were also being undermined by American oil companies, which by 1994 had become the largest customers of Iranian crude, reselling to third-country markets some 24 percent of Iran's exports, worth $4 billion a year. From Clinton's perspective, closing this loophole would only have penalized American companies because Iran would simply sell the oil to other customers. But the Europeans saw it differently, accusing us of hypocrisy since we were demanding that they prevent their corporations from doing business with Iran while our oil companies proceeded with business as usual.

In early 1995, Clinton decided to step up the pressure on Iran; he was encouraged in this by Israel's concerns about the Iranian threat, which had generated intense lobbying activity on Capitol Hill.* This pressure for a harder-line approach coincided with Iranian president Hashemi Rafsanjani's decision, in March 1995, to sign over two concessions for the Sirri offshore oil fields to Conoco, an American oil company. That generated a political furor in Washington. President Clinton quickly promulgated two executive orders banning U.S. investment in Iran's oil fields, effectively vetoing the Conoco deal.

Rafsanjani's decision may have been designed to signal his desire to engage more constructively with the United States. But the Clinton administration viewed it as an attempt to thwart our pressure on European oil companies by highlighting our hypocrisy. As Warren Christopher noted publicly, the Conoco project also had the potential to contribute to Iran's financing of international terrorism. What he could not say was that we knew Rafsanjani to be as hard-line as Ayatollah Khamenei in authorizing assassinations and terrorist operations. Rafsanjani was shrewd in playing us off against the European oil companies, who jumped at the opportunity he offered them to replace

---

* Prime Minister Rabin constantly warned Clinton about Iran's buildup of missile capabilities and its pursuit of weapons of mass destruction. He viewed Iran as a radical regional power with the motivation to threaten Israel's existence, and argued that Israel needed to make peace with its Arab neighbors the better to confront the common threat they all faced from Iran.

Conoco. Eventually, nearly a dozen foreign oil companies struck agreements with Iran, each totaling in excess of $50 million.

Senator Alfonse D'Amato and AIPAC stepped into the breach by introducing new legislation to try to block these investments. Over the loud protests of European governments, in 1996 Congress passed the Iran and Libya Sanctions Act (ILSA), which for the first time provided the president with the authority to impose secondary sanctions on any non-American company investing over $40 million in Iran. This generated even more friction in the Atlantic alliance, as European governments strove to defend the interests of their corporations and protect them from American sanctions. Consequently, the Europeans were unwilling to acknowledge Iran's active sponsorship of terrorism against the Middle East peace process for fear that we would use it as a lever to get them to act against their own oil companies. We felt they were now the ones promoting a double standard since they constantly sought to impress upon us the importance of Middle East peace to European interests. When we pointed out that one of the greatest impediments to our peacemaking efforts was Iranian support for terrorist organizations, they turned a deaf ear.

Clinton's inability to persuade our European allies of the danger Iran posed to Western interests in the Middle East was an example of a fundamental difference in attitudes. As Robert Kagan has argued, Americans and Europeans have vastly different perspectives on the role of power in international relations. The new European strategic culture emphasized "seduction over coercion." The Iranians understood the difference and effectively exploited it to counteract our containment efforts.

Nevertheless, during Clinton's first term we blocked lending to Iran by international financial institutions such as the International Monetary Fund and the World Bank, made Iran's debt rescheduling efforts more difficult, helped create a negative climate there for foreign investment, and persuaded Japan not to proceed with an aid project in southern Iran worth hundreds of millions of dollars. Through the intervention of Vice President Gore with Russia's Prime Minister Viktor Chernomyrdin, we were also able to confine new Russian arms sales to Iran to defensive categories. We slowed the transfer of missile technology from North Korea, at one point halting it altogether. And we made it more difficult for Iran to secure Russian technical assistance for its nuclear and missile programs.

We discovered an unlikely ally in the conservative-controlled Majlis (Iranian parliament), which blocked Rafsanjani's economic reforms and helped ensure a negative foreign investment climate. Combined with the threat of secondary sanctions from the United States, this managed initially to deter all but one major oil investment project. A growing national debt also forced Iran to halve its total imports, which had a particularly negative effect on its economy. Large subsidies on food and fuel, multiple exchange rates and protection for inefficient public sector businesses compounded the problems. Unilateral U.S. sanctions also succeeded in driving up the prices of some imported goods, complicated the replacement of spare parts for aging defense, industrial, aeronautical, and oil industry equipment, and brought new oil field development virtually to a standstill.

But all this did little to curb Iran's appetite for regional trouble-making. Its fingerprints seemed to be everywhere: an attempted assassination of President Mubarak in Ethiopia, the arming of Islamic insurgents in Algeria, pilgrim riots during the hajj in Saudi Arabia, and Shiite dissent in Bahrain.

Clinton had set out to moderate Iran's behavior. By now, though, the Iranians perceived a growing antagonism in American responses to their bellicosity as Clinton tightened unilateral sanctions and stepped up efforts to slow their pursuit of WMD while Congress added more fuel to the fire. When House Speaker Newt Gingrich announced in October 1995 that he would introduce legislation to provide an additional $18 million for a covert action program to unseat the Iranian regime, Iran's leaders took this as conclusive evidence of Clinton's real intentions (even though anybody with a casual acquaintance with American politics at the time would have known that Gingrich and Clinton were hardly allies). But Iranians had never forgotten the CIA role in unseating the Mosaddeq government in 1953, and Gingrich's legislation looked to them like an attempt at a repeat performance. The fact that Clinton persuaded Gingrich to modify the objectives of the legislation to fit with his declarative policy of containment rather than regime change was too fine a point for the mullahs. They would never believe that the CIA was actually unwilling even to try to recover the covert capability in Iran that it had forfeited during the first Bush administration. Instead the Iranians concluded that the United States was gunning for them.

For the first three years of the Clinton administration, the Iranians had not initiated lethal action against American targets (though they had conducted detailed surveillance of American facilities abroad and had initiated steps to place senior officials in the United States under similar surveillance). This stood in contrast to the Iranian-inspired hostage taking and murder of Americans in the 1980s.

However, in June 1996, a group of Saudi Shiites, calling themselves "Saudi Hezbollah," exploded a truck bomb outside an apartment complex in Khobar, Saudi Arabia, which killed nineteen American servicemen. With hindsight this attack could be seen as an indication of a deliberate change in Iranian policy. Later we would discover that the Iranian Revolutionary Guard Corps commander in Tehran had issued the orders for the attack. At the time, there was sufficient suspicion of Iranian instigation for President Clinton to order a plan for military retaliation should the FBI develop enough evidence to justify it. In the meantime, the CIA came up with a creative series of simultaneous intelligence actions around the world.*

This may have helped deter additional Iranian attacks against American targets but it did nothing to deter Iran's determination to exploit the other weak point in Clinton's strategy. We had always asserted, and Iran understood, that the more success the United States had with its peacemaking efforts, the more Iran would find itself isolated and contained. After the Oslo Accords were signed in September 1993, the Iranians became alarmed and even more determined to thwart Clinton's attempt to achieve a comprehensive resolution of the Arab-Israeli conflict.

Since the Iranian revolution, the Shiite clerics who ran the country had built a strategic alliance with the Alawite minority regime in Syria. Both were breakaway followers of the Imam Ali, and the Arab world's Sunni majority considered them all to be religious heretics.† Hafez

---

* As Clinton's counterterrorism chief described the message of the actions, "We have just demonstrated what we can do to hurt you. If your agents continue to engage in terrorism against us, we will hurt you in ways that will severely undermine your regime" (Richard Clarke, *Against All Enemies* (New York: Free Press, 2004), pp. 120–21).

† The Alawi sect was established in the tenth century as an offshoot of Twelver or Ismaili Shiism, which is the type practiced by most Iranians today. They are all followers of the Imam Ali, the first cousin and son-in-law of the Prophet Mohamed as well as the fourth caliph after Mohamed's death. Historically, most Muslims considered Alawites heretics. Although Iranian Shia see them as natural political allies, they also tend to look down on them religiously as a minority breakaway from their own sect.

al-Asad headed a secularist Baathist regime that had little in common with the clergy in Qom, an Iranian city central to Islamic theology. Nevertheless, he had maintained this Iranian-Syrian alliance through the eight years of the Iran-Iraq War despite the fact that the other Arab leaders (Sunnis to a man) had aligned themselves with Sunni-dominated Iraq. It was part of our calculation that if we could succeed in negotiating a Syrian-Israeli peace, we could break Damascus's alliance with Tehran.

The Iranians were aware of this, and after Arafat made peace with Rabin and Clinton, Iran urged Syria to withdraw from the peace process and cooperate in escalating attacks on Israel from southern Lebanon, offering to fund a Lebanese-Palestinian Islamic front there and supply it with heavy weapons. When Asad made clear that it was in Syria's strategic interests to remain engaged in the peace process, the Iranians became even more determined to disrupt the Israeli-Syrian negotiations.

They had a ready vehicle for doing so. Over the previous decade they had provided training, weapons, and funding for Hezbollah's guerrilla war against Israeli troops in southern Lebanon. Because Syria provided the conduit for all of this activity, the Iranians found it easy to implicate Asad by having Hezbollah provoke clashes with Israel. The United States and Israel would then blame Damascus for not controlling Hezbollah, complicating the peace negotiations.

With a significant troop presence in Lebanon and control of Hezbollah's supply lines, one would think Damascus could have exercised tighter control. But the Syrians were balancing the competing pressures from their Iranian allies to give Hezbollah a freer hand, and from their American and Israeli negotiating partners to rein them in. As a result, attacks would often come at inopportune times.

One egregious example was on the eve of President Clinton's only visit to Damascus, in October 1994 after he participated in the signing of the Israel-Jordan Peace Treaty. Clinton was taking a big political risk both because Syria was still a "state sponsor of terrorism" and because a Palestinian suicide bomber had killed twenty-two people in Tel Aviv eight days before. We had emphasized to the Syrians that the visit was conditional on them keeping the situation in Lebanon calm. Yet as Air Force One touched down in Aqaba for the signing ceremony, Hezbollah launched a dozen major mortar attacks into northern Israel, forcing residents there into air raid shelters where they listened on radios to the signing of the Israel-Jordan Peace Treaty. Despite solemn assurances from Walid Mouallem, the ambassador in Washington, that Syria would take care of the problem, the next day Hezbollah fired mortars into Israel while Clinton was meeting with Asad in Damascus.

Even then we did not fully perceive Iran's ability to sabotage the peace process because we were relying on Asad's word that he would disarm Hezbollah once Israel committed in a peace agreement to full withdrawal from Syria and Lebanon.

The Iranians used a similar tactic in sponsoring Palestinian terror operations against Israelis in the West Bank, Gaza, and behind the Green Line (demarcated in the 1949 Armistice Agreement with Arab countries, which marks Israel's pre-1967 border). During the 1990s, Hamas, as a homegrown Palestinian Sunni movement, kept its distance from Tehran. So the Iranian mullahs turned to a small Islamist Palestinian terrorist group known as Palestine Islamic Jihad (PIJ) and converted it into a wholly owned subsidiary of the Iranian Ministry of Intelligence and Security and the Revolutionary Guard Corps. PIJ cadres received payment only after killing Israelis. At Iran's command, PIJ escalated its attacks at critical junctures in Clinton's efforts to promote Israeli-Palestinian peace, thus disrupting the negotiations and eroding Israeli support for the peace process. This also strained Israeli-Syrian relations since PIJ spokesmen usually claimed responsibility from their headquarters in Damascus.

As the peace process picked up momentum, the Iranians used both Hezbollah and PIJ to block what by 1995 posed a strategic threat to their regional position. In May of that year, Israel and Syria reached agreement on an "Aims and Principles" paper, which was heralded by both sides as a "procedural breakthrough" in the negotiations over security arrangements. In June, President Clinton hosted Amnon Lipkin-Shahak, who had just succeeded Barak as the IDF's chief of staff, and General Hekmat Shehabi, the chief of staff of the Syrian army, for negotiations in the Oval Office. That dramatic event was followed by a Syrian news report of a breakthrough on the issue of a ground station on the Golan Heights to provide Israel with early warning after its withdrawal.

Iran did not attempt to conceal its concern. During his June 1995 visit to Tehran, Syrian vice president Abdul Halim Khaddam was publicly warned, "The government of Syria . . . would do well if, from now on, it does not think of anything else but the struggle until the annihi-

lation of the Zionist regime." In July, Iranian foreign minister Ali Akbar Velayati acknowledged Iran's strategic concern: "The more a
country gets close to the usurper regime [i.e., Israel], the more it will
distance itself from us."

When the Israeli-Palestinian negotiations achieved a breakthrough,
culminating in the signing of the Oslo II Accord at the White House in
September 1995, the Iranians became apoplectic. One editorial in the
Iranian press warned ominously that Asad could face "the same fate as
Anwar al-Sadat" if he too made peace. Yasser Arafat told Clinton that
after he signed the Oslo II agreement, Ayatollah Khamenei had personally ordered the Palestinian leader's assassination, taking out his
revolver and placing it on his Koran as his way of signaling his intent.
Imagine Khamenei's surprise two months later when he learned that
an Israeli assassin had done his work for him by murdering Arafat's
partner in peacemaking.

"RABIN'S BEEN SHOT. Meet me at Ichilov Hospital!" Eitan Haber,
Rabin's principal aide, had no time for words but he knew the American ambassador needed to be on hand. As I sped to the hospital down
Tel Aviv streets that were eerily empty, I called the White House to inform the president of what had just happened. It was November 4, 1995.
It had been only five weeks since the Oslo II White House signing ceremony, but suddenly the whole edifice of peace hung in the balance.

Jewish history is so burdened by tragedy and disaster that at such
traumatic times Israelis feel a collective sense of vulnerability. At those
moments, the United States has often intervened to shore up the enterprise.* Clinton understood that essential role instinctively. He had
promised Rabin in their first official meeting that the United States
would minimize the risks involved in his peacemaking efforts. Rabin
would need his American friend by his side now more than ever.

Twenty minutes after Haber's call, I was ushered into the emergency
ward in the basement of Ichilov Hospital. Eitan was there at the entrance, sitting behind a tiny receptionist desk, writing on a scrap of
paper. He was so preoccupied that he did not notice my arrival. Instead, Zvi Alderoti, the director general of the prime minister's office,
greeted me and whispered into my ear that Rabin was dead.

---

* President Harry Truman recognized the fledgling Jewish state as Arab armies
were mobilizing for a war to destroy it; President Nixon established an arms pipeline
to ferry supplies to Israel, changing the course of battle in the 1973 Yom Kippur War.

As we clutched each other in grief, Eitan left without giving me a chance to console him. He had more important business. Moments later, in front of the cameras and crowd that had gathered outside the hospital, this faithful aide, who had written every moving word that Rabin had spoken about peace over the previous twenty-six months, now declared to the Israeli nation and the world in an angry voice, "With horror, great sorrow and deep grief, the government of Israel announces the death of Prime Minister and Defense Minister Yitzhak Rabin, murdered by an assassin."

The only way I could manage my own shock and despair was to keep moving. I went in search of Rabin's wife, Leah, finding her surrounded by her family, grieving in one corner of a narrow, cold waiting room. They had barred all other Israelis from entering this makeshift mourning chamber, leaving Rabin's old rivals—Shimon Peres, the foreign minister, and Ezer Weizman, the president—outside in the corridor with a host of other officials who were steadily gathering there, silently staring at one another in shock and disbelief.

I sat with Leah, holding her hand, groping for the words that might comfort her. Dr. Barabash, the hospital chief, came into the room and gently led her to her dead husband. I rushed back to the abandoned reception desk, where I had seen a phone, and desperately tried to call the White House (we were in the hospital basement with no cell phone reception).

On religious holidays and at times of crisis, the first instinct of Israelis and their relatives abroad is to call one another. At those moments all international lines ring busy. I put the phone down in frustration and as I did so it rang. By instinct I picked it up and was startled to hear the White House operator announce that the president was on the line.

Privileged to be present in every meeting between them, I had observed firsthand how the relationship between Clinton and Rabin had developed over the last three years from wariness to a deep friendship. At first the president had been awed, even intimidated, by the older Israeli warrior, whose life had been marked by conflict, struggle, and grief. Clinton looked up to Rabin as a father figure—his own father had died in a car crash before Clinton was born and would have been the same age as Rabin. But in the aftermath of the April 1995 bombing in Oklahoma City, Rabin had expressed genuine admiration for the young president's leadership in the face of homegrown terrorism. This seemed to transform their relationship—they had become partners in adversity. Now Clinton's friend was gone and the framework of peace they had tried to construct together was about to crumble.

The president had heard Eitan's announcement. He sounded devastated. I explained that the funeral would probably be within forty-eight hours. The president did not hesitate: "I'll be there."

THE IDEA THAT Iran would exploit Rabin's assassination to thwart Clinton's peacemaking was the furthest thing from my mind at that traumatic moment. But the Iranian regime wasted no time seizing on the opening. Its clerics, alone among the world's leaders, celebrated Rabin's death, labeling him a criminal who had sought to enslave the Palestinians through the peace process.

When Shimon Peres, Rabin's successor, declared his intention to "fly high and fast" toward a peace agreement with Syria, the target became clear and the task more urgent. This was especially true when intensive Israeli-Syrian negotiations commenced at the Wye Plantation in eastern Maryland in December 1995. After the first two rounds, Dennis Ross publicly declared that "more was accomplished during these six days than in the previous four years of negotiation."

Iran decided to act.

Before the third round of Wye talks got under way in February 1996, Iran's Hezbollah proxies suddenly renewed and intensified their attacks in southern Lebanon. Then, in the middle of the negotiations, Hamas perpetrated two suicide bus bombings in the heart of West Jerusalem, killing forty-five Israelis. It is unlikely that Iran inspired those attacks.* But it exploited them through its Palestine Islamic Jihad proxy, which immediately organized an assault on Israeli children in their Purim costumes in downtown Tel Aviv. When PIJ claimed responsibility for the attack from Damascus, the Israeli-Syrian negotiations were immediately suspended.

Then in March, Hezbollah initiated attacks on Israel from civilian areas in southern Lebanon, drawing Israeli fire on Lebanese villages. Hezbollah responded by launching Katyusha rockets into villages and kibbutzim in northern Israel. This provoked further Israeli retaliation that Hezbollah again used to justify a more intensive barrage on Israel.

---

* Hamas was retaliating for Israel's assassination a month earlier of its chief terror-ist operative, the bomb-maker Yahya Ayash.

We insisted the Syrians intervene, but that only produced a temporary respite.

In the face of persistent assaults on the residents of northern Israel, Peres had to respond forcefully lest he appear, on the eve of an election, unable to protect Israelis in their homes. In April, he launched Operation Grapes of Wrath to force Lebanese civilians out of the south as a way of persuading the Lebanese and Syrian governments to rein in Hezbollah. Instead, the accidental IDF shelling at Kafr Kana, which killed some one hundred Lebanese civilians, put Israel on the defensive and angered Israel's Arab citizens. Peres had to accept a cease-fire agreement with Hezbollah, which weakened him in the eyes of Jewish voters, at the same time as his support among Israeli Arab voters plummeted.

The Iranians had achieved more than they could have hoped for. The Israeli offensive they had provoked eliminated any chance of an early resumption of Israeli-Syrian negotiations and bolstered the prospects of Benjamin "Bibi" Netanyahu—the anti-Oslo candidate. As Iranian surrogates were preparing further assaults, Clinton and Peres used every channel to send the message to Tehran to back off. Peres was successful in persuading the Germans and French of the Iranian threat at a time when we had only been met by deaf ears. Utilizing their special relationship with the Iranians, the Germans made it clear that there would be severe consequences if the attacks continued. At last the Iranians appeared to have called off their dogs. But the damage had been done.

THE ISRAELI ELECTIONS took place in May 1996, by which time I had been at my post as Clinton's ambassador in Israel for a year. Benjamin Netanyahu, the Likud's candidate, campaigned against the Clinton-sponsored peace process; his most effective ad showed Arafat walking hand in hand with a solicitous Peres—the glass overlay then shattered and the picture segued into flashes of blown-up buses and Israeli terror victims. Were Netanyahu to be elected, the process begun in Oslo would clearly be in serious jeopardy. So too would Clinton's entire Middle Eastern strategy.

The president was so concerned with that possibility that he took the unprecedented step of trying to convince Israeli voters traumatized by the recent Palestinian terrorist attacks and Hezbollah bombardments that pursuing peace should remain their highest priority. In

March 1996, Clinton organized, with only a few days' notice, an extraordinary summit of twenty-nine world leaders, thirteen of them from Arab countries, hosted by Hosni Mubarak at Sharm el-Sheikh. In the closing photo session, Bill Clinton, Boris Yeltsin, Jacques Chirac, Tony Blair, Morocco's King Hassan, Saudi foreign minister Saud al-Faisal, and Yasser Arafat joined hands with Shimon Peres to manifest their opposition to terrorism and their support for him as Israel's peacemaker. From Sharm el-Sheikh, Clinton flew Peres to Israel on Air Force One to carry his campaign directly to the Israeli people.

A month later, when Hezbollah provoked the Grapes of Wrath campaign, Clinton dispatched Christopher to put together a cease-fire that restored calm to northern Israel as quickly as possible. Then weeks before the election the president welcomed Peres to Washington to sign, with much fanfare, the "U.S.-Israel Counter-Terrorism Cooperation Accord" and speed $50 million in emergency counterterrorism assistance to Israel.

Clinton also opened a back channel to Peres's campaign through Democratic political consultants Doug Schoen and Zeev Furst, who had worked on his own campaigns. Using American political consultants in Israeli election campaigns was not in itself unusual; Netanyahu was depending on Arthur Finkelstein, another political consultant, to apply the negative campaigning techniques he had successfully developed for Republican candidates. But Clinton used the Schoen-Furst back channel to coordinate his public statements with Peres's campaign needs in the countdown to the election. For example, Netanyahu had started unjustly accusing Peres of intending to divide Jerusalem. Peres, a weak campaigner, was unable to refute this potent appeal to swing voters already deeply troubled by the terrorist attacks. Growing anxious, Clinton gave a speech the week before the election that sent an explicit message to the Israeli people that the United States would be with them if they took further risks for peace. One day before the election, he repeated the message, promising that if Israelis voted for peace—in other words, for Peres—the United States would help take care of their security.

Netanyahu was furious, sending an adviser to protest to me, but Clinton was unfazed. Bibi had earlier interfered in American politics by sending his associates to Capitol Hill to generate Republican opposition to a peace deal with Syria when Clinton and Rabin had been working on it.* Since Clinton viewed politics as a contact sport, he felt Bibi was getting his just deserts. The president was determined to boost Peres's chances just as, at the same time, he had been trying to help Yeltsin's reelection bid in Russia. In Peres's case, there was the additional sense of responsibility Clinton felt for preserving the legacy of his friend Yitzhak Rabin, who had been assassinated to stop the peace process; the president had vowed at his graveside not to let that happen.

WEDNESDAY, MAY 29, 1996, was election day in Israel. That night, knowing Clinton's intense interest in the results, I had established an election watch at the embassy in downtown Tel Aviv. Constant chattering emanated from the television sets broadcasting competing news from Israel's two TV channels as the embassy's political officers reported in from the various campaign headquarters. The din made telephone conversation difficult. Nevertheless, I immediately sensed the agitation in Ehud Yaari's voice as he called in for the third time that evening.

Yaari, a close friend, was then Channel One's commentator on Arab affairs. On election night he was following the vote count from the TV studios where the pollsters received the exit poll results. I had transmitted the information Ehud had already given me to the White House, where the president was following the Israeli election returns as closely as the citizens of Israel. Based on Ehud's reporting of the exit polls, at around midnight in Israel, 5 P.M. in Washington, I had cabled the president that Shimon Peres would be the next prime minister. Now, at 2:15 A.M. in Israel, Ehud was calling to tell me that the pollsters had revised their projections. They were about to announce that Netanyahu was the likely winner.

"How could that be?" I asked angrily. The *Chicago Daily Tribune* headline "Dewey Defeats Truman" flashed through my mind. But much more than my personal embarrassment was at stake: Clinton's entire Middle Eastern strategy hung in the balance.

In the hope that the pollsters would yet be proven wrong, I kept the

---

* Netanyahu had been fearful that if Rabin and Peres pulled off a Syrian deal, Labor would walk away with the elections. Bibi even used his Knesset immunity to leak an IDF military planning document to show that Rabin and Peres were ready to give up the Golan.

embassy's election monitoring operation going through the night. We sent in our reports to the White House every fifteen minutes as new figures for the actual vote were announced. It was like water torture. Peres kept on dropping one-tenth of a percent with every additional 2 percent of the vote tallied.

At around 7 A.M. in Israel, midnight in Washington, with 90 percent of the vote counted, Netanyahu drew even with Peres. And then, with 96.4 percent of the vote counted, Bibi passed Peres 50 to 49.9 percent. By 7:45 A.M. it was all over: Netanyahu had won the election by less than thirty thousand votes, 50.4 to 49.5 percent.

I went home and in the quiet stillness of the early morning walked alone to the Herzliya beach, where I sat and stared at the far distant horizon. Everything Clinton and the members of his peace team had worked for was now in jeopardy. Rabin's assassin, the Palestinian terrorist organizations, and Hezbollah had all contributed to this setback, but the mullahs in Tehran had reason to celebrate, too. We thought we had a strong enough alliance and a sophisticated enough strategy to overwhelm them. They had found our vulnerabilities and cleverly exploited them.

As I sat on the beach and tried to make sense of the sea change that was about to occur, the lessons eluded me. I was preoccupied with concern about my own future, since I was Clinton's ambassador and Netanyahu had just defeated his candidate. The victor would soon demand a scalp; I assumed, correctly as it turned out, that it would be mine.

Years later what happened would become clearer. The enemies of peace had proved stronger than its proponents. For Yigal Amir and the right-wing Israeli extremists who supported him, Rabin's life had become forfeit because he committed Israel to give up the West Bank, land they viewed as Judea and Samaria, their God-given birthright. Rabin had treated the larger settler movement, which shared Amir's views though not his tactics, with utter disdain. A few months before his assassination, I was with him on the podium at a Hadassah women's assembly in Jerusalem when some settlers disrupted the proceedings. Red-faced with anger, Rabin shouted at the protesters as they were dragged from the hall, "You mean *nothing* to me!" Clearly, they could not be so readily dismissed. Ariel Sharon was the only Israeli politician who proved capable of dealing with their challenge successfully, evacuating them from Sinai in 1982 and from Gaza and the northern West Bank in 2005, without major incident. Perhaps that was because he had been their greatest booster and therefore had more influence with them, understood their psychology better, and took them more seriously.

The lesson for the United States is similar. We need to take the Iranians more seriously. At the time, I would often wonder what business the Iranian clerics had interfering in the Palestinian issue. There are no Shiite shrines in the Holy Land; no Palestinian Shia to claim as their own. Why would they go to so much trouble to woo Hamas and take control of Palestine Islamic Jihad? Did they really care about liberating Jerusalem and creating a Palestinian state? Why would Ayatollah Khamenei go to the lengths of issuing a fatwa against Yasser Arafat? Why would the Iranian government be the only one to celebrate Rabin's assassination?

The explanation, I believe, lies in their perception of the Palestinian issue as a critical means both of promoting their interests in the Arab and Muslim worlds, and conversely, of preventing a hostile power from asserting dominance there. Clinton had identified the Iranian regime's motives as hostile and had therefore determined to contain its influence in the Persian Gulf. In doing so, we did calculate that containment of Iran would benefit Clinton's peacemaking efforts. But we did not imagine that they would view our peacemaking efforts as such a threat to their interests, because we did not understand that their hegemonic ambitions stretched beyond the Gulf to the Sunni heartland of the Middle East.

As Shiites, the Iranian regime views the Sunni leaders that dominate the Arab order as their competitors. As Persians, their circumstances over centuries have forced them to think in terms of a strategic struggle for power in which they will either dominate their neighborhood or be dominated by others. These elements combine to make the Iranians ambitious players across the region. And the greatest obstacle to the achievement of their aspirations is the alliance between the United States and Israel—what they call "the Great Satan" and "the little Satan." In these circumstances, a Pax Americana in the Middle East based on a resolution of the Arab-Israeli conflict represents a strategic threat to their interests. That makes the regime a far more determined opponent of peacemaking than Americans tend to recognize and it makes the achievement of Arab-Israeli peace a potent means of thwarting their radical ambitions.

10

Saddam Resurgent

The summer of 1996 represented a turning point for Bill Clinton's Middle Eastern strategy. In helping to defeat Peres, Iran had succeeded in reversing the symbiotic dynamic between the peace process and our policy of "dual containment." Now it was Saddam's turn. One month after Netanyahu's election, he rolled up the CIA-sponsored coup plotters in his armed forces. Soon after that, he put an end to the alternative overthrow option of an uprising launched from northern Iraq.

Clinton had taken on a commitment there to protect the Kurds by deterring Saddam from taking any military action. However, the State Department had failed to pay enough attention to the way feuding between the two Kurdish parties in northern Iraq could create an opening for Saddam. A dispute over the fair apportionment of revenues from the booming oil smuggling trade with Turkey led Jalal Talabani, the leader of the Patriotic Union of Kurdistan (PUK) faction, to strike a deal with Tehran for arms and military advisers from the Iranian Revolutionary Guard Corps. He then launched an attack on the positions of his archrival, Masud Barzani, the leader of the Kurdistan Democratic Party (KDP). Barzani, who had been cultivating relations with Saddam to counter Talabani's burgeoning alliance with Iran, turned to Baghdad for help.

Saddam made an uncharacteristically shrewd calculation. He attacked Talabani's capital of Erbil, which housed the headquarters of Ahmed Chalabi's Iraqi National Congress movement. Erbil was outside the northern no-fly zone the United States had maintained since the Persian Gulf War. On the night of August 31, 1996, Saddam's forces easily overran the city, executed all the INC members it could find, and then withdrew, leaving Erbil in the hands of Barzani's Kurdish forces.

Saddam could easily have overrun the rest of the northern provinces but that would have created another massive refugee crisis and provoked our military intervention. By swiftly achieving a limited victory, he left Clinton with the dilemma of how to respond. The president could not retaliate in the north because Turkey would not approve it. The Turks disliked Talabani's independence; an Iraqi move that reduced his capability for mischief suited them fine.

Similarly, the Saudis refused Clinton permission to fly strike missions out of their air bases. They only felt threatened by Saddam's activities in the south; they did not share America's commitment to the Kurds. Moreover, King Fahd had suffered a stroke in November 1995, and his successor, Crown Prince Abdullah, was much less disposed to doing Washington's bidding.

Constrained in these ways from robust action, Clinton decided instead on a naval strike designed to signal Saddam that there was a price to be paid for his aggression. Forty-four cruise missiles from U.S. warships were launched against military targets in southern Iraq, and Clinton expanded the southern no-fly zone from the 32nd to the 33rd parallel, a line that ran just south of Baghdad. What these actions in the south had to do with northern Iraq was difficult to discern, for friend and foe alike.

In one overnight battle, Saddam had managed to restore his credibility with his armed forces, even the score with Talabani, eliminate the INC operation in northern Iraq, expose Turkish and Saudi fissures in our coalition, and leave Clinton looking feckless. Combined with his success in foiling the most ambitious coup attempt the CIA had been able to mount against him, Saddam had good reason to feel that he was back in the driver's seat.

Not surprisingly, he cleverly chose this moment to rob the United States of the moral high ground we had managed to hold on to at the United Nations. In November 1996, Saddam accepted the oil-for-food resolution. The Iraqi economy felt the positive impact almost immediately, with the dinar climbing in value by more than 50 percent.

The Iraqi people also now found themselves the beneficiaries of a basic food basket supplied by the United Nations. However, because of misplaced U.N. respect for Iraqi sovereignty, Saddam's regime was allowed to handle the distribution instead of U.N. relief agencies. Rather than weakening Saddam's grip, each Iraqi family now became dependent on the regime for putting food on its table. Yet infant mortality rates remained unacceptably high—almost 10 percent of all births—

because Saddam continued to restrict the flow of medicines and equipment to hospitals. In this way, the "oil-for-food" arrangement enabled Saddam to consolidate his control of the Iraqi people at the same time as making it look as if the U.S.-sponsored sanctions were responsible for their continued suffering. Although U.N. Secretary-General Kofi Annan publicly criticized Saddam for this cynical behavior, it made little difference to Arab and Muslim public opinion.

Moreover, at France and Russia's insistence, Saddam had been allowed to retain the right to negotiate and sign the contracts for the sale of oil and purchase of goods. The United States could use its veto in the U.N. Sanctions Committee, which reviewed all the contracts. Nevertheless, as we would only subsequently discover, Saddam was able to arrange kickbacks out of the purview of this committee that netted him $7–12 billion. He was also able to allocate billions of dollars' worth of contracts to France, Russia, and China, giving these permanent members of the Security Council a strong incentive to help erode the sanctions and the inspections regime.

Clinton was now in an awkward position. He could not stop the oil-for-food arrangements without appearing to be inflicting unacceptable suffering on the Iraqi people. He could not modify the arrangements because other members of the Security Council, some with commercial interests in mind, blocked him from doing so.* And relentless American efforts to monitor Iraqi expenditures only succeeded in earning us more enmity; even the British soon tired of us and began to press for a more lenient approach. It was another of those ironies of America's engagement with the Middle East: the "oil-for-food" initiative was designed to make it easier to maintain sanctions on Saddam but instead had made it easier for Saddam to live with them.

Whereas progress on peacemaking had helped isolate Iraq and strengthen Arab support for its containment, now setbacks in Arab-Israeli relations reinforced the regression with Iraq. The peace process had turned into an endless argument with Netanyahu and Arafat over the minutiae of agreements that they both now observed in the breach.† Negotiations had stalled on the Syrian track, too. Conse-

---

* The administration's ability to know what Saddam was up to was obstructed by rules that did not require Iraq to specify the end user in its oil contracts. For what are now obvious reasons, the Russians, French, and Chinese resisted any effort in the Sanctions Committee to close that loophole.

† In August 1996, for example, when Saddam's forces attacked Erbil, I was delivering stern letters from President Clinton to Prime Minister Netanyahu in an unsuc-

quently, Arab regimes were now much less willing to associate themselves with U.S. policy, arguing that we were imposing a "double standard" by insisting that Saddam implement to the letter every U.N. resolution on Iraq, while not pressing Israel to implement the relevant U.N. resolutions with equal ardor.

At home, the American public was turning against sanctions as too harsh, while the new Republican-controlled Congress was turning against containment as too soft. In another ironic twist, Ahmed Chalabi—now homeless after Saddam's rout of the INC from northern Iraq—turned up in Washington to work with a group of dedicated Republican congressional aides in the offices of Trent Lott (the Senate majority leader) and Jesse Helms (the chairman of the Senate Foreign Relations Committee) to promote legislation that would force the Clinton administration to support his idea of a Contra-like insurgency to unseat Saddam. They teamed up with two influential Republican insiders, Paul Wolfowitz and Richard Perle, who were determined to turn Clinton's policy of containment into their policy of regime change.

The consensus on containment that Clinton had managed to maintain for the first four years of his presidency was now rapidly unraveling.

THESE UNTOWARD DEVELOPMENTS happened to coincide with my own return to Washington. Clinton had refused Netanyahu's request that I be recalled and Bibi had subsequently urged me to stay and work with him, which I did for more than a year. But the mutual trust so critical to the ambassador's role as a channel between the prime minister and the president was missing. When the new secretary of state, Madeleine Albright, asked me to serve as her assistant secretary for the Middle East, she provided me with a graceful exit. Grateful for the opportunity, I nevertheless took on this new job of managing U.S. relations with the entire region with considerable trepidation. Four years earlier, when I had joined Clinton in the White House, the wind was at our backs; now it was in our faces.

This harsh new reality was driven home to me on my first day on the job, Friday, October 27, 1997. The secretary had just concluded her

---

cessful attempt to deter him from building the new settlement/suburb of Har Homa between Jerusalem and Bethlehem, and from opening the Western Wall tunnel, which provoked a pitched battle between Palestinian protesters and Israeli soldiers.

morning meetings with her inner circle of counselors and had called an unscheduled meeting of all the senior State Department officials who dealt with Iraq.

Saddam Hussein in recent weeks had provoked a new confrontation by blocking a series of UNSCOM inspections. The United States had tried to persuade the Security Council to threaten Iraq with "serious consequences." In the process of give-and-take that Security Council diplomacy inevitably requires, the French and Russians had watered down the resolution and then perfidiously abstained on the vote, with China following suit. For the first time since his invasion of Kuwait seven years earlier, Saddam had succeeded in splitting the permanent members of the Security Council. The United States had just suffered a diplomatic rout in New York.

Albright's small private office was located next to the large, elegant formal reception room she used for meetings with foreign dignitaries. From behind her Empire mahogany desk Madeleine had a magnificent view of the Lincoln Memorial, the Potomac River, and, in the distance, the Pentagon. In front of the desk was a wing chair upholstered in a yellow pastel fabric—the "hot seat" reserved for the official responsible for the issue of the moment. Thomas Pickering, the tall, bald, bespectacled undersecretary for political affairs, former ambassador to Russia, India, Israel, and the U.N., the most senior foreign service officer in State, took that seat of dubious honor. I sat on the sofa to the right of her desk with David Welch, my principal deputy in the Near Eastern bureau. The best and brightest of the State Department's new generation of Arabists, David had been Chargé d'Affaires in Saudi Arabia following the Gulf War. His analytical acuity matched the sharpness of his bureaucratic elbows; he was lean and mean, and I was grateful that he had agreed to stay by my side. He would serve as the bureau's lead attack dog, preserving our turf in the interminable bureaucratic battles that dominate policy-making in Washington.

After all the senior officials arrived, Madeleine unleashed her anger. She was "appalled" by our incompetence in handling the UNSCOM contretemps. While we sat there like chastened schoolchildren, a phone call to her French counterpart, Hubert Védrine, went through. She scolded him, too, warning that Saddam would misread the vote as a license to misbehave.

Eventually she dismissed everyone else but me. She instructed me to come up with a strategy for dealing with Saddam's challenges to the inspectors: "I don't want ever again to find ourselves in this position."

Easier said than done. The consensus on Iraq in the Security Council during the first term of the Clinton administration had disintegrated. For our containment strategy to work now, we first had to try to reestablish that consensus among the veto-wielding permanent members.

The French had begun their drift away from us as early as June 1993, when Clinton first ordered the bombing of the intelligence headquarters in Baghdad.* When the president responded to Saddam's attack on Erbil in December 1996 with missile attacks on southern Iraq, France used the occasion to announce its air force's withdrawal from patrolling the northern no-fly zone.

From the beginning of 1997, the French decided to accentuate their differences with the United States. Jacques Chirac had come to believe that Saddam could be rehabilitated, an opinion Clinton did not share. The French president wanted the Security Council to promise Saddam "light at the end of the tunnel"; that if he complied with inspections, sanctions would be lifted.

The Russians came to the same conclusion for different reasons. The new Russian foreign minister, Yevgeny Primakov (appointed in January 1996), was an old Middle East hand from his days as the head of the Russian Foreign Intelligence Service. He had cultivated close relations with the leadership in Iraq and saw in "dual containment" an opportunity to rebuild Russia's influence in an area close to its troublesome southern border. With Iraq, there was a strong commercial motive; Saddam owed Russia $8–10 billion in pre–Gulf War debt. But Primakov also wanted to make clear that if the United States was intent on expanding the North Atlantic Treaty Organization to incorporate Russia's former Eastern European allies, then Moscow would respond by building relations with America's adversaries in the Gulf. Breaking with the United States over Iraq also played to Russian nationalist sentiment at a time when Yeltsin was facing a strong challenge in the Russian Duma from right-wing opposition parties (who were doing business with Saddam, too).

For their part, the Chinese had never liked the Security Council

---

* We had foolishly neither consulted with the French nor included them in our planning for the strike and they had been deeply offended.

resolutions on Iraq because they set a precedent for potential international intervention in Chinese affairs. As long as the other permanent members were united, China was not willing to buck the consensus. But once the Russians split from us, China did as well.

With the P5 (the five permanent members of the Security Council) now divided between a Russian-Chinese bloc and an American-British bloc, the French held the swing vote—what they no doubt identified as a "Talleyrand moment."* If they voted with us, the nonpermanent members would tend to follow and the Chinese, too, leaving the Russians isolated. If they voted against us, the United States would be stranded. Our diplomacy therefore had to focus on the French.

First we indicated to them that the United States was willing to countenance a transition from inspections to long-term monitoring of Saddam's weapons programs once he had provided a full and complete accounting of those programs. When that occurred, oil sanctions would have to be lifted. We were confident Saddam would never provide a full accounting of his WMD, but showing flexibility here enabled us to put the onus on the French to persuade Saddam to come clean if they wanted the sanctions lifted.

Second, we offered to expand the "oil-for-food" program to allow Iraq to begin to pay off its foreign debts (particularly to France and Russia). Finally, we persuaded Saudi Arabia and Kuwait to condition their commercial contracts with France, especially for lucrative arms sales, on cooperation in the U.N. Security Council against Iraq.

It didn't take long for Saddam to give us the opportunity to test the new strategy. Sensing an opportunity to drive a wedge into the crack opened up by the Russian and French abstentions in the Security Council vote, in early November 1997 Saddam blocked inspections, moved proscribed equipment out of sight of the UNSCOM-installed TV cameras, and threatened to shoot down American U-2s that were flying U.N. missions over Iraq.

The French had no good answer to our charge that their abstention had encouraged this behavior and so voted for a Security Council resolution that condemned Saddam. With the French on our side, the Russians went along and the resolution passed unanimously. Never-

---

* Charles Maurice de Talleyrand-Périgord became the legendary hero of French diplomacy when, representing defeated France at the Congress of Vienna in 1815, he succeeded in splitting the victorious European great powers, enabling him to play one bloc off against the other to secure favorable treatment for France.

theless, Saddam read the resolution as a sign of weakness since the French would not agree to include language that threatened the use of force.

Within weeks, he ordered American personnel in the UNSCOM monitoring center in Baghdad to leave Iraq. The commission's new chairman, Richard Butler, responded by withdrawing all his staff. Clinton then decided to ratchet up the military pressure to coerce Saddam into letting the inspectors back in with "unfettered access."*

Albright launched a round of consultations with her P5 counterparts, beginning with the French. Over an elaborate lunch in the elegant rococo dining salon of the Quai D'Orsay (the chateau in Paris that housed the French Foreign Ministry), Madeleine explained to Hubert Védrine that Saddam was attempting to gut UNSCOM; this time we would not accept a solution that was a "trompe l'oeil." Perhaps it was because she conducted the conversation in French, or perhaps it was the heady effect of the Pomerol and Brie, but whatever the reason, Hubert got the message that the United States was looking for an opportunity to use force against Saddam. If the French wanted to avoid that, Madeleine argued, they needed to be with us in threatening force.

The French foreign minister responded with those magical Cartesian words, "C'est logique." After lunch, in the magnificent ballroom downstairs, he told the press that Iraq had no choice but to comply with the U.N. resolutions and that "all options are open."

With the French on board, the secretary then met with Primakov in Madrid. He was adamantly opposed to our threat of force but he understood that if he didn't persuade Saddam to cooperate with UNSCOM, the United States would strike Iraq—and Russian diplomacy would be seen to have failed to protect its wayward client.

Primakov summoned Tariq Aziz to Moscow. Then he turned up at a hastily convened P5 foreign ministers' meeting in Geneva at four in the morning to announce that Iraq would allow UNSCOM to do its job unhindered; in return, Russia would work on Iraq's behalf for the speedy lifting of sanctions. It didn't seem much of a price for us to pay since Russia was already acting as Saddam's lawyer in the Security Council.

The crisis was over, for the time being. The inspectors returned to

---

* Clinton ordered B-52s to Diego Garcia, F-117s to Kuwait, and a carrier battle group to the Gulf to prepare for strikes on Saddam's known WMD or dual-use sites, then on regime targets and helicopter bases, and finally on all Iraqi air bases.

Iraq. The U.S. carrier battle group steamed out of the Gulf. We claimed a victory for the strategy of coercive diplomacy.

Within two months, however, Saddam was back blocking inspections, this time declaring his vast "presidential compounds" off-limits. Clinton responded by building up U.S. forces again in the Gulf and Albright engaged Védrine in a new round of discussions. However, this time, with Russian encouragement, U.N. Secretary-General Kofi Annan decided to rush to Baghdad and Albright could not dissuade him from making the trip.

The agreement Annan concluded with Saddam left the United States in the invidious position of having to choose between an attack on Iraq or foreign diplomats escorting UNSCOM inspectors when they entered Saddam's presidential compounds. The French were enamored with this solution and our Gulf Arab allies were not prepared to facilitate a U.S. attack on Iraq when we had no support in the Security Council. With Annan's help, Saddam had managed to isolate us again, making Clinton appear weak in the face of his recidivism.

By interfering with UNSCOM, Saddam had found a mechanism for corroding the international community's resolve. He continued to refuse to account for vast amounts of chemical weapons, biological precursors, and SCUD missiles. However, despite its best efforts, UNSCOM was unable to find much of it. The last big discovery was in 1995, when Hussein Kamel defected. Since then, repeated raids based on supposedly credible intelligence from defectors had failed to yield any results. But it seemed clear that Saddam had something important to hide. He had created the Special Security Organization with the express purpose of WMD concealment. Trucks would beat a hasty retreat out the back door of a compound when inspectors knocked on the front door. It never occurred to the U.S. intelligence community— or the avid White House and State Department consumers of its assessments, including me—that this could all be part of an elaborate bluff. Even the French believed he was hiding WMD capabilities.

Since the inspectors were also certain of this, their inspections became more aggressive. This in turn enabled Saddam to portray them as provocative and generate an international crisis at will by interfering with them.

The combined result of the aggressive inspections, Saddam's purposeful obstructionism, and Clinton's strategy of threatening force to coerce Saddam's cooperation was that Iraq and UNSCOM now had their fingers on Clinton's trigger and the United States had become, in Sandy Berger's idiom, the commission's "enforcers."

Butler understood this new reality and made sure we were comfortable with the timing of his inspections. However, Scott Ritter, the American head of the UNSCOM team responsible for uncovering Saddam's concealment mechanism, found it unacceptable to delay inspections that were bound to provoke another crisis until the United States was in a better position to respond when they did. When he resigned from the U.N. commission in protest in August 1998, he was promptly portrayed as an "American hero" by Republican congressmen looking to score political points against the Clinton administration. Ritter then demonstrated his dubious patriotism by revealing to the world the nature of UNSCOM's relations with the CIA.

Ritter's account lent credibility to Russian and Iraqi claims that the U.N. commission was just an American spy operation. By now, most members of the Security Council were more willing to give Saddam the benefit of the doubt than UNSCOM. Consequently, by the fall of 1998, the inspections had boomeranged. They were now a lever in Iraqi and Russian hands to isolate the United States in the Security Council and increase pressure for lifting sanctions.

Moreover, our Gulf Arab allies were no longer willing to support the effort to coerce Saddam. For them, standing with the United States in a confrontation with Saddam about enforcing WMD disarmament only put them on the wrong side of their public opinion.

Difficulties we were encountering at the time in our Arab-Israeli diplomacy compounded the problem. With Netanyahu stalling on the implementation of the Oslo Accords, and Clinton's efforts to budge him producing little result, taking our side against Iraq had become politically unpalatable for most Arab leaders, especially the Saudis.

Meanwhile, Republican congressmen had begun the process of impeaching the president over the Monica Lewinsky affair. They jumped on anything they could portray as weakness in his foreign policy and yet condemned his use of force as an effort to distract attention from his personal woes.

Into this mix stepped Ahmed Chalabi, who offered a simple solution: a regime change strategy that supposedly would not require a major commitment of U.S. forces, only air cover and Special Forces to support his insurgents once they had established themselves in an enclave in southern Iraq.

General Anthony Zinni, the head of Central Command at the time, and I as his diplomatic counterpart had war-gamed the various scenarios for overthrowing Saddam by force. Zinni concluded that the only viable way was to insert a ground force of 150,000 American troops. If we did that, he assessed, Saddam's forces would come apart "like an old suitcase."

Nevertheless, the Senate chose to believe Chalabi rather than Zinni and voted unanimously for the Iraq Liberation Act (ILA), which declared the overthrow of Saddam Hussein as U.S. policy.* However, Congress allocated the princely sum of $97 million in "excess defense equipment" to achieve this lofty goal.†

Notwithstanding the lack of seriousness, the fact that the ILA legislation commanded an overwhelming majority in both Houses—it passed in the Congress by 360–38—meant that Clinton had no choice but to sign it into law. This drove yet another nail into the containment coffin. The French were now able to argue that our policy was no longer *logique:* what incentive did Saddam have to comply with the U.N. resolutions if the light at the end of the tunnel shined on an American gallows?

IT WAS, AS Clinton told his advisers in a meeting on September 12, 1998, "the most difficult of problems because it is devoid of a sensible policy response." At that moment, after long months of effort, he was finally moving the Israeli-Palestinian negotiations to a potential agreement on a further Israeli withdrawal from parts of the West Bank. There was a good prospect that he would have to use force in Kosovo during the fall. He didn't have time for this distraction, but Saddam and the Congress left him no choice.

In mid-September, he approved a phased plan for responding to any future obstruction of UNSCOM by Saddam. First, we would go to

---

* As Zinni recalled the episode in a recent speech: "When I testified before Congress in 1998 . . . I told them that these guys [Chalabi and his cohorts] are not credible and they are going to lead us into something that we will regret. At that time, they were pushing a plan that Central Command would supply air support and Special Forces, and we would put it into Iraq, and they would pied-piper their way up to Baghdad and the whole place would fall apart. This plan was created by two Senate staffers and a retired general. I happened to be the commander of Central Command, [but] nobody bothered to ask me about how my troops would be used." (The two staffers Zinni was referring to were Randy Scheunemann and Danielle Pletka.)
† "Excess defense equipment" referred to whatever materiel the Pentagon no longer needed.

the Security Council to seek support for a punitive military strike. If that threat didn't change his behavior, then Clinton was prepared to use force against potential Iraqi WMD sites and regime targets. The president made his unhappiness clear: "We shouldn't be under any illusion—it's just the best of a bunch of lousy alternatives."

We spent the next six weeks in intensive efforts to secure multilateral support for the new game plan. During that period Clinton was able to complete two long-standing diplomatic efforts, both of which had a positive impact on the new Iraq strategy.

First, the secretary of state brought the two Kurdish leaders to Washington for a reconciliation summit that stabilized northern Iraq and would deny Saddam an opportunity to invade Iraqi Kurdistan in response to our planned use of force.*

Then in October 1998, at the Wye Plantation, the president brought twelve months of negotiations with Netanyahu and Arafat to a successful conclusion. The Wye Agreement's provision for a further Israeli withdrawal from the West Bank, even though only from an additional 13 percent of the territory, immediately increased the comfort level of the Arab states whose cooperation we would need. At last Clinton had managed to regenerate a positive symbiosis between the peace process and Saddam's containment.

During this same period, Crown Prince Abdullah came to the White House for a working lunch, which provided Clinton the opportunity to secure use of Saudi bases for support aircraft in the event of a confrontation with Saddam. It was a bizarre encounter, however. On one side sat the crown prince in his flowing white robes and headdress, trimmed with the finest gold threads, flanked by his similarly attired aides. On the other side sat the president, the vice president, Madeleine Albright, Secretary of Defense William Cohen, Sandy Berger, his deputy Jim Steinberg, Gore's national security adviser Leon Fuerth, and me, all in suits. Since the Saudis believed Albright and Cohen were Jewish, it must have looked to them as if Clinton and Gore were flanked entirely by Jewish advisers.† Abdullah leaned across the table and explained to Clinton in a hushed voice that he had "information"

---

* The PUK-KDP agreement provided for revenue sharing for the transport of oil from Kurdistan into neighboring Turkey and for a more explicit guarantee of U.S. protection.

† Even though neither Albright nor Cohen is Jewish, it was a common assumption in the Arab world that they were.

that Monica Lewinsky was Jewish and part of a Mossad plot to bring the president down because of his efforts to help the Palestinians. He told Clinton that he intended to share this intelligence with senators he would meet after lunch in an effort to help forestall his impeachment.*

While Clinton declined that support, he was happy to have secured the access arrangement since it positioned us well to ambush Saddam diplomatically when he predictably announced on October 31 that he was shutting down all UNSCOM operations in Iraq. In the Security Council, the French were dismayed; Chirac even told Clinton in a phone call that there should be no more carrots for Saddam. Kofi Annan told Albright he was losing his patience. The Russians went AWOL; their new foreign minister, Igor Ivanov, simply could not be found.

Yet when we started to consult about a new Security Council resolution to legitimize the use of force, the Russians and French insisted on language about lifting sanctions that would have rewarded Saddam. We instead managed to pass a simple resolution that condemned Iraq and demanded an end to its obstruction of the U.N. inspectors. The same day, Secretary of Defense Cohen reported in from a lightning tour of Saudi Arabia and the other Gulf Arab states that this time the president would have all the military access he needed.

In an unusual gesture, the Saudis decided to help us persuade Egypt and Syria to join the Gulf Cooperation Council (GCC) in a declaration of support for American use of force.† President Clinton sent a message to President Asad explaining that with the Israeli-Palestinian process moving again, he was ready to devote a new effort to the Syrian track after he dealt with Saddam. Asad was more than willing to cooperate with the Saudis against Saddam. Even Qatar, the maverick of the GCC, keen for a robust statement to legitimize its hosting of

---

* Vice President Gore was so upset by Abdullah's performance that on his next visit to Saudi Arabia he asked for a one-on-one session with the crown prince to explain to him the special relationship between the Jewish people and the United States. It may have had an impact. In March 2008, now King Abdullah launched an interfaith initiative "with our brothers who adhere to the Torah and the Bible in order to agree on a measure that would safeguard humanity against those who corrupt religions, ethics, and families." See http://www.saudiembassy.net/2008news/statements/speech detail.asp?cindex=715.

† Since the Gulf War, the GCC together with Egypt and Syria had met periodically in what became known as the "6+2 forum." It brought together the three important Arab regional powers—Saudi Arabia, Egypt, and Syria—and therefore lent considerable weight in the Arab world to its declarations.

U.S. Air Force strike aircraft, helped. On November 12, 1998, Egypt, Syria, Saudi Arabia, and the five other Gulf Arab states issued their strongest declaration on Iraq since 1994, emphasizing that Saddam alone would be responsible for the serious consequences of his failure to comply with Security Council demands. Clinton now had Arab political cover as well as access to their bases.

Everything seemed to be falling into place. Nevertheless, the president was uneasy. He was about to unleash the biggest bombing strike of his presidency, to punish Saddam for his eviction of UNSCOM. And the aftermath was unclear at best. The U.N. commission would be finished, rendering us blind to any renewed Iraqi WMD activity. Our new goal would be to overthrow Saddam, as Congress had mandated through the ILA, yet we had no effective means of achieving an objective that enjoyed neither broader domestic nor international support. Nevertheless, on November 10, the president gave the green light for launching "Desert Viper," three days of intensive air and cruise missile strikes on Saddam's potential WMD facilities and regime locations.

THE "TIME ON target" for the U.S. Air Force B-52s was 1000 hours (10 A.M.) Washington time on Saturday, November 14, 1998. On that fateful morning, my hasty breakfast was interrupted by the State Department's Operations Center: Prince Bandar bin Sultan, the Saudi ambassador, was on the line.

"What is going on?" he asked. "CNN just interviewed Tariq Aziz, who says that Saddam Hussein will accept the inspectors back into Iraq without conditions. And Kofi Annan is now telling the press that the letter he has received from Aziz is good enough for him to send the inspectors back!"

"It's too late," I responded confidently, even though I had not been watching CNN. The Joint Chiefs of Staff had briefed us that the last possible time to recall the B-52 bombers, which had been dispatched from the United States the day before, was at 0500 hours, or 5 A.M.

Bandar persisted. "Are you sure? This is a typical Saddam stunt," he said. "And if you fall for it, you'll not only look foolish but you will expose us. Saudi Arabia was with you this time because you convinced us you were serious about striking him hard. But if you don't strike him at all, you'll look weak and we'll be in trouble." To underscore his point, Bandar warned, "We won't be with you the next time."

I tried to reassure Bandar. The evening before, he had arrived at my office unannounced bearing a large bottle of the most expensive Johnny Walker whiskey. On the phone, Bandar reminded me of his investment in the "Blue Label" and the toast we had drunk to Saddam's demise. I responded that if there had been any change in plans, I would surely know.

Within minutes of that conversation, Walt Slocombe, the undersecretary of defense for policy, called to inform me that the president had just ordered the planes to turn around. I was incredulous. "Can he do that?" "Yes," Walt explained, "he can order them to abort the mission as late as three minutes from their target. They were still five minutes away."

Unbelievable. We had expected that Saddam, as he had done before, would take us to the brink and then back down, extracting concessions from the United Nations along the way. But the president had been through this sequence. Why would he now fall for this last-minute ploy that seemed designed only to forestall our attack?

By 10:30 A.M., all the principals and their aides had assembled for a crisis meeting in the White House Situation Room. The shock of the discovery that we had allowed Saddam to turn the tables on us again had cast a pall over the room. As George Tenet, recently appointed director of the CIA, and I acknowledged each other across the table, we simultaneously shook our heads in disbelief.

We were shaken out of our gloom by the entry of the president and Sandy Berger, followed by Vice President Gore. It was unusual for the president to attend principals meetings in the Situation Room, and exceptional for the vice president to accompany him.

Gore was in an agitated state. The president had not consulted him before issuing the abort order. Instead, with his secretary of state halfway around the globe in Kuala Lumpur, Malaysia, the president had called his oldest friend in the administration, Strobe Talbott, who was standing in for Madeleine. Strobe had not been involved with Iraq and did not know how rare the international acquiescence in our use of force was. Concerned that its use now would severely complicate U.S.-Russia relations at a time of flux in Moscow, Strobe reinforced Clinton's hesitation to strike. Although the secretary of defense and the chairman of the Joint Chiefs had both counseled through Sandy Berger that the attack should go forward, the president was on his own in the residence with the clock ticking.

Deciding to deploy lethal force is perhaps the most difficult and lonely judgment a president must make. Bill Clinton had ordered strikes on Baghdad in 1994. But he had agonized over the use of force in Bosnia and harbored doubts about the wisdom of simply punishing Saddam for bad behavior, as he had done unsuccessfully in 1996. At moments like these, his vice president had often bolstered his resolve; Clinton did not give him the opportunity this time. With the B-52 bombers about to unleash their lethal loads, and the American and British armada in the Gulf poised to launch hundreds of Tomahawk missiles, Clinton aborted the mission.

Now we had to figure out how to pick up the pieces. The president began the meeting by asking Sandy to brief us on the phone call he had just completed with British prime minister Tony Blair. The United Kingdom was to have been our only partner in this attack but the president had taken his decision to abort without consulting Blair, either. As it turned out, it wouldn't have mattered: Blair told Clinton that once Saddam had run up the white flag it would not be acceptable to British public opinion to go ahead and shoot him. Britain would not be with us, he warned, if Clinton now decided to use force without first testing Saddam's intentions.

The immediate question before the principals was how to deal with the letter from Tariq Aziz to Kofi Annan: test Iraqi intentions again or reorder the bombing operation without British participation? Albright (who was participating by videoconference from Kuala Lumpur), Cohen, Shelton, and Tenet all argued that the attack should proceed within the next twenty-four hours. The vice president agreed. As did Talbott. But the president was still unsure.

"The letter is bullshit," he declared. "I think we should bomb tomorrow. But how do we handle this dilemma: if we bomb we'll be fine with the Arabs but in the dock internationally; if we don't bomb we'll lose the Arabs?"

Gore could not restrain himself: "Saddam's response is of a piece with what he has been doing for seven years. We have to be strong and unequivocal in rejecting it as an inadequate response."

"But Kofi Annan will disagree with us," Clinton responded.

"He stabbed you in the back by announcing that the Iraqi letter was acceptable," Gore shot back. "You should call him and tell him, 'Listen you little . . . , you're screwing around with the national interests of the

United States and we won't put up with it!' And then you need to call
Blair and tell him that his way will only cause us more trouble. It will
be seen as a massive defeat for the United States. We'll be right back in
the soup."

The White House spent most of the day in disarray. All the president's advisers may have wanted to go ahead with the military strike
but Tony Blair was still opposed and Clinton still uncertain. In the
end, after a long three-way conversation with Blair and Chirac in the
late evening, Clinton decided he would give Saddam one last chance,
but as he explained publicly the next morning, if Saddam went back
again on his promise of full cooperation with UNSCOM, the United
States would act.

We had managed to put UNSCOM chairman Richard Butler's finger firmly back on our trigger. In thirty days he was required to report
to the Security Council on whether the Iraqis were providing his inspection teams with full cooperation. If Butler's report was negative,
the president would have to resort to force.

Saddam started obstructing the renewed inspections from the get-
go. He probably interpreted the president's decision to call off the
bombings as an indication of weakness, as Gore had predicted. His
"cheat and retreat" tactics had worked so well, why not continue them?
What he could not know was that Clinton had already decided that if
Saddam did not cooperate fully this time, the United States would au-
tomatically respond with force.

ON WEDNESDAY, DECEMBER 16, 1998, Berger summoned the
principals to a 7 A.M. meeting. He began the meeting by informing them
that the president had issued instructions to proceed with the military
offensive against Iraq unless they heard from him within the hour. No
sooner had those words left Sandy's mouth than an aide entered the
room to tell him the president was on the phone. I wondered whether
we were about to go through another last-second change of mind.

While we awaited Berger's return, each of the principals updated
their counterparts. The flint-faced Chairman of the Joint Chiefs
General Hugh Shelton reminded the meeting that the "time on target"
was 1700 hours Washington time (5 P.M.), 0100 hours Baghdad time
(1 A.M.). Coordination with the British was on track. Patriot antimissile batteries had already arrived in Kuwait and Israel to protect against

any Iraqi retaliation. On the ground in Iraq there was some unusual military activity, but Shelton believed we would still take Saddam by surprise. Twenty-foot seas in the eastern Mediterranean would necessitate a day's delay in launching some of the Tomahawks. Otherwise, he noted, "Everything is coming together as planned."

Peter Burleigh, our ambassador at the United Nations, reported via videoconference that Butler had delivered his report to U.N. Secretary-General Kofi Annan the previous evening. Within hours, Annan had circulated it to members of the Security Council noting Butler's conclusion that UNSCOM "did not enjoy full cooperation from Iraq." The Security Council would convene at 9:30 A.M. New York time to consider Butler's report.

The principals then turned to the question of briefing the congressional leadership. At that moment, the president entered the Situation Room. Two days earlier in the Gaza Strip, while Clinton was opening an international airport for the Palestinians, the House Judiciary Committee had voted to impeach him. I had been with him when he received the news. He had turned to Hillary in a panic, and she had ushered him into a holding room. After fifteen minutes there alone with the first lady, the president emerged to address hundreds of delegates to the Palestinian National Council, seamlessly departing from his text to explain eloquently what peace could mean to Palestinians and Israelis. Tears were running down the faces of the Palestinian delegates as they rose to vote overwhelmingly to annul the clauses in their covenant that called for the destruction of Israel.

Now, with the House certain to send the impeachment charge to the Senate, his presidency hung in the balance. Not surprisingly, he looked haggard. Sandy quickly briefed him on the way the game plan was unfolding.

The defense secretary tried to buck up the president. "Four weeks ago you outlined to the world the five things that Saddam Hussein had to do to avoid a military strike. He didn't measure up in any category." Cohen concluded, "We recommend going forward."

The president then looked around at his advisers. "Does anybody around this table think it should not be done?"

Tenet, Albright, and Shelton all counseled to go ahead. Leon Fuerth, representing the vice president, pointed out that Saddam had been given one last chance and had rejected it. He was clearly never going to give up his WMD as the Security Council resolutions required, "So you are left with no choice."

Clinton didn't buy Leon's implication that he had the moral high ground. "There won't be a single living soul in America who won't believe I did this because of the impeachment."

The president had pronounced the one word that none of his advisers had dared mention. But it was understandably at the forefront of his mind. *Wag the Dog*, a popular Hollywood movie playing in American theaters over the summer, had portrayed a scandal-mired president fabricating an excuse for war to divert public attention from his troubles with a young woman. The battle in the Congress over impeachment had become so bitter and partisan that it was inevitable Clinton would face that accusation if he went ahead.

Sandy Berger reminded the president that before the Judiciary Committee had voted for impeachment, he had warned Saddam that if he didn't fully cooperate with UNSCOM he would face the severest consequences. Butler, not the president, had reached the judgment of Iraqi noncooperation. Albright noted that intelligence indicated Saddam had decided to interfere with the U.N. inspections precisely because he believed that the president had been so weakened politically that he would not be able to follow through on his November warnings.

As a former, longtime Republican senator from Maine, Bill Cohen's voice carried weight with the president: "If we don't act, then you as commander in chief are emasculated."

Sandy brought the discussion to a close by gently reminding the president that they were reaching the point where he would have to make a final decision. Shelton quietly emphasized that for operational reasons he needed a decision now.

The president lowered his head, bit on his lower lip, thought for a moment, and then said, "The interesting thing is if I weren't in this bizarre political pickle there's no chance that we wouldn't attack. In fact, the only reason to hesitate is *because* of the politics. So I have to do it. There's a real danger the public won't believe me. So it's taking a big risk. But I guess that's what I get paid to do."

WITH THAT, THE president of the United States launched Operation Desert Fox. Over the next four days, 415 cruise missiles and 650 air sorties that included B-1 and B-52 bombers pounded Iraq's known WMD and dual-use sites, the Special Security Organization, and other high-value regime targets.* On cue, the Republican leadership in Congress accused Clinton of putting American lives on the line to delay the House impeachment vote. The strikes were far more successful than we imagined. According to David Kay, the former nuclear weapons inspector who headed up the effort after the Iraq War to find out what happened to Iraq's WMD capabilities, he discovered that Operation Desert Fox destroyed much of Saddam's remaining infrastructure for his chemical weapons programs.

The missile and bombing campaign was also quite effective in destabilizing Saddam's regime. Saddam apparently panicked at the extent of the attacks, ordering widespread arrests in his military, which triggered a coup attempt by Sunni generals a month later. The military strikes had also given new heart to Iraq's Shiites, who began to flock by the tens of thousands to the sermons of their charismatic grand ayatollah, Sadiq al-Sadr (the father of radical cleric Muqtada al-Sadr). Saddam responded to this threat by arranging a car "accident" for al-Sadr and two of his sons, which sparked Shiite riots in the southern suburbs of Baghdad and cities in the south.

By continuing the bombing campaign, we might have ratcheted up the pressure on Saddam's regime to compound these internal difficulties. However, Clinton's objective had been purely punitive. Rather than the start of a new and more aggressive effort to unseat Saddam, Desert Fox turned out to be the initiation of another round of containment.

In public, at least, it certainly did not sound that way. When the president appeared on television on the evening of December 16, 1998, to announce the attack on Iraq, he was forthright in his declaration of a new policy.

> The hard fact is that so long as Saddam remains in power, he threatens the well-being of his people, the peace of the region, the security of the world. The best way to end that threat once and for all is with a new Iraqi government. . . .

---

* Included in the targets were eighteen command-and-control facilities, eight Republican Guard barracks, six airfields and nineteen sites related to the WMD concealment mechanisms. See Pollack, *The Threatening Storm: The Case for Invading Iraq* (New York: Random House, 2002), p. 93.

However, Clinton and his advisers had accepted General Zinni's judgment that the only way to achieve regime change in Baghdad was through a ground invasion with at least 150,000 troops. The American people were not ready to support such a large-scale war of choice. It would take the 9/11 terrorist attacks and a good deal of exaggeration by President Bush and Vice President Cheney about the imminence of Saddam's threat to convince newly vulnerable Americans of that.

Instead, Clinton's advisers developed an "overt/covert" approach to regime change. The CIA was tasked with generating another coup plot. But in the eighteen months since Saddam Hussein had foiled the CIA's last effort, the Directorate of Operations had neither recovered its contacts with the Iraqi military nor its motivation. By the DO's estimate it would take eighteen to twenty-four months to get something going. Although they offered to help, the Egyptian, Jordanian, and Saudi intelligence services had no better ability than our own CIA to promote a coup in Baghdad.

The "overt" strategy for regime change did not fare much better. Instead of Chalabi's insurgency plan, we decided to try to reorganize the Iraqi opposition in exile and prepare it for the eventual day when Saddam was toppled. Since the Pentagon at the time wanted nothing to do with the Iraqi opposition, the task fell to us in the State Department, but the other Iraqi opposition leaders weren't prepared to follow Chalabi's lead and he wasn't about to follow any of them.

We tried hard to utilize the $97 million excess defense equipment authority but fast discovered that, having legislated the overthrow of Saddam Hussein, there was precious little interest on Capitol Hill in doing anything about it. Instead of military equipment, the Pentagon provided used desks, furniture, and computers for the offices of the Iraqi opposition exile groups, and some civil affairs training.

Finally, unable to overcome bureaucratic opposition, we came up with what we thought was a creative idea: provide Chalabi and other exile leaders cameras and communication equipment, which they could give to their contacts inside Iraq to provide information about conditions there. Little did we understand that this idea would backfire on the United States when the always artful Chalabi used the mechanism to transmit false and misleading information that the Bush administration eagerly used to make its case for the threat Saddam Hussein posed.

We also developed an active strategy to increase the pressure on

Saddam by restricting his smuggling efforts. For a time we were actually able to get the Iranians to shut down their smuggling of Iraqi oil as we shifted to a policy of engagement with their newly elected reformist president. Similarly, Dubai impounded ships coming into port carrying illicit Iraqi oil. Syria had allowed vigorous cross-border oil tanker smuggling to develop. With promises from Clinton to Asad of a renewed effort to reach an Israeli-Syrian peace agreement after the upcoming Israeli elections, we managed to shut that down completely.*

On the Jordanian front, we had been trying for years to persuade Kuwait and Saudi Arabia to provide Jordan with subsidized oil so that it could close its borders to Iraqi oil imports. Still harboring a deep resentment toward King Hussein for his alignment with Saddam, they refused to do so.†

We were unsuccessful with Turkey as well. Detailed negotiations to establish a Turkish-controlled U.N. escrow account for the proceeds of their illicit oil tanker trade with northern Iraq were scuttled for fear the Turkish parliament would vote to deny the U.S. Air Force access to Incirlik Air Base to protect the Kurds.

The results of a yearlong effort to generate the overthrow of Saddam Hussein without a military invasion thus proved limited. Ironically, instead of succeeding with regime change, we had managed to bolster the containment strategy Clinton had supposedly abandoned in December 1998. With the shutting down of Syrian and Iranian smuggling routes and greater attention to what was coming across the Jordanian border, we estimated that Saddam was now able to cream off only 5 percent of Iraq's oil revenues for his own uses.

Saddam's eviction of U.N. weapons inspectors had ensured that

---

* In April 1999, I carried a letter from Clinton to Asad conveying his promise of a renewed commitment to Israeli-Syrian peace after the Israeli elections. Once Asad expressed satisfaction with this, I raised the issue of oil smuggling from Iraq. Asad claimed the trade amounted to a few oil drums on donkeys. I offered to show him satellite photographs that depicted hundreds of tanker trucks crossing the border every day. Asad put his hands to his head in feigned agony and said, "Please don't show me the photographs!" Within a week, the cross-border tanker traffic had come to a complete halt.

† To make it possible to cut the Iraqi-Jordanian umbilical cord and close down the border to smuggling, we needed the Saudis and Kuwaitis to provide fifty thousand barrels of free oil a day to Jordan. Despite the tiny size of the requirement (Saudi Arabia and Kuwait together produce some 10 million barrels per day), and the strategic value of shutting down the Iraq-Jordan border, Kuwait and Saudi Arabia were not prepared to countenance the deal. They only did so three years later on the eve of the Iraq War.

sanctions would remain on Iraq indefinitely, but to maintain effective containment we needed to make the burden of sanctions easier on the people of Iraq. Accordingly, in December 1999, with British support, the United States introduced a Security Council resolution that removed the cap on Iraqi oil exports while continuing to capture the proceeds in a U.N. escrow account, and expanded the list of goods Iraq was allowed to import.

Without UNSCOM to push around, Saddam could only hope to provoke a crisis by constantly challenging our aircraft in the no-fly zones. He never succeeded in shooting one down, however, and in retaliation we were able to destroy what remained of his air defense systems in southern and northern Iraq.

Under U.S. protection, Iraqi Kurdistan had by now turned into a relatively prosperous safe haven. With a revenue-sharing agreement between the rival parties that we had ushered into being, they were now able to build representative government institutions.

Containment also continued to benefit from a positive symbiosis with the peace process. In May 1999, Ehud Barak was elected prime minister in Israel and, with Clinton's backing, began to pursue Syrian and Palestinian peace agreements at breakneck speed, which kept the Arabs preoccupied with Israel rather than Iraq.

But the tables soon turned on us again.

As fast as the peace process took off under Barak, the faster it began to falter and then crash, and this played directly into Saddam's hands. Once the intifada broke out in the West Bank and Gaza in October 1999 and violence escalated, he sent ostentatious amounts of money to the families of Palestine suicide bombers, making him a hero in the Palestinian street. He also dispatched five divisions west toward the Syrian border. Although the Israelis did not take the move seriously, it helped create the impression that Saddam was willing to put his army at the disposal of the Palestinian uprising. Mubarak came under pressure from Egyptian demonstrators to do the same. Two years earlier, the Arab world had been with us when we bombed Saddam's WMD facilities; but in October 2000, the Arab people were now with him, and their leaders ran for cover.

This reversal of fortunes was compounded by an increasing incidence of large-scale violations of sanctions. After Clinton's failure to achieve a breakthrough to Israeli-Syrian peace or generate a more constructive relationship with Iran, illicit oil trade across their borders with Iraq picked up in earnest. At the same time, other countries used the expansion of the "oil-for-food" process to do business with Saddam. Within a year, the amount of oil revenues finding their way into Saddam's pockets had risen from 5 to 25 percent. It had taken intense diplomacy in the aftermath of Desert Storm to resist this tide, but Clinton was now entering his presidential twilight zone and was intent on focusing his remaining energy on achieving the final breakthrough to Arab-Israeli peace. The policy of containment, which had always relied on the maintenance of sanctions, was suddenly beginning to collapse.

IN THE BLOODY aftermath of Bush's toppling of Saddam, some have argued that it was unnecessary to go to war to remove Saddam Hussein because containment was working. Containment of Iraq did indeed work surprisingly well for most of the eight years of the Clinton administration, including for a year after Clinton had supposedly abandoned it for a policy of regime change. But by the end of the Clinton administration, after some seven years of assiduous diplomacy to shore it up, Saddam's containment cage was disintegrating. The Bush administration discovered this reality for itself when, early on, Secretary of State Colin Powell tried to stave off the collapse by shoring up the sanctions on all military-related imports and closing down the smuggling across Iraq's borders in exchange for abandoning the economic sanctions. Despite all his charm, and the leverage of a new administration, Powell was unable to secure an effective "smart sanctions" resolution in the U.N. Security Council, nor seal Iraq's borders.*

Those involved in the initial design of the containment strategy had not planned for it to be a long-term policy, for we knew that support for Iraqi sanctions would inevitably erode over time. Saddam Hussein simply did not present the kind of challenge to world order posed by the aggressive communism of the Soviet Union that justified George Kennan's famous containment strategy of the 1950s. Saddam was a menace to the Middle East and to his own people, to be sure. But he was a local menace, at worst a regional threat; he did not pose sufficient danger to keep the American people let alone the international community mobilized against him for a prolonged period. Only in the

---

* Given George W. Bush's unwillingness to engage with Syria's President Bashar al-Asad, Powell could not convince him to shut down a pipeline he had opened to transport Iraqi oil to Syria in a blatant violation of the U.N. sanctions.

wake of 9/11, when Americans were persuaded by the Bush administration's claim that Saddam might give his WMD capabilities to terrorists, was there support for his removal. But few in the international
community were willing to go along with that nightmare justification
for regime change.

We originally designed containment as a medium-term policy to
force Saddam's regime to buckle and crack; it was never intended simply to keep him in a cage for as long as he survived and throw away the
keys, although that is what it morphed into.

In other cases of dealing with rogue regimes, Clinton used containment to try to change their behavior, exacting a price for their continued hostility but offering improved relations if they adjusted their
policies. In the case of Libya, this stick-and-carrot approach worked;
in the case of Iran it did not, as we shall see. But Saddam Hussein was
sui generis, so pathological and such a recidivist that from the beginning Clinton ruled out a shift from containment to engagement and
reconciliation. There would be no carrots for Saddam—only sticks designed to debilitate him to the point where he could eventually be toppled.* The containment policy certainly succeeded in weakening
Saddam, but time and again we failed in our efforts to use covert
means to topple him. The mistake lay in depending on the CIA to
overthrow him. When those efforts failed, sanctions and containment
became ends in themselves.

In the face of seven years of containment, Saddam proved that he
had more staying power than we did. The constant crises, the weekly
Iraq principals meetings, the diversion of attention from more important priorities, the image of fecklessness as Clinton marched American
forces up and then back down the hill, the thankless effort to herd the
Security Council's cats, and the constant carping from the Republican-
controlled Congress—all took their toll. This "whack-a-mole" game
eventually exhausted the president's overworked advisers. In December 1998, Clinton changed the policy from containment to "regime

---

* In eight years there were only two occasions when Clinton administration statements suggested otherwise. The first was Clinton's own words before he was sworn in
about the possibility of a "deathbed conversion" for Saddam. The second was State
Department spokesman Jamie Rubin's remark in January 1998 that we were contemplating offering Saddam a "little carrot" in exchange for compliance with the U.N.
Security Council resolutions. In both cases, the statements were immediately cor-
rected.

change" out of simple recognition that the old policy had become unsustainable.

That is why President Clinton and most of his senior advisers supported President Bush's decision to use force to topple Saddam Hussein.* But lost in the debate was what we were actually saying. Although we too believed, wrongly, that he still possessed hidden stockpiles of chemical and biological weapons, the threat we worried about was his ability to reconstitute his WMD capabilities once sanctions were gone. With sanctions already falling apart, the real concern was that Saddam would resume those programs because they were integral to his view of Iraq as the dominant power in the region. From there we had little doubt he would rise to threaten his neighbors again. In other words, the United States would eventually have to go to war with Saddam, but we did not believe Saddam posed an *imminent* threat to the region or to Americans, and we knew he had no known links to al-Qaeda. That meant Bush had time: time to finish the job in Afghanistan, time to put the Israeli-Palestinian peace process back on track, time to plan properly for overthrow's aftermath, and time to secure international approval before he launched the necessary ground invasion of Iraq.

To argue that another showdown with Saddam was inevitable is not to gainsay the utility of containment as a strategy that worked effectively for most of the Clinton administration. The lessons of that experience should have informed the Bush administration's strategy for regime change in Iraq. For example, as Clinton demonstrated time and again, assiduous American diplomacy was capable of producing international backing in a crisis even if that support could not be sustained over time. Just as the Clinton administration had repeatedly secured Security Council support for our confrontations with Saddam, so too could the Bush administration have achieved U.N. approval for its war with Saddam.

Indeed, if Bush had bothered, he would have had an easier time of it than Clinton did because the United States had the world's sympathy in the wake of 9/11. Moreover, in Clinton's days in the Security Coun-

---

* Morton Halperin was the one senior Clinton administration official who argued in favor of a renewed strategy of "containment plus" in the pre–Iraq War debate. But he had not been involved in the formulation of Iraq policy and could not have known that all his prescriptions had been tried. In every case, we either had failed to garner international support (e.g., the war crimes tribunal), or had found that the support eroded quickly (e.g., tighter policing of Iraq's borders and prevention of smuggling).

cil, the Russians were always Saddam's lawyers while the French were occasionally willing to be seduced by the logic of our arguments and the flexibility of our diplomacy. In 2002, however, the situation had reversed itself. Now Chirac and his foreign minister, in their desire to restrain the "hyperpower," had turned into the dissidents, while Russian president Vladimir Putin clearly wanted to become Bush's strategic partner in the war on terror. Had Bush not taken Putin for granted, he could quite easily have isolated France among the permanent members of the Security Council. All Putin wanted at the time was assurances of post-Saddam Iraqi debt repayments and understanding for his campaign against the Chechen rebels. Had Bush treated with Putin instead of ignoring him, he could have had three permanent member votes (United States, United Kingdom, and Russia), which would have ensured that China joined the United States or at least abstained. With a majority of the permanent members on Bush's side, the nonpermanent members would also have found it more comfortable to support us, all but guaranteeing a strong majority for a resolution authorizing the use of force. In those circumstances, France would probably have abstained.

A second lesson that emerges from Clinton's experience is that it is easier to gain Arab and international support for dealing with Middle Eastern rogue states when American diplomacy is brought effectively to bear on the Arab-Israeli front. When Clinton made progress in Arab-Israeli peacemaking, he found it much easier to secure Arab backing against Saddam; when he became bogged down in the negotiations, it proved much more difficult to get the support we needed. Had Clinton achieved an Israeli-Syrian peace agreement in April 2000, it would have given Saddam's containment a whole new lease on life, increasing his isolation as other Arab states used Syria's cover to make their own peace with Israel. Saddam's model of brutality and violence would have become increasingly anachronistic as the Arab world came to see the benefit of peaceful reconciliation.

Ironically, President Bush recognized the symbiotic relationship between Iraq and the Arab-Israeli peace process when he argued that toppling Saddam could have a ripple effect, opening a new opportunity for peacemaking. But he ignored the other side of the coin: that pushing for an end to the vicious cycle of Palestinian terror attacks and Israeli retaliations—as Tony Blair urged him to do—would have improved his ability to deal with the fallout from Saddam's removal. And then he failed to follow through on the opening that the toppling of Saddam did indeed provide for taking an initiative on the Israeli-Palestinian front.

Much of the ill will earned by the Bush administration in the international community over its Iraq policy was an unnecessary, self-inflicted wound generated by a willful disregard of the role of diplomacy in providing a cloak of international legitimacy for the strategy of preventive war that it had decided to pursue. Bush discovered belatedly that Murphy's Law applies more to the Middle East than elsewhere in the world. What can go wrong will go wrong there and when it did in post-Saddam Iraq, America found itself with few friends and supporters when we needed them most.

Of course, with Saddam dead and his regime dissolved, the United States faces a host of different problems today than Clinton had to deal with as president. The Shiite-Sunni sectarian divide that Bush's insistence on elections in January 2005 managed to generate did not exist in Clinton's time.* There was no al-Qaeda in Iraq back then. And instead of opening the gates wide to Iranian influence in Baghdad and the south—as Bush managed inadvertently to do—Clinton consciously sought to contain Iranian influence there.

There are broader lessons, however, about the uses of American diplomacy, intelligence capabilities, and force in the Middle East that can be gleaned from Clinton's experience in Iraq.

The limits on the ability of intelligence to ascertain what is happening in authoritarian states, for example, was underscored by the confident prediction that Saddam was hiding his weapons of mass destruction. That assessment was sufficiently convincing for it even to be accepted by the French and German intelligence communities, though their governments opposed acting on that judgment, and for it to be trumpeted in the U.N. Security Council by as experienced a policy maker as Colin Powell. As already noted, there were several occasions when I was convinced we would find buried WMD caches, only to be disappointed when the U.N. inspectors found nothing at the desig-

---

* Bush administration spokesmen argue that al-Qaeda was responsible for creating this Sunni-Shia divide by its bombing of the Golden Mosque in Samara in February 2006, which provoked widespread Shiite retaliation against Sunni Iraqis. However, the earlier elections that Bush insisted on had already ensconced in power a Shiite-dominated government that Sunnis refused to accept. That created the schism that al-Qaeda quickly exploited.

nated locations. To this day, some in the Israeli intelligence community remain convinced that Iraq's missing WMD were moved to Syria.

Clearly, the intelligence communities need to change the way they do business to correct for such an egregious error. But the policy makers who rely on those assessments also need to draw conclusions from this experience for their operating style. When time and again the weapons inspectors came up with nothing, we should have at least asked why. I do not recall anybody suggesting that Saddam might have been engaged in the hoax of the century. There were good reasons why that never occurred to any one of us: he had developed an elaborate concealment system; Kamel Hussein's revelations indicated that he was indeed hiding biological weapons capabilities; and chemical weapons and missiles remained unaccounted for from the 1990 war. But the one argument beyond all of those that convinced us was that his bluffing seemed to make no sense. If Saddam had only come clean, U.N. sanctions would have been lifted, notwithstanding U.S. efforts to prevent that from happening. With free access to Iraq's oil revenues and a loosened inspection regime, it would then have been only a matter of time before he had acquired again the means to advance his pathological ambitions. Since he had such an easy exit strategy at his disposal, we judged that his refusal to take it was proof positive that he had something important to hide.

The lesson for policy makers seems obvious in principle but difficult to uphold in the face of confident intelligence judgments to the contrary: it is essential to try to think like the adversary rather than assume that he thinks like we do. Time and again successive American administrations failed to understand Saddam's motivations and calculations. George H. W. Bush's administration, for example, was surprised when Saddam invaded Kuwait, surprised again when he refused to withdraw in the face of overwhelming coalition forces amassed on Kuwait's borders, and surprised a third time when his regime survived the defeat.

In Bill Clinton's administration, we failed to comprehend how crucial the image of strength was to Saddam's ability to intimidate his people and deter Iranian ambitions. Military sanctions had hindered the rebuilding of his conventional forces after their devastating defeat in Kuwait. In those circumstances, if he had admitted that he no longer possessed WMD, Saddam and his regime would have been perceived as weak and vulnerable both to his internal opponents and to his avaricious Iranian neighbor. Saddam knew, more than any other leader in the Middle East, that the weak do not survive for long in this part of the world, except by their wits, cunning, and lies. Policy makers need always to bear that in their minds when trying to fathom the motives of Middle Eastern leaders.

The limits of coercive diplomacy were also revealed by Clinton's conflict with Saddam. The threat of force should have influenced Saddam's calculus since in the Gulf War he had experienced the devastating reality of America's use of force. That memory probably persuaded him of the wisdom of withdrawing his army from the Kuwaiti border in October 1994 when Clinton amassed airpower in the Gulf. Similarly, he remained deterred from taking control of Iraqi Kurdistan throughout the Clinton years.*

The success of deterrence in containing Saddam's army, however, did not prevent him from constantly challenging American aircraft in the no-fly zones, which enabled him to demonstrate a defiance that resonated in the Iraqi and Arab streets. Nor could he be deterred from interfering with the U.N. weapons inspectors. When Clinton tried by amassing forces on Iraq's borders, Saddam would back down at the last moment, robbing the United States of its justification for using force and making Clinton appear ineffective when Saddam resumed his meddling with UNSCOM. Moreover, coercive diplomacy could not prevent diplomatic do-gooders—in this case Primakov and Annan—from using Clinton's threats of force to cut deals with Saddam that weakened UNSCOM but again robbed Washington of the justification for using force.

Those experiences suggest that coercive diplomacy has its uses in deterring rogue states from launching armed invasions across borders, but not in generating more compliant behavior at lower levels of mischief-making.

There was one other way a coercive strategy could work, at least in theory; by backing American demands with the continuous application of force, rather than just the threat of force, much the way Clinton managed to bend Yugoslav president Slobodan Milosevic's will in Kosovo. In December 1998, Clinton might have turned Operation Desert Fox into an extended bombing campaign to force Saddam to make

---

* Saddam's one-day incursion into Erbil in 1996 was the exception that proved the rule. He put Barzani's Pesh Merga forces in control there and promptly withdrew to avoid provoking American retaliation.

concessions designed to weaken his grip on power and come clean on his weapons of mass destruction. The principals considered this approach on a number of occasions in 1998 but turned it down each time. They judged Saddam to be different from Milosevic; the United States had put an end to his genocidal crimes against the Kurds and Shia much earlier.

The principals' strategy was informed instead by the experience with open-ended bombing campaigns in Vietnam, which only seemed to strengthen the resolve of the North Vietnamese and isolate the United States while eroding support for the effort at home. A prolonged bombing campaign might not have generated support for Saddam among Iraqis, but he certainly would have gained considerable sympathy in the Arab world, undermining the already shaky resolve of our Arab allies, further restricting vital access to bases, and isolating us in the international community. And in the end, to what objective would we have attached such a strategy? There was no Iraqi general we could rely on to remove Saddam from office, while Iraq's disaffected Shia did not believe they could rely on us after George H. W. Bush had let them down in 1991. In any case, we were too concerned about their dependence on Iran to turn to them. We could have tied the bombing to a demand for unfettered access for the weapons inspectors but we had lost our appetite for inspections that turned up nothing significant and therefore only increased the pressure on us to lift the sanctions.

Sanctions also proved to be a blunt weapon in the American diplomatic arsenal against Saddam, doing immense damage to Iraqi society. Yet, ironically, they have become the new lever of choice when the United States attempts to alter the policy of a rogue regime. Currently, the United States has invoked U.N. sanctions on Iran, Sudan, North Korea, the Democratic Republic of Congo, Sierra Leone, Somalia, and Syria and imposed unilateral sanctions on Iran, Syria, Belarus, Burma, Cote d'Ivoire, Cuba, the Democratic Republic of Congo, North Korea, Sudan, and Zimbabwe.

The Iraq experience shows that sanctions tend to affect the citizens of the target country much more than the regime. Saddam exacerbated this effect by using the sanctions to increase the hardship of his people and then turn the blame on the United States, the better to erode the sanctions. As long as he was able to suppress any discontent, the suffering of his people mattered little to him. Saddam of course was an egregious tyrant but this indifference to the suffering of their people generally holds true for authoritarian rogue regimes and tends to render them impervious to sanctions pressure as long as they retain the means to suppress any popular dissent the sanctions generate. Targeted sanctions can shield the people but tend to have little impact on the regime.

The effectiveness of sanctions also depends on the number of countries willing to uphold them. But even where the regime's challenge to international order is serious enough to enable the deployment of mandatory Security Council sanctions, they will erode over time as focus shifts to the next crisis, interests change, and the targeted regime finds ways to exploit the cracks in the international community's resolve.

Once imposed, however, sanctions tend to take on a life of their own. In Washington, a bureaucracy is created or expanded to police and monitor their enforcement. Regular reports must be made to the Congress, which will often impose additional sanctions and reporting requirements to assert its role and influence. A similar process takes place at the United Nations. Before long, a ratchet mechanism is in place that only allows for sanctions to be expanded as the current dosage fails to produce the desired change in behavior. Then it becomes impossible to determine the tipping point where sanctions become counterproductive and eventually ineffective.*

Looking back, we can see that the tipping point for Iraq sanctions came in the mid-1990s. That was when American leverage was greatest and Saddam's regime weakest. And that was the period when the Clinton administration shifted from using sanctions as a tactic for facilitating covert efforts to overthrow Saddam, to using them as a strategy for keeping him weak. There was little choice in the matter. Had the covert efforts been more successful, the outcome might have been different, but Saddam taught us a lesson in that regard, too. An authoritarian regime with the will to survive has a far greater ability to suppress its internal adversaries than the CIA has to promote them. When that capability for suppression is combined with a sanctions regime that becomes an end in itself, the rogue regime tends to be able

---

* Even after the United States had verified the destruction of Libya's nuclear program and that the country had ended its support for terrorism, it took almost two years to lift U.S. sanctions on Libya.

to strengthen its grip on power and thereby increase its resistance to behavior modification efforts.

Had Clinton been willing to engage Saddam, the tactical leverage generated by sanctions might have been useful in persuading him to alter his behavior—that is what the French and Russians maintained when they argued for some "light at the end of the tunnel" for Saddam. But past experience with Saddam, and his ongoing brutality toward the Iraqi people, rendered him incorrigible in our eyes and therefore we had no use for such leverage. Even if Clinton had decided to deal with the devil, however, we would probably have discovered that sanctions provided insufficient leverage to transform him from felon to favorite son. For that was indeed Clinton's experience when he alleviated sanctions in an attempt to correct the behavior of Iran's ayatollahs, the other targets of dual containment.

As Clinton had remarked in exasperation, Saddam presented a challenge to the United States that did not lend itself to a sensible policy response. Although it is very hard for Americans to accept, in the Middle East some problems don't have solutions. Sometimes, wise policy consists of waiting until something better turns up, which is what we thought happened across the Gulf in Tehran.

11

Engaging Iran

Deputy Secretary of State Strobridge Talbott III had an intimidating name and rank. But those who worked with him discovered a brainy patrician with unconventional work habits and a solicitous style. We had known each other from before government service. I had taken him on his first trip to the Middle East, in 1991, days before the outbreak of the Persian Gulf War, when he was *Time* magazine's editor at large and foreign affairs columnist. When Strobe sought Senate confirmation for the position of deputy secretary of state in 1993, I helped him secure the support of mainstream Jewish organizations in the face of an onslaught from right-wing fringe groups in the community (the same groups that subsequently opposed my nomination to be the first Jewish ambassador to Israel). Other than that, we had little interaction during Clinton's first term, his preoccupation being Russia and mine the Middle East.

I was therefore surprised to receive a phone call from him on a Saturday morning in October 1997, soon after I had returned to Washington from Israel to become assistant secretary of state for Near Eastern affairs. Strobe wanted to take me for "a walk in the woods," an expression of his desire for a private, out-of-office conversation. As we tromped along the muddy leaf-covered paths of Washington's Rock Creek Park, he wasted little time getting to the point. He had taken the measure of Madeleine Albright and decided to carve out for himself areas of responsibility that she did not consider primary turf. He thought Iran was one of them.

Five months earlier, in an upset victory, Mohammad Khatami, a reformist cleric, had been overwhelmingly elected president of Iran. Afterward, Strobe had begun to hear from friends in the Iranian exile community that Khatami was interested in a dialogue with the United States. An improvement in relations with Iran, he calculated, might in turn mitigate an emerging problem in the already difficult but vital relationship with Russia. Uncontrolled elements of the government and industry there were providing missile and nuclear technology to the Iranians; if unchecked they would likely trigger American sanctions.

Since I was the new point person for Iran in the State Department, and one of the architects of the hard-line policy of containment in the first Clinton term, Strobe wanted to know how I felt about extending an open hand to the new Iranian government. I reviewed all the problems the Iranians had caused us in the peace process and my feeling that it was only a matter of time before they acquired nuclear weapons, which might trigger an Israeli preemptive attack or a nuclear arms race in the region. But since our peacemaking diplomacy had become sluggish, and dual containment was breaking down, if Khatami's election created an opportunity to engage Iran, that might begin to turn things around, reducing Iranian pressure on Arafat and Asad while helping to isolate Saddam.

Until then, I pointed out to Strobe, the Iranians had shown no interest in the official dialogue we had been offering since 1993, and I was concerned that any engagement would require unreciprocated American gestures and concessions; that was the Iranian negotiating style. Khatami may have had popular support, but the supreme leader, Ayatollah Khamenei, was known to be deeply antagonistic to the United States and Israel. In our anxiousness to achieve a breakthrough, I cautioned, we could end up undermining Khatami by signaling Khamenei and other hard-liners that we needed reconciliation more than they did. Meanwhile our own Republican hard-liners could accuse Clinton of coddling a rogue regime.* Strobe viewed all that as a question of negotiating tactics, not strategy.

I raised two other problems. If it was true that Iran was complicit in the Khobar truck bombing in Saudi Arabia in June 1996 that killed nineteen Americans—I had not yet been briefed on the evidence— how would we justify engaging with them? Moreover, while I was serving in Israel, Congress had legislated secondary sanctions against foreign companies investing in Iran. How could we fulfill that injunction and hold out an open hand at the same time? As we climbed back

---

* Gore and Clinton had made much in their first presidential election campaign of the charge that George H. W. Bush was a coddler of dictators.

up the hill, Strobe answered simply, "If Khatami is able to moderate Iran's behavior, it will change everything."

WE CLEARLY NEEDED a change. "Dual containment" was never intended to be pursued unilaterally, and yet we had failed to maintain cohesion among our allies regarding either Iran or Iraq. In addition, the strategy had always depended on the symbiotic effect of progress in Arab-Israeli peacemaking that would have increased the isolation of the Iranian mullahs as well as Saddam. But by that time, in late 1997, negotiations with both Syria and the Palestinians had stalled.

There were certainly signs of restlessness among the Iranian people. Khatami had routed the regime's candidate, Ali Akbar Nateq-Nouri. Even the Revolutionary Guards, who had been instructed by their commander, Mohsen Rezai, to vote for Nateq-Nouri, actually cast their ballots in overwhelming numbers for Khatami. Moving quickly to take advantage of this popular mandate, the new president had ousted hard-liners from his cabinet and recruited high-profile reformers in their stead. In particular, he replaced Rezai and Ali Fallahian, the reprobate chief of the Ministry of Intelligence and Security.

During the election campaign and in interviews and speeches immediately after it, Khatami spoke of the need for a "dialogue of civilizations," even suggesting that if America changed its misguided ways, Iran could have normal relations with it. Domestically, he had promised to respect the rule of law and promote civil society and greater cultural and political freedoms. Regionally, Khatami's election coincided with a notable reduction in Iran's destabilizing activities.*

President Clinton was keen to help Khatami succeed. Clinton respected Iran's rich Persian heritage and ancient culture, and sympathized with the anger most Iranians harbored about the CIA-instigated overthrow in 1953 of Mohammad Mosaddeq, their popular, elected prime minister. Beyond that, he recognized the strategic advantage of encouraging a change in Iran's behavior, particularly if that meant reducing its opposition to his peacemaking efforts. Secretary of State

---

* After the Khobar bombing, the Iranians became more circumspect about direct involvement in terrorist attacks. In the meantime, the European Union had decided to withdraw its ambassadors from Tehran after a German judge had established Iranian involvement in the assassination in September 1992 of an Iranian-Kurdish leader and three of his colleagues at a Berlin restaurant. This had a dampening effect on Tehran's troublemaking. Iran also sought a rapprochement with Saudi Arabia, which required it to attenuate its subversion on the Arabian side of the Gulf.

Albright, frustrated by the difficulties of dealing with Arafat and Netanyahu and impatient with Saddam's time-consuming challenges, was
also looking for an initiative she could call her own.

Clinton and Albright wanted to proceed at a deliberate pace because
of Iran's pursuit of nuclear capabilities and its continuing sponsorship
of terrorism—especially problematic if evidence emerged that Tehran
had been responsible for the Khobar bombing. In that event, a consensus had formed among Clinton's advisers that we would be better off
testing Khatami's intentions than pursuing military retaliation for the
Khobar attack. Some were concerned that the use of force would provoke an Iranian terrorist response that would cost more American
lives. Others saw no way of dominating the likely escalatory cycle except through a massive use of force that American public opinion
would not support. With tension rising in relations with Saddam and
Iranian naval vessels now acting with respect and restraint when they
came across the U.S. Navy in the Gulf, an effort at engagement seemed
a more appropriate course.

It also made sense to show the international community that, unlike with Saddam, the United States could be reasonable when it came
to dealing with recalcitrant governments. The ultimate hope was to
"graduate" rogue regimes like Iran or Libya, or as Tony Lake had written during Clinton's first term, "through selective pressure perhaps
eventually [to] transform these backlash states into constructive members of the international community." We knew we could not expect
other actors in the international community forever to deny themselves trade and investment opportunities with these oil-rich countries. But we hoped that rather than earn American ire, they would
prefer to help encourage the rogues to change their behavior, thereby
rendering sanctions unnecessary.

In developing such an approach, however, Clinton had to take into
account the likely attitude of Congress as well as our Israeli and Arab
allies. A year earlier Congress had overwhelmingly approved legislation that strengthened sanctions on Iran and prohibited foreign investment there. But the instigator of that legislation, Senator Alfonse
D'Amato, was preoccupied by a tight race for reelection. Other leading
Republicans in the House and the Senate were intrigued by Khatami
and understood that the United States would be better off with a more
constructive relationship with Iran.

Netanyahu supported this approach, too. Israeli officials believed that Iran's acquisition of nuclear weapons was only a matter of time. They intended to do everything possible to delay that moment, but should it come they believed it would be better if a moderate leader like Khatami had his finger on the nuclear button rather than a hardliner obsessed with the destruction of Israel. Accordingly, the Israelis toned down their anti-Iranian rhetoric, reduced their pressure on Congress, and encouraged Clinton to pursue engagement.

Though Egypt, Jordan, Saudi Arabia, Bahrain, and the United Arab Emirates had all suffered from determined Iranian efforts to subvert their regimes, their leaders also saw in Khatami's election an opportunity to reduce tensions. Many of them met Khatami for the first time when Tehran hosted the Organization of the Islamic Conference (OIC) Summit in December 1997. They came away impressed. Crown Prince Hassan of Jordan told us that he had observed a significant change in Iranian attitudes to his country. Crown Prince Abdullah of Saudi Arabia was enthusiastic. He had already reached understandings with Iran that put an end to its long-standing disruption of the hajj pilgrimage to Mecca, and now wanted to promote a rapprochement between the United States and Iran to head off a confrontation over the Khobar Towers bombing.

CLINTON LAUNCHED HIS first attempt at engagement through what had become known as "the Swiss channel." The Swiss embassy in Tehran had represented U.S. interests there since November 1979, when the American embassy had been taken over by Iranian revolutionaries. In October 1997, Albright used this channel to send Khatami a message indicating that the U.S. government had noticed his words before and after his election and was ready to begin an official dialogue. Undersecretary of State Thomas Pickering, Bruce Riedel, now the president's special assistant for the Near East and South Asia, and David Welch, my principal deputy for Near Eastern affairs, were proposed as the interlocutors the United States would send to a first meeting. The Iranians would understand that by naming our representatives, we were signaling our seriousness about preparing the ground for a breakthrough.

Albright never received a response.

The next opportunity arose in the fall of 1997, when Albright designated thirty entities as "foreign terrorist organizations" under a recently promulgated law that banned all support for them, froze their bank accounts and other assets in the United States, and prevented their members from traveling to America. She decided to include on that list the Mujahideen-e-Khalq (MEK), an Iranian dissident organization that had been waging a violent campaign against the Iranian regime since the overthrow of the Shah. In its early actions, it had killed Americans. After its expulsion from Iran, Saddam had provided it training bases in Iraq and logistic support for terrorist attacks in major Iranian cities. The MEK returned the favor by helping Saddam crush the Shiite revolt in southern Iraq after the Gulf War.

The MEK clearly deserved to be on the terrorism list, but as an anti-Iranian organization it had managed to gain support from some influential congressmen through the sophisticated political operations of its front organization, the National Council of Resistance of Iran. In the Middle East we were always being accused of double standards. Here was one instance when Clinton could show that he applied the same standard to groups that used terrorism against our foes as well as our friends. We hoped it would be perceived in Tehran as a goodwill gesture.

It was. An Iranian news agency report called the announcement a "little victory for Iran," adding, "It is not every day the Islamic Republic can welcome a decision taken in Washington." However, in typical fashion, in a sermon at Tehran University, Rafsanjani, now head of the Expediency Council, which oversees government policies, complained erroneously that MEK was still allowed to lobby Congress and raise funds in the United States.

Nevertheless, our efforts seemed to pay off in January 1998 when Khatami gave an interview on CNN to Christiane Amanpour, which he billed as a "message to the American people." Amanpour had Iranian forebears and was engaged to Jamie Rubin, Albright's spokesman at the State Department. We were given the opportunity to suggest questions. Because of our experience a year earlier, terrorism against the peace process topped our list. On this subject Khatami told Amanpour, "I personally believe that only those who lack logic resort to violence. Terrorism should be condemned in all its manifestations." When she asked him specifically about innocent *Israeli* victims of terror, he said, "Any form of killing of innocent men and women who are not involved in confrontations is terrorism; it must be condemned and we condemn every form of it in the world."

Khatami observed that the American people had a rich and proud history that demonstrated a commitment to values that the Iranian people also held dear: religiosity, liberty, and justice. The American government, on the other hand, he said, had pursued wrongheaded policies of intervention in Iranian affairs that contradicted these values. Therefore the time was not yet ripe for official discussions. Instead, the two peoples should build their relations through exchanges of academics, intellectuals, artists, journalists, and tourists. This was what he seemed to have in mind when he spoke of a "dialogue of civilizations."

"If some day another situation is to emerge, we must definitely consider the roots and relevant factors and try to eliminate them," he said. He listed among these factors: U.S. support for the 1953 Mosaddeq coup, sanctions, and the Newt Gingrich–sponsored $18 million appropriation, which he characterized as aimed at toppling the Iranian government. He emphasized that there was grave mistrust between the U.S. and Iranian governments and argued for making "a crack in this wall . . . to prepare for a change and create an opportunity to study a new situation."

The reason for Khatami's gradualist approach became clear a week later when the supreme leader, Ayatollah Khamenei, denounced the United States as "the enemy of the Islamic Republic." Contradicting Khatami's message, he declared, "Talks with the United States have no benefit for us and are harmful to us."

Khatami sent favorable signals to us just the same. Around the time of his CNN interview, the Iranian navy began to intercept ships smuggling Iraqi oil through Iranian waters. We had been urging them to do this for some time. We read it as a quid pro quo for Clinton's actions against the MEK.

Khatami also took an initiative to address Clinton's concerns about Iranian opposition to the peace process. In January 1998, during a visit to the White House, Yasser Arafat showed Clinton a letter he had received from Khatami when they met at the OIC summit a month earlier. In the letter, Khatami repeated his call for a civilizational dialogue but also declared support for Palestinian involvement in the peace process, acknowledged Israel's existence, and spoke of the benefits to Iran of a comprehensive peace. In public, Iranian spokesmen adopted a new line that represented a significant departure from earlier Iranian interference in Palestinian affairs: Iran would accept whatever the Palestinians decided.

On January 29, 1998, in videotaped remarks addressed to the Muslim world on Id al-Fitr, the celebratory feast that marked the end of the holy month of Ramadan, President Clinton responded to Khatami's public and private messages:

> To the people of Iran I would like to say that the United States regrets the estrangement of our two nations. . . . We have real differences with some Iranian policies, but I believe these are not insurmountable. I hope that . . . the day will soon come when we can enjoy once again good relations with Iran.

In the next year, the Clinton administration would ease visa restrictions for Iranians wishing to visit the United States. It would also encourage academic and sports exchanges, the most celebrated of which was the visit by an American wrestling team to Tehran. American organizations hosted Iranian newspaper editors, film directors, musicians, scholars, and even diplomats who normally could not travel beyond New York City.* In return, Iran opened its doors to American scholars, graduate students, museum officials, and tourists. But they remained closed to any visits by U.S. officials. It appeared that Khatami had deferred to Khameini: people-to-people exchanges could proceed but anything approaching an official exchange could not. This was underscored when a Saudi attempt in February 1998 to set up a high-level channel of communication between Clinton and Khatami went unanswered.

While the anti-Iranian feelings among the American public and Congress were softening, without an official dialogue there was a limit to how far we could go in building a positive relationship. We did find a common interest in Afghanistan, where the Sunni Taliban regime was as hostile to its Shiite neighbor as it was to the United States and its opium production was creating a major drug problem among Iranian as well as American youth.† Consequently, officials from the State Department were instructed to engage with their Iranian Foreign Min-

---

* These exchanges were not always smooth. Iranians took umbrage at being fingerprinted on entry to the United States. The president sought to have this procedure amended but Louis Freeh, the director of the FBI, argued that to drop the fingerprinting would create a security risk. Clinton deferred to Freeh.

† In December 1997, in recognition of this common interest, Clinton removed Iran from the U.S. list of major narcotic-trafficking countries and supported the U.N. Drug Control Program's assistance to Iran's antidrug authorities.

istry counterparts in regular meetings of the Afghan Contact Group, a U.N. forum that brought together states with an interest in Afghanistan to coordinate policy toward Kabul. But the Iranians were under strict instructions to talk only about Afghanistan with their American colleagues.*

Nevertheless, we continued to look for opportunities to strengthen Khatami's hand. In May 1998, the president declined to impose secondary sanctions on the French oil company Total for investing in the development of an Iranian oil field and indicated that similar waivers would be extended for future deals. After that, Iran was able to conclude some twelve agreements for large-scale foreign investment in its oil fields. Clinton had effectively vitiated the ILSA legislation to send a tangible signal of his positive intent.

Secretary Albright followed up with a major speech to the Asia Society in June 1998, in which she said it was time to put the past behind us and focus on the future. She declared forthrightly that "we do not seek to overthrow [Iran's] government." Calling for a very different relationship, she endorsed Khatami's call for a "dialogue of civilizations," welcomed his denunciation of terrorism, noted the concrete actions the United States had already taken in response, and expressed a willingness to take further steps. "As the wall of mistrust comes down, we can develop with the Islamic Republic, when it is ready, a roadmap leading to normal relations."

If President Khatami was pleased by the American government's offer of normal relations, he showed no sign of it.

It took Foreign Minister Kamal Kharrazi three months to respond. In his own Asia Society speech, he insisted that the United States had to lift sanctions and apologize for past transgressions before Iran could be expected to reciprocate. Kharrazi acknowledged that Albright's speech represented a change in tone but said there was "no ground for political negotiations" until the United States dropped its sanctions against Iran, its "one-sided" support for Israel, and its attempts to interfere in Iranian affairs.

Kharrazi's rejection of a process of normalization with the United States reflected the constraints on Khatami's room for maneuver. By

---

* Ironically, in 2007 the Bush administration permitted the U.S. ambassador in Baghdad to engage with his Iranian counterpart but under strict instructions to talk only about Iraq; this time the Iranians were the ones who wanted to broaden the agenda.

the end of 1997, he and his allies were under assault: the mayor of Tehran was jailed on trumped-up charges, the interior minister was forced to resign, the cultural affairs minister was pressed by the Majlis to confine press freedoms, and two prominent reformist authors were assassinated.

In Iranian politics, relations with the United States had always served as the bellwether of the revolution. In its early days, hostility toward the United States had been one of the driving forces behind the overthrow of the Shah. The seizing of American hostages at the U.S. Embassy in Tehran in 1979 was an extreme expression of the revolutionary ardor of the Khomeini era. To engage in an official dialogue with the "Great Satan" was therefore tantamount to political heresy and was being used effectively to delegitimize its proponent.

Nevertheless, at this stage Khatami fought back, insisting on a full investigation of the killing of the writers, which exposed a widespread conspiracy to assassinate leading political figures. He was then able to purge the leadership of the MOIS. Since this was also the agency that sponsored terror abroad, Clinton's interest in backing Khatami now intensified.

In April 1999, President Clinton acknowledged the legitimacy of Iranian grievances against the United States in some seemingly impromptu remarks at a White House dinner: "I think sometimes it's quite important to tell people, look, you have a right to be angry at something my country . . . did to you fifty or sixty years ago. . . ." Later that month he announced he would lift sanctions that prevented Iran from importing food and medicines from the United States. This move also enabled the commercial export of bulk sales of U.S. grain to Iran, an action welcomed by Republican senators from farm-belt states.

WHILE CLINTON HAD been making these gestures on center stage, in the wings the FBI had finally collected evidence establishing that the Iranian Revolutionary Guard Corps had indeed instigated and facilitated the Khobar Towers attack in 1996. Something now had to be done about that. To have retaliated militarily at this point, however, would only have weakened Khatami and strengthened the hard-liners who were responsible for Khobar. Instead Clinton decided to attempt to open a back channel to Khatami to encourage him to act against the Guard Corps leadership just as he had acted against the MOIS leadership.

That was the context in which Bruce Riedel and I found ourselves on a Saturday in June 1999, seated in the parlor of the Sultan of Oman's summer chateau in Fontaine-le-Port, a township some fifty miles southeast of Paris on the banks of the Seine. The residence was decorated to suit the sultan's impeccable taste and aesthetic sensitivities. The reception room in which he granted us an audience was small and elegantly understated, except for the large medieval tapestry on the wall behind his chair, and the heating, which had been turned up despite the fact that it was summer.

The last time I had met the sultan was in the Omani desert, where he had encamped for the winter. Then he had been dressed in traditional Omani garb, his head tightly wrapped in a tribal scarf, with an ornate silver dagger at his waist. Now, the sultan greeted us in a three-piece woolen suit, the royal pate covered with a gray, Persian lamb Cossack hat—the kind that Russian gentlemen wear in Siberian winters. He seemed to be missing the desert's heat.

Clinton had chosen the sultan because of his discretion, his longstanding friendship with the United States, his readiness to work behind the scenes for our common interests, and his good relations with Oman's Iranian neighbor across the Strait of Hormuz. His foreign minister, Yusuf bin Alawi, was a shrewd and effective diplomat who hankered for a larger Omani role and worked quietly to maintain contact with all the parties to the region's various conflicts. Bin Alawi had let us know soon after Khatami's election that he had a close relationship with the new president if we should ever want to use it.

As I perspired, Bruce read aloud to the sultan and bin Alawi the message that President Clinton wanted them to transmit to President Khatami: The United States now had evidence that members of the Iranian Revolutionary Guard Corps were directly involved in the planning and execution of the Khobar bombing and were still involved in terrorist planning and activity abroad. The United States sought "good relations" with the Khatami government but could not allow the murder of American citizens to pass unaddressed. To lay a sound basis for better relations between Iran and the United States, he would need a clear commitment from Khatami that Iranian involvement in terrorist activities would stop and those responsible for the Khobar bombing would be brought to justice.

The sultan felt the message was balanced and demonstrated the president's wisdom. He was flattered that the president had asked him to convey the message; he assured us he would send his foreign minister to Tehran within ten days.

In diplomacy, timing can be critically important.

No sooner had we deposited the message with the sultan than a full-scale confrontation erupted between Khatami's student supporters and hard-line vigilantes in Tehran. Several students were killed and many others severely beaten. The riots spread from the campus of Tehran University to eighteen other cities. Khatami's nerve failed; in a deal with the supreme leader, he denounced his student supporters rather than their adversaries, making him look weak to all sides. At that moment the balance of power in Tehran shifted decisively in favor of the hard-liners.

Not surprisingly, given the circumstances, it took a month for the Omani foreign minister to secure an audience with the Iranian president. On July 20, 1999, barely a week after the riots had been suppressed, bin Alawi met with Khatami to deliver the president's message. He had set up the meeting directly with Khatami, emphasizing that he needed to meet with him alone. When he arrived at the president's office, he was surprised to be greeted by his counterpart, Foreign Minister Kharrazi, who had been invited by Khatami to join the meeting. Bin Alawi interpreted Kharrazi's presence as a sign that Khatami would inform the supreme leader about the letter.

Khatami read the message and listened carefully to bin Alawi's explanation of why acting against terrorism was so important to President Clinton's ability to build relations with him. Khatami expressed appreciation for Clinton's efforts to find the path to a more productive relationship but then noted that the United States had "huge" institutions that had made "huge mistakes." The implication was that, given the hostile state of relations, Iran should be forgiven for a few smaller mistakes.

Khatami said that as far as he knew, Iran's intelligence services had been directed to protect Iran and "not to do harm to anyone." If that were not the case, he would find out and publicize it as he had done in the case of the murdered intellectuals. As for Khobar Towers, Khatami said that, again as far as he knew, Iran was not involved, but he would look into it and get back to the sultan.

Then with some emotion he expressed gratitude for Clinton's courage in reciprocating his call for a "dialogue of civilizations."

Almost six weeks passed while we waited for Khatami's response.

Finally, in the first week of September, Kharrazi asked bin Alawi to meet with Yusif Dharifi to receive it. Dharifi was the point of contact in the Iranian Foreign Ministry for the diplomats who operated the "Swiss channel." This midlevel official emphasized to bin Alawi when they met that the response he had been asked to transmit was "a leadership position." Our efforts to set up a separate, discreet channel to Khatami had failed.

The Iranian response categorically rejected as "inaccurate and unacceptable" the president's "allegations" about the Khobar Towers attack and viewed their repetition "in the gravest terms." It accused the United States of helping terrorist elements perpetrate crimes against the Iranian people. However, it noted that Iran bore no hostile intentions toward Americans and "there exists no threat from the Islamic Republic of Iran."

While it was clear that the regime intended to take no action against those responsible for the Khobar attacks, the message seemed to indicate there would be no additional Iranian terrorist attacks on American citizens—an assurance borne out over time.

THE FAILURE TO establish a discreet channel of communication between the two presidents provides an important insight into the workings of the Iranian regime. Khatami was so much a part of that system that he would not engage with the president of the United States without the agreement of the supreme leader. He may have had the ability to moderate Tehran's tone, as in the message's references to an absence of hostile intentions and respect for the "great American people," but when it came to Iranian sponsorship of terrorism he did not have the power to address our specific concerns. Sadly, Khatami was unable to fulfill the promise of his initial intentions.

Despite the clear differences between Khatami and Khamenei they were both part of one clerical regime with a common interest in maintaining its grip on power. On highly contentious matters they would find compromises that enabled the regime to avoid splitting apart. That meant no normalization of relations with the United States (except on the "civilizational" level), no relaxation of the pursuit of weapons of mass destruction, and no reduction in support for terrorist organizations.

Nevertheless, Iran's reformers were still engaged in a bitter struggle with the hard-liners. Perhaps there was still some way we could tip the balance back in their favor. On our last trip together to the Middle East before Jamie Rubin left government and I went back to Israel to serve as ambassador for a second time, Jamie made the case to me for one more attempt to bolster the reformers. The Majlis elections scheduled for February 2000 were expected to demonstrate again the broad-based support they still enjoyed. Jamie argued that Clinton should announce a lifting of some sanctions in the aftermath of their victory, providing Khatami with a justification to respond.

We discussed whether a continuation of our policy of unilateral gestures could now make a difference, since the Khatami-Khamenei compromise was already manifesting itself in a return to hard-line troublemaking.* Jamie argued that our gestures so far had not been bold enough to enable Khatami to overcome the objections of hard-liners. He noted that Foreign Minister Kharrazi had declared that if the United States lifted sanctions on the import of Iranian rugs and food, Iran would "respond positively."

So that's exactly what we did. As Jamie predicted, the reformers swept the February Majlis elections, taking more than two-thirds of the seats. However, this precipitated a hard-line backlash in which some of the victorious reformist candidates were disqualified, the security forces enforced new rules of public behavior, and Khatami's closest adviser was shot at point-blank range. Nevertheless, Albright made a forthright apology for the U.S. role in the 1953 coup, announced the lifting of sanctions on imports of food and carpets from Iran and the export of spare parts for Iran's aging Boeing fleet, and offered to settle the outstanding legal claims on Iranian assets frozen in U.S. bank accounts since the revolution.

Within ten days the supreme leader responded by denouncing the United States as a bully, dismissing Albright's apology as worthless, her intentions as "mischievous," and her government as Iran's enemy. As for an official dialogue, Khamenei had the last word: "America's animosity will not be resolved through discussions."

·   ·   ·

---

* Khatami himself had denounced the Sharm el-Sheikh agreement that had just been struck between Arafat and newly elected Israeli prime minister Ehud Barak and signaled a relaunching of the peace process. He had also met with Palestinian terrorist leaders in Damascus and promised them more support. Iraqi oil smuggling through Iranian territorial waters had resumed and there was new evidence that the intelligence service and Revolutionary Guards were fomenting trouble in Jordan and harboring Egyptian extremists.

THE IRANIAN REVOLUTION is now entering its fourth decade. Although its ardor has cooled, power remains firmly in the hands of the hard-line clerics. Khatami's election was in many ways a false dawn that served to expose that reality rather than change it. Looking back at America's fraught relationship with the Islamic republic, the time seems always to be out of joint. Like ships passing in the night, when one side is ready for engagement, the other is not. Mohammad Khatami said as much during his first visit to the United States in 2007, nine years after his CNN interview and a year after he had stepped down as president. He regretted that "the misunderstandings and mistrust between the two sides was so deep" and "the pressure that existed on both sides" was so great that there was insufficient time, especially because "we had to proceed with caution."

In those circumstances, it's difficult to see what Clinton could have done. Perhaps if Albright's second speech had been made two years earlier in response to Khatami's CNN interview, it might have given the newly elected president an opportunity to act on relations with the United States when he was at his strongest, rather than when he had already been defeated by his hard-line opponents. Yet Khatami had explained back then that he did not believe the time was right for a breakthrough in relations. Given all the bad blood in the U.S.-Iran relationship—from the American embassy hostage taking to the Khobar Towers bombing—we could no more respond to his election with a wholesale abandonment of our previous policy than he could. He wanted to cultivate the environment through a civilizational dialogue, a proposal that Clinton and Albright fully embraced. But whereas our efforts resonated positively with the American public and the U.S. Congress, Khatami's generated a backlash from those in Iran who felt threatened by the implications of an opening to the United States.

In 2003, in the George W. Bush era, another effort at engagement was attempted, this time by the Iranians. By then, the post-9/11 American invasions of Afghanistan and Iraq had removed Iran's most antagonistic neighbors—the Taliban and Saddam—and replaced them with American forces. Witnessing our military capabilities at close quarters the hard-liners themselves sought a rapprochement with Washington, offering a "grand bargain" on all the issues that had concerned Clinton. It appears that around the same time the regime took a decision to halt its clandestine nuclear weapons program. That would have been an opportune moment to test Iran's intentions because Bush had the leverage of American forces on most of Iran's borders while Tehran's hard-liners—like Nixon with China—had an ability to deliver in a way the reformers obviously could not. This time, however, the United States was not ready to engage. Some in the Bush administration preferred to pursue regime change in Iran; others believed engagement with the ruling clerics would betray the Iranian people, who were judged wrongly to be ready to rise up against the regime.

It was a vanishing moment of opportunity. Just as the Iranians had understood that the balance of power had tilted against them, the Bush administration became caught up in Iraq, fighting a vicious insurgency in the midst of a burgeoning civil war. In the chaos, an opening was created for Iran to spread its influence to southern Iraq and to the newly elected government in Baghdad, via the close relationships it had nurtured with Iraqi Shiite political parties during their years of exile in Tehran. The internal conflict in Iraq also provided an opening for Hezbollah and the Iranian Revolutionary Guards to arm and train competing Shiite militias while supplying explosives to Sunni insurgents to help tie down U.S. forces that might otherwise have been deployed against Iran. Then, in summer 2005, Mahmoud Ahmadinejad, the hard-line Revolutionary Guards' candidate, won the presidential elections and proceeded to build his support on a populist platform of defying the United States and threatening to destroy Israel.

Although the prospects for engagement looked dismal indeed, Secretary of State Condoleezza Rice nevertheless renounced any regime change motivation and offered instead to enter negotiations with Iran over its nuclear program. For a time, more pragmatic elements in the Iranian government sought to respond to Rice's initiative, but yet again the hard-liners prevailed. Bush turned to a sanctions-based policy of pressure and containment, renewing the offer of negotiations over Iran's nuclear program in June 2008 and sending a senior diplomat to participate in the negotiations. Iran's response was to play for time.

The next American president will therefore inherit a troubled relationship with Iran. Its nuclear uranium enrichment program will be well advanced and nearing a breakout capability; its sphere of influence in Iraq consolidated; and its bid for regional dominance reinforced by its alliances with the Asad regime in Syria, Hezbollah in Lebanon, and Hamas in Gaza. Sensing that the wind is at its back, Tehran will likely feel no need to accommodate American concerns. Instead, the supreme leader has blessed Ahmadinejad's defiant stance, and as long as Iran pays no serious price for that intractability, there is little reason to hope for change.

Going forward then, the United States will find it even more necessary to counter Iranian troublemaking than in the Clinton years. The lessons of that earlier era are therefore apposite. Regrettably, Iranian reformers who are much weaker now will be no more likely to produce a sustained change in the regime's behavior than they were able to do during Khatami's heyday. Given the suppression orchestrated by Ahmadinejad, the Iranian people are also less likely to mount a successful revolt against the regime in the foreseeable future, regardless of their pro-American sentiments. It would be more realistic for American policy makers to operate on the assumption that the current clerical regime will remain capable of resisting reform, suppressing dissent, and maintaining its grip on power, while remaining ready to welcome popular resistance should it emerge from within.

There is plenty of evidence to indicate that the regime is not monolithic; at times it appears to be riven by intense power struggles. But the internal dynamics of the political warfare within the regime are normally opaque. For almost three decades, the United States has lacked an embassy in Tehran or any direct official contact. We therefore have no real ability to comprehend and thus exploit these internal divisions. Clinton's efforts to support Khatami seem only to have helped generate a hard-line backlash against him. Similarly, Bush's backing of European efforts to work with pragmatic elements in the regime to fashion a compromise on Iran's nuclear program seems only to have helped the hard-liners outflank them.* Overt efforts to fund civil society dissenters only seem to create an even greater backlash.

The challenge instead is to influence the calculus of Iran's hard-line leaders, making it clear that they are welcome to join the international community as respected members as long as they agree to abide by its rules and norms. But here too Clinton's experience shows that the impact is unpredictable. Sanctions are the preferred means of demonstrating to the regime that the costs of its outlaw behavior are greater than the benefits. But as Clinton learned from the experience with Iraq, sanctions tend to increase the suffering of the people and also

---

* In a private conversation with the author, one of Iran's negotiators with the European Union explained how Ahmadinejad had accused him of betraying Iran's national interest by even contemplating a deal that would have placed limits on its nuclear program.

help consolidate the regime's grip. And as long as oil prices, estimated to have generated $60 billion in revenues in 2007, remain exceedingly high, the Iranian regime will have a considerable ability to resist the punishing consequences of sanctions. Indeed, the regime's high cost tolerance is manifested in the three-decades long, self-inflicted American sanctions that its sustained hostility toward the United States has produced. With only a few moments of hesitation, the Iranian regime actually seems to have preferred an antagonistic relationship with the United States, with its attendant costs, to a rapprochement with the consequent benefits.

During the Clinton years, aided by our own zealots on Capitol Hill, the Iranian government deftly reduced those costs by splitting us from our European allies and that prevented the conversion of unilateral sanctions into a multilateral effort that might have had a greater impact on its calculations. Moreover, the putative economic pressure was more than offset by the improvement in oil prices from 1999 to 2001 that buoyed the Iranian economy.

Learning from these experiences, the Bush administration labored hard to secure mandatory U.N. sanctions that targeted the regime rather than the people. But the meager measures dictated by the need to achieve consensus among the five permanent Security Council members served only as grist to Ahmadinejad's mill. He used them as a foil for his acts of defiance, drowning out those in the regime who objected to the stigma of U.N. sanctions.

Offering carrots to Iran seems to work no more effectively. Tactically, the Iranians are predisposed to pocket any that are proffered and demand more. That's how they reacted to Clinton's unilateral suspension of sanctions. Moreover, because Iran has been able to get away for so long with its troublemaking without paying a meaningful price, it has come to expect much bigger carrots than the United States can possibly offer without abandoning its national interests.

For example, Iran rejected the Bush administration's offer of guaranteed nuclear fuel supplies and accession to the World Trade Organization in return for abandoning its enrichment program. Similarly, the "grand bargain" that appeared to interest Iran's leaders in 2003 would have required the United States to accept Iranian dominance in the oil-rich Persian Gulf. The Bush administration was remiss in not exploring the apparent opening, but as one who tried informally to do so, I discovered that Iranian expectations of reward were far beyond what the traffic could bear in Washington or among its Arab allies in the Gulf. And that was when the Iranians were on the defensive after Saddam's toppling. Once the United States removed two of Iran's hostile neighboring regimes for free, created a vacuum in Iraq that Iran easily filled, and helped boost the price of oil by failing to adopt a serious alternative energy policy that would have reduced U.S. demand, Iranian expectations of what it would take to buy their cooperation have naturally grown.

Nevertheless, with all of their flaws, sanctions and rewards—carrots and sticks—remain necessary means of influencing the calculus of the Iranian regime. Financial sanctions, for example, may over time increase the regime's incentive to change course as the pragmatists' warnings of the impact on Iran's international commercial relations gain credibility. Similarly, because Iran currently has limited refining capacity, an embargo on the importation of refined oil products—if it proved feasible—would also increase domestic discontent with the regime's conduct of the country's external affairs.*

As for rewards, offering to suspend sanctions as a first step toward their complete removal can help to encourage greater Iranian pragmatism. Offering investment in Iran's capital-starved oil and gas industry can also be attractive since it would meet an increasingly urgent need. It will also be important to consider whether creative technical arrangements and enhanced safeguards would make it possible for Iran to have a strictly limited indigenous enrichment capacity while providing the international community with sufficient assurances that Iran would not be able to break out and use the fuel for nuclear weapons.

In this context, the offer of direct negotiations between the United States and the government of Iran should always be on the table. Talks should not be seen as a reward for Iran, nor are they inconsistent with a policy of containment and stepped-up sanctions. The United States talked to the Soviet Union at times when its containment policy was in full swing. Similarly, from the outset the Clinton administration, like previous administrations, was willing to have an official dialogue with the Iranian regime even while it was pursuing a policy of containment. The Bush administration came around eventually to adopting the same approach.

---

* The window for a refined oil products embargo may be closing as Iran is moving rapidly to reduce its vulnerability by boosting indigenous refining capacity.

One lesson from Clinton's efforts to open a back channel to Khatami is that future presidents should avoid trying to select the Iranian leader we think we can do business with. Given American ignorance of the Byzantine complexities of regime politics in Tehran, any attempt to calibrate the message to appeal to one or another faction is likely to backfire. Instead, the message should be conveyed directly to the Iranian government, leaving its factions free to battle over the response without tainting one of them as America's favorite.

Fortunately, unlike in the Clinton era when the Iranians banned all direct contact, an official channel now exists for transmitting such initiatives. In May 2007, the Iranian government authorized its ambassador in Baghdad to meet with the U.S. ambassador there. Although the Bush administration strictly confined the agenda of this and subsequent meetings to Iraq issues, this channel could be used in the future to transmit messages on other issues as well and to feel out when and how the Iranian government would want to proceed with negotiations on those issues.

Subcontracting negotiations to the Europeans was a favorite tactic of the Bush administration, which saw diplomatic engagement with Iran as a sign of weakness. Ceding control of the negotiations to others in this way has the potential to turn them into advocates for the other side, increasing Iran's ability to play the United States off against its allies. Far better for the United States to engage directly, backed by a solid international and regional consensus.

The agenda for future negotiations should not be confined to Iraq or the nuclear file, although each issue (nuclear, peace process, terrorism, bilateral relations, regional security, etc.) could be dealt with in separate talks. The issues are and should be treated as interdependent. For example, Iran is unlikely to be willing to give up its quest for nuclear capabilities unless it is also assured that it will have a positive bilateral relationship with the United States. Dealing with one issue to the exclusion of others also robs the United States of the ability to make trade-offs, and it will be difficult to sustain domestic support for an agreement in one area if hostile Iranian behavior continues in others.

The offer of direct negotiations should not be contingent on a change in Iranian behavior since the negotiations themselves are a means of inducing that change. The Bush administration set a precondition for negotiations over Iran's nuclear program that required it first to suspend its uranium enrichment activities. This had the effect of generating neither a negotiation nor a suspension. It would have been better to make suspension the first item on the negotiating agenda while emphasizing that without it the negotiations themselves would be suspended and other options would then have to be considered.

In that context, force should never be taken off the table in dealing with Iranian behavior that threatens American interests. For all their braggadocio, Iranians respect American and Israeli force and have done their best to develop means to deter its use (deploying long-range missiles that can reach Israel, supplying medium-range rockets to Hezbollah in Lebanon, maintaining a world-wide terrorist network, building a capability to attack American forces in Iraq, and brandishing their ability to close the Strait of Hormuz to oil shipping). As strategic actors, they will not hesitate to use force to signal their interests (as in the Khobar Towers attack) but they also calculate carefully where the red lines are for their own aggressive behavior. As long as so many American forces are bogged down in Iraq, they seem to feel that they have a freer hand for mischief-making across the region. One of the benefits of drawing down the U.S. troop presence there is that it will reduce the vulnerability of American forces to Iranian-supported attacks and make the Iranians more wary of what the United States might do militarily.

On their own, however, all these measures will necessarily remain insufficient unless they are also backed by actions that manage to tilt the regional balance of power against Iran and place it in a position where its fear of isolation makes it more willing to accept the norms of international behavior. Iran lives in a strategic environment. We can see from the way the Iranian government reacted to Clinton's strategy of peacemaking and containment that it well understood the dangers and was determined to find ways to thwart it. Bush's easy initial victory over the Taliban and Saddam Hussein certainly put the Iranians on the defensive and made them momentarily more willing to consider a rapprochement. Conversely, the cockiness that Ahmadinejad displayed in declaring that Iran would "fill the vacuum" left by America's withdrawal from Iraq is a function of his belief that the balance has tilted back in Iran's favor.

Iranian hubris, however, generates a backlash internationally, which creates an opening for a future American president to organize a counteralliance and begin to roll back Iranian gains achieved during the

Bush era. In this regard, Iran's flouting of its obligations under the Nuclear Non-Proliferation Treaty, and its refusal to reach a compromise agreement with the leading European powers over its uranium enrichment program, has generated an unprecedented U.S.-European front to block Iran's nuclear ambitions, creating pressure on Russia and China to go along. During the Clinton years, the Europeans refused to take the Iranian threat seriously; now they are more open to U.N. sanctions and unilateral measures such as reducing credits for Iranian purchases, forgoing investment in Iranian oil and gas projects, blocking insurance of Iran's imports and exports, and curtailing financial dealings with Iran. The Sarkozy government in France even joined the United States in making clear that force is an option if Tehran does not respond to diplomatic entreaties.

Close coordination with Moscow will be essential to effect Iran's isolation. Vladimir Putin has already insisted that Moscow retain full control over any nuclear fuel provided for the Bushehr heavy water reactor that the Russians are building for Iran. He has also made clear to the Iranians that they need to freeze their enrichment activities if they are to hope for any sanctions relief. Allowing the Russians to play an active role in a resurrected Arab-Israeli peace process can help to consolidate a constructive Russian approach to the region. With Russia on board, it's more likely that China will join the Iranian counteralliance, too, confronting the Iranian regime with a solid bloc of the most important international actors. To achieve this kind of Russo-American partnership, however, will require future presidents to understand that they cannot expect cooperation on an issue of great strategic import to the United States if they remain unwilling to acknowledge Russia's strategic concerns.* This task has been rendered more complicated by Russia's military intervention in Georgia, but no less necessary given the threat Iran poses to U.S. interests in the Middle East.

On the regional level, the Arab world's Sunni leaders find it unacceptable to allow Iran—with its Persian, Shiite identity—to become the arbiter of Arab interests in Iraq, Lebanon, and Palestine, let alone dominate the Persian Gulf. For the first time they feel a shared sense

---

* The Bush administration's determination to press ahead on deployment of an antiballistic missile defense system in eastern Europe, despite adamant Russian objections, was a case in point. Instead of cooperating with Poland and the Czech Republic to defend against a future Iranian missile threat, Bush would have done better enlisting Russia's cooperation against the present threat of Iranian nuclear proliferation.

of threat with Israel and a common interest in countering it. As noted already, fear is a greater motivator for Arab leaders than hope. Now the enemy of their enemy has become, if not their friend, at least an acceptable partner in a regional effort to counter the emerging Iranian axis. Consequently, Saudi Arabia, Egypt, and Jordan have already expressed a greater willingness to sponsor and support an Israeli-Palestinian settlement than they did in Clinton's time, when the prospects for peacemaking were better but the threat from Iran was far less.

This creates a strategic opportunity for the United States to roll back Iran's influence that was not available to Clinton during the 1990s. But to exploit it will require a similar effort to promote an Israeli-Palestinian peace as the glue of this virtual Arab-Israeli counteralliance, and an Israeli-Syrian peace as the wedge to split the Iranian axis.

An effective attempt to resolve the Palestinian problem will enable Arab leaders to show that peace and reconciliation is a more constructive way to achieve dignity for the Arabs and justice for the Palestinians than the defiance and violence that Iran and its Hezbollah and Hamas proxies currently peddle. It will prevent Iran from exploiting the Palestinian issue to build its influence in the Middle East heartland and make its claims to dominance there look hollow. At the same time, a serious effort to bring Syria into the peace camp would strain its alliance with Iran and threaten to shut down Iran's strategic conduit to Lebanon and the Palestinian arena. Clinton's experience shows how seriously Iran views such a prospect. For this combined effort to bear fruit, however, a future president would also need to pay particular heed to the lessons of Clinton's final efforts to achieve a comprehensive Middle East peace, to which we now turn.

PART THREE

THE SECOND CHANCE

12

Syria Redux

As I watched the old, white Israeli air force Boeing 707 with an indecipherable blue insignia on its tail taxi toward the stairs and red carpet at Andrews Air Force Base, I felt a sense of great anticipation. It was January 2, 2000, the beginning of a new millennium. Fifteen minutes away, Washington waited in silent grandeur, its Roman-style architecture and imposing presence ready to greet Prime Minister Ehud Barak, just another official visitor to the capital of the most powerful nation in the world.

As assistant secretary of state for Near East affairs, it was my duty to greet Middle Eastern leaders when they arrived in Washington to meet the president. Six months earlier, I had greeted Barak on this same tarmac when he was newly elected. During that first visit, Clinton and Barak had agreed that together they would seek a comprehensive end to the Arab-Israeli conflict in Barak's first year in office and Clinton's last—the year 2000. For Clinton, this pact represented a second chance after all the difficulties of the intervening years since Rabin's assassination in November 1995. If achieved, it would be both the fulfillment of Rabin's legacy and the crowning achievement of Clinton's own now scandal-racked presidency.

It was to be a second chance for me, too. On that first visit, Barak had asked Clinton to send me back to Israel. He intended to work directly with Clinton and saw me as someone who could facilitate that purpose. The president immediately agreed. Madeleine Albright arranged to have the sitting ambassador, Ned Walker, swap jobs with me. By December 1999, the Senate had confirmed me, so at the time of this visit my family and I were already packing our bags.

My sense of anticipation, however, was driven by a more important factor. At that moment, after seven years of false starts and endless hours of fruitless negotiations, we seemed finally to be on the threshold of an Israeli-Syrian peace deal. I was convinced that this time it would be different. One month earlier, together with Albright and Ross, I had experienced one of those unique moments in the Arab-Israeli conflict when an Arab leader decides to act.

We were back in that same chamber in Asad's intimidating presidential palace on the mountainside overlooking Damascus, but this time the reception was notably different. We found Asad a sick man, his emaciated face almost skeletal, his handshake bony and weak. As he greeted me, he said, "Mr. Indyk, I haven't seen you in years. You should visit us more often." He clearly could not remember our encounter seven months earlier.

His memory failed him in more important respects, too. Once able to enthrall secretaries of state with his intellect and hold court for hours recounting events in Arab history from Saladin's defeat of the Crusaders to Sadat's supposed perfidy at Camp David, he could no longer distinguish between Clinton and Barak. He seemed so confused that at one point, Gamal Helal leaned over and whispered to me, "He doesn't understand what we are talking about!" At other points Asad seemed to withdraw completely from the conversation and then sought reentry by asking Farouq al-Sharaa, his foreign minister, what he was discussing with the secretary of state. But there were also moments of clarity in which he knew exactly what he wanted to say and do.

Asad at 69 was suffering from intermittent dementia, the hardening of the arteries in the brain that affects one's functioning to the point of confusion, memory loss, and an inability to concentrate. Years of diabetes, cancer, and heart problems had taken their toll on Asad. Six months later, he would be dead. But he still retained sufficient will and brain power to attempt two far-reaching acts that would comprise his legacy to his nation and set Syria and the Arab world on a very different course into the new millennium.

The first project was to arrange for his son Bashar to take over his presidency when he died. This had not been his original intention, but his first-born son, Basil, a lover of fast cars and women, had died in an auto crash in 1994. Bashar was an ophthalmologist, studying in London, who had managed to escape the attentions of his father until Basil's premature death. Asad had to start the grooming process all over again, knowing that this mild-mannered son would have difficulty navigating the snake pits of Syrian and inter-Arab politics. Accordingly, he had begun to remove the power brokers of his generation from the ranks of the military while sidelining the politicians he had relied on for decades, in an effort to clear the field of those who would otherwise quickly seize the space left by his son's inability to fill his father's shoes.

Asad also knew Bashar lacked the experience, negotiating skills, courage, and legitimacy among his people to make peace with the hated Zionist neighbors—Asad's second project. Yet without an Israeli peace, Syria would be isolated if the Palestinians completed their peace agreement and the rest of the Arab world normalized relations with the Jewish state. Lacking a superpower patron, Damascus could well begin losing its grip on Lebanon, and the Alawites might then lose their hold on power in Syria itself. Making peace and ensuring Bashar's succession had become the two imperatives of this dying leader.

That quickly became clear in the meeting with Albright. Perfectly lucid when it came to the peace negotiations, Asad said that he considered the differences between him and Barak to be not very great; an agreement, he said, "seemed very close." When Secretary Albright asked why Asad was insisting on defining the line of June 4, 1967, before negotiations started, he said that was not his position. When Madeleine complained that a letter he had written the president three weeks earlier had new preconditions for negotiations, he said, "I'm sure we meant what we said but if you can convince us of something else we are open to discussion. . . . I think we're lowering the bar."

Then he steered the conversation to the seniority of the negotiators. Over the years we had spent countless hours arguing with him about the need to raise the level to the political echelon and the importance of a summit meeting with the Israeli prime minister to achieve a breakthrough. The most we had been able to convince him to do was allow his army chief of staff to meet on two occasions with his Israeli counterparts. Those meetings had not been fruitful.

Now he spoke about how presidents and prime ministers should come into the negotiations "when things are at their final stage." He seemed to be envisioning a summit meeting with Barak after the terms were agreed upon at a lower level.

We had come to the meeting expecting he would say, as usual, that what he needed was a reaffirmation of the Rabin "deposit"—an Israeli readiness for full withdrawal from the Golan Heights. After months of wrangling, Barak had told Clinton he was now ready to concede it, providing us with a way forward. But, shocking to us, Asad now seemed ready to resume the negotiations without hearing the words of that previously governing requirement.

So Madeleine asked Asad point blank, "What do you need to have a formal resumption of negotiations?" He responded clearly and unconditionally: "The best thing we can do is to give a mandate to political-level people to get together. We want our territory; we want our rights." Asad had never previously agreed to a political-level negotiation. Not quite believing what we were hearing, Dennis asked, "When?" And Asad said, "We are ready now at a level below the highest level."

Asad's words did not immediately register with Madeleine, who proceeded to ask for what Asad had already granted her. Asad patiently reiterated his position.

Sharaa, equally incredulous, intervened in a way we had also never before witnessed. He challenged his president in front of the American delegation: "But this has to depend on the formula for resumption [of negotiations]. We have to have a very clear basis." When Sharaa and Dennis Ross then engaged in their usual back-and-forth on the diplomatic details, Asad grew impatient. "You're suggesting we enter a process that would not lead to a result." That was exactly what Asad had been doing for the past seven years, but now was different. "What matters is the substance," he said. "We should do something quickly."

Quickly! That was one word I never believed we would hear Hafez al-Asad utter. He had repeatedly lectured visitors from the United States on the need to move slowly and cautiously. When I had visited him in April 1999, I told him that Clinton was ready to make a new effort on the Syrian track but that without flexibility and movement from him the opportunity would be missed yet again. Asad had ended that conversation by saying, "Please tell the president I will be flexible but I will not be shot in the street by my own people, or settle for an interim deal with all the details left until later, or swap even an inch of my territory. I will not be rushed into a deal."* Yet here was Asad, seven months later, in a hurry.

Dennis asked when Asad would like to start the negotiations. Uncharacteristically, Asad said, "I'm leaving that up to the other side."

---

* Asad seemed to be referring specifically to the peace deals made by Sadat, Arafat, and King Hussein, respectively.

Dennis asked at what level the negotiations would begin. Said Asad: "It's not the highest level but it's the senior political level. I will send Farouq." Sending his foreign minister to negotiate directly with Israel would be a clear signal to all in Syria and the Arab world that the deal was about to be done.* Sharaa looked miserable but it was clear that Asad had made up his mind. He would make peace with Israel before he died.

NORMALLY, WHEN THE hatch door opens on a dignitary's plane at Andrews, the head of state or government is the first to step out. But Israelis have such a disdain for rules, especially protocol, that I could never be sure who would come down the stairs first. I was hardly disconcerted when a host of people from the Israeli delegation disembarked before the prime minister. But I did not expect that his office director would then come down and invite me to join Barak on the plane.

Israel's aging prime ministerial plane is an expression of the austerity of its residual, socialist culture as surely as the U.S. president's extravagant Boeing 747 symbolizes the power and imperial majesty of the United States. Partly refurbished in the Netanyahu era to provide sleeping quarters for the prime minister, in every other respect it was probably the most uncomfortable VIP plane in existence. Journalists and staff were stuffed into the back of the plane like cattle. Up front there were eight blue leather lounge chairs organized in two booths with tables in between them. The prime minister's seat was indistinguishable from the others, emphasizing the egalitarianism of Israeli society, in which the people always refer to their leaders by their first names. As I walked through the cabin I saw Barak sitting in the left aisle seat, facing forward. He invited me to sit opposite him. Conscious that the greeting line and motorcade were waiting for him on the tarmac, I sat anxiously on the arm of the seat and welcomed him to Washington.

"I can't do it," he responded.

· · ·

---

* When Kissinger negotiated the Israeli-Syrian separation of forces agreement in 1974, Asad had been so determined to avoid contact with Israelis that he requested that an Egyptian general sign on behalf of Syria. Since then, at Middle Eastern conferences attended by Syrian and Israeli foreign ministers, Sharaa had shunned any direct contact and made up for the awkward proximity with verbal assaults on the Israelis present.

I KNEW IMMEDIATELY what he was referring to. For six months we had been arguing with him about full withdrawal from the Golan Heights. Despite the fact that he had been Rabin's IDF chief of staff and his chosen successor, until he actually became prime minister Barak was not privy to Rabin's commitment regarding the June 4, 1967, line. From his perspective as Israel's most decorated warrior, he had little problem with the security implications, believing they could be alleviated with massive American military assistance, early warning stations, and demilitarized and limited forces zones. But as prime minister he became preoccupied with the politics of selling a Syrian deal to a skeptical Israeli public.

When Barak came to Washington in mid-July 1999 for his first official visit as prime minister, he had made clear to President Clinton that even though he wanted peace with the Syrians first, he could not reaffirm Rabin's "deposit" since he had repeatedly declared during his election campaign that the Syrians would not be on Lake Kinneret as a result of a peace agreement, and Rabin's commitment to the June 4 line would put them on the lake. His credibility with the Israeli public would be undermined if the first thing he did was renege on that commitment, Barak argued. He also felt it was bad negotiating tactics to give away Israel's strongest card before he knew what he was getting in return.

Clinton could not win him over to his view that reaffirming Rabin's "deposit" was essential to jump-starting the negotiations. A key reason was that in the summer of 1999, shortly after assuming office, Barak had been given a briefing by Ronald Lauder, scion of the Estée Lauder cosmetics conglomerate as well as Ronald Reagan's ambassador to Austria. At Netanyahu's request, Lauder had conducted a secret backchannel negotiation between him and Asad in 1998. Bibi had made it a condition of the negotiations that neither side should inform Clinton. Once defeated by Barak, Netanyahu decided that Lauder should brief the new prime minister on the Syrian mission.

Lauder told Barak that significant progress had been made toward a framework agreement with the Syrians. Most significantly for Barak, he asserted that Asad had agreed that Israel would withdraw from the Golan Heights to "a commonly agreed border based on *the international line of 1923*." If true, it meant that the Syrian leader was conceding to Israel the eastern shoreline around Lake Kinneret, since the 1923 international border was drawn ten meters from the lake, whereas the

June 4, 1967, line had the Syrians on it.* Accordingly, Barak insisted to us that there was no need for him to endorse Rabin's commitment to the June 4 line since Asad had not insisted on it in his negotiations with Netanyahu.

To bolster his argument with Clinton, Barak sent Lauder to brief the president in August 1999. Lauder brought with him a ten-point document titled "Treaty of Peace Between Israel and Syria," which he claimed Asad had accepted in August 1998. It represented a considerable advance on all the sticking points in our previous negotiations with the Syrians and Israelis and suggested that an agreement was within easy reach.†

Given our knowledge of Asad's position on the June 4 line, we should have known better than to assume that Lauder's account reflected Asad's position, but in the excitement of the moment Clinton embraced the ten points and called Asad to inform him that Barak was ready to resume negotiations on that basis.

This confounded Asad. Suspicious by nature, he saw it for what it was, an attempt by Barak to avoid a commitment to the June 4 line. Asad rejected the Lauder paper, recalled Ambassador Mouallem from Washington, and placed him under house arrest for having introduced Lauder to him. From Clinton he demanded to know whether Barak had accepted what was in the president's pocket. Clinton managed to sidestep the issue by stating that Barak was ready to conclude an agreement with Syria "within a week." Asad, giving the first sign of his new-found sense of urgency, said that perhaps they could just conclude the negotiations over the phone. The president instead suggested that they

---

* The French and British governments had drawn the 1923 border to demarcate the boundaries of the mandates given to them by the League of Nations after World War I. They drew the line ten meters from the shoreline of Lake Kinneret to preserve the water for the British Mandate of Palestine.

† According to Lauder's document, Asad had agreed to the following points: Israeli withdrawal to the international border of 1923 (since 1994, Asad had always insisted on the June 4, 1967, line); an early warning station on the Golan under U.S.-French auspices (Asad had previously rejected any early warning station on Syrian territory); Israeli withdrawal from the Golan in three stages over eighteen to thirty months (Asad had previously insisted on a two-stage withdrawal over sixteen months); and ambassadors exchanged at the beginning of the withdrawal and full normalization at the end (Asad had only been willing to agree to an end of belligerency at the beginning and ambassadors at the end). The attached map delineated on Syrian territory a demilitarized zone for the Golan, a limited forces zone behind that, and a zone that contained only defensive weapons that stretched to the outskirts of Damascus (previously Asad had only been prepared to consider the first two zones).

each send an envoy to engage in direct discussions. To our surprise, Asad immediately accepted.

At the end of August, Dennis hosted a secret meeting in Bern, Switzerland, between Asad's legal adviser, Riad Daoudi, and Barak's negotiator for Syrian matters, Uri Saguy, who had been director of military intelligence under Rabin. They made good progress on a formula for resuming the negotiations that would have given the Syrians some comfort level about Rabin's deposit "guiding" the final Israeli-Syrian agreement. However, when Daoudi checked with Sharaa, he was told to demand a direct reference to the June 4 line. This would have forced us to display publicly the deposit, which was unacceptable to both Barak and Clinton.

In the first week of September, when Albright visited Damascus for a meeting with Asad, during which he showed the first signs of confusion that became so marked in the subsequent meeting with her in December, his position hadn't changed. But he was willing to accept Albright's suggestion that the secret negotiations continue, this time in Washington.

The talks that took place at the Bethesda Hyatt on the outskirts of Washington, D.C., from September 15 to 18, 1999, were supposed to be conducted as separate U.S.-Israeli and U.S.-Syrian encounters. But both sides were keen to meet directly, which they did on the second day. By the third day, Dennis, the NSC's Rob Malley, and I bore witness to a remarkable exchange between the Israelis and Syrians as they worked together on a map to define the line of June 4, 1967. Riad Daoudi and General Ibrahim Omar, his military adviser, presented their explanation of where the line had been. General Saguy had fought on the Golan and lived all his life in the north of Israel; he knew every square meter of the contested territory. He challenged parts of the Syrian interpretation but generally accepted it, though making clear he had important reservations when it came to Israel's water needs.

The disconnect between Barak's insistence on not committing to this line and empowering his negotiator to talk about it in detail was hard for us to comprehend. But the meeting produced an extraordinary result. Saguy explained to Daoudi that he respected the Syrian claim to the June 4 line: "We need to find a way to draw the line to satisfy your principle and yet meet our needs." Daoudi responded with apparent sincerity: "We recognize Israel has needs and we are prepared to meet the needs that are based on objective principles. I fully understand the relationship between the line and the water and the vitality of water to the Israelis."

As the Israeli and Syrian negotiators traced the June 4 line from north to south on the map, identifying the large areas of agreement and the minor places where they disagreed, they finally reached Lake Kinneret. Daoudi said to Saguy, "You are interested about the lake. I know it's your main concern. . . . Israeli sources said they found certain Syrian documents claiming a territorial limit in the water. I checked with my authorities and I am authorized to tell you that the June 4 line sticks to the 1923 line."

It sounded to me like a breakthrough. If the line around the northeastern side of the lake followed the 1923 line, it meant that the Syrians would be satisfied to be ten meters from the shoreline rather than on it, as they apparently had been on June 4, 1967. Daoudi's declaration had the effect not only of ceding Syrian claims to the water in the lake, it might also allow for the possibility of an Israeli territorial strip that ran all the way around the lake, a symbol of Israeli control that would help Barak sell the agreement to his people.

On Sunday morning, September 18, Daoudi reinforced this impression by telling the U.S. team that Syria was indeed willing to accommodate Israel's water needs by a strip around the lake provided that Syria had irrigation and fishing rights for its citizens who returned to their farms on the eastern side of the lake. However, in a warning we would have done well to heed, Daoudi said, "proposals to give up Syrian territory will provoke a negative reaction." Privately, Daoudi told Dennis that Syria could accept a thirty- to fifty-meter strip around the lake as long as its farmers had the right to use the water for irrigation. We seemed to have a deal.

At the end of September, however, when Sharaa came to see Clinton, the president discovered that, notwithstanding the creative exchanges between Daoudi and Saguy, Syria still insisted on the June 4 line and every inch of Syrian territory. Secretary Albright subsequently met with Sharaa in New York and pressed him to get Asad to show more flexibility. After this meeting, and at Barak's urging, the president wrote to Asad. He first repeated his assurance that the Rabin deposit "remains in my pocket and has not been withdrawn." He said that the differences between the two sides had crystallized in a way that made it necessary for them to be bridged at the summit level, and he proposed a meeting forthwith.

It took Asad five weeks to respond to the president's proposal. This delay indicated how slowly he now functioned and how dependent he had become on his foreign minister, who had in the meantime been hospitalized by a life-threatening heart condition. What Clinton proposed in his letter to resolve at the summit—the demarcation of the border, control of water, and the arrangements for an early warning ground station—Asad now insisted had to be resolved before the summit. Asad also said that territorial swaps to solve the problem of the strip around the lake were out of the question.*

In Jerusalem, Barak was becoming impatient. After he had heard Saguy's enthusiastic debriefing, he thought he could smell and taste the agreement. He signaled the president that he was now ready to have Clinton convey to Asad his confirmation of Rabin's deposit. He also indicated that the size of the strip around the lake that he required had shrunk to one hundred meters. Barak's change of mind was facilitated by the fact that, while the Syrians were drafting Asad's hard-line response to the president's summit proposal, the Israeli prime minister found himself the unexpected beneficiary of a further report from Lauder.

Lauder was unhappy about the way Asad had rejected his account of the initiative. Netanyahu had also hung him out to dry by saying he had conveyed things Bibi had never authorized him to do. In a letter addressed to Clinton on November 12, 1999, Lauder admitted that his previous briefing of the president had outlined some points "that were never accepted by the Syrians." His November letter provided a restatement of the revised ten points of agreement. The first point was explicit about the line of withdrawal, and it was not the 1923 international border that Lauder had previously claimed:

1. Israel will withdraw from the Syrian land taken in 1967 . . . to a commonly agreed border based on the line of June 4, 1967.

Barak could now safely reaffirm the Rabin deposit knowing his archrival Netanyahu had agreed to it. Politically in Israel, he was covered.

Nevertheless, he felt strongly that his confirmation of the deposit needed to be conveyed to Asad by Clinton personally. Dennis and I

---

* Asad wrote: "I am sure that you appreciate that the Syrian Arab citizens, especially those who were uprooted from the areas and the villages on the coast of the lake, will not consider that the Golan has been returned to their country unless they make sure that the areas on the lake have been returned to them as a result of a peace agreement."

tried to disabuse Barak of this idea, arguing that the president of the United States was not likely to fly to Damascus just to get Asad to agree to resume negotiations. "What am I, chopped liver?" Albright asked us in anger when she heard of Barak's proposition, coming as it did on the eve of her own December visit to Damascus.

Barak eventually accepted a compromise. Madeleine would pop the question to Asad: What did he need to resume negotiations? If he said "the Rabin deposit," then Clinton would offer to come out to Jerusalem to get that from Barak.

In the end, of course, Asad surprised us all when in his December meeting with Albright he ignored the June 4 line question and offered high-level negotiations without preconditions. Asad had blinked and Barak had been let off the hook for the moment. But we all knew that the first thing Sharaa would insist on hearing in the negotiations was that Barak had affirmed the Rabin deposit.

"I CAN'T DO it because my political circumstances have changed," Barak said as we sat together on the plane. He could see I was incredulous. The "circumstance" was the Golan referendum law that was being discussed in the Knesset, which would require an absolute majority of registered Israeli voters to approve any territorial concession in the Golan, rather than a simple majority of those who actually voted in the referendum. Barak's pollsters were warning him that that kind of public support simply wasn't there yet and that he would have to find a way to reverse the negative mood.* Barak explained this to me and then, to underscore his point, he said, "If I commit to full withdrawal now the Israeli people will think I'm giving everything up before I know what I will be getting in return. . . . I cannot look like a *freier* in front of my people."

The rough English translation of the Hebrew word *freier* is "sucker," but its cultural connotations for Israelis are far more pejorative. Netanyahu had introduced the word into the peace process lexicon by claiming, "We are not *freiers*. We won't agree to give without receiving anything." The poll numbers convinced Barak he had to show the

---

* According to the pollsters, the public was almost evenly divided on the issue of full withdrawal (47 percent in favor, 45 percent against). However, among the new immigrant community of Russian Jews, few supported territorial concessions to the Syrians and this would "leave us way behind in regard of a Jewish majority in the referendum."

Israeli public that he was a tough negotiator when it came to dealing with Asad and that, just like Netanyahu, he was not going to give before he got.

Barak's sensitivity to the *freier* label was particularly acute with Syria because he was, for the first time, involving himself directly in the negotiations. Previously Barak had sent representatives that he could always disavow as having exceeded instructions if the public perceived them as having gone too far. However, after Asad designated Sharaa as Syria's negotiator, Sharaa had asked Madeleine to ensure that Barak led the Israeli delegation instead of his counterpart, Foreign Minister David Levy. Flattered, Barak had accepted, but the consequence was that the Israeli public could now hold him directly responsible for what was conveyed in the negotiations. This led him to switch tactics on us.

Asad was also worried about his image in the eyes of his people. His November letter to Clinton made clear his fear that he would be viewed as a traitor if he gave up an inch of territory. After waiting twenty years more than Egypt to make peace, Asad needed to justify the delay not only by being able to claim that he regained every inch of Syrian territory but that he went one better than the other Arab leaders and regained territory that was not even Syrian in 1948.

Similarly, Barak needed to show his people that he had not agreed in advance to the Syrian demand to withdraw to the June 4 line even as he recognized there would be no peace with Syria unless he conceded that principle. The way to square this circle, he thought, was to control the shoreline around the lake. Israelis would remember that the Syrians had been there before 1967. In this way, he could claim that he not only protected Israel's water sources but also gained some territory before he agreed to full withdrawal. But now that Daoudi had signaled flexibility on this critical issue, Barak had decided to stall in order to present a tough face to his public, the better to be able to sell them the far-reaching concession he was preparing to make.

From the perspective of American negotiators trying to forge a Syrian-Israeli peace agreement, these similar face-saving concerns on the part of the two protagonists made reaching a compromise particularly difficult. They both framed the negotiation as a zero-sum game in which Barak couldn't be seen as giving in to Asad's demands and Asad couldn't be seen as giving up territory. It fell to President Clinton to find a way to overcome the problem.

13

Shepherdstown Breakdown

Barak and Sharaa had had their first direct encounter two weeks earlier, on Wednesday, December 15, 1999, in the White House. Clinton had hosted events there with Rabin and Arafat, Peres and Jordan's Crown Prince Hassan, Rabin and King Hussein, and Arafat and Netanyahu. Now, finally, he had succeeded in arranging the one Arab-Israeli summit that had been his objective from the very beginning of his administration.

It began with a public ceremony in the Rose Garden. Knowing that Sharaa's performances on the public stage were always problematic if Israelis were in proximity, we had reached agreement that the only one to speak should be Clinton. Sharaa had made clear to Madeleine Albright that he would not shake hands with Barak in public; that would be left to the final summit with Asad. It fell to me to inform Barak.

As we waited in the Roosevelt Room for the president, I took Barak aside. We both feigned interest in a portrait of Teddy Roosevelt astride a galloping horse as I explained to him that Sharaa would stand next to him at the ceremony but would not shake his hand. Barak said he understood. In the few minutes that Barak and Sharaa spent with Clinton in the Oval Office while the press and delegations waited for them in the Rose Garden, Barak focused instead on the protocol for the ceremony. He suggested to the president that it would be unnatural if he and Sharaa did not say at least a few words. Sharaa had a prepared speech in his pocket so was quite willing to speak if Barak wanted to. The president said fine but cautioned them both that they should keep it short and positive.

Because Barak outranked Sharaa, he spoke first. His speech lasted thirty seconds—four sentences about the horrors of war and the imperatives of peacemaking. Sharaa went on for ten minutes. He did speak positively about peace with Israel and he made the important declaration that the conflict was about borders, not about Israel's existence. Nevertheless, he also managed to brand Israel as the aggressor in the 1967 war and complain about a supposed media campaign to mobilize sympathy for the Golan settlers at the expense of Syrians who had fled their homes in the Golan. There was no opportunity for Barak to respond and no handshake to soften the harshness of the accusations. The Israeli public's disappointment was quick and palpable, which reinforced Barak's conviction that he needed to know what concessions the Syrians would make before offering any of his own.

Above all, Barak did not want to appear to be rushing the deal. He urged us to focus the Washington talks on procedural issues and delay any discussion of substance until a subsequent round to create the impression of "a long haul." The Syrians, on the other hand, wanted to get down to business; Asad had instructed Sharaa to stay in Washington as long as necessary despite the onset of Ramadan. Typical of the shifting dynamics of Middle Eastern diplomacy, the Syrians now wanted to close the deal and the Israelis, who were usually pushing for a breakthrough, wanted to slow the process down. Moreover, Sharaa was now ready, even keen, to engage Barak in a one-on-one discussion because he expected to hear there, directly from him, about the June 4 line. Barak, in order to avoid that, refused the invitation even though this kind of discreet, high-level, direct engagement was what Israel's leaders had always insisted on.

BLAIR HOUSE, THE president's official guesthouse for foreign dignitaries, is located directly across Pennsylvania Avenue from the White House. It served as the residences of Abraham Lincoln and Harry Truman while the White House was being renovated during their presidencies. Decorated in Federal and Georgian styles, the guesthouse is actually four townhouses joined together, with four dining rooms, a library, and fourteen guest bedrooms. The entrance is covered by Blair House's signature green canopy. There is a small parlor room on the right of this vestibule, where General Robert E. Lee was offered command of the Union Army before he took control of the Confederate Army. The visiting dignitary's staff usually congregates in the dining room in the center of the main house. To the left is a large drawing room often used for official meetings between the guests and the secretary of state. Adjacent to the drawing room is a small, elegant dining room where in December 1994 Barak spent two days in negotiations with the Syrian chief of staff, General Hekmat Shehabi. Asad was so offended by Barak's shopping list of Israeli security requirements that afterward he stalled the negotiations for months.

Down a long corridor to the right there is an additional drawing room and a large dining room with a dark mahogany table and Pembroke chairs with bold blue, gold, and white striped upholstery. This is where Secretary Albright convened the first meeting between Barak, Sharaa, and their delegations.

Unlike his first Blair House appearance, this time Barak put on a virtuoso performance. He heaped lavish and extravagant praise on all things Syrian: its role as a major Middle Eastern player "since the dawn of history"; the tenacity of Syrian soldiers and their devotion to the land; the toughness with which Sharaa defended Syrian interests in international forums; his own understanding that Syria was the key to comprehensive Arab-Israeli peace; and the extraordinary statesmanship of Hafez al-Asad.

I thought he overdid it, but it was clearly music to Sharaa's ears, especially since President Clinton had just boxed them for his off-tune remarks that morning. Sharaa responded in kind, explaining that in that speech it had been his "great responsibility" to clarify publicly that Syria no longer sought to eliminate Israel. Other Arabs might counsel against making peace, but Syria now rejected that approach because it would involve too much bloodshed. Instead, he said, the time had come to make an honorable peace that would open the door wide for Israel: "After peace, in a very short period, Israelis will be able to travel throughout the Middle East." It was, Sharaa averred, "The right moment to do it."

Nevertheless, it did not take Sharaa long to bring up the Rabin deposit, making clear there could be no progress without it. He detailed the answers Warren Christopher had brought Asad concerning Rabin's acceptance of the June 4 line and his disavowal of any territorial claims. Sharaa then noted, intriguingly, that it was impossible to find this line on any historical map and therefore, he suggested, they should try together to delineate it.

Barak insisted that his government had made no commitment on territorial withdrawal. But Sharaa's admission that the line did not exist on a map opened up the possibility of drawing an Israeli-Syrian borderline that suited Barak's needs. That simple idea saved the Blair House talks.

Sharaa's statement provided Clinton with an opportunity to propose that when the negotiators reconvened in January, a committee be established to deal with the border demarcation, as well as three other committees to deal with the other aspects of the agreement (security, normalization, and water). Barak accepted, with the caveat that the committees on security and normalization would meet first and the border demarcation committee only a few days later. He wanted to use this sequence to help create the impression at home that he was negotiating Israel's concerns on security and peace before discussing Syria's demand for full withdrawal.

The president held a final meeting in the Oval Office on Thursday evening. There was a palpable sense that the people of the Middle East were on the threshold not just of a new millennium, but also of a new era in Arab-Israeli relations. Barak noted that they had just taken the first step on the road to peace together and that he was really hopeful that they would find a way to bridge the gaps.

Sharaa responded in kind, expressing the belief—extraordinary for a Syrian leader—that the last two days had "brought us closer to our Israeli neighbors." He praised Barak for his determination for peace and concluded, "There is no reason why we should not succeed."

It had taken Clinton seven long years of diplomacy to get to this moment. "The rewards of peace for both your people will be incalculable," he observed quietly as he closed the meeting. An observer of this scene could be forgiven for believing that for one brief moment it looked as if reconciliation in the Middle East was actually possible, even between Syria and Israel.

Sharaa immediately left the White House for an *iftar* (the evening meal that breaks the daily fast during the Muslim holy month of Ramadan) at the home of the Saudi ambassador. At Sharaa's request, Prince Bandar had assembled all the Arab ambassadors to Washington to hear his briefing. As Bandar recounted the event to me later, they were treated to an even more extraordinary experience than I had just witnessed in the Oval Office.

Without hesitation or caveat, Sharaa told the assembled representatives of the Arab states that they should inform their governments that Syria was about to make peace with Israel. He praised Barak as a statesman and expressed great satisfaction with the two days of talks, noting especially that they had agreed to establish a border demarcation committee and that this, together with Rabin's deposit, made him confident that all Syrian territory would be returned.

Asad was unusually positive when the president phoned him to brief him on the talks. Completely out of character, Asad agreed without hesitation to Clinton's request that he allow an American team of experts from the Pentagon, accompanied by a rabbi, to exhume bodies from four graves in a Damascus cemetery that the Israelis believed were the remains of their soldiers killed in a battle with Palestinian guerrillas near the village of Sultan Yaqub in Lebanon's Bekaa Valley in 1982. Unfortunately, the remains proved not to be those of the Israelis and Asad's humanitarian gesture went unknown and unappreciated by the Israeli public. Nevertheless, his acquiescence was an indicator of his satisfaction with what he had heard from Sharaa.

THE CLIMACTIC NEGOTIATIONS began two weeks later in Shepherdstown, West Virginia. In 1862, during the Civil War, this small, nondescript town had been the site of a minor victory for the Confederate forces after the Union Army had defeated them in the historic battle at nearby Antietam. Today, Shepherdstown is known mostly for its handsome, state-of-the-art National Conservation Training Center for the U.S. Fish and Wildlife Service. West Virginia has been the beneficiary of many such projects because its senior senator, Robert Byrd, has served for many years as the all-powerful chairman of the Senate Appropriations Committee. The training center has beautifully designed, rustic dining facilities, including a grand lounge room complete with an open fireplace, high ceilings, picture windows, and broad wooden beams.

This is where President Clinton hosted Barak and Sharaa for their dinner sessions. But most of the Israeli-Syrian negotiations took place in the adjacent hotel in which the delegations were accommodated. There the décor was modern American: plain, 1980s functional, with no frills and no charm. The sleeping quarters were cramped, hardly what the senior members of the Israeli and Syrian delegations had come to expect. The facility had been hastily chosen by the State Department when the Syrian ambassador had made clear that his countrymen were unwilling to go to Camp David because of its association with Sadat's peace agreement with Israel, which Syrians still viewed as a betrayal.

True to his tarmac turnabout, in Shepherdstown Barak refused to budge on any substantive issue; he was out to show the Israeli public that he was insisting on Israel's needs before making any territorial concessions. So instead he pressed Clinton to use his influence with the eager Syrians to generate concessions on their part. And he added a new requirement: he wanted Syria to allow negotiations with the Lebanese to resume while the Israeli and Syrian negotiators were still in Shepherdstown.

The president had received a briefing on Barak's precarious political condition from Stanley Greenberg, Clinton's pollster before he became Barak's adviser. Clinton was sympathetic to Barak's argument that if he were to sell the deal to Israelis he needed a large, attractive package to point to before he conceded on the June 4 line. In addition to Syrian concessions and Lebanese negotiations, Barak's wish list included large-scale American military assistance and Arab state recognition.* As Barak explained it to Clinton, this was like landing a moon probe: "I have only one shot and I can't afford to make a single mistake."

We dutifully went off to convince the Syrians and did so with surprising success because Sharaa, as he informed us, had a mandate from Asad to show flexibility in order to conclude the deal. Barak helped us by applying his dose of exaggerated blandishments to Sharaa's ego when the president hosted the two leaders at dinner on the second night. The next day, January 5, the normalization and security committees met and had good preliminary discussions.

That night, under pressure from Barak to secure substantive concessions from Sharaa, Madeleine Albright invoked one of her favorite tactics for getting things done: she had a woman-to-woman talk with Buthaina Shaaban. Dr. Shaaban was ostensibly Sharaa's translator but her closeness to the Asad family made her a trusted member of the Syrian team. She was well aware of Asad's frailty and his desire to conclude the deal, and she was sensitive to Sharaa's insecurity in the highest-stake negotiations he had ever conducted.

Sharaa was still recovering from his heart surgery and was feeling the political heat from those around Asad who doubted the wisdom of concluding a deal with Israel. Like Asad, he worried aloud about being

---

* Barak's request included a $23 billion compensation package for withdrawal from the Golan Heights, a memorandum of understanding that would have elevated Israel's status to that of a "strategic ally" of the United States, and enhanced intelligence cooperation.

assassinated for making peace. He had told Buthaina that he could not go home and report that he heard nothing from Barak on the line of withdrawal. So Madeleine and Buthaina cooked up an official letter from Clinton to Albright that would reiterate the existence of the Rabin deposit and emphasize that it should guide the outcome of the negotiations. Sharaa would be given a copy he could show to Asad. This side letter was a typical diplomatic ploy that we used when one side was not prepared to give the other what it needed. Without it, the negotiations would have been stuck. With it, Madeleine was able to achieve what we thought was a breakthrough.

On January 6, the secretary of state engaged the Syrian foreign minister in a discussion of all the substantive issues, using Lauder's revised ten points as the basis. Despite Asad's rebuff of Lauder, Sharaa was prepared to engage. He confirmed that Israeli withdrawal would need to be to "a line based on the line of June 4, 1967." On the water issue, Sharaa confirmed in clearer language what Daoudi had told Saguy in Bethesda in September, 1999: "sovereignty on the lake is Israel's; sovereignty on the land is ours." He also repeated that on the northeast shoreline, the line would be the same as the 1923 international boundary—that is, Syria would be at least ten meters off the shoreline. In return, Sharaa wanted the five fishing villages in that area to have access to the lake for water and fishing. In an unexpected concession, Sharaa also indicated that Kibbutz Snir, which was just to the east of the June 4 line on the Jordan River north of the lake, could be retained by Israel and the border adjusted accordingly. On the arrangements for an early warning station on the Golan, Sharaa accepted that it would be under the "total auspices and responsibility" of the United States and France for the first five years, implying what he could never say—that Israelis could have access there if the United States and France decided to grant it.

We were pleased, of course, but such quick progress put pressure on Barak to reciprocate and he was determined not to do that yet. He conceded that Sharaa was showing signs of flexibility but complained that the Syrian was refusing to agree to the resumption of the Lebanese negotiations. In his desire to create the impression of a tough, drawn-out negotiation, Barak then announced that he would have to return to Israel for a while because the prime minister could not stay out of the country for more than a week at a time.

We still had two more days of talks, however, and we hoped we would be able to persuade Barak to respond in that time. On January 7, Clinton met with both delegations to present them with an American draft of their putative peace treaty. The text was replete with brackets within which the Israeli and Syrian positions were detailed, including the concessions Sharaa had made to Albright. Since Barak had not yet responded on the critical issue of the line of withdrawal, the Israeli bracketed language at that point referred only to a commonly agreed boundary "based on consideration of the national identity and dignity of both sides, geography, security and water, as well as legal considerations." In other words, in the draft peace treaty there was no Israeli commitment to full withdrawal, let alone to the line of June 4, 1967.

As the president handed copies of the text to Barak and Sharaa, he noted that this was an American draft, which had no official standing. Its purpose was to identify the gaps as a prelude to trying to bridge them. It never occurred to us that if the document leaked we would have exposed the Syrian concessions without any indication of Israeli reciprocity. It should have.

Barak himself was obsessed with leaks. As he explained to Sharaa in a meeting they had with the president that evening, he could not talk about the line of June 4, 1967, because of his fear of them.* He knew that the agreement had to take account of Syrian dignity and thus apologized for his statement during his election campaign that Syrian feet would not splash in Lake Kinneret. But the issue was a matter of dignity for the Israeli people as well, he said. The presentation, with its oblique reference to the June 4 line, made an impact on Sharaa, who responded: "If we do it quietly we can find a way."

This mood of Israeli-Syrian partnership also manifested itself in a later meeting that night between Uri Saguy and Ibrahim Omar about security issues, in which the Syrian general indicated that his government was prepared to make minor modifications in the June 4 line and accept a 10:4 ratio in Israel's favor in dividing up the demilitarized zones along both sides of the new border. At the end of their meeting, the Israeli and Syrian generals actually shook hands.

Reality bit the next morning when the boundary demarcation committee held its first meeting. This event had been long awaited by the

---

* Barak also complained to Clinton that Shepherdstown was not the "leak-free" environment he had specifically requested because members of the delegations were free to mix with the media in the town's restaurants.

Syrians, long delayed by the Israelis, and long dreaded by the Americans. I chaired the session. Colonel Moshe Kochanovsky, deputy director general of the Ministry of Defense, led the Israeli team. I had known him to be tenacious and often infuriating in his legalistic nitpicking, but today he was conscious of the fact that he was walking on eggshells and approached his brief with courtesy and charm. Kochanovsky had instructions to talk about anything but the line of withdrawal, so he gave a long presentation on the legal concept of an international boundary, the process of demarcation, the creation of common maps, the mechanisms for boundary relations, and the management of crossing points.

General Omar listened patiently—then in a typically Syrian way, went right to the heart of the matter: "What is the territory that you are talking about? This issue must be settled today. If you're not able to address this issue, let us know so we can inform our leaders."

Kochanovsky responded that they should start with the procedural issues and then try to solve the core issues. Omar rejected that approach, so Kochanovsky switched to a legal presentation on Israel's view of Security Council Resolution 242. I should have cut him off but since the committee had only been meeting for less than thirty minutes it seemed inappropriate. Instead I let him explain his version of the intentions of the Security Council when it drafted the resolution in November 1967. According to Kochanovsky, the Security Council did not want to reestablish the insecure line of 1967.*

In a few words, Kochanovsky had managed to raise serious doubts in the minds of the Syrians about Israeli intentions to withdraw to the line of June 4. Since the Syrians had thought this was in our pocket and the only challenge was how to get it out and onto the table, they were dismayed. General Omar did not show it immediately. He politely responded that the border committee was established to draw the line,

---

* The Israeli argument is that the deliberate omission of the definite article in Resolution 242's phrasing—it only referred to "territories," not "the territories" occupied in 1967—meant that there was no requirement for complete Israeli withdrawal. This argument, combined with the reference to Israel's need to have "secure and recognized borders," forms the legal basis for Israel's insistence that it is not required to return to the 1967 lines. The Arabs, on the other hand, point to the preambular language in the resolution that refers to "the inadmissibility of the acquisition of territory by force" to argue that the resolution required Israel to give up every inch of territory it occupied in 1967. As for the borders, the Arabs argue that only recognized borders will be secure and that the only Israeli borders that they will recognize are those that do not reflect the weight of conquest.

not argue about legal interpretations of 242. Looking for some common ground, Kochanovsky was polite in return, and I quickly gaveled the meeting to a close.

Sharaa's reaction soon manifested itself. After hearing Omar's debrief, he explained to Albright that he would have to inform Asad that the Israelis had tried to manipulate the negotiations instead of putting the line of withdrawal on the table. He predicted that his president would be very upset.

Madeleine tried to placate him by emphasizing the importance of the letter she had provided him and her desire to improve bilateral relations. But Sharaa pointed out that the letter had also failed to mention explicitly the line of June 4, 1967.

Dennis tried to divert Sharaa by focusing on process: When would they reconvene? What would they say to the press? But Sharaa ignored him and complained that the Israelis now knew what they could get from the Syrians "but they and you have failed to deliver. That is what I'll have to tell President Asad. I can't report progress. June 4 was the ignition; without it the car won't start."

The president was still scheduled to host the final dinner. When he learned what had transpired, he was angry. "God damn it!" he said. "I convened this meeting now against my better judgment and Barak is gaming Sharaa and me." Then he went off into an exegesis on the latest polling data he had received from Stanley Greenberg showing that if an agreement with Lebanon was part of the deal, the Israeli voters just might vote for it.

Sandy Berger advised the president to try to get a commitment out of Barak to reaffirm the deposit in exchange for the president securing a commitment from Sharaa to allow the Lebanese negotiations to resume. The president nodded and went off to see Barak.

By Clinton's account, it was a difficult exchange. The president did his best to undermine Barak's confidence that he knew best how to handle the negotiations. Clinton argued that he was a more experienced politician than Barak and that in his judgment if Barak did a peace deal with Syria the Israeli people would support him. He promised to travel to Israel to help Barak sell it. But, in a move typical of Clinton's unwillingness to press Barak too hard, he argued that if Barak had not reaffirmed the June 4 line by the time they reconvened the negotiations, the whole process would collapse. Barak seized the opening. He said he would be ready to reaffirm the Rabin deposit if the next meeting was in a completely leakproof environment and Asad agreed to allow the Lebanese negotiations to recommence at the same time.

With that commitment from Barak, Clinton convened the dinner. It was a somber affair. Barak repeated his now worn-out words about his admiration for Syria and its great leader—the president thought that this time Barak had laid it on too thick. Sharaa responded eloquently, warning of the historic opportunity for peace they were all missing. He explained to Barak that the Israeli prime minister had made a liar out of him with his president because, after the meeting at Blair House, Sharaa had convinced Asad that Barak was serious about making peace based on full withdrawal. Now, Sharaa argued, he had done his best to meet Israel's concerns but had heard nothing in response from Barak. He concluded by saying he didn't know whether it would be possible to continue the negotiations.

After the dinner adjourned, the president took the Syrian foreign minister aside for a few minutes. He told him that he had made a great speech. Sharaa responded that he was tired and not feeling well; he would ask Asad to replace him as chief negotiator. The president applied all the charm he could muster until Sharaa expressed his willingness to come back if it was clear that the next time they would finish the agreement. The president argued passionately that the resumption of the Lebanese negotiations would have a positive impact on Barak's domestic circumstances. Since the Syrians would control the timing of the endgame of any Lebanese agreement, he didn't understand why they were against the idea.

Clinton then went back to Barak and expressed his deep disappointment: "You've gained from this round but another round like this and it will be a wholesale disaster for you, and for me."

It is not often that an American secretary of state dresses down an Israeli prime minister but the next morning Madeleine went to Barak's suite, determined to reinforce the president's message. Barak had been ready to commit to the June 4 line in order to get the negotiations started, she said. But since then, he had switched tactics.

Last night we were depressed about the lack of progress, and you were happy. You have no better friend than the president but you have played with his credibility and diminished it. I'm not sure that Sharaa will come back. We worked as hard as we could to get them to be flexible and you gave us nothing.

Barak responded calmly to this assault, repeating what he had told the president about the final round. Anything else, he argued, would result in a perception among Israelis that he had played Israel's only card before negotiations had begun.

I'm coming to the toughest decision ever made by an Israeli leader since the establishment of the state. It is an existential issue. You don't seem to understand the risks involved. It's much more complicated than what Clinton and Asad have at stake.

When Madeleine visited Sharaa, he said good-bye to her as if he would never see her again. The only way Syrians would return to the negotiations, he said, was if Clinton called Asad and convinced him that when they reconvened Barak would commit to the June 4 line. But from his perspective the talks were in crisis and he would ask Asad to send someone else to the next round. "Death is better than this," Sharaa remarked melodramatically.

Then he warmed up a little. He pledged to try to present a positive report to Asad of the hints he had heard from Barak. But unless Clinton could convince Asad about Barak's intentions there would be no third round. Yet he finally agreed to the United States announcing that the talks would resume on January 19.

GIVEN THE NARROW gaps separating the substantive positions of the Israelis and the Syrians, and the centrality of the Syrian deal to Clinton's Middle Eastern strategy, one can look back at that moment in mid-January 2000 and see that it was the right time for Clinton to have summoned Barak and Asad to a summit to conclude the agreement. Indeed, there was a lot more justification to do that on the Syrian track at that moment than there would subsequently be on the Palestinian track when the president decided to invite Barak and Arafat to Camp David. But we were led astray by our all too well-developed habit of seizing on a procedural fix to overcome a substantive roadblock. Because of Asad's dilatory tactics, this had become so ingrained in Dennis's approach to Israeli-Syrian negotiations over the twelve years that he had devoted to them that it had become a natural instinct. But it was particularly ill suited to this moment when Asad's health was so frail and he seemed so eager to make peace, when the clock on Clinton's term in office was already ticking, when Barak was rapidly losing political altitude, and when the Palestinians were growing impatient because their negotiations were being ignored.

We should have known from experience not to grasp at Sharaa's last-minute acceptance of our announcement for reconvening the talks, ignoring his warning of Asad's likely negative reaction to the results of Shepherdstown. In hindsight, we shouldn't have allowed Sharaa to go home empty-handed; Clinton should have pressed Barak to be more forthcoming at that moment, not later. But Clinton had always been particularly sensitive to the political situation in Israel. It had started with Rabin's troubles with Shas and had developed into an obsession after Clinton's failure to influence the outcome of the 1996 election between Netanyahu and Peres. He had sent Robert Shrum, Stanley Greenberg, and James Carville to Israel to help get Barak elected. These very men who had helped engineer Barak's victory so thoroughly familiarized Clinton with Barak's political difficulties that it weakened his will to persuade Barak to act now rather than later.*

There was also a predisposition in Clinton's peace team to avoid second-guessing Israeli leaders who were committed to taking risks for peace. We understood full well that Israel would have to bear the consequences of Barak's fateful decision in a way that the United States would not. And, in the end, Israel was our democratic ally, and Syria was on our list of state sponsors of terrorism. We were not prepared to push Barak any further than we did.

Instead we chose to assume that there would be another round of negotiations and focused on how to make them decisive. We forgot that in the Middle East what can go wrong usually will go wrong.

On January 13, three days after the negotiators had left Shepherdstown, the Israeli newspaper *Haaretz* published the full text of the draft peace treaty that Clinton had given to Barak and Sharaa on January 7, revealing all Sharaa's concessions and saying nothing about Israeli withdrawal from the Golan Heights. It's little wonder that when Clinton spoke to Asad the next day he was completely negative about the Shepherdstown negotiations. He dismissed Clinton's promise that Barak would reaffirm the deposit and rejected Clinton's recommendation

---

* Immediately after the conclusion of the Shepherdstown talks, we received independent confirmation of what the president's pollsters were telling Barak. According to a poll of Israeli public opinion commissioned by the U.S. government, 73 percent of Russian voters and 63 percent of Shas voters were opposed to full withdrawal from the Golan.

that the Lebanese negotiations resume, probably viewing that as an attempt to steal another card from him.

A day later Asad was unavailable to take a follow-up call from the president. The public reaction in Syria was apparently so bad that the regime had begun arresting Muslim Brotherhood and Palestinian critics. By January 18, the Arab press was reporting the arrest of some five hundred people; within a week, the number had grown to two thousand. We began to hear reports that on the streets of Damascus people were accusing Asad of selling Syrian territory to secure the succession for his son Bashar. We also received independent confirmation of the deterioration in the situation from Egypt and Saudi Arabia. In a phone call, Sharaa told Albright that every member of the leadership in Damascus was questioning the wisdom of having gone to the previous round, let alone participating in a new round. "Asad is very upset with me. He said I should not have stayed for four days without the June 4 line being put on the table. He blamed me for putting the other issues on the table without that. . . . We will not repeat this bitter experience."

LEAKS ARE A common phenomenon in diplomacy and they can be particularly damaging when they reveal the content of secret negotiations. Such publicity destroys trust between the negotiators and enables political opponents to mobilize opposition to an agreement before it has been finalized. It is no coincidence that all the Israeli-Arab negotiations that were brought to successful conclusions were based on secret diplomacy that did not leak: Sadat's visit to Jerusalem was preceded by the secret talks in Morocco; the Oslo negotiations remained secret, as did the Israel-Jordan negotiations, until the deals were finalized.

Arab governments have greater control over their media and are therefore better able to maintain secrecy than their counterparts in Israel and the United States, although this has become harder as satellite television makes it possible for independent news organizations to escape the control of the government censor.

The American peace team took extraordinary steps to protect the confidentiality of the negotiations. Only the secretary of state, the national security adviser, and their immediate peace process advisers were aware of the details. Memos, policy papers, and reporting from the region were all handled outside normal channels. The undersecretary of state for political affairs, the deputy national security adviser, the office of the secretary of defense, and the vice president's office were all kept "out of the loop," receiving only occasional oral briefings.

Unlike Rabin, Barak did not believe in compartmentalization. His large teams of negotiators were kept abreast of sensitive exchanges. Barak operated on the assumption that everything would leak and so planned accordingly, as was evident in his conduct of the Syrian negotiations. In the process, his negotiators were robbed of the ability to conduct confidential exchanges and explore the potential for compromise.

Nothing was published in Syria unless the information minister sanctioned it. There was only the occasional, inexplicable slip.* The Syrians believed that any secret meeting would be leaked by Israel so, at times, they would leak preemptively.†

Since the draft treaty was published in an Israeli newspaper, we naturally assumed someone in Barak's team had leaked it. He was, after all, obsessed with showing the Israeli public at every opportunity that he was not giving away anything to Asad without getting something first and the draft treaty certainly enabled that point to be made.

As it turned out, however, the leak came from an Israeli who was not associated with Barak. By his own account, the version that appeared in the newspaper came from Nimrod Novik. Novik, who had served as foreign policy adviser to Shimon Peres when he was prime minister in the 1980s, would often come to Washington to talk with members of the American peace team. He would then write up his discussions and circulate them to an informal network of Israelis interested in the peace process. Some of the members of this network had been involved in the original Oslo negotiations; others were providing ideas and advice to the Israeli and Palestinian negotiating teams. Novik circulated the draft peace treaty to members of this network and one of them gave the document to *Haaretz*.

Who gave the draft treaty to Novik? At the time, Barak claimed that he had launched an investigation that concluded a member of the

---

* The most memorable Syrian leak was when Syrian radio reported during the Rabin-Asad negotiations that Asad was ready to accept an early warning ground station on Mount Hermon as part of the security arrangements.

† The Syrians had in fact been responsible for a partial leak of the draft treaty's contents while we were still at Shepherdstown.

American team had leaked it. Subsequently, he publicly implicated Robert Malley, the NSC official responsible for the peace negotiations, and Aaron Miller, Dennis Ross's deputy, charging that one of them had "innocently shared his impressions with an Israeli friend."

Malley and Miller maintained close ties with Novik and his network. They all shared the view that Israeli-Palestinian negotiations should take precedence over the Syrian track. Aaron, in particular, was disconcerted by Asad's decision in December 1999 to resume negotiations, because at that time the Israelis and Palestinians were supposed to be negotiating final status issues. Since then Miller has argued vehemently against pursuing a Syrian-Israeli peace ahead of an Israeli-Palestinian accord. There is, however, no evidence that either Malley or Miller was Novik's source.

Even if one of our team did provide the draft treaty to Novik, I don't believe he intended it to appear in the Israeli press. The incident was another of those unintended consequences that so often diverted our efforts. In this case, the draft treaty's publication had the effect of sabotaging the Israeli-Syrian negotiations at a critical moment.

14

Syrian Denouement

One week after the breakdown at Shepherdstown, I arrived back at the U.S. embassy in Israel. I imagined that I was returning to help put the finishing touches on an agreement with Syria, just as Clinton had sent me to do with Yitzhak Rabin in 1995. I never considered that the process could crater again—in the same six-month time frame. The painful awakening began on the first weekend.

In our previous term, my wife Jill and I had adopted the practice of using Friday night Shabbat dinners to conduct discussions with a cross-section of Israelis about the political "crisis du jour." Israel seems to lurch from one calamity to the next at such speed that the political class rarely has time to catch its breath. When I left Israel the first time, I joked with the press that what the country really needed was a good night's sleep!

One of the endearing things about Israelis is that they all have a political opinion, which they articulate with great intelligence and passion. In the 1990s, politics had become so contentious in the country that the Shabbat family meal became the occasion for people to hone their talking points for the arguments they would have with their colleagues in the coming week.

On our first Friday night back at the U.S. ambassador's residence in Herzliya, we gathered a group of our close friends around the table in the atrium dining room. The white stucco, Mediterranean-style villa was perched on a bluff above the ocean in this seaside town north of Tel Aviv. The reception areas opened out onto a magnificent landscaped garden of flower beds and palm trees, from which we had just watched the sun sink like molten gold into an azure sea. We could have been in Cap d'Antibes, except for the tall, tilting, concrete water tower that also stood on the bluff next to the residence. Four decades earlier, Haganah soldiers had climbed this tower under the cover of darkness to signal the all-clear to the battered ships that brought illegal Jewish immigrants from the Nazi concentration camps, past British coastal patrol boats, to the shores of the promised land. It remained as a decaying monument to the founding of the Jewish state and a constant reminder to the U.S. ambassador in residence of Israel's purpose as a homeland for the Jewish people.

For this dinner we had invited a senior minister in Ehud Barak's government, several journalists, a political adviser to the prime minister, and a famous Israeli novelist. As the oversize faces of Andy Warhol's "Jewish Geniuses"—his celebrated series of lithographs of Moses, Martin Buber, Franz Kafka, Sarah Bernhardt, Louis Brandeis, Golda Meir, Albert Einstein, and other famous Jews—gazed at us from the atrium walls, our dinner guests started criticizing their new prime minister with a bitterness born of disappointment and personal slights.

Barak had barely been in office six months and yet some of his closest friends had already turned against him. They complained that he had not reached out to his constituents or attempted to broaden his base, that he was unwilling to make the case publicly for his peace strategy, that he had a high-handed manner with political colleagues, and that he had refused to listen to the advice of others. As Eitan Haber put it with ominous prescience, "I'm warning you, Martin, if he goes on like this for another six months, he will be finished."

Two days later, I had my first one-on-one meeting as ambassador with Barak, in his office in Jerusalem. By now the wood paneling and uncomfortable, low-slung blue sofa was familiar to me since I had sat there with Barak's three predecessors, Rabin, Peres, and Netanyahu. Rabin and Peres had hung pictures of themselves with Israel's legendary first prime minister, David Ben-Gurion, on the wall adjacent to the prime minister's desk. He had been their mentor. Barak, like Netanyahu, was from the next generation and had not dealt directly with "B.G." But whereas Bibi had replaced his photograph with pictures of his family, Barak had restored it alongside one of his mentor, Yitzhak Rabin. The reason became immediately clear.

Barak told me he had been elected to make the big "Ben-Gurion–size" decisions, to go for the peace summit or fall down trying. He knew that his political position was becoming precarious and his coalition fractious. He said that the reversal of his political fortunes now required a breakthrough in the peace negotiations.

Barak used his customary Cartesian logic to lay out his strategy to achieve that breakthrough. He contrasted the Syrian and Palestinian negotiations. With the Syrians, there was no intimacy but the gaps were small and the issues could be resolved in one decisive round. With the Palestinians, there was a great deal of intimacy; both sides understood each other's problems and there was a mutual desire to reach an agreement. However, the gaps were wide and the issues complicated. Therefore, he believed it was possible to reach an agreement quickly with the Syrians and take it to a referendum forty-five days later. Contrary to his unshakable conviction less than two weeks earlier in Shepherdstown, he now believed that such a deal could produce a landslide victory in the referendum and thereby act as an accelerator for the Palestinian negotiations.

He reminded me that during his election campaign he had made a commitment that the IDF would be out of Lebanon by July 2000, in six months' time. If there were no agreement with the Syrians, he would have to withdraw unilaterally, which would complicate relations with Asad and therefore reduce his chances for achieving a deal with Damascus in the near term.

Barak's analysis of his predicament was his way of explaining to me that, notwithstanding his fear of the *freier* stigma, he had decided to go for the deal with Asad. Now, Barak was in a hurry!

So was Bill Clinton as he entered his last year in office. After the Shepherdstown debacle, Asad had complained on the phone to Clinton that because of Barak's conduct he could no longer clearly identify Israel's bottom line. Clinton used this opening to generate an endgame strategy that would be quick and decisive: He explained to Asad that he wanted to meet with him and present a map that detailed Barak's best offer of withdrawal from the Golan. If this turned out to be broadly acceptable to Asad, Clinton would summon Barak to join them and conclude the agreement.

Clinton's decision was influenced by communications he received from Mubarak and Saudi ambassador Prince Bandar confirming Asad's desire to reach an agreement with Barak. On January 22, 2000, the Egyptian president traveled to Damascus to meet with his ailing Syrian counterpart. Afterward, Mubarak urgently conveyed both to Clinton and Barak that they should conclude the deal with Syria quickly because Asad was not long for this world and his son's prospects had been rendered vulnerable by the leaking of the draft treaty.

Bandar reached a similar conclusion after visiting Damascus a few days later. He reported that Asad had told him he wanted to reach agreement in one "decisive" round, but would not bargain over his territorial demands.

Barak's chief of staff, Danny Yatom, and I went to work preparing the talking points and map for Clinton's presentation of Barak's position. Although it had often been contemplated, no previous Israeli prime minister had in the end been prepared to put a detailed offer of full Israeli withdrawal from the Golan Heights on the table, let alone present the line of withdrawal in a map. But that was now our task.

In close consultation with Barak, Yatom and I developed a detailed map of the line of Israeli withdrawal, marked in red on a satellite map of the Golan Heights and the valley below. The line mostly coincided with the line of June 4, 1967, as Daoudi had explained it to Saguy (Saguy was the true expert on the June 4 line but Barak did not want him or anyone else involved in the process). It took account of Sharaa's willingness to adjust the line north of Lake Kinneret to include Kibbutz Snir on the Israeli side. However, around the northeast section of the lake, Barak insisted that the line be drawn five hundred meters from the shoreline to allow for a road to be constructed. That line went around or just through the five Syrian fishing villages that had been located there in 1967 but no longer existed. (Barak had himself drawn the line to ensure that most of the land where houses had been built in these villages would return to Syrian sovereignty.)

In compensation for this five-hundred-meter strip in the northeastern sector, Barak drew the line around the southeastern side of the lake approximately five hundred meters to the west of the June 4 line on Israeli territory that Asad did not claim, so that Syria could argue that it regained the equivalent of more than 100 percent of the Golan even as it conceded a minimal amount of territory to Israel to make the deal. In the southern sector of the lake, Barak's line put the town and hot springs of al-Hama on the Syrian side of the line, as Asad had insisted on since 1994. Barak wanted Clinton to make clear that this was a difficult concession, granted out of sensitivity to Asad's needs.* In return,

---

* Barak's argument was that Syria had taken al-Hama by force in 1964 and the Syrians were the ones arguing that the border should not reflect the acquisition of territory by force. Moreover, for more than three decades after 1967, Israelis had been bathing in the springs at al-Hama, whereas the Syrians had only been splashing their feet in the Kinneret for less than two decades before 1967.

Barak wanted Asad to consider giving Israel a sovereign corridor of ten meters on both sides of the creek that led from the springs at Banias in the northern Golan down to Lake Kinneret. Barak offered Syrians the right to fish in the lake and use its water in return for Israelis being able to visit al-Hama.

The five-hundred-meter adjustment around the lake, although considerably more than the hundred meters that Barak had previously required, was based on Sharaa's concession in the Shepherdstown talks. He had accepted Israeli sovereignty on the lake and the shoreline to a distance of ten meters (as provided by the 1923 international border). Sharaa's advisers had also been quite explicit about how that line could be drawn some fifty meters off the lake if necessary. By asking for five hundred meters, Barak was trying to build some negotiating flexibility into his position; I believed one hundred meters was still his bottom line.

I also knew that Barak had developed a "bottom, bottom" line in case Asad refused anything more than the ten meters from the shoreline allowed by the international border. He showed me pictures the IDF planning branch had juxtaposed of the shoreline before June 4, 1967, with the shoreline in 2000, which established that the lake had receded by as much as 470 meters at the northern tip where the Jordan River entered the lake, narrowing gradually to fifty meters at Kibbutz Ein Gev at the southern end of the northeastern sector of the lake. In other words, even if in the end Asad would settle for nothing less than all the territory around the lake up to ten meters off the shoreline of June 1967, there would still be enough dry land around the lake for Barak to build his all-important road.

The president's presentation needed to be comprehensive and thus it dealt with Barak's positions on all the other issues involved in a peace agreement as well—early warning, demilitarized and limited forces zones, and the timing and phasing of the Israeli withdrawal. In each case Barak indicated his requirements and signaled his flexibility.

Barak wanted the president to repeat his request that the Lebanese negotiations resume and be concluded at the same time as the Israel-Syria peace treaty. Syria would also have to prevent Hezbollah and Palestinian terror organizations under its control from resorting to violence.

Finally, Barak wanted the president to focus Asad again on the need for Syria to take confidence-building measures that would help Barak

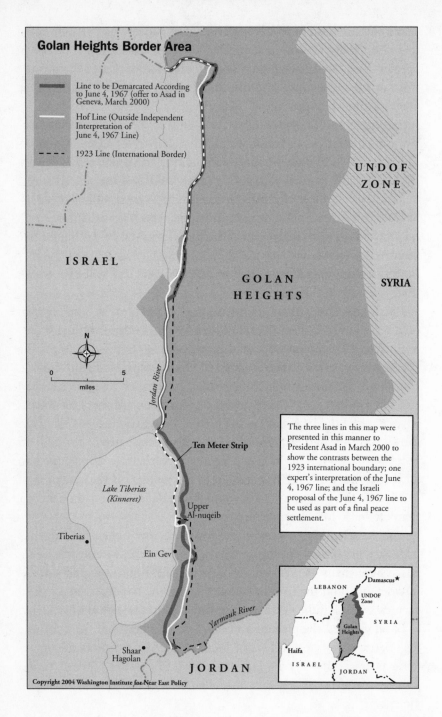

Golan Heights Border Area

Line to be Demarcated According to June 4, 1967 (offer to Asad in Geneva, March 2000)

Hof Line (Outside Independent Interpretation of June 4, 1967 Line)

1923 Line (International Border)

UNDOF ZONE

ISRAEL

GOLAN HEIGHTS

SYRIA

N

0   5
miles

Jordan River

Ten Meter Strip

The three lines in this map were presented in this manner to President Asad in March 2000 to show the contrasts between the 1923 international boundary; one expert's interpretation of the June 4, 1967 line; and the Israeli proposal of the June 4, 1967 line to be used as part of a final peace settlement.

Lake Tiberias (Kinneret)

Upper Al-nuqeib

Tiberias

Ein Gev

Yarmouk River

Shaar Hagolan

JORDAN

Damascus ★

LEBANON

UNDOF Zone

SYRIA

Golan Heights

Haifa

ISRAEL

JORDAN

Copyright 2004 Washington Institute for Near East Policy

The high point of the Middle East peace process: PLO Chairman Yasser Arafat and Israeli Prime Minister Yitzhak Rabin follow President Bill Clinton into the White House for the Oslo II Signing Ceremony on September 28, 1995.

"It seems to me Mr. Chairman, that you might be a little Jewish!" Rabin, speaking after the Oslo II Signing Ceremony, praised the impromptu speech in which Arafat had spoken of peace with his Israeli "cousins." Arafat responded to Rabin's suggestion by declaring, "Yes, Yes, Rachel [the Hebrew matriarch] is my aunt!" In his remarks, Rabin spoke for the first time about his vision of a peace in which Palestinians would have an independent state of their own. Five weeks later Rabin was assassinated.

3

Prime Minister Rabin's first meeting with President Clinton in the Oval Office, March 15, 1993 (the author was the notetaker). Rabin told Clinton that he would be prepared to commit Israel to a full withdrawal from the Golan Heights. From that moment on, Clinton knew that if he could persuade Syria's President Asad to meet Israel's peace and security requirements, Rabin would be willing to meet Asad's territorial requirements.

President Clinton greets Egypt's President Hosni Mubarak on his first visit to the White House, April 6, 1993. Clinton briefed Mubarak on his policy of "dual containment" of Iraq and Iran. As far as Mubarak was concerned, Iraq and Iran were "two of a kind."

At a press conference in Jerusalem with Secretary of State Warren Christopher on August 5, 1993, Rabin announces, "good news from Damascus." Christopher had just reported Asad's response to Rabin's offer of full withdrawal from the Golan. Unbeknownst to Christopher, Rabin was secretly negotiating with Yasser Arafat. In retrospect it became clear that Rabin was using the hint of progress on the Syrian track to pressure Arafat to make the deal.

King Hussein of Jordan and President Clinton meeting at the White House on June 22, 1994. Clinton urged the king to meet publicly with Israeli Prime Minister Rabin as a way of helping him convince Congress to approve aid to Jordan. Hussein and Rabin met at the White House on July 25, 1994, and then addressed a joint session of Congress in which Hussein declared, "Mr. Speaker, the war between Israel and Jordan is over!"

7

President Clinton witnesses the signing of the Israel-Jordan Peace Treaty at Wadi Arava on the Jordan-Israel border on October 26, 1994.

8

The Shepherdstown Showdown: Israeli Prime Minister Ehud Barak, President Clinton, and Syrian Foreign Minister Farouk Sharaa heading into their first meeting of the decisive round of Israeli-Syrian negotiations at Shepherdstown, Virginia, January 3, 2000.

Clinton, flanked by Secretary of State Madeleine Albright and National Security Adviser Sandy Berger, meets with Barak and Sharaa to deliver the American draft of an Israeli-Syrian Peace Treaty in Shepherdstown on January 7, 2000. Six days later, the draft text appeared in the Israeli newspaper *Haaretz*, severely embarrassing the Syrians because it catalogued their concessions but said nothing about the line of withdrawal Israel would make from the Golan.

10

"You've gained from this round, but another round like this and it will be a wholesale disaster for you, and for me," said Bill Clinton to Ehud Barak at Shepherdstown, January 8, 2000. The president could not convince Barak to respond to the Syrian concessions by revealing the extent of the Golan withdrawal he was prepared to make. Two months later in Geneva, Clinton would present Barak's map outlining a full withdrawal to a line based on the line of June 4, 1967, to Syria's President Asad. But by then it was too late.

11

The face of defeat: Bill Clinton and his peace team at the end of the Shepherdstown talks, January 9, 2000. From left to right: Rob Malley, Bruce Riedel, Berger, Clinton, Albright, Dennis Ross, and the author.

12

Israeli, Palestinian, and American negotiators discussing the West Bank borders of a Palestinian state at Camp David on July 13, 2000. Israel's chief negotiator, Shlomo Ben-Ami, sits to the left of Albright, opposite the Palestinian chief negotiator Abu Ala (taking notes on the right). Moments later Clinton entered the room and implored Abu Ala to respond with a counteroffer to Ben-Ami's offer of 86 percent of the West Bank. When Abu Ala refused, Clinton lost his temper and walked out.

13

Berger and Albright at Camp David explaining to Barak the offer made by Arafat on the sixth day of the summit to accept a compromise in the West Bank that would have allowed Israel to annex settlements as long as he acquired "Palestinian sovereignty in Jerusalem." Neither the Americans nor the Israelis realized it at the time, but Arafat had just laid a trap for Clinton and Barak.

Clinton confers with some of his advisers on the terrace at Aspen Lodge at Camp David, July 17, 2000. In these deliberations, Dennis Ross, the President's Middle East envoy, was always outnumbered by White House staff, contributing to a cacophony of advice and an improvised American negotiating strategy. From left to right: Clinton, Albright, Berger, Ross, Riedel, Malley, Maria Echeveste (White House Deputy Chief of Staff), and Gamal Helal (the State Department's Arabic translator).

Albright escorts Arafat to a fateful meeting with Clinton at Camp David on July 18, 2000. Clinton outlined a package deal that would have given Arafat 91 percent of the West Bank and Palestinian sovereignty over the Muslim and Christian Quarters of Jerusalem's Old City, as well as custodianship of the Muslim holy sites on the Haram al-Sharif/Temple Mount. Arafat said he would think about it, but in the early hours of the next morning, he rejected the offer.

16

Bill Clinton and George W. Bush depart the White House for Bush's inauguration as the 43rd president of the United States, January 20, 2001. Clinton had just told Bush in their hand-over meeting never to trust Arafat: "He lied to me, and he'll lie to you." Bush subsequently refused to meet with Arafat and walked away from Clinton's peace process.

"We shall remove them from our society," Israeli Prime Minister Ariel Sharon tells President Bush in their first meeting in the Oval Office, March 20, 2001, vowing to eradicate Palestinian terrorism. Bush responded, "No need to elaborate Mr. Prime Minister. I think we've got the picture." The pact they struck contrasted sharply with the one Rabin and Clinton agreed on, eight years earlier, when Rabin said he had a mandate to take risks for peace and Clinton responded, "If you're going to do that, my role is to minimize the risks."

change the increasingly negative mood in Israel toward the idea of a full withdrawal from the Golan.*

Then Clinton was supposed to tell Asad privately that this was "a moment of truth," and ask him for specific responses to Barak's positions.

I viewed it as a far-reaching, reasonable, and creative proposal that could serve as the basis for reaching an agreement that met both sides' needs. Given Asad's penchant for negotiations, neither Barak nor Clinton sought to present it as a take-it-or-leave-it proposition.

In retrospect, I should have argued with Barak that Asad would not react kindly to Barak's line of withdrawal going through the Syrian fishing villages around the lake. Asad had told me that he would never accept territorial swaps. But that idea was integral to Barak's proposal. I should have argued with Barak that presenting a demand for five hundred meters around the lake and offering territorial swaps to compensate was going to be counterproductive. I had subsequently made a similar argument to him about the need to make a complete, clean withdrawal from Lebanon and he had accepted my advice even though his army general staff was adamantly opposed to it. But in the context of the flexibility that Asad's negotiators had shown in Washington and at Shepherdstown, I believed that Barak's offer was in the ballpark, a basis for opening the give-and-take that had been the hallmark of negotiations with Asad.

ALAS, AS WE finalized our presentation, Asad no longer seemed in a responsive mood. The warning signs had started to emerge in March, when Clinton tried to call Asad to arrange for the summit meeting in Geneva. Ostensibly, this was exactly what Asad had been waiting for, yet the call was repeatedly delayed. At the time, Asad was engaged in a shakeup of his regime, but if he was so preoccupied with domestic issues that he could not meet with Clinton to negotiate peace, it was a clear indication of how his priorities had shifted. Because of the delays, the meeting that was supposed to have taken place in mid-March, before the president's trip to India and Pakistan, took place after it, on March 26, in Geneva. This meant the president would not be in top form when he met Asad. Overseas trips were exhausting for Clinton.

---

* These included a change of tone in Syrian press coverage, more efforts to locate or announce the fate of Israeli MIAs, and allowing Israelis to visit Damascus.

His schedule would be jam-packed with meetings and events, all of which energized him. Then he would have difficulty sleeping, and the next morning he would be tired and grumpy when he needed to focus.

The president's exhaustion was compounded on this particular trip by the consequences of his voracious appetite. In Pakistan, despite the warnings of his staff, he had consumed the fare with gusto. He became quite ill and had little time for his prebrief. According to some involved in that session, by the time he met Asad the president was eager to get the meeting over with.

Clinton began by asking Asad to wait until he had completed the whole presentation before he responded. He explained that Barak had limited his requirements to his vital needs. Barak was prepared for a full withdrawal "to a commonly agreed border based on the June 4, 1967, line." Given Asad's obsession with the June 4 line, Clinton's statement, delivered with emphasis for dramatic effect, should have been music to his ears. But he immediately stopped the translation and asked, "What are these words, 'commonly agreed'? I don't accept them."

Clinton pressed on. "Barak feels that sovereignty over the lake and the Jordan River are essential elements in any peace agreement with Syria," he said. Asad objected. "This is our lake. No matter how long it takes, we're not going to give up what is ours. If I were to propose this to the Syrian people, I wouldn't last for two days. . . . This is impossible." A surprised Clinton pointed out that Asad's foreign minister had explicitly stated at Shepherdstown that sovereignty over the lake would be in Israel's hands. Asad shot a withering look at Sharaa and asked him, "Did you agree to that?" Sharaa, clearly uncomfortable, avoided the question, insisting that he had demanded sovereignty over all the land.

Now Clinton *knew* he was in trouble. When he presented Barak's request for a strip of land around the lake, Asad said, "This means Barak doesn't want peace."

At this point Clinton stopped his presentation. Gamal Helal suggested that he at least finish translating Clinton's talking points. But the president was exasperated. "What's the point? He's not listening," Clinton shot back.

AT 9:20 P.M. my cell phone rang as I sat eating goulash in Fink's, an old-style Austro-Hungarian restaurant in Jerusalem established in the days of the British Mandate. I had repaired there for some comfort food as I awaited news from Geneva, expecting to fly with Barak that night when Clinton summoned him to join Asad for the final summit. Danny Yatom was calling. He had just listened in to the debriefing that Clinton had given Barak. Danny was still perfecting his English so he either tended to be long-winded and laborious or short and telegraphic. Tonight the news required the latter approach, which was just as well because it was not easy to hear over the din at Fink's: "It's not going to work," he told me tersely. I was dumbfounded. Clinton and Asad had only been meeting for an hour. How was it possible that they could already have concluded their talks and that the effort had collapsed?

I rushed to the apartment next to the David Citadel Hotel that was provided for the ambassador's overnight use in Jerusalem. There I could speak to Dennis in Geneva by secure phone. Dennis was categorical in his explanation. Asad had not been interested in anything the president had to say. Even when Dennis showed him the map with all of the Golan, al-Hama, and the additional territory to the southeast of the lake falling on the Syrian side of the line, Asad was disdainful. He was preoccupied with the fact that Barak's proposed line in the northeast sector ran to the east of the shoreline. "We can't do that," Asad had declared. It was as if he had come to Geneva to say no to the president. Clinton had emphasized that there would be no deal without the strip of land around the lake in Israel's hands. "Then things will stay as they are" was Asad's nonchalant response. Clinton agreed: "The land is in Israel's possession and they can keep it for a very long time."

When Dennis briefed Barak in his Knesset office twelve hours later, Barak's first response was emotionless and uncomplicated. "It means Asad doesn't want peace. I highly appreciate what the president did. He unveiled Asad's position. I can't see a continuation with this man. We'll have to wait for a change of power there." Barak moved immediately to a discussion of his next step: Israel's unilateral withdrawal from Lebanon. It was typical of Barak that he had developed a strategy with several branches. If one plan didn't work, he simply switched to the next, with no apparent regret and no sentimentality.

CLINTON TOLD ASAD in Geneva that given the narrowness of the differences, historians would have a hard time explaining why there was no peace deal with Syria. Looking back, on one level the explanation is straightforward: when Asad was ready, Barak was not; and when Barak was ready, it was too late for Asad. He, like Barak, had become preoccupied with internal politics, in his case ensuring the succession of his son. He no longer had the time or energy to attempt a deal with Israel as well. Just as in U.S. dealings with Iran, the time was out of joint.

Yet that explanation will not suffice. Arabs, particularly Palestinians, often argue that the Middle East conflict is caused by Israeli occupation of their land, that if only Israel would agree to withdraw fully from the territory occupied in the June 1967 war, there would be peace and security for all. But four Israeli prime ministers—Rabin, Peres, Netanyahu, and Barak—had offered Asad full withdrawal, and he had received repeated assurances from Bill Clinton that Israel would withdraw to the June 4, 1967, line. And in Geneva in March 2000, Clinton presented the Syrian leader with a map that had the Israeli line of withdrawal drawn on it, a line that was indeed based on the line of June 4, 1967, with territorial compensation for some minor adjustments that would have given Syria the equivalent of more than 100 percent of the territory it lost in 1967.

To be sure, Israel had conditions and requirements related to its security and the nature of peaceful relations that would pertain between the two countries. But these were no more onerous than those that had been agreed to by the Egyptians and Jordanians in their peace treaties.

Much of the blame, therefore, has to be attributed to the lack of leadership on the part of Hafez al-Asad. From the start of the effort in August 1993, to its demise on Lake Geneva in March 2000, Asad continually demonstrated a cautious, grudging approach to peacemaking. As one of the leading representatives of the old Arab order, which depended on conflict with Israel to sustain it, he hesitated to step beyond its bounds to make the hard and risky decisions that would have put his nation on a course to a more peaceful future.

Asad was certainly capable of such decisions. He was the unchallenged leader of Syria: he had thoroughly and ruthlessly suppressed his Sunni fundamentalist opposition. Since then the only challenge he had faced was from his brother Rifat, who spent the 1990s languishing in exile, plotting his return to power no doubt, but presenting no serious threat to Asad's leadership. Every other political challenger was in jail. There were no organizations or parties capable of threatening Asad's Baath party rule. The military officers were loyal and the army so thoroughly penetrated by Asad's intelligence apparatus that if they weren't loyal they would not have survived.

The problem was not that Asad lacked the capability of decisive leadership or that he was, as his son Bashar is today, a brash and less experienced leader. For example, his decision in 1976 to send the Syrian army into Lebanon was a momentous move that ended the civil war there and established a three-decade occupation. Similarly, Asad's decision in 1990 to side with the United States against Saddam's invasion of Kuwait, and even to send forces to the front line to appear (if not to fight) alongside coalition forces, was a risky and courageous about-face.

In other words, Asad was hardly lacking in the "right stuff," that combination of careful strategic calculation, courage to take risky decisions, and ability to persuade his people (by one means or another) to follow his lead. What was holding Asad back was a deep uncertainty about the costs and benefits of making peace with Israel. He was ever mindful of the fact that he headed a minority regime of Alawites, whose religious beliefs were regarded as heresy by mainstream Syrian Sunnis and whose iron grip on power was resented by the Sunni business elites of Damascus and Aleppo. For four decades Asad had been able to mobilize his people against the Israeli threat, justifying their economic backwardness, the diversion of resources, and most important, the maintenance of repressive state control of individual liberties. Making peace with Israel meant risking his regime in a far more fundamental way than any of his other difficult decisions had entailed.

This insecurity was evident in Asad's fear that his own people would assassinate him, not an unreasonable concern given the assassinations of Sadat and Rabin. By committing to peace, Asad would be undoing decades of unremitting hostility toward Israel that he had spoon-fed to his people on a daily basis through his government-controlled media. When Asad had apparently decided to go for a deal in 1995, this same media had been ordered to start preparing public opinion, and it did so with considerable professionalism. Billboards across Damascus proclaimed: "We fought with dignity; we will make peace with dignity." Editorials explained why it was in Syria's national interest to make peace and what Asad meant when he had declared that peace was a "strategic choice" for Syria. At the time, Farouq al-Sharaa recounted to us how he had gone before the Revolutionary Council of the Baath party to explain to them why Asad was making peace and had been well received. These activities were indicative of the way that Asad had the capability to turn Syrian public opinion around if only he had the confidence to conclude the deal with Israel.* But he did not.

The same insecurity manifested itself in his obsession with the line of June 4, 1967. This proved the greatest obstacle to the achievement of a breakthrough because it was, on the face of it, an unreasonable demand. On every other front, Arab leaders, including the Syrian-controlled Lebanese government, were prepared to accept the international boundary as the border. But Asad repeatedly insisted that if he didn't regain every inch of territory that Syria held before the 1967 war, including territory that it had taken by force since 1948, such as al-Hama, his people would not support him. The same rigidity manifested itself in Geneva, even though his usually hard-line foreign minister had adopted a more flexible approach at Shepherdstown. This concern was wrapped up with the issues of "dignity and honor," so important in Arab culture: Syrians could accept peace with Israel provided their dignity was protected, and Asad had defined Syrian dignity as synonymous with regaining every inch of territory lost in 1967.

All of these requirements were in some ways understandable. But they were also excuses for avoiding the painful compromises involved in peacemaking. Asad was never prepared to stand up in front of his people and explain why, for the sake of peace and a better future for their children, it would be necessary to accept anything other than Syria's maximum requirements. His flexibility was limited by his own insecurities more than by the demands of his people.

Peace with Israel threatened Asad's sources of legitimacy and control. It would give the Sunnis a stick to beat him with, by arguing that their president had strayed from the very pan-Arab, anti-Israel orthodoxy that he had done so much to promote in the face of other Arab leaders making peace with Israel. It would also inevitably lead to economic tensions as the opening up of Syria to American and Israeli businessmen created new opportunities for the Sunni-dominated business class to develop independent sources of capital and profits. And it would likely result in increased pressure from the Lebanese for Syrian forces to withdraw from their country once a peace deal had been signed with Israel, thereby loosening Asad's grip on Lebanon and opening himself up to further criticism from opponents in Syria.

---

* By contrast, the Syrian media launched an anti-Semitic campaign in the run-up to the Geneva summit, perhaps an early indication that Asad was not going there to consummate a peace deal with Israel.

Overall, despite moments when he seemed ready to do the deal, peacemaking was too risky a business for Asad to pursue with any vigor. He had become the prisoner of the very Arab order that he had helped to construct and maintain.

Conversely, engaging in a peace process with the United States and Israel, while stopping short of concluding an agreement, held out considerable advantages for Asad. He could avoid being treated like Iraq and Iran, which was certainly possible given Syria's sponsorship of Palestinian and Lebanese terrorism, its efforts to acquire weapons of mass destruction, and its occupation of Lebanon. He would give the United States enough of a stake in the survival of his regime that it would constrain its Israeli ally from taking advantage of Syria's loss of its superpower patron after the collapse of the Soviet Union. Moreover, active engagement in the peace process, with its summit meetings with the president and frequent visits to Damascus by the secretary of state, neutralized American pressure and legitimized Syria in the eyes of much of the world. That is probably why, in the face of Bush administration efforts to isolate and pressure Syria, Asad's son has repeatedly signaled his desire to resume peace negotiations with Israel, why he sent a representative to the Annapolis peace conference in November 2007, and why in June 2008 he began peace negotiations with Israel under Turkish auspices while insisting that the United States would have to be involved for an agreement to be reached.

This strategy suited Asad's purpose for almost all of the eight years of the Clinton administration. Accordingly, whenever we were able to meet the requirements he had leveled on the Israelis, he promptly found something else to demand.

The proof that Asad was more interested in the process than in the result came in that unique moment in December 1999 when he finally decided the time was right to go for an agreement. He simply dropped, just like that, his previous preconditions that Israel commit in advance to full withdrawal—the clearest indication that for much of the rest of the time he was using it as a procedural excuse to drag out the negotiations. He had other excuses, too: the level of the negotiators, what they would negotiate about, the inadequacy of the results of previous negotiations, or whatever else suited his purpose of stringing out the seemingly endless engagement.

His calculus only changed at the last moment when it became clear to him that his time was literally running out. Then he demonstrated that when he was in a hurry he was quite capable of flexibility on procedure and substance. But when he saw the potential backlash in Syria to peace with Israel, it was as if he were living through his worst nightmare and he backed away again.

Because securing an Israeli-Syrian peace agreement was central to Clinton's Middle Eastern strategy, he would obviously have loved to have been able to change Asad's calculus. And on the surface it seems he should have been able to. After all, Syria was in a weak and essentially isolated position, dependent on positive attention from the U.S. president and fearful that he would turn against it, unleash Israel, try to wrest Lebanon from its hands, or push ahead on other negotiations at the expense of Syria's influence. But given that Asad was never prepared to drop Syria's sponsorship of terrorist organizations, Clinton had no basis for lifting sanctions or offering Syria economic incentives. Asad was, in any case, wary of any implication that he might sell Arab "rights" for U.S. aid.

At various times Clinton tried to indicate the size of the pot of gold at the end of the peace rainbow, but to no avail. For example, in February 1996, Toni Verstandig, the deputy assistant secretary of state responsible for Middle East economic development, spent time in Damascus meeting with Asad's economic ministers and representatives of the business community. But that visit only served to underscore to Asad how far he would have to go to deregulate and loosen his control over the Syrian economy before he could hope to draw any material benefit from engagement with the United States. Similarly, after Shepherdstown we arranged for James Wolfensohn, then president of the World Bank, to discuss with Asad the idea of developing an industrial park on the Golan Heights. But this only seems to have convinced Asad that Israeli and Jewish executives were intent on moving into the Golan after the Israeli army withdrew.

As for bigger sticks, Clinton could have threatened to impose more sanctions or demanded that Syrian troops leave Lebanon, but the Syria-first strategy we were pursuing aimed to bring Damascus into the peace camp, not to isolate it. Moreover, in the peace deal Clinton envisaged, Syrian troops in Lebanon would have responsibility for disarming Hezbollah. We calculated their eviction would come over time as peace enabled the Lebanese to loosen Syria's grip.

In any case, in dealing with Asad, as in the rest of the peace process, Clinton was guided by Israeli priorities, and successive governments there clearly preferred to engage the Syrians, which meant that he couldn't set preconditions even if he had wanted to.

Ironically, ignoring Syria might have been the one approach that could have been effective. If his negotiations with Israel had been allowed to languish, Asad would have been left to cut his own deal with the Israelis, or actively oppose the Palestinians and Jordanians as they sought to make their own agreements, an option he chose not to exercise in both cases. Given Syria's strategic weakness, if the door was left open, it is more likely that Asad would have moved through it rather than hung back.

Supporting this theory is what transpired when we adopted a de facto policy of ignoring Syria during the Netanyahu era. Rather than heat up Israel's northern border with Lebanon, or support Palestinian opposition to the Arafat-Netanyahu negotiations, Asad first tried to get our attention by sending Sharaa to Washington in May 1998 to argue that focusing on Syria would help the Palestinian negotiations. Although I recommended that we respond to his invitation to restart negotiations, Madeleine and Dennis demurred because of their concern that it would provide the opportunity Netanyahu was looking for to avoid fulfilling Israel's Oslo obligations. But Asad then decided to open his own back channel to Netanyahu without our knowledge. And in that negotiation, through Ronald Lauder, Asad manifested a flexibility that had not been evident during the four previous years when Clinton and Christopher had pursued him so assiduously.

The same phenomenon occurred when the Syrians were upset that no one thought to invite them to Sharm el-Sheikh in June 2003 for George W. Bush's summit with Arab leaders that presaged the resumption of the Israeli-Palestinian peace process. Bashar al-Asad responded by calling publicly for the Israeli-Syrian negotiations to resume from where they had left off in Shepherdstown. When that offer was met by a complete lack of interest by Bush and Sharon, Bashar dropped all his preconditions. However, as soon as Israel, under Sharon's successor, Ehud Olmert, showed an interest in resuming negotiations, the conditions were reimposed. The same phenomenon asserted itself in the leadup to the November 2007 Annapolis meeting, which relaunched Israeli-Palestinian negotiations. Although barely a reference was made to Syria's issues, the deputy foreign minister showed up nevertheless and spoke of making peace with Israel.

The lesson is counterintuitive but clear: the best way to draw Syria toward peace is, ironically, to ignore it at first and focus instead on the Palestinians, and then see which negotiation holds more promise.

Clinton missed the Israeli-Syrian peace deal for another reason as well. The Israeli leaders he dealt with were constrained by domestic political complications, among them how to hold together a majority coalition in the Knesset and how to win a referendum on the agreement. The halcyon fields of the Golan Heights and snowcapped Mount Hermon were highly valued by the inhabitants of that tiny country. In the absence of real peace, there was no compelling reason to give them up. They provided a strategic advantage that had kept the Syrian front quiet, without peace, for some three decades. It's no surprise that the polling data on which Barak relied so heavily showed that there was no serious constituency for relinquishing the Golan Heights. Conversely, there is a formidable Golan settler lobby capable of playing on the sympathies of a majority of the Israeli public, which prefers the current tranquil status quo to the risks of peace with, in their view, an untrustworthy Syrian partner. It is also an axiom of Israeli politics that the system cannot tolerate concluding agreements that involve painful, tangible concessions on two fronts simultaneously. Israeli leaders have to make the calculation as to where the better opportunity lies or where the need is more pressing.

If the Syrians had been prepared to make clear the sincerity of their commitment to peace and the benefits to Israelis that would flow from it, the minds of more Israelis might have been swayed. If Asad had come to Jerusalem, as Sadat had, Barak's public opinion problem would have been solved. If Sharaa had shaken hands with Barak in the Rose Garden in December 1999, it would have helped tip public opinion in favor of peace. If the Syrians had made any effort to appeal to the Israeli public it would have been warmly received. But the Syrians would not accept that it was their responsibility to help with Israel's public opinion. Try as he might, Clinton could not change this attitude.

Considering Clinton was dealing with a reluctant and risk-averse Syrian leader and his politically challenged Israeli counterparts, one might wonder why we thought that an agreement between Israel and Syria could ever be consummated. And yet, in the winter and spring of 2000, President Clinton came very close, much closer, as we shall see, than in the effort to conclude a final status agreement with the Palestinians. But he was unable to budge Barak at Shepherdstown or Asad in Geneva two months later. What lay behind his ineffectiveness with both leaders at these critical moments?

Clinton was eloquent in warning Barak that he was making a huge mistake at Shepherdstown. Few leaders were able to resist the combination of Clinton's charismatic charm and his political experience in such circumstances. Still, it made no difference to Barak, who was convinced he knew better. Clinton did not threaten Barak with cuts in aid or a reduction in other kinds of support to change his mind because he was convinced that would have been counterproductive. An effective strategy of encouraging Israeli leaders to take risks for peace cannot be predicated on an approach that purposely increases those risks.

However, Clinton could have tried to change Barak's mind with other means. For example, Barak was depending on the president's pollsters for his political judgment. Clinton could have summoned them to Shepherdstown on that fateful last evening to argue with their ultimate boss about the implications of their results and what it would take to change Israeli public opinion. Clinton did offer to come out and campaign in Israel for the agreement, and given his popularity there (twice that of Barak's at that stage), it might have made a significant difference.

To change the perception of the Israeli public and therefore make it worthwhile for Barak to take the risk, we could have supplied new weapons systems, more intelligence sharing, or a defense alliance. That was one of America's traditional peacemaking roles, from the arms and aid package Kissinger negotiated with Rabin for the second Sinai disengagement agreement in 1975, to the huge ongoing aid commitment Carter made to Begin as part of the Israel-Egypt peace deal. Instead of threatening to cut aid at that critical moment Clinton might have actually offered Barak more.

Finally, Clinton could have used on Barak the one tactic that he was never prepared to employ with any of his Middle Eastern interlocutors: the threat to walk away from the negotiations and leave the parties to their own fate. If, on that critical last night in Shepherdstown, Clinton had told Barak—in sorrow rather than in anger—that he was no longer prepared to invest his time and the prestige of the U.S. presidency in the effort to achieve an Israeli-Syrian peace, he might well have succeeded in persuading Barak to rethink his approach. We shall see how shaken Barak was when Clinton refused to take his supposed last, best offer to Arafat at Camp David five months later. It immediately produced a dramatic concession from Barak.

Clinton did not do any of these things because he was operating under the faulty assumption that there would be another round of negotiations in which Barak had said he would reaffirm his commitment to full withdrawal and demarcate the border. We didn't listen closely enough to Sharaa's explicit warnings about Asad's likely negative reaction to his failure to come back from Shepherdstown with an Israeli commitment to withdraw to the line of June 4, 1967.

Herein lies another lesson for future American peacemaking efforts: when the rare moment arises that an Arab leader indicates a willingness to make peace, and reveals a sense of urgency, it is essential to capitalize on it immediately and pursue the opportunity relentlessly until the breakthrough is achieved and the deal is closed.

The Middle East is a region full of actors pursuing complex and obscure agendas that are not served by peacemaking. Any relaxation of the diplomatic momentum opens the door to these players to do their worst. In this case, the backlash was triggered by the unexpected leak of the draft treaty to *Haaretz,* which gave opponents in Syria the ammunition they needed to criticize a regime weakened by the ill health and insecurity of its leader.

Similarly, notwithstanding all of Asad's shortcomings, there remains the nagging sense that Clinton could have done more to move him at that critical moment in Geneva. Clinton might have focused on what we knew from long experience was Asad's stubborn approach to the line around the lake. It was predictable that Barak's requirements would become a stumbling block for Asad. But there were creative compromises that could have been tried. As we've seen, Asad's advisers were prepared to argue with him for a fifty-meter strip around the lake provided Syria's farmers had access to it. Barak seemed prepared to reduce his requirement to a hundred-meter strip or use the receding shoreline as the basis for his claim to land around the lake.

In other words, at that moment in Geneva, fifty meters separated Clinton from the Israeli-Syrian peace deal he had sought from the beginning of his presidency. Clinton could have refused to take no for an answer. He could have asked Asad to go away and consult with his advisers and given him the night to think it over. He could have told him that if the line around the lake was the problem he would summon Barak to Geneva to work up a different arrangement (Barak was waiting for the call). It should not have been beyond the capabilities of American diplomacy to bridge the gap. When we see the extraordinary lengths to which Clinton went a few months later at Camp David and after to persuade Arafat to accept his proposals, it remains puzzling why he didn't try harder.

Given what was at stake for Clinton's Middle Eastern strategy, it was not enough to lead this old Syrian horse to water. Failure would have negative consequences for Clinton's peacemaking efforts as profound as the positive ones if he had succeeded. By now he well knew Asad's rigidities and frailties. He had told us after meeting Asad in Damascus five years earlier that he would work on Asad's mind-set to get him over his insecurities. In retrospect, Clinton should have used all his persuasive powers to cajole Asad into drinking from what the dying leader viewed as a poisoned chalice, but which actually contained the elixir for his country's and the Middle East's salvation.

15

The Road to the Summit

As U.S. ambassador, I had racked up many frequent flyer miles on Israel's aging equivalent of Air Force One accompanying Israel's prime ministers as they flew the well-worn route from Ben-Gurion Airport to Andrews Air Force Base. This time, on July 10, 2000, it felt as if the winds of history were at our backs, speeding Ehud Barak toward a fateful summit at Camp David with President Clinton and Chairman Arafat.

The long flight gave me an opportunity to discuss with Barak how he planned to approach the summit. As we sat on the edge of the double bed that took up almost all of Barak's cabin, he admitted that he had not had sufficient time to prepare for the summit that he alone had insisted upon. He looked exhausted. The dark shadows under his eyes matched his casual black shirt and slacks, a reflection of his mood. He said he had slept for only five hours in the past four days because he had been engaged in a life-and-death political struggle to save his government from a no-confidence vote that would have forced its dissolution the day before his departure for Camp David. He prevailed, but it was clear to all that his government was on its last legs since he no longer commanded a majority in the Knesset.

As we talked on the plane, I therefore expected to hear about Barak's now familiar concern not to appear in front of his public as a *freier*. It would have been understandable in the circumstances. David Levy, his foreign minister, had announced on the eve of the departure for Camp David that he would not be accompanying the prime minister because he believed Barak was giving the Palestinians too much and getting nothing in return. A week earlier, Natan Sharansky, Barak's minister of interior, had taken his Russian immigrant party out of the governing coalition using a similar justification.

Instead, Barak told me that the die was now cast. He felt like an acrobat in full flight, not knowing whether there was a catcher on the other crossbar willing or able to prevent him from falling. While I was contemplating the image of Arafat in a trapeze artist's leotard, Barak explained that he was walking a very fine political line and could easily lose the core of his support in Israel. He emphasized that these issues were profound. "We're dealing with the future shape of Israel," he explained, lowering his voice. "It's essential that the president widen his lens. If you just look at the Israeli-Palestinian situation, it appears that the Palestinians are the victims and Israel has all the cards. But in the bigger picture, we are a very small country in a much larger Arab world. Jordan gives the Palestinians natural *lebensraum*—they know that they can start with a state in the West Bank and then move on to confederation with Jordan and eventually to a Palestinian state on both banks of the Jordan River. Our borders with the Arab world will be determined at Camp David. Israel will at most become a city-state with a large park in the south. These are vital decisions. We're not just dealing with moods."

Detailing his disdain for his negotiating partner, he noted that Arafat "uses his unhappiness as a tactic. He should get an Oscar for his performances." Barak wanted me to caution the president: "I don't want him to allow Arafat to pocket our concessions. We have already gone past halfway in laying out our positions and we only have a hint of his flexibility."

Barak said he was contemplating a major move on Jerusalem but could not reveal his hand early on. He intended to save his Jerusalem card for the endgame, he said. Then he asked a precise question: When is the very last moment that the president must depart for the Group of Eight summit in Okinawa?

EHUD BARAK IS Israel's most decorated soldier. He gained these accolades as a commando involved in daring operations behind enemy lines. However, his signal contribution to the defense of Israel and to the operations of the Israel Defense Forces was his development of the Sayeret Matkal, the army's elite commando unit. At the heart of Barak's concept of operations was the time factor. Operating behind enemy lines was extremely dangerous and sensitive work, given the intense interest of outside powers in the Arab-Israeli conflict. Accordingly, Barak established a strict timeline for any undercover commando operation: it would commence at the moment darkness fell and would have to be completed no later than first dawn. The troops under his command drilled repeatedly within the same time constraints, until they acted like the synchronized parts of a Swiss watch—hence Barak's pastime of dismantling and reassembling clocks. Barak also insisted that an exit strategy always had to be built into the plan, so that if the operation went awry, the unit would be able to extricate itself before dawn.*

This deeply ingrained approach to operations now informed Barak's preparations for the impending Camp David summit. He knew that Clinton was committed to attending the Okinawa G-8 summit from July 21 to 23. The equivalent of first dawn for Barak was therefore the last moment before Clinton had to leave Camp David for Okinawa. He needed to be able to calculate back from that moment to the point when he would have to make his decision to go for the deal or deploy his exit strategy. He had informed Dennis and me a few weeks earlier that, in his preliminary calculations, he expected that he would have to make this decision and put his best offer on the table on the sixth day of the summit.

Barak viewed the summit as a "high-temperature pressure cooker" in which Clinton's task was to put Arafat in the pot and turn up the heat. Based on what he had heard from other experts on Arafat and what he had observed from several of his own face-to-face meetings, Barak had concluded that Arafat would only make a difficult decision when he was cornered and had no other choice. Once Arafat had been backed into that corner, Barak would make his best offer—or have Clinton do so—which would represent Arafat's only way out. If Arafat turned the proposal down, it was essential to Barak that the United States, Europe, and the Arabs regard Israel as having made him a reasonable offer, which would strip Arafat of his much-valued international support.

---

* This planning process was evident in Barak's approach to the Israeli-Syrian negotiations. First dawn for that operation was July 2000, when Barak had promised to be out of Lebanon. If he engaged the Syrians in direct negotiations by the end of 1999, he would have six months to consummate Syrian and Lebanese peace agreements. If that mission failed, his exit strategy was a unilateral withdrawal from Lebanon. When Asad blinked in December, it fit Barak's game plan perfectly. But when Asad refused to send his negotiators back to the table after Shepherdstown, Barak became extremely agitated about the president's travel plans to South Asia and insisted that the Geneva summit had to be in March. When it became clear that there would be no deal with Syria, Barak turned immediately to his exit strategy, executing the unilateral withdrawal from Lebanon ahead of schedule.

If, however, the outcome was to be a breakthrough, Barak had to have the minimum necessary achievements to be able to sell the deal to the Israeli public. Israel still controlled most of the West Bank, a third of Gaza, all of Jerusalem, and all of the borders and airspace of the Palestinian entity, but it would have to give most of those things up to secure an agreement. Therefore, the only way to right the balance, in Barak's calculation, was to demand from the Palestinians the one thing that would enable him to say to his people, "Yes, we gave, but we will not have to give any further." That meant Arafat would have to agree, in return for Barak's tangible, far-reaching concessions to end the conflict once and for all, and end all Palestinian claims on Israel as well.

WHILE BARAK WAS calculating how to corner Arafat, the chairman was figuring out how to avoid his trap. Arafat harbored a desire to bring Barak down. Their relationship had gotten off to a bad start and had gone downhill from there. Arafat inhabited a self-made, mythical world in which he claimed to be the only undefeated Arab general, the engineer who built Kuwait's ports, and the religious expert who had prayed with the Jews at the Wailing Wall. He also believed he was responsible for Barak's victory over Netanyahu because he claimed he alone had delivered the votes of Israeli Arabs.*

But he was deeply suspicious of Barak's intentions. When Barak had served as Rabin's IDF chief of staff, Arafat regularly warned Rabin that Barak was leading a "fifth column" there. When Barak, as Rabin's minister of interior, abstained in the cabinet vote that approved the Oslo II accord in September 1995, Arafat's jaundiced eye sharpened. He also became jealous of how close Clinton and Barak had become, compared to the strains between Clinton and Netanyahu that he had managed to exploit.

Arafat's worst fears about Barak's intentions were confirmed at their first meeting on July 11, 1999. Barak argued that Arafat should consent to focus on achieving a final status agreement that would render moot the Oslo requirement of a third interim Israeli withdrawal from the West Bank (since under such an agreement the IDF would be withdrawing to final borders with the Palestinian state). Although Arafat objected vehemently to the idea, he agreed in the end because Barak

---

* In the June 1999 election, Israeli Arab voter turnout was 75 percent and 95 percent of their votes went to Barak.

promised to implement the second further redeployment that Netanyahu had signed at Wye. However, Arafat was deeply offended during
the negotiations at Sharm el-Sheikh in September 1999, which codified this trade, accusing Barak of demonstrating "the arrogance of
power."*

Arafat had learned to play his hand very effectively by exploiting the
power of the weak. Over many decades he had managed to blackmail
his stronger partners by threatening collapse. But when Barak refused
to heed the threat, Arafat had no choice but to accede and it left a bitter taste.

Arafat also felt cheated by the type of territory that Barak was prepared to offer him as part of the second further redeployment. He was
even more deeply offended when he submitted to Barak's demand that
they focus on negotiating a final status agreement but Barak stalled for
weeks on appointing his negotiators. Then Barak went off in pursuit of
the Syrian deal, neglecting his negotiations with Arafat completely in
favor of "the other woman," as the Palestinians referred to Asad. According to the Sharm el-Sheikh agreement, negotiations for a final status framework agreement were supposed to be completed by February
13, 2000. But that date came and went while Barak and Clinton were
focused on preparing for the Geneva summit with Asad.

For a time, Arafat retained his equanimity, partly because despite
the bad blood between them, Barak did deliver on the second further
redeployment, withdrawing the IDF from an additional 6.1 percent of
West Bank territory. He also released two hundred Palestinian prisoners and opened a "safe passage" for Gazans and West Bankers to travel
freely across Israel.

More important to Arafat, Barak established a back channel to him
using a former Shin Bet officer, Yossi Ginossar, who had also served in
this capacity for Rabin. This Danny Devito–like, cigar-smoking Israeli
spoke fluent colloquial Arabic and had a roguish charm and discreet
mode of operation that endeared him to Israeli prime ministers. Even
Sharon used him as a channel to Arafat in his early days as prime minister. Arafat was fond of "Joe" and trusted him, not least because he
was doing business with him on the side.

---

*   At the last moment, Arafat had demanded that a minor clause his own negotiators
had inserted be deleted from the agreement. Barak saw it as confirmation of Arafat's
manipulative character and adamantly refused to remove the offending clause, even
though it had no value to him.

In February 2000, to calm Arafat while Barak was negotiating with Asad, he used Ginossar to convey a secret commitment that he would give Arafat control of three villages bordering on the Jerusalem municipality—Abu Dis, Azariyah, and Sawahra. The villages were important to Arafat because his authority would then extend right up to the gates of Jerusalem.

Barak never delivered on this secret commitment. He did eventually bring it before the Knesset three months later and managed to pass it in the face of a storm of opposition. But for the first time since 1996, Palestinian gunmen opened fire at Israeli soldiers on the day of the Knesset vote, and Barak balked, fearing that giving Arafat the villages in these circumstances would precipitate the collapse of his government. Thus a gesture that had been intended to build confidence between the two leaders boomeranged, convincing Arafat that Barak's word was unreliable.

Arafat's concerns about Barak's intentions only deepened as the pressure began to mount on him to go to the summit at Camp David. Clinton had earlier promised him that Barak would deliver the villages. In an attempt to recoup his own credibility and ease Arafat's way to the summit, Clinton now pressed Barak to do something for Arafat. Accordingly, Barak decided in mid-June to release three Palestinian prisoners. Given his political circumstances and his belief that Arafat should have done a lot more to control the outbreak of violent Palestinian demonstrations on the day of the Knesset vote, Barak thought the gesture was generous. Arafat saw the release of three prisoners as an insult.

Now more suspicious than ever about Barak's intentions, Arafat insisted that Barak honor the Oslo requirement for a third further redeployment of the Israeli army from the West Bank before the summit was convened. Clinton told Arafat that that was a nonstarter when he came to call at the White House on June 15. Arafat reluctantly accepted Clinton's argument that they needed to use the little time left in his presidency to try to conclude the final status agreement. Arafat, no fool, told Clinton he was fearful that at a summit Barak would try to drive him into a corner and make him look like the guilty party. He therefore sought a promise from Clinton that whatever happened at Camp David, he would not be blamed. Clinton promised him, "Under no circumstances will I place the blame for failure on you."

. . .

GIVEN THE LEVEL of mistrust between Barak and Arafat, the Camp David summit was handicapped from the outset. The issues to be negotiated were so complicated and momentous that confidence and goodwill were essential to the challenge of generating compromise solutions. But mistrust on its own would not have been enough to sink the summit. What complicated matters immensely was the shift in the strategic context that the collapse of the Syrian negotiations had produced.

The failure of the Clinton-Asad summit at Geneva in March 2000, Israel's subsequent unilateral withdrawal from Lebanon in May, and then the death of Hafez al-Asad on June 10, combined to shift all the strategic vectors in the wrong direction for Clinton. In particular, he lost the advantage that peace with Asad would have brought to the negotiations with Arafat. Had he achieved an Israeli-Syrian breakthrough in Geneva, an agreement between Israel and Lebanon would have followed shortly thereafter, obviating any need for a unilateral Israeli withdrawal. And as part of that deal, Syria would have had to prevent Hezbollah from conducting military operations against Israel from a Lebanon that would have had its own peace treaty with the Jewish state.

Moreover, because of Syria's pan-Arab role, its decision to make peace with Israel would have led to normalization of relations between other Arab states and Israel, especially Saudi Arabia and the Gulf Arabs who bore no love for Arafat. Indeed, the Saudis had already stepped up their clandestine contacts with Israel as the Syrian talks moved ahead, with a Saudi promise to upgrade to public meetings once the deal with Syria was done.

All this would have put intense pressure on Arafat to settle for what he could get before the rest of the Arab world normalized relations with Israel. That had always been one of the main advantages of pursuing a "Syria-first" strategy, and it was precisely why Arafat and his negotiators had always been so threatened by the prospect of a breakthrough with Damascus.

With the failure at Geneva, however, Arafat understood that he was now the only game in town; Clinton and Barak had no alternative other than to pursue a deal with him to secure Clinton's legacy and save Barak's prime ministership. Arafat thus knew he could walk away from the deal at Camp David and still survive. Given their desperation, it was a safe bet that Clinton and Barak would pursue him with an improved offer. What he would need, however, was his own exit strategy from Camp David to counter Barak's plan to blame him for any breakdown.

So Arafat and his aides began talking about Camp David as a negotiating summit, the first of a series of meetings that would eventually produce an agreement. Arafat put this proposition to Mubarak at the end of May, when the Egyptian president sought to persuade him to go to Camp David. Palestinian negotiator Saeb Erekat made a similar case to the American peace team in advance of the summit. They were attempting to undermine Barak's concept of producing a "moment of truth" for Arafat in which he would have to make a final decision about ending the conflict.

But try as Clinton and Barak might to resist this Palestinian approach, the new reality was that without Arafat's consent, there would be no agreement, Barak's government would likely fall, and Clinton's days in the White House would end without the peace agreement he had so arduously pursued.

The second deleterious impact of the collapse of Clinton's "Syria first" strategy was indirect. Barak's willingness to offer Asad full withdrawal to a line based on the June 4, 1967, line set a precedent for the Palestinian negotiations. Arafat now had to get the same kind of deal. But on the West Bank, Barak was offering far less than the June 4 line. In addition, Israel's unilateral withdrawal from Lebanon in May 2000 meant that Israel had either withdrawn or had formally indicated a willingness to withdraw *fully* from all the remaining Arab territory occupied in 1967, except Palestinian territory. This only reinforced the Palestinians' sense of entitlement to all the territories in the West Bank and Gaza occupied by Israel in 1967.

These pressures were manifested in the shift of negotiating positions adopted by Abu Ala (Ahmed Qurei), the chief Palestinian negotiator, in the lead-up to Camp David. At the beginning of May 2000, in the first round of secret talks he held with Barak's foreign minister, Shlomo Ben-Ami, in what became known as "the Stockholm channel," Abu Ala had indicated that he could accept the concept of settlement blocs beyond the 1967 line that would be annexed to Israel. He mentioned an area of 4 percent of the West Bank for these blocs.* After the

---

* Abu Ala's fellow negotiator, Hassan Asfour, had also indicated to Ben-Ami that Gush Etzion, a settlement bloc south of Jerusalem, and Gilo, a new southern suburb of Jerusalem, could be annexed to Israel.

IDF's withdrawal from Lebanon at the end of May, Abu Ala insisted that Israel first concede the principle of withdrawal to the June 4, 1967, line. Then he would consider Israel's settlement needs. Abu Ala would maintain this approach into the Camp David summit.

Israel's withdrawal from Lebanon also complicated negotiations with Arafat because it enabled Sheikh Hassan Nasrallah, Hezbollah's leader, to argue persuasively to the Palestinian people that the IDF's retreat from Lebanon proved that the only effective way to liberate Palestine was through force, not negotiations. On May 27, when Arafat traveled to Cairo to consult with Mubarak, the Egyptians found him deeply troubled by the impact of Hezbollah's triumphalism. The master manipulator, who had played on the emotions of the Arab street for decades to pressure Arab leaders to support the Palestinian cause, now complained bitterly to Mubarak that Nasrallah was exporting his violent ideas to the streets of the West Bank and Gaza.

Arafat's sensitivity reflected a debate that had been raging for some time among Palestinian activists about the best way to liberate Palestine. The "young guard," or Tanzim, in Arafat's ruling Fatah party had grown disaffected from the Palestinian Authority and increasingly restless about the failure of the six-year-long Oslo process to end the Israeli occupation. They argued that what the Palestinian cause needed was a new revolution, an uprising not only against the Israeli occupation but also against the corrupt and arbitrary rule of Arafat and the cronies he had brought with him from Tunis. Citing the American and Israeli experience, they argued that the only way to redeem an independent Palestine was "in blood and fire."

The first indication of their inclination to violence came on May 15, 2000, the day of the aforementioned Knesset vote. Palestinians call that particular day the Naqba, or disaster, because it commemorates the establishment of the state of Israel in 1948. During the rioting in the West Bank and Gaza, Palestinian policemen opened fire on Israeli troops for the first time since the Oslo agreement had allowed them to carry Israeli-supplied weapons. When the IDF's sudden withdrawal from southern Lebanon followed soon after, it seemed to the Tanzim as if their argument for abandoning negotiations and resorting to a guerrilla war to force the liberation of Palestine had been vindicated. Hezbollah's message, trumpeted to them over Arab airwaves, had an immense resonance.

But the West Bank was not southern Lebanon and the IDF was intent on demonstrating that what happened there would not be repeated in the Palestinian territories. If the Tanzim chose to follow Hezbollah's example and launch a guerrilla war against Israel, rapid escalation was inevitable. Barak and Arafat were now sitting on a powder keg, and they both knew it.

In the process, Arafat's room for flexibility at the looming Camp David summit had been significantly narrowed. If he agreed to a deal that was rejected by the Palestinian street, violence could well erupt, threatening the survival of his increasingly unpopular regime. If he rejected the deal on offer, the frustration of the Tanzim might well lead to an explosion anyway. However, in those circumstances he would still be able to retain his legitimacy among his people as the leader who had struggled for their interests and had the courage to say No to the United States and Israel. In other words, standing up to Barak and Clinton and choosing to ride the Tanzim tiger was a surer way to survive than risking concessions that might lead him to being devoured by it. Notwithstanding all the other mistakes and failings that doomed Camp David, these adverse strategic developments foretold the outcome.

As THE PRESIDENT'S national security adviser, Sandy Berger was conscious of the broader strategic tapestry, since he dealt every day with the gamut of global and regional issues confronting the United States. Sandy, like Rob Malley and Aaron Miller, believed that the Palestinian issue was at the core of the conflict. However, he had confined his participation to orchestrating the president's participation in Middle Eastern diplomacy and playing the role of coach to the secretary of state and her peace team. Given the president's investment in Middle East peacemaking and the short time left to achieve that goal, Sandy would have loved to take the lead as the president's focus shifted to the Palestinians in the spring of 2000. But his longtime friendship with Madeleine Albright led him to respect her acute sensitivity to her prerogatives as diplomat-in-chief.

Nevertheless, in the lead-up to the Camp David Summit, Sandy was invited to receive an honorary doctorate from Tel Aviv University and this gave him a rare opportunity to make his own firsthand assessment of the chances for success. He arrived in Israel in mid-May, during the outbreak of Palestinian violence associated with the Naqba. In his meeting with Arafat, he emphasized that the president had only eight months left in office; it was therefore time to step up the pace. Arafat agreed, proposing intensive negotiations in the region before moving to the summit, while warning that the situation would explode if no progress were made. This conversation highlighted the problem: the dynamics of the process were putting pressure on the United States rather than Arafat.

Sandy's conversation with Barak was also troubling. Barak argued that the very preparations Arafat was urging on us could not possibly work because they required Israel to keep demonstrating greater flexibility while the Palestinians responded with generalities. This could only worsen Barak's domestic political position by giving his opponents ammunition to use against him when his concessions leaked, as they inevitably would.

On Jerusalem, an issue that had barely been discussed between the United States and Israel, Barak explained that he would have to be able to tell the Israeli public that Jerusalem within its municipal borders would remain the united capital of Israel. Sandy responded that Jerusalem was for the Palestinians what Lake Kinneret was for the Syrians: "We thought it was a matter of meters but for them it turned out to be a matter of principle." Barak observed that the issues surrounding Jerusalem could not be deferred if there were to be an "end of conflict" agreement. It was, he said, a conundrum.

This was driven home during a dinner I hosted for Sandy at the ambassador's residence. Around the table were many of the key Israeli and Palestinian players, Abu Mazen, Nabil Shaath, Yasser Abed Rabbo, Yossi Ginossar, Amnon Lipkin-Shahak, Haim Ramon, and Yossi Beilin among them. They were by now good friends, having spent many years trying to resolve their conflict. Tempers flared, however, as soon as Sandy raised the issue of Jerusalem. Saeb Erekat explained that the Palestinians would have to have sovereignty over all the Arab suburbs and all of the Old City with the exception of the Jewish Quarter and the Wailing Wall. Haim Ramon exploded at this suggestion, arguing vehemently that the Israeli public would never accept any division of Jerusalem let alone Palestinian sovereignty in the Old City. An agreement on Jerusalem was simply a bridge too far. It would be folly, Ramon argued, to go to a summit unless there was agreement in advance to defer the Jerusalem issue.

• • •

FOR TWO MILLENNIA, Jews had mourned the destruction of their Holy Temple in Jerusalem, had solemnly sworn never to forget the Holy City, and had constantly prayed for God to bring them back to it, "next year." When Israel's takeover of the Old City in 1967 placed the Temple Mount in Jewish hands again, many interpreted it as divine intervention. The Knesset had immediately passed a law annexing East Jerusalem, including the Old City, to Israel. And from that moment, an undivided Jerusalem as the eternal capital of Israel and the Jewish people became the essential expression of Jewish nationhood. This mantra took on such mythical proportions that any Israeli politician could jeopardize his career by daring to suggest that Israel should relinquish control over any part of it.

For Arafat, Al Quds (Jerusalem) had likewise become part of the Palestinian nationalist mantra. Palestinian aspirations were not just for an independent Palestinian state but rather an independent Palestinian state "with Jerusalem as its capital." Moreover, the Muslim world had a special connection to the al-Aqsa Mosque that had been constructed there in the seventh century. This third-holiest site in Islam had been built on the platform that the Caliph Umar, the Muslim conqueror of Jerusalem, had erected over the ruins of the Jewish Temple destroyed by the Romans in 70 C.E. A dome was also built over the rock there where the Prophet Mohamed is said to have ascended to heaven. The whole area became known as the Haram al-Sharif, the Noble Sanctuary. Christians also have their own special connection to Jerusalem since it was here that Christ is believed to have been crucified and his resurrection to have taken place. The Church of the Holy Sepulcher, just a short walk from the Temple Mount/Haram al-Sharif, houses both the place of Christ's crucifixion and his tomb.

Given the importance of these holy sites to the Arab and Muslim worlds, Arafat dared not show any willingness to compromise, especially since the Palestinian claim to control there was also hotly contested by the Jordanian, Moroccan, and Saudi kings, whom Arafat believed would not hesitate to condemn him if he accepted anything short of Muslim sovereignty.

Precisely because of these sensitivities, there was a consensus among peacemakers dating back to the 1970s that Jerusalem should be left until last. They assumed that if other contentious issues were resolved, the parties might gain the necessary confidence and trust to agree on the painful compromises that would govern any agreement on Jerusalem. Conforming to this logic, Rabin had insisted in the Oslo Accords, and Arafat had accepted, that Jerusalem should be deferred until final status negotiations were joined. Consequently, until the spring of 2000, the parties had never spoken about Jerusalem. Once they did, the issue was so sensitive that Arafat and Barak would only allow their negotiators to have the most perfunctory discussion.*

Only in mid-June, a month before the summit, did the Israelis hear from the Palestinians that they had to have sovereignty over all of Arab East Jerusalem. However, in return, the Palestinian negotiators were willing to concede Israeli sovereignty over all the Jewish suburbs that had been built there since 1967.

Gilad Sher, who represented the prime minister's office in the negotiations, told me at the time, "We don't yet have a common concept for Jerusalem." Barak was more explicit. He expressed serious doubt to me that the Jerusalem issues could be solved in a way that satisfied both sides. The agreement, in his view, had to make clear that Jerusalem remained undivided under Israeli sovereignty.

By this stage, however, Barak was quietly canvassing experts on Jerusalem for their ideas and began to understand that he could hand at least some of the Arab neighborhoods of Jerusalem over to Palestinian sovereignty. His growing confidence stemmed from the fact that in his consultations he had heard just such a proposal from Ehud Olmert, then the mayor of Jerusalem.

As mayor, Olmert had developed a well-earned reputation for being a staunch defender of a united Jerusalem under Israeli sovereignty. Yet in the spring of 2000 he suggested to Barak that an outer ring of Palestinian villages, including Shuafat, Qalandiyah, a-Ram, Azariyah, and Abu Dis, could be ceded to Palestinian sovereignty without affecting Israel's assertion of sovereignty over the Holy City. An inner ring of Arab suburbs could have shared sovereignty with the potential for them eventually coming under full Palestinian sovereignty. Olmert

---

* Shlomo Ben-Ami and Abu Ala discussed the issue as part of the "Stockholm channel." Ben Ami laid out a proposal for expanding Jerusalem's municipal boundaries to include Jewish settlements around Jerusalem. Israeli and Palestinian submunicipalities would administer the Jewish and Arab neighborhoods of the expanded city. Special arrangements would be made for Arafat to have a corridor for unimpeded access from Palestinian sovereign territory to the Haram al-Sharif and a religious committee led by Morocco, Jordan, and Saudi Arabia would oversee Palestinian administration of the Muslim holy sites.

told Barak that if he made this kind of offer at Camp David, he would support him publicly.*

Olmert was a leading member of the opposition Likud party. If he were prepared to defend such an arrangement, Barak had a much better chance of gaining broad Israeli support. By mid-June, then, the Israelis and Palestinians seemed to be moving toward an approach that might give Clinton a chance to find a workable compromise at least on the suburbs of Jerusalem.

However, on the question of the Temple Mount/Haram al-Sharif, Arafat was moving in the opposite direction. On June 25, Shlomo Ben-Ami and Amnon Lipkin-Shahak met with Arafat and, among other things, broached Barak's ideas on Jerusalem. Arafat hit the roof. When Ben-Ami then suggested deferring the issue for two years, Arafat responded by waving two of his fingers: "Not even for two hours." Arafat went running to Mubarak to complain. This occasioned a warning to Clinton from Mubarak. He emphasized that unless Arafat had real sovereignty over the Haram al-Sharif, some Muslim would assassinate him.

Mubarak's warning certainly registered with Barak. In an unusual meeting in which he briefed his coalition party heads on the presummit negotiations in the presence of Dennis Ross and me, Barak noted that Arafat would not accept Israeli sovereignty on the mosques in Jerusalem. Explaining the conundrum, he noted, "Yasser Arafat will never be able to sign an agreement that will make him a traitor in the minds of the Arab world. And [on Jerusalem] we cannot accept certain things at any price. We have vital interests related to the very roots and identity of the Jewish people—we will not be who we are if we give it up."

Because of Barak's flexibility on the East Jerusalem suburbs, we chose to focus our diplomatic energies on that issue. On June 30, Clinton suggested to his team a bridging formula that he believed he could sell to both sides at the summit: the Arab neighborhoods of Jerusalem would come under Palestinian sovereignty; the Jewish neighborhoods would remain under Israeli sovereignty; and the Old City would enjoy

---

* In the lead-up to the Annapolis meeting in 2007, Prime Minister Olmert spoke in the Knesset about this idea. Recalling the drawing of Israel's municipal borders after the Six-Day War, he said, "Was it necessary also to include the Shuafat Refugee Camp, Arab A-Sawachra, Waleja, and other villages and declare 'This too is Jerusalem'? Of this, I must confess, I am not convinced." See Prime Minister Ehud Olmert's Speech at the Knesset Session in Memory of Rehavam Zeevi, October 15, 2007.

a special status that would effectively defer the issue of sovereignty there. When Clinton called Barak on July 1, however, Barak would only agree to Palestinian sovereignty over the part of Abu Dis that was inside the Jerusalem municipal borders and the northeastern suburb of Shuafat, and only if they were necessary to close the deal.

The president did not feel this was good enough. Albright and Berger took it upon themselves to press Barak on the issue through secure phone calls. Although Barak did not give either of them anything more tangible, Berger came to understand that Barak would in the end be willing to accept the president's idea, as long as some aspects of Palestinian sovereignty on the inner suburbs were conditioned by an Israeli veto over planning and zoning issues.

These exchanges on Jerusalem were critical to the belief of Clinton and his advisers that a deal was possible on Jerusalem. Yet we had no solution—except deferral—for the problem of sovereignty over the Temple Mount/Haram al-Sharif. If Arafat managed to acquire sovereignty over the Arab suburbs of Jerusalem, I thought, it would be a huge achievement for him and for his people. Since control of the Haram al-Sharif had by then passed from Jordanian into Palestinian hands through the Palestinian-controlled *waqf*, which managed religious affairs there, deferring sovereignty would have simply led to maintenance of the status quo. If Arafat had a sovereign corridor from Palestinian territory to the Haram—as Ben-Ami had proposed to Abu Ala—then Muslim access was ensured as well. I therefore believed that we had a reasonable chance of bridging the evident gap.

This wishful thinking extended to other issues where Clinton's team believed that we had the "tools and devices" to overcome the differences. On the all-important issue of West Bank territory, Barak had introduced a formula—80 percent of the settlers absorbed into settlement blocs on some 8 percent of the West Bank—that allowed for over 90 percent of the territory to be ceded to Palestinian sovereignty.* On the Palestinian side, we had heard from two key Arafat advisers, Mohammad Dahlan and Muhammad Rachid, that 92 percent might be acceptable to Chairman Arafat as long as he was compensated with Israeli land for the West Bank territory he would have to give up.

We had also been encouraged by an unexpected development in Is-

---

* Barak told Albright when she visited him in Jerusalem at the end of June that he was ready to talk to the president about offering over 90 percent of the West Bank to the Palestinians.

raeli thinking. At the outset of the spring 2000 negotiations, Barak had been arguing that for security reasons Israel would have to retain control for a period of ten years over a strip of territory in the Jordan Valley that ran along the Jordan River, representing about 10 percent of the West Bank. However, because in early May the Palestinian negotiators had stormed out when this idea was shown to them on a map, the IDF planning branch had come up with a more reasonable approach. Israel would cede sovereignty in the Jordan Valley to the Palestinians but retain control over a strip along the Jordan River for three years. After that, control would be handed off to a U.S.-led multinational force, in which the IDF would participate. Israel would seek to alter its borders slightly in the northern part of the Jordan Valley to enable it to deploy its forces quickly southward in the event that it became necessary to cut off the valley from an advancing army coming through Jordan. The Palestinian state would also have to guarantee the IDF unimpeded access for emergency purposes into the West Bank.

We thought Barak's willingness to give the Palestinians their eastern border with Jordan provided us with a tool for persuading them to accept adjustments to their western border with Israel to allow for the settlement blocs. Indeed, as I already noted, in the first "Stockholm channel" meeting, which occurred between Abu Ala and Shlomo Ben-Ami in mid-May 2000, Abu Ala had indicated that territorial adjustments to take account of settlement blocs along the Green Line would be acceptable to the Palestinians.

The Israeli approach still left the Palestinians some 8 percent short of a full Israeli withdrawal from the West Bank to the line of June 4, 1967. In this regard, Abu Ala had introduced the idea of territorial "swaps" to make up the difference. On this basis, we thought it was reasonable to assume that the sides were close enough that the leaders at a summit meeting could resolve the territorial issues.

We engaged in the same rationalization when it came to the issue of Palestinian refugees. Here the sticking point was the Palestinian demand that their refugees be conceded the "right of return" to the homes of their forefathers in Israel. For Palestinians who had fled or had been forced from their homes during Israel's War of Independence, the dream of returning to their towns and villages had been nurtured during decades of subsistence in refugee camps scattered through Gaza, the West Bank, Lebanon, Syria, and Jordan. And descendants of these original refugees had been fed on the same myth.

Rather than arrange for their resettlement in the places where they now lived, the PLO insisted that their status as refugees be maintained and it clung to a clause in the nonbinding U.N. General Assembly Resolution 194, passed in 1948, that called for their return to their homes.

From the Israeli perspective, the Palestinian claim to a "right of return" was seen as threatening the survival of the Jewish state by swamping the country with refugees who would eventually tip the demographic balance against a Jewish majority in Israel.

The gap between the parties on this issue was obviously very wide. However, in the lead-up to Camp David we did not view it as insurmountable.

So on all the key substantive issues—Jerusalem, territory, settlements, security, and refugees—we believed we could see a way to bridge the gaps through a variety of technical mechanisms. It was the triumph of American hope over Middle Eastern experience, a victory for solutionism over defeatism.

Other factors were at play as well. Clinton was in the last six months of his presidency; it was natural for him to be thinking about his legacy. An Israeli-Palestinian peace that ended the conflict would be a lasting, historic achievement acclaimed by Americans and the international community alike. No doubt it would also wipe away the Monica Lewinsky stigma. But he needed to make his move sooner rather than later because in August the Democratic convention would select Al Gore as the party's candidate for president. Clinton did not want to look as if he was trying to steal Gore's thunder.

Barak was also relentlessly pressing Clinton to convene the summit. Compared to the political risks Barak was prepared to take, the historic decisions he was prepared to make, and the certain consequences of failure for his political future, hesitation on the president's part would have been small-minded.

Perhaps more important at that moment, however, was Clinton's realization that he really had reached the end of the negotiating road. He has been criticized for going to Camp David ill prepared. But the simple truth is that there were no more preparations to be done: Barak was not willing to offer any more concessions except at Camp David; Arafat would not move off his principles.

The president was also aware of the explosive potential of the situation: tensions were building in both Israel and the Arab world. As early as February, Ami Ayalon, the head of the Israeli general security services (Shin Bet), had cautioned me, "We can't go through the summer without an agreement because there will be an explosion of popular violence."

On July 4, 2000, with the clock ticking on Clinton's presidency and Barak's governing coalition, and with the belief that failing to act would result in an explosion, President Clinton made the decision to invite Arafat and Barak to Camp David. He made the judgment that it was better to try and fail than not to try at all.

16

Trapped at Camp David

Marine One, the president's shiny green Sikorsky Sea King helicopter, banked steeply to give its passengers a bird's-eye view of the presidential compound, where we would spend the next tumultuous fifteen days. Ehud Barak, however, wasn't paying much attention to the picturesque sight of verdant trees, manicured lawns, and log cabins. We had spoken little since transferring from his aircraft into the presidential helicopter at Andrews Air Force Base. He had asked me again when the president would have to leave for the Okinawa summit. Having checked in the meantime, I informed him it would be on July 18, eight days from then. Barak went silent.

On the other hand I couldn't suppress my excitement. I had studied and written about what transpired at Camp David in September 1978 when Jimmy Carter, Anwar Sadat, and Menachem Begin had negotiated the Israel-Egypt peace treaty. As a doctoral student in Canberra, Australia, I had pasted on my office door a poster of Sadat, who had become a hero to me for his courage to break the mold of Arab hostility to Israel. In preparation for this summit, I had written a memo to the president about the way Carter had succeeded then by pursuing the attainable rather than the unachievable—a separate Israel-Egypt peace agreement instead of one linking it to the resolution of the Palestinian issue. The sense of history was palpable even though Clinton was about to attempt what Carter dared not.

Barak was the last leader to arrive at Camp David, delayed by his domestic political crisis. Madeleine Albright was waiting to greet him at the helicopter pad and escort him to his lodgings. At Camp David, vehicle traffic is restricted and travel around the compound is either by foot, bicycle, or golf cart. Madeleine took off with Barak in one cart and I followed in another. As we rode through the woods, past quaint cabins named after the trees that grew there in abundance, it felt as if we were riding in toy cars through some halcyon magic kingdom.

It took only a few minutes to arrive at the intersection of paths that ran between the president's cabin and the lodgings of the other two leaders. Barak's cabin, Dogwood, was located up the hill, a stone's throw from the president's Aspen Lodge. Arafat's cabin, Birch, was a little farther away, some one hundred yards to the east. As we disembarked from the golf carts, Clinton emerged from the presidential lodge, golf club in hand, on his way to the driving range to practice his swing.

After welcoming Barak and directing him to his cabin, the president turned toward me and we embraced. In 1992, at our first meeting, I had told him that he would have the opportunity to achieve four peace agreements during his presidency. After the signing of the Oslo Accords in 1993, I had told him "that's one." After the signing of the Israel-Jordan Peace Treaty in 1994, I had told him, "Two down, and two to go!" Now I said to him, "Well, Mr. President, we missed the third but we can still get the fourth."

He put his arm around me, shaking his head, his words capturing his uncertainty: "At least we get the chance to bat, Martin; at least we get the chance to bat."

THE STRATEGY PREPARED for the president by his advisers was borrowed from the first Camp David summit, when President Carter's staff had prepared a framework agreement that Carter presented to Begin and Sadat; Carter then shuttled back and forth between their cabins to bridge the differences between them. We knew fairly well by now the positions of both sides and believed we had the concepts for creating bridges between them.

The initial challenge of any peacemaking plan is that it survive its first encounter with reality. Clinton's didn't. We had told both sides that on the evening of July 13 (the summit's third day), after the president returned from a speaking engagement to the NAACP in Baltimore, he would present them with an American draft of a framework agreement. In preparation for that, Albright briefed the Israeli and Palestinian teams on the contents. Her briefing was bound to generate hostile reactions from Barak and Arafat, each of whom, in advance of the president's opening gambit, wanted to demonstrate that he couldn't be pushed around.*

When the president was briefed on Barak's objections, he inexplicably decided to drop the "parameters" paper we had planned to present to both sides. Instead we were instructed to draft a new paper that outlined the positions of the two sides and suggested different options for bridging the gaps between them. This was a much softer form of intervention that allowed both parties to avoid any early concessions. Members of the Israeli team were confounded. They informed us later that Barak's strong reaction to the preview of the first paper was a bargaining tactic. They never imagined that we would respond to their negative comments by dropping the paper altogether.

The Palestinians for their part felt Clinton was trying to foist an Israeli paper on them. When we came forward on the evening of July 13 with the milder paper, the Palestinians were still suspicious. Arafat read the section on Jerusalem, saw an option of expanding Jerusalem to include Abu Dis, interpreted that as meaning Barak was trying to buy him off with a capital outside East Jerusalem, and peremptorily rejected the second paper.

Instead of holding fast in the face of predictably negative reactions, the American team caved again. When the Palestinians met with Madeleine and Dennis to express their strong objections to the description of the Palestinian positions in the second paper, they were told that they could develop their own. Saeb Erekat asked Dennis whether that meant they could reject the American paper. When Dennis answered affirmatively, they did! As Akram Haniyah, the Palestinian chronicler at Camp David, wrote in his diary, "The Palestinians won another round."

In the course of forty-eight hours, the United States had backed down twice. Barak and Arafat could only interpret this as a sign of weakness. Unfortunately, this would become a familiar pattern.

One reason for our capriciousness and improvisation lay in the asymmetrical nature of our relations with the two sides. Israel was our ally and Clinton was strongly committed to its security and well-being. The United States had no such commitment to the Palestinians, although Clinton identified with their aspirations for independent state-

---

* Barak objected to language that established the principle of Israeli withdrawal to the June 4, 1967, line; Arafat exploded when his aides told him that the issue of Jerusalem would only be addressed in general terms.

hood. The long-standing principle of "no surprises"—which Clinton had adhered to with each Israeli prime minister since the beginning of his presidency—applied at Camp David, too. Clinton would coordinate the American positions with Barak before they were presented to the Palestinians. If Israel's prime minister objected he would make adjustments, confirming the Palestinian perception that Clinton was just repackaging Israeli ideas in American wrapping.

A second problem was that the president was not the only one thinking about his legacy. This generated a jockeying for positions of influence on the American team, intensifying the tension between Madeleine Albright and Sandy Berger even though they were close friends. The only State Department participants Sandy allowed into the president's inner sanctum where strategy was deliberated were the secretary, Dennis Ross, and Gamal Helal, the Arabic translator; they were outnumbered by the five White House officials.* Dennis was the only person in this group of eight who had any experience negotiating Arab-Israeli agreements but he became just one voice in the cacophony.

In the critical bilateral meetings with Arafat and Barak, the president usually only took with him an NSC note taker (Bruce Riedel or Rob Malley). This stood in stark contrast to the way he operated at Wye Plantation during the previous Israeli-Palestinian summit, when Dennis alone accompanied him to every meeting. Sandy and Madeleine had stood on the sidelines at Wye. This time, if Dennis were to accompany Clinton to the meetings with the leaders, Albright and Berger would insist on being there, too. That meant four aides would have had to accompany the president. Barak and Arafat would then have included four of their own aides, rendering the meetings too large and formal for creative interaction. Consequently, Dennis did not attend those critical meetings; he was therefore dependent on readouts from the note-takers, who rarely had enough time to supply a fully rendered report of what had transpired. Dennis had to offer advice to the president based on partial information.

WITH HIS INITIAL approach thwarted, Clinton turned instead to pressing the two sides to improve their own offers. Since he knew that

---

* The White House team comprised Sandy Berger; John Podesta, the chief of staff; Maria Echaveste, the deputy chief of staff; Bruce Riedel, the senior Near East director at the NSC; and Riedel's deputy, Rob Malley.

Barak was willing to make bold concessions, the challenge was to persuade the Palestinians to begin to do the same. Once there was some give-and-take, things could move forward. His initial focus was on the territorial issue but negotiations on this quickly deadlocked. After three days of futile efforts to break the impasse, an increasingly frustrated president asked the two sides to meet and put maps on the table with their territorial offers.

The Israelis and Palestinians had been meeting for two hours in Holly Lodge, Anwar Sadat's accommodation during the first Camp David summit, when Clinton surprised them by joining the negotiations. Ben-Ami reported to him that he had put an Israeli map on the table that showed a Palestinian state in 86 percent of the West Bank but that Abu Ala would not put a map down because he argued that the borders of the Palestinian state had already been established by U.N. Security Council resolutions, that is, the June 4, 1967, lines. Clinton chided Abu Ala to do more than just reject the Israeli map. Abu Ala politely refused. Borrowing language from the Israeli-Syrian negotiations, Clinton then suggested that he discuss the Israeli map on the assumption that the agreements would be "based on the June 4 line." Abu Ala demurred. The president implored him, suggesting that he would get territorial swaps in return. Abu Ala again refused. Ben-Ami then asked Abu Ala how he could say no to the president of the United States, who was surely the greatest friend of the peace process. This created the impression of the United States and Israel ganging up on him. Abu Ala dug in his heels even further. The president's face reddened and he shouted at the Palestinian chief negotiator, "This is a fraud. It's not a summit. I won't have the United States covering for negotiations in bad faith. Let's quit!" And with that the president signaled Madeleine and they both stalked out.

Abu Ala's stubborn refusal to engage in a territorial give-and-take at Camp David stemmed from a complex combination of motivations. A shrewd negotiator, he believed that if he conceded on the principle of the June 4 line, the Israelis would be able to justify all manner of changes in the border based on their security concerns. Moreover, Barak was insisting on introducing another principle into the negotiations—the need for territory beyond the June 4 line to concentrate 80 percent of the settlers in three blocs. Israel controlled the territory and the Palestinians did not have the military means to force it to withdraw. Therefore, Abu Ala's most effective weapon in negotiations was what he repeatedly referred to as "international legitimacy," the principles en-shrined in U.N. resolutions. He also knew Israel needed Palestinian consent to make peace, and saying no would drive up the price.

Beyond these tactical considerations lay a particular Palestinian mind-set. From their point of view, all of historic Palestine was right-fully theirs and had been taken away from them by force. In accepting Security Council Resolution 242 they had explicitly recognized Israel's right to control 78 percent of the territories of the Palestine Mandate. Now they argued it was unfair to be expected to bargain over the 22 percent that encompassed the West Bank and Gaza. Just like Arafat, Abu Ala would be judged by his people according to one standard alone: how much of that 22 percent he gave away.

The anger and emotion expressed by the president—in front of the Israelis—left Abu Ala dazed. He was humiliated and deeply offended. He withdrew from the negotiations and repaired to his bedroom, where he stayed in his pajamas for most of the rest of the summit.

The effective sidelining of Abu Ala had a deleterious impact on the fate of the negotiations because Arafat depended on him and Abu Ma-zen, his other principal deputy, to come up with creative compromises and to lend him support in selling them to Palestinian constituents. Arafat often played them off against each other, but he needed them both in harness if he were to go for a deal at Camp David. Unfortu-nately, in the lead-up to the summit, we had managed to alienate Abu Mazen too. Dennis and Gamal Helal had arranged for his arch-rival, Mohammed Dahlan, to be hosted by Sandy Berger in the White House. This convinced Abu Mazen that the United States was supporting Dahlan for the succession to Arafat and thereby conspiring to rob him of his birthright as the number two official in the PLO. Abu Mazen's conviction was reinforced in the early days at Camp David when he witnessed how closely we worked with Dahlan, who together with his political ally, Muhammad Rachid, were the only Palestinians who seemed keen to achieve an agreement. Like Abu Ala, Abu Mazen dis-engaged from the negotiations, even departing Camp David for several days to attend his son's wedding.

NEVERTHELESS, ON THE sixth day of the summit, July 16, we fi-nally felt something give on the Palestinian side. The previous night, Clinton had orchestrated a "marathon" negotiation between Shlomo Ben-Ami and Gilad Sher on the Israeli side and Saeb Erekat and Mohammed Dahlan on the Palestinian side. The all-night session had been set up as a "simulation," so that whatever the negotiators put on the table explicitly did not commit their leaders. This stipulation had allowed Ben-Ami to go beyond his instructions—something he was wont to do anyway—and make a far-reaching offer: 90 percent of the West Bank, an eastern border on the Jordan River for the Palestinian state, sovereignty in the outer suburbs of Jerusalem, and "custodianship" for Arafat on the Haram al-Sharif. The Palestinians took down every word of the Israeli offer. Erekat said that the Palestinians could accept Israeli sovereignty over the Jewish neighborhoods of Jerusalem, including the ones built beyond the June 4 line, in East Jerusalem. But the Palestinians had again refused to respond on the West Bank territorial issue except to insist on equal territorial swaps, and had raised a new claim for damages for the years of Israeli occupation of the West Bank and Gaza.

This had provoked a harsh, formal démarche from Barak to Clinton, which Danny Yatom delivered to me on the afternoon of July 16. Noting that Ben-Ami's informal offer had seriously increased the risk to Israel's security, Barak declared apocalyptically that he did not intend to preside over the collapse of the Jewish state at Camp David. He argued that "only a sharp shaking of Arafat" by the president would change the situation. "He has to see that he has a chance to achieve an independent Palestinian state that lives in peace and cooperation with Israel or the alternative of a tragedy where the U.S. will stand by Israel."

Since the president was scheduled to leave for Okinawa in two days, Barak was operating on the assumption that we were moving into the period he had defined as the endgame and he wanted to put Clinton on notice. "It is now or never," he warned. "Only if Arafat comes to understand that this is the moment of truth will he move." Warning the president that the Palestinians were pushing him to the verge of a confrontation, he declared that when Israelis understand how far he was ready to go, "we will have the power to stand together unified in such a struggle however tough it will become. . . . There is no power in the world that can force on us collective national suicide."

The president needed no prompting from Barak to "shake" Arafat. He was at that moment having a tough confrontation with the chairman. He had hoped that the all-night negotiating session would finally generate a basis for him to shuttle between the leaders to conclude the deal. Instead the Palestinian negotiators were taking baby steps, and the consensus in the American team, from the president on down, was that Arafat was responsible.

Clinton told him as much. No other Israeli prime minister would have ever contemplated going as far as Barak, he asserted. Yet in response Barak had heard nothing meaningful from Arafat. Clinton said he saw no point in continuing and suggested ending the negotiations if that was what Arafat wanted.

Seeing the president visibly upset, Arafat resorted to one of his tactics when finding himself in a tight corner: he lied. Invoking the name of his "peace partner," Yitzhak Rabin, he claimed that Rabin had already promised him 90 percent of the West Bank years ago. He complained that the Israelis had introduced a new demand that Jews should be allowed to pray on the Haram al-Sharif, which he denounced as a perfidious Israeli scheme to undermine Muslim control there.*

Arafat should have known better than to try this out on the president. Clinton revered Rabin and had spent many hours in private conversations with him. He knew that Rabin had never contemplated giving the Palestinians more than 80 percent of the West Bank and that Palestinian sovereignty in any part of Jerusalem was out of the question for the man who had defended the city in 1948 and had reunified it under Israeli control in 1967.

The president exploded in anger. He refuted Arafat's claims and dismissed his complaint about Jewish prayer on the Temple Mount, declaring that it would not be part of the agreement. He then made an explicit threat of blame: "If you continue talking like this, I'll say [publicly] that Israel agreed to give up 90 percent of the West Bank and part of Jerusalem and your response was that no Jew can pray on the Temple Mount!" He told Arafat he was giving up an opportunity to achieve an independent Palestinian state with its capital in Jerusalem and its border on the Jordan River, insisting that Arafat respond to the Israeli concessions or he would call it quits.

Arafat was shaken by the president's anger. But his reply represented an instinctive effort to employ the tactics of the weak in the face of

---

* The idea of a place for Jews to pray on the side of the Haram al-Sharif had originated with Eli Rubinstein and Isaac Herzog, two of Barak's advisers, who were observant Jews. Barak thought it might help him secure the support of the religious parties for the deal on Jerusalem. Yossi Ginossar had raised the idea with Arafat in one of his informal meetings with the chairman early on at Camp David and reported that he was considering it.

pressure from the strong. He threatened collapse. "If I accept the Israeli offer," he said, "there'll be a revolution. I will be killed!"

Caught between Arafat's unwillingness to move forward and Barak's insistence that we force him to do so, the president convened a meeting of the American delegation to consider our strategy. At this very moment when we thought we were staring defeat in the face, Saeb Erekat interrupted our deliberations to deliver a written message from Arafat for Clinton.

The note explicitly stated that Arafat would accept a territorial compromise that would involve Israel annexing settlement blocs and compensating him with territorial swaps that were not necessarily equal in size and value. He was apparently leaving it up to the president to decide these issues. It appeared that he was also willing to accept Barak's demand for an end-of-conflict agreement. And his formula on refugees did not explicitly mention the "right of return" (although the reference to U.N. Resolution 194 was a way of introducing the right of return through the back door). There was just one catch: it was all conditioned on Palestinian sovereignty in Jerusalem.

Given the impasse that we had been confronting for the previous five days over the territorial issue, Arafat's proposal appeared to be unusually flexible. Of course, the formulations of his proposals were vague enough to leave him plenty of room to maneuver should the United States and Israel take up his offer. And it was vintage Arafat in that it raised as many questions as it answered. Indeed, Clinton's team took some time to decipher exactly what Arafat was putting forward. But in the end, the conclusion was clear and unanimous. As the president said, "We have to devote our efforts to Jerusalem."

When the president gave an upbeat report on Arafat's offer that evening, Barak had a similar response: "Good, now let's get Arafat to give up on Jerusalem." His mood had changed dramatically from the dire distemper he had displayed only a few hours earlier.

Looking back at that break point in the negotiations, it's possible to see that Arafat, ever the artful dodger, had laid a trap for Clinton and Barak. And they had now both taken the bait. Jerusalem was Arafat's escape route from what he expected would be an attempt to impose a solution on him in the last days of the summit. He could stake his flag to this cause and survive to fight another day. It was reasonable for Arafat to demand that the sovereignty issue in Jerusalem be addressed since Barak had defined this as an "end of conflict" negotiation. If by some miracle Israel would concede sovereignty in East Jerusalem and on the Haram al-Sharif, he could return from the summit a hero of the Arab and Muslim worlds. But if, as was much more likely, the American-Israeli offer on Jerusalem fell short, he would stand fast in the face of what he could describe as an attempt to deprive Muslims of their rights in the Holy City. Akram Haniyah described the Arafat mind-set:

> Yasser Arafat was aware . . . that he was fighting a battle in the name of the Palestinian people, the Arab people, the Islamic nation, and also Christians. . . . He had to defend the Holy City, with which immortal names were associated, beginning with the Caliph Umar Bin-al-Khattab, and ending with Saladin al-Ayyubi.

Arafat was narcissistic enough to imagine himself following in the footsteps of these two great heroes of Muslim history. He made repeated references to them at Camp David. Moreover, for decades he had promised his people that he would reconquer Jerusalem and that the Palestinian flag would fly over its ramparts and minarets. By invoking the names of the great caliphs, however, he was not only building his self-image as a mythological figure, he was also trying to establish a red line in the negotiations.

If he was like Umar and Saladin, he could not settle for less than conquering the Holy City. What that meant was that Israel and the United States would have to surrender the Old City to Palestinian sovereignty, just as Sophronius the Byzantine patriarch had first surrendered it to Umar in 637 C.E.

FOR THE NEXT two days, the American team labored under the illusion that we were headed for a breakthrough on Jerusalem. On the morning of July 17, the president assembled his advisers to discuss how to resolve the issues involved. It was a halcyon scene: the president encircled by all of us sitting on the stone patio at the back of Aspen Lodge, overlooking his private chipping and putting green that had been carved out of the surrounding forest. But despite the apparent calm, the president's mind had been churning. He told us he had slept badly. For a person of faith, his restlessness was understandable. We were now about to touch the holy of holies. No American president had ever taken on responsibility for trying to negotiate a solution to the highly complex, extraordinarily sensitive issues involved with Jerusalem. But Clinton had set his mind to the task.

As he listened to the briefing from Jonathan Schwartz, the State Department's deputy legal adviser, Clinton seemed to relax. Jonathan had a genius for finding legal concepts and formulations for closing seemingly unbridgeable gaps in the negotiations. In this case, he had devised a matrix of alternative versions of sovereignty in which the arrangements could differ in the various sectors of the cities.

Schwartz suggested several solutions but in the one he preferred Arafat could have a diplomatic compound on the Haram that would be inviolable Palestinian space, like an embassy, even though the overarching sovereignty would remain in Israel's hands. Under this arrangement, the U.N. Security Council could name Arafat the "custodian" of the Muslim holy sites, much as the king of Saudi Arabia was the custodian of the holy sites of Mecca and Medina.

This was a typically American way of dealing with a complex problem: break it down into categories, use functional divisions to find pragmatic solutions, and then cover these arrangements with a façade of sovereignty that was supposed to satisfy both sides' needs. As the president observed, "We've got to get the functions right and then the packaging. The Israelis will have to let Arafat have some of the symbols [of sovereignty]." Just as in the run-up to Camp David, we managed to convince ourselves that if we developed a reasonable and fair approach, the parties would accept it.

Clinton's mood was now upbeat. He called me over while he was eating lunch with his daughter, Chelsea, on the patio of the main dining facility at Laurel Lodge. He wanted to test an idea that he had been discussing with her. "I think we're going to make it," he declared. "But then we're going to have to sell it to the Israelis and Palestinians. How do you think they'd react if I spent time over there explaining the agreement to both sides?"

I encouraged him, pointing out that among Israelis and Palestinians alike he was more popular by far than their own leaders. Barak and Arafat would need all the help they could get to sell the painful compromises to their respective publics, if indeed Clinton could broker an agreement. His presence there would have a huge impact. Perhaps, I suggested, he could bring some Arab leaders to Israel, too. The president responded enthusiastically: he was ready to spend most of the

American election campaign in the Middle East, believing it would be more helpful to the Democratic candidate than if he spent that time campaigning in the Midwest (where it would turn out that Al Gore did not want his help anyway).

Clinton maintained his optimism throughout the afternoon, even when he had short meetings with Barak and Arafat to hear their opening positions on Jerusalem. Barak emphasized that he could not agree to Palestinian sovereignty in the Old City or on the Temple Mount. On the other side, Clinton heard from Arafat that he had to have sovereignty over most of the Old City, including the Haram al-Sharif.* The gap was obviously wide but Clinton still thought that a pragmatic formula on sovereignty would serve as the bridge.

From the first night at Camp David, a strictly informal back-channel exchange had been taking place. Amnon Lipkin-Shahak, Shlomo Ben-Ami, and Yossi Ginossar would sit with Muhammad Rachid and Mohammad Dahlan on a narrow, dark veranda outside the cabin that Lipkin-Shahak and Ginossar shared. There they drank scotch, smoked Yossi's Cuban Cohiba cigars, shelled pistachios, and exchanged jokes. From time to time, Dennis, Rob Malley, and I would join them. Casually, someone would raise an idea and it would generate a discussion. We were using the informal nature of the exchanges to test the limits of the other side. None of the participants in this discussion was authorized and everyone understood that they would have to sell the developing package to their principals.

In the exchanges that day, Amnon and Shlomo had suggested an arrangement in which the Palestinians would have sovereignty over two Arab suburbs in the northern reaches of Jerusalem and one in the south, a "sovereign regime" in part of the Muslim and Christian quarters of the Old City, and functional autonomy in the Arab inner suburbs. Arafat would be the custodian of the Haram al-Sharif.

When Rachid broached these ideas with Arafat, however, he sent the rivals of Dahlan and Rachid to Albright to reject them categorically. Abu Ala made clear to Madeleine that Arafat saw no point in pursuing such discussions because the basic concept was wrong—if Israel wanted an agreement, it would have to recognize the principle of Pal-

---

* In this meeting, Arafat told Clinton he was prepared to concede Israeli sovereignty over the Wailing Wall and the Jewish Quarter of the Old City.

estinian sovereignty in all of East Jerusalem, including the Old City
and the Haram al-Sharif.

Arafat was making clear in advance of the evening's climactic engagement on Jerusalem that there was no room for compromise. Madeleine was dismayed. "Failure here could open a period of violence that
could last for years," she said.

"So, we'll wait," said Abu Ala.

"That's not good enough. Sovereignty is not indivisible. It needs
some creativity from your side as well," Madeleine cajoled.

These warning signs did not seem to bother Barak any more than
Clinton. I had run into Barak on my way to Madeleine's meeting with
Abu Ala, and found him, as usual, preoccupied with the timetable for
Clinton's departure for Okinawa. Oddly, he wanted to discuss the day
after a putative agreement was reached on Jerusalem. He said that if
the president left for Okinawa before all the other issues had been finalized as well, word would leak of the Jerusalem deal, putting him in
political jeopardy at home. I tried to reassure him without revealing
that the president had just arranged to have Vice President Gore represent him at the G-8 meeting if absolutely necessary.

Since Arafat had made his counterproposal the previous afternoon,
the ball was now in Barak's court to respond. He had promised Clinton he would outline his position on Jerusalem by midnight. So, that
afternoon he convened all his aides on the back porch of Dogwood
Lodge for a marathon deliberation. In Sayeret Matkal terms, he had
reached that critical juncture when he had to decide to go forward into
the breach of battle with a daring gambit, or call the whole thing off.
The game had unfolded more or less the way Barak had expected it
would: with twenty-four hours to go before the president's departure
for Okinawa the time had come for the final act. He seemed to have no
qualms about betting everything on Jerusalem: according to several of
the participants in the discussion, Barak, like Clinton, displayed confidence that an agreement with Arafat was in reach.

Those conferring with Barak spent four hours in the most intensive
deliberations on Jerusalem in the history of Israel. Barak opened the
meeting by laying out three options: Israeli sovereignty with special
arrangements for the Palestinians; functional autonomy for Jerusalem's Palestinian residents; or painful concessions to Palestinian sovereignty that would go "all the way" to solving the problem.

Yossi Ginossar, the Israeli team's expert on Arafat, spoke up first.

He believed that Arafat's needs were for "some sovereignty in parts of the Old City" and he felt that joint sovereignty might provide an acceptable solution. Even though Yossi had seriously underestimated what Arafat would insist upon, he had nevertheless broken an Israeli taboo by putting on the table the heretical idea that sovereignty might have to be shared in the Old City.

Dan Meridor, a Jerusalemite and a former member of the right-wing Likud party, bridled at the very idea. He warned that even giving up sovereignty on the outer Arab suburbs would undercut the principle of not dividing Jerusalem; Israel certainly could not contemplate giving up sovereignty in the Old City.

Shlomo Ben-Ami disagreed strongly. Peace, he argued, could not be held hostage by an unwillingness to divide Jerusalem. The outer neighborhoods were not really part of Jerusalem anyway. Why did Israel want responsibility for the 130,000 Palestinians living there? But even if Israel were to concede the outer neighborhoods, he argued, that would not satisfy Arafat's need for some sovereignty in the Old City. Therefore, Barak should consider some kind of sovereign compound for Arafat in the Muslim Quarter with access to the Temple Mount, where Israel would retain "super-sovereignty" and the Palestinians should be offered some kind of "sub-sovereignty."

Danny Yatom, Barak's chief of staff, agreed with Shlomo that there needed to be some form of sovereignty for the Palestinians in Jerusalem but he preferred to give them "functional sovereignty" in the Old City and the inner neighborhoods, with Israel retaining full sovereignty on the Temple Mount/Haram al-Sharif.

Amnon Lipkin-Shahak argued that Israel's interest lay in separation from the Palestinians and that meant giving up responsibility for as many Arab areas in Jerusalem as possible. He agreed with Yossi that the Palestinians would have to have some form of sovereignty in the Old City; otherwise there would be no agreement. He too supported the idea of a sovereign compound for Arafat in the Muslim Quarter but, like Yatom, insisted that Israel retain sovereignty over the Temple Mount/Haram al-Sharif.

Ginossar interjected that a sovereign compound would not be enough to satisfy Arafat. This provoked Eli Rubinstein, Israel's attorney general and an Orthodox Jew, to invoke quotations from the Bible that emphasized that any concession of sovereignty in the Old City was forbidden.

Barak ended the discussion by noting that they faced a historic choice akin to David Ben-Gurion's decision to declare independence and Menachem Begin's decision at Camp David to withdraw from all of Sinai. It was impossible, in his view, to postpone the issue because without an end-of-conflict agreement the Israeli ship of state was heading for an iceberg. Therefore a decision had to be made. To agree to others having sovereignty in the Old City was "as difficult as hell," he said. Some issues, however, were "central to our being," and he therefore swore he would never sign away sovereignty over the Temple Mount.

AFTER SEVEN DAYS and nights the compound at Camp David was beginning to feel like a prison. Indeed, a high barbed-wire fence patrolled by U.S. Marines surrounded the compound. At night, in the absence of street lamps, the place took on an eerie feeling. On this particular night—Monday, July 17—dark, low-lying rain clouds had settled in, obscuring any natural illumination from the moon and stars.

Clinton was impatiently awaiting a visit from Barak, who was to give his response to Arafat's offer. The president would then incorporate Barak's ideas into a new American proposal. Depending on Arafat's response, either a deal would be in the making or the process would crater. One hundred yards away, at the Birch Lodge, Yasser Arafat was also waiting. The leaders were approaching their moment of truth.

If there was progress tonight, Clinton could delay his departure for another twenty-four hours. But if there was no breakthrough, he would leave in the morning for the G-8 summit, where he would have to explain his failure.

Where was Barak? Just after midnight, I was dispatched to find out what was going on. I walked fifty yards up the hill to Dogwood Lodge, where Barak was staying, to inform him with appropriate severity that he was keeping the president of the United States waiting. It was quite normal for the Israelis to be late; like Clinton himself, few of them had any concept of punctuality. But this was no normal night. As I stepped up onto the front deck of Barak's lodge, Gilad Sher opened the screen door and blocked my entrance. He informed me that the prime minister had almost suffocated when a peanut had become stuck in his throat. Gidi Greenstein, Sher's young, muscular deputy, had just applied the Heimlich maneuver, successfully dislodging the offending peanut but winding Barak in the process.

An hour later, Barak had recovered enough to make his way down to Aspen Lodge with Danny Yatom and Shlomo Ben-Ami to lay out his position on Jerusalem to the president. As Clinton listened his disappointment mounted. Barak said he was prepared to offer Arafat sovereignty in only one of the outer Arab suburbs of Jerusalem and a corridor through the inner suburbs to a diplomatic compound in the Muslim Quarter of the Old City adjacent to the Haram al-Sharif. From there, Arafat would have unimpeded access to the Haram and its holy mosques, over which he would be granted custodianship. Clinton knew this was far less than Arafat could be brought to accept. But what really bothered him was that Barak was now offering less than his own aides had offered the Palestinians in the back-channel exchange earlier in the day. And Arafat had already categorically rejected that offer.

Clinton exploded: "I can't go to see Arafat with a retrenchment. Maybe you can sell it to him; there's no way that I can. This is not real. This is not serious. I went to Shepherdstown and was told nothing by you for four days. I went to Geneva and felt like a wooden Indian doing your bidding. I will not let that happen here."

I watched Barak emerge from this exchange with furrowed brow. He looked stunned and perplexed as he walked back up the hill to his lodge, ignoring all of us. The president was still red-faced when I joined him. He turned to me and said, "You won't believe what your friend Barak just did to me!" He recounted what had happened. He said he would look like "an idiot" if he conveyed to Arafat what Barak was offering. I could not square this with what Amnon Lipkin-Shahak had told me after his deliberations with Barak that afternoon. He believed Barak's move on Jerusalem would be far-reaching; it might even cause the collapse of the government, "but at least we will go down fighting for peace," said Amnon.

Barak was obviously holding back his real move until what he calculated was the last possible moment. He was gaming Arafat but he had angered Clinton in the process. I suggested to the president that he call Barak back in and insist that the prime minister level with him. As Israel's best friend, Clinton had a right to know how far Barak was prepared to go, I argued. Then they could discuss the strategy for getting there.

Around 3 A.M., Barak and Clinton met again on the patio at Aspen, this time without aides present. Barak, after swearing the president to secrecy, said he was ready to divide the Old City in two, conceding complete sovereignty in the Muslim and Christian quarters to Arafat. Israel would retain sovereignty over the Jewish and Armenian quarters and the Temple Mount, although Arafat would have custodianship on the Haram al-Sharif. All the outer Arab suburbs would come under Palestinian sovereignty; in the inner Arab suburbs, Israel would only retain control over planning and zoning.

Barak's offer appeared to be so bold and so far beyond what we had expected that the president was dazzled. Surely a breakthrough was in reach.

IT IS IMPORTANT to understand just how profound a concession we believed Barak had made in the early hours of Tuesday, July 18, 2000. Since June 7, 1967, when the commander of the IDF's Paratroop Brigade announced, "The Temple Mount is in our hands," the mantra of every Israeli politician had been that Jerusalem must remain the eternal, undivided capital of Israel. Barak could invoke the memory of Ben-Gurion to justify giving up part of the Old City, as Israel's first prime minister did in accepting the U.N. Partition Plan of 1947. But united Jerusalem, in the years since its annexation by the Knesset in 1967, had become an essential part of the identity and geography of the Jewish state. To divide the Old City and give half of it to Arafat was an act either of extraordinary courage and statesmanship or of pure folly.

Personally, I considered Barak's offer a mistake; he was going too far, too fast. He had done nothing to prepare the Israeli public for such a concession and, given his already weak political position, when such a bold offer leaked it would only accelerate his downfall. Moreover, Barak's concession on sovereignty in the Old City would be the first formal offer made by the government of Israel on the subject of Jerusalem. Barak had led us to believe his opening gambit would be to offer one or two suburbs in the far northern reaches of the Jerusalem municipality to Palestinian sovereignty. Having shared his bottom line with Clinton, he should have stuck with this approach. They could have agreed among themselves that Clinton would offer Arafat something short of that: perhaps Palestinian sovereignty in all the outer suburbs as the first move. Then Clinton might have been able to convince Arafat that he had achieved a huge negotiating victory when the prime minister eventually and seemingly reluctantly conceded sovereignty in two sectors of the Old City.

Instead Barak now wanted Clinton to persuade Arafat that his first offer was in fact his last, best offer. And in Clinton's rush to achieve the breakthrough, and his delight at hearing the extent of Barak's real offer, he wasn't about to hold back. But Arafat's mind did not work like that; such an opening bid was only likely to whet his appetite for more, especially for sovereignty over the Haram al-Sharif.

Still, I felt admiration for Barak's boldness and courage. He had broken the Israeli taboo on the idea of dividing Jerusalem between its Jewish and Arab areas, just as Rabin had broken the taboo on dealing with the PLO. Barak had stretched beyond his political limits; the president's challenge was now to get Arafat to do the same.

Clinton postponed his departure by twenty-four hours and on the evening of Tuesday, July 18, summoned Arafat to Aspen Lodge. The president spoke in somber tones. He emphasized to Arafat the historic nature of the opportunity. He said that Barak had moved well beyond what he had expected him to do. The Palestinians had a chance now to achieve their national aspirations, including in Jerusalem. If they missed this moment, he said, it might never come again. Barak would not survive and another American president might not be willing to engage in the same way.

Clinton pointed out that at the time of the first Camp David agreement there were only five thousand Jewish settlers in the West Bank; now they numbered over 170,000. If there were no agreement, their numbers would continue to grow until there would be no hope for an independent Palestinian state. The president then laid out the elements of a package deal that would constitute the basis for concluding an agreement: 91 percent of the West Bank; a satisfactory solution to the refugee problem; an end-of-conflict agreement; and in Jerusalem, Palestinian sovereignty in all the outer Arab suburbs, a special system of divided authorities for the inner Arab suburbs, Palestinian sovereignty in the Muslim and Christian quarters of the Old City, and Palestinian custodianship of the Haram al-Sharif.

Arafat promised to think about it and went back to his lodge. During the early morning hours of July 19, Saeb Erekat came back with a series of questions about the details of Clinton's proposal. Madeleine and Dennis had already gone to bed. Instead of consulting them, Sandy Berger responded to the questions. Worrying about getting Clinton to

Okinawa, Sandy then told Saeb that the president needed to know whether Arafat would accept his ideas as the basis for concluding an agreement. Saeb responded with a letter signed by the chairman stating that the ideas the president had put forward contradicted the terms of reference for the negotiations and therefore did not constitute a basis for continuing the talks.

Clinton, unlike in his meeting with Asad in Geneva, refused to take Arafat's no for an answer. That morning he visited Arafat at Birch Lodge and did his best to cajole and coerce him to change his position. Arafat "blew me off," the president told us in exasperation. But he postponed his departure for Okinawa by yet another twelve hours and dispatched Madeleine and Dennis to Birch to try again. That ended in a shouting match, with Madeleine stalking out of Birch Lodge after accusing Arafat of "blowing it."

The president called Mubarak, Saudi Arabia's Crown Prince Abdullah, King Abdullah of Jordan, and President Ben Ali of Tunisia, seeking their support as a way of providing Arab cover for Arafat to accept the Jerusalem offer. But when their aides checked with the Palestinian delegation and heard that the Haram would remain under Israeli sovereignty, the effort came to naught. Only King Abdullah and President Ben Ali called the chairman, but they ended up conveying Arafat's complaints to us rather than pressing him to accept Clinton's proposal.

Critics of the American approach at Camp David make much of our failure to involve the Arab states in the summit. They argue that Arafat would have been more responsive had he known that Egypt and Saudi Arabia would support a compromise on Jerusalem. Certainly, we were remiss in our overall approach to the Arabs in the run-up to Camp David and once there. Although they had been briefed in general, no serious effort was made to involve them in the summit preparations. Because Ned Walker, the assistant secretary of state for Near Eastern affairs, who had day-to-day responsibility for dealing with these Arab governments, had been excluded from the Camp David team, he had no way to keep them apprised of what was occurring. And until they received the president's phone calls, nine days into the summit, no other member of the American delegation had bothered to brief them. This was folly indeed, especially since the Palestinians were providing them with a negative spin on what we were doing in their daily updates. Even Barak provided regular briefings to President Mubarak and King Abdullah of Jordan while they heard nothing from us.

Nevertheless, it is unlikely that even if we had actively sought to recruit Arab leaders into the Camp David process, the end result would have been any different when it came to persuading Arafat to accept Clinton's proposal on Jerusalem. Mubarak and Crown Prince Abdullah did not trust Arafat. They would never put themselves in a position where Arafat could accuse them in front of their own people of pressuring him to give up Muslim rights in Jerusalem.

Clinton now sent out his aides to engage with Arafat's advisers in the hope that they might persuade him to change his mind. It was to no avail. Clinton then decided to try one last time with Arafat on the afternoon of July 19. The president again invoked the "historic opportunity" that Arafat was forsaking, the political risk that Barak was taking, the unprecedented nature of the offer on the table, and his own inability to do anything more for the Palestinians if Arafat continued to reject the proposals as a basis for negotiations. Arafat was unmovable; he argued emotionally that he would rather kill himself than accept Clinton's proposal: "The Palestinian leader who can sign the relinquishment of Jerusalem has not been born yet. I will not betray the trust. I will not betray my people."

Then Arafat made a baffling claim: as a religious expert, he said, he knew the ruins of the Jewish Temple were not under the Haram al-Sharif; they were in Nablus! He knew better.* But if he were to admit any Jewish claim to the area under the Haram al-Sharif, it would undermine his insistence that the Palestinians alone had the right to sovereignty there. That would breach the defense he had created for himself.

Critics and defenders of Arafat alike have made much of the fact that he did not make a counterproposal during those critical days at Camp David. This is often ascribed to Arafat's character. As Shlomo Ben-Ami describes it, "He is . . . always fleeing from decision-making." Arafat's defenders, on the other hand, argue that he was preoccupied

---

* Caliph Umar had built the al-Aqsa Mosque on the Temple Mount because he believed that was where Solomon's Temple had stood. Muslims refer to Jerusalem—not Nablus—as the *Madinat Bayt al-Maqdis,* the City of the Temple. Arafat was fond of claiming that when he was growing up in Jerusalem he had prayed with the Jews at the Wailing Wall, part of the Western Wall of the Temple compound.

with avoiding any dilution of the U.N. resolutions that formed the terms of reference for the solution of the Palestinian problem.

The real explanation, in my view, is more straightforward. Arafat had been seeking an escape route from the moment he arrived at Camp David. He found it in the issue of sovereignty over the Haram al-Sharif. What Clinton and Barak viewed as an unprecedented, far-reaching, and generous offer, Arafat saw as a way to avoid an imposed solution. And that is why he rejected it out of hand.

Following this meeting with Clinton, Arafat ordered his delegation to pack their bags.

17

The Collapse

The presidential motorcade was lined up along the semicircular tarmac that connected the lodges of the three principals. The black limousines and SUVs had been waiting for three hours to spirit Clinton and his staff down the fogged-in mountain to Andrews Air Force Base, where Air Force One would fly him to Okinawa. Rain clouds had settled in over the Catoctin Mountains that Wednesday night, July 19, drenching the presidential retreat in an unrelenting downpour. To keep warm, the drivers had left their engines idling, pumping steam from their exhausts into the foggy darkness that had enveloped the lodges. Aides milled around under black umbrellas, like undertakers at a funeral.

Arafat may have concluded the summit was over but Bill Clinton was not yet willing to give up. While the motorcade waited, Clinton shuttled between Arafat's and Barak's cabins trying to arrange for the summit negotiations to continue until he returned from Okinawa. In the twenty-four hours since Arafat first rejected the American proposal, Clinton and Barak had come to the realization that their respective strategies had failed. In fact, all three leaders had been forced to contemplate their options. It was easiest for Arafat to live with the failure. He could walk away as the hero who said no to the United States and Israel over Jerusalem. He also knew that if Barak wanted to save his political skin, he would have to continue to pursue an agreement. Similarly, if Clinton wanted to salvage his presidential legacy, he too would have to try again. That is why in his meeting with Clinton that afternoon he had suggested that the negotiators continue to meet, perhaps in Washington, for another two weeks, after which the leaders could return for another summit.

This proposal was anathema to Barak. He would lose all the advantages of the pressure-cooker environment he had wanted to create at

Camp David and be exposed to a barrage of criticism at home for the far-reaching concessions he had offered. He would look truly like a *freier*, chasing Arafat after the latter had rejected such an unprecedented offer. He wanted to make sure Arafat was seen to be responsible for the summit's failure. Continuing the negotiations after the summit would muddy the waters of blame.

Clinton had felt all along that Arafat would try to drag the United States toward his position without reaching an agreement at this summit. He feared Arafat would then allow the pressure to build as the September 13, 2000, milestone approached, marking five years since final status negotiations had been set to begin under the Oslo process. At that time, Arafat had threatened to make a unilateral declaration of independent Palestinian statehood, which would provoke a confrontation with Israel. In this context, Arafat's proposal to continue negotiations confirmed Clinton's assessment of his tactics. And if Clinton allowed everybody to depart Camp David when he left for Okinawa, he would be confronted with the dramatic headlines of his failure when he arrived at the G-8 summit. The president therefore proposed that everybody keep working at Camp David until he returned from Okinawa.

Barak was only prepared to accept Clinton's proposal on condition that the continuing negotiations would be based on the ideas Clinton had laid out to Arafat the night before. This was of course unacceptable to Arafat. So, in a second meeting with Arafat, Clinton suggested that the two sides focus on Jerusalem in his absence; if that issue could be resolved, they could then focus on all the other issues when he returned. Arafat had no hesitation in accepting this proposal. He would never say no to the continuation of negotiations because then he would look unreasonable. There was always the chance that the Israelis would improve their offer, as they had been doing ever since the inception of the final status talks. If they didn't, he had no problem sticking to his guns on Jerusalem. He had nothing to lose.

Clinton then returned to Barak and told him that *if* Arafat achieved a satisfactory solution on Jerusalem, he would accept the U.S. ideas on the other issues. That wasn't quite true. But Barak understood from this explanation that Arafat had accepted the American proposal from the night before as the basis for continuing the negotiations, and Barak therefore agreed to stay.

Within minutes, Clinton was gone. He had left both leaders believing different things about the basis for continuing the negotiations. Madeleine Albright was left to clean up the mess.

The president had achieved a last-minute reprieve, for which the Israeli and Palestinian delegations were grateful. They had been congregating in the dining hall at Laurel Lodge to say their good-byes when they heard that they were not leaving after all. They spontaneously embraced one another and recommitted themselves to finding a solution. But as Albright set out to clarify the murky premises Clinton had established for continuing the negotiations, the goodwill dissipated.

First she told Barak the truth: "Yasser Arafat did not know acceptance of the American proposals was a condition for staying, while you were told it was." Barak expressed his "deep disappointment," but said he would not make things difficult for the secretary. He accepted her suggestion of informal discussions but emphasized that he would not agree to formal negotiations until Arafat accepted Clinton's proposals.

When Arafat heard from Albright that there would be no formal negotiations in the president's absence, he flew into a rage. He claimed that Barak had tricked him into staying so that he could buy time to form a national unity government at home that would enable him to confront the Palestinians rather than negotiate with them. He said he was offended by the way the Israeli prime minister was ignoring him. "I will not be a slave to Barak," he declared theatrically.

That evening at dinner, in the presence of both leaders and their delegations, Albright fell on her sword for the president: "This was a bad day and it's our fault. The American proposals are now off the table while groups engage in informal discussions." Barak looked suicidal; Arafat looked pleased. As soon as the dinner was over Barak excused himself and walked out. As he stormed past me he muttered, "I'm fed up with this improvisation!"

We had followed Barak's lead but we had failed to deliver the goods. For the third time since the beginning of the summit we had backed down, setting a precedent that would prove impossible to undo.

Barak had good reason to be upset. Both Asad and Arafat had slipped from his grip, leaving him politically exposed, with no gains to show for it. He plunged into what appeared to be a deep depression, isolating himself in his cabin and refusing to see anybody. Two days later he emerged, accepting Madeleine's invitation to visit the Gettysburg battlefield where he expressed great interest in the details of the battle that changed the course of American history. He avoided drawing any parallels with his own battle at Camp David.

MADELEINE, DENNIS, AND the State Department team were now back in control of what was left of the negotiating process, but as we tried to salvage the summit before the president's return on July 23, we soon discovered that neither leader would make any serious concession in Clinton's absence.

Since we were only able to engage in informal discussions, on July 21, Dennis convened in his cabin the most constructive individuals from the two sides to tackle the intractable issue of sovereignty in Jerusalem. Dahlan, Rachid, Lipkin-Shahak, Ben-Ami, and Ginossar joined the deliberations. Both Shlomo and Amnon emphasized to the Palestinians that the Temple Mount was a question of national identity for Israelis. Amnon was eloquent in his anguish. "The Temple Mount is the lock and we don't have the key. All that we have is our heritage and our beliefs. I can't put myself in Palestinian shoes; I have only my own shoes. And I can't give it up. You will have control; your flag will fly there. But if we give up our sovereignty, we give up our dreams— we'll be thrown out of office."

Shlomo spoke of "practical sovereignty" on the Haram for the Palestinians that would upgrade their role, including an office for the chairman, a change in the legal status, and flags. In return, Jews would have to have the ability to pray on the perimeter and a mechanism would need to be established to ensure no excavations took place.

Dahlan said Arafat believed the prayer issue would inject an explosive element into any agreement. Amnon responded that perhaps the only viable solution was to freeze the status for five years. Rachid said that would be dangerous for both leaders. Finally, Dennis ended the emotional but ultimately inconclusive two-hour discussion by declaring that if we didn't find a way to defer the issue we would leave Camp David with nothing.

Unable to break that logjam, Dennis decided to test whether progress was at least possible on the security issues. To lead the discussions, Madeleine pressed George Tenet, the director of the CIA, into service. During the Oslo period, Tenet had developed unique relationships with both the Israelis and Palestinians. Arafat liked to deal with

George because in his mind the CIA was all-powerful and he considered himself Tenet's equivalent as director of the nine competing security organizations he had established in the West Bank and Gaza. Arafat seemed dazzled by George's cigar-chomping, back-slapping, New York City hard talk.

The Israeli relationship with the CIA had also deepened under George's leadership and the Israeli security establishment had worked closely with him on a number of vital issues, including countering Palestinian terrorism. George had put these relationships to good effect during the Wye Plantation negotiations, where the deal he fashioned on security arrangements had enabled Clinton to break through to a wider agreement. We had hopes that he could work the same magic now at Camp David.

Tenet was helped by the fact that he was dealing with pragmatists on both sides. Mohammed Dahlan, as the head of the Gaza Preventive Security Service, was the only one in the Palestinian delegation with security credentials and had already proved to be one of its most constructive members. Shlomo Yanai, the IDF's head of military planning, had developed the concept that would enable the Israeli army to withdraw from the Jordan Valley.

The security negotiations that took place on July 21–22 demonstrated what was possible when people who trusted each other were allowed to work quietly on an understanding. In return for Israeli withdrawal from the Jordan Valley, the Palestinian negotiators agreed to three Israeli early warning sites that would remain in the Judean hills, unimpeded Israeli use of West Bank airspace, and IDF access to designated areas in the Jordan Valley on specified roads in the event of an emergency arising from an eastern front threat. Other issues remained to be resolved but these understandings represented a conceptual breakthrough.*

On the refugee issue, the Palestinians appeared to be ready to consider trading the "right of return" for the reality of a fixed number of refugees actually returning to Israel. In the border negotiations, however, the gap actually widened with Abu Ala offering a 1.5 percent adjustment to the borders and the Israelis countering with 13.5 percent.

---

* They still needed to agree on the definition of an "emergency" that would trigger the IDF's use of West Bank highways. The Israelis also demanded a residual military presence in the Jordan Valley for twelve years, alongside the third-party force that the Palestinians had been prepared to accept.

But in these informal exchanges Abu Ala was at least prepared now to discuss territorial adjustments to the 1967 line.

Accordingly, on the eve of the president's return, Madeleine sent him an upbeat briefing. While she conceded that we had not found an acceptable solution to the sovereignty issue on the Temple Mount/ Haram al-Sharif, she thought that building up Arafat's "custodial" functions there and possibly agreeing to a division of "religious sovereignty" might yet produce the elusive middle way. She told the president that a full deal still remained possible.

Just in case we were unable to resolve the Temple Mount issue, though, she asked us to prepare a fallback: a framework agreement in which the parties would resolve all other issues but defer the sovereignty issues in the Old City for state-to-state negotiations that would be concluded within two years.* We also prepared a no-agreement contingency. In that case, the president could propose that Israel and the United States recognize a Palestinian state with provisional borders in the 42 percent of the West Bank that was already under Palestinian control. State-to-state negotiations would then continue to determine the final borders as well as to resolve all the other issues.

However, in the twenty-four hours between sending Madeleine's positive assessment to the president and his early return to Camp David on July 23, Barak and Arafat made clear that her optimism was not grounded in reality.

Barak told Albright that since Arafat had rejected the ideas proposed by the president before he left, they were now off the table. He wanted Arafat to understand that there was a price to be paid for his refusal of the earlier proposal. Instead of sovereignty over the Muslim and Christian quarters in the Old City, Barak now went back to his old offer of a "sovereign corridor" from the outer suburbs where the Palestinians would have sovereignty through one inner suburb to a "sovereign compound" in the Old City, adjacent to the Haram al-Sharif, where Arafat would have custodianship.

Barak's mind was clearly focused on preparing for the breakdown of the summit. He warned Madeleine that if Arafat declared indepen-

---

* In this proposal the status quo in East Jerusalem would have to be reliably frozen while the northern neighborhoods would come under Palestinian sovereignty in return for Palestinian acceptance of Israeli sovereignty over the Jewish neighborhoods of East Jerusalem. The inner Arab neighborhoods could have self-governing arrangements in the two-year interim period.

dence unilaterally, he would respond with his own unilateral annexation of West Bank territory.

While Albright was meeting with Barak, Tenet was struggling with Arafat, who repeated his by now well-worn talking points on Jerusalem. When George raised the idea of deferring the issue, Arafat said he would be accused by the Muslim world of having "sold Jerusalem to achieve my state." After that meeting, Arafat sent Clinton a letter to greet him on his arrival that cataloged his complaints about Israeli "intransigence" on all the key issues.

The last round of presidential engagement had left both leaders bruised and resentful of each other. While some of their negotiators had used the interval as an opportunity to try to bridge the gaps,* with Clinton's imminent homecoming their leaders' only interest seemed to be to pin the blame on the other for the approaching breakdown.

Upon the president's return, Barak and Arafat repeated to him their indictments of each other, Barak adding for the first time a request that if the negotiations broke down Clinton should move the U.S. embassy from Tel Aviv to Jerusalem. But both were prepared to accept a new round of negotiations between their aides and the president to see if he could resolve the outstanding issues. Clinton felt he could now make more progress with the negotiators than with their leaders, since they respected and appreciated his engagement and, unlike the leaders, they had been attempting to bridge the gaps. For the first time at Camp David, Dennis was brought in to sit by the president's side to help him deal with the details.

The president plunged himself into an all-night session with the security experts, emerging at 5:30 A.M. with agreement on everything except the question of the residual Israeli presence in the Jordan Valley. After a few hours sleep, Clinton was up and at the negotiators again, this time over the refugee issue. But, in contrast to the security talks, the negotiators—Abu Mazen, Nabil Shaath, Dan Meridor, and Eli Rubinstein—were unwilling to translate what little progress they had made in their informal negotiations during his absence into any formal understanding. Clinton's presence could not bridge the gap between the Palestinian demand for the "right of return" and Israeli in-

---

* Dahlan and Yanai were discussing a territorial deal that would have conceded 4 percent of the West Bank for settlement blocs. Saeb Erekat and Gilad Sher were discussing the idea of Israeli sovereignty over Jewish-owned property in the Armenian Quarter of the Old City.

sistence that the numbers of returning refugees be strictly limited and under their unilateral control.*

In the border negotiations, Shlomo Ben-Ami and Abu Ala each presented maps to the president. The Palestinian maps offered the Israelis less than 2 percent of the West Bank for settlement blocs. They had drawn the borders around the blocs as tightly as possible so that they looked like clover leafs or balloons on strings, in which each settlement would be connected to Israel by a road through Palestinian territory rather than incorporated into a block of contiguous Israeli terrain. And the territorial swaps the Palestinians demanded in exchange were no longer adjacent to the Gaza Strip (in the Halutza Dunes) but rather on the Israeli side of the border with the West Bank. This was nowhere near the adjustment Barak or Clinton had in mind, nor close to the "compromise" offer of 4 percent suggested by Dahlan in the earlier informal discussions.

The early morning bloom generated by the all-night security session had now faded. Negotiators who wanted to reach agreement, such as Dahlan and Yanai, were able to make progress as long as their leaders were indulgent or ignorant of what they were doing. But this phenomenon was the exception to the rule at Camp David. In most of the negotiations that took place there, one or the other side was looking to protect a principle rather than find the compromise. That was the hallmark of the refugee and border negotiations. And in those cases, the president learned that to overcome the gaps there he had no choice but to try again to fashion a compromise with the two leaders. Indeed, Arafat had already indicated to Clinton that he would leave it to him to decide the territorial compromise.

At 4 P.M. on Monday afternoon, Clinton therefore decided to take another run at Arafat. The chairman was summoned to the Aspen Lodge, where a stormy meeting ensued. The president threatened to wash his hands of the Palestinian cause. He said ties with the United States would be frozen, there would be no more aid, and Arafat would find himself isolated. "You have been here for fourteen days and said no to everything," he said to Arafat. "These things have consequences;

---

* The Palestinians insisted on recognition of the "right of return" and repatriation of refugees from Lebanon to their former homes in the Galilee and rejected the Israeli demand for compensation to be paid to Jewish refugees who had fled from Arab countries. The Israeli negotiators rejected the "right of return," and would accept only a limited number of refugees—ten thousand over ten years—under family reunion arrangements.

failure will mean an end to the peace process. . . . Let's let hell break loose and live with the consequences."

Arafat was unmoved. With the practiced fury of an accomplished actor, he swore again that he would never relinquish Jerusalem. With rising emotion, he reminded Clinton that he was not just the leader of the Palestinian people; he was also the permanent vice president of the Organization of the Islamic Conference and the defender of Christian rights in Jerusalem! He repeated that the Israelis had no rights on the Haram. The ruins of the Temple were not there, he insisted, and the demand for Jewish prayer there was nothing but a plot to steal Palestinian rights. When Clinton suggested deferral, Arafat said, "Not for one minute!" When Clinton offered Barak's idea of a "sovereign compound" for Arafat adjacent to the Haram, the chairman demanded full sovereignty there. Finally, the performance reached its climax: "Do you want to attend my funeral? I will not wait for them to come and shoot me, I will shoot myself if I agree to relinquish Jerusalem and its holy places."

Exasperated, the president told his aides to think about last-minute ploys that might make a difference. I sought out Shlomo Ben-Ami, who had been one of the most flexible and creative members of the Israeli delegation. We met alone. I told him in grave tones that the summit was ending unless we came up with something. He unleashed a tirade against the Palestinians, who he said suffered from "a surfeit of international legitimacy." But he had been contemplating how to break the Gordian knot over sovereignty in Jerusalem. He outlined to me a new idea: in return for Jewish prayer in the "Moroccan compound" on the Temple Mount and a mechanism to prevent any excavation, Arafat should be offered *"sovereign* custodianship" on the Haram, a kind of mandate or trusteeship that should also include responsibility for security there. Shlomo's idea was to use the word *sovereignty* to describe situations that actually involved encumbrances on its exercise. He extended the concept to the inner Arab suburbs, where the Palestinians could be offered "limited sovereignty," but Israel would have its interests in law enforcement, security, planning, and zoning protected.

It wasn't much to go on but enough to convince the president that he should give it one last try with the Jerusalem negotiators. Erekat and Ben-Ami were summoned to Aspen Lodge at 10 P.M. Clinton reviewed the options before them: declare failure, try to find a compromise on Jerusalem, try to reach agreement by deferring some or all of the Jerusalem issues, or end the summit but announce the continuation of negotiations. Erekat played with the idea of deferring both Jerusalem and refugees. Ben-Ami expressed amazement that a Palestinian negotiator would be prepared to delay solving a humanitarian issue when the president was offering to raise tens of billions of dollars for refugee resettlement and compensation. Saeb then focused on the option he had preferred from the outset—end the summit but continue the negotiations.

Finally, at around midnight, the president put back on the table Barak's original offer to divide sovereignty in the Old City but enhance it by borrowing Ben-Ami's concept of a Palestinian "sovereign mandate" on the Haram al-Sharif with residual sovereignty remaining in Israel's hands.* The president turned to Ben-Ami and asked him whether he could accept the package. Shlomo suggested that Erekat reply first. The president turned to Saeb, who said his instructions were to accept nothing less than full Palestinian sovereignty. Clinton asked him to convey the proposal to Arafat.

Saeb returned from that consultation at 1 A.M. on Tuesday, July 25, with a letter from Arafat thanking the president for his efforts and urging him to continue the negotiations after the summit. "Peace will remember your role," he wrote. In the letter Arafat emphasized that the president's proposals on Jerusalem "do not lead us in the right direction because we cannot accept any Israeli sovereignty in the Muslim and Christian holy places."

At 8:45 A.M. the president summoned the American team to Aspen Lodge for a final meeting. As he went over the draft we had prepared announcing the failure of the summit, he shared with us his gut assessment of what went wrong. "Arafat wanted 100 percent of Jerusalem and gave Barak nothing. He was prepared to give up on a state and a solution for the refugees for Jerusalem. He's no different than any other Arab leader when it comes to doing something for the refugees. Barak on the other hand was courageous and creative. He was willing to take less than one hundred percent and Arafat wasn't. People criti-

---

* In addition, Clinton proposed that the outer suburbs become part of the Palestinian state. In the Old City and the inner suburbs he offered two options: either Palestinian "sovereign self-rule" on the inner suburbs and a special regime for the Old City, or functional autonomy in the inner neighborhoods and Palestinian sovereignty in the Muslim and Christian quarters of the Old City.

cize him for not meeting with Arafat but he was right because the Palestinians were just sitting back and doing nothing."

The president agreed that we had to find a way to continue the talks if we wanted to avoid an explosion, the very thing that had driven us to the summit in the first place. He decided that rather than criticize Arafat directly, he would laud Barak's efforts and damn Arafat with faint praise. As he would tell the press at the White House later that day, "Prime Minister Barak showed particular courage, vision, and an understanding of the historical importance of this moment. Chairman Arafat made it clear that he, too, remains committed to the path of peace."

The conversation turned to what Barak wanted from Clinton to protect him from the political fallout he would encounter when word leaked of his willingness to concede 91 percent of the West Bank and divide Jerusalem. Barak was pressing Clinton hard to move the U.S. embassy to West Jerusalem, at least recognizing that part of the city as Israel's capital to cover for the offer Barak had made to cede East Jerusalem to Arafat. Clinton was concerned about how Arafat would react. "How can I stop Arafat's unilateral declaration of independence if I act unilaterally by moving the embassy?" Nobody felt like answering him. He must have seen the deflated and exhausted looks on all our faces so he tried to encourage us: "We must remain undeterred. I don't want any hangdog expressions out there."

As Sandy Berger and I accompanied the president for his farewell call on Barak, Clinton started swearing: "Goddamnit, I'm going to get outflanked by the Republicans in Congress on the embassy issue. They're going to ram it down my throat. This time I'm going to get out ahead of them." The president had shifted in his own mind from peacemaker back to politician, where Arafat had always been and Barak had never known how to be.

THERE IS A common belief that "we came close" to agreement at Camp David, but the truth is that we were not close at all. Looking back, however, Clinton did make some important progress. Complex final status issues were discussed seriously for the first time, including Jerusalem and refugees. The Israeli negotiators came to understand that there would be no final agreement without giving up almost all of the West Bank and providing compensation for the rest; the Palestinian negotiators conceded that a majority of the settlers would remain in settlement blocs that would be annexed to Israel. Israel found a way to secure its eastern border without retaining control of the Jordan Valley; Palestinians accepted that there would have to be a residual Israeli security presence and other security constraints to make it possible for Israel to withdraw from almost all of the West Bank.

Arafat also made some important concessions that will not be forgotten in any future final status agreement: that the Palestinians would recognize Israeli sovereignty in all the newly built Jewish suburbs of East Jerusalem all the way from Givat Zeev in the north to Giloh in the south and Maale Adumim in the east; that Israel would have sovereignty over the Jewish Quarter of the Old City; and that the Wailing Wall would remain in Israel's hands. Similarly, Barak broke Israeli taboos on Jerusalem by accepting the concept of Palestinian sovereignty over all the outer Arab suburbs, more limited sovereignty over the inner Arab suburbs, and even Palestinian sovereignty in two quarters of the Old City.

Indeed, if Camp David had been billed and organized as a preliminary summit, it might have been treated as a great success rather than a miserable failure. But none of the concessions made by either side at Camp David would probably have been contemplated if this had been just a preparatory summit. Barak was only prepared to make his far-reaching moves in the context of an endgame that he mistakenly believed he was in.

Given the broader strategic circumstances, and the personalities involved, it is difficult to see how any combination of deft diplomacy and negotiating tactics could have succeeded in producing an agreement at Camp David. Arafat went to Camp David to avoid a trap, not to make a deal. Because of the collapse of the Syrian track some three months earlier, he was under no real pressure to change his mind. That frustrated Clinton and provoked his eruptions of anger.

Barak could not understand how it was possible for a weak player like Arafat to resist the importuning and blandishments of the mightiest power in the world. At one point, he asked me: "Tell me, is it possible that the president promised Arafat that if he came to the summit he would not be pressured? Why doesn't he make clear to Arafat that if he doesn't say yes it will be the end of his relationship with the United States?"

Barak was fixated on the idea that Clinton could impose a solution on Arafat. But Arafat found the escape route he was seeking by wrapping himself in the flag of Jerusalem's sovereignty.

Barak has since argued that the real Arafat was unmasked at Camp David: a leader who lacked the character or will to make a historic compromise. He would not accept an end-of-conflict agreement with Israel because his real purpose was the demise of the Jewish state. But Camp David was hardly a good laboratory test for that proposition. In Arafat's response to Clinton on the sixth day, he explicitly accepted the idea of a "finalization of the conflict." But it was not reasonable to expect that Arafat, or any Arab leader for that matter, would agree to an end-of-conflict agreement that left sovereignty over the Haram al-Sharif in Israeli hands forever. Barak explicitly recognized this reality before Camp David. He told Sandy Berger at that time that he had no answer for this conundrum.

Camp David revealed Arafat's true capabilities rather than his true intentions. The master of tactical maneuvering, instead of walking into Barak's trap he managed to set one of his own. He did so not for any grand principle but rather for the base purpose of jumping out unscathed from the Camp David cauldron, to live to fight another day.

There was one approach that might have prevented the breakdown at Camp David. On the territorial and related security issues the two sides were very close to agreement; with concentrated effort the differences could have been bridged (as the president demonstrated on the security issues the night he returned from Okinawa). In the preparations for Camp David, if we had admitted the improbability of resolving all the issues in one summit, we could perhaps have conditioned both sides to the concept of a partial agreement that resolved the West Bank and Gaza territorial issues, ended Palestinian and Israeli claims to each other's land, established a Palestinian state, and set a framework and timetable for agreeing on the other issues.

Clinton did try for a partial solution at Camp David, but only when the effort to achieve agreement on Jerusalem failed. By then it was too late. Here the comparison with Camp David I is instructive. Carter's aides told him that Sadat would never sign an Israeli-Egyptian agreement that met Egypt's territorial requirements unless it were linked to a West Bank agreement for the Palestinians. But at the outset of the summit negotiations, and against the advice of his aides, Carter deleted the linkage from the American proposal. Consequently, he was able to persuade Begin to make a complete withdrawal from Sinai and solve the related security issues, which led to the signing of the Camp David Accords and the Israel-Egypt peace treaty. The Palestinian issues were simply deferred at Camp David I as the Jerusalem and refugee issues might have been deferred in advance at Camp David II.

For the comparison to hold, Clinton would have had to give up on the idea of ending the conflict on his presidential watch—and he would have had to convince Barak to do the same. That would not have been easy. Arafat, in turn, would have had to possess the courage that Sadat showed, and for which he paid with his life. Arafat had none of that stuff. His repeated references to his fear of assassination show how the issue of survival, rather than the idea of putting an end to the conflict, was central to his calculations. And so, in the final analysis, the combination of a flawed strategic context and a lack of leadership would still likely have doomed any alternative approach.

18

Intifada!

By mid-October 2000, Bill Clinton was coming to the end of his presidency; Ehud Barak was fighting for his political survival; and Yasser Arafat was facing a storm of Palestinian resentment. They had come a long way from Camp David three months earlier, all of it downhill.

Barak and Arafat looked sullen and preoccupied at the Sharm el-Sheikh Marriott Golf Resort as they sat in cream leather boardroom chairs around a grandiose semicircular conference table. Back in Gaza and the West Bank a battle had been raging between the IDF and armed Palestinians in what would become known as the al-Aqsa intifada. Already almost one hundred Palestinians and seven Israelis had been killed in the nineteen days that had passed since Israel's leader of the opposition in the Knesset, Ariel Sharon, had visited the Temple Mount/Haram al-Sharif under heavy Israeli police escort. The visit sparked violent demonstrations and exchanges of fire that spread from Jerusalem to every major city in the West Bank and Gaza and even to Arab villages in Israel.

This emergency summit had been organized in an effort to curtail the violence so that a peace agreement might yet be negotiated before Clinton's term expired and Barak's government collapsed. It was reminiscent of March 1996 at Sharm el-Sheikh, when Hosni Mubarak and Bill Clinton had summoned world leaders to an antiterror summit designed to bolster the peacemaking efforts of Shimon Peres and Arafat. At that time, the symbolism of Arab and world leaders holding hands with Israel's prime minister in front of the cameras did little to salvage Peres's candidacy for prime minister.

At least the 1996 summit resulted in a serious effort by Arafat to confront the terrorists in his midst and stop their operations. This time, his glum silence as President Clinton announced the summit results to the assembled press gaggle was indicative of a different approach. Clinton declared that Barak and Arafat had agreed to issue statements calling for an end to the violence and to take concrete measures to stop the confrontations. An American-led fact-finding commission would be established to report on the events and "how to prevent their recurrence," Clinton explained.

While the commission, led by former senator George Mitchell, would begin its work by the end of the year, and Barak would issue his call for an end to the violence, Arafat would do nothing serious to stop the killing. Indeed, one senior Arab diplomat informed me afterward that during the summit Arafat actually sent a message to his Fatah Tanzim youth to "continue to do what you have to do." Within forty-eight hours, the Tanzim were waging a prolonged gun battle with the IDF in Nablus and had killed a rabbi from the West Bank settlement of Kedumim.

Nevertheless, Clinton left Sharm el-Sheikh that afternoon content with the promise he had received from Arafat. "It was the most incredible conversation," he had recounted to us. "Really! No whining. Arafat was sincere. He wasn't gaming me," he said, responding to my skeptical look. His talking points had called for him to tell Arafat in no uncertain terms that if he didn't stop the violence he could forget about any American peacemaking effort for the rest of Clinton's presidency. The president had not followed the script.

Five days earlier, a wild Palestinian mob had stormed the Palestinian police station in Ramallah and brutally murdered two Israeli reservists being held there, dipping their hands in Israeli blood and displaying it to the screaming hordes. Clinton had called Arafat and urged him to condemn the violence but he did not press him to take further action, even though he had received reports that Arafat had released Mohammed Deif from prison on the same day. Deif was the most notorious Hamas terrorist ringleader, responsible for the kidnapping and killing of Nachshon Wachsman, a dual American-Israeli citizen. Deif was also the mastermind of the terrorist bombings that had occasioned the first Sharm el-Sheikh summit where Clinton had personally pressed Arafat to find and arrest him. His release now, in the midst of the violence, could only be read as a signal from Arafat to Hamas to continue their operations, and as a rebuff to the president of the United States.

Clinton nonetheless believed that sympathy rather than pressure was the best way to deal with Arafat at Sharm el-Sheikh this time around. Perhaps he felt he had gone too far in publicly blaming Arafat for Camp David's failure. Perhaps he considered the Israeli army's response in the opening days of the intifada excessive; he questioned me intently on that point in the briefing before his Sharm el-Sheikh meetings with Barak and Arafat. Whatever the reason, instead of up-braiding Arafat when he had the opportunity, he told the chairman how concerned he was at the loss of Palestinian lives. This seems to have triggered a charm offensive in which Arafat, by Clinton's account, praised him as the great hope for peace and expressed his deep appre-ciation for the support he had given to the Palestinian cause. Arafat then made him a solemn promise that he would conclude a peace agreement with Israel while Clinton was still president. Arafat sug-gested Clinton bring the two leaders together again after the American elections in November to consummate the deal.

It was a cunning move that diverted Clinton from pressing Arafat to stop the violence. From that point on, until his last day in office, Clinton would believe in Arafat's promise and it would affect all his calculations as he struggled to find a way to complete the peace agree-ment we had failed to achieve at Camp David.

CLINTON FOUND A willing partner in this effort in Ehud Barak, who, despite supposedly unmasking Arafat at Camp David, neverthe-less still clung to the belief that political salvation lay in the achieve-ment of a peace agreement with him. In retrospect, Barak's decision to pursue an agreement in the face of sustained Palestinian violence and terrorism appears as mistaken a political calculation as Clinton's judg-ment was about Arafat's sincerity.

While Clinton may have been blinded by his desire to complete the job he had begun in the first days of his presidency, Barak continued with his strategy in the belief that it would resolve his political prob-lems. His governing coalition had been reduced to only forty-two seats and the Knesset had passed the first reading of a bill calling for early elections. To survive he had to assemble at least nineteen other votes to pass a budget by the end of the year. He could have sought a national unity government with Ariel Sharon and the Likud; quiet talks between Labor and Likud representatives had been ongoing since August. But the price of that accommodation was abandonment of the positions Ba-rak had adopted at Camp David—something he was not willing to do.

The alternative was to pursue the peace process to its logical conclu-sion. That had the virtue of keeping the left of the political spectrum on board since their raison d'être was the peace process. But it also had the consequence of turning Barak into their hostage; if he abandoned this course, they would turn against him and his government would collapse.

Barak was convinced that if he achieved a breakthrough, he could take the agreement to a referendum or an early election and the Israeli public's desire for peace would result in a renewal of his mandate. However, as the intifada wore on and undermined the public's trust in Arafat and the Palestinians, this became an ever more dubious proposition. But by then his political circumstances had become so dire that he had no choice but to plunge ahead or give up his office.

A more typical politician would have compromised with Sharon even though it meant abandoning the peace process for a while. But, as Barak explained it to me at the time, he was not interested in staying in power just for the sake of it. If he failed to achieve the breakthrough to peace now, he was confident the people would return him to power later.

So Clinton and Barak, having struck their pact at their first meeting in July 1999, now rededicated themselves to the effort. By August 10, barely three weeks after the Camp David collapse, they were already conferring on the dates for a new summit.

Arafat's calculus was at that moment just as desperate. While he returned from Camp David to a tumultuous welcome in Gaza, his reception elsewhere was decidedly chilly. In August, he had embarked on an exhausting tour to make his case in the world's capitals, visiting fifteen countries in eighteen days.* But after marching down all those red carpets and reviewing all those honor guards in his military-style uniform, he had precious little to show for his efforts.

Everywhere he went, Arafat discovered that the United States and Israel had been there ahead of him. Through phone calls or urgent visits by emissaries, Barak and Clinton had prebriefed the leaders Arafat met, explaining their version of what had happened at Camp David.†

---

* France came first, followed by Saudi Arabia, Yemen, Morocco, Tunisia, Algeria, Jordan, and Egypt. Then he made a rare trip to Tehran followed by visits to Moscow, Beijing, New Delhi, Dhaka, Jakarta, and Kuala Lumpur.

† Albright had dispatched Ned Walker on a fourteen-nation tour that included the important capitals of Europe and the Arab world. Barak visited Cairo, Amman, and Ankara; Danny Yatom discreetly briefed the leaders of Bahrain, Oman, Qatar, and the United Arab Emirates; Efraim Halevy briefed Saudi Arabia's Prince Bandar; Shlomo Ben-Ami was dispatched to Morocco, Tunisia, and Europe; and even Shimon Peres played a role, providing briefings in New Delhi and Jakarta.

All the leaders he met with counseled him to return to the negotiating table. The Arabs in particular were unsympathetic. Instead, the leaders of Tunisia, Morocco, Egypt, and Jordan all began to engage with the United States and Israel in efforts to find acceptable compromises, particularly on the Jerusalem issue. Iran was willing to call for an emergency meeting of the Organization of the Islamic Conference to back Arafat's demand for full sovereignty in Jerusalem, but the Arabs would not go along.

In Cairo Arafat discovered that Mubarak, his most important patron, would not even support his call for an Arab League summit. Instead, with the help of Morocco's King Mohammed VI, Mubarak diverted him to a low-profile meeting of the Arab League's Jerusalem Committee, which issued a weakly-worded confirmation of his claim to sovereignty in Jerusalem. Rather than endorsing his demand for full Palestinian sovereignty over the Haram al-Sharif, Mubarak involved himself in an effort to achieve a compromise on this issue.

In an early August meeting between Secretary Albright and Archbishop Tauran, the pope's foreign minister, Tauran clarified that the Vatican had never agreed to Arafat taking control of the Christian holy sites in Jerusalem and preferred that an international regime assume responsibility. When Arafat turned up in Moscow, he was warned by Vladimir Putin, Russia's new president, not to make a unilateral declaration of independence.

So meager was the backing that Arafat managed to garner and so strong the pressure on him to return to negotiations that he quietly shelved his long-threatened unilateral declaration of independence, which it was thought he would make on September 13, 2000.

Discontent was also beginning to surface in the streets of the West Bank and Gaza. Before Camp David there was still some hope that negotiations could produce the dream of unencumbered statehood that Arafat had been feeding his people on for generations. But the word of failure there left Palestinians to contemplate a never-ending continuation of Arafat's corrupt and arbitrary rule, combined with Israeli settlement expansion and the daily humiliation of IDF checkpoints. Increasingly, Arafat found himself caught between the demands of the international community for compromise and the demands of his people for delivery on his promises. True to form, Arafat took advantage of whatever turned up.

· · ·

THE FIRST OPPORTUNITY was a new American initiative. Dennis Ross visited Arafat in Gaza at the end of August to explain that the president was willing to convene a new summit in five weeks, but before he did, he had to know that an agreement was achievable. To test that proposition, Dennis said, the American peace team would consult with both sides and prepare a paper that the president would present to the two leaders. A compromise on Jerusalem would have to be worked out before the summit. The president proposed to meet separately with Barak and Arafat in New York at the U.N. Millennium Summit during the first week of September to see whether that compromise was possible.

This initiative was a mixed blessing for Arafat. Although it confirmed Clinton's and Barak's continued interest in him, Dennis's talk of compromise on Jerusalem signaled that their offer would still fall short of Arafat's requirements. That just reinforced his dilemma of being blamed by his people if he compromised, and blamed by the international community if he did not.

Clinton imagined that he could solve the Jerusalem sovereignty problem one month after we had failed to do so at Camp David in part because he and his advisers were convinced that a little creativity would generate a practical solution. This time also we had the positive engagement of Egypt, the one country that could give Arafat the necessary political cover to compromise on such a sensitive issue.

And amazingly, Barak was willing to be more flexible. In mid-August, he indicated to me that for the first time since Israel had annexed the Old City of Jerusalem in 1967, an Israeli prime minister was ready to give up Israeli sovereignty on the Temple Mount. Sitting in his Defense Ministry office in Tel Aviv, he uncapped his black Waterman fountain pen and sketched a matrix for me with two intersecting axes that created four quadrants. The vertical axis measured degrees of sovereignty, between full "political sovereignty" (P) at the bottom and full "divine sovereignty" (G) at the top. The horizontal axis measured the amount of time allowed for resolving the issue, from open-ended deferral at the far left (D) to immediate resolution at the far right (I). Barak said that any proposal that fell in the outer corners was unacceptable to one side or the other. He then drew a rectangle that overlapped the intersecting axes primarily in the top right-hand quadrant of God's sovereignty, agreed upon immediately. In his assessment this was the domain in which the solution for the Temple Mount lay. It in-

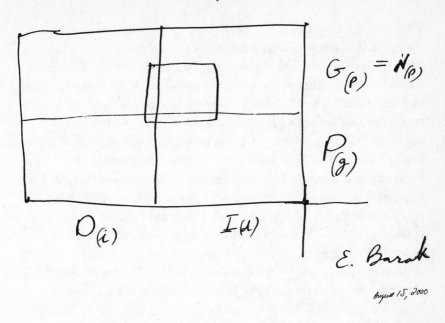

$$G_{(p)} = \dot{N}_{(p)}$$

$$P_{(g)}$$

$$O_{(i)} \qquad I_{(\mu)}$$

E. Barak

August 15, 2000

cluded some lesser elements of political sovereignty along with some elements of deferral.

Although the presentation was abstract, the meaning was unmistakable: he was signaling that he was now prepared to explore the idea that Israel would cede its claim of sovereignty on the Temple Mount to God, provided Arafat was prepared to do the same with his claim to Palestinian sovereignty on the Haram al-Sharif.

The chief Sephardic rabbi of Israel, Rabbi Eliyahu Bakshi-Doron, endorsed Barak's new approach. In a meeting at the end of August he informed me that from a Jewish religious perspective it was vital to ensure that nothing disrupted the ruins of the Second Temple. The place was so sacred, he explained, that it was forbidden for Jews to set foot there for fear of desecrating holy ground. Therefore, in his view, sovereignty was and should remain in the hands of God, and the challenge was to find "guardians of God" who would protect the site and prevent any change in the status quo.* That was precisely the formula

---

* The chief Ashkenazi rabbi, Yisrael Meir Lau, would later tell me that giving up sovereignty on the Temple Mount would betray Zionism and the Jewish people. But Rabbi Bakshi-Doron's opinion carried much more political weight at the time because of the importance of Sephardic religious voters.

King Hussein had advanced in July 1994 in his joint appearance with Yitzhak Rabin before a special session of Congress.

The challenge now was to convince Arafat to relinquish his claim, too. Armed with this new concession from Barak, and its rabbinical sanctification, we went to work on the Egyptians. Barak had already paved the way by sending Israel Hasson, a low-key Shin Bet official who was fluent in Arabic, to meet with Mubarak and his advisers, Amre Moussa and Osama el-Baz. The Egyptian president did not know where the Temple Mount/Haram al-Sharif and the Wailing Wall were actually located. So, armed with maps and aerial photographs, Hasson provided the Egyptians with a detailed briefing. Suitably impressed, Mubarak expressed a willingness to support the idea of sovereignty being assigned to God. But when Mubarak discussed the idea with Arafat in mid-August, he was told that God's sovereignty on the Haram al-Sharif was unacceptable because that might lead to an argument over whose God had the sovereignty. Arafat-inspired commentary in the pan-Arab press suddenly began to accuse Egypt of acting as an "impartial arbiter" rather than serving as "the champion of Arab rights in the face of Israeli expansionism."

Since Foreign Minister Amre Moussa was particularly sensitive to his standing in Arab public opinion, he promptly shifted Egypt's position from supporting God's sovereignty on the Haram al-Sharif to proposing that the whole area be declared "sacred space" in which nobody would have sovereignty. As Moussa explained it, Barak would have to give up Israeli sovereignty over the Wailing Wall if he expected Arafat to give up his claim to Palestinian sovereignty over the Haram al-Sharif.

From Barak's point of view, of course, it was the Haram al-Sharif that was in dispute, not the wall—Arafat had already conceded it to Israel's sovereignty at Camp David. To avoid backsliding, Dennis proposed that the Palestinians have "sovereign jurisdiction" or "religious sovereignty" over the two mosques and that there would be no mention of the wall. Barak then insisted that if the Palestinians were going to have any kind of sovereignty on the Temple Mount, Israel had to have the "residual sovereignty" there. The idea of dissolving the sovereignty had morphed into sharing it.

At the end of August, President Clinton stopped in Cairo on his way back from a trip to Africa and instead proposed to Mubarak to internationalize sovereignty by putting the holy sites in the hands of the

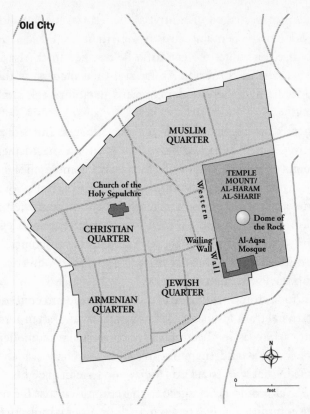

Old City

MUSLIM
QUARTER

TEMPLE
MOUNT/
AL-HARAM
AL-SHARIF

Church of the
Holy Sepulchre

Western

Dome of
the Rock

CHRISTIAN
QUARTER

Wailing
Wall

Al-Aqsa
Mosque

W a l l

JEWISH
QUARTER

ARMENIAN
QUARTER

N

0
feet

JERUSALEM

Security Council, which would take the sovereignty but confer author-ity on the two sides for their respective sites.

Meanwhile, Arafat's mood was darkening. Any formula that re-quired him to dilute his claim to sovereignty over the Haram al-Sharif fueled his anger. He rejected Clinton's proposal of U.N. Security Coun-cil control because none of the permanent members were Islamic states and he would therefore be accused of giving Jerusalem up to the "Cru-saders." He also denied ever more vehemently that the Temple Mount was actually under the Haram. So he did not take it kindly when Den-nis bluntly laid out four choices for him: either he took sovereignty on the Haram and acknowledged Israel's sovereignty on the Temple ruins below it, or he took sovereign jurisdiction of the mosques and Israelis had the same for the wall, or he gave sovereignty up to God, or he ac-cepted that nobody would have sovereignty. Since none of these gave

Arafat the uncontested sovereignty that he felt was his due, he arrived in New York in early September ready for a fight.* Barak's tactics made matters worse. En route to New York, he bragged to the Israeli press about his success in cornering Arafat and then made sure that every world leader he met there understood his flexibility and Arafat's intransigence.

Arafat took his anger out on Madeleine Albright in their preparatory meeting. When she asked him how he could expect Israel to give up sovereignty over the site where the Jewish Temple once stood, he rejected the notion that ruins could legitimize a claim to sovereignty and stormed out of the room. Later, when Clinton suggested a modified version of his Security Council idea, Arafat countered with the suggestion that the Organization of the Islamic Conference's Jerusalem Committee take sovereignty instead and confer "sovereign jurisdiction" on the Palestinian Authority.

Clinton took from this that Arafat was now ready to concede sovereignty on the Haram al-Sharif. But as Arafat would often remind his interlocutors, he was the "*permanent* vice president of the Jerusalem Committee" and would therefore maintain one hand on the sovereignty issue in that way. Israel was to have no sovereign rights. Clinton, knowing Barak would never agree to that, proposed that the membership of the committee be expanded to include other nations that would clearly protect Israeli interests. Arafat left it up to Clinton to convince the members of the Jerusalem Committee to agree to that, knowing that they could not accept non-Muslim nations having a say in the ownership of Jerusalem's Muslim holy sites.

Nevertheless, Clinton and Barak came away from the Millennium Summit meetings with the feeling that Arafat had moved on the Jerusalem issue, and that prospects for an agreement were still good. Clinton now estimated that he had only about five weeks left to reach an agreement. In the third week of September, he told his peace team he was ready to put an American paper on the table as the basis for concluding an agreement.

Barak's strategy still called for maximizing the pressure on Arafat

---

* The pressure Arafat felt at that moment was on display for the world to see when he stalked off the set of a live CNN interview with Christiane Amanpour after she challenged his decision not to sign a deal at Camp David, noting that Barak had gone farther than any previous Israeli prime minister. See Arafat interview with Christiane Amanpour, CNN, September 8, 2000.

to accept or reject the deal in the coming weeks. After his round of New York meetings with world leaders, Barak was satisfied that he had succeeded in costing Arafat his international legitimacy. But in advance of consultations on the American paper he urged Clinton again to threaten Arafat. And he mobilized French president Jacques Chirac, on a rare visit to Israel, to press Arafat to accept divided sovereignty on the Haram/Temple Mount. Arafat was still not buying and, by the accounts of his aides, was becoming more angry and paranoid as the pressure mounted.

But Arafat was capable of disguising his true feelings when it suited him. On the eve of dispatching their negotiators to Washington to consult on the package that Clinton had ordered the American peace team to prepare, Arafat had a rare but cordial dinner with Barak at his home in Kochav Yair. Together they mandated their negotiators to reach agreement. On the way out the door, Arafat gave Barak a friendly warning about the danger of Sharon's imminent visit to the Haram al-Sharif.

The consultations in Washington also appeared to go well. The Palestinians were briefed on the broad details of the positions that the president would advance and, from Dennis's perspective, went home satisfied with the direction of American thinking. Shlomo Ben-Ami, on returning to Israel, assessed that a historic deal was just weeks away.

According to the paper Dennis prepared for Clinton, the Palestinians would get the equivalent of 93–97 percent of the West Bank (in contrast to the 91 percent offered at Camp David). The security arrangements were adjusted to take greater account of Palestinian concerns. Dennis proposed an arrangement for some Palestinian refugees to return to Israel with priority given to refugees from Lebanon but the "right of return" would only apply to the state of Palestine, not Israel. Arafat would have sovereignty over all the Arab neighborhoods of Jerusalem.

However, on the issue of critical importance to Arafat—sovereignty over the Haram al-Sharif—the new offer still fell short of his aspiration. Dennis wanted Clinton to propose a "special regime" for the Holy Basin, which would include the Old City, Mount Zion, the Mount of Olives, and the Garden of Gethsemane. Arafat would have sovereignty over the Muslim, Christian, and two-thirds of the Armenian Quarters of the Old City (compared with only the Christian and Muslim quarters offered to him at Camp David). But on the Haram al-Sharif, an international body would take control; at most, Arafat would have "sovereign jurisdiction" there.*

From Arafat's perspective, we had only managed to heighten his dilemma. If the president presented these proposals and he did not accept them, he would surely face the condemnation of most of the world's leaders, including many in the Arab world. And if he did accept, he would surely be condemned by Muslim critics for giving up sovereignty over the Haram al-Sharif. In other words, if Clinton tabled the paper, Arafat would be trapped with his back against the wall.

Palestinian academic Yezid Sayigh, perhaps the most astute observer of Arafat's behavior, has explained that in such circumstances the chairman would resort to a tactic honed throughout his long career known as *al-huroub ila al-amam*—an escape by running forward. And that seems to have been exactly what he did after Sharon's visit to the Temple Mount.

That visit actually passed without any serious incident, with Sharon respecting an understanding worked out between Shlomo Ben-Ami and West Bank Palestinian security chief Jibril Rajoub that he would not enter the mosque. The Palestinian demonstrations on the Haram al-Sharif ended without serious incident. But the next day, when twenty thousand Palestinians crowded the Haram al-Sharif for Friday prayers, the protesters ran amok and Jewish worshipers at the Wailing Wall below were stoned. The Israeli police moved in and were also greeted by a barrage of stones. Heavily outnumbered, they opened fire, killing four Palestinians and injuring some two hundred others. The following day, protests erupted all over Gaza and the West Bank. The Israeli army faced firing from within the crowds of demonstrators and fired back, killing four in Gaza and another six in the West Bank.

Instead of moving quickly to tamp down the violence for fear that it would render impossible the agreement that was about to be hatched, Arafat sat with arms folded. As he explained to Terje Roed-Larsen, Kofi Annan's special representative for the Middle East, at the time, "The [Israelis] suffer because of casualties. I don't. My people are glorified as martyrs."

Allowing the violence to escalate and the Palestinian casualty count

---

* Israel would have sovereignty over the Jewish Quarter, the Wailing Wall, and the Jewish parts of the Armenian Quarter, the City of David, Mount Zion, and the cemetery on the Mount of Olives.

to climb meant Clinton would have to shelve his proposal (in fact he never had a chance to discuss the paper with his advisers). Arafat could then use the image of Israeli soldiers shooting at Palestinian demonstrators to mobilize the Arab world and generate international condemnation of Israel.* All this would increase the pressure on Clinton and Barak to be more forthcoming as they tried to induce Arafat to turn off the violence. As Yezid Sayigh noted, "Arafat's instinctive reaction was to maintain this advantage, which in a crude sense required a daily death toll." In an Egyptian newspaper interview, Marwan Barghouti, one of the leaders of the intifada, explained that Arafat wanted him to continue the uprising so as to reap the political benefits.

Arafat's ability in this way to turn the tables on Barak almost drove the Israeli prime minister to distraction. "What the hell is happening?" he asked George Tenet, who was visiting Israel at the time. "Arafat initiated violence and the leaders of the world can't tell the truth?"

Unfortunately, Barak now made his own contribution to the deteriorating situation by giving the IDF a free hand in responding to the deliberate use of firearms by the Tanzim. In fact, the Israeli army had prepared for the uprising in meticulous fashion. Military intelligence had issued an assessment in March 2000 in which it judged that the Palestinians were likely to resort to violence to further their objectives. The lesson the IDF wanted to teach the Palestinians was that anyone who opens fire on Israeli soldiers or citizens will be killed. Accordingly, snipers were trained and assigned to IDF units serving in the territories, military positions were reinforced, soldiers were equipped with the latest Kevlar flak jackets, and patrol vehicles were up-armored. Since the army had assessed that the threat would come from armed Palestinians, they did not equip their forces with crowd control equipment such as water cannons and tear gas.

On the Palestinian side, the Tanzim, knowing that the IDF was likely to open fire on those firing at them, decided to take up positions among the stone-throwing demonstrators so that Palestinian casualties would mount.

The impact on the environment for peacemaking was devastating. Palestinians were furious at Israel for the loss of life inflicted on their

---

* The apparent IDF shooting of Mohammed al-Dura, a twelve-year-old child in Gaza, which had supposedly been captured on video by France 2 television, generated widespread international sympathy for the Palestinians.

youth and the increased road closures and army checkpoints that now made normal life impossible. Israelis were furious with the Palestinians for betraying them, using the guns Israel had allowed them to acquire under the Oslo agreements to open fire on their peace partners, desecrating a Jewish holy site (Joseph's Tomb in Nablus), and murdering Israeli civilians.

Arafat discovered fairly quickly that in this instance using violence as a pressure tactic worked quite well. The Arab street grew angry, Arab regimes condemned Israel and demanded American action to curb the IDF response, and the international community rallied around the Palestinians rather than pressing Arafat to compromise. Sure enough, Barak and Clinton started making him better offers.

Israeli military intelligence assessed that Arafat could easily bring the violence under control if he wanted to. Other Israeli security experts, like Ami Ayalon, a former head of the Shin Bet, and Amnon Lipkin-Shahak, a former IDF chief of staff, believed that Arafat was now riding on the back of a furious tiger. At the outset he had every reason to avoid reining it in but as the intifada picked up steam they believed he had become reluctant to try for fear of exposing his diminished authority. This made Arafat unwilling to issue clear-cut orders to his security chiefs to stop the violence and they therefore stood idly by, afraid that their competitors would outbid them if they dared to try. The rivalry Arafat had purposely created between them now helped increase the havoc.

Barak eventually came to understand that allowing the IDF a free hand to teach the Palestinians a lesson only played into Arafat's strategy of exploiting Palestinian casualties to secure greater Arab and international support. By November, Barak was exercising much greater control over his army and police. But by then Arafat had much less control. On their own, they were now unable to end the uprising and return to the negotiating table.

Clinton tried to intervene. Within seven days of Sharon's visit to the Temple Mount, Madeleine Albright was meeting with Barak and Arafat in Paris, attempting to broker a cease-fire agreement that included mechanisms to deal with incidents as they arose and a "fact-finding" commission to investigate the causes of the violence. But at the last moment, French president Jacques Chirac intervened on Arafat's side making him think he should hold out for a better deal.

As soon as Arafat returned to the West Bank, all hell broke loose again.* Clinton then led an intense international diplomatic effort to get him to calm things down. Arafat promised to issue strict orders to stop the violence, but he never did.

Clinton understood he could not proceed with his plan for presenting American ideas to the two parties while the ground was burning under their feet. Instead, after consulting with Mubarak, who had become increasingly worried about the reaction in his own streets, Clinton decided to summon the leaders to Sharm el-Sheikh. His basic objectives were to get Arafat and Barak to declare a mutual cease-fire, agree on the fact-finding commission, and issue a call for resumption of negotiations. The initial vehicle for negotiating this agreement at Sharm was a meeting between the secretary of state, the foreign ministers of Israel, Jordan, and Egypt, and their counterparts in the Palestinian Authority, the European Union, and the United Nations. Within minutes it descended into a shouting match between the Israelis and Palestinians, with the encouragement of Amre Moussa. It was evident that nothing would be agreed on in that forum.†

It was left to the president to work his magic on Arafat and Barak, using Mubarak and George Tenet for reinforcement. That evening, Mubarak, Clinton, Arafat, and Tenet sat out on the porch, with the cool breeze coming off the Sinai Desert. Earlier in the day Tenet had developed a security protocol with Jibril Rajoub, Arafat's West Bank preventive security chief, and Avi Dicter, the Shin Bet head. The president reviewed the steps the Palestinians would take to stop the violence. Arafat, never one for details, especially when it came to controlling his fighters at a time when he had neither the desire nor incentive to do so, simply responded, "Yes, yes! Yes, yes!"

Barak was worried that Arafat would violate the agreement and Israel would have to live with a fact-finding commission that Barak ex-

---

* IDF headquarters were attacked, Joseph's Tomb in Nablus was ransacked by a Palestinian mob, Jewish settlers were fired upon during a funeral, setting off gun battles between Palestinians and Israeli soldiers in the Nablus area that raged for hours, and then the two Israeli army reservists were lynched by a mob in Ramallah. In retaliation, IDF helicopters attacked Palestinian police offices and TV and radio stations in downtown Ramallah and Gaza City.
† This experience provided concrete evidence of the problems involved in trying to negotiate Israeli-Palestinian issues in an international forum. The Arabs would always line up behind the Palestinians in an effort to put Israel in the corner, and the United States would have no choice but to come to Israel's defense. This would lead to a polarization that made rational discussion, never mind reasonable compromises, impossible.

pected would condemn it for its response to the Palestinian-initiated violence. So he insisted that the commission be established by Clinton and headed by an American who would report to the next president.

Clinton accepted both points and persuaded an amenable Arafat. The next morning the press assembled to hear the president read the agreement. Afterward, Clinton returned immediately to Washington, taking George, Madeleine, and Dennis with him. Nobody from Washington stayed on in the region to follow up. Indeed, with the exception of an overnight visit by Dennis to Israel in November for the funeral of Leah Rabin, we would not see a single senior member of the Clinton administration in Israel again. For the next three months, the two sides were left to implement the Sharm el-Sheikh agreement by themselves.

Given Arafat's promise to reach an agreement before Clinton left office, something the president was determined to achieve, it was odd that Clinton now reduced his efforts to bring the violence to an end. The Israeli people were turning against the Oslo deal. They would hardly be willing to hand over half the Old City of Jerusalem to Arafat when he couldn't even protect one Jewish holy site in Nablus from the Palestinian mob. Palestinian gunmen were now shooting at Gilo, a southern suburb of Jerusalem. Israelis asked themselves, What would the gunmen do from the ramparts of the Old City if they gained control of East Jerusalem? If the violence continued, there was no chance the Israeli public would support the far-reaching agreement Barak and Clinton still had in mind.

Unless we succeeded in putting an end to Israeli retaliations, the Palestinians would hardly be ready to accept the compromises at the heart of Clinton's plan either. Inflicting maximum pain on the other side to force it to submit was growing more popular with both sides than seeking a negotiated reconciliation. Only an outside party with the influence of the United States had a chance of pressing the leaders to stand against these tides of anger and desire for revenge. Yet the Clinton administration failed to do so.

The president seems to have assumed that if we were able to get the deal, the fighting would stop, much as a lack of oxygen suffocates a fire. This was an assumption that Barak made, too. Subsequently, Clinton would admit his regret "that I was not strong or wise or eloquent or persuasive enough to head [the violence] off."

At the time, Madeleine Albright was finishing up other diplomatic initiatives in Bosnia and North Korea. She had already had two run-ins with Arafat, in New York and Paris, when he walked out on her. She had no desire to repeat the exercise. When I pleaded with her and Sandy Berger in a meeting in Washington in November that they urgently needed to send a senior person to Israel to get Barak and Arafat to implement George Tenet's cease-fire plan, she responded by suggesting that our translator, Gamal Helal, should go to Egypt for consultations.

Tenet, for his part, now preferred to leave the implementation to his people on the ground. The USS *Cole* had just been attacked in Yemen in what he suspected was another al-Qaeda raid and there had been a spike in reports of other planned terror attacks on U.S. targets. These demanded his attention. In addition, in this early stage of the intifada, Tenet and his Agency staff in Israel and the territories were alarmed to see Palestinian security officials join the ranks of the uprising. Under the Oslo Accords it had been the Agency's job to train and equip them. The issue simply became too hot to handle politically at a time of transition to a new administration in Washington.

By this time Dennis Ross had decided to retire at the end of the Clinton administration. The period through January 20, 2001, represented the last window for him to achieve what had eluded his considerable diplomatic skills for the twelve years he had been responsible for U.S. peacemaking efforts. He seems to have judged that rather than try to stop the intifada, he would be better off spending his remaining weeks working on the final attempt to secure the outlines of a peace agreement.

The net effect was that no senior American official in Washington took responsibility for implementing the cease-fire plan in the Sharm el-Sheikh communiqué. That left it up to Arafat and Barak.

EVEN THOUGH THE Sharm el-Sheikh communiqué had been issued in Arafat's name, it quickly became clear that he did not intend to implement it. Palestinian attacks on Israeli civilians ensured Israeli retaliations, keeping the streets of the Arab world roiling with indignation. The Arab leaders who had refused to convene after Camp David had now agreed to hold an Arab League summit meeting in Cairo to provide support.

Barak, on the other hand, had every reason to want to implement the Tenet arrangements. He needed a restoration of calm if he was to go ahead with the negotiations. Thus, as soon as he returned from Egypt, he issued the requisite declaration calling for an end to the violence. None was forthcoming from Arafat. Barak sent his security chiefs to a trilateral security meeting with the CIA and the Palestinians to work out an implementation schedule for all of the measures announced by Clinton. Arafat's security chiefs did not show up.*

The result was predictable. Fighting flared first in Gaza and then in the West Bank; the IDF retaliated by killing ten Palestinians. The Egyptians then hosted a meeting of Israeli and Palestinian security chiefs in Cairo that produced understandings on a series of reciprocal steps consistent with the Sharm el-Sheikh agreement. The Israelis lifted the closures in response but the Palestinians escalated the violence to between thirty and sixty attacks a day.

It became evident to the Israeli security chiefs that their Palestinian counterparts would not take action without clear orders from Arafat, but he refused to issue them. The Israelis concluded that the only answer was to tighten the closure and respond with force.

During this escalation of violence, Clinton called Arafat to say he could not persuade Barak to restrain the Israeli army unless Arafat stopped the shooting from the Tanzim. But when Arafat ranted about the excesses of the IDF, Clinton softened his approach and simply asked whether Arafat might do more to restrain his fighters.

Barak of course pressed Clinton to get Arafat to stop the violence. But time was running out for their joint peace endeavor. In his phone conversations with Clinton, therefore, Barak's focus quickly shifted to the negotiations. One week after their meeting in Sharm el-Sheikh, with the violence raging, Barak and Clinton agreed that Clinton would invite both leaders to Washington separately to prepare for a summit meeting between the three of them a few weeks later.

As long as Arafat was making a "good-faith effort" to stop the violence, Barak was ready to come. But he warned ominously that if Arafat didn't cooperate, he would have to form a national unity government with Sharon and target the Palestinian Authority as well as Arafat's leadership. Clinton warned Barak that he was setting up a choice "between total peace and total war."

---

* Five days later, when the CIA finally managed to bring Dicter (the Shin Bet head) together with Mohammed Dahlan and Amin al-Hindi (the head of the Palestinian Mukhabarat), they knew nothing about what Arafat had agreed they would do in the Sharm el-Sheikh protocol. Dicter had to brief them.

Despite these warnings, both Barak and Clinton now seemed to believe that if they did not press on, all would be lost. Arafat was invited to a meeting at the White House on November 9; Barak a few days later. Arafat had done nothing to fulfill his Sharm el-Sheikh commitments yet he was now to be welcomed in Washington to receive a better peace offer.

The president emerged from his November meeting with Arafat very pleased with the discussion because Arafat had repeated his commitment to achieve an agreement before Clinton left office. The president indicated that at the summit they were working toward, around 95 percent of the West Bank would go to the Palestinians, with territorial swaps. This represented an advance on the 91 percent offered by Clinton and Barak at Camp David. When Arafat insisted again that he must have sovereignty on the Haram al-Sharif, the president said he understood how important this was for Arafat, that Israel also had needs, and that he would work on a formula that took both into account. On the Palestinian refugees' "right of return," the president discussed a formula that would recognize the right in some fashion but restrict the actual numbers going to Israel. Overall, Arafat said that he could not give a definitive yes until he knew all the details, but he volunteered, "We are in the ballpark!"

In Clinton's subsequent meeting with Barak, the Israeli leader did not object to the president's description of what the "ballpark" would have to look like on all the major issues, indicating that he was ready to go back to Camp David for another summit by Christmas if the level of violence had been lowered by then.

Barak complained of Arafat's success in manipulating Clinton into improving the offer he had made him at Camp David and insisted that something had to be done to lessen the violence. The president and Barak agreed to press Amnon Lipkin-Shahak into service as a go-between with Arafat. They calculated that with a better offer on the table and an agreement in reach, Arafat would have the incentive to tamp down the violence. But it seems that for Arafat the Washington meeting was yet another indication that violence could be used to extract further concessions. If so, Barak and Clinton had only given him further incentive to keep it going.

From the outset, Amnon was skeptical about his chances for success. The problem, as he saw it, was that nobody was in control of the Palestinian arena anymore. Arafat's mood changed from day to day with whatever tactical advantages he might be able to gain from the moment. Moreover, while the chairman liked to portray himself as a general in complete command of the situation, in Amnon's view he actually had no accurate picture of what was going on.

Nevertheless, Amnon was prepared to try. In a series of midnight meetings in mid-November, he and Arafat reached an understanding: Arafat would first attempt to stop the shooting from Bethlehem onto the Jerusalem suburb of Gilo by sending his policemen to arrest the perpetrators. In return, Israel would allow goods to flow into and out of Gaza. But just as the situation seemed to be calming down, a roadside bomb exploded near an Israeli school bus in Gaza, killing two Israelis and seriously wounding nine, most of them children. The attack generated outrage in Israel. In reprisal, Barak authorized helicopter and naval gunboat attacks on eleven Palestinian Authority targets in Gaza.

Arafat as usual denied any responsibility. He blamed a splinter Fatah group based in Damascus and promised a full investigation. The Israelis and the CIA, however, confirmed that senior people in Mohammed Dahlan's Gaza Preventive Security force were actually responsible for the attack. Within days, the firing from Bethlehem on Gilo resumed. Amnon gave up in disgust.

Successive efforts to pressure Arafat to stop the intifada ended similarly. It would take more than five years for the Palestinian tiger to exhaust itself. By that time almost one thousand Israelis and some 3,400 Palestinians would be killed and the edifice of peacemaking that Clinton had constructed would be completely destroyed.

19

The End of the Peace Process

There is a tide in the affairs of men
Which taken at the flood, leads on to fortune;
Omitted, all the voyage of their life
Is bound in shadows and in miseries.
—Brutus in William Shakespeare's
Julius Caesar

Although it was a Friday night, when other families in Rehavya, a tony neighborhood of West Jerusalem, were hosting Shabbat dinners, the prime minister's residence was buzzing with the activity of a normal business day. The residence itself is hard to see from the outside; high walls surround it for security reasons. A modest, Bauhaus-style stucco villa, typical of the clean lines of the modernist architecture that dominated residential building in the early years of the Jewish state, it had been renovated during Rabin's era with furniture and decorations that matched the building's design. On its walls hung beautiful landscape paintings of Jerusalem and other parts of the Holy Land painted by Reuven Rubin, Israel's most celebrated landscape artist.

It was December 8, 2000. Despite the onset of Shabbat, I had been scheduled for a 9 P.M. meeting with the prime minister. When I arrived he was engaged in intense conversation with one of his staunchest allies, Ophir Pines-Paz, the Labor Party whip in the Knesset. I could easily imagine why he was meeting with Ophir: ten days earlier, Barak had surprised the nation by announcing there would be early general elections in three months' time—more than two years ahead of the expiration of the Knesset's term.

In one sense, his announcement was the logical consequence of the steady decline in his political circumstances. Benjamin Netanyahu, whom Barak had beaten in a landslide in 1999, had now opened up a nineteen-point lead in the polls.* With only thirty members now left in his minority coalition, he had purchased a three-month "safety net" from Shas (the Sephardic religious party) by agreeing to provide more funding for their school network. But the pact had expired on November 28, 2000. In the meantime, Palestinian terror attacks were succeeding in driving up the Israeli casualty toll and Barak's government seemed incapable of stopping them.

I had sought this meeting with Barak because the president wanted to understand how his decision to go to early elections would affect their efforts to achieve peace. Barak explained that he had decided to move up the elections to the earliest possible date—February 6, 2001—virtually to coincide with Clinton's departure from office on January 20. In this way, he thought he could create the ultimate moment of truth both for Arafat and for himself. The only way for him to win the election, he felt, was to bring a peace agreement to the people and make the vote a referendum on peace. True to form, he now proposed a timetable for reaching that agreement before the end of Clinton's term: ten days of intensive Israeli-Palestinian negotiations; ten days of negotiations with American mediators present; and then ten days of summitry with President Clinton, this time in the region, if the chances of getting a deal looked promising.

As a political high-wire act, it was breathtaking. Barak was now depending on Clinton and Arafat to save him. But with five weeks left in office, the president had little ability to do so; given his relationship with Barak, the chairman had little incentive.

Nevertheless, Clinton was willing to sign up for Barak's "blitz" strategy for achieving an agreement in thirty days. And both Clinton and Barak were prepared to believe that Arafat was a willing partner in this sprint to the finish line.

Although in retrospect this looks like wishful thinking, at the time Arafat appeared to be in earnest. On November 9, when Arafat visited Washington, he had insisted to Clinton that it was time to go for the

---

* Barak would later change his decision, resign, and call for elections for prime minister only, driving Netanyahu from the race because the law at the time allowed only members of Knesset to run in a special election for the prime ministership. Bibi had resigned his Knesset seat after his electoral defeat eighteen months earlier.

complete agreement. At that meeting, Arafat had flattered the president by telling him that only he could make the deal; that after he was gone it would take a year or two to put it together again, "and we don't have a year or two."

He subsequently met with the normally skeptical Dennis Ross in Morocco in mid-December and convinced him of his seriousness, too. Afterward, Dennis asked me to tell Barak that Arafat's whole demeanor had indicated a sense of urgency that he hadn't seen before. Dennis said he had been frank with him about Israel's minimum requirements for the deal, including no Palestinian "right of return" to Israel. Then he had asked Arafat directly, "Is it possible to do a deal?" Arafat had answered, "Yes, it's possible to do a deal because I am serious and they are serious."

Amnon Lipkin-Shahak was sent by Barak to meet with Arafat three days later and he too came back convinced that Arafat wanted an agreement. Arafat even told Amnon he wanted to be directly involved in the summit preparations, suggesting that the two of them should meet every forty-eight hours to review the negotiators' progress and give them instructions. For Amnon, this was the clearest sign that Arafat wanted to reach an agreement.

Both Dahlan and Rachid also told me that Arafat was convinced he should do the deal. They said he understood that the trade was sovereignty in Jerusalem for the "right of return" to Israel; he just wanted a solution for the Palestinian refugees in Lebanon that included the absorption of some of them in Israel.*

The explanation for these common assessments of Arafat's upbeat mood and his apparent willingness to reach agreement may lie in the major concession he had secured from Shlomo Ben-Ami. On December 10, two days before Dennis's meeting with Arafat in Morocco, Ben-Ami had told Arafat's negotiators that Israel would agree to the Palestinians having "some kind of sovereignty" on the Haram al-Sharif in exchange for Israeli sovereignty over the Western Wall and language that would signify Palestinian acknowledgment of the attachment of the Jewish people to the Temple Mount.

---

* Separately, Shlomo Ben-Ami told me that Arafat had said he was prepared to give up 5 percent of the West Bank as long as he was compensated with swaps, and his negotiators conceded that the calculation of the territorial swaps could include their extraterritorial needs in Israel (including safe passage between the West Bank and Gaza, port access, and a desalination plant on the coast for water to be used in the West Bank).

Arafat had good reason to be happy. Israel's foreign minister had just yielded on the issue that had caused the collapse of the talks at Camp David. Ben-Ami confirmed this new position on Palestinian sovereignty on the Temple Mount directly to Arafat in a December 14 meeting at the Erez crossing point in Gaza, the night before Arafat met with Amnon. Not surprisingly, Ben-Ami also became convinced that Arafat was now intent on making the deal.

Ben-Ami's move also had a dramatic influence on Clinton's calculations. If Israel was now willing to accept Palestinian sovereignty on the Haram al-Sharif, he thought he could cut Jerusalem's Gordian knot. And when Clinton spoke to Arafat by phone after these meetings, Arafat said he wanted the deal done now. Dennis was convinced; in debriefing me on that call, he declared flatly, "Arafat has decided to do it!"

Confidence in the outcome built for several more days as the Israeli and Palestinian negotiators transferred their engagement to Bolling Air Force Base outside Washington. These talks with the American peace team were designed to lay the groundwork for the president's presentation of a package of bridging proposals that would constitute the basis for a summit meeting. On the second day, Ben-Ami again said that Israel would be prepared to accept Palestinian sovereignty on the Haram al-Sharif, sparking a revolt in the Israeli delegation.* Not surprisingly, the Palestinian negotiators were delighted. Yasser Abed Rabbo, the head of the Palestinian delegation, declared publicly, "Concerning sovereignty over Arab Jerusalem, . . . we are very close on this point."

Ben-Ami had always been more forward-leaning than the other Israeli negotiators on the sovereignty issue, but his explicit offer at Bolling was the consequence of Israeli domestic politics much more than the product of some carefully developed negotiating strategy to which the rest of the Israeli delegation was not privy. At that very moment, Shimon Peres was threatening to run against Barak in the elections, splitting the center-left's vote and guaranteeing Barak's defeat. According to the electoral law, candidates could compete for the prime ministership in the special election Barak had called if they had the support of ten Knesset members from one faction. The leftist Meretz Party

---

* The two members of the Israeli delegation from Barak's office—Gilad Sher and Pini Meidan—both told the Palestinian and American negotiators that Ben-Ami had exceeded Barak's instructions.

happened to have ten Knesset members. Their dislike for Barak was palpable but their one hesitation in supporting Peres's bid was that it would disrupt Barak's efforts to achieve a peace agreement with the Palestinians before the elections. To convince them that such an agreement was possible, however, they needed to hear it from the Palestinians.

Ben-Ami was like a man possessed when it came to a possible Peres candidacy. If Barak were to be forced out by the electorate, he considered himself the rightful successor. But the only way to thwart Peres at this juncture was to have the Palestinians certify that the negotiations were making real progress; Ben-Ami's offer on the Haram al-Sharif ensured that declaration. The next day, the Meretz Knesset members resolved not to support Peres. It was a salutary reminder of Henry Kissinger's maxim that Israel doesn't have a foreign policy, only domestic politics.

At the same time as Ben-Ami was apparently exceeding his authority in Washington, I was meeting with Barak to review the ideas Clinton was about to table. Barak emphasized to me that the sovereignty issue should be put aside in favor of the establishment of a special regime that would put the holy sites under international control. He warned, "The most assured way to destroy the agreement is to have the president say that the Temple Mount is going to be under Palestinian sovereignty." This was confusing, to say the least, because Barak had done nothing to rein in his foreign minister.

Barak of course had a more intense interest than Ben-Ami in blocking Peres's candidacy, which would doom his already doubtful chances for reelection. Shlomo was his stalking horse. Barak could use him both to block Peres and help produce a breakthrough to an agreement. At the same time, he could maintain plausible deniability and thereby hope to avoid the immediate political fallout from being seen to have ceded the Temple Mount to Arafat.

Since this was mostly about domestic politics, Barak's warning to me was necessary to deter the president from actually incorporating the offer in the proposals he was about to put to both parties. That would prove to be too clever by half. Once Israel's foreign minister had made the concession of Palestinian sovereignty explicit, Clinton judged that there was little point in the United States offering less, especially if it could be the catalyst for an agreement. My report to Dennis of Barak's warning went unheeded.

From the president's point of view, the last piece of the puzzle had now fallen into place. Ben-Ami had shown the Palestinians a map at Bolling that offered them 95.5 percent of the West Bank. The Israeli and American negotiators had made clear that there would be no "right of return" to Israel and that this would be the trade for whatever was offered them on Jerusalem.

On Saturday, December 23, 2000, the president summoned the Israeli and Palestinian negotiators into the Cabinet Room to present the Clinton Parameters—his best judgment of what it would take to conclude an agreement. He made it clear he was prepared to discuss his ideas with both leaders. However, he warned that he would only accept refinement "within the boundaries I will set forth." He would give the leaders four days to respond but emphasized that "if these ideas are not accepted by either side they will be off the table and have no standing in the future. . . . They go with me when I leave office."

The president then proceeded to outline his parameters: an independent Palestinian state in all of Gaza and 94–96 percent of the West Bank, with 1-3 percent territorial compensation for the rest; a capital in East Jerusalem with Palestinian sovereignty on all Arab suburbs and the Arab quarters of the Old City; Palestinian refugees would have the "right of return" to Palestine but not to Israel; and the Palestinians would have sovereignty on the Haram al-Sharif (see Appendix D, page 441, for the full text of the Clinton Parameters). It was a carefully crafted presentation, a formal American proposal from the president himself, of what constituted a fair and reasonable solution to the Israeli-Palestinian conflict.*

Unlike at Camp David, this document had been meticulously prepared after extensive consultations with Israeli and Palestinian negotiators and their leaders. All the important Arab leaders had been briefed on the details and had endorsed the plan. Barak and Arafat now had to make historic decisions: the one to give up Jewish sovereignty on the Temple Mount/Haram al-Sharif, the other to abandon the Palestinian "right of return" to Israel.

· · ·

---

* President George W. Bush later would claim that he was the first U.S. president to support an independent Palestinian state. But President Clinton had done that quite explicitly in his parameters. The difference was that Clinton had conditioned his support on Palestinian acceptance of the other parameters, including the settlement blocs and a "right of return" only to the state of Palestine.

ON DECEMBER 28, 2000, after a daylong debate, the Israeli cabinet resolved to accept Clinton's parameters as the basis for negotiating an agreement, provided the Palestinians accepted them, too. That was a huge achievement not just for the Palestinians but also for the Arab and Muslim worlds. Arafat should have been satisfied.

Much to the dismay of Clinton and his team, instead of promptly accepting the parameters, Arafat equivocated.

The first indication that we had a problem came from King Mohammed VI of Morocco, who, at our request, had phoned Arafat on December 26 to urge him to accept. Arafat told him that he needed more time to secure the approval of the Palestinian Legislative Council. Since the council had never amounted to more than a rubber stamp for Arafat's decisions, it was a transparent excuse for delay.

On December 27, when it was clear that the Israeli cabinet would approve the acceptance of the parameters, Barak called Arafat and suggested that if he was ready to accept as well they should go together to see Mubarak in Sharm el-Sheikh and deliver their responses to him. Arafat demurred.

On December 28, Arafat sent a long letter to Clinton outlining Palestinian requirements, including that Palestinian sovereignty over the Haram al-Sharif "in its entirety, is indivisible."

In Washington, the letter caused consternation. Clinton was out of time. If Arafat was doing his usual last-minute maneuver to extract more concessions, the whole process would unravel as Palestinian demands were countered by Israeli demands. The president responded immediately, expressing his deep disappointment and noting that all the Arab leaders whom Arafat had asked him to consult had agreed that the American ideas were fair and that those leaders would support an agreement that was based on them. If Arafat accepted them, clarifications would follow. But if not, the president warned, the process would come to an end.

What followed was all too familiar to us. Everyone set to work to bring Arafat around. First and most importantly, Mubarak got into the act. But instead of pressing Arafat to accept the parameters, he urged him to discuss his concerns with Clinton. Then U.N. Secretary-General Kofi Annan, the king of Morocco, and the president of Tunisia all spoke to Arafat. But when they urged him to accept the parameters, they heard a litany of questions about them, and complaints about supposed Israeli interpretations of them.

Map Reflecting Clinton Ideas

Proposed Palestinian State

Israeli Settlement Blocs Annexed to Israel

Haifa

*Sea of
Galilee*

*MEDITERRANEAN
SEA*

Jordan River

0   15
miles

N

Jenin

Tulkarm

Nablus

Qalqilya

Tel Aviv

WEST BANK

Ramallah

Jericho

Jerusalem   Maale
Adumim

ISRAEL

Bethlehem

Gaza

Hebron

GAZA
STRIP

*Dead
Sea*

JORDAN

EGYPT

No formal map was presented to the Israelis and Palestinians in
December 2000 by President Clinton, but this map illustrates the
Clinton ideas—a Palestinian state in 95% of the West Bank and
100% of Gaza. This map actually understates the Clinton ideas by
not showing an additional 1 to 3% of territorial swaps to the
Palestinian state from areas within Israel.

Copyright 2004 Washington Institute for Near East Policy

These reservations appeared in a second, even longer letter from Arafat to Clinton on December 30, requesting maps and further clarifications. This time he was told that most of his questions fit within the parameters but that the president was not prepared to answer them until Arafat accepted the parameters themselves. Arafat responded by asking for a meeting with Clinton, which was set for January 2, 2001.

The delay in securing a response from Arafat had left the arena wide open to other actors. On December 29, the IDF's chief of staff, General Shaul Mofaz, took the extraordinary step of publicly warning that the Clinton Parameters would leave Israel vulnerable to an attack from the east. On December 31, the Tanzim killed the son of Meir Kahane, who had inherited his father's leadership of Kach, the extreme right-wing settler organization. His wife also died and five of their daughters were injured, prompting right-wing demands for retaliation and revenge. In the context of the dramatic concessions to which Barak had now formally acceded, the public mood in Israel was turning dramatically against Clinton's parameters. As Barak explained to some visiting U.S. senators, "We are losing the public's trust because they feel we are not protecting them."

Without Arafat's acceptance of Clinton's parameters, Barak's concessions in the face of continued Palestinian violence were convincing Israelis that he was indeed Arafat's *freier*. Barak's political advisers were arguing that he should pull the plug on the peace process immediately to stanch the hemorrhaging of his support. But if he did so, he could face a revolt in his own party; they still had time to replace him with Peres as their candidate.

On January 2, the day Arafat arrived in the Oval Office to give his answer to the president, Barak informed Clinton that the country was so shaken by Palestinian violence that he was now beyond the point where he could participate in the negotiations without causing fatal damage to his candidacy. "I can't dive into an empty pool hoping that Arafat will put the water in," he said. Yet, notwithstanding his almost hopeless political circumstances, Barak would not change course. When the president asked him whether he should go ahead with his meeting with Arafat, Barak grasped at the thinnest of straws. Perhaps he could still win the elections, he told the president, if he could get an agreement in ten days.

In the meeting, Arafat told Clinton that he accepted the parameters but had some views that he also wanted to express. He then took each

of the critical parameters and sought to expand them. He rejected Israeli sovereignty on the Western Wall. He said there would have to be
a whole new formula for refugees. He objected to a residual IDF presence in the Jordan Valley as an infringement on Palestinian sovereignty. And then he reiterated to the president that he still wanted to
get the deal done on Clinton's watch, but suggested that the two sides
should continue the negotiations based not just on the president's parameters but also on Arafat's "views." That was a sure recipe for an
extended negotiation rather than an agreement before the president
departed office.

As Dennis Ross would subsequently explain, by seeking to expand
or alter the parameters, Arafat's response was tantamount to a rejection of them. But no one in Washington was prepared to say so at the
time. Instead, Jake Siewert, the White House spokesman, said that the
president had answered Arafat's questions. He refused to characterize
Arafat's response. Dennis asked Barak to send Gilad Sher to Washington to receive a debriefing and discuss next steps. Then he proposed to
bring the Palestinian negotiators back for another round of negotiations at Bolling. In other words, even though Arafat had just slipped
past his ultimate moment of truth, and even though Clinton had less
than three weeks left in office, the peace team carried on as if it were
peace process business as usual.

Keeping the hope of peace alive, however, quickly turned into a fiasco. The Israeli and Palestinian negotiating teams met at Erez, on the
border between Gaza and Israel, on January 10 and spent most of their
time arguing about an earlier statement made by Yasser Abed Rabbo
accusing Barak of war crimes. The Palestinians repeated the "views"
Arafat had offered Clinton. The Israelis said they were outside the parameters and the Palestinians should revise their positions to bring
them inside. The Palestinians refused and the Israelis in turn refused
to outline their positions. Instead they said they would come back with
positions outside the parameters, just as the Palestinians had done.

In the next week, the parameter exercise would fall apart completely.
To reduce Peres's opposition, Barak sent him to try to persuade Arafat,
but Peres promptly introduced new ideas not mentioned in Clinton's
parameters. Then Barak dispatched Amnon Lipkin-Shahak and Yossi
Ginossar to talk to Arafat. Both reported that Arafat had taken several
steps back from where he had been in previous discussions with them.
On territory, Jerusalem, and refugees, both sides were now ignoring

the Clinton Parameters, and Clinton was powerless to do anything to constrain them.

As we approached the deadline for Clinton's departure from the Oval Office, Barak had taken to calling me in the early hours of the morning. On January 13, 2000, he called at 7 a.m., much later than usual. He said he had slept only one hour in the last two days. He sounded exhausted, his voice hoarse from the speechmaking required for his reelection campaign.

He told me he had just been updated on Lipkin-Shahak's meeting with Arafat. He now saw no chance of a breakthrough. He wanted Clinton to understand that the rise in the level of violence and his difficult political situation left him with no choice but to suspend the negotiations and focus on security. To stand a chance of winning, he explained, he had to close a gap of 1 percent each day before the elections; calling off the negotiations would help him do that because the Israeli public now detested Arafat.

Barak went on to speak about a plan to "separate" Israelis and Palestinians that he was developing in his mind, which he intended to implement unilaterally after the elections—the precursor of Sharon's subsequent unilateral withdrawal from Gaza. He noted yet again that Arafat had succeeded in manipulating him and us. He now asked only that the president credit him publicly for trying and express understanding for his decision to stop the negotiations. He had paid with his political credibility but at least now, he comforted himself, no one could say that Arafat was ready for the endgame. Barak, always conscious of the clock, ended the conversation by noting in a matter-of-fact way, "I believe time has run out."

That is the way eight years of peace process diplomacy ended, at least for me. Ten days later, Clinton left the Oval Office. Three weeks later, Ariel Sharon defeated Barak in a landslide.

There was a postscript. Notwithstanding the decision that he told me about, Barak sent all the "peaceniks" in his cabinet—including Yossi Sarid, the leader of the leftist Meretz party, and Yossi Beilin, one of the original architects of Oslo—to the Egyptian resort town of Taba, to see for themselves that no agreement with the Palestinians was possible. A good deal of mythology surrounds the negotiations that took place there from January 21 to 27, 2001, after Clinton had left office.

Even today, would-be peacemakers call for picking up the negotiations where they left off at Taba, although there is no agreement about what happened there and no written record of the proceedings.

The United States has no firsthand account of the meeting because the incoming secretary of state, Colin Powell, setting the default position of the Bush administration, did not want the United States involved. Instead we dispatched political officers to sit around the swimming pools at Taba and in neighboring Eilat and pick up what they could from the participants returning to their hotels at the end of each negotiating session. From those reports and from the briefings I subsequently received from the negotiators themselves, it is clear that limited progress was made.

The Palestinians did present a West Bank map that for the first time outlined their acceptance of the incorporation of key settlements into Israel on 3 percent of the West Bank. However, the border drawn by the Palestinians again vitiated the concept of settlement blocs.

Nabil Shaath, the Palestinian foreign minister, and Yossi Beilin discussed a formula in which Israel would be able to claim it did not agree to a "right of return" while the Palestinians would be able to claim they had secured that right. They were far apart on the number of refugees who would return to Israel.

The Palestinians rejected Clinton's proposal that Israeli sovereignty extend beyond the Western Wall to the area under the Haram al-Sharif. As Yossi Sarid explained it to me, there were five or six major issues on Jerusalem that could not be resolved. Beilin, the irrepressible optimist, admitted to me that even if they had solved the refugee issue, the problem of Jerusalem would remain.

Not surprisingly, violence disrupted the negotiations, with Barak recalling the Israeli delegation after two Israelis were shot, execution style, while they ate lunch in a West Bank restaurant. In an attempt to keep the hope of peace alive, the chief negotiators—Shlomo Ben-Ami and Abu Ala—announced to the press as they packed their bags that "we have never before been so close to attaining an agreement." While that may have been true in relative terms, in absolute terms they were not close at all.

WHY DID SOMETHING that held such promise go so badly wrong? The prevailing view in Israel has been shaped by Barak's denunciation of Arafat as a man who sought Israel's destruction in phases, using violence to promote his ends and maintaining the "right of return" issue as a way of perpetuating the conflict until demography eventually sank the Jewish state.

Arafat's defenders have argued that he was never made a formal offer, or that the offer was unacceptable, or that he in fact accepted Clinton's parameters but was misunderstood.

The truth is that the Camp David summit in July 2000 failed because Arafat rejected Clinton's offer on Jerusalem, an offer that Americans and Israelis regarded as generous but that fell short of Arafat's minimum requirements of Palestinian sovereignty on the Haram al-Sharif. Those negotiations manifestly did not break down over the issue of the Palestinian "right of return."

But the final status negotiations did not end at Camp David. That summit actually marked the beginning of intensive negotiations that continued through January 2001, when they came to an inconclusive end at Taba. During that period, many of Arafat's concerns that were left unaddressed at Camp David were dealt with in detail. In particular, at the end of 2000, President Clinton formally offered Arafat Palestinian sovereignty over the Haram al-Sharif as one of the parameters for the final agreement. If that is what he had been holding out for at Camp David, why did he turn down Clinton's offer? The answer, to my mind, is straightforward: rather than breaking through into a new world, he clung to what he knew best—the ways of the old Arab order.

In Shakespeare's *Julius Caesar*, Brutus speaks eloquently of that moment when leaders must take their fate and the destiny of their people in their hands. Shimon Peres uses a different analogy. He describes history as a galloping horse running past the window. At that critical moment, the leader must decide whether to jump on or let history pass him by. True statesmanship is the courage to take the leap without the certainty of a secure landing.

Arafat had played an inherently weak hand masterfully, cynically exploiting the spontaneous eruption of the intifada and the urgent desires of Clinton and Barak to achieve a peace agreement to extract a far better offer than he had received at Camp David. But the deal presented to him in the Clinton Parameters was not cost-free or without considerable risk. He appeared willing to contemplate those consequences in the abstract when both Clinton and Dennis Ross presented their proposals to him. But when confronted by the reality of the deal, he balked.

Had he accepted the offer, Arafat would have had to stand before his people and tell them that he had secured a great victory in Jerusalem. But he also would have had to tell the Palestinian refugees that they would have a right to return to the Palestinian state, that they would be compensated for all their years of suffering, that some of them would be able to join their families in the Jewish state, but that they would have no "right" to return to homes their families had left behind fifty years before in Israel.

This would have been no simple task. For five decades Arafat had kept these refugees in camps and fed them on the illusion that one day they would return to a Palestine that had long ago become Israel. Anger and rage were roiling the streets of the West Bank and Gaza, especially in those back alleys that ran through the refugee camps where the casualty toll had been highest. It would have taken courage indeed for Arafat to stand before them at that moment and explain that they would not be going back to the homes of their forefathers, few of which existed anymore, even though they had known that in their hearts for a long time.

Every speech by every Palestinian politician emphasized the "right of return." Only Sari Nuseibeh, the professorial scion of a leading Jerusalem family, had ever dared suggest that this was an unrealistic mythology. Arafat was too scared to tell them the truth. Indeed, the Palestinian people were subsequently misled into believing that Clinton had proposed a noncontiguous state consisting of three cantons in the West Bank, based on a map that the Israelis had put forward at Camp David that bore no resemblance to what Clinton actually offered Arafat in his parameters.

Always prone to miscalculation because of the mythical world that he inhabited, Arafat chose to listen to those around him who whispered in his ear that Clinton was finished and he would do better waiting for George W. Bush. The new president, they assured him, would be like his father and pressure Israel into making him an even better offer. In fact, Bush's people had signaled Arafat that if he accepted the Clinton Parameters the new administration would honor them. Though Arafat fancied himself an expert on American and Israeli politics, he was oblivious to the rightward shift in the Republican Party, which now had a Christian evangelical base that was hard-line in its support for Israel. He was just as wrong in believing Barak would beat Sharon, his nemesis from his Beirut days.*

Arafat thought, in any case, that he was immune from the consequences because Rachid had secured a supposed safety net for him from the Israeli right wing. After Camp David, with Arafat's approval, Rachid had initiated a dialogue with Avigdor Lieberman, the leader of Yisrael Beiteinu, the right-wing Russian immigrant party, and Ehud Olmert, then the Likud mayor of Jerusalem. According to Rachid's account, Lieberman had indicated that the broad outlines of Barak's territorial offer would be acceptable to the national (right-wing) bloc and Olmert had said that he would not oppose giving up Israeli sovereignty over the Temple Mount/Haram al-Sharif. This had provided Arafat with the illusion that what was on offer by Barak and Clinton would still be on offer if Sharon became prime minister.

Since Arafat always chose the way that secured his survival to fight another day, rather than make the decisions that would secure the interests of his people, he chose to let history's horse gallop past his window. Four years later, after over three thousand Palestinians and almost a thousand Israelis were sacrificed to his tactical game, Arafat passed away stateless in a French hospital, still waiting for something better to turn up. To his dying day, Arafat had consoled himself with the conviction that he was, after all, "Yasser Arafat! The only undefeated Arab general!" That is what he angrily shouted at me, waving his finger in the air, during our last official meeting at his headquarters in June 2001.

IT IS TOO easy, though, to put all the blame on Arafat. After eight years, Clinton and our team surely should have known with whom we were dealing. Near the end of his second term, Clinton had become dependent on the statesmanship of Yasser Arafat, a characteristic that he had only exhibited once when, in truly desperate straits, he had accepted the Oslo deal.

Had Clinton been able to conclude the Israeli-Syrian peace deal, Arafat would have found himself in similar circumstances, scrambling to secure Palestinian interests. He just might then have grabbed at the

---

* Arafat only woke up to the near certainty of Barak's defeat one week before the vote. At that point he attempted to warn Jewish voters that Sharon would destroy the peace and urged Israeli Arab voters to set aside their enmity for Barak and vote for him.

lifeline offered him at Camp David, or afterward. But without the Syrian deal, achieving an Israeli-Palestinian final status agreement at the end of the Clinton administration had become impossible.

Clinton and his advisers had all become so keen to salvage an agreement in the last six months of the administration that we suspended disbelief when the artful dodger promised Clinton the moon. Clinton also repeatedly signaled to Arafat that he was in a hurry. For the bazaar merchant, customers in a hurry are the most vulnerable to extortion, especially when he senses, as Arafat did, that time was on his side. Then we repeatedly made him better offers when he failed to live up to his promises to stop the violence. Clinton wrongly assumed that achieving the deal would end the violence rather than understanding that only by ending the violence would there be any chance of closing the deal.

Had Barak refused to continue the negotiations until the violence stopped, he might have spurred Clinton into a more serious effort to achieve a lasting cease-fire. But Barak's willingness to continue the negotiations and to keep on improving the Israeli offer enabled Clinton to focus instead on the diplomacy of the deal and encouraged Arafat to keep the violence going while demanding a higher price.

It would prove to be an immense tragedy whose proportions are still being defined. Clinton's successor, George W. Bush, judged that it was better not to try at all than to try and fail; but he drew the wrong conclusion. The problem was not in daring to make peace; it was in how Clinton chose to do it and with whom he had to work.

Therein lies the lesson.

20

Epilogue

In politics, what begins in fear usually ends in folly.
—Samuel Taylor Coleridge

On Tuesday, March 20, 2001, I found myself in the Bush White House, the outgoing American ambassador accompanying the incoming Israeli prime minister, Ariel Sharon, on his first official visit to Washington. I felt like a spectator from a different era.

They had wasted no time changing the furniture and décor in the Oval Office. Instead of the familiar bright yellow, blue, and crimson color scheme emblematic of the Clinton era, the presidential seal was now embroidered in a pale peach carpet, tastefully offset by pale orange roses on the coffee table. The couch felt strange and uncomfortable, probably because of my own uneasiness as a Clinton administration interloper.

On the president's desk, the two bronze busts of Truman and Roosevelt were gone. So too was Clinton's collection of memorabilia—the medallions, paperweights, and the simple pebble that I had given him from Rabin's graveside, which he had kept on that desk for five years. In their place was nothing now but a Tiffany clock and three blue leather folders embossed with the presidential seal. Not a lot of work done here, I thought.

George W. Bush had been president for eight weeks. He had just concluded a luncheon meeting with Ariel Sharon in his private dining room, the same place where Clinton and Rabin had dined on September 13, 1993, after the historic handshake with Arafat on the lawn outside.

Sharon had gone to pains to prepare properly for this meeting. For a decade he had been persona non grata in Washington after his exploits in Lebanon in the early 1980s, and his encouragement of settlement building in the early 1990s, had damaged his relationships with the Reagan and earlier Bush administrations. Now, returning as prime minister, Sharon was determined to avoid any show of daylight between himself and the new president. He had taken note of how both Yitzhak Shamir and Bibi Netanyahu, the two previous Likud leaders, had mismanaged relations with American presidents, which had contributed significantly to their electoral defeats. He understood that this president was not interested in picking up where Clinton had left off in the peace process, which suited Sharon fine. But he wanted to find common ground with Bush.

Sharon calculated that the best way to approach the new president was to talk about terrorism, which he did at some length as the two leaders lunched alone in the president's private dining room. Afterward, in the Oval Office, as Bush reviewed their discussion in front of Sharon and the American and Israeli delegations, he mocked the portly prime minister. He noted to the group that Sharon had talked so much he had little time to eat. Turning to Sharon, he asked him whether he could manage without a meal, and then added, "But I noticed you polished off the dessert!"

Sharon took food seriously. He once told me that as an army general he used to carry a pistol on one side of his belt and a salt shaker on the other, "just in case I came across some *shishlik* on the grill!" He was oblivious to Bush's frat-boy humor. He just took it as a cue to launch again into his terrorism talking points.

Terror posed the greatest danger not just to Israel but also to the United States and the West, Sharon explained. He identified Osama bin Laden, Hezbollah, and Iran as the major protagonists. "Terror," he declared, rolling his *r*'s and drawing out the last syllable, "is a strategic threat to regional stability in the Middle East." As the leader of the free world, he argued, it was incumbent on Bush to lead a coalition of Western states in fighting this imminent threat because only he had the power and influence to mount such a campaign. Sharon warned that a failure to do so would leave the West exposed to great danger.

It was a cogent presentation. But it was springtime in Washington; September 11 was still five months off. When he had discussed his terrorism talking points with me before the White House visit, I had suggested to Sharon that the new president would probably be more interested in what Israel could do for Bush's cherished ballistic missile defense program.

Sharon's appeal fell on deaf ears. The president simply smiled and said nothing. Then Sharon warned that he knew how to deal with Palestinian terrorists because he had been fighting them all his life. "Mr. President," Sharon said with a twinkle in his eye and the delicate lifting of his right hand, pinkie extended, "we shall remove them from our society." Now Bush smiled back and said, "No need to elaborate, Mr. Prime Minister. I think we've got the picture."

As the meeting drew to a close and the Israeli and American delegations filed out of the room, the president stopped me at the door to the outer office. We had never met before, but he knew me by reputation as a member of Clinton's peace team. He asked, "Why didn't Arafat take the deal?" I responded that there was enough blame to go around. However, if I had to give the most important reason, I would say it was a lack of leadership on Arafat's part.

"That's exactly right. No leadership," said the president. Then he gave me his own take on the situation: "Clinton and Barak were two men who were desperate to make a deal. They made Arafat an incredible offer but he turned them down and resorted to violence. The Israelis elected Sharon. Now there's nothing to be done because Arafat already rejected an offer that Sharon is not going to repeat." Giving me that smug smile that would become his trademark, the president concluded, "There's no Nobel Peace Prize to be had here." He obviously felt that he had figured it out.

GEORGE W. BUSH, however, went on to develop the wrong prescription. Clinton's diplomatic effort had failed but that did not mean there was no role for American diplomacy. Still, Bush entered the White House with no desire to engage in Arab-Israeli peacemaking, or any other diplomatic initiative in the Middle East for that matter. To be sure, he was influenced by the ongoing intifada and by the warning Clinton had given him as he exited, on the dangers of trusting Arafat. But Bush's answer was to stand back and let the parties fight it out. All the members of Clinton's peace team were either let go or sidelined. The words *peace process* were literally expunged from the State Department's lexicon.* Any argument for political engagement was consistently dismissed with the derogatory adjective *Clintonesque*. "We don't do diplomacy," one of Bush's senior aides boasted to me at the time. "We do policy!"

Bush did let George Tenet, still the CIA director, negotiate a new cease-fire plan, and George Mitchell put forward his fact-finding commission's recommendations for ending the violence and restarting the negotiations. However, notwithstanding the fact that both Sharon and Arafat accepted these proposals, Bush would do nothing serious to ensure their implementation. He vetoed any hint of an American diplomatic initiative. As ambassador, for example, I received authorization to shuttle between Sharon and Arafat to try to stop the violence. But I was explicitly instructed by the president not to be involved in any political effort. When Sharon offered a freeze on all settlement activity for six months if Arafat would make a serious attempt to stop the intifada violence, Bush showed no interest in taking him up on it.

Understanding his boss's disdain for Middle Eastern diplomacy, America's chief diplomat, Secretary of State Colin Powell, was unwilling to commit any of his considerable prestige to the effort. On his first visit to the region, in February 2001, Powell told me that he thought the Bush administration would just "park this problem for a while." He ignored my protest that the car had no brakes and could not just be left on such a steep hill. Powell returned in June 2001, supposedly to launch a timetable for implementing the Tenet cease-fire plan and the Mitchell recommendations that his advisers and I had worked to prepare both sides for. He left them confused about what they were supposed to do and did not return for nine months. As the violence escalated, Bush sent General Anthony Zinni out with instructions to secure a cease-fire but stay away from any political process. Powell said Zinni would remain on the ground until the job was done; he came home within three weeks after a series of terrorist bombings were allowed to derail his mission.

In June 2002, President Bush did put forward his vision of a two-state solution in which a secure Israel would live alongside a viable, democratic Palestine. But he still remained aloof, conditioning his involvement on the Palestinians finding new leadership. On the eve of

---

* In the Bush administration the Middle East peace process was referred to simply as "the Middle East" to underline its rejection of Clinton's way of doing business.

the Iraq War, Bush hastily blessed the Quartet's Road Map, drawn up by others to provide the very political dimension his administration had so determinedly thwarted. He did that only as a sop to British prime minister Tony Blair, who needed the president's endorsement of an Israeli-Palestinian peace initiative to bolster support within his Labor Party for the Iraq War effort.

After Saddam had been toppled, and the other Quartet members had successfully pressured Arafat to appoint Abu Mazen as his prime minister, Bush decided to host a Sharon–Abu Mazen summit in Aqaba, Jordan, in June 2003. Bush had previously proudly boasted to the press that he "didn't do [Middle East] summits," but he wanted to savor the fruits of his apparent victory in Iraq. With the renewal of Palestinian terror attacks, and the foundering of the post-Saddam effort in Iraq, however, Bush soon walked away from Abu Mazen and returned to his default position of disengagement.

At least eight times as many Israelis and Palestinians were killed during Bush's first four years than in Clinton's last four years—3,822 as opposed to 446. Palestinian terrorist attacks and Israeli retaliations accounted for most of those deaths. But rather than intervene to stop the killing, Bush left Arafat and Sharon to their own devices and, with no American initiative to respond to, each came to see the defeat of the other as the only acceptable outcome. The killing would only diminish when both sides exhausted themselves.

All those years of terrorism and violence destroyed any semblance of trust between Israelis and Palestinians. Even after Arafat died, Israelis still saw no point in negotiating with Abu Mazen, his more moderate replacement. Arafat's rejection of Clinton's final offer and his resort to violence had led most Israelis to conclude that they had no partner for peace on the Palestinian side and that their survival in a Jewish state now depended on separating from the Palestinians—not out of respect, as Rabin had wanted, but out of the very hatred that his peace initiative had been designed to expunge.

Sharon responded to this overwhelming sentiment with unilateral acts, building a separation barrier between the West Bank and Israel and withdrawing completely from Gaza. While Bush watched from the sidelines, the basic compact of the Arab-Israeli peace process—the exchange of territory for peace—was discredited and abandoned. Instead, Hamas claimed a victory for violence and Sharon's critics argued that he too had become a *freier*, yielding all the Gaza settlements without getting anything from the Palestinians in return, an argument that was reinforced when rocket attacks from Gaza on nearby Israeli towns and kibbutzim became a regular occurrence.

Five years of intifada violence and Israeli retaliation also destroyed the institutions of Palestinian governance. These had already been weakened by years of mismanagement and the kleptocratic tendencies that Arafat had encouraged among his acolytes. But now the security services disintegrated, warlords emerged to challenge the Palestinian Authority, armed gangs loosed havoc in the main Palestinian towns, and the Islamist terror organizations took advantage of the anarchy to strengthen their popular support and organizational capabilities. When Bush finally got around to doing something about the deteriorating situation by appointing General William Ward to help with the restructuring and retraining of the Palestinian security services, and former World Bank president James Wolfensohn to rebuild the Palestinian economy, it was too late. The Palestinian Authority's inability to establish order in Gaza in the wake of Israel's withdrawal only underscored the extent of the disintegration.

It should not have been surprising in these circumstances that when Bush, in pursuit of his vision of a democratic Palestine, insisted that the Palestinians undergo an election in January 2006, Hamas won control of the Palestinian government, marking the first time that an Islamist party had come to power in the Arab world. It was another of those Middle Eastern ironies that George W. Bush, who regarded Islamist extremists as mortal enemies of the United States, would be the midwife of that untoward development.

The elections for the Palestinian Legislative Council were supposed to take place in July 2005, but Abu Mazen postponed them for six months in the hope that circumstances would improve for Fatah. As the new date for elections loomed and Hamas appeared set to win a significant proportion of the seats, Abu Mazen considered a further postponement. Sharon was willing to cooperate in this effort to deny Hamas a victory at the ballot box. They reached an understanding that Sharon would ban Hamas candidates from running in East Jerusalem and Abu Mazen would then declare that the elections could not proceed. Sharon was ready to do his part, provided Bush did not criticize him for disrupting a democratic process. Israeli and Palestinian envoys were dispatched to Washington and returned with a very clear message: the president himself had decided that the elections should go ahead as planned. According to two of the senior American officials who discussed the issue with Bush, the president believed that it would be good for Hamas to participate in the elections because it would make them accountable to the people.

The rest is history. Hamas won an upset victory in what was by all accounts a free and fair election. George W. Bush's application of democratic principles had succeeded in bringing an Islamist party with its own militia and terrorist cadres to power. This was not the first time that his insistence on the "purple thumb" principle of using elections to promote democracy had advantaged extremist parties.* In Iraq, Shiite parties entered the democratically elected government with their militias intact. Similarly, in Lebanon, despite the passage of the American-sponsored U.N. Security Council Resolution 1559, which called on Hezbollah to disarm, Bush chose elections over fulfillment of the Security Council's requirements.

In each case, Bush ignored a fundamental democratic tenet: the "one gun" principle that a monopoly of force must reside in the hands of the elected government. The results were predictable. The Shiite militias took over the various Iraqi ministries and established a reign of terror. In Lebanon, Hezbollah took advantage of the opening to build its parliamentary strength and its alliance with disaffected Christian factions, which enabled it to paralyze the Lebanese government. And in the most sensitive part of the Middle East, on the seam line between Israel and the Arab world, Hamas first took over the interior ministry forces and then used their newly uniformed cadres to take power in Gaza by military putsch.

Bush's dream of an independent, democratic Palestinian state was turning into the nightmare of a rump state in Gaza, ruled by Islamist forces, and a West Bank under Israeli occupation.

Bush's refusal to engage had profoundly negative consequences for America's standing in the Arab and Islamic world. Clinton's efforts to solve the Israeli-Palestinian problem ultimately failed but at least he had gained America a good deal of credit for trying. This in itself did nothing to stop extremist violence. However, Bush's insensitivity to the Palestinians fed the narrative of humiliation in the Muslim world that Osama bin Laden sought to exploit. A fundamental objective of

---

* Voters in recent Arab elections, most notably in Iraq, have their thumbs stamped with purple ink to indicate that they have voted. It was treated by most as a badge of honor.

al-Qaeda's terror campaign was to turn Muslims against the United States. As their anger grew at the Israeli military response to the intifada, bin Laden started espousing the Palestinian cause. Bush's decision to reverse America's involvement in settling the Israeli-Palestinian conflict had played into bin Laden's hands.

Antagonism toward the United States in the Arab world was also fueled by a sense that Bush was promoting a double standard, condemning human rights abuses across the region while practicing his own in Guantanamo and Abu Ghraib. Bush's insistence that the authoritarian leaders of Egypt and Saudi Arabia open the political space in their countries might have enabled him to recoup much of America's lost ground, since the president seemed to be siding with the people against these unpopular leaders. However, sectarian warfare in Iraq, soaring oil prices, and a growing challenge from Iran brought Bush back to the reality of America's dependence on the Egyptian and Saudi regimes to help stabilize the region. These same leaders used the success of Islamist parties in the elections demanded by Bush to justify suppressing those small voices of a new Arab liberalism that had emerged, while Bush stood by, opting for stability over freedom. Having promised those courageous Arab democrats steadfast support, Bush's abandonment of them deepened public doubts about American sincerity and reliability.

There was one positive unintended consequence of Bush's unwillingness to engage. Crown Prince Abdullah of Saudi Arabia became so frustrated with his failure to persuade Bush to intervene to stop the Israeli-Palestinian violence, and so fearful of its destabilizing consequences in the Arab world, that he launched his own initiative. In February 2002, in an interview with Thomas L. Friedman of the *New York Times,* he offered Israel his own version of a territories-for-peace deal in which Israel would receive peace, recognition, normalization, and an end to the conflict from the whole Arab world if it agreed to withdraw to the 1967 lines. Abdullah told television interviewer Barbara Walters that Israeli flags would fly over embassies in every Arab capital. The Arab League subsequently amended and endorsed the offer in its Beirut Declaration of March 28, 2002, putting twenty-two Arab states on record in support of ending the Arab-Israeli conflict. Bush paid lip service to the initiative but would do nothing at the time to test it.

· · ·

GIVEN BUSH'S DETACHED approach, it was baffling that in November 2007 he should have reversed almost seven years of virtual neglect and convened an international conference in Annapolis to launch a new effort to resolve the Israeli-Palestinian conflict. Forty-nine countries and international organizations were represented, including fifteen Arab states, the G-8, the permanent members of the U.N. Security Council, members of the Organization of the Islamic Conference, and representatives of the International Monetary Fund and the World Bank, as well as the Israeli and Palestinian leaderships. Bush seemed to be conceding that diplomacy did have its uses after all. As Churchill famously noted, "Americans can always be counted on to do the right thing . . . after they have exhausted all other possibilities."

This was Clintonesque indeed, although the president and his secretary of state took umbrage at the suggestion. First, they launched their peace initiative at the end of Bush's term in office. When Olmert and Abbas agreed on a negotiating timeline that would have them reach an agreement by the end of the Bush administration, they created a deadline for the president that he embraced. Bush had derided Clinton for being desperate to achieve a deal by the end of his presidency but now endorsed an effort that would put him in a similar situation.

Bush's putative Israeli partner, Prime Minister Ehud Olmert, like Ehud Barak in Clinton's time, entered the process in very poor political condition—his approval rating among Israeli voters was actually within the margin of error. His political weakness was compounded by police investigations into alleged corrupt practices which made it difficult for him to secure the necessary support from the Israeli people for the bold steps required to resolve the conflict. Like Barak, as he moved into negotiations his ruling coalition began to fall apart, forcing him to increase settlement building as a way to maintain the support of the Shas party. And like Barak, as his situation became more severe he would come to view the peace process as his only route to political salvation.

On the Palestinian side, Abu Mazen entered the process even weaker than Olmert. What Arafat had lacked in courage, Abu Mazen lacked in capability. He had inherited a corrupt and rudderless Fatah political organization and the disintegrating institutions of the Palestinian Authority and would do little to repair the situation. Having lost Gaza to Hamas, he had become dependent on the Israeli army to help him maintain his hold on the West Bank. He was hardly the courageous and imaginative leader needed to produce a historic breakthrough, but the fear that Hamas would take control of the West Bank propelled him forward.

Bush was a weakened president, just as Clinton had become in his second term. Clinton had to fight off impeachment; Bush was besieged by a hostile Congress that second-guessed his every move and weighed down by a debilitating war in Iraq. In addition, the memory of American power had faded during the last years of both presidencies. For Clinton, the containment of Iraq was collapsing and the effort to engage Iran had failed. His ability to wield American influence through the practice of diplomacy had diminished accordingly. Bush had squandered his influence on ill-fated efforts to promote democracy that had only served to empower America's enemies.

Nevertheless, this belated return to diplomatic means at least enabled Secretary of State Rice to create a credible peace process architecture after seven years of watching while the previous one was burned to the ground. On the first level of this constuct, Israeli and Palestinian negotiators grappled with the final status issues of borders, refugees, and Jerusalem that would define the endgame of a two-state solution. If nothing else, this had the virtue of restoring some credibility to the notion of partnership. On the second level, both sides were supposed to implement their Road Map commitments under the watchful eye of an American general.* Meanwhile, on the third level, another American general was overseeing the rebuilding of the capabilities of the Palestinian security services to enable them to police the territory that Israel would hand over to the Palestinian Authority in any agreement. On the fourth level, Bush and Rice drafted former British prime minister Tony Blair to work with Salam Fayyad, the Palestinians' technocratic prime minister, on jump-starting the West Bank Palestinian economy with a variety of housing, infrastructure, and industrial park projects. And on the fifth level, the Arab states and international donors were encouraged to support the process by fulfilling $7 billion in pledges to the Palestinian Authority and by backing Abu Mazen against his Hamas challengers.

Nevertheless, with so many moving parts, this process could only

---

* Among other obligations, Israel was supposed to freeze all settlement activity and dismantle illegal settlement outposts while the Palestinian Authority was supposed to end incitement and violence as well as begin dismantling the infrastructure of terror.

work if progress were made simultaneously on each level, thereby creating a reinforcing synergy between all of them. For example, fulfilling Road Map commitments would do much to restore the deeply damaged confidence of Israelis and Palestinians in the intentions of the other. That in turn would lubricate the negotiations and encourage Arab states in particular to engage more actively in support of the process. Similarly, providing the Palestinian security services with the ability to take control of policing the main cities and towns of the West Bank could lead to the easing of Israeli security restrictions, which would enable the Blair-Fayyad economic projects to take off.

The condition precedent for all that, however, was active diplomatic engagement by Bush and Rice on all of these levels, something that Clinton and his peace team had undertaken for seven years before they attempted the final push in 2000. Bush had never been prepared to do that, and this last time around would prove no exception to the rule he had established for himself from the beginning of his administration. Even though he had made the Annapolis process his own and declared in January 2008 that he intended to achieve nothing short of a peace treaty by the end of his term in office, he then stood back and cheered the parties on from the sidelines.

Lacking presidential backing for a robust American diplomatic engagement, Rice made many trips to the region, but they yielded little progress on the various levels of the process she had constructed. And, as Clinton discovered, a failure to advance in one arena impeded movement in the others. The perception of increased Israeli settlement activity embarrassed Arab leaders, making some of them unwilling to provide capital for jump-starting the West Bank economy and others wary about more active political engagement. Palestinian inability to deal with the West Bank terror infrastructure made the IDF reluctant to dismantle roadblocks and relax other security measures that would have enabled a return to normalcy for Palestinians. As both sides lost confidence in the negotiations, achieving compromises on the final status issues became more difficult. Finally, the effort had to be suspended in September 2008 when Prime Minister Ehud Olmert was forced to resign because of unrelated allegations of corruption.

Nevertheless, Rice did succeed in putting the peace process back on track. By the end of the Bush administration, economic conditions in the West Bank had started to improve, and Palestinian security forces had managed to reestablish order in major West Bank cities, earning the grudging respect of their Israeli counterparts. Negotiations yielded no concrete results, but they at least brought the parties full circle back to the same gaps on territory, refugees, and Jerusalem that had separated them at the end of the Clinton administration.* Yet neither Bush nor Rice would attempt to bridge those gaps.

DESPITE THE FACT that Bush identified the ideological battle taking place across the region by the end of his presidency as one between Islamist extremists and pro-Western moderates, he nevertheless showed little concern for the way his diplomatic detachment was actually playing into the hands of his enemies. Iran's Mahmoud Ahmadinejad, Hezbollah's Hassan Nasrallah, and Hamas's Khaled Mashal had crafted a message that resonated in the Arab street: "our way works," they would repeatedly proclaim, pointing out that violence, terrorism, and defiance were the only effective ways to provide the Palestinians with justice and revenge and the Arab and Muslim world with dignity. As evidence, they claimed that violent "resistance" had forced Israel to withdraw unilaterally from Lebanon in May 2000 and from Gaza in September 2005, and had enabled Hezbollah to stand undefeated before the mighty IDF, unlike any Arab army, in the Lebanese war of summer 2006. Meanwhile, Iran's defiance in the face of international sanctions had enabled the revolutionary Islamic republic to develop an independent nuclear enrichment capability.

Arab leaders who found themselves subject to constant criticism for hiding between Uncle Sam's legs while cohabiting with the "Zionist entity" had only one means of responding to the ideological assault. They had to prove that their way of negotiation, reconciliation, and normalization under American auspices could deliver more effectively for the Palestinians, Arabs, and Muslims.

President Bush raised the stakes in this contest quite dramatically by declaring in January 2008 that he intended to resolve the Palestin-

---

* Olmert is reliably reported to have offered Abu Mazen 93 percent of the West Bank with 5.5 percent of Israeli territory adjacent to Gaza as compensation, but the Palestinians were holding out for 97 percent with 1:1 territorial swaps. On refugees, Olmert apparently offered to take in 20,000 over ten years while Abu Mazen wanted 200,000 and Israeli Foreign Minister Tzipi Livni objected to even one. And on Jerusalem, Olmert offered a special regime in the Old City while the Palestinians insisted on sovereignty on the Temple Mount/Haram al-Sharif. See Aluf Benn, "PA Rejects Olmert's Offer to Withdraw from 93% of West Bank," *Haaretz*, August 12, 2008.

ian issue by the time he left office. His failure to achieve that objective did much to strengthen the argument of the extremists, while undermining the credibility of all those involved in the Annapolis process.

Bush's effort was handicapped by more than just his unwillingness to engage; his ideological convictions led him to exclude both Hamas and Syria from his belated peace initiative, two key players that could do much to thwart or facilitate the process.

Hamas's exclusion was the more understandable since it made clear at every opportunity that it opposed any peace agreement with Israel. But Hamas's control of Gaza gave it an ability to disrupt the process by launching attacks against Israel or by threatening to deny Abu Mazen the support of Gazans for any deal he might conclude with Israel. That put an additional premium on demonstrating to Palestinians that Bush's initiative could produce positive results for them since real progress in the negotiations would put pressure on Hamas to go along. But instead of pressing Olmert and Abbas to conclude their deal and live up to their commitments, Bush pressed the Arab states to cease their efforts to reconcile Hamas with the Palestinian Authority. The futility of that effort was demonstrated in June 2008, when the Israeli government, with Egyptian mediation, entered into an informal cease-fire with Hamas. That forced Abu Mazen to declare his desire for reconciliation with Hamas, leaving Bush out on a limb of his own creation.

Syria's Bashar al-Asad, by contrast with Hamas, had been signaling his desire to engage in peace negotiations with Israel for several years. He sent a delegation to the Annapolis conference to underscore this peaceful intent. Moreover, Olmert also saw an advantage in including Syria because, like Rabin and Barak, he wanted to play both tracks off against each other, while giving Asad an alternative to retaliation for the Israeli strike, in September 2007, on Syria's clandestine nuclear reactor. Olmert even went so far as to convey to Asad, via Turkish prime minister Recep Tayyip Erdogan, that he was ready for a full withdrawal from the Golan Heights, which in May 2008 produced indirect Israeli-Syrian peace negotiations under Turkish auspices for the first time since the breakdown in Geneva at the end of the Clinton administration.

But Bush would have none of it, despite the fact that his policy of isolating Syria had been rendered inoperable by Israel and Turkey, two of America's closest allies in the broader Middle East. He was unwilling to recognize both the clear advantages for his own peace initiative of engaging in the Israeli-Syrian negotiations and the unprecedented awkwardness of an American president refusing to support an effort by his Israeli ally to make peace.

Bush's failure to undertake serious diplomatic engagement left the United States, at the end of his presidency, in a much more difficult situation in the Middle East, with all of its allies weakened, the bulk of its armed forces tied down in Iraq, and Iran and its proxies aggressively attempting to fill the vacuum he had created. The unintended consequence of Bush's determined detachment was a newfound and powerful interest—both in America and in the Middle East—in a reinvigorated U.S. diplomacy. Indeed, in the last six months of his presidency most of the Middle East's actors seemed to be positioning themselves for that new era. It would be the ultimate irony if that were to be his only lasting positive bequest to the region.

21

The Lantern on the Stern

We cannot play innocents abroad in a world that is not innocent.
—Ronald Reagan

The contrast between Bush's indifference to the details of peacemaking and Clinton's obsession with them could not have been
more profound. Nevertheless, there was something quintessentially
American about their common belief in the need to make the Middle
East over in America's image. Clinton's vision was of a peaceful, har-
monious region where its people would live "the quiet miracle of a
normal life." Bush's vision was of a Middle East "where the extremists
are marginalized by millions of moms and dads who want the same
opportunities for their children that we have for ours."

They were both motivated by an idealism that has become the hallmark of America's post–Cold War engagement in the Middle East, a
confidence that the United States knows the remedy for the ills that
plague such a troubled region. Almost two centuries earlier, American
missionaries were some of the first to try their hand, in a romantic attempt to promote American values in the Muslim heartland. But since
World War II, successive administrations found their reformist impulses constrained by the Cold War requirements of sphere of influence politics and balance of power diplomacy.

When the collapse of the Soviet Union left the United States as the
world's only superpower, and the eviction of Saddam Hussein's army
from Kuwait elevated it to dominance in the Middle East, American
presidents found themselves able to contemplate doing more than just
maintaining stability in a volatile region. Clinton set himself a trans-

formational objective: to move the Middle East into the twenty-first century by ending the Arab-Israeli conflict.

Bush would succumb to a similar temptation after his toppling of Saddam. Whereas Clinton had sought to transform the Middle East into a place where the lion could lie down with the lamb, Bush declared America's objective to be a free and democratic Middle East, an even more idealistic notion given the lack of any such experience in the traditional, tribal societies of the Arab world.

This idealism seems to generate a troubling naïveté in the American approach to the Middle East that is part innocence, part ignorance, and part arrogance. Clinton's willingness to believe Arafat was matched by Bush's belief that, once in power, democratic accountability would moderate Hamas. Clinton was willing to invest in Iran's reformers, only to discover that they were fronting for the hard-line mullahs. Bush was willing to believe that the Iranian people were true liberals who wanted nothing better than to be able to overthrow their reactionary leadership, only to see them vote into office a hard-line president.

In Clinton's peace team, we assumed that if we could just find the right legal formula, a centuries-old conflict between Jewish and Muslim claims to sovereignty on the Temple Mount/Haram al-Sharif would be resolved. Secretary of State Condoleezza Rice imagined that it would be as easy to take the big steps involved in resolving the Jerusalem and refugees issues as it would be to focus on the small steps of establishing a viable cease-fire.

This American naïveté is a product of circumstance and experience. Providence has infused Americans with a generosity of spirit that finds expression in their desire to spread their good fortune to others and to believe that others will want to receive it as openly as they give it.

The American experience has also generated the conviction that every problem has a solution—that it just takes determination, creativity, and resources to achieve the necessary result. And as America's power has grown, its belief in its democratic way of government, its free-market economy, and its problem-solving capabilities has only been reinforced.*

---

* The Bush administration thought, for example, that the best way to rebuild the Iraqi army was to dismiss all its officers and start recruitment from scratch. That was the American way, but the effect was to deprive large numbers of officers and soldiers of their jobs, dignity, and income, boosting the ranks of the Sunni insurgency.

Without the influence of this naïve idealism, no American president could imagine that he might transform the Middle East. But if such efforts are inevitable, it is also predictable that they will run up against the same structural impediments detailed in this book: the resistance of Arab leaders to change; the fractiousness of Israeli politics; Palestinian dysfunctionalism; and the vulnerability of any political process to endemic violence and terrorism. Together they make the Middle East a uniquely difficult arena for the practice of American statecraft.

One could easily conclude from the experiences of Clinton and Bush that the United States is simply unsuited to handle the complexities of Middle Eastern politics given the gaps in history, culture, and experience. The American impulse to transform this region seems bound to lead the United States into quixotic enterprises. Indeed, after the trauma of the adventure in Iraq, it would be natural for Americans to declare the situation hopeless, come home, construct a virtual barrier, and attempt to quarantine this troublesome part of the world.

Unfortunately, the United States does not have the luxury of turning its back on the Middle East. If American leaders were willing to take seriously the challenge of energy independence, the United States might be able to detach itself somewhat from affairs there. But for now, the Middle East will continue to play a vital role in fueling the global economy, the wellbeing of which is a vital U.S. interest.*

The geostrategic location of the Middle East, astride the world's major communication routes and shipping lanes, also makes it impossible to cut America off from it. And the United States has taken on the obligation of ensuring Israel's survival and the security of critical Arab allies. To abandon them to their fate in such a dangerous neighborhood would have damaging consequences for the credibility of American commitments worldwide.

And then there's the siren song of Arab-Israeli peacemaking, which has proven to be irresistible even to an American president like George W. Bush, who was determined to ignore it.

IF, FOR THE foreseeable future then, American presidents are bound to intervene in the Middle East, how can they do so more effectively than in recent history?

---

* Some 60 percent of the world's proven oil reserves are buried in the Middle East. The region has also become the supply basin for the energy needs of the emerging economic giants of India and China.

First we need to remember that American involvement in the Middle East has had a positive side. The Israel-Egypt and Jordan-Israel peace treaties are the enduring products of sustained American diplomatic engagement. Similarly, the eviction of Iraqi forces from Kuwait, the withdrawal of Syrian forces from Lebanon, and the elimination of Libya's nuclear weapons program are illustrative of the role of American power in stabilizing the region and changing it for the better.

The lesson of American failures is not to give up, or to move into a purely crisis management mode, but rather to adopt a wiser approach by making our reformist goals more modest and our assumptions more realistic. Lowering our sights is also a requirement of America's reduced regional influence—the result of squandering our resources and attention on the ill-fated adventure in Iraq. Especially at a time when American credibility has been so damaged by the missteps of the Bush administration, it is important to avoid raising regional expectations that the president then fails to fulfill. That will only benefit the radical voices who argue that the United States and its regional allies can no longer deliver. Instead, the emphasis should be on toning down the rhetoric and allowing the results of American diplomacy to speak for themselves.

In pursuing a more realistic approach, it is critical that American policy makers avoid the assumption that their Middle Eastern counterparts think and act like Americans and will play by American rules. Why should they? Whether Arab, Israeli, or Iranian, as weaker players their instinct will be to resist American stratagems or divert them to their own purposes. Seldom will they follow our wishes, let alone surrender to American diktat—a lesson George W. Bush learned the hard way. And since they will usually have a bigger stake in the outcome than the United States does, their approaches will normally prevail.

Most authoritarian leaders in the Middle East face no term limit, except that of their natural lives. They have little incentive to take risks unless they feel they can no longer abide the status quo, or circumstances have so changed that they must adjust their approach. In most cases, when they decide to make peace or alter their behavior in other fundamental ways, it is because they believe their own survival is on the line, not because the U.S. president demands it. When those rare moments occur, however, they do provide the opportunity for U.S. diplomacy to achieve breakthroughs because the particular leader is, perhaps only for a fleeting instant, ready to take risks and make momentous decisions.

This rare willingness to move beyond the constraints of the existing Middle Eastern order is not necessarily an indication of statesmanship. Neither Hafez al-Asad nor Yasser Arafat possessed the necessary courage and vision to qualify for that distinction. Their people's well-being was not their first priority. When they decided to act, it was about survival, not leadership.

Anwar Sadat and King Hussein had nobler motives, but they, too, were concerned for their own survival. Nevertheless, their tactical decisions to move at a particular moment were based on longer-term strategies to secure the future of their countries and the salvation of their people. Arafat's and Asad's strategic purpose was simply to stay in place, but when the survival of their regimes was threatened, they too were willing to move. They quickly altered course, however, when the discomfort of the particular moment passed or they found what they thought were less risky ways to ensure their survival.

Israeli leaders are necessarily less committed to the status quo because their political time horizon is set by a four-year cycle of democratic elections and the difficulties of keeping their coalition governments together. Already by their third year in office, the law of coalition erosion asserts itself as partners depart the government to position themselves for the coming electoral contest. That dynamic means that Israeli governments rarely survive for their full terms and that Israeli prime ministers, like American presidents, only have a narrow window within which to act.

Taking peace initiatives can accelerate the coalition-fraying process quite dramatically, as Ehud Barak discovered after only one year in office. Barak of course was the exception; most Israeli prime ministers are made of more cautious stuff. Yet, given the tragic history of attempts to destroy the Jewish people over the last two millennia, they are highly sensitive to issues that could affect Israel's existence and will often be prompted to take the initiative out of concern for the state's survival, if not their own.*

---

* Sharon, for example, believed that the greatest danger to Israel's survival lay in a return to Israel's 1967 borders in the West Bank and the redivision of Jerusalem. He gave up Gaza in order to prevent that from happening. Olmert believed that the demographic threat to Israel's survival required it to relinquish control of the West Bank and the Arab parts of East Jerusalem. It motivated him to launch final status negotiations with Mahmoud Abbas in 2007.

In other words, for one reason or another the Middle East's leaders are always maneuvering even if it is just to stay in place. When a naïve American interventionism connects with these already turbulent currents, the impact on the survivalist instincts of the region's leaders often generates unpredictable results. Even trained and experienced American experts on the Middle East have difficulty playing the role of prophet. Rarely have any of them accurately forecast war or peace in this region.* That will be even more the case for an American president unschooled in the complexities of the Middle East. He should therefore be alert to the law of unintended consequences that seems to adhere particularly in the Middle East: when an American president pushes on one door in this neighborhood, another may well open.

Even a man as attuned to the forces of history as Henry Kissinger did not perceive the way that his policy of détente with the Soviet Union overlooked Egyptian interests and thereby helped generate Anwar Sadat's decision to launch war in October 1973. Jimmy Carter was unaware that his efforts in 1977 to bring Syria to an international conference so threatened Sadat's interests that he decided to fly to Jerusalem and deal directly with Israel instead. Bill Clinton's efforts to pursue a Syria-first strategy helped push Yasser Arafat and King Hussein into their deals with Israel. George W. Bush's determination to avoid engaging in peace-process diplomacy helped convince Saudi Arabia's Crown Prince Abdullah to launch his peace initiative in February 2002. Condoleezza Rice's focus on the Palestinian issue, and Bush's focus on isolating Damascus, helped create conditions for relaunching Israeli-Syrian negotiations, which was not at all what they intended.

Therefore, some of the most important requirements of successful American Middle Eastern diplomacy are humility, flexibility, and agility. Presidents need to expect the unexpected and attempt to put themselves in the shoes of their Arab and Israeli counterparts. Their advisers need to listen carefully to what Middle Eastern leaders say to their people in public, not just what they whisper to American officials in private to ingratiate themselves with the great power. They need to have their radars tuned for those unusual moments when Middle Eastern leaders break the mold of anticipated behavior and act in sur-

---

* The American intelligence community's track record on Iraq's WMD is the most egregious example, but they also failed to predict the 1973 Arab-Israeli war, Sadat's visit to Jerusalem in 1977, Saddam's invasion of Kuwait in 1990, or the Oslo Accords in 1993.

prising ways—when Rabin extends his arm to Arafat and the PLO chairman grasps it, when King Hussein decides to deal openly with Israel, when Asad drops all his preconditions and asks only that Clinton conclude the deal quickly, when Saudi Arabia's King Abdullah offers to end the conflict with Israel, and when Iran's hardliners propose a "grand bargain" to Bush. Timing is vital. The president must be prepared to act immediately when an opportunity presents itself. If that moment is seized and quickly exploited, the president can reshape the calculations of all the other Middle Eastern players to America's advantage.

FUTURE PRESIDENTS CAN do more, however, than merely waiting for that moment to ripen or appear. If they are inclined to try, they have the power to shape the strategic context that affects the calculations of Middle Eastern leaders. Those leaders inhabit a dangerous neighborhood. If they fail to read accurately the changes in regional dynamics, they can put themselves and their people in great peril. They pay particular attention to the impact of external forces on their political environment, especially the United States because of its immense power.

This gives an American president the ability to help create the critical sense of urgency that is at the heart of any change in the behavior of Middle Eastern leaders and to provide the safety net when they decide to undertake the risky business of moving forward. To do that effectively, however, future presidents will need to develop clear and realistic objectives and an integrated strategy to achieve them that like-minded regional leaders can identify with and support.

A central lesson of Clinton's experience in the Middle East is that everything is connected there. What happens in the Persian Gulf will have an impact on the shores of the Mediterranean and vice versa. What happens in one Arab-Israeli negotiation will influence the others. Therefore it is essential that the president's strategy for the region takes account of the positive synergy that can be generated between the various policy branches, as well as the negative impact on efforts in one arena produced by setbacks or failures in another.

This is easier said than done. As we have seen, Bill Clinton developed an integrated strategy that combined "dual containment" of Iran and Iraq with a push for comprehensive Arab-Israeli peace in an attempt to exploit the symbiosis between the two. But we did not anticipate that Clinton's focus on a Syrian-Israeli peace deal would provoke such Iranian-backed violent opposition. Nor did we expect that setbacks in the Arab-Israeli peace process would so complicate the effort to contain Saddam Hussein. And had Clinton been more cognizant of the deleterious impact on Israeli-Palestinian negotiations of the failure to clinch the deal between Asad and Barak in Shepherdstown and Geneva in early 2000, he would surely have pushed harder for the agreement.

George W. Bush identified the potential "ripple effect" of toppling Saddam Hussein on the prospects for advancing Israeli-Palestinian peace, but he failed to follow through. At least Bush took advantage of the impact of Saddam's demise on Muammar Qadhafi's calculations to secure abandonment of his nuclear ambitions, but Bush ignored the impact on Iranian calculations, spurning their short-lived interest in settling differences with the United States.* He then argued that promoting democracy in the Palestinian territories and the Arab states would redound to the benefit of Arab-Israeli peace, but that ended up strengthening the radical opponents of peacemaking instead.

Bush would have been better off following the example set by his father, who used the regional impact of America's 1991 eviction of the Iraqi army from Kuwait to generate an Arab-Israeli negotiating process with all of Israeli's Arab neighbors. Clinton also understood the beneficial impact on America's standing across the region of a sustained effort to resolve the Arab-Israeli conflict, and he used that to good effect. It took George W. Bush seven years to connect these dots, and America paid a high price in devalued influence in the Middle East and the tarnishing of its brand name in the meantime. He finally acknowledged the connection in his last year in office, but by then it was too late to repair the damage. Future presidents would do well to focus on the interconnected nature of regional politics from the outset.

WHEN A FUTURE American president resolves to embark on diplomatic initiatives to change the Middle East, he or she will need to main-

---

* As the November 2007 National Intelligence Estimate indicated, the Iranians decided to stop their efforts to design a nuclear bomb in 2003, after the American invasion of neighboring Iraq. See the National Intelligence Council's National Intelligence Estimate, "Iran: Nuclear Intentions and Capabilities," http://www.dni.gov/press_releases/20071203_release.pdf.

tain focus on the big picture and resist the efforts of the region's actors to drag the United States down into their swamps. They will be assiduous in their attempts at this because it reduces the asymmetry in power between these smaller states and the mighty superpower. American presidents should be wary of the sucking sound that accompanies the descent into endless details; it signals a squandering of their influence.

However, without presidential attention to the details, leaders in the Middle East will prefer to avoid risky concessions and shirk politically dangerous obligations. And by doing so they will either fail to reach agreement or erode accords made under American auspices.* A balance needs to be struck. In his last year, Clinton became too involved in the details and reduced his leverage as a result. By contrast, throughout his presidency, Bush remained focused on what he liked to call "the big picture" and therefore never used his leverage effectively.

The president's involvement needs to be reserved for those critical moments when the deal has to be closed or Middle Eastern leaders must take risky decisions. Then they will need the reassurance that comes from dealing directly with the president of the United States. At other times, the details should be left to the president's assistants, who must be empowered to speak for him. Unfortunately, Middle Eastern leaders have grown accustomed to direct presidential engagement, and White House aides are attracted to the idea of back channels that bypass the president's diplomats. The president has enough problems wielding his influence effectively in the Middle East; he should not let it be undermined by allowing Israeli or Arab leaders to end-run his envoys.†

IF A PRESIDENT sees an opportunity to take the diplomatic initiative, how should his team be structured? The Clinton administration's Middle Eastern operation was initially well organized but became quite dysfunctional by the end. The appointment of Dennis Ross as Middle East envoy reporting to the secretary of state had the advantage of a

---

* There are no better examples of this than the way Palestinian leaders handled their obligations to stem violence and incitement, or Israeli leaders approached their obligation to freeze settlement activity.

† Clinton was careful to keep the right balance until his last year in office, when he made himself available to Barak whenever the prime minister picked up the phone, and hosted or met with Arafat whenever he asked for a meeting. Bush encouraged the use of White House back channels with Israeli and Saudi leaders, undermining the roles of his secretaries of state and ambassadors.

senior-level official devoting his full-time energies to the president's peacemaking priorities. But Dennis operated independently of the people tasked with responsibility for the rest of the Middle East, and they were usually excluded from the policy deliberations.* This deprived the operation of planning resources and much-needed expertise on the Arab world and tended to leave Arab leaders disconnected from the American effort, especially at the critical Camp David summit.

If the Middle East is likely to be a high priority on the president's foreign policy agenda, the secretary of state will normally want to keep control of the issue.† As the country's highest diplomat, the secretary's involvement then serves as an indicator of the president's commitment. There is no need to appoint a presidential envoy unless the secretary of state does not wish to be involved in the effort (which in itself would send the wrong signal to the region and the Washington bureaucracy). However, if the secretary of state takes on the task, then he or she will need a high-level team of specialists empowered to deal with the details of any presidential initiative. A special Middle East envoy, reporting to the president through the secretary of state, is probably the best way to organize for a presidential peace initiative, as Clinton did. However, that envoy needs to partner with the assistant secretary who runs the State Department's Near East Bureau and needs to be staffed by that bureau and its ambassadors in the field, rather than operating independently of it.

THE QUESTION OF whose side time is on is critical in judging the political dynamics of the Middle East. The answer should always inform presidential decision-making on the region's issues. Osama bin Laden is credited with asserting, "You Americans have the watches, but we Arabs have the time." That is usually correct, although as this book has noted, those rare moments when Arab leaders feel a sense of urgency provide critical break points for American diplomacy. In comparison, American presidents, limited to a maximum of two four-year terms, have barely any time at all to achieve the ambitions they seem bound to set for themselves in the Middle East. That reality dictates an

---

* The only period when this was not the case was for the two years that I served as Assistant Secretary for Near East Affairs because of the friendship and partnership that Dennis and I had previously established. But when I left again for Israel, the bureaucratic rivalries reemerged in full force.
† This has been true of every secretary of state since Henry Kissinger introduced the concept of "shuttle diplomacy" to the Middle East.

early start for a president with ambitions to reform this part of the world. It can take a new president six to nine months to get a team in place, consult with regional and world leaders, and develop a suitable strategy. Unfortunately, the Middle East will not wait patiently for the president to decide its fate. The gearing-up and policy review process therefore needs to be compressed into the president's first three months.

Because Middle Eastern leaders usually move at a much slower pace than Washington, rarely respect a deadline imposed from abroad, fear that haste will be taken as a sign of weakness, and always want to haggle over the details, the president should expect that whatever he seeks to achieve will always take longer than he plans. He needs to avoid creating a deadline that only applies to the United States, since that puts pressure on the wrong party. Thus the ideal time to attempt breakthroughs is in the second and third years of the president's term. As bin Laden's warning suggests, however, the president cannot expect the Middle East to fit his timetable and, as already emphasized, he needs to be ready to seize the moment whenever it might arise.

Nevertheless, an attempt to reach a Middle Eastern agreement in the last year of the president's second term is probably the worst timing of all. The fact that both Clinton and Bush set those deadlines for themselves had more to do with their desire to burnish their tarnished presidencies than good policy sense. Clinton, in contrast to Bush, had at least spent the previous seven years working the process. But in both cases, their Middle Eastern counterparts could see the sand running out of Washington's hourglass and conclude that they would be better off making their concessions to a new president.

In this context, the way the president hands over policy to the next administration is critically important. George H. W. Bush's handoff to Clinton was a good model. Bush had invested his efforts in establishing a functioning negotiating process that Clinton could then quickly pick up and move forward. Clinton's handoff to George W. Bush, by contrast, left a lot to be desired. Negotiations had broken down, and the Palestinian territories were in flames. For good measure, Clinton warned his successor against dealing with Arafat. And when he left office he took with him all the work he had done to develop the parameters of the Israeli-Palestinian peace agreement. How different things might have looked if, after Camp David, Clinton had concentrated on ending the intifada violence and had then in his last days in office laid out—as U.S. policy—his judgment of what an agreement should look like. Bush would then have been bound by convention to promote Clinton's parameters rather than conclude that it was all hopeless and turn away.

Bush's father, of course, was expecting to win a second term and therefore had every reason to keep the process alive and little need to try to drive the negotiations to a conclusion. Bill Clinton and George W. Bush had already used up their two terms in office. The desire to achieve something before they left trumped the need to hand over policy to their successors in good working order. Ironically, their legacies would have been better served had they not tried to reach for the brass ring at the end of their rides.

OVER THE NEXT decade, American presidents will need to draw on these principles and lessons as they set course in the Middle East. They are likely to find that the waters there are exceedingly rough. The removal of Saddam and Bush's insistence on elections in Iraq propelled a Shiite majority into government in Baghdad for the first time in five hundred years, generating Sunni-Shia tensions across the region. The civil war that ensued effectively removed Iraq from the balance of power equation in the Gulf and therefore tilted it in favor of Iran, with repercussions beyond the Persian Gulf to the wider Middle East.

In Lebanon, Iran's Shiite proxy Hezbollah filled the vacuum left by Bush's success in forcing Asad to remove Syrian troops. Meanwhile, in the Palestinian arena, Iranian backing for Hamas helped the group first win the elections and then take Gaza by force. Iran's leaders have left little doubt that their intention is to assert Iranian dominance across the region. Meanwhile their determination to proceed with large-scale uranium enrichment sends the signal to their neighbors that they intend to back this bid with a nuclear option.

This creates the strategic context for the Middle Eastern leaders that future presidents will have to deal with. For the Sunni leaders of the Arab world it represents a frightening change in strategic circumstances. King Abdullah of Jordan has warned of a Shiite arc that stretches from its base in Iran through Iraq to Syria and Lebanon. For him, as well as Hosni Mubarak of Egypt and King Abdullah of Saudi Arabia, it is simply unacceptable that Iran should become the arbiter of Arab interests in Iraq and the Middle Eastern heartland—areas that have been dominated by the Sunnis for fourteen centuries.

Israel too cannot abide a hostile Iranian hegemon in its neighborhood, especially one with nuclear ambitions that calls for its destruction and provides support to Hezbollah and Hamas on Israel's northern and southern borders respectively. Turkey—a non-Arab, Sunni neighbor of Iran, Iraq, and Syria—is similarly concerned about the consequences of Iran's destabilizing behavior in its neighborhood.

Concern about the security implications of an Iranian nuclear capability is already pressuring Iran's Arab neighbors, with their immense wealth, to develop their own nuclear programs. Meanwhile, Israel is considering a preventive military strike on Iran's nuclear facilities that would, at best, delay Iran's program and could, at worst, ignite the flames of a new, open-ended conflict.

The first challenge therefore is to reshape the strategic context in a way that gets Iran's attention. An energetic effort to engage Iran in direct negotiations over its nuclear program and regional role needs to be combined with a concerted effort to rollback its influence in Iraq and the Middle Eastern heartland.

The reduction in violence in Iraq generated by Bush's "surge" and the resulting slow but certain progress toward political reconciliation between Iraq's Shia and Sunni factions, has begun to lay the groundwork for reducing Iran's influence there. Although still fragile, the reconciliation process will necessarily make the Shiite parties less dependent on Iran. At the same time, the reduction in violence in Iraq makes it possible to start withdrawing American forces. As the strain on the U.S. defense forces is eased, and troops are freed up for deployment elsewhere, Iran will begin to take more seriously the threat of American military action against its interests. Reducing the footprint of U.S. forces in Iraq will also make them less vulnerable to Iranian retaliation in the event of a U.S. or Israeli military strike on Iran's nuclear facilities, which will in turn make the Iranians less sure that they can deter such action.

A renewed American initiative to resolve the Arab-Israeli conflict should lie at the heart of this rollback strategy because it can serve as the cement for a virtual alliance between America's regional partners. It is important, however, that this effort to reshape the strategic context not be portrayed as an attempt to build an anti-Iranian alliance or to exploit Sunni-Shiite tensions, which the American intervention in Iraq inadvertently unleashed. The purpose of attempting to engage with Iran's government on the diplomatic playing field is to persuade it that the United States and our regional allies would welcome a responsible Iranian regional role. At the same time, successful Arab-Israeli peacemaking will undoubtedly reduce Iran's opportunities to play an irresponsible role in the Middle Eastern heartland and perhaps reduce its cockiness.

The common interest that can unite America's regional allies is likely to be matched by their common sense of urgency to resolve the Palestinian problem. The growing Palestinian demographic threat is spurring Israel's leaders to find a way to end the West Bank occupation. The growing Islamist threat encourages moderate Arab leaders to demonstrate that through negotiations with Israel they can address Palestinian grievances more effectively than through the extremists' formula of "resistance" (that is, violence and terrorism). And there is a growing awareness among Middle Eastern leaders that a failure to achieve a two-state solution will generate over time Israel's detachment from the West Bank as well as Gaza, leaving two failed terror statelets on the seam line between Israel and Egypt, and between Israel and Jordan—a nightmare for all three of America's allies in the region's heartland.

A successful effort to roll back Iran's influence in the Arab-Israeli arena by attempting to resolve the Israeli-Palestinian conflict will also require a more effective strategy for dealing with Hamas, which rules in Gaza. Arab leaders see Hamas as a Sunni Islamist movement that Shiite Iran has managed to hijack. Most of them would prefer to co-opt than confront Hamas, thereby weaning it from dependence on Iran and returning it to the Sunni side of the divide. After Hamas took over Gaza by military putsch in June 2007, however, the combined opposition of the United States, Israel, and the Palestinian Authority managed to persuade these Sunni leaders to restrain their instinct for reconciliation and go along with a policy of isolating Hamas and besieging Gaza.

A year later, Israel, with the assistance of Egypt, negotiated a cease-fire with Hamas. The essence of their new approach was to put Hamas in the dilemma of deciding whether it is a "resistance" movement or a government responsible for providing for the needs of Gaza's citizens. Under pressure to relieve the Israeli-Egyptian siege, Hamas decided to stop its rocketing of Israeli towns and kibbutzim and instead enforce a cease-fire by arresting those who were still pursuing its original violent intent.

The challenge for the next president is to build on the cease-fire to effect a real change in Hamas's intentions. This will require keeping Hamas in its dilemma. But the president should leave this task to Israel, Egypt, and the Palestinian Authority because, as the custodian of the peace process, the United States needs to uphold the principle of not engaging with parties that are fundamentally opposed to peacemaking. However, if Hamas continues to police the cease-fire with Israel, the president should support Abu Mazen's efforts to reconcile with Hamas on the basis of its continued rejection of violence and its willingness to respect political agreements negotiated by the PLO with Israel. The goal should be a unified Palestinian partner for negotiations with Israel that is capable of fulfilling its commitments in the West Bank and Gaza, especially by preventing violent opposition to peace.

Because all that will take time, the rollback effort will need to be buttressed by a serious attempt to bring the Israeli-Syrian negotiations to a successful conclusion. Syria serves as the principal conduit for Iran's influence in the Lebanese and Palestinian arenas, yet on the subject of what to do about Israel there is a deep divergence between Iran and Syria, captured in the fact that at the same time as Iran's president threatens to wipe Israel off the map, his Syrian ally is attempting to make peace with Israel. Israeli-Syrian engagement can threaten to crimp Iran's pipeline into Lebanon and Gaza, generating friction between Tehran and Damascus and perhaps increasing the pressure to take the possibility of Iran's own engagement with the United States more seriously. Should negotiations yield a peace agreement, it would likely cause the breakup of the Iranian-Syrian axis. But that could happen only if the next president decides to involve the United States in the negotiations, since Syria will not abandon its strategic relations with Iran unless it knows that normalized relations with the United States would replace them.

FUTURE PRESIDENTS WOULD need to reinforce this strategy by developing a new Middle Eastern security framework to deal with the combined threats of growing instability and a potential nuclear arms race. The United States already has strong security relationships with every state in the Middle East except Syria and Iran.* The challenge is

---

* The United States has built strategic relationships with Israel, Egypt, Turkey, Jordan, Saudi Arabia, and the other Gulf Cooperation Council states. It is also developing security ties with Iraq, Lebanon, and the Palestinian Authority.

to knit these separate relationships together for the common purpose of preventing regional nuclear proliferation, deterring aggression by any regional power, managing instability in Iraq, and resolving regional conflicts.

As part of this effort to build a regional security architecture, the United States will need to begin consulting with our Middle Eastern allies about the idea of extending a nuclear umbrella to all of them in the event that diplomacy with Iran fails to head off its nuclear program. This NATO-like security framework for the Middle East would represent a major commitment on America's part but it may be the only way to prevent a highly destabilizing nuclear arms race in the region. In return, regional members would have to commit to policies that bolster this nascent moderate alliance: nonproliferation, support for a peaceful settlement of the Arab-Israeli conflict, security cooperation, counterterrorism cooperation, and meaningful internal reform. As Iraq stabilizes it will be important to include it in this security framework. If diplomacy succeeds in establishing effective international control of Iran's nuclear program, Iran should also be invited to join the club.

Despite America's diminished regional influence brought on by Bush's missteps in Iraq and his failure to promote Arab-Israeli peace or block Iran's nuclear ambitions, Arabs and Israelis alike still look to Washington to play a critical balancing role. But it would be a mistake for future American presidents to revert only to the balance of power diplomacy of the earlier Cold War era. For that would indicate that Washington had learned little from the failures of its post–Cold War engagement in the headier game of transformational politics in the Middle East. Instead, future American presidents need to utilize the workable elements from both approaches.

They will have to discard the policy of regime change. The removal of Saddam was so mishandled that the American people will be wisely skeptical of any new attempt and the region's leaders will not want to be associated with it. In any case, Saddam was unique—no other Middle Eastern regime is both that much of an international outlaw and that vulnerable to overthrow.

Similarly, the United States needs to adjust its approach to promoting democratic change in the Middle East, an immensely difficult, long-term project. Although it would be tempting to focus only on promoting Middle Eastern stability in such uncertain times, future presidents should not abandon the effort to encourage political and economic reform. Instead a new balance needs to be struck between stability and progress, one that recognizes American interests in supporting friendly authoritarian regimes while encouraging them to embark on serious liberalization programs. This should not be understood just as an attempt to promote American values; increasingly, internal reform in these countries is becoming an American strategic interest because continued repression by their regimes is weakening liberal, secular voices and strengthening radical, Islamist alternatives.

Egypt and Saudi Arabia, America's two most important Arab allies, are both likely to face successions to a new generation of leaders in the next decade. The United States will have an intense interest in ensuring that these successions are smooth and broadly accepted by the people. If Washington becomes identified with candidates for succession who do not enjoy legitimacy with their own people, it will be sowing the seeds of future trouble. Supporting the expansion of basic political freedoms in these societies can serve as a means of putting the United States on the right side of change when it comes.

Bush did succeed in establishing a well-funded bureaucratic infrastructure for Middle Eastern democracy-promotion efforts. It should be preserved and used in a sustained effort to help build democratic institutions—political parties, a free press, women's rights, civil society organizations, and independent judiciaries. When elections do take place, it is essential to uphold one democratic standard Bush ignored—the elected government must have a monopoly on the use of force. That means the United States should oppose parties with militias or terrorist infrastructures participating in elections unless they first disarm.

WHEN FUTURE AMERICAN presidents turn again to Arab-Israeli peacemaking as an integral part of an effective American strategy for the Middle East, they will discover that the Arabs still look to Washington as the main address for resolving their conflict with Israel. No matter how unpopular the United States becomes in the region, that remains the abiding reality because of the special relationship of trust and influence we have cultivated with Israel through five decades of ever-growing support. How to use that influence remains a hotly debated topic, with critics of America's pro-Israel bias arguing that if only the United States would be more "even-handed," or if only the United States would pressure Israel to give up occupied territory, the problem could be readily resolved.

Israelis are certainly cognizant of their dependence on the United States and expect their leaders to manage the relationship with Washington effectively.* They will resist, however, any American attempt to dictate what is in Israel's best interest. That only leads the Israeli government to dig in its heels and mobilize its formidable support in the American Jewish community and now in the Christian evangelical community as well. Because of this support, American presidents will be wary of confronting Israel. But if they do so and fail, they will undermine the Arab perception that the United States is the only power that can move Israel. That in turn would help legitimize the Iranian/Hezbollah/Hamas argument that "resistance" is the only way to liberate Arab territory.

In fact, the issue is miscast. Whenever Israel and an Arab state have engaged in peace negotiations, Israel's leaders have been prepared to offer or agree to full withdrawal to the pre–June 1967 lines. That was true for negotiations with Egypt, Jordan, and Lebanon. It is also true for negotiations with Syria, where five Israeli prime ministers—Rabin, Peres, Netanyahu, Barak, and now Olmert—have offered full withdrawal from the Golan Heights.† In recent years, Israelis also supported the complete unilateral withdrawals from southern Lebanon and Gaza. In all these cases, American diplomatic engagement and support helped make the Israeli withdrawals possible. The record therefore suggests that American presidents can be more successful when they put their arms around Israeli prime ministers and encourage them to move forward, rather than attempt to browbeat them into submission.

Other than the Golan Heights, the only Arab territories left in contention now are the West Bank and East Jerusalem. However, a large majority of Israelis have already accepted the idea of leaving the West Bank, much as they left Gaza in their minds long before Sharon began

---

* Yitzhak Shamir and Bibi Netanyahu lost their reelection bids in large part because the Israeli electorate saw them as ignoring or flouting the concerns of American presidents.

† In April 2008, Syria's Information Minister, Buthaina Shaaban, announced that Turkish prime minister Recep Tayyip Erdogan had conveyed to President Asad that Prime Minister Olmert was willing to make a full withdrawal from the Golan Heights. Olmert's office did not deny the claim.

the evacuation of the settlers there. They have forced their government unilaterally to define the proximate border with the West Bank by completing the construction of the separation barrier that incorporates 8.5 percent of the West Bank and leaves most of the settlements on the other side. Polls show they would support the territorial arrangements for the West Bank in the Clinton Parameters provided that the settlement blocs are incorporated into Israel. Moreover, Clinton's proposal that the Arab suburbs of Jerusalem be in Palestinian hands and the Jewish suburbs in Israeli hands is no longer heretical, as it was when Barak first proposed it at Camp David.*

Israelis now have an offer of peace and normalization from all the Arab state members of the Arab League and a Palestinian negotiating partner committed to peaceful reconciliation. What they need is to see a Palestinian ability to control and police the territory from which Israel withdraws. In retrospect, most Israelis view the unilateral withdrawals from Lebanon and Gaza as mistakes because violent attacks continued. They fear the same thing will happen in the West Bank, leaving Ben-Gurion Airport and Israel's main cities vulnerable to Palestinian attacks.

In contrast, the Israeli withdrawals from Egyptian, Syrian (in 1974), and Jordanian territory left strong central governments in control of the evacuated territory that scrupulously policed the agreements. Israelis need a Palestinian government in the West Bank that will maintain the peace in a similar fashion. Absent a Palestinian ability to control the territory within its ambit and prevent hostile acts emanating from there, no potential agreement could be implemented. Therefore the capacity of the Palestinian security services needs to be rebuilt in transparent ways that put power in responsible and capable hands. However, that process will take time, while the need to show tangible progress is an urgent priority. Here the role of outside powers becomes critical.

If the Arab states are serious about playing a more active role in settling the conflict, they need to become custodians and guarantors of Palestinian commitments to live in peace with Israel. As states, they have capabilities the stateless Palestinians lack and can help make up

---

* In October 2007, Deputy Prime Minister Haim Ramon raised the idea in the Israeli cabinet. In the ensuing discussion, the right-wing Russian leader Avigdor Lieberman supported Ramon. Prime Minister Olmert subsequently supported the proposal in a speech to the Knesset. His coalition remained intact.

for the weakness of Palestinian institutions even as they help to rebuild them. Egypt and Jordan, as neighbors of Gaza and the West Bank respectively, have a particular responsibility in this regard.* Other Arab leaders can provide political cover for weak Palestinian counterparts who will otherwise face difficulties defending political compromises with Israel. This is the opposite function to the interested-bystander role they all adopted in the 1990s when they put the onus on Arafat to make the compromises with Israel and live up to them. Then they feared they would be accused of betraying Palestinian rights; in the future they will need to stand together to defend their collective compromises.

Nevertheless, the contribution of Arab states will always be constrained by the reluctance of their leaders to appear in the role of policing the Palestinians. In the best case, therefore, there will still be a deficit in the capacity of the Palestinian government to control the territory Israel is supposed to withdraw from. International forces will have to fill this gap. Israelis have long resisted this idea out of concern that international forces will not be willing to police the Palestinians either. Lately, however, some Israeli officials have come to accept that such forces may be able to play a useful complementary role in policing borders and passages, as Barak and Clinton envisaged at Camp David when the West Bank security arrangements were being negotiated. International forces could also be used for internal security functions in the Palestinian territories, such as helping to man roadblocks and passages until Palestinian security forces are in a position to assume these responsibilities on their own.

These international forces will have to be prepared to do more than just serve as observers. As partners to the Palestinian security forces they will have to be willing to undertake policing functions, including arresting terrorist suspects. In playing this role, it is important that the Palestinian people see them as facilitating the creation of an independent Palestine, rather than as replacing one occupying power with another. It is essential therefore that the international forces have a political chapeau to legitimize their operations—ideally an Israeli-Palestinian peace agreement endorsed by a U.N. Security Council resolution.

---

* Egypt and Jordan already have heightened their involvement by providing weapons and training to forces loyal to the Palestinian president and by attempting to prevent arms smuggling into Palestinian territories.

Settlement activity will need to be addressed effectively in any renewed peace process. Neither Clinton nor Bush found a way to prevent it from interfering with their efforts. Each was sympathetic to Israeli leaders who argued that, since most settlements would be evacuated after the final agreement was struck, it should be acceptable that during the negotiations they placate their domestic opposition by allowing selective settlement activity to continue.* In the process they downplayed the fact that additional settlement activity seriously undermines the credibility of their Palestinian interlocutors and exposes Arab leaders to the charge that their involvement is facilitating the takeover of more Palestinian land. Successive Israeli governments have already committed to the Quartet's Road Map, which requires a freeze on all settlement activity, including "natural growth," but George W. Bush allowed them to observe that commitment in the breach. Future presidents need to insist that during final status negotiations all settlement activity be frozen, including in the settlement blocs, unless it is done in agreement with the Palestinians.†

WHEN THE UNITED States takes up Middle East peacemaking in earnest again, it will inevitably return to many of the bridging proposals developed by Bill Clinton in 2000 during negotiations with Barak and Arafat. Two issues, however, still have to be resolved that do not lend themselves to simple or creative solutions, as Clinton's efforts revealed.

Although Barak accepted Clinton's proposal for Palestinian sovereignty on the Haram al-Sharif, it is highly unlikely that this will ever be acceptable to a majority of Israelis, who know the area as the Temple Mount. And Palestinians will not be willing to accept Israeli sover-

---

* Rabin and Peres built in Jerusalem's environs and the Jordan Valley while freezing activity in other settlements in the West Bank and Gaza. Netanyahu used the "natural growth" loophole to justify widespread expansion of existing West Bank settlements. Sharon and Olmert built in the settlement blocs (Ariel, Jerusalem, and Gush Etzion) that they assumed would be incorporated into Israel in the final status agreement. Neither of them was willing to dismantle unauthorized settlement outposts, despite their promises to President Bush.

† One way for the president to approach settlement activity is to promote a six-month "time-out" during which the final borders between Israel and the Palestinian state should be finalized through negotiations. Only after agreement is reached could settlement activity resume in the areas that Palestinians have agreed will be incorporated into Israel. Prime Minister Begin agreed to a three-month freeze at Camp David I, and Prime Minister Sharon offered George W. Bush a similar "time-out" in April 2001, in response to the Mitchell Report's call for a full settlement freeze.

eignty on the entire Western Wall (which runs beneath the Muslim Quarter of the Old City), let alone the area that lies behind the wall (which runs under the Haram al-Sharif). Any attempt to produce a creative formula for dividing or dissolving sovereignty is bound to come up against the reality that the sovereignty issue is simply too sensitive, even explosive, to lend itself to a rational solution.

Instead, the Holy Basin—the Old City and the religious sites around it—could be put under an international regime responsible for maintaining the status quo in which control of the religious sites remains in the hands of the relevant religious authorities, in perpetuity.*

Alternatively, the walls of the Old City of Jerusalem could demarcate the borders of a "special regime" in which the Israeli and Palestinian governments would share sovereignty over the territory within, under a joint condominium. The holy sites inside the walls would remain under the control of the respective religious authorities but there would be no specific designation of sovereignty for these places. Any effort to change the status quo would be subject to mutual veto power.†

The desire for recognition of a "right of return" for Palestinian refugees to Israel is a highly emotional issue for both sides. Most Palestinian refugees by now understand that they are not going to be returning to their forefathers' homes in Israel and will be prepared to accept practical arrangements for compensation and resettlement. But after so many decades of suffering, they are not prepared to have what they regard as their "right" ignored. From their perspective, it is a matter of dignity and justice.

On the other side, Israelis see this Palestinian insistence on the recognition of their "right" to return to Israel as the thin end of a wedge that will be used in the future to perpetuate Palestinian grievances against Israel. As Clinton learned in 2000, Israelis will support far-reaching concessions provided they know that there will be no further

---

* Under this arrangement, the Haram al-Sharif would remain in the hands of the *waqf*, which is controlled by the Palestinians; the Wailing Wall and the tunnels along the Western Wall would remain in the hands of the Israeli Ministry of Religious Affairs; and the Christian holy sites would remain in the hands of the various Christian sects. The international regime would guarantee free access to all and establish a system for handling excavations by any party.

† Israelis and Palestinians would be free to enter the Old City through Israeli- and Palestinian-controlled gates, respectively. They would not be able to exit to the other's territory without travel permits. The special regime would need a third-party or joint police force to maintain law and order inside the Old City.

claims on Israel, especially not one that carries with it a demographic threat to Israel's existence as a Jewish state. While willing to allow some Palestinian refugees to enter under a family reunion scheme, no Israeli government would accept that they have a "right" to go there. Neither side has shown any willingness to budge on what appear to be their minimal requirements.

Ideally, Israeli and Palestinian leaders would have the courage to stand in front of their people and explain that in order to achieve peace both have bitter pills to swallow: Palestinians would have to give up their claim to a right of return to Israel in return for the implementation of that right in their Palestinian homeland; Israelis would have to concede their claim to Arab parts of Jerusalem. Absent that straight talk, the only alternative is to find an acceptable legal formula that concedes the right to the Palestinians while vitiating it at the same time.*

AS ALREADY NOTED, the strategic imperative that drives the return to peacemaking will require the United States to reengage with Syria and become the sponsor again of the Israeli-Syrian negotiations. This does not mean, however, that the next president should return to the "Syria first" policy that Bill Clinton pursued for much of his administration. Given the urgency of the Palestinian situation, it will be important for him to focus his efforts there while encouraging the Israeli-Syrian negotiations to move forward at their own pace. One of the important though counterintuitive lessons of Clinton's experience is that the United States is more likely to achieve a breakthrough on the Syrian track if the president focuses American attention on the Palestinian one.

Bashar al-Asad is all too aware that he rules over a Sunni country whose alliance with Iran is not viewed as natural by most of his citizens at a time of heightened Sunni-Shiite tensions. A Sunni Arab state coalition engaging with the United States and Israel to resolve the Palestinian problem can reinforce the fear in Damascus of being left behind. That concern can in turn help overcome the natural preference

---

* Under such an arrangement Palestinians could apply to go to Israel, but Israel would have the sovereign right to decide who could enter its territory. Refugees could be given a set period—say three years—to exercise their right to compensation and/ or resettlement. After that, they would no longer be recognized as refugees and their claims would expire.

of Syria's leaders for a process for its own sake. As Bill Clinton learned the hard way, a drawn-out process enables Damascus to reduce its isolation and rebuild relations with Washington while maintaining its strategic relationship with Iran and pursuing efforts to regain control in Lebanon. Indeed, although Bashar al-Asad made repeated peace overtures to Israel during the Bush administration, he made clear that he would only conclude a peace deal with Israel if the United States were in the room. He thus exhibits little pretense about his process-driven interest.

However, the president can use an Israeli-Syrian negotiating process to American advantage, too. It could facilitate the Israeli-Palestinian negotiations in several indirect ways: Hamas and Palestine Islamic Jihad would feel under far greater pressure to go along with the negotiations if they felt their Syrian patron was about to make a deal with Israel and shut down their Damascus headquarters; the Palestinian negotiators would have greater political cover in the Arab world; and the United States could take advantage of the competition between the two tracks to advance progress on both.

The next president can also make clear that a condition for American involvement this time is that Lebanon is off the table since, in the intervening Bush years, the United States has taken on responsibility for ensuring Lebanon's independence. Instead of making Syria responsible for disarming Hezbollah in Lebanon, as Barak and Clinton had tried to do, the president should insist that Syria close its borders to the shipment of arms to Hezbollah and other Lebanese irregulars. Disarming Hezbollah, however, should be a Lebanese responsibility, perhaps in the context of an Israeli-Lebanese peace negotiation that resolves the remaining minor border issues.

One lesson from Clinton's experience with the Israeli-Syrian negotiations is that the Syrians will need to be able to credibly claim that Israel withdrew to the June 4, 1967, line. Under that heading, the issue of the fifty meters of disputed territory around the northeast sector of Lake Kinneret will need to be resolved. One suggestion is that while sovereignty on the lake would be Israel's, the area of land on the northeastern side could revert to Syrian sovereignty but be turned into a park under international supervision, which would provide Israelis and Syrians with open access.

A fatal flaw in Clinton's efforts to achieve an Israeli-Syrian peace agreement was that the trade of territories for peace never seemed that attractive to Israelis, given the stability of the Golan Heights status quo and the unwillingness of Syria's leader to make demonstrable gestures that would signify his truly peaceful intentions. The change in strategic circumstances occasioned by Iran's bid for nuclear weapons and regional hegemony, however, has altered the stakes for Israelis who now perceive an existential threat. If Syria were prepared to swap its strategic alliance with Iran for the return of the Golan Heights, many Israelis would likely see that as making a more tangible contribution to their security than the "warm peace" that they no longer believe in. "Territories for strategic realignment" could, in this way, provide a critical incentive that was missing in Clinton's time, turning the Israeli leader who made such a deal from a *freier* into the nation's savior.

LAUNCHING A NEW attempt to reshape the Middle East is bound to be a difficult enterprise, especially at a time of deep doubts about the credibility of American leadership. Yet the combination of vital interests and opportunities to do good is likely to be as irresistible to future American presidents as it was to Bill Clinton and George W. Bush. But if they embark on new endeavors to promote change in a region that is so resistent to it, they will need a lantern on the stern, which this book has attempted to provide, to illuminate the troubled route that Bill Clinton took and thereby provide them with a surer way forward. They will also need Arab and Israeli leaders like Sadat, Begin, Rabin, and Hussein, leaders with the vision and courage to break the mold of conflict and hatred that has left the Middle East bound in shadows and misery for so long, notwithstanding the transformational instincts of American presidents. With such leaders, there is much that U.S. diplomacy can achieve, hopefully drawing upon the wisdom and humility generated by the light which experience provides.

Appendixes

A. THE OSLO AGREEMENT
September 13, 1993

The Government of the State of Israel and the P.L.O. team (in the Jordanian-Palestinian delegation to the Middle East Peace Conference) (the "Palestinian Delegation"), representing the Palestinian people, agree that it is time to put an end to decades of confrontation and conflict, recognize their mutual legitimate and political rights, and strive to live in peaceful coexistence and mutual dignity and security and achieve a just, lasting and comprehensive peace settlement and historic reconciliation through the agreed political process. Accordingly, the two sides agree to the following principles:

ARTICLE I: AIM OF THE NEGOTIATIONS

The aim of the Israeli-Palestinian negotiations within the current Middle East peace process is, among other things, to establish a Palestinian Interim Self-Government Authority, the elected Council (the "Council"), for the Palestinian people in the West Bank and the Gaza Strip, for a transitional period not exceeding five years, leading to a permanent settlement based on Security Council Resolutions 242 and 338.

It is understood that the interim arrangements are an integral part of the whole peace process and that the negotiations on the permanent status will lead to the implementation of Security Council Resolutions 242 and 338.

ARTICLE II: FRAMEWORK FOR THE INTERIM PERIOD

The agreed framework for the interim period is set forth in this Declaration of Principles.

ARTICLE III: ELECTIONS

1. In order that the Palestinian people in the West Bank and Gaza Strip may govern themselves according to democratic principles, direct, free and general political elections will be held for the Council under agreed supervision and international observation, while the Palestinian police will ensure public order.
2. An agreement will be concluded on the exact mode and conditions of the elections in accordance with the protocol attached as Annex I, with the goal of holding the elections not later than nine months after the entry into force of this Declaration of Principles.
3. These elections will constitute a significant interim preparatory step toward the realization of the legitimate rights of the Palestinian people and their just requirements.

ARTICLE IV: JURISDICTION

Jurisdiction of the Council will cover West Bank and Gaza Strip territory, except for issues that will be negotiated in the permanent status negotiations. The two sides view the West Bank and the Gaza Strip as a single territorial unit, whose integrity will be preserved during the interim period.

ARTICLE V: TRANSITIONAL PERIOD AND PERMANENT STATUS NEGOTIATIONS

1. The five-year transitional period will begin upon the withdrawal from the Gaza Strip and Jericho area.
2. Permanent status negotiations will commence as soon as possible, but not later than the beginning of the third year of the interim period, between the Government of Israel and the Palestinian people representatives.
3. It is understood that these negotiations shall cover remaining issues, including: Jerusalem, refugees, settlements, security arrangements, borders, relations and cooperation with other neighbors, and other issues of common interest.
4. The two parties agree that the outcome of the permanent status negotiations should not be prejudiced or preempted by agreements reached for the interim period.

ARTICLE VI: PREPARATORY TRANSFER OF POWERS AND RESPONSIBILITIES

1. Upon the entry into force of this Declaration of Principles and the withdrawal from the Gaza Strip and the Jericho area, a transfer of authority from the Israeli military government and its Civil Administration to the authorised Palestinians for this task, as detailed herein, will commence. This transfer of authority will be of a preparatory nature until the inauguration of the Council.

2. Immediately after the entry into force of this Declaration of Principles and the withdrawal from the Gaza Strip and Jericho area, with the view to promoting economic development in the West Bank and Gaza Strip, authority will be transferred to the Palestinians on the following spheres: education and culture, health, social welfare, direct taxation, and tourism. The Palestinian side will commence building the Palestinian police force, as agreed upon. Pending the inauguration of the Council, the two parties may negotiate the transfer of additional powers and responsibilities, as agreed upon.

ARTICLE VII: INTERIM AGREEMENT

1. The Israeli and Palestinian delegations will negotiate an agreement on the interim period (the "Interim Agreement").

2. The Interim Agreement shall specify, among other things, the structure of the Council, the number of its members, and the transfer of powers and responsibilities from the Israeli military government and its Civil Administration to the Council. The Interim Agreement shall also specify the Council's executive authority, legislative authority in accordance with Article IX below, and the independent Palestinian judicial organs.

3. The Interim Agreement shall include arrangements, to be implemented upon the inauguration of the Council, for the assumption by the Council of all of the powers and responsibilities transferred previously in accordance with Article VI above.

4. In order to enable the Council to promote economic growth, upon its inauguration, the Council will establish, among other things, a Palestinian Electricity Authority, a Gaza Sea Port Authority, a Palestinian Development Bank, a Palestinian Export Promotion Board, a Palestinian Environmental Authority, a Palestinian Land Authority and a Palestinian Water Adminis-

tration Authority, and any other Authorities agreed upon, in accordance with the Interim Agreement that will specify their
powers and responsibilities.

5. After the inauguration of the Council, the Civil Administration
will be dissolved, and the Israeli military government will be
withdrawn.

ARTICLE VIII: PUBLIC ORDER AND SECURITY

In order to guarantee public order and internal security for the Palestinians of the West Bank and the Gaza Strip, the Council will establish
a strong police force, while Israel will continue to carry the responsibility for defending against external threats, as well as the responsibility for overall security of Israelis for the purpose of safeguarding their
internal security and public order.

ARTICLE IX: LAWS AND MILITARY ORDERS

1. The Council will be empowered to legislate, in accordance with
the Interim Agreement, within all authorities transferred to it.
2. Both parties will review jointly laws and military orders pres-
ently in force in remaining spheres.

ARTICLE X: JOINT ISRAELI-PALESTINIAN
LIAISON COMMITTEE

In order to provide for a smooth implementation of this Declaration of
Principles and any subsequent agreements pertaining to the interim
period, upon the entry into force of this Declaration of Principles, a
Joint Israeli-Palestinian Liaison Committee will be established in order to deal with issues requiring coordination, other issues of common
interest, and disputes.

ARTICLE XI: ISRAELI-PALESTINIAN COOPERATION
IN ECONOMIC FIELDS

Recognizing the mutual benefit of cooperation in promoting the development of the West Bank, the Gaza Strip and Israel, upon the entry
into force of this Declaration of Principles, an Israeli-Palestinian Economic Cooperation Committee will be established in order to develop
and implement in a cooperative manner the programs identified in the
protocols attached as *Annex III* and *Annex IV.*

ARTICLE XII: LIAISON AND COOPERATION
WITH JORDAN AND EGYPT

The two parties will invite the Governments of Jordan and Egypt to participate in establishing further liaison and cooperation arrangements between the Government of Israel and the Palestinian representatives, on the one hand, and the Governments of Jordan and Egypt, on the other hand, to promote cooperation between them. These arrangements will include the constitution of a Continuing Committee that will decide by agreement on the modalities of admission of persons displaced from the West Bank and Gaza Strip in 1967, together with necessary measures to prevent disruption and disorder. Other matters of common concern will be dealt with by this Committee.

ARTICLE XIII: REDEPLOYMENT OF ISRAELI FORCES

1. After the entry into force of this Declaration of Principles, and not later than the eve of elections for the Council, a redeployment of Israeli military forces in the West Bank and the Gaza Strip will take place, in addition to withdrawal of Israeli forces carried out in accordance with Article XIV.

2. In redeploying its military forces, Israel will be guided by the principle that its military forces should be redeployed outside populated areas.

3. Further redeployments to specified locations will be gradually implemented commensurate with the assumption of responsibility for public order and internal security by the Palestinian police force pursuant to Article VIII above.

ARTICLE XIV: ISRAELI WITHDRAWAL FROM THE GAZA STRIP
AND JERICHO AREA

Israel will withdraw from the Gaza Strip and Jericho area, as detailed in the protocol attached as *Annex II.*

ARTICLE XV: RESOLUTION OF DISPUTES

1. Disputes arising out of the application or interpretation of this Declaration of Principles, or any subsequent agreements pertaining to the interim period, shall be resolved by negotiations through the Joint Liaison Committee to be established pursuant to Article X above.

2. Disputes which cannot be settled by negotiations may be resolved by a mechanism of conciliation to be agreed upon by the parties.

3. The parties may agree to submit to arbitration disputes relating to the interim period, which cannot be settled through conciliation. To this end, upon the agreement of both parties, the parties will establish an Arbitration Committee.

ARTICLE XVI: ISRAELI-PALESTINIAN COOPERATION CONCERNING REGIONAL PROGRAMS

Both parties view the multilateral working groups as an appropriate instrument for promoting a "Marshall Plan," the regional programs and other programs, including special programs for the West Bank and Gaza Strip, as indicated in the protocol attached as *Annex IV*.

ARTICLE XVII: MISCELLANEOUS PROVISIONS

1. This Declaration of Principles will enter into force one month after its signing.

2. All protocols annexed to this Declaration of Principles and Agreed Minutes pertaining thereto shall be regarded as an integral part hereof.

Done at Washington, D.C., this thirteenth day of September, 1993.

For the Government of Israel
For the P.L.O.

Witnessed By:

The United States of America
The Russian Federation

ANNEX I: PROTOCOL ON THE MODE AND CONDITIONS OF ELECTIONS

1. Palestinians of Jerusalem who live there will have the right to participate in the election process, according to an agreement between the two sides.

2. In addition, the election agreement should cover, among other things, the following issues:

a. the system of elections;

b. the mode of the agreed supervision and international observation and their personal composition; and

c. rules and regulations regarding election campaign, including agreed arrangements for the organizing of mass media, and the possibility of licensing a broadcasting and TV station.

3. The future status of displaced Palestinians who were registered on 4th June 1967 will not be prejudiced because they are unable to participate in the election process due to practical reasons.

ANNEX II: PROTOCOL ON WITHDRAWAL OF ISRAELI FORCES FROM THE GAZA STRIP AND JERICHO AREA

1. The two sides will conclude and sign within two months from the date of entry into force of this Declaration of Principles, an agreement on the withdrawal of Israeli military forces from the Gaza Strip and Jericho area. This agreement will include comprehensive arrangements to apply in the Gaza Strip and the Jericho area subsequent to the Israeli withdrawal.

2. Israel will implement an accelerated and scheduled withdrawal of Israeli military forces from the Gaza Strip and Jericho area, beginning immediately with the signing of the agreement on the Gaza Strip and Jericho area and to be completed within a period not exceeding four months after the signing of this agreement.

3. The above agreement will include, among other things:

a. Arrangements for a smooth and peaceful transfer of authority from the Israeli military government and its Civil Administration to the Palestinian representatives.

b. Structure, powers and responsibilities of the Palestinian authority in these areas, except: external security, settlements, Israelis, foreign relations, and other mutually agreed matters.

c. Arrangements for the assumption of internal security and public order by the Palestinian police force consisting of police officers recruited locally and from abroad holding Jordanian passports and Palestinian documents issued by Egypt. Those who will participate in the Palestinian police force coming from abroad should be trained as police and police officers.

    d. A temporary international or foreign presence, as agreed upon.

    e. Establishment of a joint Palestinian-Israeli Coordination and Cooperation Committee for mutual security purposes.

    f. An economic development and stabilization program, including the establishment of an Emergency Fund, to encourage foreign investment, and financial and economic support. Both sides will coordinate and cooperate jointly and unilaterally with regional and international parties to support these aims.

    g. Arrangements for a safe passage for persons and transportation between the Gaza Strip and Jericho area.

4. The above agreement will include arrangements for coordination between both parties regarding passages:

    a. Gaza–Egypt; and

    b. Jericho–Jordan.

5. The offices responsible for carrying out the powers and responsibilities of the Palestinian authority under this Annex II and Article VI of the Declaration of Principles will be located in the Gaza Strip and in the Jericho area pending the inauguration of the Council.

6. Other than these agreed arrangements, the status of the Gaza Strip and Jericho area will continue to be an integral part of the West Bank and Gaza Strip, and will not be changed in the interim period.

ANNEX III: PROTOCOL ON ISRAELI-PALESTINIAN COOPERATION IN ECONOMIC AND DEVELOPMENT PROGRAMS

The two sides agree to establish an Israeli-Palestinian continuing Committee for Economic Cooperation, focusing, among other things, on the following:

1. Cooperation in the field of water, including a Water Development Program prepared by experts from both sides, which will also specify the mode of cooperation in the management of water resources in the West Bank and Gaza Strip, and will include proposals for studies and plans on water rights of each party, as well as on the equitable utilization of joint water resources for implementation in and beyond the interim period.

2. Cooperation in the field of electricity, including an Electricity

Development Program, which will also specify the mode of co-operation for the production, maintenance, purchase and sale of electricity resources.

3. Cooperation in the field of energy, including an Energy Development Program, which will provide for the exploitation of oil and gas for industrial purposes, particularly in the Gaza Strip and in the Negev, and will encourage further joint exploitation of other energy resources. This Program may also provide for the construction of a Petrochemical industrial complex in the Gaza Strip and the construction of oil and gas pipelines.

4. Cooperation in the field of finance, including a Financial Development and Action Program for the encouragement of international investment in the West Bank and the Gaza Strip, and in Israel, as well as the establishment of a Palestinian Development Bank.

5. Cooperation in the field of transport and communications, including a Program, which will define guidelines for the establishment of a Gaza Sea Port Area, and will provide for the establishing of transport and communications lines to and from the West Bank and the Gaza Strip to Israel and to other countries. In addition, this Program will provide for carrying out the necessary construction of roads, railways, communications lines, etc.

6. Cooperation in the field of trade, including studies, and Trade Promotion Programs, which will encourage local, regional and inter-regional trade, as well as a feasibility study of creating free trade zones in the Gaza Strip and in Israel, mutual access to these zones, and cooperation in other areas related to trade and commerce.

7. Cooperation in the field of industry, including Industrial Development Programs, which will provide for the establishment of joint Israeli-Palestinian Industrial Research and Development Centers, will promote Palestinian-Israeli joint ventures, and provide guidelines for cooperation in the textile, food, pharmaceutical, electronics, diamonds, computer and science-based industries.

8. A program for cooperation in, and regulation of, labor relations and cooperation in social welfare issues.

9. A Human Resources Development and Cooperation Plan, providing for joint Israeli-Palestinian workshops and seminars, and

for the establishment of joint vocational training centers, research institutes and data banks.

10. An Environmental Protection Plan, providing for joint and/or coordinated measures in this sphere.

11. A program for developing coordination and cooperation in the field of communication and media.

12. Any other programs of mutual interest.

ANNEX IV: PROTOCOL ON ISRAELI-PALESTINIAN COOPERATION CONCERNING REGIONAL DEVELOPMENT PROGRAMS

1. The two sides will cooperate in the context of the multilateral peace efforts in promoting a Development Program for the region, including the West Bank and the Gaza Strip, to be initiated by the G-7. The parties will request the G-7 to seek the participation in this program of other interested states, such as members of the Organisation for Economic Cooperation and Development, regional Arab states and institutions, as well as members of the private sector.

2. The Development Program will consist of two elements:

   a. an Economic Development Program for the West Bank and the Gaza Strip.

   b. a Regional Economic Development Program.

   A. The Economic Development Program for the West Bank and the Gaza Strip will consist of the following elements:

      1. A Social Rehabilitation Program, including a Housing and Construction Program.

      2. A Small and Medium Business Development Plan.

      3. An Infrastructure Development Program (water, electricity, transportation and communications, etc.).

      4. A Human Resources Plan.

      5. Other programs.

   B. The Regional Economic Development Program may consist of the following elements:

      1. The establishment of a Middle East Development Fund, as a first step, and a Middle East Development Bank, as a second step.

2. The development of a joint Israeli-Palestinian-Jordanian Plan for coordinated exploitation of the Dead Sea area.
3. The Mediterranean Sea (Gaza)—Dead Sea Canal.
4. Regional Desalinization and other water development projects.
5. A regional plan for agricultural development, including a coordinated regional effort for the prevention of desertification.
6. Interconnection of electricity grids.
7. Regional cooperation for the transfer, distribution and industrial exploitation of gas, oil and other energy resources.
8. A Regional Tourism, Transportation and Telecommunications Development Plan.
9. Regional cooperation in other spheres.

3. The two sides will encourage the multilateral working groups, and will coordinate towards their success. The two parties will encourage intersessional activities, as well as pre-feasibility and feasibility studies, within the various multilateral working groups.

AGREED MINUTES TO THE DECLARATION OF PRINCIPLES ON INTERIM SELF-GOVERNMENT ARRANGEMENTS

A. GENERAL UNDERSTANDINGS AND AGREEMENTS

Any powers and responsibilities transferred to the Palestinians pursuant to the Declaration of Principles prior to the inauguration of the Council will be subject to the same principles pertaining to Article IV, as set out in these Agreed Minutes below.

B. SPECIFIC UNDERSTANDINGS AND AGREEMENTS

Article IV
It is understood that:
1. Jurisdiction of the Council will cover West Bank and Gaza Strip territory, except for issues that will be negotiated in the perma-

nent status negotiations: Jerusalem, settlements, military locations, and Israelis.

2. The Council's jurisdiction will apply with regard to the agreed powers, responsibilities, spheres and authorities transferred to it.

Article VI (2)

It is agreed that the transfer of authority will be as follows:

1. The Palestinian side will inform the Israeli side of the names of the authorised Palestinians who will assume the powers, authorities and responsibilities that will be transferred to the Palestinians according to the Declaration of Principles in the following fields: education and culture, health, social welfare, direct taxation, tourism, and any other authorities agreed upon.

2. It is understood that the rights and obligations of these offices will not be affected.

3. Each of the spheres described above will continue to enjoy existing budgetary allocations in accordance with arrangements to be mutually agreed upon. These arrangements also will provide for the necessary adjustments required in order to take into account the taxes collected by the direct taxation office.

4. Upon the execution of the Declaration of Principles, the Israeli and Palestinian delegations will immediately commence negotiations on a detailed plan for the transfer of authority on the above offices in accordance with the above understandings.

Article VII (2)

The Interim Agreement will also include arrangements for coordination and cooperation.

Article VII (5)

The withdrawal of the military government will not prevent Israel from exercising the powers and responsibilities not transferred to the Council.

Article VIII

It is understood that the Interim Agreement will include arrangements for cooperation and coordination between the two parties in this regard. It is also agreed that the transfer of powers and responsibilities to the Palestinian police will be accomplished in a phased manner, as agreed in the Interim Agreement.

Article X

It is agreed that, upon the entry into force of the Declaration of Principles, the Israeli and Palestinian delegations will exchange the names of the individuals designated by them as members of the Joint Israeli-Palestinian Liaison Committee.

It is further agreed that each side will have an equal number of members in the Joint Committee. The Joint Committee will reach decisions by agreement. The Joint Committee may add other technicians and experts, as necessary. The Joint Committee will decide on the frequency and place or places of its meetings.

Annex II

It is understood that, subsequent to the Israeli withdrawal, Israel will continue to be responsible for external security, and for internal security and public order of settlements and Israelis. Israeli military forces and civilians may continue to use roads freely within the Gaza Strip and the Jericho area.

Done at Washington, D.C., this thirteenth day of September, 1993.

For the Government of Israel
For the P.L.O.

Witnessed By:

The United States of America
The Russian Federation

B. THE WASHINGTON DECLARATION
(ISRAEL—JORDAN—THE UNITED STATES)
July 25, 1994

A. After generations of hostility, blood and tears and in the wake of years of pain and wars, His Majesty King Hussein and Prime Minister Yitzhak Rabin are determined to bring an end to bloodshed and sorrow. It is in this spirit that His Majesty King Hussein of the Hashemite Kingdom of Jordan and Prime Minister and Minister of Defense, Mr. Yitzhak Rabin of Israel, met in Washington today at the invitation of President William J. Clinton of the United States of America. This initiative of President William J. Clinton constitutes an historic landmark in the United States' untiring efforts in promoting peace and stability in the Middle East. The personal involvement of the President has made it possible to realise agreement on the content of this historic declaration.

The signing of this declaration bears testimony to the President's vision and devotion to the cause of peace.

B. In their meeting, His Majesty King Hussein and Prime Minister Yitzhak Rabin have jointly reaffirmed the five underlying principles of their understanding on an Agreed Common Agenda designed to reach the goal of a just, lasting and comprehensive peace between the Arab States and the Palestinians, with Israel.

1. Jordan and Israel aim at the achievement of just, lasting and comprehensive peace between Israel and its neighbours and at the conclusion of a Treaty of Peace between both countries.

2. The two countries will vigorously continue their negotiations to arrive at a state of peace, based on Security Council Resolutions 242 and 338 in all their aspects, and founded on freedom, equality and justice.

3. Israel respects the present special role of the Hashemite Kingdom of Jordan in Muslim Holy shrines in Jerusalem. When negotiations on the permanent status will take place, Israel will give high priority to the Jordanian historic role in these shrines. In addition the two sides have agreed to act together to promote interfaith relations among the three monotheistic religions.

4. The two countries recognise their right and obligation to live in peace with each other as well as with all states within secure and recognised boundaries. The two states affirmed their respect for and acknowledgment of the sovereignty, territorial integrity and political independence of every state in the area.

5. The two countries desire to develop good neighbourly relations of cooperation between them to ensure lasting security and to avoid threats and the use of force between them.

C. The long conflict between the two states is now coming to an end. In this spirit the state of belligerency between Jordan and Israel has been terminated.

D. Following this declaration and in keeping with the Agreed Common Agenda, both countries will refrain from actions or activities by either side that may adversely affect the security of the other or may prejudice the final outcome of negotiations. Neither side will threaten the other by use of force, weapons, or any other means, against each other and both sides will thwart threats to security resulting from all kinds of terrorism.

E. His Majesty King Hussein and Prime Minister Yitzhak Rabin took note of the progress made in the bilateral negotiations within the Jordan-Israel track last week on the steps decided to implement the sub-agendas on borders, territorial matters, security, water, energy, environment and the Jordan Rift Valley.

In this framework, mindful of items of the Agreed Common Agenda (borders and territorial matters) they noted that the boundary sub-commission has reached agreement in July 1994 in fulfillment of part of the role entrusted to it in the sub-agenda. They also noted that the sub-commission for water, environment and energy agreed to mutually recognise, as the role of their negotiations, the rightful allocations of the two sides in Jordan River and Yarmouk River waters and to fully respect and comply with the negotiated rightful allocations, in accordance with agreed acceptable principles with mutually acceptable quality. Similarly, His Majesty King Hussein and Prime Minister Yitzhak Rabin expressed their deep satisfaction and pride in the work of the trilateral commission in its meeting held in Jordan on Wednesday, July 20th 1994, hosted by the Jordanian Prime Minister, Dr. Abdessalam al-Majali, and attended by Secretary of State Warren Christopher and Foreign Minister Shimon Peres. They voiced their pleasure at the association and commitment of the United States in this endeavour.

F. His Majesty King Hussein and Prime Minister Yitzhak Rabin believe that steps must be taken both to overcome psychological barriers and to break with the legacy of war. By working with optimism towards the dividends of peace for all the people in the region, Jordan and Israel are determined to shoulder their responsibilities towards the human dimension of peace making. They recognise imbalances and disparities are a root cause of extremism which thrives on poverty and unemployment and the degradation of human dignity. In this spirit His Majesty King Hussein and Prime Minister Yitzhak Rabin have today approved a series of steps to symbolise the new era which is now at hand:

1. Direct telephone links will be opened between Jordan and Israel.

2. The electricity grids of Jordan and Israel will be linked as part of a regional concept.

3. Two new border crossings will be opened between Jordan and Israel—one at the southern tip of Aqaba–Eilat and the other at a mutually agreed point in the north.

4. In principle free access will be given to third country tourists traveling between Jordan and Israel.

5. Negotiations will be accelerated on opening an international air corridor between both countries.

6. The police forces of Jordan and Israel will cooperate in combating crime with emphasis on smuggling and particularly drug smuggling. The United States will be invited to participate in this joint endeavour.

7. Negotiations on economic matters will continue in order to prepare for future bilateral cooperation including the abolition of all economic boycotts.

All these steps are being implemented within the framework of regional infrastructural development plans and in conjunction with the Jordan-Israel bilaterals on boundaries, security, water and related issues and without prejudice to the final outcome of the negotiations on the items included in the Agreed Common Agenda between Jordan and Israel.

G. His Majesty King Hussein and Prime Minister Yitzhak Rabin have agreed to meet periodically or whenever they feel necessary to review the progress of the negotiations and express their firm intention to shepherd and direct the process in its entirety.

H. In conclusion, His Majesty King Hussein and Prime Minister Yitzhak Rabin wish to express once again their profound thanks and appreciation to President William J. Clinton and his Administration for their untiring efforts in furthering the cause of peace, justice and prosperity for all the peoples of the region. They wish to thank the President personally for his warm welcome and hospitality. In recognition of their appreciation to the President, His Majesty King Hussein and Prime Minister Yitzhak Rabin have asked President William J. Clinton to sign this document as a witness and as a host to their meeting.

His Majesty King Hussein
Prime Minister Yitzhak Rabin
President William J. Clinton

C. DRAFT TREATY OF PEACE BETWEEN
ISRAEL AND SYRIA

The draft peace treaty presented by President Clinton to Israeli Prime Minister Ehud Barak and Syrian Foreign Minister Farouq Sharaa, Shepherdstown, Virginia, January 7, 2000. First published by Akiva Eldar in the Israeli daily Ha'aretz, January 13, 2000.

TREATY OF PEACE BETWEEN THE STATE OF ISRAEL
AND THE SYRIAN ARAB REPUBLIC

(Note: January 7, 2000. This draft text, prepared by the American side, has no official or legal status and does not necessarily reflect the views of any party. Its purpose is to serve as a tool in discussions.)

The Government of the State of Israel and the Government of the Syrian Arab Republic:

Aiming at the achievement of a just, lasting and comprehensive peace in the Middle East based on Security Council resolutions 242 and 338 and within the framework of the peace process initiated at Madrid on 31 October 1991;

Reaffirming their faith in the purposes and principles of the Charter of the United Nations and recognizing their right and obligation to live in peace with each other, as well as with all states, within secure and recognized boundaries;

Desiring to establish mutual respect and to develop honorable, friendly and good neighborly relations;

Resolved to establish permanent peace between them in accordance with this Treaty.

Have agreed as follows:

ARTICLE I: ESTABLISHMENT OF PEACE AND SECURITY WITHIN RECOGNIZED BOUNDARIES.

1. The state of war between Israel and Syria (hereinafter "the Parties") is hereby terminated and peace is established between them. The Parties will maintain normal, peaceful relations as set out in Article III below.

2. The permanent secure and recognized international boundary between Israel and Syria is the boundary set forth in Article II

below. The location of the boundary has been commonly agreed (Syrian position: and is based on the June 4, 1967 line) (Israeli position: taking into account security and other vital interests of the Parties as well as legal considerations of both sides). Israel will (S: withdraw) (I: relocate) all its armed forces (S: and civilians) behind this boundary in accordance with the Annex of this Treaty. (S: Thereafter, each Party will exercise its full sovereignty on its side of the international boundary, including as agreed in this Treaty.)

3. To enhance the security of both Parties, agreed security measures will be implemented in accordance with Article IV below.
4. The time line at the Annex sets forth an agreed schedule for synchronized implementation of this and the other Articles of this Treaty.

ARTICLE II: INTERNATIONAL BOUNDARY

1. The international boundary between Israel and Syria is as shown on the mapping materials and co-ordinates specified in the Annex. This boundary is the permanent, secure and recognized international boundary between Israel and Syria and supersedes any previous boundary or line of demarcation between them.
2. The Parties will respect the inviolability of this boundary and of each other's territory, territorial waters and airspace.
3. A Joint Boundary Commission is hereby established. Its functions and activities are set out in the Annex.

ARTICLE III: NORMAL PEACEFUL RELATIONS

1. The Parties will apply between them the provisions of the Charter of the United Nations and the principles of international law governing relations among states in time of peace.

In particular:

   a. they recognize and will respect each other's sovereignty territorial integrity and political independence and right to live in peace within secure and recognized boundaries; and
   b. they will establish and develop friendly and good neighborly relations, will refrain from the threat or use of force, directly or indirectly, against each other, will cooperate in promoting peace, stability and development in their region and will settle all disputes between them by peaceful means.

2. The Parties will establish full diplomatic and consular relations, including the exchange of resident ambassadors.
3. The Parties recognize a mutuality of interest in honorable and good neighborly relations based on mutual respect and for this purpose will:
    a. promote beneficial bilateral economic and trade relations including by enabling the free and unimpeded flow of people, goods and services between the two countries.
    b. remove all discriminatory barriers to normal economic relations, terminate economic boycotts directed at the other Party, repeal all discriminatory legislation, and cooperate in terminating boycotts against either Party by third parties.
    c. promote relations between them in the sphere of transportation. In this regard, the Parties will open and maintain roads and international border crossings between the two countries, cooperate in the development of rail links, grant normal access to its ports for vessels and cargoes of the other or vessels or cargoes destined for or coming from that Party, and enter into normal civil aviation relations.
    d. establish normal postal, telephone, telex, data facsimile, wireless and cable communications and television relay services by cable, radio and satellite between them on a non-discriminatory basis in accordance with relevant international conventions and regulations; and
    e. promote cooperation in the field of tourism in order to facilitate and encourage mutual tourism and tourism from third countries. The Annex sets forth the agreed procedures for establishing and developing these relations, (I: including the schedule for the attainment of relevant agreements as well as arrangements concerning the Israelis and Israeli communities in areas from which Israeli forces will be relocated pursuant to Article I).
4. The Parties undertake to ensure mutual enjoyment by each other's citizens of due process of law within their respective legal systems and before their courts.

    Notes (I) Components of normal peaceful relations which require further discussion: cultural relations; environment; interconnection of electricity grids; energy; health and medicine; and agriculture.

(II) Other possible areas for consideration: combating crime and drugs; anti-incitement cooperation; human rights; places of historical and religious significance and memorials; legal cooperation in the search for missing persons.

ARTICLE IV: SECURITY

A. *Security Arrangements*

Recognizing the importance of security for both Parties as an important element of permanent peace and stability, the Parties will employ the following security arrangements to build mutual confidence in the implementation of this Treaty and to provide for the security needs of both Parties:

1. Areas of limitation of forces and capabilities, including limitations on their readiness and activities, and on armaments, weapon system and military infrastructure, as described in the Annex.

2. Within the areas of limitation of forces and capabilities, the establishment of a demilitarized zone (I: encompassing both the area from which Israeli forces will be relocated and the existing Area of Separation established under the Agreement on Disengagement between Israeli and Syrian Forces of 31 May 1974) (S: of equal scope on both sides of the border). As described in the Annex, no military forces, armaments, weapon systems, military capabilities, or military infrastructure will be introduced into the demilitarized zone by either Party and only a limited civil police presence may be deployed in the area. (I: Both sides agree not to fly over the demilitarized zone without special arrangements.)

3. Early warning capabilities, including an early warning ground station on Mt. Hermon (I: with an effective Israeli presence) (S: operated by the United States and France under their total auspices and responsibilities). Arrangements for the unimpeded, efficient and continuous operation of this station are as detailed in the Annex.

4. A monitoring, inspection and verification mechanism (I: composed of the two Parties and a multinational component and including on-site technical means) (S: through an international

presence), to monitor and supervise the implementation of the security arrangements. Details regarding these security arrangements, including their scope, positioning and nature, as well as other security arrangements, are specified in the Annex.

B. *Other Security Measures*

As further steps to ensure a permanent cessation of hostilities of any form between the Parties or from their territories against each other.

1. Each Party undertakes to refrain from cooperating with any third party in a hostile alliance of a military character and will ensure that territory under its control is not used by any military forces of a third party (including their equipment and armaments) in circumstances that would adversely affect the security of the other Party.

2. Each Party undertakes to refrain from organizing, instigating, inciting, assisting or participating in any acts or threats of violence against the other Party, its citizens or their property wherever located, and will take effective measures to ensure that no such acts occur from, or are supported by individuals on, its territory or territory under its control. In this regard, without prejudice to the basic rights of freedom of expression and association, each Party will take necessary and effective measures to prevent the entry, presence and operation in its territory of any group or organization, and their infrastructure, which threatens the security of the other Party by the use of, or incitement to the use of, violent means.

3. Both Parties recognize that international terrorism in all its forms threatens the security of all nations and therefore share a common interest in the enhancement of international cooperative efforts to deal with this problem.

C. *Cooperation and Liaison in Security Matters*

The Parties will establish a direct liaison and coordination mechanism between them as described in the Annex to facilitate implementation of the security provisions in this Treaty. Its responsibilities will include: direct and real-time communication on security issues, minimization of friction along the international border, addressing any problems arising during the implementation process, helping to prevent errors or misinterpretations, and maintaining direct and continuous contacts with the monitoring, inspection and verification mechanism.

ARTICLE V: WATER

1. The Parties recognize that full resolution of all water issues between them constitutes a fundamental element in ensuring a stable and lasting peace. (S: Based on relevant international principles and practices), the Parties have agreed to establish (I: arrangements that will ensure the continuation of Israel's current use in quantity and quality of all) (S: mutually agreeable arrangements with respect to water quantities and quality from) the surface and underground waters in the areas from which Israeli forces will (I: relocate) (S: withdraw) pursuant to Article I, as detailed in the Annex. (I: The arrangements should include all necessary measures to prevent contamination, pollution or depletion of the Kinneret/Tiberias and Upper Jordan River and their sources.)

2. For the purposes of this Article and the Annex, the Parties will establish (I: a Joint Water Committee and a supervision and enforcement mechanism) (S: a Joint Administrative Board). The composition, mandate and mode of operations of the (I: Joint Water Committee and the supervision and enforcement mechanism) (S: Joint Administrative Board) will be as detailed in the Annex.

3. The Parties have agreed to cooperate on water-related matters, as detailed in the Annex, (I: including ensuring the quantity and quality of water allocated to Israel under other agreements concerning water originating in Syria.)

ARTICLE VI: RIGHTS AND OBLIGATIONS

1. This Treaty does not affect and shall not be interpreted as affecting in any way the rights and obligations of the Parties under the Charter of the United Nations.

2. The Parties undertake to fulfill in good faith their obligations under this Treaty, without regard to action or inaction of any other Party and independently of any instrument external to this Treaty.

3. The Parties will take all the necessary measures for the application in their relations of the provisions of the multilateral conventions to which they are Parties, including the submission of appropriate notification to the Secretary General of the United Nations and other depositories of such conventions. They will also abstain from actions that would curtail the rights of either Party to participate in international organizations to which they belong in accordance with the governing provisions of those organizations.

4. The Parties undertake not to enter into any obligation in conflict with this Treaty.

5. Subject to Article 103 of the United Nations Charter, in the event of a conflict between the obligations of the Parties under the present Treaty and any of their other obligations, the obligations under this Treaty will be binding and implemented.

ARTICLE VII: LEGISLATION

The Parties undertake to enact any legislation necessary in order to implement the Treaty, and to repeal any legislation that is inconsistent with the Treaty.

ARTICLE VIII: SETTLEMENT OF DISPUTES

Disputes between the Parties arising out of the interpretation or application of the present Treaty shall be settled by negotiation.

ARTICLE IX: FINAL CLAUSES

1. This treaty shall be ratified by both Parties in conformity with their respective constitutional procedures. It shall enter into force on the exchange of instruments of ratification and shall supersede all previous bilateral agreements between the Parties.

2. The Annexes and other attachments attached to this Treaty shall constitute integral parts thereof.

3. The Treaty shall be communicated to the Secretary General of the United Nations for registration in accordance with the provisions of Article 102 of the Charter of the United Nations.

Done this day——in————in the English, Hebrew and Arabic languages, all languages being equally authentic. In case of any divergence of interpretation, the English text will be authoritative.

D. THE CLINTON PARAMETERS

President Clinton's Parameters as Presented by Him to the Israeli and Palestinian Negotiators on December 23, 2000.

On Wednesday, I went over general parameters to help focus your negotiations and gave you specific tasks. I know you have been working hard. I have heard reports from Madeleine and Dennis, and frankly, I believe that at this rate you will not get there. We are running out of time and cannot afford to lose this opportunity.

I believe it is my responsibility to give you my best judgment of what it will take to narrow your differences on key issues so that leaders can take final decisions. Obviously, you will have to resolve other issues; but if you can resolve these core ones, I believe you will reach a deal.

I want to make clear this is not a U.S. proposal. Rather, it reflects my best judgment of what it will take to conclude an agreement in the next two weeks. If these ideas are not accepted by either side, they will be off the table and have no standing in the future.

I ask you to take these ideas back to your leaders. I am prepared to meet with them separately to further refine them and plan for a summit to conclude an agreement. But it should be clear to them that they should not come here to renegotiate these ideas. They should come here to try to refine them within the boundaries I will set forth. I would like to know by Wednesday if they are prepared to come on that basis.

TERRITORY

You heard from me last time that I believe the solution will need to provide for Palestinian sovereignty over somewhere between 90 and 100 percent of West Bank territory, and that there will need to be swaps and other territorial arrangements to compensate for the land Israel annexes for its settlement blocs.

Based on what I have heard since we last met, I believe the solution should be in the mid-90 percents; I believe you should work on the basis of a solution that provides between 94 and 96 percent of West Bank territory to the Palestinian state with a land swap of 1 to 3 percent; you will need to work out other territorial arrangements such as permanent

Safe Passage. As you work out the territorial arrangements, you might also consider the swap of leased land to meet your respective needs.

Given these parameters, you should lose no time in developing final maps consistent with the criteria I laid out last time (e.g., 80 percent of the settlers in blocs, contiguity of territory for each side, minimize annexation and the number of Palestinians affected).

SECURITY

As I said on security the last time, the challenge is to address legitimate Israeli security concerns while respecting Palestinian sovereignty. The key lies in an international presence that can only be withdrawn by the agreement of both sides. My best judgment is that Israeli withdrawal should be phased over thirty-six months while the international force is gradually introduced into the area. At the end of this period, a small Israeli presence in fixed locations would remain in the Jordan Valley under the authority of the international force for another thirty-six months. This period could be reduced in the event of favorable regional developments that diminish the threats to Israel.

On early-warning stations, I believe that Israel should maintain three facilities on the West Bank with a Palestinian liaison presence; the stations would be subject to review after three years, with any change in status to be mutually agreed.

On the emergency deployments, I understand you still have work to do on developing maps of the relevant areas and routes. In defining what would constitute an "emergency," I suggest you think about formulations that refer to "an imminent and demonstrable threat to Israel's national security that requires Israel to declare a national state of emergency." Of course, the international forces would need to be notified of any such determination.

On airspace, I suggest that the state of Palestine will have sovereignty over its airspace but that the two sides should work out special arrangements for Israeli training and operational needs.

I understand that the Israeli position is that Palestine should be defined as a "demilitarized state," while the Palestinian side has proposed "a state of limited arms." As a possible compromise formula I suggest you think in terms of a "non-militarized state." This would be consistent with the fact that, as well as a strong Palestinian security force, Palestine will have an international force for border security and deterrence purposes. Whatever the terminology, you need to work out specific understandings on the parameters of the Palestinian security forces.

JERUSALEM AND REFUGEES

I am acutely aware how difficult the Jerusalem and refugee issues are to both sides. My sense, however, is that the remaining gaps are more in formulations than in the practical realities.

JERUSALEM

On Jerusalem, as I said last time the most promising approach is to follow the general principle that what is Arab in the City should be Palestinian and what is Jewish should be Israeli; this would apply to the Old City as well. I urge you to work on maps to create maximum contiguity for both sides within this framework.

We have all spent a lot of energy trying to solve the issue of the Haram/Temple Mount. One thing seems clear to me—the gap does not relate to practical administration of the area but to symbolic issues of sovereignty and finding a way to accord respect to the religious beliefs of both sides. This is nevertheless clearly one of your most sensitive issues and concerns the interests of religious communities beyond Israel and Palestine.

I know you have been speaking about a number of formulations. Perhaps you can agree on one. But I want to suggest two additional approaches that I believe would formalize Palestinian de facto control over the Haram while respecting the convictions of the Jewish people. Under each, there could be an international monitoring system to provide mutual confidence.

1. Your agreement could provide for Palestinian sovereignty over the Haram, and for Israeli sovereignty over either "the Western Wall and the space sacred to Judaism of which it is a part" or "the Western Wall and the holy of holies of which it is a part." There would be a firm commitment by both not to excavate beneath the Haram or behind the Western Wall.

2. Alternatively, the agreement could provide for Palestinian sovereignty over the Haram and Israeli sovereignty over the Western Wall and for "shared functional sovereignty over the issue of excavation under the Haram or behind the Western Wall." That way, mutual consent would be required before any excavation takes place in these areas.

One of these formulations should be acceptable to you both.

REFUGEES

The issue of Palestinian refugees is no less sensitive than Jerusalem. But here again my sense is that your differences are focused mostly on how to formulate your solutions, not on what will happen on the practical level.

I believe Israel is prepared to acknowledge the moral and material suffering caused to the Palestinian people as a result of the 1948 War and the need to assist the international community in addressing the problem. I also believe the Palestinian side is prepared to join in such an international solution and that we have a pretty good idea of what it would involve.

The fundamental gap seems to be how to handle the concept of the right of return. I know the history and how hard it would be for the Palestinian leadership to appear to be abandoning this principle. At the same time, I know the Israeli side cannot accept any reference to a right of return that would imply a right to immigrate to Israel in defiance of Israel's sovereign policies on admission or that would threaten the Jewish character of the State.

Any solution will have to address both of these needs. It will also have to be consistent with the two-state approach that both sides have accepted as the way to end the Israeli-Palestinian conflict. A new State of Palestine is about to be created as the homeland of the Palestinian people, just as Israel was established as the homeland of the Jewish people. Under this two-state solution, our guiding principle has to be that the Palestinian state will be the focal point for the Palestinians who choose to return to the area, without ruling out that Israel will accept some of these refugees.

I believe you need to adopt a formulation on the right of return that will make clear there is no specific right of return to Israel, itself, but that does not negate the aspirations of Palestinian refugees to return to the area. I propose two alternatives:

Both sides recognize the right of Palestinian refugees to return
to historic Palestine.
Both sides recognize the right of Palestinian refugees to a
homeland.

The agreement would define the implementation of this general right in a way that is consistent with the two-state solution. It would list the five possible homes for refugees: 1) The State of Palestine; 2)

Areas in Israel being transferred to Palestine in the land swap; 3) Re-habilitation in host country; 4) Resettlement in third country; 5) Admission to Israel.

In listing these five options, you would make clear that return to the West Bank, Gaza, or the areas acquired through the land swap would be a right for all Palestinian refugees, while rehabilitation in their host countries, resettlement in third countries, or absorption into Israel would depend upon the policies of those countries. Israel could indicate in the agreement that it intended to establish a policy so that some of the refugees could be absorbed into Israel, consistent with Israel's sovereign decision.

I believe that priority should be given to the refugee population in Lebanon. Taken together the parties would agree that these steps implement Resolution 194.

END OF CONFLICT

I propose that the agreement clearly mark the end of the conflict and its implementation put an end to all claims. This could be implemented through a UN Security Council Resolution that notes that resolutions 242 and 338 have been implemented and through the final release of Palestinian prisoners.

WRAP-UP

I believe this is the outline of a fair and lasting agreement. It gives the Palestinian people the ability to determine their future on their own land, a sovereign and viable state recognized by the international community, al-Quds as its capital, sovereignty over the Haram, and new lives for the refugees.

It gives the people of Israel a genuine end to the conflict, real security, the preservation of sacred religious ties, the incorporation of 80 percent of the settlers into Israel, and the largest Jewish Jerusalem in history, recognized by all as your capital.

This is the best I can do. I would ask you to brief your leaders and let me know if they are prepared to come for discussions based on these ideas. I want to be very clear on one thing. These are my ideas. If they are not accepted they are not just off the table. They go with me when I leave office.

E. THE ARAB LEAGUE'S BEIRUT DECLARATION
ON THE SAUDI PEACE INITIATIVE
March 28, 2002

The Arab Peace Initiative

The Council of Arab States at the Summit Level at its 14th Ordinary Session, reaffirming the resolution taken in June 1996 at the Cairo Extra-Ordinary Arab Summit that a just and comprehensive peace in the Middle East is the strategic option of the Arab countries, to be achieved in accordance with international legality, and which would require a comparable commitment on the part of the Israeli government.

Having listened to the statement made by his royal highness Prince Abdullah bin Abdul Aziz, crown prince of the Kingdom of Saudi Arabia, in which his highness presented his initiative calling for full Israeli withdrawal from all the Arab territories occupied since June 1967, in implementation of Security Council Resolutions 242 and 338, reaffirmed by the Madrid Conference of 1991 and the land-for-peace principle, and Israel's acceptance of an independent Palestinian state with East Jerusalem as its capital, in return for the establishment of normal relations in the context of a comprehensive peace with Israel.

Emanating from the conviction of the Arab countries that a military solution to the conflict will not achieve peace or provide security for the parties, the Council:

1. Requests Israel to reconsider its policies and declare that a just peace is its strategic option as well.

2. Further calls upon Israel to affirm:

    I—Full Israeli withdrawal from all the territories occupied since 1967, including the Syrian Golan Heights, to the June 4, 1967 lines as well as the remaining occupied Lebanese territories in the south of Lebanon.

    II—Achievement of a just solution to the Palestinian refugee problem to be agreed upon in accordance with UN General Assembly Resolution 194.

    III—The acceptance of the establishment of a sovereign independent Palestinian state on the Palestinian territories occupied since June 4, 1967 in the West Bank and Gaza Strip, with East Jerusalem as its capital.

3. Consequently, the Arab countries affirm the following:

I—Consider the Arab-Israeli conflict ended, and enter into a peace agreement with Israel, and provide security for all the states of the region.

II—Establish normal relations with Israel in the context of this comprehensive peace.

4. Assures the rejection of all forms of Palestinian patriation which conflict with the special circumstances of the Arab host countries.

5. Calls upon the government of Israel and all Israelis to accept this initiative in order to safeguard the prospects for peace and stop the further shedding of blood, enabling the Arab countries and Israel to live in peace and good neighbourliness and provide future generations with security, stability and prosperity.

6. Invites the international community and all countries and organisations to support this initiative.

7. Requests the chairman of the summit to form a special committee composed of some of its concerned member states and the secretary general of the League of Arab States to pursue the necessary contacts to gain support for this initiative at all levels, particularly from the United Nations, the Security Council, the United States of America, the Russian Federation, the Muslim states and the European Union.

Notes

1. Syria First

PAGE

14 *Rabin had ignored diplomatic protocol:* "Israeli Preference for Nixon Hinted," *Washington Post,* June 11, 1972, p. A1.

15 *"sucker punched":* See Tom Fiedler, "Clinton: Don't Fall for GOP Labels," *Miami Herald,* August 12, 1992.

2. Dual Containment

PAGE

31 *"If [Saddam] wants a different relationship":* Thomas L. Friedman, "The New Presidency: Clinton Backs Raid but Muses about a New Start," *New York Times,* January 14, 1993.

31 *"no intention of normalizing relations":* Thomas L. Friedman, "Clinton Affirms U.S. Policy on Iraq," *New York Times,* January 15, 1993.

32 *Even Muammar Qadhafi:* See Anthony Lake, "Confronting Backlash States," *Foreign Affairs* 73, no. 2 (March/April 1994), pp. 45–55.

34 *on arms from the United States:* The United States sold Saddam sixty Hughes helicopters and encouraged its European allies to provide everything from air defense radar to Exocet missiles and ballistic missile technology. From 1985 to 1990, the U.S. Department of Commerce approved $1.5 billion in exports to Iraq of American high technology and other equipment with potential military uses—some of it shipped directly to such Iraqi agencies as the Ministry of Defense, Atomic Energy Commission, and air force. U.S. firms provided such products as advanced computers, electronic instruments, and high-grade graphics terminals for rocket testing and analysis; flight simulators and test equipment; microwave communications gear; radar maintenance equipment, and computer mapping systems. See Henry Weinstein and William C. Rempel, "Iraq Arms: Big Help From U.S.; Technology was Sold with Approval—And Encouragement—From the Commerce Department but often Over Defense Officials' Objections," *Los Angeles Times,* February 13, 1991, p. A1.

34 *clashes with the Iranian navy:* Dilip Hiro, Introduction to *Neighbors, Not Friends: Iraq and Iran after the Gulf Wars* (New York: Routledge, 2001); and Ken Pollack, *The Persian Puzzle: The Conflict between Iran and America* (New York: Random House, 2004), pp. 224–27.

36 *April Glaspie:* See "Confrontation in the Gulf; Excerpts from Iraqi Document on Meeting With U.S. Envoy," *New York Times,* September 23, 1990, sec. 1, part 1, p. 19.

38 *clothe its policy:* As Secretary of State Christopher explained it, "Our policy is that all the U.N. resolutions should be faithfully and fully obeyed by Saddam Hussein. It's just inconceivable to me that he can obey those resolutions and stay in power" (*This Week with David Brinkley,* ABC News, April 4, 1993).

42   *the* New York Times: See Douglas Jehl, "U.S. Seeks Ways to Isolate Iran; Describes Leaders as Dangerous," *New York Times,* May 27, 1993, p. A1.

42   *the* Washington Post: R. Jeffrey Smith and Daniel Williams, "White House to Step Up Plans to Isolate Iran, Iraq; Administration to Try 'Dual Containment,'" *Washington Post,* May 23, 1993, p. A26.

42   *As I outlined in the speech:* Martin Indyk, "The Clinton Administration's Approach to the Middle East," Soref Symposium, May 18, 1993, www.washington institute.org/pubs/indyk.

3. "That's What Kings Do"

PAGE

47   *As a child growing up:* See Warren Christopher, *Chances of a Lifetime* (New York: Scribner, 2001), chapter 1.

54   *they paid from $35 to 50 billion:* See Shahram Chubin and Charles Tripp, *Iran and Iraq at War* (Boulder, Colo.: Westview Press, 1988), p. 154; R. King, "The Iran-Iraq War: the Political Implication," *Adelphi Papers* No. 219 (London: International Institute for Strategic Studies, 1987), pp. 17–18, 33.

55   *American dependence:* In the 1990s, for example, Saudi Arabia accounted for between 15 and 18 percent of all U.S. oil imports. See Department of Energy, Energy Information Administration, Annual Energy Review 2003 data, Table 5.7, Petroleum Net Imports by Country of Origin, 1960–2003, http://www.eia.doe .gov/emeu/aer/txt/ptb0507.html.

58   *leave well enough alone:* For a wider discussion of the Clinton administration's approach to the issue of political change in the Arab world, see Martin Indyk, "Back to the Bazaar," *Foreign Affairs* 81, no. 1 (January/February 2002), pp. 75–88.

59   *vitiated the impact:* Steven Heydemann, "Upgrading Authoritarianism in the Arab World," Saban Center for Middle East Policy at the Brookings Institution, *Analysis Paper* 13 (October 2007).

4. September 13, 1993

PAGE

65   *Arafat sent Rabin a letter:* For the full text of the letter see David Makovsky, *Making Peace with the PLO: The Rabin Government's Road to the Oslo Accord* (Boulder, Colo.: Westview Press, 1996), appendix 12.

65   *prepared announcement:* Transcript of remarks by President Bill Clinton on the Mideast Peace Agreement, the Rose Garden, the White House, Washington, D.C., September 10, 1993, Federal News Service.

66   *As he told the* New York Times: Thomas L. Friedman, "Mideast Accord: U.S. Policy; Clinton Seeks to Buoy Israelis, Saying U.S. Backing Is Firm," *New York Times,* September 12, 1993, p. A1.

67   *having second thoughts:* Leah Rabin put the time of his decision at 5:30 P.M. on Friday evening, which was 10:30 A.M. in Washington, the time that Clinton was beginning his remarks in the Rose Garden. See Leah Rabin, *Rabin: Our Life, His Legacy* (New York: G. P. Putnam's Sons, 1997), pp. 251–52.

67   *As Christopher tells it:* Christopher, *Chances of a Lifetime,* p. 202.

70   *little-noticed letter:* For the details of these negotiations see Uri Savir, *The Process: 1,100 Days That Changed the Middle East* (New York: Vintage, 1999), chapter 3, and Makovsky, *Making Peace with the PLO,* pp. 79–81.

70   *"strong police force":* See "Article VIII: Public Order and Security," *The Israeli-Palestinian Declaration of Principles on Interim Self-Government Arrangements,* September 1993, in Appendix A, p. 418.

70   *Dennis Ross suggested to Shimon Peres:* See Shimon Peres, *Battling for Peace* (New York: Random House, 1995), p. 306.

70 *Christopher also raised the issue:* Abu Mazen, who was in the meeting, published an embellished account of this statement by Christopher. See Mahmoud Abbas (Abu Mazen), *Through Secret Channels* (London: Garnet, 1995), p. 214.

74 *Asad's intelligence service:* See Jillian Becker, *The PLO: The Rise and Fall of the Palestine Liberation Organization* (London: Wiedenfeld & Nicolson, 1984), pp. 46–47.

74 *By one account:* Abu Iyad, *Palestinien sans Patrie* (Paris: Edition Fayolle, 1978), pp. 80–84. By another account, Asad was unhappy about releasing Arafat because he suspected him of being under the influence of the Muslim Brotherhood and too independent of Syria. See Patrick Seale, *Asad: The Struggle for the Middle East* (London: I. B. Tauris, 1988), p. 125.

5. The Anatomy of Rabin's Oslo Decision
PAGE

79 *Rabin openly expressed:* See Itamar Rabinovich, *The Brink of Peace: The Israeli-Syrian Negotiations* (Princeton, N.J.: Princeton University Press, 1999), p. 83.

80 *ninth round of the Oslo negotiations:* The ninth round took place in Gressheim, Oslo, from July 4 to 6, 1993; the tenth round took place in Halvorsbole, Oslo, from July 11 to 12, 1993. See Savir, *The Process*, pp. 35–44, and Mahmoud Abbas, *Through Secret Channels*, pp. 159–66.

80 official *negotiation:* For the details of these negotiations see Savir, *The Process*. Savir says that the Clinton administration was "aware" of the negotiations but doubted they would yield results. And he admits that Peres turned up at Point Mugu "out of the blue" with an agreement, worried that we would be piqued at being left out of the negotiations (pp. 65–67). Peres is deliberately vague about what happened but claims that he had an enthusiastic green light from Dan Kurtzer and Warren Christopher. Peres says that during the months of intensive official negotiations in Oslo he found it "strange" not to have heard anything from the United States. He says he assumed it was due to our discretion and skepticism. He also admits he "initiated no direct contact with the Americans regarding the Oslo process." See Peres, *Battling for Peace*, p. 296.

81 *a letter:* For the text of the letter from Arafat to Rabin see Abbas, *Through Secret Channels*, pp. 81–82.

81 *answered Rabin's concerns:* As Dennis recalls, "Arafat made clear he would defer all the sensitive issues, especially Jerusalem and jurisdiction, in order to reach an interim agreement." Ross, *The Missing Peace* (New York: Farrar, Straus and Giroux, 2004), p. 108.

83 *Christopher would remember:* As Christopher recounts it, "Our meeting ended with Asad having given me little of consequence to bring to Rabin, apart from a willingness to talk further." For Christopher's account see his *Chances of a Lifetime*, pp. 220–22.

83 *Rabin went out to the assembled press:* See David Makovsky, Bill Hutman, and Michal Yudelman, "Rabin 'convinced Syria wants peace,'" *Jerusalem Post*, August 6, 1993.

83 *strange way to show disappointment:* Rabinovich recounts that he too only learned of Rabin's real disappointment later on: "I had been aware of his disappointment with Asad's initial reaction, but it was only later that I learned the full extent of his disappointment" (Rabinovich, *The Brink of Peace*, p. 107).

83 *what we thought were unofficial:* Christopher notes in his account that he had been aware of the talks in Oslo "but because of Rabin's open skepticism, had never thought much would come of them" (*Chances of a Lifetime*, p. 199).

84 *"which is what the Americans prefer":* Savir, *The Process*, p. 50.

84 *Shimon Peres wrote:* Peres wrote: "The vacuum may be filled by opposing forces with other initiatives, *including the possibility of desired progress between Israel*

and Syria. Secretary Christopher is at this very moment visiting our region" [emphasis added] (*Battling for Peace,* p. 296).

84 *It was one or the other:* Ibid., p. 299.

85 *Rabin did not reveal:* Interview with Itamar Rabinovich, New York, February 27, 2002.

85 *Rabin had reminded him:* Ibid.

86 *in crisis:* According to Savir's account, the Oslo talks broke down on July 26. They did not resume until August 13, when the breakthrough was achieved. See Savir, *The Process,* pp. 44–53.

87 *He had promised voters:* On June 10, 1992, Rabin told the Golan settlers, "The Golan is a strategic asset and Israel will never come down from the Heights." *Voice of Israel,* June 10, 1992, accessed through *BBC Summary of World Broadcasts,* June 13, 1992.

90 *This has led some analysts:* See John J. Mearsheimer and Stephen M. Walt, *The Israel Lobby and U.S. Foreign Policy* (New York: Farrar, Straus & Giroux, 2007).

6. Detour on the Road to Damascus
PAGE

92 *the president gave a lengthy interview:* "Time and again . . . the President hammered at a single point: Israeli public opinion. That was the key, he said, because Israel is the country that will have to trade tangible security assets for promises." See Thomas L. Friedman, "Mideast Accord: U.S. Policy; Clinton Seeks to Buoy Israelis, Saying U.S. Backing is Firm," *New York Times,* September 12, 1993, p. A1.

93 *clandestine meeting with King Hussein:* The account of this meeting comes from author's interview with Efraim Halevy, who was present.

94 *their first meeting:* This account also comes from an interview with Efraim Halevy, who attended the meeting. He elaborates in his book, *Man in the Shadows: Inside the Middle East Crisis with a Director of Israel's Mossad* (New York: St. Martin's, 2006).

96 *Mark Twain had observed:* The Innocents Abroad, or, The New Pilgrims' Progress (New York: Modern Library, 2003), p. 336.

97 *"high regard":* See Henry Kissinger, *Years of Upheaval* (Boston: Little, Brown, 1985), pp. 781–82.

97 *constructive and flexible:* Jimmy Carter, *Keeping Faith: Memoirs of a President* (New York: Bantam, 1982), p. 286.

97 *"intellectually engaging":* James Baker, *The Politics of Diplomacy* (New York: G. P. Putnam's Sons, 1995), p. 427.

98 *none of his acuity:* Bill Clinton, *My Life* (New York: Knopf, 2004), pp. 574–75.

102 *set of principles:* The points in the Peres-Hussein agreement were:
  • immediate commencement of secret, bilateral negotiations to reach a peace agreement;
  • a U.S./Jordan/Israel committee on economic development that would meet at ministerial level;
  • a quadrilateral committee including the PLO would address joint development projects and refugee issues;
  • a Jordan/Palestinian/Israel committee would be established to promote trade and development;
  • Jordan's international debt burden would be addressed;
  • security coordination would be enhanced to foil any attempt to menace the peace process;
  • no interference in the religious status quo in Jerusalem would be permitted;
  • Jordan/Israel free trade zones would be established on a gradual basis; and
  • the two sides would cooperate in the Red Sea.

103 *Peres started sending:* On November 1, 1993, for example, Peres declared on Is-

rael Radio, "There is an impression as though Israel doesn't want to continue the peace negotiations with Syria. It's totally unfounded." *Voice of Israel,* Jerusalem, November 1, 1993, accessed as "Peres affirms desire to pursue negotiations with Syria," *BBC Summary of World Broadcasts,* November 3, 1993.

104 *with Syria rather than Jordan:* Rabinovich refers to three gestures toward the Syrians: a cabinet reaffirmation of a government decision of June 19, 1967, that provided for return of all occupied territory except Jerusalem; a public statement that the Golan law of 1981 did not actually provide for the annexation of the Golan; and a statement that Israel did not seek or claim sovereignty in the Golan (Itamar Rabinovich, *The Road Not Taken* [New York: Oxford University Press, 1991], p. 128).

104 *one thing they would be listening for:* Clyde Haberman, the *New York Times* correspondent in Israel, came up with the same conclusion in a front-page story written on the day of the Geneva summit: "Clinton in Europe: The Mideast Poker Game; After Asad's Play, the Pressure is Now on Israel," *New York Times,* January 17, 1994, p. A1.

105 *Syria seeks a just and comprehensive peace:* "The President's News Conference with President Hafez al-Asad," Public Papers of the Presidents, January 16, 1994. Emphasis added.

106 *foremost exponent:* Contrast this with Asad's position as he espoused it only six months earlier, before he knew about the Oslo deal: "Our call for a comprehensive solution stems from the fact that we are concerned with what is offered to our Palestinian brothers and with what they accept or reject. We cannot proceed without them or overtake them." See interview with President Hafez al-Asad by Talal Salman, *Al Safir,* August 12, 1993, Foreign Broadcast Information Service, NES-93-156, August 16, 1993, p. 56.

106 *"shrink Israel's influence":* Patrick Seale with Linda Butler, "Asad's Regional Strategy and the Challenge from Netanyahu," *Journal of Palestine Studies* 26 no. 1 (Autumn 1996), pp. 36–37.

115 *The White House promptly announced:* On March 18, 1994, the White House released the following statement: "President Asad informed the President that he had consulted with the leaders of Syria, Jordan and Lebanon and that they had agreed that bilateral peace process negotiations with Israel would resume in April. President Asad noted that the Arab leaders took this decision in the context of their support for the UN Security Council resolution on Hebron and to enhance efforts to improve the security of the Palestinians and to advance the overall negotiating process toward a comprehensive and lasting peace." See "Presidential Statement on Presidential Calls to Asad and Hussein," Office of the Press Secretary, March 18, 1994, accessed April 28, 2005 through the Clinton Foundation, http://www.clintonfoundation.org/legacy/031894-presidential -statement-on-presidential-calls-to-asad-and-hussein.htm.

115 *Rabin had not expected:* Interview with Amnon Lipkin-Shahak, Washington, D.C., January 16, 2003.

7. Peace with Jordan

PAGE

127 *needed America's military backing:* See Asher Susser, "Jordan," in *Middle East Contemporary Survey,* vol. XVIII, Westview Press, 1994.

128 *debt relief for Jordan:* At the time, Jordan's foreign debt amounted to some $6.9 billion, of which $951 million was owed to the United States ($398 million in military debt and $553 million in nonmilitary obligations).

129 *Dennis asked him:* As Dennis recounts, "Efraim, I know what's going on here: The Jordanians are using you to convince us that we must do more for them. At one level, that's great. It is wonderful that they see the value of using you with

us; that certainly indicates that they have a high stake in good relations with you. On the other hand, it makes me wonder who is manipulating whom." See Ross, *The Missing Peace*, p. 173.

131 *Asad would not try to block:* A year later Asad would explain his thinking at the time he discovered the pending Israeli-Jordanian breakthrough. He criticized the Jordanians: "The sight with which they measure their steps is very short." He noted that King Hussein's decision had put pressure on Syria, but as long as he was engaged in negotiations with Israel, he said it would not alter his strategy. "We cannot change what had happened. . . . We have also decided not to wage battles among us because this is actually in the interest of those who plan for our misery." See Asad interview with *al-Ahram* newspaper, quoted in "Asad says peace should be fair," United Press International, October 11, 1995.

136 *Peres was humiliated:* See Samuel Segev, *Crossing the Jordan* (New York: St. Martin's, 1998), p. 305.

141 *According to a poll:* See "Israeli Right Ahead in Polls," Agence France-Presse, November 18, 1994.

8. Dual Containment and the Peace Process
PAGE

149 *followed the advice of the chairman:* See Clinton, *My Life*, pp. 525–26.

152 *Saddam's regime had resorted:* Kenneth Pollack, *The Threatening Storm: The Case for Invading Iraq* (New York: Random House, 2002), pp. 68–71.

153 *tough battle in the Security Council:* See John M. Goshko, "Sentiment Against U.N. Sanctions on Iraqis Grows," *Washington Post*, October 7, 1994, p. A30.

158 *Bush dismissed Franklin Roosevelt's meeting:* "President Discusses Freedom and Democracy in Latvia," transcript, May 7, 2005, http://www.whitehouse.gov/news/releases/2005/05/20050507-8.html.

160 *viewed himself as a "cowboy":* This is how Baer described himself in his autobiography, and the way he was portrayed in the movie *Syriana*. See Robert Baer, *See No Evil: The True Story of a Ground Soldier in the CIA's War on Terrorism* (New York: Crown, 2002), p. 173.

162 *"The action you have planned":* Ibid., p. 173.

163 *"outlined the coup":* Ibid., p. 174. Emphasis added.

163 *"operating at the edge of my orders":* Ibid., p. 199.

165 *defected to Jordan:* Amatzia Baram, *Building Toward Crisis: Saddam Husayn's Strategy for Survival*, Washington Institute for Near East Policy, 1998, Policy Paper No. 47, pp. 8–10; Pollack, *The Threatening Storm*, pp. 76–77.

166 *promote a military putsch:* See Pollack, *The Threatening Storm*, p. 80; and Baram, *Building Toward Crisis*, pp. 50–51.

9. Iran's Breakout
PAGE

168 *undermined by American oil companies:* When President Clinton finally shut off this avenue in 1995, European and Asian companies wasted little time filling the gap. See Meghan L. O'Sullivan, *Shrewd Sanctions: Statecraft and State Sponsors of Terrorism* (Washington, D.C.: Brookings Institution, 2002), pp. 64–67.

168 *two executive orders:* Executive Order 12957, *Prohibiting Certain Transactions with Respect to the Development of Iranian Petroleum Resources*, 60 Fed. Reg. 14, 615 (March 17, 1995), and Executive Order 12959, *Prohibiting Certain Transactions with Respect to Iran*, 60 Fed. Reg. 24, 757 (May 9, 1995).

168 *engage more constructively:* See, for example, an op-ed by the former deputy assistant secretary of state for international energy policy, Edward L. Morse, "Misguided Sanctions," *New York Times*, March 22, 1995, p. A19.

168 *As Warren Christopher noted:* Christopher noted at the time: "We feel Iran is an

outlaw nation, that they have projected terror throughout the region and they have sought to undermine the peace process. . . . Wherever you look, you find the evil hand of Iran in the region." See Norman Kempster, "Christopher Ends His Role in Debate on Conoco-Iran Deal," *Los Angeles Times,* March 13, 1995, and Sid Balman Jr., "U.S. May Block Conoco-Iran Deal," United Press International, March 9, 1995.

169 *nearly a dozen foreign oil companies:* Rex J. Zedalis, "The Total S.A. Case: Meaning of 'Investment' Under the ILSA," *American Journal of International Law* 92, no. 3 (July 1998), p. 539; "Shell Decides Not to Develop Iran Oilfields," *New York Times,* July 4, 1995.

169 *secondary sanctions:* In May 1998, after a year of negotiations, the Clinton administration struck a deal with the European Union in which ILSA sanctions were waived on three companies from France, Russia, and Malaysia involved in a $2 billion investment in Iran's South Pars gas field. In return, parent countries of the companies involved pledged to cooperate with the "broad objectives" of American law, which meant they would work to deny Iran access to nuclear or other WMD technology and oppose its sponsorship of terrorism. See Douglas Jehl, "Iran Smiles After U.S. Waives Sanctions Against 3 Companies," *New York Times,* May 20, 1998, p. A13; Elizabeth Shogren and Robin Wright, "U.S. Waives Sanctions On Iran Gas Deal," *Los Angeles Times,* May 19, 1998, p. A1; James Bennet, "To Clear Air With Europe, U.S. Waives Some Sanctions," *New York Times,* May 19, 1998, p. A6.

169 *As Robert Kagan has argued:* Robert Kagan, *Of Paradise and Power: America and Europe in the New World Order* (New York: Knopf, 2004), p. 55.

170 *driving up the prices:* As Jahangir Amuzegar, a former Iranian finance minister, noted, during this period inflation was unacceptably high, cost and price distortions enormous, and unemployment and underemployment politically explosive. See "Adjusting to Sanctions," *Foreign Affairs* 76, no. 3 (May/June 1997), p. 31.

170 *forfeited during the first Bush:* According to Richard Perle's congressional testimony in February 2005, "in a display of unbelievable, careless management we put pressure on agents operating in Iran to report with greater frequency and didn't provide improved communications. . . . When the CIA's sources stepped up their reporting, the Iranian intelligence authorities quickly saw the surge in traffic and, as I understand it, virtually our entire network in Iran was wiped out." See Greg Miller, "C.I.A. Operation in Iran Failed When Spies Were Exposed," *Los Angeles Times,* February 12, 2005, p. A1.

171 *change in Iranian policy:* The indication of a change in Iranian policy may have come earlier, in the November 1995 terrorist attack on the Riyadh headquarters of the U.S. military training mission for the Saudi National Guard, which killed five Americans. However, the Saudis promptly arrested and executed four men before we were able to gain access to them, making it impossible to determine whether they were acting on Iranian instructions. See Richard Clarke, *Against All Enemies* (New York: Free Press, 2004), pp. 112–13.

171 *determined to thwart Clinton's attempt:* See Anoushiravan Ehteshami and Raymond A. Hinnebusch, *Syria and Iran: Middle Powers in a Penetrated Regional System* (New York: Routledge, 1997), pp. 188–89.

173 *"The government of Syria":* Voice of the Islamic Republic of Iran Network 1, Tehran (Persian), June 24, 1995, in *BBC Summary of World Broadcasts,* June 26, 1995.

174 *"The more a country":* See "Iran, Syria differ on Mideast peace process," Agence France-Presse, June 25, 1995.

174 *One editorial in the Iranian press:* See "The Ungratefulness of Damascus," *Abrar,* Tehran (Persian), December 30, 1995, in *BBC Summary of World Broadcasts,* January 9, 1996.

176 *celebrated Rabin's death:* See Pollack, *The Persian Puzzle*, p. 276.

176 *Dennis Ross publicly declared:* Rabinovich, *The Brink of Peace*, p. 210.

178 *Clinton gave a speech:* The president said, "So I say this to the people of Israel: We've been with you every step of the way for the last three years. As Israel takes further risks for peace in the future, it can count on further manifestations of American support. We must be with you every step of the way until there is a comprehensive, lasting peace in the Middle East. Now is not the time to turn back, and the United States must do its part." See Remarks by the President at United States Coast Guard Academy Commencement, May 22, 1996, accessed through FDCH Federal Department and Agency Documents.

178 *he repeated the message:* The president said, "I think we all recognize that that election tomorrow is a very important election for the future of Israel and the future of the Middle East. Israel is a great democracy, and the people are fully capable of making their own judgments. The United States supports the peace process. And we have made it clear that if further steps are taken that entail risks for peace, we will stand with the government and the people of Israel, and the leaders of Israel, in minimizing those risks. We will do everything we possibly can to do it. That is the important thing that I want the people of Israel to know. They have to make the decision whether they want to pursue the peace process or not. That is their decision. We believe that, ultimately, it's the only way to bring peace and security. And we want both peace and security. I think that's what they all want. I think that's why the race is so close. But I can tell you this. If they decide to stay on the path of peace, we will share the risk. We will do what we can to minimize the risk. They can make the decision. Whatever decision they make, we obviously—all countries—will accept and respect. But if they decide to stay with peace, we will do what we can to make sure they can have security, as well." See Remarks by President Clinton in Veterans Announcement, May 28, 1996, accessed through U.S. Newswire.

179 *trying to help Yeltsin's reelection bid:* Cf. Strobe Talbott, *The Russia Hand* (New York: Random House, 2002), pp. 191–97. Talbott quotes Clinton as saying, "I know . . . we've got to stop short of giving a nominating speech for the guy. But we've got to go all the way in helping in every other respect" (p. 195).

10. Saddam Resurgent

PAGE

183 *infant mortality rates:* Department of Economic and Social Affairs, 2000 Demographic Yearbook: fifty-second issue (New York: United Nations, 2002), p. 384.

184 *Annan publicly criticized Saddam:* Annan said that "the Iraqi leadership must understand that if it wants sanctions to be ended and to see the light at the end of the tunnel, it must comply fully. . . . We did not get the kind of cooperation we expected from the Iraqis." See Christopher S. Wren, "U.N. Council Asked to Raise Limit on Sale of Iraqi Oil," *New York Times*, February 3, 1998, p. A8.

184 *netted him $7–12 billion:* The Government Accountability Office estimated that from 1997 through 2002, Hussein received between $7.43 billion and $12.8 billion in illicit revenue. The Iraq Survey Group put the number at $8.53 billion and the Independent Inquiry Committee put it at $10.23 billion for the years 1997–2002. See U.S. Government Accountability Office, "United Nations, Lessons Learned from Oil for Food Program Indicate the Need to Strengthen U.N. Internal Controls and Oversight Activities," April 2006, Appendix III, http://www.gao.gov/new.items/d06330.pdf.

184 *able to allocate:* The Volcker Committee, appointed by Kofi Annan, reported in October 2005 how Iraq systematically rewarded companies within those countries it viewed as friendly, particularly those on the U.N. Security Council. Russian companies purchased about one-third of the oil during the program. French

companies were second only to the Russians. All in all, more than 2,253 companies paid $1.8 billion in illegal surcharges and kickbacks to Saddam. See Independent Inquiry Committee, *Report on the Manipulation of the Oil-for-Food Programme,* October 27, 2005, pp. 2, 9, 47.

190 *vast amounts:* According to a December 1998 report by the Wisconsin Project on Nuclear Arms Control, Iraq had not accounted for at least 3.9 tons of VX nerve gas; 550 artillery shells filled with mustard gas; 107,500 casings for chemical arms; 157 aerial bombs filled with germ agents; 25 missile warheads containing germ agents such as anthrax, aflotoxin, and botulinum; and components for three to four implosion-type nuclear weapons missing only uranium fuel. See "What the Inspectors Can't Find and Why they Can't Find it," Report by the Wisconsin Project on Nuclear Arms Control, December 20, 1998 at http://www.wisconsinproject.org/pubs.html#reports.

192 *Zinni concluded:* See Remarks at Center for Defense Information Board of Directors Dinner by General Anthony Zinni, U.S.M.C. (Ret.), May 12, 2004, available at http://www.cdi.org/program/document.cfm?DocumentID=2208.

195 *Egypt, Syria, Saudi Arabia:* See Thomas W. Lippman and Bradley Graham, "Support for U.S. Stance on Iraq Grows; 8 Arab States Hold Baghdad Responsible for Crisis as Military Buildup Continues," *Washington Post,* November 13, 1998, p. A38.

201 *According to David Kay:* See James Risen, "Ex-Inspector Says C.I.A. Missed Disarray in Iraq's Arms Programs," *New York Times,* January 26, 2004.

201 *The hard fact:* Address to the Nation, President William J. Clinton, December 16, 1998, Office of the Press Secretary.

202 *backfire on the United States:* See Jane Mayer, "The Manipulator," *The New Yorker,* June 7, 2004, which details how Chalabi exploited partisan divisions between the Republican Congress and the Clinton administration to build support for his operations. Mayer notes that the "Information Collection Program" set up in the State Department was transferred to the Pentagon's Defense Intelligence Agency after the 9/11 attacks, thereby ensuring that Chalabi's "intelligence" was fed directly into the U.S. intelligence system.

205 *some have argued:* See George A. Lopez and David Cortright, "Containing Iraq: Sanctions Worked," *Foreign Affairs* 83, no. 4 (July/August 2004), p. 1, and Joseph Cirincione and Dipali Mukhopadhyay, "Why Pollack is Wrong: We Have Contained Saddam," *Carnegie Analysis,* February 21, 2003, at http://www.ceip.org/files/nonprolif/templates/article.asp?NewsID=4379.

207 *ability to reconstitute:* See, for example, the testimony of a former senior Iraqi intelligence officer who ran Saddam's WMD procurement network. He told Bob Drogin of the *Los Angeles Times* that in 2001 he went to Jordan, Cyprus, Morocco, South Africa, and Argentina, using phony passports to help arrange the secret purchase of "dual-use" items, such as medical laboratory equipment, to be used to build chemical and biological weapons if the United Nations one day declared Iraq WMD-free and lifted sanctions. The intelligence officer also claimed that in 1996, Saddam ordered his intelligence services to create a series of secret cells of Iraqi scientists and technicians to formulate plans on how to build WMD when the United Nations lifted sanctions. "We could start again anytime," the intelligence officer said. "It's very easy. Especially biological." See Bob Drogin, "The Vanishing: What Happened to the WMD?" *The New Republic,* July 21, 2003.

207 *achieved U.N. approval:* See Martin Indyk, "We Forgot the Russians," *Washington Post,* March 23, 2003, and James P. Rubin, "Stumbling Into War," *Foreign Affairs* 82, no. 5 (September/October 2003), p. 46.

209 *unnecessary, self-inflicted wound:* This argument is also made by one of the leading neoconservative advocates of regime change in Iraq. See Robert Kagan,

"America's Crisis of Legitimacy," *Foreign Affairs* 83, no. 2 (March/April 2004), pp. 65–87.

213 *render them impervious to sanctions:* For the way that sanctions are being used by Iranian president Mahmoud Ahmadinejad to consolidate his grip on power, see Michael Slackman, "Hard Times in Iran Help Leaders Tighten Their Hold," *New York Times,* September 5, 2007.

11. Engaging Iran
PAGE
217 *Even the Revolutionary Guards:* See Pollack, *The Persian Puzzle,* p. 314.
217 *Khatami spoke of the need:* In what appeared to be a deliberate effort to mirror our own approach, Khatami explained in a press conference after his election that "our policies towards the U.S.A. depends on changes in the attitude and positions of the U.S.A. concerning Iran's Islamic revolution." See Ibid., pp. 314–15.
218 *as Tony Lake had written:* Lake, "Confronting Backlash States."
219 *reached understandings with Iran:* Since the 1980s, Shiite pilgrims from Iran had staged often violent demonstrations during the hajj. By the 1990s, confrontations between Iranian demonstrators and Saudi riot police had become a regular feature of the pilgrimage. Abdullah negotiated an understanding with the Iranian government that allowed increased numbers of Iranians to make the pilgrimage if they behaved themselves in an appropriate manner. The Iranian government demonstrated its goodwill by sending organizers who worked with the Saudi police to keep the crowd under control. See Henner Fürtig, *Iran's Rivalry with Saudi Arabia Between the Gulf Wars* (Reading, U.K.: Ithaca Press, 2002).
220 *"little victory for Iran":* Islamic Republic News Agency (IRNA), Tehran (English), October 13, 1997, in *BBC Summary of World Broadcasts,* October 14, 1997.
221 *"If some day another situation":* Interview with President Mohammad Khatami, January 7, 1998, http://www.cnn.com/WORLD/9801/07/iran/interview.html.
221 *Arafat showed Clinton a letter:* See Madeleine Albright, *Madam Secretary: A Memoir* (New York: Miramax, 2003), p. 320.
223 *Secretary Albright followed up:* Remarks by Secretary of State Madeleine K. Albright at the 1998 Asia Society Dinner, New York, June 17, 1998, http://www.asiasociety.org/speeches/albright.html.
223 *showed no sign of it:* The day after the speech, Iranian radio claimed that Washington's offer was "inadequate." Foreign Minister Kamal Kharrazi said a few days later, "If the United States is serious, it must prove it by . . . changing its hostile stand toward Iran." See Voice of the Islamic Republic of Iran, external service, Tehran (English), June 18, 1998, in BBC Worldwide Monitoring, October 18, 1998; Christophe de Roquefeuil, "Guarded Iranian Reaction to US Normalization Offer," Agence France-Presse, June 19, 1998; and Voice of the Islamic Republic of Iran, Tehran (English), June 20, 1998, in *BBC Monitoring Middle East,* June 21, 1998.
223 *In his own Asia Society speech:* Remarks by H.E. Dr. Kamal Kharrazi, Foreign Minister of the Islamic Republic of Iran at the Asia Society, New York, September 28, 1998, www.asiasociety.org/speeches/kharrazi.html.
224 *he and his allies were under assault:* See Pollack, *The Threatening Storm,* pp. 327–31.
224 *collected evidence:* The evidence came from two perpetrators of the attack who had been imprisoned in Saudi Arabia. For years the Saudis had refused to provide the FBI with access to these culprits, for fear that it would precipitate an American retaliatory attack on Tehran that would destabilize the Saudi kingdom. With Clinton now seeking to engage Khatami, however, the chances of

such an attack had receded, so Crown Prince Abdullah relented. In June 2001, the U.S. District Court in Alexandria, Virginia, indicted thirteen Saudis and one Lebanese on charges of murder, attempted murder, conspiracy to kill U.S. nationals and employees, and the use of weapons of mass destruction. The indictment refers to the suspects as "inspired, supported and directed by elements in the Iranian government."

228 *"respond positively":* Cited in Puneet Talwar, "Iran in the Balance," *Foreign Affairs* 80, no. 4 (July/August 2001), p. 68.

228 *Albright made a forthright apology:* See Secretary of State Madeleine K. Albright, Remarks before the American-Iranian Council, March 17, 2000, Washington, D.C., as released by the Office of the Spokesman, U.S. Department of State, http://secretary.state.gov/www/statements/2000/000317.html.

228 *supreme leader responded:* See Supreme Leader's Speech on the Day of Eid Ghadir, Mashhad, March 25, 2000, http://www.khameini.de/speeches/speech 2000.htm#25.3.2000.

229 *Khatami said as much:* See Guy Dinmore and Najmeh Bozorgmehr, "FT Interview: Mohamed Khatami," *Financial Times,* September 5, 2006; Robin Wright, "Interview with Mohamed Khatami," *Washington Post,* September 5, 2006.

229 *another effort at engagement:* In May 2003, Sadegh Kharazi, Iran's ambassador to France, faxed a two-page letter to the State Department that outlined steps that both the United States and Iran might take. The letter called for cooperation on nuclear issues and said Iran would cease supporting terrorist groups and would recognize Israel in exchange for the United States abolishing sanctions. See Glenn Kessler, "In 2003, U.S. Spurned Iran's Offer of Dialogue; Some Officials Lament Lost Opportunity," *Washington Post,* June 18, 2006, p. A16. For the text of the letter see http://www.armscontrol.org/pdf/2003 Spring Iran Proposal .pdf.

229 *decision to halt:* National Intelligence Council, "Iran: Nuclear Intentions and Capabilities," National Intelligence Estimate, November 2007.

230 *offered instead to enter negotiations:* On May 31, 2006, Secretary of State Rice announced that if Iran suspended its nuclear program, the United States would join Europe in direct negotiations with Iran. Statement by Secretary of State Condoleezza Rice, May 31, 2006.

231 *sanctions tend to:* Michael Slackman, "Hard Times Help Leaders in Iran Tighten Their Hold," *New York Times,* September 5, 2007, p. A1.

232 *preferred an antagonistic relationship:* As Meghan O'Sullivan noted in her comprehensive study of the impact of American sanctions on Iran, "the most important reason why sanctions failed to elicit any change in Iran's actions was that the stakes associated with the behavior in question were high and the costs of Iranian noncompliance with U.S. demands were low. . . . Because of the importance of these activities to Iran, the choice between ending them or enduring the comparatively small costs associated with U.S. sanctions has been an easy one." See Meghan L. O'Sullivan, *Shrewd Sanctions,* pp. 91–92.

232 *improvement in oil prices:* Iranian oil revenues rose from $16.09 billion in 1999 to $25.44 billion in 2000 and $21.42 billion in 2001. See 2003 Annual Statistical Bulletin, http://www.opec.org.

235 *cockiness that Ahmadinejad displayed:* In a speech in Tehran, Ahmadinejad declared that "the political power of the occupiers is being destroyed rapidly and very soon we will be witnessing a great power vacuum in the region. We, with the help of regional friends and the Iraqi nation, are ready to fill this void." See Megan Greenwell, "Riots at Iraqi Religious Festival Leave 28 Dead," *Washington Post,* August 29, 2007, p. A13.

12. Syria Redux

246 *the Syrian mission:* Netanyahu had been looking for a breakthrough with Syria to avoid Clinton's insistence that he implement the Oslo Accords. For five weeks in mid-1998, Lauder conducted nine separate negotiating sessions with Asad on Netanyahu's behalf. Negotiations deadlocked in September 1998, when Asad told Lauder not to come back to Damascus without a map from Netanyahu showing the line of Israeli withdrawal. Bibi wanted to draw a line with a thick marker pen on a small map in order to leave room for negotiations about the exact positioning of the border. However, he could not produce it without the involvement of the IDF, which required the consent of Yitzhak Mordechai, his defense minister.

As the former commander of Northern Command, Mordechai objected to the security arrangements Lauder had worked out with Asad and considered the whole negotiation behind Clinton's back improper. He consulted with Ariel Sharon, then foreign minister. An old-fashioned infantry general, Sharon would not be party to an offer of full withdrawal from the Golan that would cede the high ground to Syria. Netanyahu was stymied. If he gave the map to Lauder without Mordechai's and Sharon's approval it would probably have brought his government down. Without the map, Lauder could not return to Damascus and his mission ended.

Bibi tried to resurrect it a month later. En route to the Wye Plantation summit with Clinton and Arafat in October 1998, he met with Lauder in Washington and asked him to convey to Asad through Syrian ambassador Walid Mouallem his willingness to travel from Wye to Damascus to deliver in person the map Asad was demanding. This appears to have been a last-minute attempt by Netanyahu to prepare an escape route from the Wye deal he expected to have to conclude with Arafat. But Asad would not countenance the heretical idea of hosting an Israeli prime minister in Damascus based on a map he had not yet seen. See Zev Schiff, "Syria agreed to foreign troops on Hermon," *Haaretz*, May 28, 1999; Daniel Pipes, "What Netanyahu almost gave away," *The New Republic*, July 5, 1999, p. 18; Ross, *The Missing Peace*, pp. 509–15.

251 freier: As Israeli psychologist Raphi Rothstein explains it, the *freier* is the symbol of gullibility, naïveté, and in the last account, stupidity. Overall, a *freier* is a weak, pathetic, laughable person in the harsh Darwinist struggle for existence that characterizes life in Israel.

13. Shepherdstown Breakdown

266 *Arab press was reporting:* See "Islamists Report Upsurge in Arrest of Opposition," *al-Quds al-Arabi,* January 18, 2000, *BBC Summary of World Broadcasts,* January 20, 1998.

268 *he publicly implicated:* See Barak's speech in Shimon Shamir and Bruce Maddy-Weitzman, eds., *The Camp David Summit—What Went Wrong* (Brighton, U.K.: Sussex Academic Press, 2005), pp. 133–34.

268 *Miller has argued vehemently:* When Dennis and I briefed Aaron in Damascus after the breakthrough meeting with Asad, he went into a funk. His critique of the "Syria first" strategy can be found at http://www.dayan.org/commentary/ Miller-Tel%20Aviv%20University.pdf. See also Aaron David Miller, "A 'Syria-First' Peace Plan Can Only Be a Distraction," *Los Angeles Times,* January 11, 2004, part M, p. 5, and *The Much Too Promised Land: America's Search for Arab-Israeli Peace* (New York: Bantam, 2008), pp. 252–57.

14. Syrian Denouement

270 *They complained:* Seven years later, as Barak attempted to win back leadership of the Labor Party, he wrote about his "lack of maturity" during his tenure as prime minister: "It is possible that I became prime minister too soon. I made many mistakes, and my lack of experience was to my detriment. Today I know that there are no shortcuts . . . and that leadership is a shared burden, not a solo mission." See Mazal Mualem, "Barak Announces He Will Run for Labor Leadership," *Haaretz,* January 8, 2007.

273 *Barak's positions:* Because the Syrians insist that any future negotiation begin from the point where they last left off, the details of Barak's proposal are worth noting:

- The early warning ground station on the Golan Heights should be under the total control of the United States with nine Israelis manning that site for no more than seven years.
- In return, Barak would accept the same kind of early warning ground station on Israeli territory, manned in part by Syrians for the same period.
- The Golan Heights area from which the Israeli army withdrew would be demilitarized.
- Limited forces zones would be established on each side of this demilitarized zone of the border based on a ratio of four kilometers of Israeli territory for every ten kilometers of Syrian territory.
- A U.S. monitoring group would operate on both sides of the border to check key military locations to ensure that no preparation were being made for offensive operations.
- Syrian strike forces could be deployed around Damascus provided the United States had the ability to inspect them at any time.
- Israel's withdrawal would be completed in three phases over three years and three months.
- All the settlers would be withdrawn during this period but the settlements would not be dismantled.
- Embassies would be established, ambassadors exchanged, and the borders opened in the first phase; complete normalization would be achieved by the end of the third phase.

283 *Bashar al-Asad responded:* See "Key Passages from Interview with Syria's President," *New York Times,* December 1, 2003, p. A12.

283 *the conditions were reimposed:* Aron Heller, "Israel Cannot Meet Syria Demand to Commit in Advance to Full Withdrawal from Golan," Associated Press, July 22, 2007.

286 *stumbling block for Asad:* In his memoir, Dennis Ross remembers that he had deep reservations before the Geneva summit: "I felt that Asad would not accept what we were bringing from Barak" (*The Missing Peace,* p. 578).

15. The Road to the Summit

288 *Barak told me:* For emphasis, Barak referenced a letter he had received from Supreme Court President Justice Moshe Landau, the lead judge in the trial of Adolf Eichmann, the chief architect of the Holocaust. Landau warned Barak that "succeed or fail, there are certain things you should not do because they affect the very identity of the Zionist state." See Shragai Nadav, "Look who's hoisting Yesha's banner," *Haaretz,* July 18, 2000.

289 *daring operations:* In May 1972, Barak led a group of Israeli commandos that stormed a hijacked Sabena airliner on the Tarmac at Lod Airport, Tel Aviv, freeing ninety-seven passengers and ten crew who had been held hostage for twenty-

three hours. In 1973, Barak disguised himself as a woman, wearing a wig and packing explosives in his purse, to lead an assassination squad into Beirut to kill three senior Palestinian figures in revenge for the murder of eleven Israeli athletes at the 1972 Munich Olympics. Barak and his team landed in rubber dinghies on the Lebanese shore, executed the Palestinians, and escaped unharmed. Barak helped organize the July 4, 1976, storming of Entebbe Airport in Uganda to rescue passengers from a hijacked Air France jet. Israeli commandos rescued one hundred hostages. Barak is also thought to have masterminded the 1988 assassination of the PLO's military commander, Khalil al-Wazir, otherwise known as Abu Jihad, in his Tunisian villa.

292 *doing business with him on the side:* During Rabin's time, Ginossar had helped to arrange the monopolies on cement, gas, tobacco, and flour for Arafat, whereby commissions would be paid by the Israeli suppliers to the Palestinian Authority and directly deposited in Arafat-controlled bank accounts in Israel. Subsequently, Ginossar arranged for most of the proceeds of these funds to be transferred to Swiss bank accounts, as Peter Hirschberg reported in 1996. In December 2002, Ozrad Lev, a former partner to Ginossar, disclosed that $300 million in Palestinian Authority funds was transferred to Arafat through a secret Swiss account managed by Ginossar. Lev claimed Ginossar made $10 million through the deal. See Peter Hirschberg, "Playing Monopoly," *Jerusalem Report,* February 22, 1996, p. 14; Laurie Copans, "Israeli former envoy says he helped transfer funds illegally to Arafat and his top aide," Associated Press, December 5, 2002.

293 *storm of opposition:* The National Religious Party leader Yitzhak Levi said his party, which had five seats, would leave the coalition because of the vote. Shas and Yisrael Baaliya voted against the move, raising fears they would bolt, too. See Mike O'Connor and Lee Hockstader, "Riots Sweep West Bank and Gaza; Palestinian Protesters, Police Battle Israelis in Bloodiest Clashes in 4 Years," *Washington Post,* May 16, 2000, p. A1; Deborah Sontag, "Palestinian Forces Exchange Gunfire With Israeli Troops," *New York Times,* May 16, 2000, p. A1.

296 *argue persuasively:* Four months before the outbreak of the intifada, Nasrallah proclaimed on Syrian television that "with resistance and steadfastness we can force on our enemy whatever we want. . . . The Lebanese example, I believe, will prompt the Palestinian people to adopt the option of resistance and intifada." Syrian Arab Television, Damascus (Arabic), June 1, 2000, accessed through *BBC Summary of World Broadcasts,* June 3, 2000.

300 *outer ring of Palestinian villages:* During the 2006 election campaign, when Olmert was running for prime minister, one of his spokesmen reiterated the same ideas in public. As Otniel Schneller explained Olmert's plan, "The Old City, Mount Scopus, the Mount of Olives, the City of David, Sheikh Jarra will remain in our hands, but Kafr Akeb, A-Ram, Shuafat, Hizma, A-Zaim, A-Tur, Abu Dis are not part of historic Jerusalem, and in the future, when the Palestinian state is established, they will become its capital." The Old City and its environs would be under international religious-political rule. See Nadav Shragai, *Haaretz,* March 23, 2006.

301 *"Not even for two hours":* As quoted by Shlomo Ben-Ami in an interview with Ari Shavit, *Haaretz,* October 3, 2001.

303 *a more reasonable approach:* Under the proposal, the IDF would be able to move swiftly from Israel eastward down specified highways to designated deployment areas in the Jordan Valley, where it could marshal its tanks for defense against an eastern front coalition. Shlomo Yanai has since outlined his security concept in "Israel's Core Security Requirements for a Two State Solution," *Analysis Paper Number 3,* Saban Center for Middle East Policy, Brookings Institution, January 2005.

304 *U.N. General Assembly Resolution 194:* Section 11 of Resolution 194 states, ". . . the refugees wishing to return to their homes and live at peace with their neighbors should be permitted to do so at the earliest practicable date, and that compensation should be paid for the property of those choosing not to return and for loss of or damage to property which, under principles of international law or in equity, should be made good by the governments or authorities responsible. . . ."

304 *explosive potential of the situation:* In March, Mandy Orr, the Israeli general in charge of West Bank Palestinians not yet under Arafat's control, briefed me in detail on the growing despair in the West Bank: "The trend is very bad. Either there will be an agreement and things will change or Yasser Arafat will have to avoid becoming the target by channeling the hatred towards us." And in a meeting in the same month, Abu Ala warned me in dire terms that if something didn't move in the negotiations, the situation in the West Bank and Gaza would erupt.

16. Trapped at Camp David

PAGE

308 *were confounded:* As Dan Meridor, a former Likud minister of justice and member of the Israeli delegation, wrote in his diary, "The president dropped the paper because the Americans were afraid. It sent the signal that the United States is not prepared to risk anything" (Interview with Dan Meridor, Tel Aviv, August 7, 2003).

314 *written message from Arafat:* Arafat's response contained five points:
   1. If the Palestinians have sovereignty in Jerusalem, we will leave it to the president to decide the percentage for the settlement blocs and the ratio of territorial swaps.
   2. On the Jordan River, we must have control over the entire border but will accept an international presence there under U.S. leadership.
   3. We are ready to enter into immediate discussions on security arrangements.
   4. The finality of conflict will come at the conclusion of the Comprehensive Agreement on Permanent Status but we will deal with any formula you propose.
   5. We need a just solution for the refugees based on U.N. Resolution 194.

315 *Yasser Arafat was aware:* Akram Haniyah, "Camp David Papers," *al-Ayyam,* August 6, 2000, pp. 1, 15.

315 *Caliph Umar Bin-al-Khattab:* The Caliph Umar was one of the Companions of the Prophet who, after his death, had helped spread the Muslim domain to Persia, Iraq, Syria, and Palestine. Umar's conquest of Jerusalem in 638 had been a peaceful affair; Saladin's capture of Crusader-controlled Jerusalem in 1187 was a similarly bloodless encounter. Umar insisted on being led to the Temple Mount, where King Solomon had built the first Jewish Temple and Herod had built the second. Umar was horrified to see that the ruins had been used by the Christians as the city rubbish dump. He directed that a mosque be built at the southern end of the platform—away from the Temple ruins—where Herod had built his palace. That is where the al-Aqsa Mosque—the third-holiest mosque in Islam—stands today. Saladin was also purposeful in his determination to turn Jerusalem into a Muslim holy city. But Saladin invited the Jews, who had been banished by the Crusaders, to return to Jerusalem, providing them with their own district within the city walls adjacent to the Temple Mount. See Karen Armstrong, *Jerusalem: One City, Three Faiths* (New York: Ballantine, 1996), chapters 11, 14; Kanan Makiya, *The Rock: A Tale of Seventh-Century Jerusalem* (New York: Pantheon, 2001), pp. 317–19.

316 *diplomatic compound on the Haram:* Although this was Schwartz's preferred so-

lution, he outlined other ways of dealing with the sovereignty issue: sovereignty over the Temple Mount/Haram al-Sharif could be shared in a condominium-like arrangement; by agreement the sovereignty could be left in dispute (both sides would disagree over who held sovereignty but that would not disrupt the day-to-day functional arrangements); or sovereignty could be divided, with the Palestinians acquiring sovereignty over the surface of the Haram and the Israelis retaining sovereignty over the Western Wall.

318 *most intensive deliberations:* This account is based on interviews with some of the participants in the discussion and the diary of Dan Meridor.

321 *"I can't go to see Arafat":* As quoted in Robert Malley and Hussein Agha, "Camp David: The Tragedy of Errors," *New York Review of Books,* August 9, 2001, p. 8.

322 *he was going too far, too fast:* After the next night, walking back to my cabin at 4 A.M., I bumped into Shlomo Ben-Ami, who asked me whether I thought it was necessary for Barak to go so far on Jerusalem. As Shlomo recalls our meeting in the dark woods, we agreed that "Ehud was nuts." See Ari Shavit interview with Shlomo Ben-Ami, "End of a Journey," *Haaretz,* October 3, 2001.

325 *argue that he was preoccupied:* A counterproposal from Arafat would have been "tantamount to gambling with what the Palestinians considered their most valuable currency, international legality." Malley and Agha, "Camp David," p. 15.

17. The Collapse

PAGE

328 *keep working at Camp David:* Haniyah remembers his boss's response to Clinton's new proposal: "Yasser Arafat showed a light smile. He got the message. Bill Clinton did not want to go to Okinawa a failure." See Akram Haniyah, "Camp David Diary—6th Installment," *al-Ayyam,* August 8, 2000, pp. 1, 15, English version accessed through World News Connection.

329 *left both leaders believing:* In his memoirs, Clinton admits the fault was his: "Apparently, I had not been as clear with Arafat as I thought I had been about what the terms of staying on should be" (Clinton, *My Life,* p. 915).

333 *with agreement:* The areas of agreement included:
   • Palestinian acceptance of three Israeli-manned early warning sites with one Palestinian present in each site.
   • The Palestinians would have sovereignty over the West Bank airspace; however, the Israelis would be entrusted to run a unified air control system with a regime that guaranteed nondiscrimination against the Palestinians.
   • The "emergency" situation that could prompt IDF reentry into the West Bank along designated routes would be defined as "an imminent and demonstrable threat."
   • The Palestinians agreed to a demilitarized state but wanted a different term to describe it.
   • The passageways between the Palestinian state and Egypt and Jordan would be controlled by the Palestinians with an Israeli "invisible presence."
   • The Israelis were prepared to be part of a multinational force that would remain in the Jordan Valley after the three-year period in which Israel would complete its withdrawal from the West Bank; the Palestinians rejected a residual Israeli presence. However, the president made clear to the Palestinian negotiators that if they wanted control over their border with Jordan they would have to concede a strictly limited Israeli military presence as part of the multinational force.

334 *"You have been here":* As quoted in Malley and Agha, "Camp David," pp. 62–63.

339 *Barak has since argued:* See Benny Morris, "Camp David and After: An Exchange

(1. An Interview with Ehud Barak)," *New York Review of Books,* June 13, 2002, p. 49.

18. Intifada!

PAGE

342 *publicly blaming Arafat:* His fainthearted praise of Arafat in the press conference announcing the failure at Camp David was followed by an interview with Israel TV in which Clinton was much more explicit in praising Barak and blaming Arafat. In that interview, he threatened to move the U.S. embassy to West Jerusalem and "review" the bilateral relationship with the Palestinians if Arafat were to make a unilateral declaration of independence. See John F. Burns, "Arafat, on Diplomatic Tour, Accuses Israelis of 'Big Lies,' " *New York Times,* July 30, 2000, sec. 1, p. 6, and James Gerstenberg, "Clinton Tells Israel TV He May Move Embassy From Tel Aviv to Jerusalem," *Los Angeles Times,* July 29, 2000, p. A3.

348 *commentary in the pan-Arab press:* See *Mideast Mirror* summary of Abdel Bari al-Atwan in *al-Quds al-Arabi,* August 31, 2000. An editorial in the Palestinian newspaper *al-Quds* at the time lamented "the absence of a united and firm Arab and Muslim stand. This is especially true on the issues of Jerusalem in general and Al-Aqsa in particular. . . . This message should say that Jerusalem is indeed a red line for the Arabs from the ocean to the Gulf and that Jerusalem is the real yardstick to measure the success or failure of the peace process." See "Al-Aqsa Mosque and the Absence of an Arab-Muslim Stand," *al-Quds,* August 21, 2000, accessed through World News Connection.

351 *French president Jacques Chirac:* Charles Enderlin reprints the transcript of a conversation between Chirac and Arafat on September 20. Chirac urges Arafat to accept a form of divided sovereignty in which he would have active sovereignty over the surface of the Haram to a depth of some meters while Israel would have passive sovereignty over the area beneath where the Temple ruins were presumed to be. Chirac's reference to the Temple ruins triggered the now standard Arafat tirade about the nonexistence of the Temple ruins under the Haram, and his rejection of the idea of divided sovereignty. Chirac tried to explain to him using French logic: "It's the *idea* of the ruins in the mind of the Israeli people that has to be reckoned with, not so much the ruins themselves." Chirac's effort was fruitless. See Charles Enderlin, *Shattered Dreams: The Failure of the Peace Process in the Middle East, 1995–2002* (New York: Other Press, 2003), p. 281.

351 *Sharon's imminent visit:* Barak had Shlomo Ben-Ami, who was the minister of police, coordinate Sharon's visit with Jibril Rajoub, Arafat's West Bank preventive security chief. Barak subsequently testified in front of a state inquiry commission that Rajoub had assured Ben-Ami that "if Sharon steered clear of the Muslim shrines on the Temple Mount, the visit would be peaceful." Barak also said Rajoub had told him that while the Palestinians didn't like Sharon visiting the holy site, they "wouldn't use it as a pretext for riots." See Joel Greenberg, "Barak Testifies on Israeli Arab Violence," *New York Times,* November 21, 2001, p. A10; Jack Katzenell, "Barak: blaming Mideast violence on Sharon visit to holy site 'not a bad pretext,' " Associated Press, November 20, 2001. For Ben-Ami's account, see Nina Gilbert and Lamia Lahoud, "Ben-Ami: Rajoub said Sharon Temple Mount visit would pose no problem," *Jerusalem Post,* Wednesday, October 4, 2000, p. 2.

351 *security arrangements were adjusted:* We reduced, by at least half, the number of years the IDF would remain in the Jordan Valley, we granted the Israeli air force access to Palestinian airspace for defensive purposes only, and we provided for a joint air traffic control system that would ensure no discrimination.

352 *a tactic honed:* "Neither an initiator nor a planner," Sayigh argued, "[Arafat] has

instead seized upon the fortuitous eruption of a major crisis or other dramatic event brought about by external agency to obscure and escape a strategic predicament." See Yezid Sayigh, "Arafat and the Anatomy of a Revolt," *Survival* 43, no. 3 (Autumn 2001), p. 47.

353 *In an Egyptian newspaper interview:* "Interviewer: So you believe that Arafat does not want to stop the *intifada*? Marwan Barghouti: Yes, although I did not want to spell it out, but you forced me to say it. The continuation of the *intifada* serves the interests of the Palestinian Authority, which had reached a deadlock in the negotiations." See "Fatah's Marwan Al-Barghouti on Intifada, Peace Talks," *al-Musawwar* (Arabic), November 10, 2000, pp. 18–19, accessed through World News Connection.

353 *the Israeli army had prepared:* As Major General Amos Malka, the head of military intelligence at the time, noted in a subsequent newspaper article, "By the beginning of 1999 we already succeeded in understanding that there was a chance for a confrontation as a result of a chain of events, rather than a premeditated move. We emphasized time and again that the turn to violence would be a last step after a political deadlock, and its goal would be to return to the political route in an improved position." See "Not Distortion, But Rather Rewriting with Hindsight," *Yedioth Ahronoth,* June 30, 2004, p. B11.

354 *allowing the IDF a free hand:* The chief of staff, Lieutenant General Moshe "Boogie" Yaalon, expressed this objective publicly when he declared that it was necessary to "sear into the consciousness" of the Palestinians that terrorism and violence "have no chance of leading to any achievement." See Haim Shapiro, "Ya'alon: PA doesn't recognize our right to exist," *Jerusalem Post,* August 26, 2002, p. 1.

356 *Clinton would admit his regret:* "Clinton Laments Lack of Progress in the Middle East," Reuters, September 8, 2001. He made the remarks in a speech in Sydney, Australia.

357 *Arab League summit meeting:* Arafat's strategy did produce some gains from the Arab League summit: new pledges of economic aid, condemnation of Israeli "atrocities," and a freezing of all non-formal diplomatic contacts with Israel. Arafat also picked up a stronger endorsement of Palestinian demands for sovereignty over East Jerusalem. See Susan Sachs, "Arab States Take Diplomatic Steps to Punish Israel," *New York Times,* October 23, 2000, p. A1; Deborah Sontag, "Barak Formally Declares Timeout in the Peace Effort," *New York Times,* October 23, 2000, p. A12.

19. The End of the Peace Process
PAGE

362 *nineteen-point lead:* According to a poll published in *Maariv* on December 8, 27 percent of respondents supported Barak whereas 46 percent supported Netanyahu. See "Mother of all electoral upheavals on the cards," *Mideast Mirror,* December 8, 2000, Section: Israel, Vol. 14, No. 238.

363 *Dennis said he had been frank:* In Dennis's account of this encounter, he recalls his uncertainty at the time about Arafat's seriousness. But there was no uncertainty in his instructions as to what to tell Barak. See Ross, *The Missing Peace,* pp. 746–47.

367 *Israeli cabinet resolved to accept:* The decision was officially transmitted to me by fax that night by Zvi Shtauber, Barak's foreign policy adviser. On January 5, 2001, Gilad Sher addressed an official letter to Sandy Berger noting some elements in Israel's positions that were different than the president's but emphasizing that addressing these points in future negotiations "should not call into question the internal logic of the President's ideas." For example, Sher's letter pointed out that to incorporate 80 percent of the settlers within settlement blocs

would need more than the 4–6 percent of West Bank territory allocated in the president's parameters. On Jerusalem, it expressed Israel's preference for a special regime for the Holy Basin and noted the need for further elaboration of the sovereign and functional arrangements in and around the Temple Mount to take adequate account of the three-thousand-year ties of Judaism to the site. However, the letter did not challenge the principle of sovereignty on the Haram al-Sharif going to the Palestinians.

369 *publicly warning:* Mofaz had previously given his consent to his subordinate, General Yanai, presenting these same arrangements to the Palestinians. Now he declared publicly that giving up the Jordan Valley would impair the IDF's ability "to defend the strategic front of the State of Israel and its ability to deal appropriately with threats from the East." See John Kifner, "All Sides Resist Plan by Clinton For the Mideast," *New York Times*, December 31, 2000, p. A1.

370 *tantamount to a rejection:* Prince Bandar recounts his own anger at the White House for refusing to bring the hammer down on Arafat's head. He met with Arafat in his hotel immediately after Arafat's meeting with the president. By that time, Arafat was already lying, claiming that he had reached agreement. When Bandar discovered from Sandy Berger that it was not true, he bade farewell to the chairman, boarded his plane, and flew off to his retreat in Aspen. See Elsa Walsh, "The Prince," *The New Yorker*, March 24, 2003, pp. 57–58.

370 *Jake Siewert:* Press briefing by White House spokesman Jake Siewert, January 2, 2001, Federal News Service transcript, accessed through Lexis-Nexis.

370 *Peres promptly introduced:* Peres had long believed that no Israeli prime minister would be able to pass an agreement that gave sovereignty to the Palestinians on the Temple Mount. Instead, in a January 13 meeting at Erez, he proposed to Arafat a grandiose scheme for turning Jerusalem into the headquarters of the United Nations, with sovereignty dissolved. Arafat said he'd have to consult with the Muslim and Christian worlds. Peres also proposed negotiations in Europe in the coming week, under Norwegian auspices, to work out a new formula on refugees. Since this is what Arafat had proposed to Clinton in response to his refugee parameters, Arafat was more than willing to have Nabil Shaath work on that.

370 *had taken several steps back:* Arafat now demanded 98 percent of the territory and rejected more of the security arrangements. And in a subsequent meeting between the negotiators, Abu Ala rejected the idea of putting all the Jewish suburbs of East Jerusalem under Israeli sovereignty and Gilad Sher reciprocated by rejecting Palestinian sovereignty on the Temple Mount.

372 *call for picking up the negotiations:* King Abdullah of Jordan, in a speech before a joint session of Congress in March 2007, declared, "At Taba, as in the Geneva Accords, the parties have outlined the parameters of the solution." See Remarks by King Abdullah II of Jordan in an Address to a Joint Session of the U.S. Congress, March 07, 2007, transcript through Federal News Service.

372 *vitiated the concept of settlement blocs:* Instead of 80 percent of the settlers being incorporated in these blocs, as the Clinton Parameters provided, the Palestinian map would account for only 30 percent. In addition, the Palestinian negotiators insisted that the settlement of Efrat in the Gush Etzion bloc would have to be removed. See David Makovsky, "Taba Mythchief," *The National Interest*, Spring 2003, pp. 119–29.

372 *"we have never before":* Aluf Benn, Nadav Shragai, and Yossi Verter, "Israel-PA: Peace Pact Never So Close," *Haaretz*, January 28, 2001.

374 *an unrealistic mythology:* In a speech at Hebrew University on October 15, 2001, Nuseibeh said Palestinians should end their call for a right of return: "The Palestinians have to realize that if we are to reach an agreement on two states, then those two states will have to be one for the Israelis and one for the Palestinians,

not one for the Palestinians and the other also for the Palestinians." See Joel Greenberg, "Palestinian Offers Idea: Get Israelis On Our Side," *New York Times,* October 17, 2001, p. A7.

374 *would do better waiting:* Both Rachid and Dahlan told me that Arafat had heard this from Palestinians who had met with Bush people during the campaign. Colin Powell, however, told me that specific assurances were conveyed from the campaign to Arafat that, if he accepted the Clinton deal, the Bush administration would stand by it. Elsa Walsh gives a similar account from Powell ("The Prince," p. 49).

20. Epilogue
PAGE

380 *he still remained aloof:* See Neil MacFarquhar, "President's Speech Is Criticized for Lacking Specific Proposals," *New York Times,* June 25, 2002, p. A11.

381 *Quartet's Road Map:* The Road Map was produced by representatives of the European Union, United Nations, and Russia, with input from the State Department.

382 *rebuild the Palestinian economy:* Wolfensohn later expressed his frustration at the way the Bush administration undermined his efforts, noting "I was never given the mandate to negotiate the peace." See Shahar Smooha, "All the dreams we had are now gone," *Haaretz,* July 21, 2007.

384 *bin Laden started espousing:* For example, in November 2002, al-Qaeda suicide bombers crashed an explosive-laden vehicle into an Israeli-owned resort hotel in Mombasa, Kenya, and shot two antiaircraft missiles at an Israeli plane taking off for Tel Aviv. In claiming responsibility for the attacks, al-Qaeda member Sulaiman Abu Ghaith threatened more attacks against Israel and the United States saying, "Liberation of our holy places, led by Palestine, is our central issue." In a striking response, Yasser Arafat spoke out against bin Laden: "Why is bin Laden talking about Palestine now? Bin Laden never—not ever—stressed this issue. He never helped us. . . . I'm telling him directly not to hide behind the Palestinian cause." See "Al Qaeda Claims Role in Kenya Attacks," Reuters, *Washington Post,* December 9, p. A19; Marie Colvin, "Bin Laden's no friend, says Arafat," *Sunday Times* (London), December 15, 2002, p. 23.

384 *in an interview:* See Thomas L. Friedman, "An Intriguing Signal From the Saudi Crown Prince," *New York Times,* February 17, 2002, p. 11.

384 *Beirut Declaration:* See "Extracts from the text of the 'Beirut Declaration' (final communiqué) issued on March 28, 2002," Arab League, http://www.al-bab .com/arab/docs/league/communique02.htm.

385 *This was Clintonesque indeed:* See Steven Lee Meyers, "Bush's Clintonesque Mideast Strategy," *International Herald Tribune,* November 27, 2007.

386 *Road Map commitments:* See "A Performance-Based Roadmap to a Permanent Two-State Solution to the Israeli-Palestinian Conflict," Press Statement, Office of the Spokesman, U.S. Department of State, April 30, 2003, http://www.state .gov/r/pa/prs/ps/2003/20062.htm.

389 *the Israeli strike:* For the details of Israel's strike see David Sanger, "Government Releases Images of Syrian Reactor," *New York Times,* April 25, 2008, and Robin Wright, "U.S. Details Reactor in Syria," *Washington Post,* April 25, 2008, p. A12.

The Lantern on the Stern
PAGE

391 *"the quiet miracle of a normal life":* See Transcript of Remarks by President Bill Clinton at the Middle East Peace Signing Ceremony for the Israeli-PLO Accord, September 13, 1993, Federal News Transcript, accessed through Lexis-Nexis.

391 *"where the extremists are marginalized":* "President Bush Discusses Importance

of Freedom in the Middle East," Abu Dhabi, U.A.E., January 13, 2008, http://www.whitehouse.gov/news/releases/2008/01/20080113-1.html.

391 *American missionaries:* As Michael Oren, who chronicled these early missionary efforts, has noted, "Common to all of these communities was the conviction that America had a divinely assigned role to act as a "light unto nations," and to strive for global peace." See Michael B. Oren, *Power, Faith, and Fantasy: America in the Middle East, 1776 to the Present* (New York: Norton, 2007), pp. 80–97.

399 *details should be left:* See Daniel C. Kurtzer and Scott B. Lasensky, *Negotiating Arab-Israeli Peace* (Washington, D.C.: U.S. Institute of Peace, 2008), pp. 47–51.

399 *back channels that bypass:* See Nahum Barnea and Ariel Kastner, "Backchannel: Bush, Sharon, and the Uses of Unilateralism," Saban Center for Middle East Policy at the Brookings Institution, *Monograph Series* 2 (December 2006).

406 *extending a nuclear umbrella:* See Martin Indyk and Tamara Cofman Wittes, "Back to Balancing in the Middle East," *The American Interest* 3, no. 2 (November/December 2007), pp. 42–51.

407 *should not abandon the effort:* See Tamara Cofman Wittes, *Freedom's Unsteady March: America's Role in Building Arab Democracy* (Washington, D.C.: Brookings Institution, 2008).

409 *separation barrier:* See B'Tselem, "Separation Barrier Statistics," available at http://www.btselem.org/english/Separation_Barrier/Statistics.asp.

410 *International forces:* See Martin Indyk, "A Trusteeship for Palestine," *Foreign Affairs* 82, no. 3 (May/June 2003), pp. 51–60.

411 *observe that commitment:* See Glenn Kessler, "Israelis Claim Secret Agreement with U.S., Americans Insist No Deal Made on Settlement Growth," *Washington Post*, April 24, 2008, p. A14.

414 *turned into a park:* This idea was first floated just before Clinton's meeting with Asad in Geneva in April 2000 by Patrick Seale, Hafez al-Asad's biographer. In January 2007, Israeli media reported on secret track II negotiations between a former director general of Israel's Foreign Ministry and a Syrian-American with close ties to the Asad regime. Among the provisions of their agreement was a buffer zone on the eastern side of Lake Kinneret where a park would be established for joint use by Israelis and Syrians. See Akiva Eldar, "Syrian Representatives Reach Secret Understandings," *Haaretz*, January 16, 2007.

Acknowledgments

From the day I entered the White House to take on the responsibility of advising President Clinton on the Middle East, I expected that I would one day write a book about the history that I would try to help him make. I took meticulous notes of the conversations and meetings I participated in. But I had no idea just how long it would take and what a challenge it would become to convert those experiences into what I hope is a readable book.

I have carried this work around with me in my head and on my shoulders for more than six years. It has been a long, rich, and often painful journey of reassessment and self-discovery, which would not have been possible without the support and encouragement so many offered along the way. Each one made a special contribution for which I am deeply grateful.

Bill Clinton gave me the opportunity of my life by appointing me as his special assistant for the Middle East, and twice as his ambassador to Israel. I hope any criticism of him, and his advisers, will be read in the context of my deep admiration and appreciation for his profound commitment to peacemaking in the Middle East, his immense humanity, and his loyalty and friendship to me.

Over my eight years in government, many people befriended, guided, supported, and protected me. They include my bosses Sandy Berger, Warren Christopher, and Tony Lake; my colleagues Ed Djerijian, Ellen Laipson, Rob Malley, Mark Parris, Tom Pickering, Bruce Riedel, Gideon Rose, Jamie Rubin, Jonathan Schwartz, George Tenet, and in particular, Dennis Ross; my staff in the Near East Bureau and Embassy Tel Aviv, Jeff Feltman, James Larocco, the late Stan Moskowitz, Ron Neumann, Richard Roth, David Satterfield, Jake Walles, Tony Verstandig, and David Welch; and my dedicated Israeli security detail.

During my time in government, I worked closely with many Arab,

Israeli, and European diplomats and politicians who taught me much about the Middle East as well as the value of friendship in the midst of conflict. They include Mahmoud Abbas, Ehud Barak, Mohammed Bassiouny, Saeb Erekat, Salam Fayyad, Avi Gil, Eitan Haber, Efraim Halevy, Sheikh Hamad bin-Jassem, Abdel Ilah Khatib, Amnon Lipkin-Shahak, David Manning, Dan Meridor, Sallai Meridor, Marwan Muasher, Ahmed Maher, Walid Mouallem, Itamar Rabinovich, Mohamed Rachid, Terje Roed-Larsen, Uri Savir, and Gilad Sher.

The wives of senior government officials and ambassadors pay a high price for their husbands' public service, with little recognition for their own contributions. My former wife, Jill Collier Indyk, took to the unreasonable demands of representing the United States in Israel with unflagging enthusiasm and flair. She was the one who decided that we should go back there "to finish the job." How she convinced Bill Clinton and Ehud Barak to send us remains somewhat of a mystery but is testament to her determination and commitment for which I will always remain grateful.

I wrote this book while establishing and directing the Saban Center for Middle East Policy at the Brookings Institution. Haim Saban made both activities possible and I owe him, and his wife Cheryl, a great debt of gratitude for their extraordinary generosity, friendship, and faith in me. I came to know Strobe Talbott as a steadfast colleague in government, but as President of Brookings he gave me the space to write this book and the constant encouragement to complete it. Different in so many respects, Haim and Strobe were the common godfathers of this enterprise.

Several people at Brookings and beyond read and critiqued the manuscript and helped to make it a much better book. They include Nahum Barnea, Hirsh Goodman, Sarah Indyk, Ken Pollack, William Quandt, Itamar Rabinovich, Bruce Riedel, and Strobe Talbott. The responsibility for the contents of this book, however, rests on my shoulders alone.

Haim Malka and Ariel Kastner were my research assistants at the Saban Center at Brookings during this effort. My gratitude to them for their unwavering commitment to the project and conscientious devotion to completing the mammoth tasks involved cannot be overstated. They were ably assisted by a group of eager interns who included Nir Artzi, Joel Branaman, Andrew Colvin, Shai Gruber, Amanda Rizkala, Sara Robinson, and Emily Solis-Cohen.

Many others at the Saban Center eased my workload so that I could devote time to writing. I am particularly grateful to Ken Pollack, my partner there, as well as Andrew Horesh, Ross Johnson, Ellen McHugh, Hayden Morel, Yinnie Tse, and Mitchell Wunsh.

I drew inspiration for this book from the many places where I worked on it, in Washington, East Hampton, Nantucket, Martha's Vineyard, Gibson Island, and Saint-Paul de Vence. None was more inspiring than Mishkenot Sh'ananim in Jerusalem, where I spent six weeks in the summer of 2004. Special thanks to Michael Shiloh, the Mishkenot staff, and the Jerusalem Foundation for making that possible.

When it came to publishing the manuscript, Gloria Loomis, my agent, did an exceptional job promoting and protecting my interests with perseverance and patience. I wrote this book long because I had so much to tell. Jonathan Segal devoted many hours to cutting and trimming the manuscript to readable length; in the process, he taught me much about writing and undoubtedly made it a better book. The amazing Alice Mayhew and the team at Simon & Schuster, including Roger Labrie, Karen Thompson, Gypsy da Silva, Tom Pitoniak, and Victoria Meyer took over the task of shepherding the manuscript to publication with enthusiasm and conviction.

Without the love and encouragement of my family and friends, this book would never have been completed. They were my solace and my salvation. They include Dan and Joanna Rose, Tom and Anne Friedman, Hirsh Goodman and Isabel Kershner, Jane Perlez and Ray Bonner, Nancy Delston, Ivor and Evelyn Indyk, Micha Nussinov and Shelley Indyk, Ehud and Dagmar Ya'ari, and Sarah Schiff. Sadly Zeev Schiff, my mentor in all things, died before he could see this work in print.

My partner, Gahl Hodges Burt, came into my life when I was already experiencing the birth pains of this book. That she opened her heart to me, offered unselfish encouragement, and read and commented on every draft, is testament to the idea that love conquers all.

My children, Sarah and Jake, had to give up their father to the unreasonable demands of public service in their formative years, and then had to cope with the distractions of my struggle to come to terms with what happened there. I hope they know now that none of it ever detracted from my love for them and that they will come to understand through reading this book why it is better to try and fail than not to try at all.

My parents, John and Mary Indyk, were anything but absent in my formative years in Sydney, Australia. Their understanding and encouragement of my ambitious pursuit, even though it took me far away from them, has made everything else possible in my life. My father was a great surgeon who now battles the onset of Parkinson's disease with inspiring dignity and the loving care of my mother. It is to his triumph of spirit that I dedicate this book.

Index

Page numbers in *italics* refer to illustrations and maps. Page numbers beginning with 448 refer to notes.

Abbas, Mahmoud, *see* Abu Mazen
Abdullah, King of Saudi Arabia, 183,
   193–94, 397, 458
   Camp David II and, 324, 325
   Gore's meeting with, 194*n*
   G. W. Bush's relations with, 50–51,
      384
   Iranian leadership role rejected by,
      402
   Iran policy and, 219, 457
   Iraq War and, 50–51
   peace initiative of, 384, 396
Abdullah I, King of Jordan, 94, 100, 101,
   127, 138
Abdullah II, King of Jordan, 13, 26*n*,
   133*n*, 324, 325, 402, 466
Abu Ala (Ahmed Qurei), 84, 372, 462,
   466
   Camp David II and, 295–96, 300*n*,
      302, 303, 310–11, 317–18, 331–32,
      334
Abu Dis, 293, 300, 302, 308
Abu Jihad (Khalil al-Wazir), 112, 461
Abu Mazen (Mahmoud Abbas), 111, 298,
   388, 395*n*, 450
   Annapolis Conference and, 385–86
   at Aqaba Summit, 381
   Camp David II and, 311, 333
   elections and, 382
   Hamas reconciliation attempted by,
      405
   Oslo Accords and, 60, 63, 65
adversaries, thinking like, 210
Afghanistan, 207, 222–23
   Soviets in, 53, 55
   Taliban in, 222, 229, 235
Against All Enemies (Clarke), 171*n*
Ahmadinejad, Mahmoud, 230–32, 235,
   388, 457, 458
"Aims and Principles" paper, 173
Airbus, 56, 57*n*

Air Force, U.S., 33*n*, 195, 203
Air Force One, 138–40, 172, 178, 327
Air France, 461
al-Aqsa intifada, *see* intifada, second
Alawites, 125, 171, 243, 279
Albright, Madeleine, 6, 185–87, 241–44,
   344*n*, 350, 356–57
   Asia Society speech of, 223
   Camp David II and, 302, 306–10,
      317–18, 323, 324, 329–30, 332–33
   Iran policy and, 215, 218, 219–20, 223,
      228, 229
   Iraq policy and, 157, 164, 186–87,
      189, 190, 193, 194, 196, 197, 199,
      200
   Paris talks held by, 354–55, 356–57
   Shaaban's talk with, 258–59
   Syrian-Israeli peace process and,
      242–44, 248, 249, 251, 252, 253,
      255, 258–59, 260, 262, 263–64,
      266, 283
   Tauran's meeting with, 345
Alderoti, Zvi, 174
Algeria, 4, 47, 57, 58, 68, 170
al-Hama, 272, 277, 280
Ali, Imam, 171
Allawi, Ayad al-, 152, 166
Allenby Bridge, 122*n*
al-Nida division, 153
al-Qaeda, 53, 207, 209, 357, 384, 467
Amanpour, Christiane, 220, 350*n*
American Israel Public Affairs
   Committee (AIPAC), 90, 114, 169
Amir, Yigal, 180
Amman, 45, 102, 103, 132–34
   Hashimiya Palace in, 132–33
   Middle East North Africa Economic
      Summit in, 142*n*
Amuzegar, Jahangir, 454
Andrews Air Force Base, 66, 68, 241, 245,
   288, 306, 327

Annan, Kofi, 455
  Iraq policy and, 184, 190, 194, 197–98,
    199, 211, 353
  Palestinian-Israeli peace efforts and,
    13, 367
  son of, 165
Annapolis Peace Conference (2007), 9,
    67, 117, 281, 283, 301*n*, 385–89
antiballistic missile defense system, 236*n*
anti-Semitism, 280*n*
Aoun, Michel, 75
Aqaba, 93, 138–39, 172
Aqaba, Gulf of, 127*n*
Aqaba Summit (June 2003), 381
Arab Americans, 130*n*
Arab League, 52–53, 101, 345, 409
  Jerusalem Committee of, 345
  Summit of (2002), 357, 465
  see also Beirut Declaration on the
    Saudi Peace Initiative
Arabs, Arab world, 25, 26, 27, 35, 44–59,
    204, 212, 278, 355*n*, 412
  Camp David II and, 324–25, 345, 400
  Christopher's disdain for, 44, 47–48
  Clinton Parameters and, 367
  corrupt regimes of, 4
  dignity and honor in, 280
  Egypt's role in, 51, 52
  G. W. Bush administration and, 26*n*,
    383–84, 388
  hospitality in, 47
  intifada and, 354, 357–58, 464
  Iran's destabilizing of, 30, 34, 51, 53,
    55, 236–37
  Israel economic boycott of, 136
  Israeli, 291, 300, 375*n*
  Marsh, 157
  Palestinian-Israeli peace process and,
    237, 296, 384, 409–10
  public opinion in, 90, 164, 184, 191,
    348
  Resolution 242 and, 261*n*
  Syrian-Israeli peace and, 243, 255,
    256–57
  time in, 47–48, 142, 400
  Twain's views on, ix
  U.S. compared with, 48–49
  see also specific people and places
Arad, Ron, 104*n*
Arafat, Yasser, 58, 60–81, 110–23, 216,
    218, 244*n*, 286–360, 362–76, 379–82,
    392, 396, 397, 411, 462
  Abu Mazen compared with, 385
  Asad's relationship with, 74–76, 78,
    92–93, 114, 117, 450
  assassination fears of, 340
  Barak's first meeting with, 291–92
  Barak's frustration with, 108, 292*n*

bin Laden criticized by, 467
Camp David II and, 264, 286–340,
    343, 348, 350*n*, 373, 376, 462, 463,
    464
Christopher's relationship with, 23, 32
Clinton Parameters and, 5, 13–14,
    366–71, 373–74, 466
Clinton's letters from, 333, 336, 367
Clinton's meetings with, 13, 73,
    359–60, 369–70, 399*n*
Clinton's payback to, 13–14, 379, 401
death of, 375, 381
fatwa against, 181
Ginossar's business with, 292, 461
Goldstein massacre and, 111–17
Gulf War and, 19–20, 75, 88
gun of, 68–69, 70
international recognition craved by,
    66
intifada and, 341–43, 345–46, 353–60,
    373, 374, 380, 381, 464–65
Israeli elections and, 177
King Hussein's relationship with,
    94–95, 100, 114, 117, 126, 133, 135,
    136, 142–43
kissing of, 68, 70
lack of leadership of, 379, 395
Mubarak's influence with, 56, 295,
    296, 301, 345, 367
Netanyahu's negotiations with, 67, 184,
    283
Oslo Accords and, 1–2, 14, 56, 60–73,
    76–81, 88–89, 92–95, 102, 106, 110,
    118, 120–23, 132, 135, 137, 140,
    142–45, 172, 291, 293, 300, 328,
    375, 450
post-Camp David tour of, 344–45
"power of the weak" and, 123
Rabin's correspondence with, 81, 86
self-made mythical world of, 291, 374
Sharm el-Sheikh Summits and, 13,
    178, 228*n*, 341–43, 355–59
in Tunis, 27, 28, 66, 79, 111–17
unwillingness to accept responsibility
    of, 71
waqf and, 101, 102, 135, 136
in Washington, 1–2, 19, 46, 60–62,
    134, 359–60, 362–63, 369–70, 377
Wye Agreement and, 67, 193, 459
Armistice Agreement with Arab
    countries (1949), 173
Army, U.S., 18, 30, 163
Asad, Bashar al-, 7, 279, 402, 408*n*, 413
  Annapolis Conference and, 117, 281,
    389
  father's takeover plans for, 242–43,
    266, 271
  Iraq policy of, 151, 205*n*

Syrian-Israeli negotiations and, 117, 128*n*, 151, 266, 271, 281, 282–83, 389, 414–15
Asad, Basil al-, 242
Asad, Hafez al-, 58, 73–76, 78–89, 95–100, 102–10, 216
  Arafat's relationship with, 74–76, 78, 92–93, 114, 117, 450
  assassination feared by, 279
  Christopher's meetings with, 21*n*, 48, 79–83, 283
  Clinton's calls to, 114–15, 131, 257, 264, 265–66, 275
  Clinton's letters and messages to, 194, 203*n*, 249–50, 252
  Clinton's meetings with, 104–8, 110, 141, 173, 275–78, 280, 284–85, 286–87, 292, 294, 321, 324
  concessions made by, 106, 107, 124, 131, 141
  death of, 294
  health problems of, 97*n*, 98, 242, 250, 258, 264, 271
  image fears of, 252
  insecurity of, 279–80
  Iranian-Syrian alliance and, 171–72
  Israeli-Jordanian peace and, 141, 143, 453
  Israeli-Syrian peace efforts and, 3, 17–18, 20–22, 28–29, 62, 76, 79–89, 92, 96, 114, 117, 118, 124–26, 135, 141–45, 155, 173–74, 194, 203, 242–55, 258–59, 262–68, 271–87, 290*n*, 292, 293, 294, 329, 397, 450, 452, 459
  King Hussein's relationship with, 95, 129, 131, 142–43, 453
  lack of leadership by, 278–79, 395
  Oslo Accords and, 92–93, 99, 452
  palace of, 97, 98, 242
  Saddam's antagonism toward, 151
  thuggish instincts of, 99
Asad, Rifat, 96, 97*n*, 278
Asfour, Hassan, 295*n*
Asia Society speeches, 223
Aspin, Les, 15–17, 36, 38, 153
Associated Press, 105
Atwood, Brian, 68*n*
Australia, 23, 62, 63, 306
Ayalon, Ami, 304–5, 354
Ayash, Yahya, 176*n*
Azariyah, 293, 300
Aziz, Tariq, 156, 189, 195, 197
Azoulay, André, 46

B-1 bomber, 200–201
B-52 bomber, 154, 189*n*, 195, 197, 200–201

Baathists, in Syria, 74, 151, 172, 278–80
back channel, 178, 246, 283, 399*n*
  Barak-Arafat, 292–93
  importance of, 143–44
  Khatami and, 225–27, 234
  Stockholm, 295–96, 300*n*, 303
Badr Brigade, 161
Baer, Bob, 160–63, 453
BAE Systems, 56*n*
Baghdad, 48–49, 160, 164, 197, 201
  Annan in, 190
  intelligence headquarters in, 149–50, 187
  Iranian ambassador in, 234
  Iranian influence in, 209, 230
  UNSCOM in, 189
  U.S. occupation of, 163
Bahrain, 33, 170, 219
Baker, James, 23, 24, 48, 79, 97
Bakshi-Doron, Eliyahu, 347, 347*n*
balance of power, 15–16, 22, 143, 145, 391, 406
  dual containment and, 32–36, 42, 43
  Iran and, 22, 33–36, 40, 42, 230, 235, 402–3
Bandar bin Sultan, Prince, 56–57, 139*n*, 195–96, 344*n*
  Arafat and, 66, 68, 69–70, 466
  Syrian-Israeli peace efforts and, 256, 271, 272
Barabash, Dr., 175
Barak, Ehud, 6, 173, 204, 288–344, 346–51, *347*, 353–76, 379, 395, 399*n*, 411, 465
  Arafat's first meeting with, 291–92
  Arafat's suspicions about, 291–94
  Camp David II and, 264, 285–86, 288–340, 343, 344, 348, 359, 409, 410, 463, 464
  Clinton Parameters and, 366–71
  daring commando operations of, 289, 460–61
  in election of 1999, 271, 291*n*, 362, 362*n*
  election of 2001 and, 361–62, 364–65, 370, 371, 375, 465
  freier label and, 251–52, 271, 288, 328, 369, 459
  Golan Heights as viewed by, 124*n*, 251
  intifada and, 341–44, 353–60, 369–70
  lack of maturity of, 460
  leaks and, 260, 267–68
  Olmert compared with, 385, 389
  Oslo Accords and, 291, 293, 307
  Sayeret Matkal and, 289–90
  Sharaa's negotiations with, 252–60
  Sharm el-Sheik Summit (2000) and, 13, 228*n*, 341–42, 355–59

Barak, Ehud (*cont.*)
  in Shepherdstown talks, 257–60,
    262–64, 271, 284–86, 398
  Syrian peace process and, *see* Syrian-
    Israeli peace process, Barak in
Barghouti, Marwan, 353, 465
Barzani, Masud, 182
Baz, Osama el-, 348
Bedouins, 49, 54
Begin, Menachem, 67, 75, 145, 285
  at Camp David I, 306, 307, 320, 340,
    411*n*
Beilin, Yossi, 298, 371–72
Beirut, 88, 111, 461
Beirut Declaration on the Saudi Peace
    Initiative (2002), 384, 446–47
Ben Ali, Zine El Abidine, 324
Ben-Ami, Shlomo, 13–14, 344*n*, 351,
    363–66, 363*n*, 372
  Camp David II and, 295, 300–303, 310,
    311–12, 317, 319, 321, 325, 330, 334,
    335–36, 463
  Sharon's visit to Temple Mount and,
    352, 464
Ben-Gurion, David, 89, 270, 320, 322
Berger, Samuel (Sandy), 41, 191, 193,
    196–98, 200, 262, 357
  Arafat's message from, 113–14
  Camp David II and, 297–98, 302, 309,
    311, 323–24, 337, 339
  in Clinton campaign, 15, 31
  Sher's letter to, 465–66
Berlin, 217*n*
Bern meeting (1999), 248
Bethesda Hyatt talks (Sept. 1999),
    248–49, 259
Bethlehem, 360
Bible, 60, 319
bin Alawi, Yusuf, 225–27
bin Laden, Osama, 150, 378, 383–84,
    467
  time warning of, 400, 401
biological weapons, 165–66, 190, 207,
    210, 456
Blair, Tony, 178, 197, 198, 208, 381
  Fayyad's work with, 386, 387
Blair House, 254–56, 263
Blitzer, Wolf, 62, 105
Boeing, 56, 98–99, 228, 241, 245
Bolling Air Force Base, 364–66, 370
Bosnia, 17, 38, 197
Burleigh, Peter, 199
Bush, George H. W., 19, 22, 23, 26–27, 56,
    58, 98, 378
  Arafat's relations with, 88
  assassination attempt against, 149
  in election of 1992, 14–15, 216*n*
  Iran policy of, 32, 170, 229–36

Iraq policy of, 30, 31, 35, 36, 38, 157,
    210, 212, 398
Israeli policy of, 14–15, 118–19
Operation Provide Comfort and, 159*n*
Oslo Accords and, 69, 73
policy handover by, 401, 402
Bush, George W., 3–10, 14, 17, 37, 51,
    377–93, 401–4, 415
  Annapolis Conference and, 9, 117,
    385–87, 389
  Arabs alienated by, 26*n*, 383–84
  Clinton compared with, 3, 4–5, 7–10,
    24*n*, 78, 232–36, 366*n*, 378, 381, 385,
    386, 387, 391, 401, 411
  Clinton's policy handover to, 14, 401–2
  international ill will toward, 209
  Iran policy of, 157, 223*n*, 229–36, 384,
    392, 397, 398
  Iraq War and, *see* Iraq War
  Israeli-Palestinian peace process and,
    9, 117, 207, 283, 366*n*, 372, 374, 376,
    378–82, 384–90, 411
  Israeli settlements and, 411
  Israeli-Syrian peace and, 151, 283, 389,
    396
  Palestinian elections and, 382–83
  regime change and, 5, 8, 151, 205–9,
    230
  stability vs. freedom and, 58–59, 158
  successes of, 7
Bushehr heavy water reactor, 236
Butler, Richard, 189, 191, 198, 199

Cairo, 44, 45, 48–49, 116, 357
  Arafat in, 296, 345
  Christopher-Mubarak meeting in,
    52–53
  Clinton in, 348–49
  Gaza-Jericho signing ceremony in,
    120–23
  Israeli-Palestinian security chiefs
    meeting in, 357
Cairo West Air Base, 52*n*
California, 56
Camp David Accords, 340
Camp David Summit (1978), 257, 306,
    307, 310, 320, 323, 411*n*
  Camp David II compared with,
    339–40
Camp David Summit (2000), 138, 264,
    285–341, 343–46, 351, 359, 376, 400,
    410
  border issues in, 296, 303, 308*n*, 310,
    312, 334
  collapse of, 327–40, 343, 344, 345,
    350*n*, 373, 464
  collapse of "Syria first" and, 294–95
  critics of U.S. approach at, 324–25

Jerusalem issue and, *see* Jerusalem, Camp David II and
maps and, 303, 310, 334, 374
mistrust in, 291–94
as negotiating summit, 295
progress at, 337–38
refugee issue in, 303–4, 314, 331, 333–34, 336, 462
road to, 288–305
U.S. draft of framework agreement for, 307–9
"can-do" problem-solving attitude, U.S., 49
Carter, Jimmy, 33, 59, 67, 97, 144, 285, 396
at Camp David, I, 306, 307, 339–40
Oslo Accords and, 69, 73
Carville, James, 265
Chalabi, Ahmed, 38, 162–63, 182, 185, 456
regime change strategy of, 191–92, 202
Chechen rebels, 208
chemical weapons, 30, 34, 152, 190, 201, 207, 210, 456
Cheney, Dick, 14, 35, 162, 202
Chernomyrdin, Viktor, 169
China, 184, 187–88, 208, 230, 393*n*
Iran's relations with, 40, 236
Chirac, Jacques, 178, 187, 194, 198, 208, 354
Jerusalem issue and, 351, 464
Christians, 335, 345, 412*n*, 462
evangelicals, 90, 374–75, 408
in Lebanon, 75, 383
Christopher, Warren, 6, 21*n*, 28, 44–49, 78–80, 120–26, 283
Arab food and, 44, 121, 122
background of, 47
at Dead Sea ceremonies, 132, 133
dual containment and, 51, 56
in Egypt, 52–53, 55–56, 120–22
Fahd's meeting with, 55–56
Husseini negotiations and, 27, 86
on Iranian terrorism, 168, 453–54
Iraq policy and, 38, 448
in Israel, 44–45, 85, 86, 114, 126, 178
King Hussein's meetings with, 103–4, 128–29, 132
in Morocco, 44–47
NSC and, 16–18, 38, 154
Oslo Accords and, 60, 62, 63, 66–67, 70–71, 72, 120–22, 450
"Syria first" and, 23–24, 27, 62, 79–83, 85, 93, 96, 450
"Syria second" and, 93, 99, 100, 103, 105, 114, 116, 123–26
U.S.-Syrian relations and, 105–6

Washington Declaration and, 132, 134, 135, 136
Churchill, Winston, 158, 385
CIA, 16, 152, 154, 159–63
Camp David II and, 330–31
Directorate of Operations (DO) of, 160, 161, 162, 202
intifada and, 357, 358, 360
Iran policy and, 170, 171, 217, 454
overthrow of Saddam and, 36, 37, 38, 160–63, 166, 182, 183, 202, 206, 213
UNSCOM's relations with, 191
Clarke, Richard, 171*n*
Clinton, Bill, 2–10, 13–20, 23–32, 53, 56–59, 76–79, 103–15, 118–19, 127–31, 134–41, 288–344, 346, 348–60, 362–79, 389, 391–93, 396–402, 410–15
aircraft deals and, 56–57
Arab culture and, 48–50
Asad's relations with, *see* Asad, Hafez al-budget deficit and, 128
Camp David II and, 264, 285–86, 287, 288–340, 343, 344, 346, 359, 373, 410, 463, 464
coddling-a-rogue-regime charges against, 216
continuity maintained by, 23–24
dual containment and, 30–32, 35–43, 57, 149–85, 190–214, 397–98, 453
in election of 1992, 14–15, 31*n*, 216*n*
in election of 1996, 56
Goldstein impasse and, 111–15, 120
G. W. Bush compared with, 3, 4–5, 7–10, 24*n*, 78, 232–36, 366*n*, 378, 381, 385, 386, 387, 391, 401, 411
impeachment and, 194, 199, 200, 201, 386
innocence of, 76–77
intifada and, 13, 341–43, 353–60, 401
Iran engaged by, 216–29, 231–37
Israeli elections (1996) and, 177–80, 182, 265, 455
Jordanian-Israeli peace and, 4, 130, 131, 134–40, 143, 144–45, 151, 172
King Hussein's meetings with, 107, 109–10, 127–30
Lewinsky affair and, 191, 194, 304
Middle East ills and, 3–4
New York Times interviews of, 31, 32, 66, 92
at NSC meetings, 16–19, 149–50, 158, 196–200
Okinawa Summit and, 289, 290, 306, 312, 318, 320, 323, 324, 327–30, 339
Oslo Accords and, 2–3, 4, 60–73, 76–77, 82, 89, 92, 111–15, 120, 131, 191, 459

Clinton, Bill (*cont.*)
  Pakistan trip of, 275, 276
  policy handover by, 14, 401–2
  Rabin's assassination and, 175–81
  regime change and, 205, 206–7
  Sharm el-Sheikh Summits and, 13,
    178, 341–43, 355–59
  successes of, 4
  on sucker punch, 14, 15
  "Syria first" and, 17–20, 25, 28–29,
    76–79, 85, 88, 89, 91–93, 145, 246,
    282, 294–95, 396, 413
  Syrian-Israeli peace process and, 3, 4,
    208, 241–60, 262–66, 271–78,
    281–87, 292, 294, 375–76, 397, 398,
    414–15, 459
  "Syria second" and, 93, 98, 99, 103–8,
    126, 131
  Washington Summit and, 130, 131,
    134–35, 136
Clinton, Chelsea, 316
Clinton, Hillary Rodham, 15, 139, 199
Clinton Parameters (Dec. 23, 2000), 5,
    13–14, 366–71, *368*, 373–74, 401–2,
    409
  Sher's letter about, 465–66
  text of, 441–45
CNN, 62, 68, 105, 195, 350*n*
  Khatami's interview with, 220–21, 229
Cohen, William, 193, 194, 197, 199, 200
Cold War, 52, 391, 406
Cole, USS, 357
Coleridge, Samuel Taylor, 1, 377
Commerce Department, U.S., 448
Congress, U.S., 99, 213, 337, 386
  Iran policy and, 170, 216, 218, 219, 220,
    222, 229
  Iraq policy and, 185, 192, 195, 206
  Israel policy and, 18, 90, 136
  Jordan policy and, 109, 128, 129, 130,
    134, 138
  King Hussein-Rabin appearance at,
    137–38, 348
  see also House of Representatives, U.S.;
    Senate, U.S.
Congress of Vienna, 188*n*
Conoco, 168–69
containment, *see* dual containment;
  specific countries
"containment plus" strategy, 207*n*
cruise missiles, 183, 195, 200–201
Czech Republic, 236*n*

Dahlan, Mohammed, 358*n*, 360, 363, 467
  Camp David II and, 302, 311–12, 317,
    330, 331, 333*n*, 334
  Gaza Preventive Security Service of,
    331, 360

Damascus, 48–49, 96–100, 106, 173,
    247*n*, 266, 360
  Albright in, 242–44, 248, 251
  Arafat's trip to, 93
  Bandar's trip to, 272
  bodies exhumed in, 257
  business community of, 279, 282
  Christopher's trips to, 45, 79–83, 99,
    100, 104, 114, 116, 123–26
  Clinton in, 139*n*, 141, 172, 173, 287
  descriptions of, 96
  Israeli visits to, 275*n*
  Khatami in, 228*n*
  King Hussein's visit to, 103, 129
  Kissinger's trips to, 20, 79, 97
  Mubarak's trip to, 271
  Palestinian rejectionist groups in, 21,
    71
  strike forces around, 460
D'Amato, Alfonse, 169, 218
Daoudi, Riad, 248–49, 252, 259, 272
Dayan, Moshe, 144
debt relief, for Jordan, 127*n*, 128–29, 130,
    131*n*, 141, 452
Defense Department, U.S., 36, 42, 94,
    129*n*, 192*n*, 202, 257
  Chalabi and, 162–63
Deif, Mohammed, 342
democracy, 49, 59
  in Israel, 90, 455
  in Palestine, 382–83
  U.S. spreading of, 7, 9, 57, 382–83, 384,
    386, 392, 398, 406–7
Democrats, 178, 304, 317
Deri, Aryeh, 87*n*
Deutsch, John, 166
Dharifi, Yusif, 227
Dicter, Avi, 355, 358*n*
diplomacy:
  balance of power, 32–36, 406
  Clinton's emphasis on, 3, 4, 5, 8, 9–10,
    207
  G. W. Bush's neglect of, 8, 207, 209,
    379–80, 386–89, 396
direct engagement, in peacemaking,
    144–45
Directorate of Military Intelligence,
    Israeli, 95–96
Djerejian, Ed, 68
Doral Country Club, 15
Draft Treaty of Peace between Israel and
    Syria (Jan. 2000), 434–40
Drogin, Bob, 456
drugs, 222
Druze, Syrian, 21
dual containment, 5, 30–43, 51, 56–57,
    87, 149–214, 397–98
  author's speech on, 41–43

breakdown of, 216
Iran's breakout and, 167–82
origin of term, 41–42
peace process and, 42, 43, 149–66, 208, 217
Saddam's resurgence and, 182–214
traditional U.S. approach vs., 32–36
Dura, Mohammed al-, 353n

early warning stations:
Israeli, 82n, 124n, 173, 247n, 250, 259, 267n, 331, 460, 463
Syrian, 124n
East Bank, 100, 101, 102
Eastern Europe, 187, 236n
East Jerusalem, 86, 113, 356, 395n, 408, 465
Camp David II and, 299–301, 308, 312, 315, 317, 318, 332n, 337, 338
in Clinton Parameters, 366, 466
Hamas candidates banned in, 382
Jordanian control in, 100, 102
Echaveste, Maria, 309n
economy, U.S., 9, 59
Egypt, 13, 20, 50–59, 139, 324, 389, 463
border crossings to, 110n
economy of, 57–58
G. W. Bush relations with, 384
Hamas cease-fire and, 404
intelligence service of, 202
intifada and, 355, 357, 358
Iranian threat and, 237, 402
Iran's relations with, 53, 219, 228n
Iraq's relations with, 52–53, 155, 194, 195, 202
Israeli-Jordanian peace and, 141–42
Israel's relations with, 52, 55, 141–42, 237, 345, 396, 409, 410
Jerusalem issue and, 345, 346, 348–49
Oslo Accords and, 2, 120–23
Palestinian-Israeli peace process and, 56, 237, 295, 301, 345, 367
in Six-Day War, 145
Soviet relations with, 52, 89
Syria's relations with, 74, 84, 271, 396
U.S. relations with, 26, 27, 50–53, 55–58, 89, 141, 155, 194, 266, 345, 384, 404–7
Yom Kippur War and, 89, 396
Egyptian-Israeli peace process, 18, 19, 28–29, 52, 67, 82, 84, 125, 130, 141, 142n, 278, 285, 408
Camp David I and, 257, 306, 307, 310, 339–40
Sadat's trip to Jerusalem and, 29, 45, 87, 266, 284, 396
see also Israel-Egypt peace treaty
Eisenhower, Dwight D., 89, 128

Ekéus, Rolf, 152–53, 165, 166
elections, 407
in Egypt, 51
in Iran, 215–17, 219, 225, 228, 229, 230
in Iraq, 209, 230, 383, 402
Palestinian, 382–83
in Russia, 179
elections, Israeli, 95, 119, 141, 203, 344, 408n
of 1992, 26, 79, 87
of 1996, 67, 177–80, 182, 265, 455
of 1999, 271, 291n, 362
of 2001, 361–62, 364–65, 370, 371, 375, 465
of 2006, 461
elections, U.S.:
of 1992, 14–15, 31n, 216n
of 1996, 56
of 2000, 304, 317
Erbil, 182, 184n, 187
Erdogan, Recep Tayyip, 389, 408n
Erekat, Saeb, 295, 298, 308, 311–12, 314, 323–24, 333n, 335–36
Erez, 364, 370, 466
Europe, U.S. tensions with, 167–69
European Union, 217n, 231n, 355, 454, 467
evangelicals, 90, 374–75, 408

Fahd, King of Saudi Arabia, 50, 51, 54–58, 139n, 155–56
aircraft deal and, 56–57
stroke of, 183
Faisal, King of Saudi Arabia, 54, 55
Faisal, Saud al-, 67, 178
Fallahian, Ali, 217
Fatah, 75, 360, 382, 385
Tanzim in, 296–97, 342, 353–54, 358, 369
Fayyad, Salam, 386, 387
FBI, 171, 222n, 224, 457
Finkelstein, Arthur, 178
Foley, Tim, 138
Fontaine-le-Port, 225
Foreign Ministry, Iranian, 222–23, 226–27
France, 54, 177, 259
colonialism of, 48–49, 124
intelligence of, 209
Iran policy of, 236, 454
Iraq policy of, 31, 164, 184, 186–90, 192, 194, 208, 209, 214
mandate of, 247n
Saddam's contracts to, 184, 455–56
Freeh, Louis, 222n
Friedman, Thomas L., 31, 42, 92, 384
Fuerth, Leon, 17, 38, 193, 199–200
Furst, Zeev, 178

Gamyat Islamiya, 53
gas industry, Iranian, 233, 236, 454
Gaza, 4, 68n, 180–81, 291, 341–46, 363n, 395n
  Arafat–Ben-Ami meeting in, 364
  Arafat's return to, 151
  Camp David II and, 295, 296, 311, 312, 331, 334, 339
  Clinton in, 199
  in Clinton Parameters, 366, *368*
  economy of, 72, 73
  Hamas in, 8, 17n, 230, 381–82, 383, 385, 389, 404–5
  intifada in, 204, 341–43, 345, 352–60, 374
  Israeli withdrawal from, 110, 371, 381–82, 388, 404, 408–9
  maps of, 121–23
  Muwassi in, 121, 122n
  Oslo Accords and, 71, 83, 86, 89, 90, 110, 118, 120–23
  Palestinians in, 21, 26, 70, 71, 78–79, 80, 88, 110, 117, 118, 303, 405
  Palestinian state in, 3
  Syrian peace and, 118
  terrorism in, 173
Gaza City, 355n
"Gaza first" deal, 86n
Gaza Preventive Security Service, 331, 360
Gemayel, Beshir, 99
Geneva, 189
  Clinton-Asad meetings in, 104–8, 110, 275–78, 280, 284–85, 286–87, 290n, 292, 294, 321, 324, 398, 460
Germany, 177, 209, 217n
Ghaith, Sulaiman Abu, 467
gifts, 139–40
Gilo, 295n, 356, 360
Gingrich, Newt, 170, 221
Ginossar, Yossi, 144, 370
  Arafat's business with, 292, 461
  Camp David II and, 292–93, 298, 313n, 317, 318–19, 330
Ginsberg, Marc, 44
Glaspie, April, 36
God, 21, 90, 138, 346–48
Golan Heights, 26, 74, 84n, 94, 135, 408
  early warning sites on, 82n, 124n, 173, 247n, 259, 460
  industrial park for, 282
  Israeli settlements in, 87
  Syrian peace and, 17–19, 21–22, 23, 28–29, 62, 79–82, 85–89, 91, 99, 103, 105, 108, 109, 118, 124, 125, 129, 151, 179n, 245–51, 254–58, 262–63, 265, 271–75, *274*, 277, 284, 389, 415, 451, 452, 459
  U.S. troops proposed for, 18, 23, 29, 106

Golan Heights Separation of Forces Agreement (1974), 21, 86, 97
Goldstein, Baruch, 111–18, 120
Gore, Al, 2, 138, 193, 216n, 318
  Egypt's economy and, 57–58
  in election of 2000, 304, 317
  Iran policy and, 169
  at NSC meetings, 15–17, 195–98
  in Saudi Arabia, 194n
Government Accountability Office, U.S., 455
Great Britain, 54, 56n
  colonialism of, 48–49, 94, 101, 124
  Hashemites influenced by, 132–33
  Iraq policy of, 31, 184, 188, 197, 198, 204, 208
  mandate of, 124, 247n
  public opinion in, 197
Greenberg, Stanley, 262, 265
Green Line, 173, 303
Greenstein, Gidi, 320–21
Group of Eight (G-8), 385
  Summit of (2000), 289, 290, 306, 312, 318, 320, 323, 324, 327–30, 339
Gulf Cooperation Council (GCC), 33, 194, 405n
Gulf War, first, 33, 37, 55, 153, 154, 155, 391, 396n
  Arafat and, 19–20, 75, 88
  defeat of Saddam's army in, 15–16, 30, 35, 36, 398
  failure to overthrow Saddam in, 35
  funding of victims of, 164
  Jordan and, 109, 128, 133, 145
  Kurds and, 159n
  Mubarak's views on, 52–53
  no-fly zone and, 182
  Syria and, 22, 75, 98, 279
  WMD and, 210
Gulf War, second, *see* Iraq War
Gush Etzion, 295n, 411n

Ha'aretz, 107, 265, 267, 286
Haber, Eitan, 63, 64, 67, 69–70, 122, 270
  Rabin's death and, 174–76
  Washington Declaration and, 132, 134, 135, 136, 138
Haberman, Clyde, 452
Halevy, Efraim, 95, 103, 126–27, 129, 144, 344n, 451, 452–53
Halperin, Morton, 207n
Hama, 99
Hamas, 8, 17n, 70, 237, 342, 381–83, 385–89, 392, 402–5, 408, 414
  elections of 2006 and, 382–83
  Iran's relations with, 173, 181, 230, 403
  in West Jerusalem, 176
Hammurabi division, 153

Hamza, Prince of Jordan, 133*n*
handshaking, 1, 46, 67–68, 137
   Syrian-Israeli peace process and, 67,
     253, 254, 284
Haniyah, Akram, 308, 315, 463
Harawi, Ilyas, 115
Hashemite rulers, 54, 101, 104, 132–33,
   140*n*, 141
Hassan, Crown Prince of Jordan, 127,
   128, 132, 133–34, 142*n*, 219
Hassan II, King of Morocco, 44–47, 50,
   135*n*, 178
Hasson, Israel, 348
"headroom," use of term, 130*n*–31*n*
Hebrew University, 5
Hebron, 452
   Goldstein massacre in, 111–18, 120
Hebron Agreement (1997), 6, 68*n*
Hejaz region, 54, 100
Helal, Gamal, 25, 242, 276, 309, 311, 357
Helms, Jesse, 185
Hermon, Mount, 267*n*, 284
Herzliya, 94*n*, 269–70
Herzog, Isaac, 313*n*
Hezbollah, 87, 98, 141, 180, 273, 378, 408
   Camp David II and, 296–97
   elections and, 383
   Iran's links with, 39, 40, 43, 172–73,
     176–78, 230, 235, 237, 403
   Iraqi conflict and, 230
   in Lebanon, 7–8, 43, 95, 172, 176–78,
     230, 235, 282, 383, 388, 402, 414
   Saudi, 171
Hindi, Amin al-, 358*n*
Hirschberg, Peter, 461
Hirschfeld, Yair, 80
Holst, Jorgen, 84
hostages, 460–61
   U.S., 33, 40*n*, 171, 224, 229
House of Representatives, U.S., 201, 218
   Judiciary Committee of, 199, 200
human rights, 37, 59, 384
Hussein, Kamel, 210
Hussein, Saddam, 3, 6, 30–42, 216, 218,
   456
   Arafat's siding with, 19–20, 75, 88
   Asad's antagonism toward, 151
   assassination attempts against, 152
   containment of, 30–32, 36–42,
     149–66, 182–214, 216, 217, 398
   death of, 209
   Gulf War and, *see* Gulf War, first
   illicit revenue of, 184, 455
   importance of image of strength to,
     210–11
   Iran-Iraq War and, 34–37, 54, 157
   Kurds and, 34, 35, 159–63, 182–83,
     211, 212

MEK aided by, 220
palaces and compounds of, 150, 164,
   190
removal of, 7, 30, 36, 37, 38, 41, 50–51,
   53, 149, 151, 159–64, 166, 182,
   191–92, 202, 203, 205–9, 213, 229,
   233, 235, 381, 392, 398, 402, 406
resurgence of, 182–214
second Kuwait invasion threat of,
   153–55, 159, 211
smuggling efforts of, 203
technology of, 34, 448
U.N. weapons inspectors evicted by,
   189, 194, 195, 203–4
Hussein, Sharif, 100
Hussein bin Talal, King of Jordan, 2, 4,
   27, 74, 112, 115, 126–45, 151, 166,
   203, 244*n*, 396, 397
   Arafat's relationship with, 94–95,
     100, 114, 117, 126, 133, 135, 136,
     142–43
   Asad's relationship with, 95, 129, 131,
     142–43, 453
   Clinton's meetings with, 107, 109–10,
     127–30
   death of, 130, 133*n*
   flight over Israel of, 143*n*
   Jerusalem as viewed by, 138, 348
   parliament speech of (July 9, 1994),
     130, 131
   Peres's meetings with, 100–104, 451
   Rabin's relationship with, 93–95, 100,
     109, 129
   Saddam's aggression rejected by,
     155–56
   survival motive of, 395
   Washington Summit and, 130, 131,
     132–38, 143*n*
Husseini, Abdel Qader al-, 27*n*
Husseini, Faisal, 27, 28, 79, 85, 86

idealism, U.S., 49, 391–93
IDF, *see* Israel Defense Forces
Ikhwan, 54
ILSA, *see* Iran and Libya Sanctions Act
   (ILSA)
Incirlik Air Base, 159, 203
Independent Inquiry Committee, 455
India, 393*n*
Indyk, Jill, 5, 269
Indyk, Martin (author):
   as ambassador to Israel, 6–7, 174–76,
     179–80, 185, 215, 241, 269–73,
     288–89, 298, 371, 377, 380
   as assistant secretary for the Middle
     East, 6, 185–90, 192, 215–17, 241–46,
     400*n*
   Australian upbringing of, 23

Indyk, Martin (*cont.*)
  Camp David II and, 288–89, 290,
    306–7, 322
  career path of, 5–6
  in Clinton campaign, 15–16, 31*n*
  dual containment speech of, 41–43
  Israeli elections and, 179–80
  Israel-Jordan peace efforts and, 102–3,
    132, 133–34, 139
  Israel-Syria peace efforts and, 23,
    62–63, 80–81, 93, 98, 107, 125, 131,
    141, 241–46
  Jewish identity of, 23, 25
  Jordan policy and, 95
  in Morocco, 44–47
  Netanyahu-Clinton correspondence
    and, 184*n*–85*n*
  in NSC, 5, 17, 37–38, 41, 156–57,
    160–61
  Oslo Accords and, 62–70
  Rabin's death and, 6, 174–76
  in Tunis, 111–12, 115
Indyk, Sarah, 5
innocence, U.S., 49–50, 391, 392
Innocents Abroad, The (Twain), ix
intelligence, limits of, 209–10
  see also CIA; *specific countries*
inter-Arab rivalries, 142–43
International Atomic Energy Agency
    (IAEA), 152, 165
International Monetary Fund, 169, 385
intifada, first, 19, 27, 70, 86
intifada, second, 7, 204, 341–43, 345–46,
    352–60, 369–70, 373, 379–82, 384,
    401, 461, 464–65
  Paris talks and, 354–55, 357
  Sharm el-Sheik Summit and, 13,
    341–43, 355–59
Iran, 4–7, 19, 32–37, 53, 58, 204, 215–37,
    281, 388, 390, 402–6, 408
  Afghan relations with, 222–23
  aircraft needs of, 56, 57
  bid for regional dominance by, 7, 39,
    181, 230, 232, 235, 236–37, 402–4
  Chalabi's connection with, 163
  containment of, 5, 6, 30, 32, 39–43, 56,
    57, 86–87, 149, 151, 157, 167–82, 206,
    216, 233, 397–98
  drug problem in, 222
  economy of, 40, 167–70
  Egypt's relations with, 53, 219, 228*n*
  Germany's relations with, 177
  G. W. Bush policy for, 157, 223*n*,
    229–36, 384, 392, 397, 398
  Hezbollah's links with, 39, 40, 43,
    172–73, 176–78, 230, 235, 237, 403
  intelligence service of, 161, 228*n*,
    454

international backlash against,
    235–36
  Iraqi influence of, 37, 157, 161, 209,
    230, 403
  Iraqi oil smuggling of, 203
  Iraq's relations with, 34–37, 54, 151,
    157, 167, 172, 211, 236
  Islamists in, 4, 53
  Israel's relations with, 216, 218–19,
    235, 403
  Jordan's relations with, 219, 228*n*
  in Khobar truck bombing, 171, 216,
    217*n*, 218, 219, 224–27, 229, 235,
    457–58
  Lebanon's relations with, 236, 237,
    378
  Mosaddeq overthrown in, 170, 217,
    221, 228
  navy of, 34, 218, 221
  nuclear program of, *see* nuclear
    programs, of Iran
  oil of, 40, 167, 168–69, 223, 232, 233,
    236, 453
  Omani diplomatic role with, 225–27
  parliament of (Majlis), 170, 224, 228
  peace process subverted by, 39,
    176–81
  Rabin's assassination exploited by,
    176–81
  revolution in, 32, 33–34, 39, 53, 59,
    171, 224, 228, 229
  Russia's relations with, 40, 169, 236,
    454
  sanctions and, 167–70, 212, 216, 218,
    223, 228, 231–33, 236, 388, 454,
    457, 458
  Saudi relations with, 54, 55, 195,
    217*n*
  Syrian-Israeli peace efforts and, 22,
    43, 172–73, 237, 398, 413
  Syria's relations with, 151, 171–74, 230,
    237
  Talabani's deal with, 182
  U.S. hostages in, 33, 171, 224, 229
  U.S. idealism and, 392
  U.S. seen as "Great Satan" by, 19, 32,
    181, 224
  U.S. weak points exploited by, 167–74,
    180, 182
Iran Air, 56
Iran and Libya Sanctions Act (ILSA),
    169, 223, 454
Iranian Ministry of Intelligence and
    Security (MOIS), 53, 173, 217, 224,
    226
Iranian Revolutionary Guard Corps
    (IRGC), 39, 40, 53, 173, 217, 228*n*
  Iraq War and, 230

Khobar truck bombing and, 171, 224, 225
Talabani's relations with, 182
Iran-Iraq War, 34–37, 54, 151, 157, 172
Iraq, 3–7, 58, 113, 281
  civil war in, 230, 384, 402
  Clinton's use of force against, 149–50, 183, 187, 193–201, 211–12
  containment of, 5, 30–32, 36–43, 56, 86–87, 149–66, 182–214, 216, 217, 386, 398
  coup plots in, 159–64, 166, 182, 183, 201, 202
  economy of, 152, 183
  Egypt's relations with, 52–53, 155, 194, 195, 202
  elections in, 209, 230, 383, 402
  fragmentation of, 37
  Gulf War and, *see* Gulf War, first
  infant mortality in, 183–84
  insurgency in, 151, 230, 392*n*
  intelligence service of, 149–50, 187, 456
  Iran's influence in, 37, 157, 161, 209, 230, 403
  Iran's relations with, 34–37, 54, 151, 157, 167, 172, 211, 236
  Israeli-Syrian peace and, 22
  Israel's relations with, 35, 140*n*
  Jordan's relations with, 94, 109, 128, 155–56, 202, 203
  no-drive zone option for, 156–57
  no-fly zone of, 30–31, 38, 154, 156, 157, 160, 182, 183, 187, 204, 211
  oil of, 33, 35, 151–52, 164–65, 182, 183–84, 188, 203, 204–5, 210, 221
  sanctions against, 30, 127, 150–53, 158–59, 164–65, 184–85, 188, 194, 204–5, 207, 210, 212–14, 455, 456
  Saudi relations with, 54, 55, 183, 202
  Shiite-Sunni divide in, 209, 403
  Syria's relations with, 16, 151, 194, 195, 204
  UNSCOM and, 152–53, 164–66, 186–95, 198–200, 204
  U.S. security ties with, 405*n*, 406
  WMD and, *see* weapons of mass destruction, Iraq and
Iraqi army, 55, 152, 154, 158, 159, 204, 211, 391, 398
  in coup attempt, 160
  destruction of, 15, 19, 30, 35, 36
  rebuilding of, 392*n*
  size of, 34–35
Iraqi National Accord (al-Wifaq al-Watani), 166
Iraqi National Congress (INC), 38, 162, 182, 183, 185
Iraqi War Crimes Tribunal, 38

Iraq Liberation Act (ILA), 192, 195
Iraq Survey Group, 455
Iraq War, 381, 386, 390, 392, 393, 394, 398, 406
  destabilizing consequences of, 50–51, 59, 235, 404
  lessons of, 9, 393, 394
  Sunni-Shiite tensions unleashed in, 403
  "surge" in, 403
  U.S. invasion in, 50, 152, 158, 163, 202, 207, 229
  U.S. withdrawals in, 235, 403
Irish Republican Army, 63
Islam, Muslims, 39, 54, 100, 184, 392
  G. W. Bush administration and, 383–84, 388
  see also Shiites; Sunni
Islamic fundamentalists, 57, 58, 97, 99
Islamists, 58, 387
  in Iran, 4, 53
  Palestinian, 173, 382–83, 404
  see also Hamas; Hezbollah
Israel, 13–29, 40*n*, 49, 403–15, 467
  air force of, 81*n*, 143*n*, 241, 464
  antimissile batteries in, 198–99
  Arab economic boycott of, 136
  Arabs' shared threat with, 237
  author as ambassador to, 6–7, 174–76, 179–80, 185, 215, 241, 269–73, 288–89, 298, 371, 377, 380
  Berger's visit to, 297–98
  coalition politics in, 4, 87, 90, 118, 284, 288, 305, 359, 385, 395
  elections in, *see* elections, Israeli
  establishment of, 94, 112, 296
  Hamas cease-fire with, 404
  intelligence in, 210
  Knesset in, *see* Knesset
  leaks and, 81, 103, 132, 134, 179*n*
  nuclear power of, 112
  public opinion in, 21, 26, 87, 125, 130, 246, 251–52, 257, 265*n*, 267, 284, 298, 371, 451
  right wing in, 101, 116, 117, 180, 369, 375, 409*n*
  security of, 20, 22, 25, 70, 80, 81, 82*n*, 92, 105, 106, 110*n*, 114, 255, 256, 278, 303, 308, 331, 338, 340, 371, 461, 466
  U.S. relations with, 14–15, 18, 26, 28, 82, 89–91, 118–19, 127–28, 141, 174, 178, 258*n*, 265, 285, 308, 355*n*, 374–75, 404, 405*n*, 406–8
  see also Palestinian-Israeli peace process; *specific events, organizations, sites, and Middle East states*

Israel Defense Forces (IDF), 108, 110, 112, 115, 118, 173, 273, 291, 322, 355*n*, 459
  Arafat's warning of fifth column in, 291
  in Gaza, 296, 345
  Golan Heights and, 17–19, 74, 94, 109, 179*n*, 282, 460
  intifada and, 341, 342, 353, 354, 358, 360
  in Jordan Valley, 303, 331, 333, 338, 370, 461, 463, 464, 466
  in Lebanon, 75, 177, 257, 271, 290*n*, 294, 295, 296
  planning branch of, 303, 331
  Sayeret Matkal in, 289–90, 318
  in West Bank, 1, 71, 296–97, 303, 345, 387, 463
  West Bank withdrawal of, 292
Israel-Egypt Peace Treaty (1978), 18, 67, 141, 144, 257, 278, 306, 340, 394
Israel-Jordan Peace Treaty (1994), 2, 131–32, 138–45, 278, 394
  lessons of, 142–45
  signing of, 138–41, 172–73, 307
"Israel lobby," 90
Israel Radio, 14*n*, 67, 451–52

Japan, 41, 169
Jericho, 94, 110
  Oslo Accords and, 71, 80, 83, 86, 89, 110, 118, 120–23
Jerusalem, 20, 21, 27, 79, 93, 95, 104, 106, 125, 128, 178, 181, 345–52, 356, 386, 395*n*, 411*n*, 412, 452, 464
  al-Aqsa Mosque in, 100, 101, 299, 325*n*, 349, 462
  Albright's visit to, 302*n*
  Barak's concession on, 322–23
  Camp David II and, 289, 291, 293, 298–302, 308, 312–28, 330, 332, 333, 335–40, 345, 348, 373, 409, 462–63
  as capital of Palestinian state, 89, 299, 313, 461
  Christopher in, 44–45, 85, 86, 114, 126
  Church of the Sepulchre in, 349
  Clinton Parameters and, 366–67, 370–71, 374, 409, 466
  Dome of the Rock in, 101, 299, 349
  Fink's in, 276–77
  King Hussein's flight over, 143*n*
  move of U.S. embassy to, 337, 464
  as occupied territory, 113–14
  Oslo Accords and, 71, 72, 80, 81, 86, 89, 93*n*, 113, 135, 300, 450
  Palestinians in, 27, 79, 88, 101
  Sadat's trip to, 28–29, 45, 87, 266, 284, 396
  Saladin's conquest of, 462
  Security Council and, 113–14
  siege of, 27*n*, 78
  Temple Mount/Haram al-Sharif in, 14, 101, 299–302, 308, 312, 313, 315, 317, 319–26, 330, 332, 335, 336, 339, 341, 345–52, 349, 354, 359, 363–67, 372, 373, 375, 388*n*, 392, 411–12, 462, 463, 464, 466
  Umar's conquest of, 462
  Wailing Wall in, 291, 298, 317*n*, 325*n*, 338, 348, 352, 412*n*
  waqf in, 101, 102, 127, 135, 136, 302, 412*n*
  Western Wall in, 363, 370, 372, 411–12
Jerusalem Committee, 135*n*
Jewish Agency, 94
Jews, 2, 3, 6, 21, 23, 193, 194, 282, 323
  on Clinton peace team, 24, 25
  Hebron and, 117–18
  Moroccan, 45, 46
  psychology of, 143
  Russian, 251*n*
  Sephardic, 87*n*, 265, 347, 362, 461
  Syrian, 98–99, 104
  in U.S., 15, 98, 113, 128, 130*n*, 134, 215, 408
Joint Chiefs of Staff (JCS), 36, 159, 161, 195, 197, 198–99
  Powell as chairman, of, 14, 16–18, 38, 149–50, 153
  Shalikashvili as chairman of, 153–55
Jordan, 4, 24, 84, 289, 355, 463
  army of, 128, 129*n*
  banks of, 102
  border crossings to, 110*n*, 122*n*, 123, 135*n*
  borders of, 123, 127
  British ways in, 132–33
  Clinton in, 138–40
  debt relief for, 127*n*, 128–29, 130, 131*n*, 141, 452
  Gulf War and, 109, 128, 133, 145
  hospitality in, 47
  intelligence service of, 202
  Iranian threat and, 237, 402
  Iran's relations with, 219, 228*n*
  Iraqi relations with, 94, 109, 128, 155–56, 202, 203
  Israeli peace process with, 2, 4, 19, 84, 88, 95, 100–104, 106–10, 114, 124*n*, 126–45, 151, 155, 172–73, 266, 278, 283, 307, 394, 397, 408, 451, 452–53
  Israeli relations with, 93–96, 345, 409, 410
  Jerusalem and, 100–101, 102, 127, 135, 136, 299, 300*n*, 302, 345
  Kamel's defection to, 165

Madrid Conference and, 20, 102
oil imports of, 203
Oslo process and, 2, 94–95
as Palestine, 101
Palestinians in, 74, 75, 100, 109, 133, 303
parliament of, 130, 131
PLO challenge to, 94, 100, 133, 143
in Six-Day War, 145
in Syria, 124
Syria's relations with, 74, 94, 95, 141
U.S. relations with, 26, 27, 57, 109, 127–29, 141, 151, 166, 345, 404, 405n
Jordan River, 94, 100, 101, 127, 259, 273, 274, 276, 289
bridges of, 121
Camp David II and, 303, 312, 313, 462
Jordan Valley, 411n
IDF in, 303, 331, 333, 338, 370, 461, 463, 464, 466
Julius Caesar (Shakespeare), 361, 373
Jumblatt, Kamal, 99

Kach movement, 116, 369
Kafr Kana, 177
Kagan, Robert, 169
Kahane, Meir, son of, 369
Kahane Chai movement, 116
Kamel, Hussein, 165, 190
Kay, David, 201
Kennan, George F., 38, 205
Kennedy, John F., 32
Kenya, al-Qaeda in, 467
Kerr, Malcolm, 24
Khaddam, Abdul Halim, 173–74
Khamenei, Ayatollah Ali, 51, 168, 174, 181, 216, 221, 222, 227–28
Kharazi, Sadegh, 458
Kharrazi, Kamal, 223, 226–27, 228, 457
Khatami, Mohammad, 215–29, 231, 457
assaults on allies of, 224, 226
attempt to open Omani channel to, 225–27, 234
call for civilizational dialogue made by, 221, 223, 227, 229
CNN interview of, 220–21, 229
peace process supported by, 221
U.S. visit of, 229
Khobar truck bombing, 171, 216, 217n, 218, 219, 224–27, 229, 235, 457–58
Khomeini, Ayatollah, 32, 39, 55, 224
Khrushchev, Nikita, 32
Kibbutz Ein Gev, 273, 274
Kibbutz Snir, 259, 272
Kinneret, Lake, 246–47, 249, 259, 260, 272–77, 274, 286
Jerusalem compared with, 298
park at, 414, 468

Kiryat Arba, 111, 117
Kissinger, Henry, 6, 14, 21, 23, 82, 86, 245n, 365, 396
second Sinai disengagement deal and, 94, 285
shuttle diplomacy of, 20, 48, 79, 400n
Knesset, 87n, 130, 179n, 251, 284, 288, 293, 296, 341
elections and, 343, 361–62, 365
Jerusalem annexed by, 299, 322
Olmert's speech to, 301n, 409n
Kochanovsky, Moshe, 261–62
Kosovo, 192, 211–12
Kozyrev, Andrey, 60, 122
Kurdistan Democratic Party (KDP), 182, 193n, 204
Kurds, 34, 35, 37, 38, 159–64, 182–83, 211
Clinton's protection of, 159, 203, 204, 212
Iranian, 217n
Washington reconciliation Summit of, 193
Kurtzer, Daniel, 24, 80, 111, 450
Kuwait, 30, 36n, 37, 57, 61, 139, 188, 189n, 291, 394
antimissile batteries in, 198–99
G. H. W. Bush's visit to, 149
oil of, 33, 34, 157, 203
Saddam's invasion of, 19–20, 22, 33, 35, 52–53, 55, 75, 88, 145, 153, 155, 164, 210, 279, 391, 396n, 398
Saddam's second invasion threat against, 153–55, 159, 211
Syrian aircraft deal and, 98–99

Labor Party, Israeli, 22, 64, 87, 95, 102, 141, 343, 361–62, 460
Laipson, Ellen, 159, 161
Lake, Anthony (Tony), 15, 36, 41, 81n, 218
Iran policy and, 167
Iraq policy and, 153, 154, 160–62
in NSC, 16, 37–38, 156, 160
Oslo Accords and, 62–63, 68
Landau, Moshe, 460
Lau, Yisrael Meir, 347n
Lauder, Ronald, 246–47, 250, 259, 283, 459
leadership, in peacemaking, 145, 278–79
League of Nations, 247n
leaks, 162, 298
Israel and, 81, 103, 132, 134, 179n
in Syrian-Israeli peace talks, 260, 263, 265–68, 271, 286
Lebanese-Palestinian Islamic front, 172

Lebanon, 7–8, 18, 24, 84, 104*n*, 172, 405
  civil war in, 75, 279
  elections in, 383
  Hezbollah in, 7–8, 43, 95, 172, 176–78,
    230, 235, 282, 383, 388, 402, 414
  IDF withdrawal from, 271, 290*n*, 294,
    295, 296, 388, 408, 409, 461
  Iran's relations with, 236, 237, 378
  Israeli invasion of, 75
  Israeli peace with, 106, 124*n*, 140, 173,
    258, 262, 263, 266, 273, 294, 408, 414
  Palestinians in, 74–75, 88, 95, 111, 257,
    303, 334*n*, 351
  in Syria, 124
  Syria's influence on, 21, 74–75, 87, 243,
    280–83
  Syria's occupation of, 75, 98, 99,
    279–83
  Syria's withdrawal from, 7, 394, 402
  U.S. relations with, 405*n*
Lev, Ozrad, 461
Levi, Yitzhak, 461
Levy, David, 252, 288
Lewinsky, Monica, 191, 194, 304
Lewis, Sam, 28
Libya, 4, 32, 218
  containment of, 206
  nuclear program of, 213*n*, 394, 398
  sanctions and, 169, 213*n*
Lieberman, Avigdor, 375, 409*n*
Likud party, 27, 102, 141, 301, 343, 375,
  378
  in election of 1996, 177–80
Lincoln, Abraham, 254
Lineberry, Liz, 44
Lipkin-Shahak, Amnon, 115–16, 173,
  354, 359–60, 363, 364, 370
  Camp David II and, 298, 301, 317, 319,
    321, 330
Livni, Tzipi, 388*n*
London, 102, 109, 127, 129
Lott, Trent, 185

Mabus, Ray, 155
McDonnell Douglas, 56, 57
Madrid, 189
Madrid Peace Conference (1991), 20, 22,
  76, 79, 84, 88, 97, 98, 102
Majali, Abdel Salaam, 132, 133
Malaysia, 454
Malka, Amos, 465
Malley, Robert, 24, 25, 248, 268, 297, 309,
  317
maps, 364*n*, 366, 372
  Camp David II and, 303, 310, 334, 374
  Clinton Parameters and, *368*, 374
  of Middle East, *x–xi*
  Oslo Accords and, 121–23

Syrian-Israeli peace efforts and, 247*n*,
  255–56, 271, 272, *274*, 277, 459
March of Folly, The (Tuchman), 10
Marine One, 306
Maronite Christians, 75
Marsh Arabs, 157
Mashal, Khaled, 388
Mayer, Jane, 456
Mecca, 54, 100, 101, 135*n*, 219, 316
Medina, 54, 100, 101, 135*n*, 316
Mediterranean Sea, 94, 151, 199, 397
Meidan, Pini, 364*n*
Meir, Golda, 94
Meretz Party, 364–65, 371
Meridor, Dan, 319, 333, 462
Middle East:
  advantage of time in, 400–402
  balance of power in, *see* balance of
    power
  Clinton's trips to, 48, 138–41, 172–73,
    348–49
  end of peace process in, 361–76
  map of, *x–xi*
  more effective U.S. interventions in,
    393–97
  regional security architecture in,
    405–6
  Soviet foothold in, 52
  U.S. dominance in, 19, 22, 36, 42,
    391–92
  U.S. shaping of strategic context in,
    397–99
  U.S. team structure for, 399–400
  see also specific places and topics
Middle East North Africa Economic
  Summit (1995), 142*n*
Miller, Aaron, 24, 25, 72, 111, 268, 297
Milosevic, Slobodan, 211–12
Ministry of Religious Affairs, Israeli,
  412*n*
Mitchell, Andrea, 65
Mitchell, George, 342, 380
Mitchell Report, 411*n*
Mofaz, Shaul, 369, 466
Mohamed, Crown Prince of Morocco,
  46
Mohamed, Prophet, 101, 133, 171*n*, 299,
  462
Mohammed VI, King of Morocco, 345,
  367
MOIS, *see* Iranian Ministry of
  Intelligence and Security
Mombasa, al-Qaeda in, 467
Mordechai, Yitzhak, 459
Morocco, 4, 44–47, 50, 57, 135*n*, 144, 266
  Arafat-Ross meeting in, 363, 465
  Israel's relations with, 45, 46, 345
  Jerusalem and, 299, 300*n*, 345

Mosaddeq, Mohammad, 170, 217, 221, 228
Moscow, 189, 345
Mossad, 94n, 95, 144, 194
Mouallem, Walid, 92, 131, 173, 247, 459
Moulay, Prince, 46
Moussa, Amre, 122, 142n, 348, 355
Mubarak, Gamal, 51
Mubarak, Hosni, 27, 41, 58, 115, 155, 204, 355
    Arafat's consulting with, 295, 296, 301, 345, 367
    assassination attempt against, 170
    Camp David II and, 295, 296, 301, 324, 325
    Clinton Parameters and, 367
    Iranian leadership role rejected by, 402
    Jerusalem issue and, 345, 348–49
    Jordanian-Israeli peace and, 141–42
    Oslo deal and, 1–2, 56, 120–23
    at Sharm el-Sheikh Summits, 13, 178, 341
    Syrian-Israeli peace efforts and, 155, 271
    as upholder of status quo, 50–54
Mujahideen-e Khalq (MEK), 220, 221
Munich Olympics, 461
Muslim Brotherhood, 266, 450
Muwassi, 121, 122n

Nablus, 325, 342, 355n
    Joseph's Tomb in, 354, 355n, 356
Naqbaq (disaster), 296–97, 298
Nasrallah, Hassan, 296, 388, 461
Nasser, Gamal Abdel, 52, 74
Nateq-Nouri, Ali Akbar, 217
National Conservation Training Center, 257
National Council of Resistance of Iran, 220
National Guard, Saudi, 454
National Intelligence Estimate, 398n
National Religious Party, 461
National Security Council, 5, 24, 37–38, 41, 309
    Iraq policy and, 37–38, 149–50, 153–54, 156–61, 196–200
    March 3, 1993, meeting of, 16–19
National Security Decision Directives, 41
Navy, U.S., 33n, 52n, 155, 183, 218
NBC, 65
Neriah, Jacques, 123
Netanyahu, Benjamin "Bibi," 6, 185, 191, 218, 245, 270, 378, 408n, 411n
    Arafat's negotiations with, 67, 184, 283
    in election of 1996, 177–80, 265
    in election of 1999, 291, 362, 362n
    in election of 2001, 362, 362n, 465
    Iran policy and, 218–19

Oslo Accords and, 283, 459
    Syrian peace efforts and, 246–47, 250, 252, 278, 283, 408, 459
    Wye Agreement and, 193, 292, 459
New York Times, 41, 42, 384
    Clinton interviews in, 31, 32, 66, 92
Nile River, 51, 53
Nixon, Richard, 14, 15, 94, 174n, 230
Noor, Queen of Jordan, 133n, 139
North Atlantic Treaty Organization, 187
Northern Ireland, 63
North Korea, 9, 212
North Vietnam, 212
Norway, 80, 115
Nour, Ayman, 51n
Novik, Nimrod, 267–68
Nuclear Non-Proliferation Treaty, 39, 40, 236
nuclear programs, 9, 405–6
    of Iran, 7, 9, 39, 40, 167, 168, 169, 216, 219, 229–36, 398n, 403, 405–6, 415, 454, 458
    of Iraq, 30, 152, 165
    of Libya, 213n, 394, 398
    of Syria, 81n, 389, 405–6
Nuseibeh, Sari, 374, 466–67

Office of Management and Budget, U.S., 131n
oil, 9, 20, 32–35, 40, 48, 59, 393
    price of, 59, 232, 233, 384
    Straits of Hormuz and, 235
    see also specific countries
oil embargo, 55
oil-for-food program, 151–52, 164–65, 183–84, 188, 205
Okinawa, Group of Eight Summit in, 289, 290, 306, 312, 318, 320, 323, 324, 327–30, 339
Oklahoma City bombing, 175
Olmert, Ehud, 67, 283, 300–301, 388, 395n, 408, 411n, 461, 463
    Annapolis Conference and, 385, 389
    Rachid's dialogue with, 375
Oman, 33, 47, 57, 225–27
Oman, Sultan of, 225–26
Omar, Ibrahim, 248, 260–62
OPEC, 55
Operation Desert Fox, 195–201, 211–12
Operation Desert Storm, 205
Operation Desert Viper, 195
Operation Grapes of Wrath, 177, 178
Operation Provide Comfort, 159n
opium, 222
Oren, Michael, 468
Organization of the Islamic Conference (OIC), 135n, 335, 345, 350, 385
    1997 Summit of, 219, 221

Orr, Mandy, 462
Oslo Accords, 1–4, 60–95, 131, 134–35,
    142–45, 177, 191, 266, 267, 291, 293,
    300, 328, 330, 354, 356, 357, 375,
    396*n*
  Agreement (Sept. 13, 1993), 1, 417–29
  anatomy of Rabin's decision and,
    78–91, 450–51
  Asad's questions about, 93
  Asad's view of, 99, 106, 452
  breakdown of talks for, 86, 451
  flaws in, 71–72
  four-stage process in, 71
  Gaza-Jericho and, 71, 83, 86, 89, 110,
    118, 120–23
  Goldstein impasse and, 111–17, 120
  hints about negotiations for, 80
  II (Sept. 28, 1995), 1–3, 174, 291
  implementation of, 56, 110, 120, 121,
    459
  interim agreement in, 71, 72, 93*n*,
    110
  Iranian response to, 171, 172
  Jordan's displeasure and, 94–95, 102
  kissing, gun, and uniform issues and,
    68–70
  signing ceremonies, 1–2, 45, 46, 60–71,
    87*n*, 92, 93, 110, 120–23, 132, 134,
    137, 140, 174, 307
  "track II" dialogue and, 80
O'Sullivan, Meghan, 458

Pakistan, Clinton's trip to, 275, 276
Palestine, Palestinians, 52, 84, 155, 278,
    461
  Asad's concession on, 106, 107
  British Mandate for, 124, 247*n*
  British withdrawal from, 94
  Camp David I and, 339–40
  debate over liberation strategy for,
    296–97
  East Bank and, 101
  economy of, 102, 128, 382
  Goldstein massacres and, 111–14, 116,
    117
  Gulf War and, 19–20
  intifadas of, *see* intifada, first; intifada,
    second
  Iran's relations with, 236, 237
  Madrid Conference and, 20, 76, 79, 88,
    102
  refugees, *see* refugees, Palestinian
  self-determination of, 2–3, 101
  Twain in, ix
  victim image of, 289
  see also specific sites
Palestine Islamic Jihad (PIJ), 39, 70, 173,
    176, 181, 414

Palestine Liberation Organization (PLO),
    101–2, 304, 405, 461
  establishment of, 84
  finances of, 88
  King Hussein challenged by, 94, 100,
    133, 143
  in Lebanon, 74–75, 88, 111
  terrorism and, 19, 21, 61, 63, 65, 70–71,
    75, 88
Palestinian Authority, 56, 70, 144, 296,
    350, 382, 389, 461
  Hamas's relations with, 385, 386, 404–5
  intifada and, 359, 360, 465
  U.S. relations with, 405*n*
Palestinian-Israeli peace process, 1–5,
    8–9, 13–14, 18–28, 42, 192, 194, 204,
    243, 267, 268, 283, 285–376, 396,
    404, 408–13
  Annapolis Conference and, 9, 67, 117,
    281, 283, 301*n*, 385–89
  Aqaba Summit and, 381
  Arab support for, 237, 296, 384, 409–10
  Crown Prince Abdullah's initiative for,
    384, 396
  G. W. Bush and, 9, 117, 207, 283, 366*n*,
    372, 374, 376, 378–82, 384–90, 411
  Khatami's support for, 221
  Madrid Conference and, 20
  PIJ disruption of, 173
  Sharm el-Sheikh (2000) and, 13, 228*n*,
    341–43, 355–59
  Sharm el-Sheikh (2003) and, 283
  stalling of, 217, 265
  Syrian talks contrasted with, 271
  Syria separated from, 18, 29
  Taba negotiations and, 371–72, 373, 466
  see also Camp David Summit; Clinton
    Parameters; Oslo Accords
Palestinian Legislative Council, 367,
    382–83
Palestinian National Council, 199
Palestinian prisoners, Barak's release of,
    292, 293
Palestinian state, 89, 101, 102, 181, 351
  Barak's views on, 289
  Camp David II and, 289, 291, 299, 310,
    311, 313, 323, 328, 332, 336, 339, 345
  in Clinton Parameters, 366
  Clinton's identification with, 308–9
  G. W. Bush's views on, 366*n*, 380
  Jerusalem as capital of, 89, 299, 313, 461
  Rabin's views on, 2–3, 28, 95
  Security Council and, 310, 311
pan-Arabism, 20, 74, 280, 294, 348
Paris, 102, 189, 354–55, 357
Parris, Mark, 36–37
Patriotic Union of Kurdistan (PUK), 161,
    182–83, 193*n*, 204

Pentagon, *see* Defense Department, U.S.
Peres, Shimon, 6, 44–45, 73, 81, 267, 270, 344*n*, 411*n*
 Clinton Parameters and, 370–71, 466
 election of 1996 and, 67, 177–80, 182, 265
 election of 2001 and, 364–65
 Jordan's peace efforts and, 95–96, 100–104, 109, 128, 132, 133, 136–37, 451
 Oslo Accords and, 60, 62–65, 67, 70, 71, 80, 82, 84, 86, 95, 110, 120–22, 137, 144, 450
 Palestinian economy and, 128
 Rabin's death and, 175–80
 Rabin's rivalry with, 64, 67, 87, 136–37, 175
 at Sharm el-Sheik Summit (1996), 178, 341
 Syrian peace efforts and, 84, 99, 103, 176, 179*n*, 278, 408, 450–51
Perle, Richard, 185, 454
Perry, William, 153–54
Persian Gulf, 5, 20, 21, 52, 59, 151, 154, 218, 397, 402
 failure of traditional U.S. approach in, 32–36
 Iran's attempt at dominance of, 39, 181, 232, 236–37
 Russia's building of relations in, 187
 U.S. warships in, 150, 189*n*, 190
 see also Gulf War, first
Pesh Merga troops, 161, 163
Pickering, Thomas, 186, 219
Pines-Paz, Ophir, 361–62
Pletka, Danielle, 192*n*
PLO, *see* Palestine Liberation Organization
Podesta, John, 309*n*
Point Mugu, 62, 63, 70, 72, 450
Poland, 236*n*
Powell, Colin, 24*n*, 38, 209
 in Bush administration, 14, 38, 205, 372, 380
 as JCS chairman, 14, 16–18, 38, 149–50, 153
 at NSC meetings, 16–18
Primakov, Yevgeny, 187, 189, 211
prisoners of war, 151*n*
Pundak, Ron, 80
Putin, Vladimir, 208, 236, 345

Qadhafi, Muammar, 4, 32, 398
Qalandiyah, 300
Qatar, 33, 57, 194–95
Qurei, Ahmed, *see* Abu Ala

Rabat, 44–47
 Arab Summit in (1974), 101

Rabbo, Yasser Abed, 298, 364, 370
Rabin, Leah, 7, 44–45, 67, 175, 356
Rabin, Yitzhak, 1–6, 8, 14–18, 21, 23, 32, 102–10, 140–45, 267, 270, 291, 313, 348, 381, 397, 411*n*
 Arafat's correspondence with, 81, 86
 assassination of, 3, 5, 7, 29, 144, 174–81, 241, 279
 back channel of, 144
 Barak compared with, 323
 elections and, 26, 79, 87, 95
 funeral of, 81, 176, 377
 Hebron crisis and, 114–18
 Iran as viewed by, 168*n*
 Jordan peace efforts and, 95–96, 102, 104, 128–38, 140, 141, 143, 155
 King Hussein's relationship with, 93–95, 100, 109, 129
 Kissinger's negotiations with, 285
 Oslo Accords and, 1–3, 45, 46, 56, 60–73, 76, 78–91, 99, 106, 114–18, 121–23, 132, 135, 137, 140, 142, 143, 144, 172, 300
 public opinion and, 21, 26
 Rabat visit of, 45
 "Syria first" and, 17–18, 21, 22, 26–29, 62, 79–89, 91, 96, 450
 Syrian peace and, 178–79, 243–44, 246, 248–51, 255, 257, 259, 262–63, 267*n*, 278, 389, 408
 "Syria second" and, 99, 103, 106–9, 114, 124–26, 135
 Washington Declaration and, 132–38
 Washington Summit and, 130–38
 Washington visits of, 1–3, 27–29, 45, 46, 84, 85, 87*n*, 88, 94, 114, 377
Rabinovich, Itamar, 63, 81, 125, 450, 452
Rachid, Muhammad, 302, 311, 317, 330, 363, 375, 467
Rafsanjani, Hashemi, 168–70, 220
Rahman, Omar Abdel, 53
Rajoub, Jibril, 352, 355
Ramallah, 342, 355*n*
Ramon, Haim, 81, 86, 298, 409*n*
"ratchet" strategy, 156–58, 189, 201, 213
Reagan, Ronald, 26–27, 34, 88, 157, 378, 391
refugees:
 Jewish, 334*n*
 Kurdish, 159*n*, 183
refugees, Palestinian, 71, 82*n*, 96, 333, 336, 351, 386, 392, 466
 Clinton Parameters and, 366, 367, 370–71, 374
 in Jordan, 100, 133
 "right of return" for, 303–4, 314, 331, 333–34, 351, 359, 363, 366, 372, 373, 374, 412–13, 462, 466–67

refugees, in Syria, 88, 96
regime change, 151, 203, 205–9
  Chalabi's strategy for, 191–92, 202
  G. W. Bush and, 5, 8, 151, 205–9, 230
  Iran and, 230
  "overt/covert" approach to, 202
  Parris and, 36–37
  Zinni's views on, 192, 202
Republican Guard, Iraqi, 35, 153, 154, 156, 159, 163, 201*n*
Republicans, 178, 337, 374
  Iran policy and, 216, 218, 224
  Iraq policy and, 185, 191, 200, 201, 456
Rezai, Mohsen, 217
Reza Pahlavi, Shah of Iran, 33, 59, 220, 224
Rice, Condoleezza, 9, 230, 386, 387–88, 392, 396
Riedel, Bruce, 41, 156, 159, 219, 309
Ritter, Scott, 191
Riyadh, 45, 139*n*, 155, 454
Road Map, 381, 386, 387, 411, 467
Rodham, Hugh, 15
Rodham, Tony, 15
Roed-Larsen, Terje, 84, 352
Roosevelt, Franklin D., 54–55, 73, 158, 377
Roosevelt, Theodore, 253
Ross, Dennis, 23–24, 25, 95, 102, 346, 348–51, 356, 357, 364, 366
  appointed Middle East envoy, 399–400
  Camp David II and, 290, 301, 308, 309, 311, 317, 323, 324, 330, 333
  Clinton Parameters and, 370, 373
  Jordanian-Israeli peace efforts and, 129, 452–53
  in Morocco, 44, 47, 363, 465
  Oslo Accords and, 62, 69, 70, 72, 81, 122, 283, 450
  Syrian-Israeli peace efforts and, 79–80, 81*n*, 82, 85, 93, 99, 107, 108, 124, 125, 131, 141, 176, 242, 244–45, 248–51, 262, 268, 277, 283, 459, 460
  in Tunis, 111, 113–14, 115
Rothstein, Raphi, 459
Rubin, Jamie, 206*n*, 220, 228
Rubin, Reuven, 361
Rubinstein, Eli, 127, 136, 137, 313*n*, 319, 333
Rumsfeld, Donald, 162
Rushdie, Salman, 39
Russia, 60, 345, 467
  Iran's relations with, 40, 169, 236, 454
  Iraq policy and, 152, 153, 157, 164, 184, 186–91, 194, 196, 208, 214
  Saddam's contracts with, 184, 455
  U.S. relations with, 179, 187, 191, 196, 208

Sadat, Anwar, 19, 28–29, 55, 67, 84, 89, 94, 145, 244*n*
  Arab rejection of peace moves by, 20
  assassination of, 51, 144, 174, 279, 340
  as author's hero, 23, 306
  back channel of, 144
  at Camp David I, 257, 306, 307, 310, 339–40
  Jerusalem visit of, 28–29, 45, 87, 266, 284, 396
  King Hussein compared with, 130, 143
  made president, 52
  survival motive of, 395
Sadr, Muqtada al-, 201
Sadr, Sadiq al-, 201
Saguy, Uri, 107, 108, 248–49, 250, 259, 260, 272
Sahhaf, Mohammed al-, 158
Saladin, 315, 462
Salah ad-Din, 160
Samara, Golden Mosque bombing in, 209*n*
Samarrai, Wafiq al-, 160–63
Sarid, Yossi, 371–72
Sarkozy, Nicolas, 236
Saud, Abdul Aziz al-, 54–55, 100–101
Saud, Muhammed bin, 54
Saudia Airlines, 56–57
Saudi Arabia, 33, 37, 78*n*, 135*n*, 139, 316
  Annapolis meeting and, 67
  creation of, 54, 101
  dual containment and, 56–57
  French relations with, 188
  G. W. Bush relations with, 50–51, 384
  hajj in, 54, 170, 219, 457
  hospitality in, 47
  intelligence service of, 202
  Iranian threat and, 237, 402
  Iran's relations with, 219, 457
  Iraq's relations with, 54, 55, 183, 202
  Israel's relations with, 56, 294
  Jerusalem and, 299, 300*n*, 324
  Khobar bombing in, *see* Khobar truck bombing
  oil of, 33, 53, 54, 55, 155, 157, 203, 449
  Oslo II and, 2
  Palestinian relations with, 20
  security purchased by, 54–55
  U.S. relations with, 26, 33, 50–51, 53–59, 155–56, 183, 188, 193–96, 266, 384, 405*n*, 407
  U.S. use of bases and airspace in, 154, 155, 183, 193, 194
"Saudi Hezbollah," 171
Savir, Uri, 80, 84, 102, 450, 451
Sawahra, 293
Sayeret Matkal, 289–90, 318
Sayigh, Yezid, 352, 353, 464–65

Scheunemann, Randy, 192*n*
Schneller, Otniel, 461
Schoen, Doug, 178
Schwartz, Jonathan, 316, 462–63
Schweid, Barry, 105
Sciolino, Elaine, 41
SCUD missiles, 190
Seale, Patrick, 106, 468
"Second Coming, The" (Yeats), 123
Secret Service, U.S., 69, 139
Senate, U.S., 192, 199, 215, 218, 241
Sephardic Jews, 87*n*, 265, 347, 362, 461
September 11, 2001, terrorist attacks, 4,
    58, 150, 202, 206, 207, 229, 378
settlements, Israeli, 180–81, 355*n*, 369,
    386*n*, 411, 460, 466
  Camp David II and, 314, 323, 334,
    337–38, 462
  in Golan Heights, 86, 87, 254, 451
  Hebron crisis and, 111, 112, 115–19
  Oslo Accords and, 71, 72, 86, 114, 118,
    123
  Sharon and, 180–81, 378, 380, 381–82,
    408–9, 411*n*
  in West Bank, 302, 323, 372, 408–9,
    411*n*
Shaaban, Buthaina, 98, 258–59, 408*n*
Shaath, Nabil, 120, 298, 333, 372, 466
Shakespeare, William, 361, 373
Shalikashvili, John (Shali), 153–58
Shamir, Yitzhak, 27*n*, 102, 118–19, 378,
    408*n*
Sharaa, Farouq al-, 79, 105–6
  aircraft deal of, 98–99
  Barak's negotiations with, 252–60
  in Shepherdstown talks, 257–60,
    262–65, 273, 276, 280, 286
  Syrian-Israeli peace efforts and, 79,
    242, 244, 245, 248, 249, 252–60,
    262–66, 272, 273, 276, 279, 283,
    286
Sharansky, Natan, 288
Sharm el-Sheikh, 367
Sharm el-Sheikh agreement, 228*n*, 292,
    355–59
Sharm el-Sheikh Summit (1996), 178,
    341, 342
Sharm el-Sheikh Summit (2000), 13,
    228*n*, 341–43, 355–59
Sharm el-Sheikh Summit (2003), 283
Sharon, Ariel, 6, 67, 75, 145, 292, 343,
    344, 359, 377–82, 395*n*, 459
  in election of 2001, 375
  freier label and, 381
  Gaza withdrawal of, 371, 381–82
  settler relations of, 180–81, 378, 380,
    381–82, 408–9, 411*n*
  at Sharm el-Sheik Summit (2003), 283

Temple Mount visited by, 341, 352, 354
  in Washington, 377–79
Shas Sephardi party, 87*n*, 265, 362, 385,
    461
Shatt al-Arab waterway, 54
Shehabi, Hekmat, 173, 255
Shelton, Hugh, 197–200
Shepherdstown talks, 257–67, 271, 273,
    276, 280, 283, 284–86, 290*n*, 321,
    398
Sher, Gilad, 300, 311–12, 320, 333*n*, 364*n*
  Clinton's Parameters and, 370, 465–66
Sheves, Shimon, 64
Shiites, 53, 170, 171, 402–4, 413
  Iranian, 33, 34, 37, 171, 181, 222, 236,
    457
Shiites, Iraqi, 201, 209, 230, 383, 402, 403
  Iranian influence on, 37, 157, 161, 230
  no-fly zone and, 31*n*, 38
  Saddam's brutality toward, 34*n*, 35,
    212, 220
Shrum, Robert, 265
Shuafat, 300, 301*n*, 302
shuttle diplomacy, 20, 48, 79–80, 114,
    126, 400*n*
Siewert, Jake, 370
Sinai Peninsula, 18, 89, 128, 180–81, 320,
    340
  second disengagement deal and, 94,
    285
Singapore, 73
Singer, Joel, 81, 122
Sirri offshore oil fields, 168
"6+2 forum," 194*n*
Six-Day War (1967), 88, 100, 101, 145,
    254, 301*n*
  Camp David II and, 296, 303, 308*n*,
    310, 312
  Syrian-Israeli border issues and,
    124–26, 131, 246–50, 252, 259, 260,
    261, 272, 273, 278, 280, 286, 295, 414
Sixth Fleet, 94
Slocombe, Walt, 196
smuggling, 203, 204–5, 207*n*, 221, 228*n*
Solana, Javier, 13
Solomon, King, 462
Sophronius, 315
Soviet Union, 22, 34, 396
  in Afghanistan, 53, 55
  collapse of, 15, 19, 22, 36, 38–39, 391
  containment of, 38–39, 205
  Egypt's relations with, 52, 89
  immigrants from, 14–15
Special Forces, U.S., 191
Special Middle East Coordinator
    (SMEC), 23–24
Special Security Organization, Iraqi, 190,
    201

Stalin, Joseph, 158
State Department, U.S., 42, 44, 105, 257,
    467
  Arabists vs. Zionists in, 24–25
  Camp David II and, 309, 316, 330
  Iran policy and, 215–20, 222–23, 458
  Iraq policy and, 36–37, 182, 185–90,
    202, 206n
  Near East Bureau of, 400
  Palestinians and, 19, 20, 61, 63, 68, 92n
  terrorism list of, 19, 21, 34, 61, 63, 99,
    219–20
  Washington Summit and, 130n, 134
  the words *peace process* expunged
    from, 379–80
Stealth F-117 fighters, 154
Steinberg, Jim, 193
Stephanopoulos, George, 60–61
Stethem, Robert, 40n
Stockholm channel, 295–96, 300n, 303
Studeman, William, 154, 161–62
Sudan, 53, 212
Suez Canal, 52, 155
Suez Crisis (1956), 89, 128
Sultan Yaqub, 104n, 257
Sunni, 34, 55, 166, 171, 172, 181, 402–4
  in Afghanistan, 222
  in Egypt, 51
  Iran as viewed by, 236–37
  in Iraq, 37, 152, 172, 201, 209, 230,
    392n, 402
  in Lebanon, 75
  Palestinian, 173
  in Syria, 88, 279, 280, 413
"Swiss channel," 219, 227
Syria, 73–89, 139, 176–79
  aircraft deal and, 98–99
  Annapolis Conference and, 117, 283
  economy of, 88, 106, 279, 280, 282
  Egypt's relations with, 74, 84, 271, 396
  Gulf War and, 22, 75, 98, 279
  intelligence in, 279
  Iran's relations with, 151, 171–74, 230,
    237, 413, 415
  Iraq's relations with, 16, 151, 194, 195,
    204
  Israeli-Jordanian peace and, 129, 141
  Israel's relations with, 84, 245n,
    389–90, 409
  Jordan's relations with, 74, 94, 95, 141
  Lebanon's relations with, *see*
    subheadings under Lebanon
  Madrid Conference and, 22, 76, 84, 97,
    98
  nuclear power of, 81n, 389
  Oslo Accords and, 92–93, 99, 106
  Palestinians in, 21, 71, 96, 98, 124, 303
  public opinion in, 280

  sanctions against, 212, 282
  smuggling in, 203
  treaty obligations and, 21
  U.S. relations with, 22, 75, 98, 99,
    105–6, 109, 114–15, 131, 141, 151,
    194, 203, 281, 282, 396, 405–6,
    413–15
Syrian Arab Airlines, 98–99
Syrian-Israeli peace process, 3, 4, 6, 91–
    100, 151, 155, 184, 194, 208, 241–87,
    375–76, 408, 413–15, 451–52
  Barak in, 108, 109, 124n, 204, 241–60,
    262–65, 267–68, 270–78, 284–87,
    290n, 292, 293, 295, 329, 389, 397,
    398, 408, 460
  Bern meeting and, 248
  Bethesda Hyatt talks in, 248–49, 259
  Blair House talks in, 254–56, 263
  borders issues in, 124–26, 131, 246–52,
    255–56, 259–64, 271–76, *274*, 278,
    280, 286, 295
  draft treaty in, 260, 265, 267–68, 271,
    434–40
  explanations for failure of, 277–87
  Geneva talks and, 104–8, 110, 275–78,
    280, 284–85, 286–87, 290n, 292,
    294, 321, 324, 398, 460
  Golan Heights and, *see* Golan Heights,
    Syrian peace and
  G. W. Bush's lack of interest in, 151,
    283, 389
  handshaking and, 67, 253, 254, 284
  Iranian interference in, 172–73, 176,
    237, 398
  Israeli elections and, 178–79, 203
  Jordanian-Israeli peace and, 129, 135,
    140–45, 453
  leaks in, 260, 263, 265–68, 271, 286
  maps and, 247n, 255–56, 271, 272, *274*,
    277, 459
  Palestinian talks contrasted with, 271
  revised ten points of agreement and,
    250
  Shepherdstown talks in, 257–67, 271,
    273, 276, 280, 283, 284–85, 286,
    290n, 321, 398
  stalling of, 117, 184, 217, 283, 294, 338
  "Syria first" and, 17–29, 43, 62–63,
    76–89, 91, 93, 145, 246, 282, 294–95,
    396, 413
  Syrian denouement in, 269–87
  "Syria second," 93, 96–100, 103–9,
    114–17, 123–26
  "Treaty of Peace Between Israel and
    Syria" in, 247
  water resources and, 21, 82n, 246–50,
    259, 260, 286–87
Wye talks and, 176

Taba negotiations, 372, 373, 466
Talabani, Jalal, 161, 163, 182–83
Talbott, Strobridge, III (Strobe), 154, 196, 215–17
"Talleyrand moment," 188
Talleyrand-Périgord, Charles Maurice de, 188*n*
Tanzim, 296–97, 342, 353–54, 358, 369
Tarawneh, Fayez, 136
Tauran, Archbishop, 345
technology, 34, 40, 169, 448, 454
Tehran, 217*n*, 222, 224, 231
    Iraqi exiles in, 230
    Khaddam's visit to, 173–74
    Swiss embassy in, 219
Tehran University, 220, 226
Tel Aviv, 46, 106, 107, 135, 346
    hostages freed in, 460–61
    Ichilov Hospital in, 3, 6, 174–75
    terrorism in, 176
    U.S. embassy in, 179–80, 333
Tel Rumeida, 112, 115–16
Temporary International Presence in Hebron (TIPH), 115
Tenet, George, 159, 161, 196–97, 199
    Camp David II and, 330–31, 333
    intifada and, 353, 355–58, 380
terrorism, 378–79, 393
    in Egypt, 58
    Iran and, 39, 40, 167–69, 171, 172–73, 216–20, 223–27, 228*n*, 235, 237, 378, 453–54, 457–58
    Iraq and, 34, 150, 206, 383
    Israel and, 130, 135*n*, 141, 172–73, 175–77
    Jordan and, 100, 128, 135*n*
    in Lebanon, 95, 176–77
    Libya and, 4, 32, 213*n*
    Palestinian, 141, 173, 180, 204, 208, 228*n*, 273, 281, 343, 362, 379, 381–82, 387, 404
    PLO and, 19, 21, 61, 63, 65, 70–71, 75, 88
    in Saudi Arabia, 171, 454
    Syria and, 21, 58, 98, 99, 105, 172, 177, 265, 281, 282
    in U.S., 4, 58, 150, 175
    see also al-Qaeda; Hamas; Hezbollah; September 11, 2001, terrorist attacks
Tibi, Ahmed, 81
Tomahawk missiles, 150, 197, 199
Total, 223
Tripoli, 75
Truman, Harry, 174*n*, 179, 254, 377
Tuchman, Barbara, 10
Tuhami, Hassan, 144
Tunis, 21, 112
    Arafat in, 27, 28, 66, 79, 111–17

Tunisia, 75, 324, 345
Turabi, Hassan al-, 53
Turkey, 203, 403, 405*n*
    Iraqi coup attempt and, 161, 162
    Israeli-Syrian negotiations and, 117, 281, 389
    Kurds and, 35, 159, 161, 182, 183
TWA, 40*n*
Twain, Mark, ix, 96
Twelver (Ismaili) Shiism, 171*n*

U-2 aircraft, 188
Ubayd tribe, 152
Uganda, storming of Entebbe Airport in, 461
Umar, Caliph, 299, 315, 325*n*, 462
United Arab Emirates, 33, 219
United Nations (U.N.), 13, 355, 466, 467
    Afghan Contact Group at, 223
    Arafat at, 68–69
    Drug Control Program of, 222*n*
    Iran and, 40, 168, 232, 236
    Iraq and, 19, 30, 31, 37, 38, 40–41, 42, 113, 151–53, 158, 164–65, 183–200, 203–12, 448, 456
    Palestinians and, 68–69, 112–15
    Partition Plan of, 322
    Sanctions Committee of, 165, 184
    Turkey and, 203
United Nations General Assembly, 68–69, 112
    Resolution 194 of, 304, 314, 462
United Nations Security Council, 38, 112–15, 157, 158, 204–9, 213, 316, 385, 410, 452
    Iran and, 232
    Iraq sanctions and, 30, 40–41, 184, 194, 205
    Iraq weapons inspections and, 30, 152, 153, 184, 186–91, 193–95, 198–200
    Jerusalem issue and, 349, 350
    Palestinian state and, 310, 311
    Resolution 242 of, 124, 261, 311
    Resolution 904 of, 115
    Resolution 949 of, 158
    Resolution 986 of, 164–65
    Resolution 1559 of, 383
    Resolution 3379 of, 112
    Saddam's awarding of contracts and, 184, 455
    Syria and, 23, 117
United Nations Special Commission (UNSCOM), 152–53, 164–66, 186–95, 198–200, 204, 211
    Clinton plan for response to Iraqi obstruction of, 192–93
U.N. Millennium Summit (2000), 346–51

uranium enrichment program, Iranian, 230, 232, 235, 236
"U.S.-Israel Counter-Terrorism Cooperation Accord," 178

Vatican, 345
Védrine, Hubert, 186, 189, 190
Velayati, Ali Akbar, 174
Verstandig, Tony, 282
Vietnam War, 212
Volcker Committee, 455–56

Wachsman, Nachshon, 342
Wag the Dog (movie), 200
Wahhab, Muhammad Abd al-, 54
Wahhabi, 54
Walker, Ned, 241, 324, 344*n*
Walters, Barbara, 384
waqf (Islamic trust), 101, 102, 127, 135, 136, 302, 412*n*
Ward, William, 382
War of Independence (1948), 27*n*, 78, 100, 303
Washington Declaration (July 25, 1994), 132–38, 430–33
  draft text of, 135–36
Washington Institute for Near East Policy, 15, 23, 41–43
Washington Post, 14*n*, 42
Washington Summit (1994), 130–38
Washington Summit (1998), 193
water resources, 71, 247*n*
  of Jordan, 109, 127, 140
  Syrian-Israeli talks and, 21, 82*n*, 246–50, 259, 260, 286–87
Wazir, Khalil al-, *see* Abu Jihad
weapons of mass destruction (WMD), 4, 458
  Iran and, 168*n*, 170, 454
  Iraq and, 19, 30, 152, 153, 165–66, 188–201, 204, 206, 207, 209–10, 396*n*, 456
  Syria and, 210, 281
Weizman, Ezer, 175
Welch, David, 186, 219
West Bank, 1, 4, 86, 104, 128, 291, 351, 363*n*, 366, 372, 395*n*, 408–11
  Camp David I and, 339–40
  Camp David II and, 295, 296, 302–3, 311, 312, 313, 331–34, 337, 338, 339, 351, 359, 410, 463
  in Clinton Parameters, 366, *368*, 409, 466

economy of, 387–88
Hamas in, 17*n*, 386
intifada in, 204, 341–43, 345, 352–60, 374
Israeli separation barrier with, 381
Israeli settlers in, 22, 87, 180–81
Israeli withdrawal from, 180–81, 192, 193, 292, 293, 404, 408–9
Jordanian control in, 94, 95, 100, 102
maps of, 121–23
Oslo Accords and, 71, 291
Palestinians in, 21, 26, 70, 71, 78–79, 88, 100, 101, 118, 126, 142, 296–97, 303, 385–86, 405, 409, 462
Palestinian state in, 3, 289
Syrian peace and, 118
terrorism in, 173
Wye Agreement and, 193
West Jerusalem, 176, 337, 361–62, 464
White House, 311, 359
  Barak-Sharaa ceremony at, 253–54, 284
  signing ceremonies at, 1–2, 60–71, 87*n*, 137, 174, 377
Wisconsin Project on Nuclear Arms Control, 456
WMD, *see* weapons of mass destruction
Wolfensohn, James, 282, 382, 467
Wolfowitz, Paul, 185
Woolsey, James, 16, 38
World Bank, 169, 282, 385
World Trade Organization, 232
Wye Agreement (Oct. 1998), 6, 193, 292, 331, 459
Wye negotiations, 67, 176, 193, 459

Yaalon, Moshe (Boogie), 465
Yaari, Ehud, 179
Yalta Conference, 158
Yanai, Shlomo, 331, 333*n*, 334, 461, 466
Yarmuk River, 127
Yatom, Danny, 272, 277, 344*n*
  Camp David II and, 312, 319, 321
Yeats, William Butler, 123
Yeltsen, Boris, 178, 179, 187
Yemen, 57, 357
Yisrael Baaliya, 461
Yisrael Beiteinu, 375
Yom Kippur War (1973), 6, 89, 174*n*, 396

Zinni, Anthony, 192, 202, 380
Zionism, Zionists, 25, 42, 81, 113, 347n, 460

Photo Credits

About the Author

Martin S. Indyk is the Director of the Saban Center for Middle East Policy at The Brookings Institution and a Senior Fellow in its Foreign Policy Studies Program. Twice U.S. Ambassador to Israel, Special Assistant to the President, and Senior Director for Near Eastern and South Asian Affairs in the National Security Council, and Assistant Secretary of State for Near East Affairs, Indyk lives in Washington, D.C.